RACE, CLASS, AND GENDER IN THE UNITED STATES

RACE, CLASS, AND GENDER IN THE UNITED STATES

AN INTEGRATED STUDY

Tenth Edition

Paula S. Rothenberg

with
Soniya Munshi

Borough of Manhattan
Community College

worth publishers
Macmillan Learning

New York

Publisher, Psychology and Sociology: Rachel Losh
Associate Publisher: Jessica Bayne
Senior Associate Editor: Sarah Berger
Development Editor: Thomas Finn
Assistant Editor: Kimberly Morgan Smith
Executive Marketing Manager: Katherine Nurre
Media Producer: Hanna Squire
Director, Content Management Enhancement: Tracey Kuehn
Managing Editor, Sciences and Social Sciences: Lisa Kinne
Senior Project Editor: Kerry O'Shaughnessy
Photo Editor: Robin Fadool
Permissions Associate: Chelsea Roden
Director of Design, Content Management: Diana Blume
Senior Design Manager: Vicki Tomaselli
Cover and Interior Design: Kevin Kall
Senior Production Supervisor: Stacey B. Alexander
Composition: Jouve North America
Printing and Binding: LSC Communications
Cover Photo: Silberkorn/Shutterstock

Library of Congress Control Number: 2016932674

ISBN-13: 978-1-4641-7866-5
ISBN-10: 1-4641-7866-6

© 2016, 2014, 2010, 2007 by Worth Publishers

All rights reserved

Printed in the United States of America

Third printing

Worth Publishers
One New York Plaza
Suite 4500
New York, NY 10004-1562
www.worthpublishers.com

CONTENTS

PART VII   How It Happened: Race and Gender Issues in U.S. Law   469

PART VIII Maintaining Race, Class, and Gender Hierarchies: Reproducing "Reality"   537

PREFACE

Reflections from the First to the Tenth Edition of *Race, Class, and Gender*

When the first edition of *Race, Class, and Gender in the United States* was published in 1988 under the title *Racism and Sexism: An Integrated Study*, there was no World Wide Web. There were no smart phones. Smoking was still allowed on airplanes. China was one of the poorest nations in the world, the Soviet Union still existed, and apartheid was alive—if not well—in South Africa. In fact, the next president of South Africa and famed civil rights leader Nelson Mandela was still in prison in 1988, serving the 25th year of his sentence.

In the United States, the Reagan Administration was defending the secret sale of U.S. arms to Iran, while the Supreme Court was asked to decide whether one of the largest associations of "businessmen"—the Rotary Club—had a constitutional right to refuse to admit women as members. Scholars were arguing over the relationship between race and intelligence—a debate that was about to get even more heated in the decade that followed. Three quarters of the American population thought homosexual relations between two consenting adults was *always* wrong and the state had the right to outlaw such conduct.* As for the issue of economic inequality, it was nowhere to be found in the public discourse.

Much has happened in the intervening years. With a surge in voter turnout in 2008, a black man was elected president, and as of this writing, a woman is leading the polls for—and, by the time you are reading this, may even have won—the presidency of the United States. Given the setbacks for the feminist, black, and Latino/a movements of the 1960s and 1970s, most Americans in the 1980s did not expect to witness this type of cultural and political change in their lifetime. Even more inconceivable, given the cultural landscape, was that a growing LGBT (lesbian, gay, bisexual, and transgender) movement would help make gay marriage legal, and gender reassignment would enter the popular culture. An Occupy Wall Street movement helped put the issue of economic inequality squarely on the national and international agenda, seemingly overnight. And while many had hoped for a growing environmental movement, few anticipated the emergence of a global approach to climate change.

On the other hand, nearly three decades after the first edition of this book was published, so much has stayed the same or worsened. In 1988, the richest 20% of Americans held 83% of total household wealth: today, that 20% holds 93% of the nation's wealth. Women have made significant strides politically, socially, and economically, yet they still make only 77 cents for every dollar a man makes—and the

---

* Smith, Tom W. "Public Attitudes toward Homosexuality." NORC/University of Chicago: September, 2011.

The right of states to outlaw acts of homosexuality by consenting adults was based on the 1986 Supreme Court decision *Bowers* v. *Hardwick.*

gap is even greater for women of color (64 cents for African American women). While racial profiling has finally caught the attention of the media, its persistence—and its expansion to Muslim and Sikh communities—continues to destroy lives and families. Policies, like affirmative action, that were designed to remedy inequities have been deeply weakened. So too, have organizations, like unions, that had for so long been such an important check on inequality and injustice. Twenty-two percent of the children in the United States live in poverty, a proportion nearly identical to what it was 30 years ago. How ironic that so much change can co-exist with so much stagnation.

How do we make sense of all of this? In the introduction to the first edition of the book, I put it simply: "An integrated approach to the study of racism and sexism within the context of class provides us with a more comprehensive, more accurate, more useful analysis of the world in which we live out our lives." This is as true now as it was nearly three decades ago.

New to *Race, Class, and Gender*, Tenth Edition

The tenth edition of *Race, Class, and Gender*, like previous editions, views the problems facing our country and our communities as structural, and seeks to contribute to the conversation about fairness and justice. Like its predecessors, this edition undertakes the study of race, gender, and sexuality within the context of class. We look at racism, sexism, heterosexism, class privilege, and the concepts of patriarchy and white privilege, and explore the interlocking nature of these systems of oppression as they work in combination and impact virtually every aspect of life in U.S. society today. New to Part II of this edition, we revisit Kimberlé Crenshaw's work on intersectionality, a term she coined in 1989. In an interview, Crenshaw reflects on the continued need for an accessible metaphor that captures the complexity of multiple and simultaneous forms of oppression. This intersectional framework is one that we rely on throughout the book to illustrate the complex dimensions of race, gender, sexuality, and class.

Part I introduces these different categories by examining the ways each of them has been socially and hierarchically constructed to the benefit of some and to the disadvantage of others. Susan Stryker's work, new to this edition, explores the relationship between sex, gender, and gender identity. This excerpt lays a foundation for later pieces that address trans lives, identities, and experiences, all showing us how gender identity is shaped by race, class, sexuality, and other factors. For example, additional writings include a piece on violence against trans women ("The Transgender Crucible" by Sabrina Rubin Erdely in Part IV), the role of economic access in living as a trans person ("'I am Alena': Life as a Trans Woman Where Survival Means Living as Christopher" by Ed Pilkington in Part V), and a reflection on how recent public attention on trans communities is mediated by privilege so that many stories and experiences continue to be omitted ("The Unbearable (In)visibility of Being Trans" by Chase Strangio in Part VI).

This edition includes an intentional, focused, and intersectional engagement with current public conversations about mass incarceration, police violence, and racial and other forms of profiling. We have included an excerpt from Michelle Alexander's *The New Jim Crow* (Part IV), which addresses mass incarceration and racial targeting of Black and Latino communities. "The Ghosts of Stonewall: Policing Sex, Policing Gender" by Joey L. Mogul, Andrea J. Ritchie, and Kay Whitlock and the above-mentioned "Transgender Crucible" both discuss how the actions and identities of LGBT people, especially people of color, come under greater scrutiny by the law and are more vulnerable to punishment. Julianne Hing's article, "Race, Disability and the School-to-Prison Pipeline," illustrates the relationship between educational institutions, systems of punishment, and the risks involved for marginalized students.

In Part VI, "Many Voices, Many Lives," Claudia Rankine, Ta-Nehisi Coates, and Kiese Laymon each offer a poetic reflection on how structural racism, specifically anti-black racism, operate on a deeply personal, everyday level of experience. Also in this part, Edwidge Dandicat shares a beautiful and difficult meditation on the concurrences of anti-black racism by linking the white supremacist killings of black churchgoers in Charleston, South Carolina, to the state policies of the removal of Haitians in the Dominican Republic. Finally, in Part VIII's exploration of the role of the media and stereotypes in maintaining race, class, and gender hierarchies, Ta-Nehisi Coates and Tressie McMillan Cottom each reflect on the police killings of two unarmed black men, Michael Brown and Jonathan Ferrell. Coates and Cottom challenge "respectability politics," or the idea that it is the responsibility of those individuals and groups that are being racially targeted to change their behavior to prevent such targeting. Coates and Cottom are concerned with how safety and protection from violence are distributed in our society and argue that one's basic humanity is not something that must be earned. In our final part, Part IX, we include a selection by Tasbeeh Herwees about the founders of the Black Lives Matter movement. Herwees explores how gender and sexuality are integral to social justice organizing, even when it is explicitly centered on race.

As in previous editions, we pay substantive attention to the complex and evolving dynamics of identity. For example, we feature Christina Greer's research on the relationship between native-born black Americans and black ethnic immigrants, illuminating the heterogeneity within black communities. We also include Angelo N. Ancheta's seminal essay "Neither Black nor White" in Part II, which illustrates how Asians have been racially positioned in the United States. Scot Nakagawa's "On Solidarity, 'Centering Anti-Blackness' and Asian Americans" in Part IX brings Ancheta's analysis into the present, reflects on how Asian Americans are racially positioned today, and offers suggestions for how Asian Americans should participate in contemporary racial justice struggles.

This edition includes several pieces about the experiences of communities that are, or are perceived to be, Arab and/or Muslim. Moustafa Bayoumi's work with Arab- and Muslim-American youth in the post-9/11 period illustrates how contemporary examples of the racialization and exclusion of Arab and Muslim Americans reflects a history of these processes in the United States. Jon Ronson's work (Part VIII) looks at stereotypical representations of terrorists in the media and how typecasting limits the opportunities available for Muslim-American actors.

Additionally, this edition includes two new pieces that address the racialized experience of indigenous populations in the United States. In Part IV, Brian Bienkowski documents how environmental racism affects Native American populations in Michigan, and in Part VIII, David Zirin examines how cultural racism is enacted against indigenous communities through professional sports team mascots.

Several essays in this new edition take a look at immigration policies. Faye Hipsman and Doris Meissner (Part III) provide a helpful overview of how the U.S. immigration system works, its historical context, and contemporary trends in immigration. Tim Henderson's piece (Part IV) looks at the fear of deportation in undocumented communities. In his article, Henderson notes that even when the rate of deportation went down, the level of fear in undocumented immigrant communities remained. He shows our feelings of fear and insecurity operate beyond the concrete risks we face. At the time of this writing, in early 2016, the Obama administration has prioritized a new wave of removal operations, conducting raids of mostly Central American individuals and families, making Henderson's work even more poignant. Douglas Massey's work ("Immigration Enforcement as a Race-Making Institution" in Part V) shows how immigration policy shapes the demographics of communities in the United States—in this case, Latino immigrants. Moving from the structural to the individual, E. Tammy Kim's writing (Part VI) tells the story of an undocumented immigrant and the everyday struggles she faces.

This edition includes many new pieces that approach issues of class and the economy from an intersectional perspective. In Part I, we include a short essay by Susan Greenbaum that challenges the persistent myth that poor people are to blame for their economic conditions, by looking at government, corporate, and other structural factors that shape poverty. In the next part, Robin DiAngelo provides a personal reflection on how her experience of poverty and class oppression did not negate her white privilege. In Part V, Rakesh Kochhar and Richard Fry offer an updated overview of inequality and wealth distribution by racial category. Seth Freed Wessler challenges stereotypes about Asian "model minority" success, painting a more complete picture of class distribution in Asian immigrant communities. Linda Burnham's research shows how black women, facing both racism and sexism in the workplace, were more affected than others by the last recession and continue to struggle during the economic recovery. Ai-jen Poo writes about how domestic workers, organizing as a workforce of mostly immigrant women of color, challenge unfair and unjust workplace conditions. Organizing on the basis of "women's work" makes visible the often-erased caring labor that is essential to our economy. Finally, Tracie McMillan writes about hunger in the United States, challenging assumptions about what the everyday experience of being without sufficient food looks like.

We close this edition with essays that encourage readers to redefine difference and to think in broad terms about the kind of society we wish to live in and the kinds of relationships we wish to have with others. These essays in Part IX, "Social Change: Revisioning the Future and Making a Difference," by Audre Lorde, bell hooks, and Cooper Thompson, as well as the new pieces by Tasbeeh Herwees and Scot Nakagawa about the current movement for Black Lives, demonstrate how people who care about the issues of inequality, privilege, and injustice can, and are, making a difference in the world. Faculty using this book will find that this section allows them to end their courses in a very positive way. This is important because students who study social problems often end up feeling overwhelmed by the extent and severity of these issues. The articles in the last section leave students with an understanding that ordinary people acting on their principles really can make a difference!

Acknowledgments

Many people contributed to *Race, Class, and Gender*—and its evolution over the course of nearly three decades. First, I owe a profound debt to the old 12th Street study group, with whom I first studied black history and first came to understand the centrality of the issue of race. I am also indebted to the group's members, who provided me with a lasting example of what it means to commit one's life to the struggle for equality and justice for all people.

Next, I owe an equally profound debt to my friends and colleagues in the New Jersey Project on Inclusive Scholarship, Curriculum, and Teaching, and to friends, colleagues, and students at William Paterson University who have been involved in the various race and gender projects we have carried out over the years. I have learned a great deal from all of them. I would also like to thank the faculty and students, too many to name, at the many colleges and universities where I have lectured over the years.

In addition I am grateful to the reviewers of this and previous editions for their insightful feedback. They include: Mildred Anterior, New Jersey City University; Maral N. Attallah, Humboldt State University; Adriana Leela Bohm, Delaware Community College; Nancy F. Browning, Lincoln University of Missouri; Debra Butterfield, Boston College; Natalie Smith Carslon, North Dakota State University; Margaret Crowdes, California State University–San Marcos; Helen Dedes, William Paterson University; Margie Kitter Edwards, Temple University; Miriam Rheingold Fuller, University of Central Missouri; Lawrence Andrew Gill, William Paterson University; Tonya Huber-Warring, St. Cloud State University; Denise Isom, California Polytechnic State University–San Luis Obispo; Kelly F. Jackson, Arizona State University; Navita Cummings James, University of South Florida; Michelle L. Johnson, Ramapo College of New Jersey; Mary Kelley, University of Central Missouri; Deborah L. Little, Adelphi University; Enid Logan, University of Minnesota; David Lucander, Rockland Community College; Michele Murphy, William Patterson University; Julie Norflus-Good, Ramapo College of New Jersey; Archana Pathak, Virginia Commonwealth University; Viji Sargis, William Paterson University; Rashad Shabazz, University of Vermont; Roger Simpson, California State University, Fresno; and Rebeckah Zincavage, Boston College.

This edition would not have been possible without the work of three collaborators to whom I am deeply indebted: Soniya Munshi for her research, writing, and revisions to this edition; Sarah Berger, my hands-on editor, for her insights, sensitivity,

perseverance, and deep commitment to the project; and Greg Mantsios for his invaluable assistance and good judgment about all things related to this and all previous
editions.

Finally, I want to thank Greg for being such a remarkable partner as well as collaborator; our children, Alexi Mantsios and Andrea Mantsios; and their partners,
Caroline Donohue and Luis Armando Ocaranza Ordaz, for their insights, observations, and most of all, their extraordinary support through thick and thin.

ABOUT THE AUTHOR

Paula Rothenberg has been writing, teaching, and consulting on a variety of topics for over five decades. Her areas of expertise include multicultural curriculum transformation, issues of inequality, equity, and privilege, globalizing the curriculum, and white privilege. From 1989 to 2006, she served as Director of the New Jersey Project on Inclusive Scholarship, Curriculum, and Teaching, and Professor of Philosophy and Women's Studies at The William Paterson University of New Jersey. She is the author of *Invisible Privilege: A Memoir about Race, Class, and Gender* (University Press of Kansas). Her anthology, *White Privilege: Readings on the Other Side of Racism,* is now in its fifth edition. *Beyond Borders: Thinking Critically About Global Issues* was published by Worth in 2005, and her anthology, *What's the Problem? A Brief Guide to Critical Thinking,* was published in 2009. Paula Rothenberg is also co-editor of a number of other anthologies, including *Creating an Inclusive College Curriculum: A Teaching Sourcebook* from the New Jersey Project; *Feminist Frameworks: Alternative Theoretical Accounts of the Relations between Women and Men*; and *Philosophy Now.* Her articles and essays appear in journals and anthologies across the disciplines, and many have been widely reprinted.

About the Contributor

Soniya Munshi is Assistant Professor of Sociology at the Borough of Manhattan Community College of the City University of New York, where she also teaches Asian American Studies in the Center for Ethnic Studies. Her research examines the racial politics of antiviolence work, the role of legal and medical institutions in constructing and responding to social problems, and social movements that build strategies of accountability outside punishment. Soniya Munshi is a member of the National Collective of INCITE! Women, Gender Non-Conforming, and Trans People of Color Against Violence and the Critical Ethnic Studies Association Working Group.

INTRODUCTION

It is impossible to make sense out of either the past or the present without using race, class, gender, and sexuality as central categories of description and analysis. Yet many of us are the products of an educational system that has taught us to ignore these categories and thus not to see the differences in power and privilege that surround us. As a result, events that some people identify as clear examples of sexism or racism appear to others to be simply "the way things are." Understandably, this difference in outlook often makes conversation difficult and frustrating. A basic premise of this book is that much of what passes for a neutral perspective across the disciplines and in cultural life smuggles in elements of class, race, and gender bias and distortion. Because the so-called neutral point of view is so pervasive, it is often difficult to identify. One of the goals of this text is to help the reader learn to recognize some of the ways in which issues of race, class, and gender are embedded in ordinary discourse and daily life. Learning to identify and employ race, class, and gender as fundamental categories of description and analysis is essential if we wish to understand our own lives and the lives of others.

The Challenges of Studying Race, Class, and Gender

As we begin our study together, some differences from other academic enterprises are immediately apparent. Whereas students and faculty in an introductory literature or chemistry class rarely begin the semester with deeply felt and firmly entrenched attitudes toward the subject, almost every student in a course that deals with issues of race, class, gender, and sexuality enters the room on the first day with strong feelings, and almost every faculty member does so as well. The consequences can be either very good or very bad. Under the best conditions, if we acknowledge our feelings head on, those feelings can provide the basis for a passionate and personal study of the topics and can make this course something out of the ordinary, a class that has real long-term meaning both for students and for teachers.

This material presents many challenges. Racism, sexism, heterosexism, and class privilege are all systems of oppression with their own particular history and their own intrinsic logic (or illogic). Therefore it is important to explore each of these systems on its own terms; at the same time, these systems operate in conjunction with one another to form an enormously complex set of interlocking and self-perpetuating relations of domination and subordination. It is essential that we understand the ways in which these systems overlap, intersect, and play off one another. For purposes of analysis, it may be necessary to talk as if it were possible to abstract race or sexuality from, say, gender and class, and for a time subject a dimension to exclusive scrutiny, even though such distinctions are never possible in reality. When we engage in this kind of abstraction, we should never lose sight of the fact that any particular individual has an ethnic background, a class location, an age, a sexual orientation, a religious orientation, a gender, and that all these characteristics are inseparable from the person and from one another. Always, the particular combination of these identities shapes the individual and locates him or her in society.

It is also true that in talking about racism, sexism, and heterosexism in the context of class, we may have to make generalizations about the experience of different groups of people, even as we affirm that each individual is unique. For example, in order to highlight similarities in the experiences of some individuals, this book often talks about "people of color" or "women of color," even though these terms are somewhat problematic. When I refer to "women" in this book instead of "white women" or "women of color," it is usually in order to focus on the particular experiences or the legal status of women as women. Yet for the purposes of discussion and analysis, it is often necessary to make artificial distinctions in order to focus on particular aspects of experience that may not be separable in reality. Language both mirrors reality and helps to structure it. No wonder, then, that it is so difficult to use our language in ways that adequately address our topics.

Structure of the Book

This book begins with an examination of the ways in which race, class, gender, and sexuality have been socially constructed in the United States as "differences" in the form of hierarchies. What exactly does it mean to claim that someone or some group of people is "different"? What kind of evidence might be offered to support this claim? What does it mean to construct differences? And how does society treat people who are categorized in this way? The readings in Parts I, II, III, and IV are intended to initiate a dialogue about the ways in which U.S. society constructs difference, and the social, political, and personal consequences that flow from that construction. These readings encourage us to think about the meaning of racism, sexism, heterosexism, and class privilege, and how these systems intersect.

Part I treats the idea of difference itself as a social construct, one that underlies and grounds racism, sexism, class privilege, and homophobia. Each of the authors included would agree that while some of these differences may appear to be "natural" or given in nature, they are in fact socially constructed, and the meanings and values associated with these differences create a hierarchy of power and privilege which, precisely because it does appear to be "natural," is used to rationalize inequality.

Part II introduces the concept of "oppression" in order to examine racism, sexism, heterosexism, and class privilege as intersecting systems of oppression that ensure advantages for some and diminished opportunities for others. Part III moves us beyond a black/white paradigm for thinking about issues of race and examines some of the complexities of the experiences and the challenges that arise from living in a genuinely diverse, multicultural society in which white privilege continues to play a major role in shaping economic, political, and social life.

Part IV provides us with concrete examples of how the systems of oppression operate in contemporary society. Through news articles and other materials, we get a first-hand look at the kinds of discrimination that are faced by members of groups subject to unequal and discriminatory treatment.

Defining racism and sexism is always a volatile undertaking. Most of us have strong feelings about race and gender relations and have a stake in the way those relations are portrayed and analyzed. Definitions are powerful. They can focus attention on certain aspects of reality and make others disappear. Parts I through IV are intended to examine the process of definition. The readings allow us to discuss the ways in which we have been taught to think about race, class, and gender difference and to examine how these differences manifest themselves in daily life.

Part V provides statistics and analyses that demonstrate the impact of economic structures on race, class, and gender differences in people's lives. Whereas previous selections depend primarily on narrative to define and illustrate discrimination and oppression, the material in Part V presents current data, much of it drawn from U.S. government sources, that document the ways in which socially constructed differences mean real differences in opportunity, expectations, and treatment. These differences are brought to life in the articles, poems, and stories in Part VI, offering glimpses into the lives of women and men of different ethnic and class backgrounds, who express their sexuality and cultures in a variety of ways. Although many selections are highly personal, each points beyond the individual's experience to social policy or practice or to culturally conditioned attitudes.

When people first begin to recognize the enormous toll that racism, sexism, heterosexism, and class privilege takes, they often are overwhelmed. How can we reconcile our belief that the United States extends liberty and justice and equal opportunity for all with the reality presented in these pages? How has the disconnect between our beliefs and our actual experiences happened? At this point we must turn to history.

Part VII highlights important aspects of the history of subordinated groups in the United States by focusing on historical documents that address race and gender issues in U.S. law since the beginning of the Republic. When these documents are read in the context of the earlier material describing race, gender, and class differences in contemporary society, they give us a way of using the past to make sense of the present. Focusing on the legal status of women of all colors and men of color allows us to distill hundreds of years of history down to a manageable size, while still providing the historical information needed to make sense of contemporary society.

Our survey of racism and sexism in the United States, past and present, has shown that these phenomena can assume different forms in different contexts. For some, these experiences are still all too real today; for others they reflect a crude, blatant racism that seems incompatible with contemporary life. But racism, sexism, homophobia, and class privilege are in fact perpetuated in contemporary society—why do these divisions and the accompanying differences in opportunity and achievement continue? How are they reproduced? Part VIII offers some suggestions.

The selections in Part VIII focus on how our conceptions of others—and, equally important, our conceptions of ourselves—help perpetuate racism, sexism, heterosexism, and class privilege. The discussion moves beyond the specificity of stereotypes; it analyzes how modes of conceptualizing reality itself are conditioned by forces that are not always obvious. Racism, sexism, heterosexism, and classism are not only systems of oppression that provide advantages and privileges to some, they are not simply identifiable attitudes, policies, and practices that affect individuals' lives; racism, sexism, heterosexism, and classism operate on a basic level to structure what we come to think of as "reality." As such, they limit our possibilities and personhood. They cause us to internalize beliefs that distort our perspectives and expectations and make it more difficult to identify the origins of unequal and unjust distribution of resources. This hierarchy of privilege and opportunity has been institutionalized throughout our society, and in this way it has been rationalized and normalized. We grow up being taught that the prevailing hierarchy in society is natural and inevitable, perhaps even desirable, and so we fail to identity that unequal and unjust distribution as a problem.

Finally, Part IX offers some suggestions for moving beyond racism, sexism, heterosexism, and classism. These selections are intended to stimulate discussion about the kinds of change we might wish to explore in order to transform society. Some of the articles offer ideas about the causes of and cures for the pervasive social and economic inequality and injustice that are documented in this volume and suggest ways to revise our society and our social relationships. Others move from theory to practice by offering very specific suggestions about, and concrete examples of, interrupting the cycle of oppression and bringing about social change. Some of these articles suggest things that individuals can do in the course of everyday life in order to make a difference; others provide examples of people working together to bring about social change. The task is enormous, time is short, and our collective future is at stake.

PART I

The Social Construction of Difference: Race, Class, Gender, and Sexuality

Every society grapples with the question of how to distribute its wealth, power, resources, and opportunities. In some cases, the distribution is relatively egalitarian; in others, it is dramatically unequal. Those societies that tend toward a less egalitarian distribution have adopted various ways to apportion privilege; some have used age, others have used ancestry. U.S. society, like many others, places a priority on sex, race, and class. To this end, race and gender differences have often been portrayed as unbridgeable and immutable.

Men and women have historically been portrayed as polar opposites with innately different abilities and capacities. The very traits that are considered positive in a man are seen as signs of dysfunction in a woman, and the qualities that are praised in women are often ridiculed in men. We need only look at the representation of women in U.S. politics where, despite making up a majority of the population, women hold less than 20 percent of congressional seats, or at the small percentage (9 percent[2]) of male nurses in the profession to see that ideas about gender differences shape our view of what men and women can and cannot do.

Race difference has been portrayed in a similarly binary fashion. White-skinned people of European origin have viewed themselves as innately superior in intelligence and ability to people with darker skin or different physical characteristics. As both the South Carolina Slave Code of 1712 and the Dred Scott Decision, in Part VII of this text, make clear, "Negroes" were believed to be members of a different and lesser race. Their enslavement, like the genocide carried out against Native Americans, was justified on the basis of these assumed differences. In the Southwest, Anglo landowners claimed that "Orientals" and Mexicans were naturally suited to perform certain kinds of brutal, sometimes crippling, farm labor to which whites were "physically unable to adapt."[3]

Class status, too, has been correlated with supposed differences in innate ability and moral worth. Property qualifications for voting have been used not only to prevent African Americans from exercising the right to vote, but also to exclude poor whites. From the beginnings of U.S. society, owning property was considered an indication of superior intelligence and character.

We begin this book with an entirely different premise. All the readings in this first part argue that far from reflecting natural and innate differences among people, the categories of gender, race, and class are socially constructed. Rather than being "given" in nature, they reflect culturally constructed differences that maintain the prevailing distribution of power and privilege in a society, and they change in relation to changes in social, political, and economic life.

At first this may seem to be a strange claim. On the face of it, whether a person is male or female or a member of a particular race seems to be a straightforward question of biology. But like most differences that are alleged to be "natural" and "immutable," or unchangeable, the categories of race and gender are far more complex than they might seem.

Social scientists often distinguish between "sex" as a category that is assigned at birth and "gender" as the particular set of socially constructed meanings that are associated with each sex. Although "sex" is often assumed to be natural or biological, even sex is socially constructed. As Susan Stryker shows in this part, sex collapses complex and diverse physiology, biology, and genetics into only two available options: male or female.

The meaning of classification as a man or as a woman differs from culture to culture and within each society as well as over different periods of time. It is this difference in connotation or meaning that theorists point to when they claim that gender is socially constructed. What is understood as "naturally" masculine or feminine behavior in one society may be the exact opposite of what is considered "natural" for women or men in another culture. Furthermore, while it is true that most societies have sex-role stereotypes that identify certain jobs or activities as appropriate for women and others for men, and claim that these divisions reflect "natural" differences in ability and/or interest, there is little consistency in the kinds of task that have been so categorized. In some societies it is women who are responsible for agricultural labor, and in others it is men. Even within cultures that claim that women are unsuited for heavy manual labor, some women (usually women of color and poor white working women) have always been expected and required to perform backbreaking physical work—on plantations, in factories, on farms, in commercial laundries, and in their homes. Anthropologist Gayle Rubin explains it this way:

Gender is a socially imposed division of the sexes. . . . Men and women are, of course, different. But they are not as different as day and night, earth and sky, yin and yang, life and death. In fact, from the standpoint of nature, men and women are closer to each other than either is to anything else—for instance, mountains, kangaroos, or coconut palms. The idea that men and women are more different from one another than either is from anything else must come from somewhere other than nature.[4]

In fact, we might go on to argue, along with Rubin, that "far from being an expression of natural differences, exclusive gender identity is the suppression of natural similarities."[5] Boys and girls, women and men, are under enormous pressure from the earliest ages to conform to sex-role stereotypes that divide basic human attributes between the two sexes. In Selection 4, Judith Lorber argues that differences between women and men are never merely differences but are constructed hierarchically so that women are always portrayed as different in the sense of being deviant and deficient. Central to this construction of difference is the social construction of sexuality, a process Jonathan Ned Katz and Michael Kimmel analyze in Selections 5 and 6. In Selection 7, Susan Stryker asks us to evaluate our assumptions about the relationship among sex, gender, and sexuality, and posits that transgender feminism reveals the limits of theorizing about gender on the basis of sexed bodies.

The idea of race has been socially constructed in similar ways. The claim that race is a social construction challenges the once-popular belief that people are born into different races that have innate, biologically based differences in intellect, temperament, and character. The idea of ethnicity, in contrast to race, focuses on the shared social/cultural experiences and heritages of various groups and divides or categorizes them according to these shared experiences and traits. The important difference here is that those who talk of race and racial identity believe that they are dividing people according to biological or genetic similarities and differences, whereas those who talk of ethnicity simply point to commonalities that are understood as social, not biological, in origin.

Contemporary historian Ronald Takaki suggests that in the United States, "[r]ace . . . has been a social construction that has historically set apart racial minorities from European immigrant groups."[6] Michael Omi and Howard Winant, authors of Selection 1, would agree. They maintain that race is more a political categorization than a biological or scientific category. They point to the relatively arbitrary way in which the category has been constructed and suggest that changes in the meaning and use of racial distinctions can be correlated with economic and political changes in U.S. society. Dark-skinned men and women from Spain were once classified as "white" along with fair-skinned immigrants from England and Ireland, whereas early Greek immigrants were often classified as "Orientals" and subjected to the same discrimination that Chinese and Japanese immigrants experienced under the laws of California and other Western states. In South Africa, Japanese immigrants were categorized as "white," not "black" or "colored," presumably because the South African economy depended on trade with Japan. In contemporary U.S. society, dark-skinned Latin people are often categorized as "black" by those who continue to equate something called "race" with skin color. In Selection 2, Pem Davidson Buck argues that whiteness and white privilege were constructed historically along with race difference in order to divide working people from each other and in this way protect the wealth and power of a small, privileged elite. In Selection 3, "How Jews Became White Folks," Karen Brodkin provides a detailed account of the specific ways in which the status and classifications of one group, Jewish immigrants to the United States, changed over time as a result of and in relation to economic, political, and social changes in our society.

The claim that race is a social construction is not meant to deny the obvious differences in skin color and physical characteristics that people manifest. It simply sees these differences on a continuum of diversity rather than as reflecting innate genetic differences among peoples. Scientists have long argued that all human beings are descended from a common stock.

Writing about racism, Algerian-born French philosopher Albert Memmi once explained that racism consists of stressing a difference between individuals or populations. The difference can be real or imagined and in itself doesn't entail racism (or, by analogy, sexism). It is not difference itself that leads to subordination, but the interpretation of difference. It is the assigning of a value to a particular difference in a way that discredits an individual or group to the advantage of another that transforms mere difference into deficiency.[7] In this country, both race and gender differences have been carefully constructed as hierarchy. This means that in the United States, it is not merely that women are described as different from men, but also that the difference is understood to leave women deficient. Similarly with race: People of color are described as different from white people, and that difference too is understood as deviance from an acceptable norm—even as pathology—and in both cases, difference is used to rationalize racism and sexism.

In Selection 6, Michael Kimmel argues that homophobia is "intimately interwoven with both sexism and racism." According to Kimmel, the ideal of masculinity that prevails in U.S. society today is one that reflects the needs and interests of capitalism. It effectively defines "women, nonwhite men, nonnative-born men, homosexual men" as "other" and deficient, and in this way renders members of all these groups as well as large numbers of white working class and middle class men powerless in contemporary society.

Our understanding of the ways in which race and gender differences have been constructed is further enriched by Douglas Baynton's analysis in Selection 9. Baynton argues that the idea of disability has functioned historically to justify unequal treatment for women and minority groups as well as to justify inequality for disabled people themselves. In his essay, he explores the ways in which the concept of disability has been used at different moments in history to disenfranchise various groups in U.S. society and to legitimize discrimination against them.

The social construction of class is analogous, but not identical, to that of race and gender. Differences between rich and poor, which result from particular ways of structuring the economy, are socially constructed as innate differences among people. These differences are then used to rationalize or justify the unequal distribution of wealth and power that results from economic decisions made to perpetuate privilege. In addition, straightforward numerical differences in earnings are rarely the basis for conferring class status. For example, school teachers and college professors are usually considered to have a higher status than plumbers and electricians, even though the earnings of plumbers and electricians are often significantly higher. Where people are presumed to fit into the class hierarchy has less to do with clear-cut numerical categories than it does with the socially constructed superiority of those who perform mental labor (i.e., work with their heads) over those who perform manual labor (i.e., work with their hands). In addition, the status of various occupations and the class position the occupations imply often change depending on whether the occupation is predominantly female or male and on its racial composition.

Equally significant, differences in wealth and family income have been overladen with value judgments and stereotypes to the extent that identifying someone as a member of the middle class, working class, or underclass carries implicit implications about his or her moral character and ability. In the nineteenth century, proponents of Calvinism and social Darwinism maintained that being poor in itself indicated that an individual was morally flawed and thus deserved his or her poverty—relieving society of any responsibility for social ills. More recently, as Susan Greenbaum discusses in Selection 8, the idea that poverty can be blamed on family structure and cultural values was brought to the fore again in the 1965 government-issued Moynihan Report, which claimed that African American family values were producing a "tangle of pathology." This approach to blaming the poor for being poor refuses to see poverty as a social and economic problem that we can collectively address.

Finally, class difference can be said to be socially constructed in a way that parallels the construction of race and gender as difference. In this respect, the organization of U.S. society makes hierarchy or class itself appear natural and inevitable. We grade and rank children from their earliest ages and claim to be sorting them according to something called "natural ability." The tracking that permeates our system of education both reflects and creates the expectation that there are A people, B people, C people, and so forth. Well before high school, children come to define themselves and others in just this way and accept this kind of classification as natural. Consequently, quite apart from accepting the particular mythology or ideology of class difference prevalent at any given moment (i.e., "the poor are lazy and worthless" versus "the poor are meek and humble and will inherit the earth"), we come to think it natural and inevitable that there should be class differences in the first place. In the final essay in Part I, Jean Baker Miller asks and answers the question "What do people do to people who are different from them and why?"

NOTES

1. Steve Hill, "Why Does the US Still Have So Few Women in Office?" *The Nation.* March 7, 2014.
2. American Nurses Association. The Practice of Professional Nursing Work Force. "Fast Fact 2014" Retrieved November 25th, 2015 (http://www.nursingworld.org /MainMenuCategories/ThePracticeofProfessionalNursing/workforce/Fast-Facts-2014 -Nursing-Workforce.pdf)
3. Ronald Takaki, *A Different Mirror: Multicultural American History* (Boston: Little, Brown, 1993), p. 321.
4. Gayle Rubin, "The Traffic in Women," in *Toward an Anthropology of Women*, Rayna R. Reiter, ed. (New York: Monthly Review Press, 1975), p. 179.
5. Ibid., p. 180.
6. Takaki, *Different Mirror.*
7. Albert Memmi, *Dominated Man* (Boston: Beacon Press, 1968).

1 Racial Formations

Michael Omi and Howard Winant

In 1982–83, Susie Guillory Phipps unsuccessfully sued the Louisiana Bureau of Vital Records to change her racial classification from black to white. The descendant of an eighteenth-century white planter and a black slave, Phipps was designated "black" in her birth certificate in accordance with a 1970 state law which declared anyone with at least one-thirty-second "Negro blood" to be black. The legal battle raised intriguing questions about the concept of race, its meaning in contemporary society, and its use (and abuse) in public policy. Assistant Attorney General Ron Davis defended the law by pointing out that some type of racial classification was necessary to comply with federal record-keeping requirements and to facilitate programs for the prevention of genetic diseases. Phipps's attorney, Brian Begue, argued that the assignment of racial categories on birth certificates was unconstitutional and that the one-thirty-second designation was inaccurate. He called on a retired Tulane University professor who cited research indicating that most whites have one-twentieth "Negro" ancestry. In the end, Phipps lost. The court upheld a state law which quantified racial identity, and in so doing affirmed the legality of assigning individuals to specific racial groupings.[1]

The Phipps case illustrates the continuing dilemma of defining race and establishing its meaning in institutional life. Today, to assert that variations in human physiognomy are racially based is to enter a constant and intense debate. *Scientific* interpretations of race have not been alone in sparking heated controversy; *religious* perspectives have done so as well.[2] Most centrally, of course, race has been a matter of *political* contention. This has been particularly true in the United States, where the concept of race has varied enormously over time without ever leaving the center stage of US history.

What Is Race?

Race consciousness, and its articulation in theories of race, is largely a modern phenomenon. When European explorers in the New World "discovered" people who looked different than themselves, these "natives" challenged then existing conceptions of the origins of the human species, and raised disturbing questions as to whether *all* could be considered in the same "family of man."[3] Religious debates flared over the attempt to reconcile the Bible with the existence of "racially distinct" people. Arguments took place over creation itself, as theories of polygenesis questioned whether God had made only one species of humanity ("monogenesis"). Europeans wondered if the natives of the New World were indeed human beings

From Michael Omi and Howard Winant, "The Social Construction of Difference: Race, Class, Gender, and Sexuality" in *Racial Formations in the United States: From the 1960s to the 1980s*. Copyright © 1986. Reprinted by permission of the authors.

with redeemable souls. At stake were not only the prospects for conversion, but the types of treatment to be accorded them. The expropriation of property, the denial of political rights, the introduction of slavery and other forms of coercive labor, as well as outright extermination, all presupposed a worldview which distinguished Europeans—children of God, human beings, etc.—from "others." Such a world-view was needed to explain why some should be "free" and others enslaved, why some had rights to land and property while others did not. Race, and the interpreta-tion of racial differences, was a central factor in that worldview.

In the colonial epoch science was no less a field of controversy than religion in attempts to comprehend the concept of race and its meaning. Spurred on by the classificatory scheme of living organisms devised by Linnaeus in *Systema Naturae,* many scholars in the eighteenth and nineteenth centuries dedicated themselves to the identification and ranking of variations in humankind. Race was thought of as a *biological* concept, yet its precise definition was the subject of debates which, as we have noted, continue to rage today. Despite efforts ranging from Dr. Samuel Morton's studies of cranial capacity[4] to contemporary attempts to base racial classification on shared gene pools,[5] the concept of race has defied biological definition. . . .

Attempts to discern the *scientific meaning* of race continue to the present day. Although most physical anthropologists and biologists have abandoned the quest for a scientific basis to determine racial categories, controversies have recently flared in the area of genetics and educational psychology. For instance, an essay by Arthur Jensen which argued that hereditary factors shape intelligence not only revived the "nature or nurture" controversy, but raised highly volatile questions about racial equality itself.[6] Clearly the attempt to establish a *biological* basis of race has not been swept into the dustbin of history, but is being resurrected in various scientific are-nas. All such attempts seek to remove the concept of race from fundamental social, political, or economic determination. They suggest instead that the truth of race lies in the terrain of innate characteristics, of which skin color and other physical attributes provide only the most obvious, and in some respects most superficial, indicators.

Race as a Social Concept

The social sciences have come to reject biologistic notions of race in favor of an approach which regards race as a *social* concept. Beginning in the eighteenth cen-tury, this trend has been slow and uneven, but its direction clear. In the nineteenth century Max Weber discounted biological explanations for racial conflict and instead highlighted the social and political factors which engendered such conflict.[7] The work of pioneering cultural anthropologist Franz Boas was crucial in refuting the scientific racism of the early twentieth century by rejecting the connection between race and culture, and the assumption of a continuum of "higher" and "lower" cultural groups. Within the contemporary social science literature, race is assumed to be a variable which is shaped by broader societal forces.

Race is indeed a pre-eminently *sociohistorical* concept. Racial categories and the meaning of race are given concrete expression by the specific social relations and historical context in which they are embedded. Racial meanings have varied tremendously over time and between different societies.

In the United States, the black/white color line has historically been rigidly defined and enforced. White is seen as a "pure" category. Any racial intermixture makes one "nonwhite." In the movie *Raintree County*, Elizabeth Taylor describes the worst of fates to befall whites as "havin' a little Negra blood in ya'—just one little teeny drop and a person's all Negra."[8] This thinking flows from what Marvin Harris has characterized as the principle of *hypo-descent*:

> By what ingenious computation is the genetic tracery of a million years of evolution unraveled and each man [sic] assigned his proper social box? In the United States, the mechanism employed is the rule of hypo-descent. This descent rule requires Americans to believe that anyone who is known to have had a Negro ancestor is a Negro. We admit nothing in between. . . . "Hypo-descent" means affiliation with the subordinate rather than the superordinate group in order to avoid the ambiguity of intermediate identity. . . . The rule of hypo-descent is, therefore, an invention, which we in the United States have made in order to keep biological facts from intruding into our collective racist fantasies.[9]

The Susie Guillory Phipps case merely represents the contemporary expression of this racial logic.

By contrast, a striking feature of race relations in the lowland areas of Latin America since the abolition of slavery has been the relative absence of sharply defined racial groupings. No such rigid descent rule characterizes racial identity in many Latin American societies. Brazil, for example, has historically had less rigid conceptions of race, and thus a variety of "intermediate" racial categories exists. Indeed, as Harris notes, "One of the most striking consequences of the Brazilian system of racial identification is that parents and children and even brothers and sisters are frequently accepted as representatives of quite opposite racial types."[10] Such a possibility is incomprehensible within the logic of racial categories in the US.

To suggest another example: the notion of "passing" takes on new meaning if we compare various American cultures' means of assigning racial identity. In the United States, individuals who are actually "black" by the logic of hypo-descent have attempted to skirt the discriminatory barriers imposed by law and custom by attempting to "pass" for white.[11] Ironically, these same individuals would not be able to pass for "black" in many Latin American societies.

Consideration of the term "black" illustrates the diversity of racial meanings which can be found among different societies and historically within a given society. In contemporary British politics the term "black" is used to refer to all nonwhites. Interestingly this designation has not arisen through the racist discourse of groups such as the National Front. Rather, in political and cultural movements, Asian as well as Afro-Caribbean youth are adopting the term as an expression of self-identity.[12] The wide-ranging meanings of "black" illustrate the manner in which racial categories are shaped politically.[13]

The meaning of race is defined and contested throughout society, in both collective action and personal practice. In the process, racial categories themselves are formed, transformed, destroyed and re-formed. We use the term *racial formation* to refer to the process by which social, economic and political forces determine the content and importance of racial categories, and by which they are in turn shaped by racial meanings. Crucial to this formulation is the treatment of race as a *central axis* of social relations which cannot be subsumed under or reduced to some broader category or conception.

Racial Ideology and Racial Identity

The seemingly obvious, "natural" and "common sense" qualities which the existing racial order exhibits themselves testify to the effectiveness of the racial formation process in constructing racial meanings and racial identities.

One of the first things we notice about people when we meet them (along with their sex) is their race. We utilize race to provide clues about *who* a person is. This fact is made painfully obvious when we encounter someone whom we cannot conveniently racially categorize—someone who is, for example, racially "mixed" or of an ethnic/racial group with which we are not familiar. Such an encounter becomes a source of discomfort and momentarily a crisis of racial meaning. Without a racial identity, one is in danger of having no identity.

Our compass for navigating race relations depends on preconceived notions of what each specific racial group looks like. Comments such as, "Funny, you don't look black," betray an underlying image of what black should be. We also become disoriented when people do not act "black," "Latino," or indeed "white." The content of such stereotypes reveals a series of unsubstantiated beliefs about who these groups are and what "they" are like.[14]

In US society, then, a kind of "racial etiquette" exists, a set of interpretative codes and racial meanings which operate in the interactions of daily life. Rules shaped by our perception of race in a comprehensively racial society determine the "presentation of self,"[15] distinctions of status, and appropriate modes of conduct. "Etiquette" is not mere universal adherence to the dominant group's rules, but a more dynamic combination of these rules with the values and beliefs of subordinated groupings. This racial "subjection" is quintessentially ideological. Everybody learns some combination, some version, of the rules of racial classification, and of their own racial identity, often without obvious teaching or conscious inculcation. Race becomes "common sense"—a way of comprehending, explaining and acting in the world.

Racial beliefs operate as an "amateur biology," a way of explaining the variations in "human nature."[16] Differences in skin color and other obvious physical characteristics supposedly provide visible clues to differences lurking underneath. Temperament, sexuality, intelligence, athletic ability, aesthetic preferences and so on are presumed to be fixed and discernible from the palpable mark of race. Such diverse questions as our confidence and trust in others (for example, clerks or salespeople, media figures, neighbors), our sexual preferences and romantic images, our tastes in music, films, dance, or sports, and our very ways of talking, walking, eating and dreaming are ineluctably shaped by notions of race. Skin color "differences" are thought to explain perceived differences in intellectual, physical and artistic temperaments, and to justify distinct treatment of racially identified individuals and groups.

The continuing persistence of racial ideology suggests that these racial myths and stereotypes cannot be exposed as such in the popular imagination. They are, we think, too essential, too integral, to the maintenance of the US social order. Of course, particular meanings, stereotypes and myths can change, but the presence of a *system* of racial meanings and stereotypes, of racial ideology, seems to be a permanent feature of US culture.

Film and television, for example, have been notorious in disseminating images of racial minorities which establish for audiences what people from these groups look like, how they behave, and "who they are."[17] The power of the media lies not only in their ability to reflect the dominant racial ideology, but in their capacity to shape that ideology in the first place. D. W. Griffith's epic *Birth of a Nation,* a sympathetic treatment of the rise of the Ku Klux Klan during Reconstruction, helped to generate, consolidate and "nationalize" images of blacks which had been more disparate (more regionally specific, for example) prior to the film's appearance.[18] In US television, the necessity to define characters in the briefest and most condensed manner has led to the perpetuation of racial caricatures, as racial stereotypes serve as shorthand for scriptwriters, directors and actors, in commercials, etc. Television's tendency to address the "lowest common denominator" in order to render programs "familiar" to an enormous and diverse audience leads it regularly to assign and reassign racial characteristics to particular groups, both minority and majority.

These and innumerable other examples show that we tend to view race as something fixed and immutable—something rooted in "nature." Thus we mask the historical construction of racial categories, the shifting meaning of race, and the crucial role of politics and ideology in shaping race relations. Races do not emerge full blown. They are the results of diverse historical practices and are continually subject to challenge over their definition and meaning.

Racialization: The Historical Development of Race

In the United States, the racial category of "black" evolved with the consolidation of racial slavery. By the end of the seventeenth century, Africans whose specific identity was Ibo, Yoruba, Fulani, etc. were rendered "black" by an ideology of exploitation based on racial logic—the establishment and maintenance of a "color line." This of course did not occur overnight. A period of indentured servitude which was not rooted in racial logic preceded the consolidation of racial slavery. With slavery, however, a racially based understanding of society was set in motion which resulted in the shaping of a specific *racial* identity not only for the slaves but for the European settlers as well. Winthrop Jordan has observed: "From the initially common term *Christian,* at mid-century there was a marked shift toward the terms *English* and *free.* After about 1680, taking the colonies as a whole, a new term of self-identification appeared—*white*."[19]

We employ the term *racialization* to signify the extension of racial meaning to a previously racially unclassified relationship, social practice or group. Racialization is an ideological process, an historically specific one. Racial ideology is constructed from pre-existing conceptual (or, if one prefers, "discursive") elements and emerges from the struggles of competing political projects and ideas seeking to articulate similar elements differently. An account of racialization processes that avoids the pitfalls of US ethnic history[20] remains to be written.

Particularly during the nineteenth century, the category of "white" was subject to challenges brought about by the influx of diverse groups who were not of the same Anglo-Saxon stock as the founding immigrants. In the nineteenth century, political and ideological struggles emerged over the classification of Southern Europeans, the Irish and Jews, among other "non-white" categories.[21] Nativism was only effectively curbed by the institutionalization of a racial order that drew the color line *around,* rather than *within,* Europe.

By stopping short of racializing immigrants from Europe after the Civil War, and by subsequently allowing their assimilation, the American racial order was recon-solidated in the wake of the tremendous challenge placed before it by the abolition of racial slavery.[22] With the end of Reconstruction in 1877, an effective program for limiting the emergent class struggles of the later nineteenth century was forged: the definition of the working class *in racial terms*—as "white." This was not accomplished by any legislative decree or capitalist maneuvering to divide the working class, but rather by white workers themselves. Many of them were recent immigrants, who organized on racial lines as much as on traditionally defined class lines.[23] The Irish on the West Coast, for example, engaged in vicious anti-Chinese race-baiting and committed many pogrom-type assaults on Chinese in the course of consolidating the trade union movement in California.

Thus the very political organization of the working class was in important ways a racial project. The legacy of racial conflicts and arrangements shaped the definition of interests and in turn led to the consolidation of institutional patterns (e.g., segregated unions, dual labor markets, exclusionary legislation) which perpetuated the color line *within* the working class. Selig Perlman, whose study of the development of the labor movement is fairly sympathetic to this process, notes that:

> The political issue after 1877 was racial, not financial, and the weapon was not merely the ballot, but also "direct action"—violence. The anti-Chinese agitation in California, culminating as it did in the Exclusion Law passed by Congress in 1882, was doubtless the most important single factor in the history of American labor, for without it the entire country might have been overrun by Mongolian [sic] labor and *the labor movement might have become a conflict of races instead of one of classes.*[24]

More recent economic transformations in the US have also altered interpretations of racial identities and meanings. The automation of southern agriculture and the augmented labor demand of the postwar boom transformed blacks from a largely rural, impoverished labor force to a largely urban, working-class group by 1970.[25]

When boom became bust and liberal welfare statism moved rightwards, the majority of blacks came to be seen, increasingly, as part of the "underclass," as state "dependents." Thus the particularly deleterious effects on blacks of global and national economic shifts (generally rising unemployment rates, changes in the employment structure away from reliance on labor intensive work, etc.) were explained once again in the late 1970s and 1980s (as they had been in the 1940s and mid-1960s) as the result of defective black cultural norms, of familial disorganization, etc.[26] In this way new racial attributions, new racial myths, are affixed to "blacks."[27] Similar changes in racial identity are presently affecting Asians and Latinos, as such economic forces as increasing Third World impoverishment and indebtedness fuel immigration and high interest rates, Japanese competition spurs resentments, and US jobs seem to fly away to Korea and Singapore.[28]. . .

Once we understand that race overflows the boundaries of skin color, super-exploitation, social stratification, discrimination and prejudice, cultural domination and cultural resistance, state policy (or of any other particular social relationship we list), once we recognize the racial dimension present to some degree in *every* identity, institution and social practice in the United States—once we have done this, it becomes possible to speak of *racial formation*. This recognition is hard-won; there is a continuous temptation to think of race as an *essence,* as something fixed, concrete and objective, as (for example) one of the categories just enumerated. And there is also an opposite temptation: to see it as a mere illusion, which an ideal social order would eliminate.

In our view it is crucial to break with these habits of thought. The effort must be made to understand race as *an unstable and "decentered" complex of social meanings constantly being transformed by political struggle.* . . .

NOTES

1. *San Francisco Chronicle,* 14 September 1982, 19 May 1983. Ironically, the 1970 Louisiana law was enacted to supersede an old Jim Crow statute which relied on the idea of "common report" in determining an infant's race. Following Phipps's unsuccessful attempt to change her classification and have the law declared unconstitutional, a legislative effort arose which culminated in the repeal of the law. See *San Francisco Chronicle,* 23 June 1983.

2. The Mormon church, for example, has been heavily criticized for its doctrine of black inferiority.

3. Thomas F. Gossett notes:

> Race theory . . . had up until fairly modern times no firm hold on European thought. On the other hand, race theory and race prejudice were by no means unknown at the time when the English colonists came to North America. Undoubtedly, the age of exploration led many to speculate on race differences at a period when neither Europeans nor Englishmen were prepared to make allowances for vast cultural diversities. Even though race theories had not then secured wide acceptance or even sophisticated formulation, the first contacts of the Spanish with the Indians in the Americas can now be recognized as the beginning of a struggle between

conceptions of the nature of primitive peoples which has not yet been wholly settled. (Thomas F. Gossett, *Race: The History of an Idea in America* [New York: Schocken Books, 1965], p. 16).

Winthrop Jordan provides a detailed account of early European colonialists' attitudes about color and race in *White Over Black: American Attitudes Toward the Negro, 1550–1812* (New York: Norton, 1977 [1968]), pp. 3–43.

4. Pro-slavery physician Samuel George Morton (1799–1851) compiled a collection of 800 crania from all parts of the world which formed the sample for his studies of race. Assuming that the larger the size of the cranium translated into greater intelligence, Morton established a relationship between race and skull capacity. Gossett reports that:

In 1849, one of his studies included the following results: The English skulls in his collection proved to be the largest, with an average cranial capacity of 96 cubic inches. The Americans and Germans were rather poor seconds, both with cranial capacities of 90 cubic inches. At the bottom of the list were the Negroes with 83 cubic inches, the Chinese with 82, and the Indians with 79. (Ibid., p. 74).

On Morton's methods, see Stephen J. Gould, "The Finagle Factor," *Human Nature* (July 1978).

5. Definitions of race founded upon a common pool of genes have not held up when confronted by scientific research which suggests that the differences *within* a given human population are greater than those *between* populations. See L. L. Cavalli-Sforza, "The Genetics of Human Populations," *Scientific American* (September 1974), pp. 81–9.

6. Arthur Jensen, "How Much Can We Boost IQ and Scholastic Achievement?" *Harvard Educational Review,* vol. 39 (1969), pp. 1–123.

7. Ernst Moritz Manasse, "Max Weber on Race," *Social Research,* vol. 14 (1947), pp. 191–221.

8. Quoted in Edward D. C. Campbell, Jr., *The Celluloid South: Hollywood and the Southern Myth* (Knoxville: University of Tennessee Press, 1981), pp. 168–70.

9. Marvin Harris, *Patterns of Race in the Americas* (New York: Norton, 1964), p. 56.

10. Ibid., p. 57.

11. After James Meredith had been admitted as the first black student at the University of Mississippi, Harry S. Murphy announced that he, and not Meredith, was the first black student to attend "Ole Miss." Murphy described himself as black but was able to pass for white and spent nine months at the institution without attracting any notice (ibid., p. 56).

12. A. Sivanandan, "From Resistance to Rebellion: Asian and Afro-Caribbean Struggles in Britain," *Race and Class,* vol. 23, nos. 2–3 (Autumn–Winter 1981).

13. Consider the contradictions in racial status which abound in the country with the most rigidly defined racial categories—South Africa. There a race classification agency is employed to adjudicate claims for upgrading of official racial identity. This is particularly necessary for the "coloured" category. The apartheid system considers Chinese as "Asians" while the Japanese are accorded the status of "honorary whites." This logic nearly detaches race from any grounding in skin color and other physical attributes and nakedly exposes race as a juridical category subject to economic, social and political influences. (We are indebted to Steve Talbot for clarification of some of these points.)

14. Gordon W. Allport, *The Nature of Prejudice* (Garden City, New York: Doubleday, 1958), pp. 184–200.

15. We wish to use this phrase loosely, without committing ourselves to a particular position on such social psychological approaches as symbolic interactionism, which are outside

the scope of this study. An interesting study on this subject is S. M. Lyman and W. A. Douglass, "Ethnicity: Strategies of Individual and Collective Impression Management," *Social Research*, vol. 40, no. 2 (1973).

16. Michael Billig, "Patterns of Racism: Interviews with National Front Members," *Race and Class*, vol. 20, no. 2 (Autumn 1978), pp. 161–79.

17. "Miss San Antonio USA Lisa Fernandez and other Hispanics auditioning for a role in a television soap opera did not fit the Hollywood image of real Mexicans and had to darken their faces before filming." Model Aurora Garza said that their faces were bronzed with powder because they looked too white. "'I'm a real Mexican [Garza said] and very dark anyway. I'm even darker right now because I have a tan. But they kept wanting me to make my face darker and darker'" (*San Francisco Chronicle*, 21 September 1984). A similar dilemma faces Asian American actors who feel that Asian character lead roles inevitably go to white actors who make themselves up to be Asian. Scores of Charlie Chan films, for example, have been made with white leads (the last one was the 1981 *Charlie Chan and the Curse of the Dragon Queen*). Roland Winters, who played in six Chan features, was asked by playwright Frank Chin to explain the logic of casting a white man in the role of Charlie Chan: "'The only thing I can think of is, if you want to cast a homosexual in a show, and you get a homosexual, it'll be awful. It won't be funny . . . and maybe there's something there . . .'" (Frank Chin, "Confessions of the Chinatown Cowboy," *Bulletin of Concerned Asian Scholars*, vol. 4, no. 3 [Fall 1972]).

18. Melanie Martindale-Sikes, "Nationalizing 'Nigger' Imagery Through 'Birth of a Nation'," paper prepared for the 73rd Annual Meeting of the American Sociological Association, 4–8 September 1978, in San Francisco.

19. Winthrop D. Jordan, op. cit., p. 95; emphasis added.

20. Historical focus has been placed either on particular racially defined groups or on immigration and the "incorporation" of ethnic groups. In the former case the characteristic ethnicity theory pitfalls and apologetics such as functionalism and cultural pluralism may be avoided, but only by sacrificing much of the focus on race. In the latter case, race is considered a manifestation of ethnicity.

21. The degree of antipathy for these groups should not be minimized. A northern commentator observed in the 1850s: "An Irish Catholic seldom attempts to rise to a higher condition than that in which he is placed, while the Negro often makes the attempt with success." Quoted in Gossett, op. cit., p. 288.

22. This analysis, as will perhaps be obvious, is essentially DuBoisian. Its main source will be found in the monumental (and still largely unappreciated) *Black Reconstruction in the United States, 1860–1880* (New York: Atheneum, 1977 [1935]).

23. Alexander Saxton argues that:

> North Americans of European background have experienced three great racial confrontations: with the Indian, with the African, and with the Oriental. Central to each transaction has been a totally one-sided preponderance of power, exerted for the exploitation of nonwhites by the dominant white society. In each case (but especially in the two that began with systems of enforced labor), white workingmen have played a crucial, yet ambivalent, role. They have been both exploited and exploiters. On the one hand, thrown into competition with nonwhites as enslaved or "cheap" labor, they suffered economically; on the other hand, being white, they benefited by that very exploitation which was compelling the nonwhites to work for low wages or for nothing. Ideologically they were drawn in opposite directions. *Racial identification cut at right angles to class consciousness.* (Alexander Saxton, *The*

Indispensable Enemy: Labor and the Anti-Chinese Movement in California (Berkeley and Los Angeles: University of California Press, 1971), p. 1; emphasis added.)

24. Selig Perlman, *The History of Trade Unionism in the United States* (New York: Augustus Kelley, 1950), p. 52; emphasis added.
25. Whether southern blacks were "peasants" or rural workers is unimportant in this context. Sometime during the 1960s blacks attained a higher degree of urbanization than whites. Before World War II most blacks had been rural dwellers and nearly 80 percent lived in the South.
26. See George Gilder, *Wealth and Poverty* (New York: Basic Books, 1981); Charles Murray, *Losing Ground* (New York: Basic Books, 1984).
27. A brilliant study of the racialization process in Britain, focused on the rise of "mugging" as a popular fear in the 1970s, in Stuart Hall *et al., Policing the Crisis* (London: Macmillan, 1978).
28. The case of Vincent Chin, a Chinese American man beaten to death in 1982 by a laid-off Detroit auto worker and his stepson who mistook him for Japanese and blamed him for the loss of their jobs, has been widely publicized in Asian American communities. On immigration conflicts and pressures, see Michael Omi, "New Wave Dread: Immigration and Intra–Third World Conflict," *Socialist Review,* no. 60 (November–December 1981).

2 Constructing Race, Creating White Privilege

Pem Davidson Buck

Constructing Race

Improbable as it now seems, since Americans live in a society where racial characterization and self-definition appear to be parts of nature, in the early days of colonization before slavery was solidified and clearly distinguished from other forms of forced labor, Europeans and Africans seem not to have seen their physical differences in that way.[1] It took until the end of the 1700s for ideas about race to develop until they resembled those we live with today. Before Bacon's Rebellion, African and European indentured servants made love with each other, married each other, ran away with each other, lived as neighbors, liked or disliked each other according to individual personality. Sometimes they died or were punished together for resisting or revolting. And masters had to free both Europeans and Africans if they survived to the end of their indentures. Likewise, Europeans initially did not place all Native Americans in a single racial category. They saw cultural, not biological, differences among Native Americans as distinguishing one tribe from another and from themselves.

Given the tendency of slaves, servants, and landless free Europeans and Africans to cooperate in rebellion, the elite had to "teach Whites the value of whiteness" in order to divide and rule their labor force.[2] After Bacon's Rebellion they utilized their domination of colonial legislatures that made laws and of courts that administered them, gradually building a racial strategy based on the earlier tightening and lengthening of African indenture. Part of this process was tighter control of voting. Free property-owning blacks, mulattos, and Native Americans, all identified as *not* of European ancestry, were denied the vote in 1723.[3]

To keep the racial categories separate, a 1691 law increased the punishment of European women who married African or Indian men; toward the end of the 1600s a white woman could be whipped or enslaved for marrying a Black. Eventually enslavement for white women was abolished because it transgressed the definition of slavery as black. The problem of what to do with white women's "black" children was eventually partially solved by the control of white women's reproduction to prevent the existence of such children. The potentially "white" children of black women were defined out of existence; they were "black" and shifted from serving a thirty-year indenture to being slaves. To facilitate these reproductive distinctions and to discourage the intimacy that can lead to solidarity and revolts, laws were passed requiring separate quarters for black and white laborers. Kathleen Brown points out that the control of women's bodies thus became critical to the maintenance of whiteness and

From *Worked to the Bone.* Copyright © Monthly Review Press, 2001. Reprinted by permission.

to the production of slaves.[4] At the same time black men were denied the rights of colonial masculinity as property ownership, guns, and access to white women were forbidden. Children were made to inherit their mother's status, freeing European fathers from any vestiges of responsibility for their offspring born to indentured or enslaved African mothers. This legal shift has had a profound effect on the distribution of wealth in the United States ever since; slaveholding fathers were some of the richest men in the country, and their wealth, distributed among *all* their children, would have created a significant wealthy black segment of the population.

At the same time a changing panoply of specific laws molded European behavior into patterns that made slave revolt and cross-race unity more and more difficult.[5] These laws limited, for instance, the European right to teach slaves to read. Europeans couldn't use slaves in skilled jobs, which were reserved for Europeans. Europeans had to administer prescribed punishment for slave "misbehavior" and were expected to participate in patrolling at night. They did not have the legal right to befriend Blacks. A white servant who ran away with a Black was subject to additional punishment beyond that for simply running away. European rights to free their slaves were also curtailed.

Built into all this, rarely mentioned but nevertheless basic to the elite's ability to create and maintain whiteness, slavery, and exploitation, was the use of force against both Blacks and Whites. Fear kept many Whites from challenging, or even questioning, the system. It is worth quoting Lerone Bennett's analysis of how the differentiation between black and white was accomplished:

> The whole system of separation and subordination rested on official state terror. The exigencies of the situation required men to kill some white people to keep them white and to kill many blacks to keep them black. In the North and South, men and women were maimed, tortured, and murdered in a comprehensive campaign of mass conditioning. The severed heads of black and white rebels were impaled on poles along the road as warnings to black people and white people, and opponents of the status quo were starved to death in chains and roasted slowly over open fires. Some rebels were branded; others were castrated. This exemplary cruelty, which was carried out as a deliberate process of mass education, was an inherent part of the new system.[6]

Creating White Privilege

White privileges were established. The "daily exercise of white personal power over black individuals had become a cherished aspect of Southern culture," a critically important part of getting Whites to "settle for being white."[7] Privilege encouraged Whites to identify with the big slaveholding planters as members of the same "race." They were led to act on the belief that all Whites had an equal interest in the maintenance of whiteness and white privilege, and that it was the elite—those controlling the economic system, the political system, and the judicial system—who ultimately protected the benefits of being white.[8]

More pain could be inflicted on Blacks than on Whites.[9] Whites alone could bear arms; Whites alone had the right of self-defense. White servants could own livestock; Africans couldn't. It became illegal to whip naked Whites. Whites but not Africans had to be given their freedom dues at the end of their indenture. Whites were given the right to beat any Blacks, even those they didn't own, for failing to show proper respect. Only Whites could be hired to force black labor as overseers. White servants and laborers were given lighter tasks and a monopoly, for a time, on skilled jobs. White men were given the right to control "their" women without elite interference; Blacks as slaves were denied the right to family at all, since family would mean that slave husbands, not owners, controlled slave wives. In 1668, all free African women were defined as labor, for whom husbands or employers had to pay a tithe, while white women were defined as keepers of men's homes, not as labor; their husbands paid no tax on them. White women were indirectly given control of black slaves and the right to substitute slave labor for their own labor in the fields.

Despite these privileges, landless Whites, some of them living in "miserable huts," might have rejected white privilege if they saw that in fact it made little *positive* difference in their lives, and instead merely protected them from the worst *negative* effects of elite punishment and interference, such as were inflicted on those of African descent.[10] After all, the right to whip someone doesn't cure your own hunger or landlessness. By the end of the Revolutionary War unrest was in the air. Direct control by the elite was no longer politically or militarily feasible. Rebellions and attempted rebellions had been fairly frequent in the hundred years following Bacon's Rebellion.[11] They indicated the continuing depth of landless European discontent. Baptist ferment against the belief in the inherent superiority of the upper classes simply underscored the danger.[12]

So landless Europeans had to be given some *material* reason to reject those aspects of their lives that made them similar to landless Africans and Native Americans, and to focus instead on their similarity to the landed Europeans—to accept whiteness as their defining characteristic. Landless Europeans' only real similarity to the elite was their European ancestry itself, so that ancestry had to be given real significance: European ancestry was identified with upward mobility and the right to use the labor of the non-eligible in their upward climb. So, since land at that time was the source of upward mobility, land had to be made available, if only to a few.

Meanwhile, Thomas Jefferson advocated the establishment of a solid white Anglo-Saxon yeoman class of small farmers, who, as property owners, would acquire a vested interest in law and order and reject class conflict with the elite. These small farmers would, by upholding "law and order," support and sometimes administer the legal mechanisms—jails, workhouses and poorhouses, and vagrancy laws—that would control other Whites who would remain a landless labor force. They would support the legal and illegal mechanisms controlling Native Americans, Africans, and poor Whites, becoming a buffer class between the elite and those they most exploited, disguising the elite's continuing grip on power and wealth. . . .

The Psychological Wage

The initial construction of whiteness had been based on a material benefit for Whites: land, or the apparently realistic hope of land. By the 1830s and 1840s, most families identified by their European descent had had several generations of believing their whiteness was real. But its material benefit had faded. Many Whites were poor, selling their labor either as farm renters or as industrial workers, and they feared wage slavery, no longer certain they were much freer than slaves.[13] But this time, to control unrest, the elite had no material benefits they were willing to part with. Nor were employers willing to raise wages. Instead, politicians and elites emphasized whiteness as a benefit in itself.

The work of particular white intellectuals, who underscored the already existing belief in white superiority and the worries about white slavery, was funded by elites and published in elite-owned printing houses.[14] These intellectuals provided fodder for newspaper discussions, speeches, scientific analysis, novels, sermons, songs, and blackface minstrel shows in which white superiority was phrased as if whiteness in and of itself was naturally a benefit, despite its lack of material advantage. This sense of superiority allowed struggling northern Whites to look down their noses at free Blacks and at recent immigrants, particularly the Irish. This version of whiteness was supposed to make up for their otherwise difficult situation, providing them with a "psychological wage" instead of cash—a bit like being employee of the month and given a special parking place instead of a raise.

Many Whites bought into the psychological wage, expressing their superiority over non-Whites and defining them, rather than the capitalists, as the enemy. They focused, often with trade union help, on excluding Blacks and immigrants from skilled trades and better-paying jobs. Employers cooperated in confining Blacks and immigrants to manual labor and domestic work, making a clear definition of the work suitable for white men.[15] Native white men began shifting away from defining themselves by their landowning freedom and independence. Instead they accepted their dependence on capitalists and the control employers exercised over their lives, and began to define themselves by their class position as skilled "mechanics" working for better wages under better working conditions than other people. They became proud of their productivity, which grew with the growing efficiency of industrial technology, and began using it to define whiteness—and manhood. The ethic of individual hard work gained far wider currency. Successful competition in the labor marketplace gradually became a mark of manhood, and "white man's work" became the defining characteristic of whiteness.[16] Freedom was equated with the right to own and sell your own labor, as opposed to slavery, which allowed neither right. Independence was now defined not only by property ownership but also by possession of skill and tools that allowed wage-earning men to acquire status as a head of household controlling dependents.[17]

This redefinition of whiteness was built as much on changing gender as on changing class relationships.[18] Many native white men and women, including workers, journalists, scientists, and politicians, began discouraging married women from working for wages, claiming that true women served only their own families. Despite this claim—the cult of domesticity, or of true womanhood—many wives of working class men actually did work outside the home. They were less likely to do so in those cases where native men were able, through strikes and the exclusion of women, immigrants, and free Blacks, to create an artificial labor shortage. Such shortages gave native working class men the leverage to force employers to pay them enough to afford a non-earning wife. Women in the families of such men frequently did "stay home" and frequently helped to promote the idea that people who couldn't do the same were genetically or racially or culturally inferior.

But native Whites whose wages actually weren't sufficient struggled on in poverty. If a native woman worked for wages, particularly in a factory, the family lost status. Many female factory workers were now immigrants rather than native Whites. Many had no husband or had husbands whose wages, when they could get work, came nowhere near supporting a family.[19] It is no wonder immigrant women weren't particularly "domestic." Such families didn't meet the cultural requirements for white privilege—male "productivity" in "white man's work" and dependent female "domesticity." These supposed white virtues became a bludgeon with which to defend white privilege and to deny it to not-quite-Whites and not-Whites, helping to construct a new working class hierarchy. This new hierarchy reserved managerial and skilled jobs for "productive" native Whites. So, for the price of reserving better jobs for some native Whites, the capitalist class gained native white consent to their own loss of independence and to keeping most of the working class on abysmally low wages.

In the South, where there was less industry, the psychological wage slowly developed an additional role. It was used not only to gain consent to oppressive industrial relations, but also to convince poor farming Whites to support Southern elites in their conflict with Northern elites. Du Bois points out that by the Civil War

> . . . it became the fashion to pat the disenfranchised poor white man on the back and tell him after all he was white and that he and the planters had a common object in keeping the white man superior. This virus increased bitterness and relentless hatred, and after the war it became a chief ingredient in the division of the working class in the Southern States.[20]

REFERENCES

1. My discussion of the construction of race and racial slavery is deeply indebted to Lerone Bennett, *The Shaping of Black America* (New York: Penguin Books, 1993 [1975]), 1–109. See also Theodore Allen, *Invention of the White Race*, vol. II, *The Origin of Racial Oppression in Anglo-America* (New York: Verso, 1997), 75–109; Audrey Smedley, *Race in North America: Origin and Evolution of a Worldview* (Boulder: Westview Press, 1993), 100–1, 109, 142–3, 198; Kathleen Brown, *Good Wives, Nasty Wenches, and Anxious Patriarchs: Gender, Race, and Power in Colonial Virginia* (Chapel Hill: University of North Carolina Press, 1996), 107–244; bell hooks, *Ain't I a Woman: Black Women and Feminism* (Boston: South End Press, 1981), 15–51.

2. Bennett, *Shaping of Black America*, 74–5.

3. Allen, *Invention*, vol. II, 241.

4. Brown, *Good Wives*, pays particular attention to control of women's bodies and status in producing slavery and race (see especially 181, 129–33, 116); also see Allen, *Invention*, vol. II, 128–35, 146–7, 177–88; Bennett, *Shaping of Black America*, 75.

5. For this section see Bennett, *Shaping of Black America,* 72; Edmund Morgan, *American Slavery, American Freedom: The Ordeal of Colonial Virginia* (New York: W. W. Norton and Co, 1975), 311–3; Allen, *Invention,* vol. II, 249–53.

6. Bennett, *Shaping of Black America,* 73–4.

7. The first quote is from Smedley, *Race in North America,* 224; the second is from David Roediger, *The Wages of Whiteness: Race and the Making of the American Working Class* (New York: Verso, 1991), 6.

8. Allen, *Invention,* vol. II, 162, 248–53, emphasizes that elites invented white supremacy to protect their own interests, although working-class Whites did much of the "dirty work" of oppression.

9. Morgan, *American Slavery,* 312–3. On white privileges see Ronald Takaki, *A Different Mirror: A History of Multicultural America* (Boston: Little, Brown, 1993), 67–8; Allen, *Invention,* vol. II, 250–3; Brown, *Good Wives,* 180–3.

10. The quote is from Allen, *Invention,* vol. II, 256, citing a contemporary traveler.

11. Howard Zinn, *A People's History of the United States* (New York: HarperCollins, 1995, 2nd ed.), 58.

12. Smedley, *Race in North America,* 174–5.

13. Bennett, *Shaping of Black America,* 10, 44–5.

14. Allen, *Invention,* vol. I, 109.

15. On runaways see Morgan, *American Slavery, American Freedom,* 217; Smedley, *Race,* 103–5; Bennett, *Shaping of Black America,* 55.

16. On the tendency to make common cause, see Allen, *Invention,* vol. II, 148–58; Bennett, *Shaping of Black America,* 19–22, 74. On increasing anger and landlessness see Allen, *Invention,* vol. II, 208–9, 343 n. 33; Ronald Takaki, *A Different Mirror: A History of Multicultural America* (Boston: Little, Brown, 1993), 62.

17. Berkeley is quoted in Takaki, *Different Mirror,* 63.

18. On Bacon's Rebellion see Takaki, *Different Mirror,* 63–5; Morgan, *American Slavery, American Freedom,* 254–70; Allen, *Invention,* vol. II, 163–5, 208–17, 239; Brown, *Good Wives,* 137–86. Although interpretations of the rebellion vary widely, it does seem clear that the frightening aspect of the rebellion for those who controlled the drainage system was its dramatic demonstration of the power of a united opposition to those who monopolized land, labor, and trade with Native Americans.

19. Allan Kulikoff, *Tobacco and Slaves: The Development of Southern Cultures in the Chesapeake 1680–1800* (Chapel Hill: University of North Carolina Press, 1986), 77, 104–17.

20. Morgan, *American Slavery, American Freedom,* 271–9.

How Jews Became White Folks

And What That Says About Race in America

Karen Brodkin

> The American nation was founded and developed by the Nordic race, but if a few more million members of the Alpine, Mediterranean and Semitic races are poured among us, the result must inevitably be a hybrid race of people as worthless and futile as the good-for-nothing mongrels of Central America and Southeastern Europe.
> —KENNETH ROBERTS, "WHY EUROPE LEAVES HOME"

It is clear that Kenneth Roberts did not think of my ancestors as white, like him. The late nineteenth century and early decades of the twentieth saw a steady stream of warnings by scientists, policymakers, and the popular press that "mongrelization" of the Nordic or Anglo-Saxon race—the real Americans—by inferior European races (as well as by inferior non-European ones) was destroying the fabric of the nation.

I continue to be surprised when I read books that indicate that America once regarded its immigrant European workers as something other than white, as biologically different. My parents are not surprised; they expect anti-Semitism to be part of the fabric of daily life, much as I expect racism to be part of it. They came of age in the Jewish world of the 1920s and 1930s, at the peak of anti-Semitism in America.[1] They are rightly proud of their upward mobility and think of themselves as pulling themselves up by their own bootstraps. I grew up during the 1950s in the Euro-ethnic New York suburb of Valley Stream, where Jews were simply one kind of white folks and where ethnicity meant little more to my generation than food and family heritage. Part of my ethnic heritage was the belief that Jews were smart and that our success was due to our own efforts and abilities, reinforced by a culture that valued sticking together, hard work, education, and deferred gratification.

I am willing to affirm all those abilities and ideals and their contribution to Jews' upward mobility, but I also argue that they were still far from sufficient to account for Jewish success. . . . Instead I want to suggest that Jewish success is a product not only of ability but also of the removal of powerful social barriers to its realization.

It is certainly true that the United States has a history of anti-Semitism and of beliefs that Jews are members of an inferior race. But Jews were hardly alone. American anti-Semitism was part of a broader pattern of late-nineteenth-century racism against all southern and eastern European immigrants, as well as against Asian immigrants, not to mention African Americans, Native Americans, and Mexicans. These views

Brodkin, Karen. *How Jews Became White Folks and What That Says About Race in America*. Copyright © 1998 by Karen Brodkin. Reprinted by permission of Rutgers University Press.

justified all sorts of discriminatory treatment, including closing the doors, between 1882 and 1927, to immigration from Europe and Asia. This picture changed radically after World War II. Suddenly, the same folks who had promoted nativism and xenophobia were eager to believe that the Euro-origin people whom they had deported, reviled as members of inferior races, and prevented from immigrating only a few years earlier, were now model middle-class white suburban citizens.[2]

It was not an educational epiphany that made those in power change their hearts, their minds, and our race. Instead, it was the biggest and best affirmative action program in the history of our nation, and it was for Euromales. That is not how it was billed, but it is the way it worked out in practice. I tell this story to show the institutional nature of racism and the centrality of state policies to creating and changing races. Here, those policies reconfigured the category of whiteness to include European immigrants. There are similarities and differences in the ways each of the European immigrant groups became "whitened." I tell the story in a way that links anti-Semitism to other varieties of anti-European racism because this highlights what Jews shared with other Euro-immigrants.

Euroraces

The U.S. "discovery" that Europe was divided into inferior and superior races began with the racialization of the Irish in the mid-nineteenth century and flowered in response to the great waves of immigration from southern and eastern Europe that began in the late nineteenth century. Before that time, European immigrants—including Jews—had been largely assimilated into the white population. However, the 23 million European immigrants who came to work in U.S. cities in the waves of migration after 1880 were too many and too concentrated to absorb. Since immigrants and their children made up more than 70 percent of the population of most of the country's largest cities, by the 1890s urban America had taken on a distinctly southern and eastern European immigrant flavor. Like the Irish in Boston and New York, their urban concentrations in dilapidated neighborhoods put them cheek by jowl next to the rising elites and the middle class with whom they shared public space and to whom their working-class ethnic communities were particularly visible.

The Red Scare of 1919 clearly linked anti-immigrant with anti-working-class sentiment—to the extent that the Seattle general strike by largely native-born workers was blamed on foreign agitators. The Red Scare was fueled by an economic depression, a massive postwar wave of strikes, the Russian Revolution, and another influx of postwar immigration. . . .

Not surprisingly, the belief in European races took root most deeply among the wealthy, U.S.-born Protestant elite, who feared a hostile and seemingly inassimilable working class. By the end of the nineteenth century, Senator Henry Cabot Lodge pressed Congress to cut off immigration to the United States; Theodore

Roosevelt raised the alarm of "race suicide" and took Anglo-Saxon women to task for allowing "native" stock to be outbred by inferior immigrants. In the early twentieth century, these fears gained a great deal of social legitimacy thanks to the efforts of an influential network of aristocrats and scientists who developed theories of eugenics—breeding for a "better" humanity—and scientific racism. . . .

By the 1920s, scientific racism sanctified the notion that real Americans were white and that real whites came from northwest Europe. Racism by white workers in the West fueled laws excluding and expelling the Chinese in 1882. Widespread racism led to closing the immigration door to virtually all Asians and most Europeans between 1924 and 1927, and to deportation of Mexicans during the Great Depression.

Racism in general, and anti-Semitism in particular, flourished in higher education. Jews were the first of the Euro-immigrant groups to enter college in significant numbers, so it was not surprising that they faced the brunt of discrimination there. The Protestant elite complained that Jews were unwashed, uncouth, unrefined, loud, and pushy. Harvard University President A. Lawrence Lowell, who was also a vice president of the Immigration Restriction League, was open about his opposition to Jews at Harvard. The Seven Sister schools had a reputation for "flagrant discrimination.". . .

Columbia's quota against Jews was well known in my parents' community. My father is very proud of having beaten it and been admitted to Columbia Dental School on the basis of his skill at carving a soap ball. Although he became a teacher instead because the tuition was too high, he took me to the dentist every week of my childhood and prolonged the agony by discussing the finer points of tooth-filling and dental care. . . .

My parents believe that Jewish success, like their own, was due to hard work and a high value placed on education. They attended Brooklyn College during the Depression. My mother worked days and went to school at night; my father went during the day. Both their families encouraged them. More accurately, their families expected it. Everyone they knew was in the same boat, and their world was made up of Jews who were advancing just as they were. . . .

How we interpret Jewish social mobility in this milieu depends on whom we compare them to. Compared with other immigrants, Jews were upwardly mobile. But compared with nonimmigrant whites, that mobility was very limited and circumscribed. The existence of anti-immigrant, racist, and anti-Semitic barriers kept the Jewish middle class confined to a small number of occupations. Jews were excluded from mainstream corporate management and corporately employed professions, except in the garment and movie industries, in which they were pioneers. Jews were almost totally excluded from university faculties (the few who made it had powerful patrons). Eastern European Jews were concentrated in small businesses, and in professions where they served a largely Jewish clientele. . . .

My parents' generation believed that Jews overcame anti-Semitic barriers because Jews are special. My answer is that the Jews who were upwardly mobile were special among Jews (and were also well placed to write the story). My generation might well respond to our parents' story of pulling themselves up by their own bootstraps with "But think what you might have been without the racism and with some affirmative action!" And that is precisely what the post-World War II boom, the decline of systematic, public, anti-Euro racism and anti-Semitism, and governmental affirmative action extended to white males let us see.

Whitening Euro-ethnics

By the time I was an adolescent, Jews were just as white as the next white person. Until I was eight, I was a Jew in a world of Jews. Everyone on Avenue Z in Sheepshead Bay was Jewish. I spent my days playing and going to school on three blocks of Avenue Z, and visiting my grandparents in the nearby Jewish neighborhoods of Brighton Beach and Coney Island. There were plenty of Italians in my neighborhood, but they lived around the corner. They were a kind of Jew, but on the margins of my social horizons. Portuguese were even more distant, at the end of the bus ride, at Sheepshead Bay. The *shul,* or temple, was on Avenue Z, and I begged my father to take me like all the other fathers took their kids, but religion wasn't part of my family's Judaism. Just how Jewish my neighborhood was hit me in first grade, when I was one of two kids to go to school on Rosh Hashanah. My teacher was shocked—she was Jewish too—and I was embarrassed to tears when she sent me home. I was never again sent to school on Jewish holidays. We left that world in 1949 when we moved to Valley Stream, Long Island, which was Protestant and Republican and even had farms until Irish, Italian, and Jewish ex-urbanities like us gave it a more suburban and Democratic flavor.

Neither religion nor ethnicity separated us at school or in the neighborhood. Except temporarily. During my elementary school years, I remember a fair number of dirt-bomb (a good suburban weapon) wars on the block. Periodically, one of the Catholic boys would accuse me or my brother of killing his god, to which we'd reply, "Did not," and start lobbing dirt bombs. Sometimes he'd get his friends from Catholic school and I'd get mine from public school kids on the block, some of whom were Catholic. Hostilities didn't last for more than a couple of hours and punctuated an otherwise friendly relationship. They ended by our junior high years, when other things became more important. Jews, Catholics, and Protestants, Italians, Irish, Poles, "English" (I don't remember hearing WASP as a kid), were mixed up on the block and in school. We thought of ourselves as middle class and very enlightened because our ethnic backgrounds seemed so irrelevant to high school culture. We didn't see race (we thought), and racism was not part of our peer consciousness. Nor were the immigrant or working-class histories of our families.

As with most chicken-and-egg problems, it is hard to know which came first. Did Jews and other Euro-ethnics become white because they became middle-class? That is, did money whiten? Or did being incorporated into an expanded version of whiteness open up the economic doors to middle-class status? Clearly, both tendencies were at work.

Some of the changes set in motion during the war against fascism led to a more inclusive version of whiteness. Anti-Semitism and anti-European racism lost respectability. The 1940 Census no longer distinguished native whites of native parentage from those, like my parents, of immigrant parentage, so Euro-immigrants and their children were more securely white by submersion in an expanded notion of whiteness.[3]

Theories of nurture and culture replaced theories of nature and biology. Instead of dirty and dangerous races that would destroy American democracy, immigrants became ethnic groups whose children had successfully assimilated into the mainstream and risen to the middle class. In this new myth, Euro-ethnic suburbs like mine became the measure of American democracy's victory over racism. Jewish mobility became a new Horatio Alger story. In time and with hard work, every ethnic group would get a piece of the pie, and the United States would be a nation with equal opportunity for all its people to become part of a prosperous middle-class majority. And it seemed that Euro-ethnic immigrants and their children were delighted to join middle America.

This is not to say that anti-Semitism disappeared after World War II, only that it fell from fashion and was driven underground. . . .

Although changing views on who was white made it easier for Euro-ethnics to become middle class, economic prosperity also played a very powerful role in the whitening process. . . .

. . . The postwar period was a historic moment for real class mobility and for the affluence we have erroneously come to believe was the American norm. It was a time when the old white and the newly white masses became middle class.[4]

The GI Bill of Rights, as the 1944 Serviceman's Readjustment Act was known, is arguably the most massive affirmative action program in American history. It was created to develop needed labor force skills and to provide those who had them with a lifestyle that reflected their value to the economy. The GI benefits that were ultimately extended to 16 million GIs (of the Korean War as well) included priority in jobs—that is, preferential hiring, but no one objected to it then—financial support during the job search, small loans for starting up businesses, and most important, low-interest home loans and educational benefits, which included tuition and living expenses. This legislation was rightly regarded as one of the most revolutionary postwar programs. I call it affirmative action because it was aimed at and disproportionately helped male, Euro-origin GIs.[5] . . .

Education and Occupation

It is important to remember that, prior to the war, a college degree was still very much a "mark of the upper class," that colleges were largely finishing schools for Protestant elites. Before the postwar boom, schools could not begin to accommodate the American masses. Even in New York City before the 1930s, neither the public schools nor City College had room for more than a tiny fraction of potential immigrant students.[6]

Not so after the war. The almost 8 million GIs who took advantage of their educational benefits under the GI Bill caused "the greatest wave of college building in American history." White male GIs were able to take advantage of their educational benefits for college and technical training, so they were particularly well positioned to seize the opportunities provided by the new demands for professional, managerial, and technical labor. . . .

The reason I refer to educational and occupational GI benefits as affirmative action programs for white males is because they were decidedly not extended to African Americans or to women of any race. Theoretically they were available to all veterans; in practice women and black veterans did not get anywhere near their share. Women's Army and Air Force units were initially organized as auxiliaries, hence not part of the military. When that status was changed, in July 1943, only those who reenlisted in the armed forces were eligible for veterans' benefits. Many women thought they were simply being demobilized and returned home. The majority remained and were ultimately eligible for veterans' benefits. But there was little counseling, and a social climate that discouraged women's careers and independence cut down on women's knowledge and sense of entitlement. The Veterans Administration kept no statistics on the number of women who used their GI benefits.[7]

The barriers that almost completely shut African American GIs out of their benefits were even more formidable. In Neil Wynn's portrait, black GIs anticipated starting new lives, just like their white counterparts. Over 43 percent hoped to return to school, and most expected to relocate, to find better jobs in new lines of work. The exodus from the South toward the North and West was particularly large. So it was not a question of any lack of ambition on the part of African American GIs. White male privilege was shaped against the backdrop of wartime racism and postwar sexism. . . .

The military, the Veterans Administration, the U.S. Employment Services (USES), and the Federal Housing Administration effectively denied African American GIs access to their benefits and to new educational, occupational, and residential opportunities. Black GIs who served in the thoroughly segregated armed forces during World War II served under white officers. African American soldiers were given a disproportionate share of dishonorable discharges, which denied them veterans' rights under the GI Bill. Between August and November 1946, for example, 21 percent of white soldiers and 39 percent of black soldiers were dishonorably discharged. Those who did get an honorable discharge then faced the Veterans Administration and the USES. The latter, which was responsible for job placements, employed very few African Americans, especially in the South. This meant that black veterans did not receive much employment information and that the offers they did receive were for low-paid and menial jobs. "In one survey of 50 cities, the movement of blacks into peacetime employment was found to be lagging far behind that of white veterans: in Arkansas ninety-five percent of the placements made by the USES for Afro-Americans were in service or unskilled jobs."[8] African Americans were also less likely than whites, regardless of GI status, to gain new jobs commensurate with their wartime jobs. For example, in San Francisco, by 1948, black Americans "had dropped back halfway to their prewar employment status."[9]

Black GIs faced discrimination in the educational system as well. Despite the end of restrictions on Jews and other Euro-ethnics, African Americans were not welcome in white colleges. Black colleges were overcrowded, but the combination of segregation and prejudice made for few alternatives. About 20,000 black veterans attended college by 1947, most in black colleges, but almost as many, 15,000, could not gain entry. Predictably, the disproportionately few African Americans who did gain access to their educational benefits were able, like their white counterparts, to become doctors and engineers, and to enter the black middle class.[10]

Suburbanization

In 1949, ensconced in Valley Stream, I watched potato farms turn into Levittown and Idlewild (later Kennedy) airport. This was the major spectator sport in our first years on Long Island. A typical weekend would bring various aunts, uncles, and cousins out from the city. After a huge meal, we'd pile into the car—itself a novelty—to look at the bulldozed acres and comment on the matchbox construction. During the week, my mother and I would look at the houses going up within walking distance. . . .

At the beginning of World War II, about one-third of all American families owned their houses. That percentage doubled in twenty years. . . .

The Federal Housing Administration (FHA) was key to buyers and builders alike. Thanks to the FHA, suburbia was open to more than GIs. People like us would never have been in the market for houses without FHA and Veterans Administration (VA) low-down-payment, low-interest, long-term loans to young buyers. . . .

The FHA believed in racial segregation. Throughout its history, it publicly and actively promoted restrictive covenants. Before the war, these forbade sales to Jews and Catholics as well as to African Americans. The deed to my house in Detroit had such a covenant, which theoretically prevented it from being sold to Jews or African Americans. Even after the Supreme Court outlawed restrictive covenants in 1948, the FHA continued to encourage builders to write them in against African Americans. FHA underwriting manuals openly insisted on racially homogeneous neighborhoods, and their loans were made only in white neighborhoods. . . .

The result of these policies was that African Americans were totally shut out of the suburban boom. An article in *Harper's* described the housing available to black GIs.

> On his way to the base each morning, Sergeant Smith passes an attractive air-conditioned, FHA-financed housing project. It was built for service families. Its rents are little more than the Smiths pay for their shack. And there are half-a-dozen vacancies, but none for Negroes.[11]

. . . Urban renewal was the other side of the process by which Jewish and other working-class Euro-immigrants became middle class. It was the push to suburbia's seductive pull. The fortunate white survivors of urban renewal headed disproportionately for suburbia, where they could partake of prosperity and the good life. . . .

If the federal stick of urban renewal joined the FHA carrot of cheap mortgages to send masses of Euro-Americans to the suburbs, the FHA had a different kind of one-two punch for African Americans. Segregation kept them out of the suburbs, and redlining made sure they could not buy or repair their homes in the neighborhoods in which they were allowed to live. The FHA practiced systematic redlining. This was a practice developed by its predecessor, the Home Owners Loan Corporation (HOLC), which in the 1930s developed an elaborate neighborhood rating system that placed the highest (green) value on all-white, middle-class neighborhoods, and the lowest (red) on racially nonwhite or mixed and working-class neighborhoods. High ratings meant high property values. The idea was that low property values in redlined neighborhoods made them bad investments. The FHA was, after all, created by and for banks and the housing industry. Redlining warned banks not to lend there, and the FHA would not insure mortgages in such neighborhoods. Redlining created a self-fulfilling prophesy. . . . The FHA's and VA's refusal to guarantee loans in redlined neighborhoods made it virtually impossible for African Americans to borrow money for home improvement or purchase. Because these maps and surveys were quite se-cret, it took the civil rights movement to make these practices and their devastating consequences public. As a result, those who fought urban renewal, or who sought to make a home in the urban ruins, found themselves locked out of the middle class. They also faced an ideological assault that labeled their neighborhoods slums and called them slumdwellers.[12]

Conclusion

The record is very clear. Instead of seizing the opportunity to end institutional-ized racism, the federal government did its level best to shut and double-seal the postwar window of opportunity in African Americans' faces. It consistently refused to combat segregation in the social institutions that were key to upward mobility in education, housing, and employment. Moreover, federal programs that were themselves designed to assist demobilized GIs and young families system-atically discriminated against African Americans. Such programs reinforced white/nonwhite racial distinctions even as intrawhite racialization was falling out of fashion. This other side of the coin, that white men of northwest European ancestry and white men of southeastern European ancestry were treated equally in theory and in practice with regard to the benefits they received, was part of the larger postwar whitening of Jews and other eastern and southern Europeans.

The myth that Jews pulled themselves up by their own bootstraps ignores the fact that it took federal programs to create the conditions whereby the abilities of Jews and other European immigrants could be recognized and rewarded rather than deni-grated and denied. The GI Bill and FHA and VA mortgages, even though they were advertised as open to all, functioned as a set of racial privileges. They were privileges because they were extended to white GIs but not to black GIs. Such privileges were forms of affirmative action that allowed Jews and other Euro-American men to be-come suburban homeowners and to get the training that allowed them—but much less so women vets or war workers—to become professionals, technicians, salesmen, and managers in a growing economy. Jews and other white ethnics' upward mobility was due to programs that allowed us to float on a rising economic tide. To African Americans, the government offered the cement boots of segregation, redlining, urban renewal, and discrimination.

Those racially skewed gains have been passed across the generations, so that racial inequality seems to maintain itself "naturally," even after legal segregation ended. Today, I own a house in Venice, California, like the one in which I grew up in Valley Stream, and my brother until recently owned a house in Palo Alto much like an Eichler house. Both of us are where we are thanks largely to the postwar benefits our parents received and passed on to us, and to the educational benefits we received in the 1960s as a result of affluence and the social agitation that developed from the black Freedom Movement. I have white, African American, and Asian American colleagues whose parents received fewer or none of America's postwar benefits and who expect never to own a house despite their considerable academic achievements. Some of these colleagues who are a few years younger than I also carry staggering debts for their education, which they expect to have to repay for the rest of their lives.

Conventional wisdom has it that the United States has always been an affluent land of opportunity. But the truth is that affluence has been the exception and that real upward mobility has required massive affirmative action programs. . . .

NOTES

1. Gerber 1986; Dinnerstein 1987, 1994.

2. Not all Jews are white or unambiguously white. It has been suggested, for example, that Hasidim lack the privileges of whiteness. Rodriguez (1997, 12, 15) has begun to unpack the claims of white Jewish "amenity migrants" and the different racial meanings of Chicano claims to a crypto-Jewish identity in New Mexico. See also Thomas 1996 on African American Jews.

3. This census also explicitly changed the Mexican race to white (U.S. Bureau of the Census 1940, 2:4).

4. Nash et al. 1986, 885–886.

5. On planning for veterans, see F. J. Brown 1946; Hurd 1946; Mosch 1975; "Post-war Jobs for Veterans" 1945; Willenz 1983.

6. Willenz 1983, 165.

7. Willenz 1983, 20–28, 94–97. I thank Nancy G. Cattell for calling my attention to the fact that women GIs were ultimately eligible for benefits.

8. Nalty and MacGregor 1981, 218, 60–61.

9. Wynn 1976, 114, 116.

10. On African Americans in the U.S. military, see Foner 1974; Dalfiume 1969; Johnson 1967; Binkin and Eitelberg 1982; Nalty and MacGregor 1981. On schooling, see Walker 1970, 4–9.

11. Quoted in Foner 1974, 195.

12. See Gans 1962.

REFERENCES

Anderson, Karen. 1981. *Wartime Women.* Westport, Conn.: Greenwood.

Barkan, Elazar. 1992. *The Retreat of Scientific Racism: Changing Concepts of Race in Britain and the United States Between the World Wars.* New York: Cambridge University Press.

Berman, Marshall. 1982. *All That Is Solid Melts into Air: The Experience of Modernity.* New York: Simon and Schuster.

Binkin, Martin, and Mark J. Eitelberg. 1982. *Blacks and the Military.* Washington, D.C.: Brookings Institution.

Brown, Francis J. 1946. *Educational Opportunities for Veterans.* Washington, D.C.: Public Affairs Press American Council on Public Affairs.

Cockcroft, Eva. 1990. *Signs from the Heart: California Chicano Murals.* Venice, Calif.: Social and Public Art Resource Center.

Dalfiume, Richard M. 1969. *Desegregation of the U.S. Armed Forces: Fighting on Two Fronts, 1939–1953.* Columbia: University of Missouri Press.

Dinnerstein, Leonard, 1987. *Uneasy at Home: Anti-Semitism and the American Jewish Experience.* New York: Columbia University Press.

———. 1994. *Anti-Semitism in America.* New York: Oxford University Press.

Dobriner, William M. 1963. *Class in Suburbia.* Englewood Cliffs, N.J.: Prentice-Hall.

Eichler, Ned. 1982. *The Merchant Builders.* Cambridge, Mass.: MIT Press.

Foner, Jack. 1974. *Blacks and the Military in American History: A New Perspective.* New York: Praeger Publishers.

Gans, Herbert. 1962. *The Urban Villagers.* New York: Free Press of Glencoe.

Gerber, David, ed. 1986. *Anti-Semitism in American History.* Urbana: University of Illinois Press.

Gilman, Sander. 1996. *Smart Jews: The Construction of the Image of Jewish Superior Intelligence.* Lincoln: University of Nebraska Press.

Gordon, Milton. 1964. *Assimilation in American Life: The Role of Race, Religion and National Origins.* New York: Oxford University Press.

Gould, Stephen J. 1981. *The Mismeasure of Man.* New York: Norton.

Grant, Madison. 1916. *The Passing of the Great Race: Or the Racial Basis of European History.* New York: Charles Scribner.

Greer, Scott. 1965. *Urban Renewal and American Cities.* Indianapolis: Bobbs-Merrill.

Hartman, Chester. 1975. *Housing and Social Policy.* Englewood Cliffs, N.J.: Prentice-Hall.

Havighurst, Robert J., John W. Baughman, Walter H. Eaton, and Ernest W. Burgess. 1951. *The American Veteran Back Home: A Study of Veteran Readjustment.* New York: Longmans, Green and Co.

Higham, John. 1955. *Strangers in the Land.* New Brunswick, N.J.: Rutgers University Press.

Hurd, Charles. 1946. *The Veterans' Program: A Complete Guide to Its Benefits, Rights and Options.* New York: McGraw-Hill Book Company.

Jackson, Kenneth T. 1985. *Crabgrass Frontier: The Suburbanization of the United States.* New York: Oxford University Press.

Johnson, Jesse J. 1967. *Ebony Brass: An Autobiography of Negro Frustration Amid Aspiration.* New York: The William Frederick Press.

Markowitz, Ruth Jacknow. 1993. *My Daughter, the Teacher: Jewish Teachers in the New York City Schools.* New Brunswick, N.J.: Rutgers University Press.

Milkman, Ruth. 1987. *Gender at Work: The Dynamics of Job Segregation by Sex During World War II.* Urbana: University of Illinois Press.

Mosch, Theodore R. 1975. *The GI Bill: A Breakthrough in Educational and Social Policy in the United States.* Hicksville, N.Y.: Exposition Press.

Nalty, Bernard C., and Morris J. MacGregor, eds. 1981. *Blacks in the Military: Essential Documents.* Wilmington, Del.: Scholarly Resources, Inc.

Nash, Gary B., Julie Roy Jeffrey, John R. Howe, Allen F. Davis, Peter J. Frederick, and Allen M. Winkler. 1986. *The American People: Creating a Nation and a Society.* New York: Harper and Row.

Pardo, Mary. 1990. "Mexican-American Women Grassroots Community Activists:'Mothers of East Los Angeles'."*Frontiers* 11, 1:1–7.

Patterson, Thomas C. 1997. *Inventing Western Civilization.* New York: Monthly Review Press.

"Postwar Jobs for Veterans." 1945. *The Annals of the American Academy of Political and Social Science* 238 (March).

Ripley, William Z. 1923. *The Races of Europe: A Sociological Study.* New York: Appleton.

Rodriguez, Sylvia. 1997. "Tourism, Whiteness, and the Vanishing Anglo." Paper presented at the conference "Seeing and Being Seen: Tourism in the American West." Center for the American West, Boulder, Colorado, 2 May.

Schoener, Allon. 1967. *Portal to America: The Lower East Side 1870–1925.* New York: Holt, Rinehart, and Winston.

Sowell, Thomas. 1981. *Ethnic America: A History.* New York: Basic Books.

Squires, Gregory D., ed. 1989. *Unequal Partnerships: The Political Economy of Urban Redevelopment in Postwar America.* New Brunswick, N.J.: Rutgers University Press.

Steinberg, Stephen. 1989. *The Ethnic Myth: Race, Ethnicity and Class in America.* 2d ed. Boston: Beacon Press.

Thomas, Laurence Mordekhai. 1996. "The Soul of Identity: Jews and Blacks." In *People of the Book,* ed. S. F. Fishkin and J. Rubin-Dorsky. Madison: University of Wisconsin Press, 169–186.

U.S. Bureau of the Census. 1940. *Sixteenth Census of the United States,* V.2. Washington, D.C.: U.S. Government Printing Office.

Walker, Olive. 1970. "The Windsor Hills School Story." *Integrated Education: Race and Schools* 8, 3:4–9.

Willenz, June A. 1983. *Women Veterans: America's Forgotten Heroines.* New York: Continuum.

Wynn, Neil A. 1976. *The Afro-American and the Second World War.* London: Paul Elek.

"Night to His Day"

The Social Construction of Gender
Judith Lorber

Talking about gender for most people is the equivalent of fish talking about water. Gender is so much the routine ground of everyday activities that questioning its taken-for-granted assumptions and presuppositions is like thinking about whether the sun will come up.[1] Gender is so pervasive that in our society we assume it is bred into our genes. Most people find it hard to believe that gender is constantly created and re-created out of human interaction, out of social life, and is the texture and order of that social life. Yet gender, like culture, is a human production that depends on everyone constantly "doing gender" (West and Zimmerman 1987).

And everyone "does gender" without thinking about it. Today, on the subway, I saw a well-dressed man with a year-old child in a stroller. Yesterday, on a bus, I saw a man with a tiny baby in a carrier on his chest. Seeing men taking care of small children in public is increasingly common—at least in New York City. But both men were quite obviously stared at—and smiled at, approvingly. Everyone was doing gender—the men who were changing the role of fathers and the other passengers, who were applauding them silently. But there was more gendering going on that probably fewer people noticed. The baby was wearing a white crocheted cap and white clothes. You couldn't tell if it was a boy or a girl. The child in the stroller was wearing a dark blue T-shirt and dark print pants. As they started to leave the train, the father put a Yankee baseball cap on the child's head. Ah, a boy, I thought. Then I noticed the gleam of tiny earrings in the child's ears, and as they got off, I saw the little flowered sneakers and lace-trimmed socks. Not a boy after all. Gender done.

Gender is such a familiar part of daily life that it usually takes a deliberate disruption of our expectations of how women and men are supposed to act to pay attention to how it is produced. Gender signs and signals are so ubiquitous that we usually fail to note them—unless they are missing or ambiguous. Then we are uncomfortable until we have successfully placed the other person in a gender status; otherwise, we feel socially dislocated. . . .

For the individual, gender construction starts with assignment to a sex category on the basis of what the genitalia look like at birth.[2] Then babies are dressed or adorned in a way that displays the category because parents don't want to be constantly asked whether their baby is a girl or a boy. A sex category becomes a gender status through naming, dress, and the use of other gender markers. Once a child's gender is evident, others treat those in one gender differently from those in the other, and the children respond to the different

From " 'Night to His Day': The Social Construction of Gender," in *Paradoxes of Gender*, pp. 13–18, 22, 23–27, 29, 30, 32–35, and notes on pp. 304–305. Copyright © 1994 by Yale University. All Rights Reserved. Reprinted by permission of Yale University Press as publisher treatment by feeling different and behaving differently. As soon as they can talk, they start to refer to themselves as members of their gender. Sex doesn't come into play again until puberty, but by that time, sexual feelings and desires and practices have been shaped by gendered norms and expectations. Adolescent boys and girls approach and avoid each other in an elaborately scripted and gendered mating dance. Parenting is gendered, with different expectations for mothers and for fathers, and people of different genders work at different kinds of jobs. The work adults do as mothers and fathers and as low-level workers and high-level bosses, shapes women's and men's life experiences, and these experiences produce different feelings, consciousness, relationships, skills—ways of being that we call feminine or masculine.[3] All of these processes constitute the social construction of gender.

Gendered roles change—today fathers are taking care of little children, girls and boys are wearing unisex clothing and getting the same education, women and men are working at the same jobs. Although many traditional social groups are quite strict about maintaining gender differences, in other social groups they seem to be blurring. Then why the one-year-old's earrings? Why is it still so important to mark a child as a girl or a boy, to make sure she is not taken for a boy or he for a girl? What would happen if they were? They would, quite literally, have changed places in their social world.

To explain why gendering is done from birth, constantly and by everyone, we have to look not only at the way individuals experience gender but at gender as a social institution. As a social institution, gender is one of the major ways that human beings organize their lives. Human society depends on a predictable division of labor, a designated allocation of scarce goods, assigned responsibility for children and others who cannot care for themselves, common values and their systematic transmission to new members, legitimate leadership, music, art, stories, games, and other symbolic productions. One way of choosing people for the different tasks of society is on the basis of their talents, motivations, and competence—their demonstrated achievements. The other way is on the basis of gender, race, ethnicity—ascribed membership in a category of people. Although societies vary in the extent to which they use one or the other of these ways of allocating people to work and to carry out other responsibilities, every society uses gender and age grades. Every society classifies people as "girl and boy children," "girls and boys ready to be married," and "fully adult women and men," constructs similarities among them and differences between them, and assigns them to different roles and responsibilities. Personality characteristics, feelings, motivations, and ambitions flow from these different life experiences so that the members of these different groups become different kinds of people. The process of gendering and its outcome are legitimated by religion, law, science, and the society's entire set of values. . . .

Western society's values legitimate gendering by claiming that it all comes from physiology—female and male procreative differences. But gender and sex are not equivalent, and gender as a social construction does not flow automatically from genitalia and reproductive organs, the main physiological differences of females and males. In the construction of ascribed social statuses, physiological differences such as sex, stage of development, color of skin, and size are crude markers. They are not the source of the social statuses of gender, age grade, and race. Social statuses are carefully constructed through prescribed processes of teaching, learning, emulation, and enforcement. Whatever genes, hormones, and biological evolution contribute to human social institutions is materially as well as qualitatively transformed by social practices. Every social institution has a material base, but culture and social practices transform that base into something with qualitatively different patterns and constraints. The economy is much more than producing food and goods and distributing them to eaters and users; family and kinship are not the equivalent of having sex and procreating; morals and religions cannot be equated with the fears and ecstasies of the brain; language goes far beyond the sounds produced by tongue and larynx. No one eats "money" or "credit"; the concepts of "god" and "angels" are the subjects of theological disquisitions; not only words but objects, such as their flag, "speak" to the citizens of a country.

Similarly, gender cannot be equated with biological and physiological differences between human females and males. The building blocks of gender are *socially constructed statuses*. . . .

Genders, therefore, are not attached to a biological substratum. Gender boundaries are breachable, and individual and socially organized shifts from one gender to another call attention to "cultural, social, or aesthetic dissonances" (Garber 1992, 16). . . .

For Individuals, Gender Means Sameness

Although the possible combinations of genitalia, body shapes, clothing, mannerisms, sexuality, and roles could produce infinite varieties in human beings, the social institution of gender depends on the production and maintenance of a limited number of gender statuses and of making the members of these statuses similar to each other. Individuals are born sexed but not gendered, and they have to be taught to be masculine or feminine.[4] As Simone de Beauvoir said: "One is not born, but rather becomes, a woman . . . ; it is civilization as a whole that produces this creature . . . which is described as feminine" (1953, 267).

Children learn to walk, talk, and gesture the way their social group says girls and boys should. Ray Birdwhistell, in his analysis of body motion as human communication, calls these learned gender displays *tertiary* sex characteristics and argues that they are needed to distinguish genders because humans are a weakly dimorphic species—their only sex markers are genitalia (1970, 39–46). Clothing, paradoxically, often hides the sex but displays the gender.

In early childhood, humans develop gendered personality structures and sexual orientations through their interactions with parents of the same and opposite gender. As adolescents, they conduct their sexual behavior according to gendered scripts. Schools, parents, peers, and the mass media guide young people into gendered work and family roles. As adults, they take on a gendered social status in their society's stratification system. Gender is thus both ascribed and achieved (West and Zimmerman 1987). . . .

Gender norms are inscribed in the way people move, gesture, and even eat. In one African society, men were supposed to eat with their "whole mouth, wholeheartedly, and not, like women, just with the lips, that is halfheartedly, with reservation

and restraint" (Bourdieu [1980] 1990, 70). Men and women in this society learned
to walk in ways that proclaimed their different positions in the society:

> The manly man . . . stands up straight into the face of the person he approaches, or
> wishes to welcome. Ever on the alert, because ever threatened, he misses nothing of
> what happens around him. . . . Conversely, a well brought-up woman . . . is expected
> to walk with a slight stoop, avoiding every misplaced movement of her body, her head
> or her arms, looking down, keeping her eyes on the spot where she will next put her
> foot, especially if she happens to have to walk past the men's assembly. (70)

. . . For human beings there is no essential femaleness or maleness, femininity or
masculinity, womanhood or manhood, but once gender is ascribed, the social order
constructs and holds individuals to strongly gendered norms and expectations. Individuals may vary on many of the components of gender and may shift genders temporarily or permanently, but they must fit into the limited number of gender statuses
their society recognizes. In the process, they re-create their society's version of women
and men: "If we do gender appropriately, we simultaneously sustain, reproduce, and
render legitimate the institutional arrangements. . . . If we fail to do gender appropriately, we as individuals—not the institutional arrangements—may be called to account
(for our character, motives, and predispositions)" (West and Zimmerman 1987, 146).

The gendered practices of everyday life reproduce a society's view of how women
and men should act (Bourdieu [1980] 1990). Gendered social arrangements are justified by religion and cultural productions and backed by law, but the most powerful means of sustaining the moral hegemony of the dominant gender ideology is
that the process is made invisible; any possible alternatives are virtually unthinkable
(Foucault 1972; Gramsci 1971).[5]

For Society, Gender Means Difference

The pervasiveness of gender as a way of structuring social life demands that gender
statuses be clearly differentiated. Varied talents, sexual preferences, identities, personalities, interests, and ways of interacting fragment the individual's bodily and social
experiences. . . . In the social construction of gender, it does not matter what men
and women actually do; it does not even matter if they do exactly the same thing. The
social institution of gender insists only that what they do is *perceived* as different. . . .

If gender differences were genetic, physiological, or hormonal, gender bending and
gender ambiguity would occur only in hermaphrodites, who are born with chromosomes and genitalia that are not clearly female or male. Since gender differences are
socially constructed, all men and all women can enact the behavior of the other, because
they know the other's social script: " 'Man' and 'woman' are at once empty and overflow-
ing categories. Empty because they have no ultimate, transcendental meaning. Overflow-
ing because even when they appear to be fixed, they still contain within them alternative,
denied, or suppressed definitions" (Scott 1988, 49). . . .

For one transsexual man-to-woman, the experience of living as a woman changed
his/her whole personality. As James, Morris had been a soldier, foreign correspondent,
and mountain climber; as Jan, Morris is a successful travel writer. But socially, James

was superior to Jan, and so Jan developed the "learned helplessness" that is supposed to characterize women in Western society:

> We are told that the social gap between the sexes is narrowing, but I can only report that having, in the second half of the twentieth century, experienced life in both roles, there seems to me no aspect of existence, no moment of the day, no contact, no arrangement, no response, which is not different for men and for women. The very tone of voice in which I was now addressed, the very posture of the person next in the queue, the very feel in the air when I entered a room or sat at a restaurant table, constantly emphasized my change of status.
>
> And if other's responses shifted, so did my own. The more I was treated as woman, the more woman I became. I adapted willy-nilly. If I was assumed to be incompetent at reversing cars, or opening bottles, oddly incompetent I found myself becoming. If a case was thought too heavy for me, inexplicably I found it so myself. . . . Women treated me with a frankness which, while it was one of the happiest discoveries of my metamorphosis, did imply membership of a camp, a faction, or at least a school of thought; so I found myself gravitating always towards the female, whether in sharing a railway compartment or supporting a political cause. Men treated me more and more as junior, . . . and so, addressed every day of my life as an inferior, involuntarily, month by month I accepted the condition. I discovered that even now men prefer women to be less informed, less able, less talkative, and certainly less self-centered than they are themselves; so I generally obliged them. (1975, 165–66)[6]

Gender as Process, Stratification, and Structure

As a social institution, gender is a process of creating distinguishable social statuses for the assignment of rights and responsibilities. As part of a stratification system that ranks these statuses unequally, gender is a major building block in the social structures built on these unequal statuses.

As a *process*, gender creates the social differences that define "woman" and "man." In social interaction throughout their lives, individuals learn what is expected, see what is expected, act and react in expected ways, and thus simultaneously construct and maintain the gender order: "The very injunction to be a given gender takes place through discursive routes: to be a good mother, to be a heterosexually desirable object, to be a fit worker, in sum, to signify a multiplicity of guarantees in response to a variety of different demands all at once" (Butler 1990, 145). Members of a social group neither make up gender as they go along nor exactly replicate in rote fashion what was done before. In almost every encounter, human beings produce gender, behaving in the ways they learned were appropriate for their status, or resisting or rebelling against these norms. Resistance and rebellion have altered gender norms, but so far they have rarely eroded the statuses.

Gendered patterns of interaction acquire additional layers of gendered sexuality, parenting, and work behaviors in childhood, adolescence, and adulthood. Gendered norms and expectations are enforced through informal sanctions of gender-inappropriate behavior by peers and by formal punishment or threat of punishment by those in authority should behavior deviate too far from socially imposed standards for women and men. . . .

As part of a *stratification* system, gender ranks men above women of the same race and class. . . .

The further dichotomization by race and class constructs the gradations of a heterogeneous society's stratification scheme. . . . The dominant categories are the hegemonic ideals, taken so for granted as the way things should be that white is not ordinarily thought of as a race, middle class as a class, or men as a gender. The characteristics of these categories define the Other as that which lacks the valuable qualities the dominants exhibit.

In a gender-stratified society, what men do is usually valued more highly than what women do because men do it, even when their activities are very similar or the same. In different regions of southern India, for example, harvesting rice is men's work, shared work, or women's work: "Wherever a task is done by women it is considered easy, and where it is done by [men] it is considered difficult" (Mencher 1988, 104). A gathering and hunting society's survival usually depends on the nuts, grubs, and small animals brought in by the women's foraging trips, but when the men's hunt is successful, it is the occasion for a celebration. Conversely, because they are the superior group, white men do not have to do the "dirty work," such as housework; the most inferior group does it, usually poor women of color (Palmer 1989). . . .

Societies vary in the extent of the inequality in social status of their women and men members, but where there is inequality, the status "woman" (and its attendant behavior and role allocations) is usually held in lesser esteem than the status "man." Since gender is also intertwined with a society's other constructed statuses of differential evaluation—race, religion, occupation, class, country of origin, and so on—men and women members of the favored groups command more power, more prestige, and more property than the members of the disfavored groups. Within many social groups, however, men are advantaged over women. . . .

As a *structure,* gender divides work in the home and in economic production, legitimates those in authority, and organizes sexuality and emotional life (Connell 1987, 91–142). . . .

When gender is a major component of structured inequality, the devalued genders have less power, prestige, and economic rewards than the valued genders. In countries that discourage gender discrimination, many major roles are still gendered; women still do most of the domestic labor and child rearing, even while doing full-time paid work; women and men are segregated on the job and each does work considered "appropriate"; women's work is usually paid less than men's work. Men dominate the positions of authority and leadership in government, the military, and the law; cultural productions, religions, and sports reflect men's interests. . . .

Gender inequality—the devaluation of "women" and the social domination of "men"—has social functions and a social history. It is not the result of sex, procreation, physiology, anatomy, hormones, or genetic predispositions. It is produced and maintained by identifiable social processes and built into the general social structure and individual identities deliberately and purposefully. The social order as we know it in Western societies is organized around racial ethnic, class, and gender inequality. I contend, therefore, that the continuing purpose of gender as a modern social institution is to construct women as a group to be the subordinates of men as a group. The life of everyone placed in the status "woman" is "night to his day—that has forever been the fantasy. Black to his white. Shut out of his system's space, she is the repressed that ensures the system's functioning" (Cixous and Clément [1975] 1986, 67).

NOTES

1. Gender is, in Erving Goffman's words, an aspect of *Felicity's Condition:* "any arrangement which leads us to judge an individual's . . . acts not to be a manifestation of strangeness. Behind Felicity's Condition is our sense of what it is to be sane" (1983, 27). Also see Bem 1993; Frye 1983, 17–40; Goffman 1977.

2. In cases of ambiguity in countries with modern medicine, surgery is usually performed to make the genitalia more clearly male or female.

3. See Butler 1990 for an analysis of how doing gender is gender identity.

4. For an account of how a potential man-to-woman transsexual learned to be feminine, see Garfinkel 1967, 116–85, 285–88. For a gloss on this account that points out how, throughout his encounters with Agnes, Garfinkel failed to see how he himself was constructing his own masculinity, see Rogers 1992.

5. The concepts of moral hegemony, the effects of everyday activities (praxis) on thought and personality, and the necessity of consciousness of these processes before political change can occur are all based on Marx's analysis of class relations.

6. See Bolin 1988, 149–50, for transsexual men-to-women's discovery of the dangers of rape and sexual harassment. Devor's "gender blenders" went in the opposite direction. Because they found that it was an advantage to be taken for men, they did not deliberately cross-dress, but they did not feminize themselves either (1989, 126–40).

REFERENCES

Almquist, Elizabeth M. 1987. Labor market gendered inequality in minority groups. *Gender & Society* 1:400–14.

Amadiume, Ifi. 1987. *Male daughters, female husbands: Gender and sex in an African society.* London: Zed Books.

Barkalow, Carol, with Andrea Raab. 1990. *In the men's house.* New York: Poseidon Press.

Bem, Sandra Lipsitz. 1993. *The lenses of gender: Transforming the debate on sexual inequality.* New Haven: Yale University Press.

Bernard, Jessie. 1981. *The female world.* New York: Free Press.

Bérubé, Allan. 1989. Marching to a different drummer: Gay and lesbian GIs in World War II. In Duberman, Vicinus, and Chauncey.

Birdwhistell, Ray L. 1970. *Kinesics and context: Essays on body motion communication.* Philadelphia: University of Pennsylvania Press.

Blackwood, Evelyn. 1984. Sexuality and gender in certain Native American tribes: The case of cross-gender females. *Signs: Journal of Women in Culture and Society* 10:27–42.

Bolin, Anne. 1987. Transsexualism and the limits of traditional analysis. *American Behavioral Scientist* 31:41–65.

_____. 1988. *In search of Eve: Transsexual rites of passage.* South Hadley, Mass.: Bergin & Garvey.

Bourdieu, Pierre. [1980] 1990. *The logic of practice.* Stanford, Calif.: Stanford University Press.

Butler, Judith. 1990. *Gender trouble: Feminism and the subversion of identity.* New York and London: Routledge.

Cixous, Hélène, and Catherine Clément. [1975] 1986. *The newly born woman,* translated by Betsy Wing. Minneapolis: University of Minnesota Press.

Collins, Patricia Hill. 1990. *Black feminist thought: Knowledge, consciousness, and the politics of empowerment.* Boston: Unwin Hyman.

Connell, R.[Robert] W. 1987. *Gender and power: Society, the person, and sexual politics.* Stanford, Calif.: Stanford University Press.

Coser, Rose Laub. 1986. Cognitive structure and the use of social space. *Sociological Forum* 1:1–26.

De Beauvoir, Simone. 1953. *The second sex,* translated by H. M. Parshley. New York: Knopf.

Devor, Holly. 1989. *Gender blending: Confronting the limits of duality.* Bloomington: Indiana University Press.

Duberman, Martin Bauml, Martha Vicinus, and George Chauncey, Jr. (eds.). 1989. *Hidden from history: Reclaiming the gay and lesbian past.* New York: New American Library.

Durova, Nadezhda. 1989. *The cavalry maiden: Journals of a Russian officer in the Napoleonic Wars,* translated by Mary Fleming Zirin. Bloomington: Indiana University Press.

Dwyer, Daisy, and Judith Bruce (eds.). 1988. *A home divided: Women and income in the Third World.* Palo Alto, Calif.: Stanford University Press.

Faderman, Lillian. 1991. *Odd girls and twilight lovers: A history of lesbian life in twentieth-century America.* New York: Columbia University Press.

Foucault, Michel. 1972. *The archeology of knowledge and the discourse on language,* translated by A. M. Sheridan Smith. New York: Pantheon.

Freeman, Lucy, and Alma Halbert Bond. 1992. *America's first woman warrior: The courage of Deborah Sampson.* New York: Paragon.

Frye, Marilyn. 1983. *The politics of reality: Essays in feminist theory.* Trumansburg, N.Y.: Crossing Press.

Garber, Marjorie. 1992. *Vested interests: Cross-dressing and cultural anxiety.* New York and London: Routledge.

Garfinkel, Harold. 1967. *Studies in ethnomethodology.* Englewood Cliffs, N.J.: Prentice-Hall.

Goffman, Erving. 1977. The arrangement between the sexes. *Theory and Society* 4:301–33.

_____. 1983. Felicity's condition. *American Journal of Sociology* 89:1–53.

Gramsci, Antonio. 1971. *Selections from the prison notebooks,* translated and edited by Quintin Hoare and Geoffrey Nowell Smith. New York: International Publishers.

Groce, Stephen B., and Margaret Cooper. 1990. Just me and the boys? Women in local-level rock and roll. *Gender & Society* 4:220–29.

Jacobs, Sue-Ellen, and Christine Roberts. 1989. Sex, sexuality, gender, and gender variance. In *Gender and anthropology,* edited by Sandra Morgen. Washington, D.C.: American Anthropological Association.

Jay, Nancy. 1981. Gender and dichotomy. *Feminist Studies* 7:38–56.

Matthaei, Julie A. 1982. *An economic history of women's work in America.* New York: Schocken.

Mencher, Joan. 1988. Women's work and poverty: Women's contribution to household maintenance in South India. In Dwyer and Bruce.

Morris, Jan. 1975. *Conundrum.* New York: Signet.

Nanda, Serena. 1990. *Neither man nor woman: The hijras of India.* Belmont, Calif.: Wadsworth.

New York Times. 1989. Musician's death at 74 reveals he was a woman. 2 February.

Palmer, Phyllis. 1989. *Domesticity and dirt: Housewives and domestic servants in the United States, 1920–1945.* Philadelphia: Temple University Press.

Reskin, Barbara F. 1988. Bringing the men back in: Sex differentiation and the devaluation of women's work. *Gender & Society* 2:58–81.

Rogers, Mary F. 1992. They were all passing: Agnes, Garfinkel, and company. *Gender & Society* 6:169–91.

Rubin, Gayle. 1975. The traffic in women: Notes on the political economy of sex. In *Toward an anthropology of women,* edited by Rayna R[app] Reiter. New York: Monthly Review Press.

Scott, Joan Wallach. 1988. *Gender and the politics of history.* New York: Columbia University Press.

West, Candace, and Don Zimmerman. 1987. Doing gender. *Gender & Society* 1:125–51.

Wheelwright, Julie. 1989. *Amazons and military maids: Women who cross-dressed in pursuit of life, liberty and happiness.* London: Pandora Press.

Wikan, Unni. 1982. *Behind the veil in Arabia: Women in Oman.* Baltimore, Md.: Johns Hopkins University Press.

Williams, Christine L. 1989. *Gender differences at work: Women and men in nontraditional occupations.* Berkeley: University of California Press.

Williams, Walter L. 1986. *The spirit and the flesh: Sexual diversity in American Indian culture.* Boston: Beacon Press.

5 The Invention of Heterosexuality

Jonathan Ned Katz

Heterosexuality is old as procreation, ancient as the lust of Eve and Adam. That first lady and gentleman, we assume, perceived themselves, behaved, and felt just like today's heterosexuals. We suppose that heterosexuality is unchanging, universal, essential: ahistorical.

Contrary to that common sense conjecture, the concept of heterosexuality is only one particular historical way of perceiving, categorizing, and imagining the social relations of the sexes. Not ancient at all, the idea of heterosexuality is a modern invention, dating to the late nineteenth century. The heterosexual belief, with its metaphysical claim to eternity, has a particular, pivotal place in the social universe of the late nineteenth and twentieth centuries that it did not inhabit earlier. This essay traces the historical process by which the heterosexual idea was created as ahistorical and taken-for-granted. . . .

By not studying the heterosexual idea in history, analysts of sex, gay and straight, have continued to privilege the "normal" and "natural" at the expense of the "abnormal" and "unnatural." Such privileging of the norm accedes to its domination, protecting it from questions. By making the normal the object of a thoroughgoing historical study we simultaneously pursue a pure truth and a sex-radical and subversive goal: we upset basic preconceptions. We discover that the heterosexual, the normal, and the natural have a history of changing definitions. Studying the history of the term challenges its power.

Contrary to our usual assumption, past Americans and other peoples named, perceived, and socially organized the bodies, lusts, and intercourse of the sexes in ways radically different from the way we do. If we care to understand this vast past sexual diversity, we need to stop promiscuously projecting our own hetero and homo arrangement. Though lip-service is often paid to the distorting, ethnocentric effect of such conceptual imperialism, the category heterosexuality continues to be applied uncritically as a universal analytical tool. Recognizing the time-bound and culturally-specific character of the heterosexual category can help us begin to work toward a thoroughly historical view of sex. . . .

I'm grateful to Lisa Duggan, Judith Levine, Sharon Thompson, Carole S. Vance, and Jeffrey Weeks for comments on a recent version of this manuscript, and to Manfred Herzer and his editor, John DeCecco, for sharing, prepublication, Herzer's most recent research on Kertbeny. I'm also indebted to John Gagnon, Philip Greven, and Catharine R. Stimpson for bravely supporting my (unsuccessful) attempts to fund research for a full-length study of heterosexual history.

From *Socialist Review, 20* (January–March 1990): 7–34. Copyright © 1990 by Jonathan Ned Katz. Reprinted by permission of the author.

Before Heterosexuality: Early Victorian True Love, 1820–1860

In the early nineteenth-century United States, from about 1820 to 1860, the heterosexual did not exist. Middle-class white Americans idealized a True Woman-hood, True Manhood, and True Love, all characterized by "purity"—the freedom from sensuality.[1] Presented mainly in literary and religious texts, this True Love was a fine romance with no lascivious kisses. This ideal contrasts strikingly with late nineteenth- and twentieth-century American incitements to a hetero sex.*

Early Victorian True Love was only realized within the mode of proper procreation, marriage, the legal organization for producing a new set of correctly gendered women and men. Proper womanhood, manhood, and progeny—not a normal male-female eros—was the main product of this mode of engendering and of human reproduction.

The actors in this sexual economy were identified as manly men and womanly women and as procreators, not specifically as erotic beings or heterosexuals. Eros did not constitute the core of a heterosexual identity that inhered, democratically, in both men and women. True Women were defined by their distance from lust. True Men, though thought to live closer to carnality, and in less control of it, aspired to the same freedom from concupiscence.

Legitimate natural desire was for procreation and a proper manhood or womanhood; no heteroerotic desire was thought to be directed exclusively and naturally toward the other sex; lust in men was roving. The human body was thought of as a means towards procreation and production; penis and vagina were instruments of reproduction, not of pleasure. Human energy, thought of as a closed and severely limited system, was to be used in producing children and in work, not wasted in libidinous pleasures.

The location of all this engendering and procreative labor was the sacred sanctum of early Victorian True Love, the home of the True Woman and True Man—a temple of purity threatened from within by the monster masturbator, an archetypal early Victorian cult figure of illicit lust. The home of True Love was a castle far removed from the erotic exotic ghetto inhabited most notoriously then by the prostitute, another archetypal Victorian erotic monster. . . .

Late Victorian Sex-Love: 1860–1892

"Heterosexuality" and "homosexuality" did not appear out of the blue in the 1890s. These two eroticisms were in the making from the 1860s on. In late Victorian Amer-ica and in Germany, from about 1860 to 1892, our modern idea of an eroticized universe began to develop, and the experience of a heterolust began to be widely documented and named. . . .

---

*Some historians have recently told us to revise our idea of sexless Victorians: their experience and even their ideology, it is said, were more erotic than we previously thought. Despite the revisionists, I argue that "purity" was indeed the dominant, early Victorian, white middle-class standard. For the debate on Victorian sexuality see John D'Emilio and Estelle Freedman, *Intimate Matters: A History of Sexuality in America* (New York: Harper & Row, 1988), p. xii.

In the late nineteenth-century United States, several social factors converged to cause the eroticizing of consciousness, behavior, emotion, and identity that became typical of the twentieth-century Western middle class. The transformation of the family from producer to consumer unit resulted in a change in family members' relation to their own bodies; from being an instrument primarily of work, the human body was integrated into a new economy, and began more commonly to be perceived as a means of consumption and pleasure. Historical work has recently begun on how the biological human body is differently integrated into changing modes of production, procreation, engendering, and pleasure so as to alter radically the identity, activity, and experience of that body.[2]

The growth of a consumer economy also fostered a new pleasure ethic. This imperative challenged the early Victorian work ethic, finally helping to usher in a major transformation of values. While the early Victorian work ethic had touted the value of economic production, that era's procreation ethic had extolled the virtues of human reproduction. In contrast, the late Victorian economic ethic hawked the pleasures of consuming, while its sex ethic praised an erotic pleasure principle for men and even for women.

In the late nineteenth century, the erotic became the raw material for a new consumer culture. Newspapers, books, plays, and films touching on sex, "normal" and "abnormal," became available for a price. Restaurants, bars, and baths opened, catering to sexual consumers with cash. Late Victorian entrepreneurs of desire incited the proliferation of a new eroticism, a commoditized culture of pleasure.

In these same years, the rise in power and prestige of medical doctors allowed these upwardly mobile professionals to prescribe a healthy new sexuality. Medical men, in the name of science, defined a new ideal of male-female relationships that included, in women as well as men, an essential, necessary, normal eroticism. Doctors, who had earlier named and judged the sex-enjoying woman a "nymphomaniac," now began to label women's *lack* of sexual pleasure a mental disturbance, speaking critically, for example, of female "frigidity" and "anesthesia."*

By the 1880s, the rise of doctors as a professional group fostered the rise of a new medical model of Normal Love, replete with sexuality. The new Normal Woman and Man were endowed with a healthy libido. The new theory of Normal Love was the modern medical alternative to the old Cult of True Love. The doctors prescribed a new sexual ethic as if it were a morally neutral, medical description of health. The creation of the new Normal Sexual had its counterpart in the invention of the late Victorian Sexual Pervert. The attention paid the sexual abnormal created a need to name the sexual normal, the better to distinguish the average him and her from the deviant it.

Heterosexuality: The First Years, 1892–1900

In the periodization of heterosexual American history suggested here, the years 1892 to 1900 represent "The First Years" of the heterosexual epoch, eight key years in which the idea of the heterosexual and homosexual were initially and tentatively formulated

---

*This reference to females reminds us that the invention of heterosexuality had vastly different impacts on the histories of women and men. It also differed in its impact on lesbians and heterosexual women, homosexual and heterosexual men, the middle class and working class, and on different religious, racial, national, and geographic groups.

by U.S. doctors. The earliest-known American use of the word "heterosexual" occurs in a medical journal article by Dr. James G. Kiernan of Chicago, read before the city's medical society on March 7, 1892, and published that May—portentous dates in sexual history.[3] But Dr. Kiernan's heterosexuals were definitely not exemplars of normality. Heterosexuals, said Kiernan, were defined by a mental condition, "psychical hermaphroditism." Its symptoms were "inclinations to both sexes." These heterodox sexuals also betrayed inclinations "to abnormal methods of gratification," that is, techniques to insure pleasure without procreation. Dr. Kiernan's heterogeneous sexuals did demonstrate "traces of the normal sexual appetite" (a touch of procreative desire). Kiernan's normal sexuals were implicitly defined by a monolithic other-sex inclination and procreative aim. Significantly, they still lacked a name.

Dr. Kiernan's article of 1892 also included one of the earliest-known uses of the word "homosexual" in American English. Kiernan defined "Pure homosexuals" as persons whose "general mental state is that of the opposite sex." Kiernan thus defined homosexuals by their deviance from a gender norm. His heterosexuals displayed a double deviance from both gender and procreative norms.

Though Kiernan used the new words heterosexual and homosexual, an old procreative standard and a new gender norm coexisted uneasily in his thought. His word heterosexual defined a mixed person and compound urge, abnormal because they wantonly included procreative and non-procreative objectives, as well as same-sex and different-sex attractions.

That same year, 1892, Dr. Krafft-Ebing's influential *Psychopathia Sexualis* was first translated and published in the United States.[4] But Kiernan and Krafft-Ebing by no means agreed on the definition of the heterosexual. In Krafft-Ebing's book, "heterosexual" was used unambiguously in the modern sense to refer to an erotic feeling for a different sex. "Homo-sexual" referred unambiguously to an erotic feeling for a "same sex." In Krafft-Ebing's volume, unlike Kiernan's article, heterosexual and homosexual were clearly distinguished from a third category, a "psycho-sexual hermaphroditism," defined by impulses toward both sexes.

Krafft-Ebing hypothesized an inborn "sexual instinct" for relations with the "opposite sex," the inherent "purpose" of which was to foster procreation. Krafft-Ebing's erotic drive was still a reproductive instinct. But the doctor's clear focus on a different-sex versus same-sex sexuality constituted a historic, epochal move from an absolute procreative standard of normality toward a new norm. His definition of heterosexuality as other-sex attraction provided the basis for a revolutionary, modern break with a centuries-old procreative standard.

It is difficult to overstress the importance of that new way of categorizing. The German's mode of labeling was radical in referring to the biological sex, masculinity or femininity, and the pleasure of actors (along with the procreant purpose of acts). Krafft-Ebing's heterosexual offered the modern world a new norm that came to dominate our idea of the sexual universe, helping to change it from a mode of human reproduction and engendering to a mode of pleasure. The heterosexual category provided the basis for a move from a production-oriented, procreative imperative to a consumerist pleasure principle—an institutionalized pursuit of happiness. . . .

Only gradually did doctors agree that heterosexual referred to a normal, "other-sex" eros. This new standard-model heterosex provided the pivotal term for the modern regularization of eros that paralleled similar attempts to standardize masculinity and femininity, intelligence, and manufacturing.[5] The idea of heterosexuality as the master sex from which all others deviated was (like the idea of the master race) deeply authoritarian. The doctors' normalization of a sex that was hetero proclaimed a new heterosexual separatism—an erotic apartheid that forcefully segregated the sex normals from the sex perverts. The new, strict boundaries made the emerging erotic world less polymorphous—safer for sex normals. However, the idea of such creatures as heterosexuals and homosexuals emerged from the narrow world of medicine to become a commonly accepted notion only in the early twentieth century. In 1901, in the comprehensive *Oxford English Dictionary*, "heterosexual" and "homosexual" had not yet made it.

The Distribution of the Heterosexual Mystique: 1900-1930

In the early years of this heterosexual century the tentative hetero hypothesis was stabilized, fixed, and widely distributed as the ruling sexual orthodoxy: The Heterosexual Mystique. Starting among pleasure-affirming urban working-class youths, southern blacks, and Greenwich-Village bohemians as defensive subculture, hetero-sex soon triumphed as dominant culture.[6]

In its earliest version, the twentieth-century heterosexual imperative usually continued to associate heterosexuality with a supposed human "need," "drive," or "instinct" for propagation, a procreant urge linked inexorably with carnal lust as it had not been earlier. In the early twentieth century, the falling birth rate, rising divorce rate, and "war of the sexes" of the middle class were matters of increasing public concern. Giving vent to heteroerotic emotions was thus praised as enhancing baby-making capacity, marital intimacy, and family stability. (Only many years later, in the mid-1960s, would heteroeroticism be distinguished completely, in practice and theory, from procreativity and male-female pleasure sex justified in its own name.)

The first part of the new sex norm—hetero—referred to a basic gender divergence. The "oppositeness" of the sexes was alleged to be the basis for a universal, normal, erotic attraction between males and females. The stress on the sexes' "oppositeness," which harked back to the early nineteenth century, by no means simply registered biological differences of females and males. The early twentieth-century focus on physiological and gender dimorphism reflected the deep anxieties of men about the shifting work, social roles, and power of men over women, and about the ideals of womanhood and manhood. That gender anxiety is documented, for example, in 1897, in *The New York Times'* publication of the Reverend Charles Parkhurst's diatribe against female "andromaniacs," the preacher's derogatory, scientific-sounding name for women who tried to "minimize distinctions by which manhood and womanhood are differentiated."[7] The stress on gender difference was a conservative response to the changing social-sexual division of activity and feeling which gave rise to the independent "New Woman" of the 1880s and eroticized "Flapper" of the 1920s.

The second part of the new hetero norm referred positively to sexuality. That novel upbeat focus on the hedonistic possibilities of male-female conjunctions also reflected a social transformation—a revaluing of pleasure and procreation, consumption and work in commercial, capitalist society. The democratic attribution of a normal lust to human females (as well as males) served to authorize women's enjoyment of their own bodies and began to undermine the early Victorian idea of the pure True Woman—a sex-affirmative action still part of women's struggle. The twentieth-century Erotic Woman also undercut nineteenth-century feminist assertion of women's moral superiority, cast suspicions of lust on women's passionate romantic friendships with women, and asserted the presence of a menacing female monster, "the lesbian."[8] . . .

In the perspective of heterosexual history, this early twentieth-century struggle for the more explicit depiction of an "opposite-sex" eros appears in a curious new light. Ironically, we find sex-conservatives, the social purity advocates of censorship and repression, fighting against the depiction not just of sexual perversity but also of the new normal heterosexuality. That a more open depiction of normal sex had to be defended against forces of propriety confirms the claim that heterosexuality's predecessor, Victorian True Love, had included no legitimate eros. . . .

The Heterosexual Steps Out: 1930–1945

In 1930, in *The New York Times,* heterosexuality first became a love that dared to speak its name. On April 30th of that year, the word "heterosexual" is first known to have appeared in *The New York Times Book Review.* There, a critic described the subject of André Gide's *The Immoralist* proceeding "from a heterosexual liaison to a homosexual one." The ability to slip between sexual categories was referred to casually as a rather unremarkable aspect of human possibility. This is also the first known reference by *The Times* to the new hetero/homo duo.[9]

The following month the second reference to the hetero/homo dyad appeared in *The New York Times Book Review,* in a comment on Floyd Dell's *Love in the Machine Age.* This work revealed a prominent antipuritan of the 1930s using the dire threat of homosexuality as his rationale for greater heterosexual freedom. *The Times* quoted Dell's warning that current abnormal social conditions kept the young dependent on their parents, causing "infantilism, prostitution and homosexuality." Also quoted was Dell's attack on the "inculcation of purity" that "breeds distrust of the opposite sex." Young people, Dell said, should be "permitted to develop normally to heterosexual adulthood." "But," *The Times* reviewer emphasized, "such a state already exists, here and now." And so it did. Heterosexuality, a new gender-sex category, had been distributed from the narrow, rarified realm of a few doctors to become a nationally, even internationally, cited aspect of middle-class life.[10] . . .

Heterosexual Hegemony: 1945–1965

The "cult of domesticity" following World War II—the reassociation of women with the home, motherhood, and child-care; men with fatherhood and wage work outside the home—was a period in which the predominance of the hetero norm went almost unchallenged, an era of heterosexual hegemony. This was an age in which conservative mental-health professionals reasserted the old link between heterosexuality and procreation. In contrast, sex-liberals of the day strove, ultimately with success, to expand the heterosexual ideal to include within the boundaries of normality a wider-than-ever range of nonprocreative, premarital, and extramarital behaviors. But sex-liberal reform actually helped to extend and secure the dominance of the heterosexual idea, as we shall see when we get to Kinsey.

The postwar sex-conservative tendency was illustrated in 1947, in Ferdinand Lundberg and Dr. Marnia Farnham's book, *Modern Woman: The Lost Sex*. Improper masculinity and femininity were exemplified, the authors decreed, by "engagement in heterosexual relations . . . with the complete intent to see to it that they do not eventuate in reproduction."[11] Their procreatively defined heterosex was one expression of a postwar ideology of fecundity that, internalized and enacted dutifully by a large part of the population, gave rise to the postwar baby boom.

The idea of the feminine female and masculine male as prolific breeders was also reflected in the stress, specific to the late 1940s, on the homosexual as sad symbol of "sterility"—that particular loaded term appears incessantly in comments on homosex dating to the fecund forties.

In 1948, in *The New York Times Book Review*, sex liberalism was in ascendancy. Dr. Howard A. Rusk declared that Alfred Kinsey's just published report on *Sexual Behavior in the Human Male* had found "wide variations in sex concepts and behavior." This raised the question: "What is 'normal' and 'abnormal'?" In particular, the report had found that "homosexual experience is much more common than previously thought," and "there is often a mixture of both homo and hetero experience."[12]

Kinsey's counting of orgasms indeed stressed the wide range of behaviors and feelings that fell within the boundaries of a quantitative, statistically accounted heterosexuality. Kinsey's liberal reform of the hetero/homo dualism widened the narrow, old hetero category to accord better with the varieties of social experience. He thereby contradicted the older idea of a monolithic, qualitatively defined, natural procreative act, experience, and person.[13]

Though Kinsey explicitly questioned "whether the terms 'normal' and 'abnormal' belong in a scientific vocabulary," his counting of climaxes was generally understood to define normal sex as majority sex. This quantified norm constituted a final, society-wide break with the old qualitatively defined reproductive standard. Though conceived of as purely scientific, the statistical definition of the normal as the-sex-most-people-are-having substituted a new, quantitative moral standard for the old, qualitative sex ethic—another triumph for the spirit of capitalism.

Kinsey also explicitly contested the idea of an absolute, either/or antithesis between hetero and homo persons. He denied that human beings "represent two discrete populations, heterosexual and homosexual." The world, he ordered, "is not to be divided into sheep and goats." The hetero/homo division was not nature's doing: "Only the human mind invents categories and tries to force facts into separated pigeonholes. The living world is a continuum."[14]

With a wave of the taxonomist's hand, Kinsey dismissed the social and historical division of people into heteros and homos. His denial of heterosexual and homosexual personhood rejected the social reality and profound subjective force of a historically constructed tradition which, since 1892 in the United States, had cut the sexual population in two and helped to establish the social reality of a heterosexual and homosexual identity.

On the one hand, the social construction of homosexual persons has led to the development of a powerful gay liberation identity politics based on an ethnic group model. This has freed generations of women and men from a deep, painful, socially induced sense of shame, and helped to bring about a society-wide liberalization of attitudes and responses to homosexuals.[15] On the other hand, contesting the notion of homosexual and heterosexual persons was one early, partial resistance to the limits of the hetero/homo construction. Gore Vidal, rebel son of Kinsey, has for years been joyfully proclaiming:

> there is no such thing as a homosexual or a heterosexual person. There are only homo- or heterosexual acts. Most people are a mixture of impulses if not practices, and what anyone does with a willing partner is of no social or cosmic significance.
>
> So why all the fuss? In order for a ruling class to rule, there must be arbitrary prohibitions. Of all prohibitions, sexual taboo is the most useful because sex involves everyone. . . . we have allowed our governors to divide the population into two teams. One team is good, godly, straight; the other is evil, sick, vicious.[16]

Heterosexuality Questioned: 1965–1982

By the late 1960s, anti-establishment counterculturalists, fledgling feminists, and homosexual-rights activists had begun to produce an unprecedented critique of sexual repression in general, of women's sexual repression in particular, of marriage and the family—and of some forms of heterosexuality. This critique even found its way into *The New York Times*.

In March 1968, in the theater section of that paper, freelancer Rosalyn Regelson cited a scene from a satirical review brought to New York by a San Francisco troupe:

> a heterosexual man wanders inadvertently into a homosexual bar. Before he realizes his mistake, he becomes involved with an aggressive queen who orders a drink for him. Being a broadminded liberal and trying to play it cool until he can back out of the situation gracefully, he asks, "How do you like being a ah homosexual?" To which the queen drawls drily, "How do you like being ah whatever it is you are?"

Regelson continued:

> The Two Cultures in confrontation. The middle-class liberal, challenged today on many fronts, finds his last remaining fixed value, his heterosexuality, called into question. The theater . . . recalls the strategies he uses in dealing with this ultimate threat to his world view.[17]

Heterosexual History: Out of the Shadows

Our brief survey of the heterosexual idea suggests a new hypothesis. Rather than naming a conjunction old as Eve and Adam, heterosexual designates a word and concept, a norm and role, an individual and group identity, a behavior and feeling, and a peculiar sexual-political institution particular to the late nineteenth and twentieth centuries.

Because much stress has been placed here on heterosexuality as word and concept, it seems important to affirm that heterosexuality (and homosexuality) came into existence before it was named and thought about. The formulation of the heterosexual idea did not create a heterosexual experience or behavior; to suggest otherwise would be to ascribe determining power to labels and concepts. But the titling and envisioning of heterosexuality did play an important role in consolidating the construction of the heterosexual's social existence. Before the wide use of the word "heterosexual," I suggest, women and men did not mutually lust with the same profound, sure sense of normalcy that followed the distribution of "heterosexual" as universal sanctifier.

According to this proposal, women and men make their own sexual histories. But they do not produce their sex lives just as they please. They make their sexualities within a particular mode of organization given by the past and altered by their changing desire, their present power and activity, and their vision of a better world. That hypothesis suggests a number of good reasons for the immediate inauguration of research on a historically specific heterosexuality.

The study of the history of the heterosexual experience will forward a great intellectual struggle still in its early stages. This is the fight to pull heterosexuality, homosexuality, and all the sexualities out of the realm of nature and biology [and] into the realm of the social and historical. Feminists have explained to us that anatomy does not determine our gender destinies (our masculinities and femininities). But we've only recently begun to consider that *biology does not settle our erotic fates.* The common notion that biology determines the object of sexual desire, or that physiology and society together cause sexual orientation, are determinisms that deny the break existing between our bodies and situations and our desiring. Just as the biology of our hearing organs will never tell us why we take pleasure in Bach or delight in Dixieland, our female or male anatomies, hormones, and genes will never tell us why we yearn for women, men, both, other, or none. That is because desiring is a self-generated project of individuals within particular historical cultures. Heterosexual history can help us see the place of values and judgments in the construction of our own and others' pleasures, and to see how our erotic tastes—our aesthetics of the flesh—are socially institutionalized through the struggle of individuals and classes.

The study of heterosexuality in time will also help us to recognize the *vast historical diversity of sexual emotions and behaviors*—a variety that challenges the monolithic heterosexual hypothesis. John D'Emilio and Estelle Freedman's *Intimate Matters: A History of Sexuality in America* refers in passing to numerous substantial changes in sexual activity and feeling: for example, the widespread use of contraceptives in the nineteenth century, the twentieth-century incitement of the female orgasm, and the recent sexual conduct changes by gay men in response to the AIDS epidemic. It's now a commonplace of family history that people in particular classes feel and behave in substantially different ways under different historical conditions.[18] Only when we stop assuming an invariable essence of heterosexuality will we begin the research to reveal the full variety of sexual emotions and behaviors.

The historical study of the heterosexual experience can help us *understand the erotic relationships of women and men in terms of their changing modes of social organization.* Such modal analysis actually characterizes a sex history well underway.[19] This suggests that the eros-gender-procreation system (the social ordering of lust, femininity and masculinity, and baby-making) has been linked closely to a society's particular organization of power and production. To understand the subtle history of heterosexuality we need to look carefully at correlations between (1) society's organization of eros and pleasure; (2) its mode of engendering persons as feminine or masculine (its making of women and men); (3) its ordering of human reproduction; and (4) its dominant political economy. This General Theory of Sexual Relativity proposes that substantial historical changes in the social organization of eros, gender, and procreation have basically altered the activity and experience of human beings within those modes.[20]

A historical view locates heterosexuality and homosexuality in time, helping us distance ourselves from them. This distancing can help us formulate new questions that clarify our long-range sexual-political goals: What has been and is the social function of sexual categorizing? Whose interests have been served by the division of the world into heterosexual and homosexual? Do we dare not draw a line between those two erotic species? Is some sexual naming socially necessary? Would human freedom be enhanced if the sex-biology of our partners in lust was of no particular concern, and had no name? In what kind of society could we all more freely explore our desire and our flesh?

As we move [into the year 2000], a new sense of the historical making of the heterosexual and homosexual suggests that these are ways of feeling, acting, and being with each other that we can together unmake and radically remake according to our present desire, power, and our vision of a future political-economy of pleasure.

NOTES

1. Barbara Welter, "The Cult of True Womanhood: 1820–1860," *American Quarterly*, vol. 18 (Summer 1966); Welter's analysis is extended here to include True Men and True Love.

2. See, for example, Catherine Gallagher and Thomas Laqueur, eds., "The Making of the Modern Body: Sexuality and Society in the Nineteenth Century," *Representations,* no. 14 (Spring 1986) (republished, Berkeley: University of California Press, 1987).

3. Dr. James G. Kiernan, "Responsibility in Sexual Perversion," *Chicago Medical Recorder,* vol. 3 (May 1892), pp. 185–210.

4. R. von Krafft-Ebing, *Psychopathia Sexualis, with Especial Reference to Contrary Sexual Instinct: A Medico-Legal Study*, trans. Charles Gilbert Chaddock (Philadelphia: F. A. Davis, 1892), from the 7th and revised German ed. Preface, November 1892.

5. For the standardization of gender see Lewis Terman and C. C. Miles, *Sex and Personality, Studies in Femininity and Masculinity* (New York: McGraw Hill, 1936). For the standardization of intelligence see Lewis Terman, *Stanford-Binet Intelligence Scale* (Boston: Houghton Mifflin, 1916). For the standardization of work, see "scientific management" and "Taylorism" in Harry Braverman, *Labor and Monopoly Capital: The Degradation of Work in the Twentieth Century* (New York: Monthly Review Press, 1974).

6. See D'Emilio and Freedman, *Intimate Matters*, pp. 194–201, 231, 241, 295–96; Ellen Kay Trimberger, "Feminism, Men, and Modern Love: Greenwich Village, 1900–1925," in *Powers of Desire: The Politics of Sexuality*, ed. Ann Snitow, Christine Stansell, Sharon Thompson (New York: Monthly Review Press, 1983), pp. 131–52; Kathy Peiss, "'Charity Girls' and City Pleasures: Historical Notes on Working Class Sexuality, 1880–1920," in *Powers of Desire*, pp. 74–87; and Mary P. Ryan, "The Sexy Saleslady: Psychology, Heterosexuality, and Consumption in the Twentieth Century," in her *Womanhood in America*, 2nd ed. (New York: Franklin Watts, 1979), pp. 151–82.

7. [Rev. Charles Parkhurst], "Woman. Calls Them Andromaniacs. Dr. Parkhurst So Characterizes Certain Women Who Passionately Ape Everything That Is Mannish. Woman Divinely Preferred. Her Supremacy Lies in Her Womanliness, and She Should Make the Most of It—Her Sphere of Best Usefulness the Home," *The New York Times*, May 23, 1897, p. 16:1.

8. See Lisa Duggan, "The Social Enforcement of Heterosexuality and Lesbian Resistance in the 1920s," in *Class, Race, and Sex: The Dynamics of Control*, ed. Amy Swerdlow and Hanah Lessinger (Boston: G. K. Hall, 1983), pp. 75–92; Rayna Rapp and Ellen Ross, "The Twenties Backlash: Compulsory Heterosexuality, the Consumer Family, and the Waning of Feminism," in *Class, Race, and Sex*; Christina Simmons, "Companionate Marriage and the Lesbian Threat," *Frontiers*, vol. 4, no. 3 (Fall 1979), pp. 54–59; and Lillian Faderman, *Surpassing the Love of Men* (New York: William Morrow, 1981).

9. Louis Kronenberger, review of André Gide, *The Immoralist, New York Times Book Review*, April 20, 1930, p. 9.

10. Henry James Forman, review of Floyd Dell, *Love in the Machine Age* (New York: Farrar & Rinehart), *New York Times Book Review*, September 14, 1930, p. 9.

11. Ferdinand Lundberg and Dr. Marnia F. Farnham, *Modern Woman: The Lost Sex* (New York: Harper, 1947).

12. Dr. Howard A. Rusk, *New York Times Book Review*, January 4, 1948, p. 3.

13. Alfred Kinsey, Wardell B. Pomeroy, Clyde E. Martin, *Sexual Behavior in the Human Male* (Philadelphia: W. B. Saunders, 1948), pp. 199–200.

14. Kinsey, *Sexual Behavior*, pp. 637, 639.

15. See Steven Epstein, "Gay Politics, Ethnic Identity: The Limits of Social Constructionism," *Socialist Review* 93/93 (1987), pp. 9–54.

16. Gore Vidal, "Someone to Laugh at the Squares With" [Tennessee Williams], *New York Review of Books*, June 13, 1985; reprinted in his *At Home: Essays, 1982–1988* (New York: Random House, 1988), p. 48.

17. Rosalyn Regelson, "Up the Camp Staircase," *The New York Times*, March 3, 1968, Section II, p. 1:5.

18. D'Emilio and Freedman, *Intimate Matters*, pp. 57–63, 268, 356.

19. Ryan, *Womanhood*; John D'Emilio, "Capitalism and Gay Identity," in *Powers of Desire*, pp. 100–13; Jeffrey Weeks, *Coming Out: Homosexual Politics in Britain from the Nineteenth Century to the Present* (London: Quartet Books, 1977); D'Emilio and Freedman, *Intimate Matters*;

Katz, "Early Colonial Exploration, Agriculture, and Commerce: The Age of Sodomitical Sin, 1607–1740," *Gay/Lesbian Almanac,* pp. 23–65.

20. This tripartite system is intended as a revision of Gayle Rubin's pioneering work on the social-historical orgainization of eros and gender. See "The Traffic in Women: Notes on the Political-Economy of Sex," in *Toward an Anthropology of Women,* ed. Rayna R. Reiter (New York: Monthly Review Press, 1975), pp. 157–210, and "Thinking Sex: Notes for a Radical Theory of the Politics of Sexuality," in *Pleasure and Danger: Exploring Female Sexuality,* ed. Carole S. Vance (Boston: Routledge & Kegan Paul, 1984), pp. 267–329.

6 Masculinity as Homophobia
Fear, Shame, and Silence in the Construction of Gender Identity
Michael S. Kimmel

We think of manhood as eternal, a timeless essence that resides deep in the heart of every man. We think of manhood as a thing, a quality that one either has or doesn't have. We think of manhood as innate, residing in the particular biological composition of the human male, the result of androgens or the possession of a penis. We think of manhood as a transcendent tangible property that each man must manifest in the world, the reward presented with great ceremony to a young novice by his elders for having successfully completed an arduous initiation ritual. . . .

In this chapter, I view masculinity as a constantly changing collection of meanings that we construct through our relationships with ourselves, with each other, and with our world. Manhood is neither static nor timeless; it is historical. Manhood is not the manifestation of an inner essence; it is socially constructed. Manhood does not bubble up to consciousness from our biological makeup; it is created in culture. Manhood means different things at different times to different people. We come to know what it means to be a man in our culture by setting our definitions in opposition to a set of "others"—racial minorities, sexual minorities, and, above all, women. . . .

Classical Social Theory as a Hidden Meditation of Manhood

Begin this inquiry by looking at four passages from that set of texts commonly called classical social and political theory. You will, no doubt, recognize them, but I invite you to recall the way they were discussed in your undergraduate or graduate courses in theory:

> The bourgeoisie cannot exist without constantly revolutionizing the instruments of production, and thereby the relations of production, and with them the whole relations of society. Conservation of the old modes of production in unaltered form, was, on the contrary, the first condition of existence for all earlier industrial classes. Constant revolutionizing of production, uninterrupted disturbance of all social conditions, everlasting uncertainty and agitation distinguish the bourgeois epoch from all earlier ones. All fixed, fast-frozen relations, with their train of ancient and venerable

Republished with permission of Sage Publications, Inc., from *Theorizing Masculinities*, Harry Brod and Michael Kaufman, eds., Men's Studies Association (U.S.), pp. 119–141. Copyright © 1994; permission conveyed through Copyright Clearance Center, Inc. I am grateful to Tim Beneke, Harry Brod, Michael Kaufman, Iona Mara-Drita, and Lillian Rubin for comments on earlier versions of the chapter.

prejudices and opinions are swept away, all new-formed ones become antiquated before they can ossify. All that is solid melts into air, all that is holy is profaned, and man is at last compelled to face with sober senses, his real conditions of life, and his relation with his kind. (Marx & Engels, 1848/1964)

An American will build a house in which to pass his old age and sell it before the roof is on; he will plant a garden and rent it just as the trees are coming into bearing; he will clear a field and leave others to reap the harvest; he will take up a profession and leave it, settle in one place and soon go off elsewhere with his changing desires. . . . At first sight there is something astonishing in this spectacle of so many lucky men restless in the midst of abundance. But it is a spectacle as old as the world; all that is new is to see a whole people performing in it. (Tocqueville, 1835/1967)

Where the fulfillment of the calling cannot directly be related to the highest spiritual and cultural values, or when, on the other hand, it need not be felt simply as economic compulsion, the individual generally abandons the attempt to justify it at all. In the field of its highest development, in the United States, the pursuit of wealth, stripped of its religious and ethical meaning, tends to become associated with purely mundane passions, which often actually give it the character of sport. (Weber, 1905/1966)

We are warned by a proverb against serving two masters at the same time. The poor ego has things even worse: it serves three severe masters and does what it can to bring their claims and demands into harmony with one another. These claims are always divergent and often seem incompatible. No wonder that the ego so often fails in its task. Its three tyrannical masters are the external world, the super ego and the id. . . . It feels hemmed in on three sides, threatened by three kinds of danger, to which, if it is hard pressed, it reacts by generating anxiety. . . . Thus the ego, driven by the id, confined by the super ego, repulsed by reality, struggles to master its economic task of bringing about harmony among the forces and influences working in and upon it; and we can understand how it is that so often we cannot suppress a cry: "Life is not easy!" (Freud, "The Dissection of the Psychical Personality," 1933/1966)

If your social science training was anything like mine, these were offered as descriptions of the bourgeoisie under capitalism, of individuals in democratic societies, of the fate of the Protestant work ethic under the ever rationalizing spirit of capitalism, or of the arduous task of the autonomous ego in psychological development. Did anyone ever mention that in all four cases the theorists were describing men? Not just "man" as in generic mankind, but a particular type of masculinity, a definition of manhood that derives its identity from participation in the marketplace, from interaction with other men in that marketplace—in short, a model of masculinity for whom identity is based on homosocial competition? Three years before Tocqueville found Americans "restless in the midst of abundance," Senator Henry Clay had called the United States "a nation of self-made men."

What does it mean to be "self-made"? What are the consequences of self-making for the individual man, for other men, for women? It is this notion of manhood—rooted in the sphere of production, the public arena, a masculinity grounded not in land ownership or in artisanal republican virtue but in successful participation in marketplace competition—this has been the defining notion of American manhood.

Masculinity must be proved, and no sooner is it proved than it is again questioned and must be proved again—constant, relentless, unachievable, and ultimately the quest for proof becomes so meaningless that it takes on the characteristic, as Weber said, of a sport. He who has the most toys when he dies wins. . . .

Masculinity as History and the History of Masculinity

The idea of masculinity expressed in the previous extracts is the product of historical shifts in the grounds on which men rooted their sense of themselves as men. To argue that cultural definitions of gender identity are historically specific goes only so far; we have to specify exactly what those models were. In my historical inquiry into the development of these models of manhood[1] I chart the fate of two models for manhood at the turn of the 19th century and the emergence of a third in the first few decades of that century.

In the late 18th and early 19th centuries, two models of manhood prevailed. The *Genteel Patriarch* derived his identity from landownership. Supervising his estate, he was refined, elegant, and given to casual sensuousness. He was a doting and devoted father, who spent much of his time supervising the estate and with his family. Think of George Washington or Thomas Jefferson as examples. By contrast, the *Heroic Artisan* embodied the physical strength and republican virtue that Jefferson observed in the yeoman farmer, independent urban craftsman, or shopkeeper. Also a devoted father, the Heroic Artisan taught his son his craft, bringing him through ritual apprenticeship to status as master craftsman. Economically autonomous, the Heroic Artisan also cherished his democratic community, delighting in the participatory democracy of the town meeting. Think of Paul Revere at his pewter shop, shirtsleeves rolled up, a leather apron—a man who took pride in his work.

Heroic Artisans and Genteel Patriarchs lived in casual accord, in part because their gender ideals were complementary (both supported participatory democracy and individual autonomy, although patriarchs tended to support more powerful state machineries and also supported slavery) and because they rarely saw one another: Artisans were decidedly urban and the Genteel Patriarchs ruled their rural estates. By the 1830s, though, this casual symbiosis was shattered by the emergence of a new vision of masculinity, *Marketplace Manhood.*

Marketplace Man derived his identity entirely from his success in the capitalist marketplace, as he accumulated wealth, power, status. He was the urban entrepreneur, the businessman. Restless, agitated, and anxious, Marketplace Man was an absentee landlord at home and an absent father with his children, devoting himself to his work in an increasingly homosocial environment—a male-only world in which he pits himself against other men. His efforts at self-making transform the political and economic spheres, casting aside the Genteel Patriarch as an anachronistic feminized dandy—sweet, but ineffective and outmoded, and transforming the Heroic Artisan into a dispossessed proletarian, a wage slave.

As Tocqueville would have seen it, the coexistence of the Genteel Patriarch and the Heroic Artisan embodied the fusion of liberty and equality. Genteel Patriarchy was the manhood of the traditional aristocracy, the class that embodied the virtue of liberty. The Heroic Artisan embodied democratic community, the solidarity of the urban shopkeeper or craftsman. Liberty and democracy, the patriarch and the artisan, could, and did, coexist. But Marketplace Man is capitalist man, and he makes both freedom and equality problematic, eliminating the freedom of the aristocracy and proletarianizing the equality of the artisan. In one sense, American history has been an effort to restore, retrieve, or reconstitute the virtues of Genteel Patriarchy and Heroic Artisanate as they were being transformed in the capitalist marketplace.

Marketplace Manhood was a manhood that required proof, and that required the acquisition of tangible goods as evidence of success. It reconstituted itself by the exclusion of "others"—women, nonwhite men, nonnative-born men, homosexual men—and by terrified flight into a pristine mythic homosocial Eden where men could, at last, be real men among other men. The story of the ways in which Marketplace Man becomes American Everyman is a tragic tale, a tale of striving to live up to impossible ideals of success leading to chronic terrors of emasculation, emotional emptiness, and a gendered rage that leave a wide swath of destruction in its wake.

Masculinities as Power Relations

Marketplace Masculinity describes the normative definition of American masculinity. It describes his characteristics—aggression, competition, anxiety—and the arena in which those characteristics are deployed—the public sphere, the marketplace. If the marketplace is the arena in which manhood is tested and proved, it is a gendered arena, in which tensions between women and men and tensions among different groups of men are weighted with meaning. These tensions suggest that cultural definitions of gender are played out in a contested terrain and are themselves power relations.

All masculinities are not created equal; or rather, we are all *created* equal, but any hypothetical equality evaporates quickly because our definitions of masculinity are not equally valued in our society. One definition of manhood continues to remain the standard against which other forms of manhood are measured and evaluated. Within the dominant culture, the masculinity that defines white, middle class, early middle-aged, heterosexual men is the masculinity that sets the standards for other men, against which other men are measured and, more often than not, found wanting. Sociologist Erving Goffman (1963) wrote that in America, there is only "one complete, unblushing male":

> a young, married, white, urban, northern heterosexual, Protestant father of college education, fully employed, of good complexion, weight and height, and a recent record in sports. Every American male tends to look out upon the world from this perspective. . . . Any male who fails to qualify in any one of these ways is likely to view himself . . . as unworthy, incomplete, and inferior. (p. 128)

This is the definition that we will call "hegemonic" masculinity, the image of masculinity of those men who hold power, which has become the standard in psychological evaluations, sociological research, and self-help and advice literature for teaching young men to become "real men" (Connell, 1987). The hegemonic definition of manhood is a man *in* power, a man *with* power, and a man *of* power. We equate manhood with being strong, successful, capable, reliable, in control. The very definitions of manhood we have developed in our culture maintain the power that some men have over other men and that men have over women.

Our culture's definition of masculinity is thus several stories at once. It is about the individual man's quest to accumulate those cultural symbols that denote manhood, signs that he has in fact achieved it. It is about those standards being used against women to prevent their inclusion in public life and their consignment to a devalued private sphere. It is about the differential access that different types of men have to those cultural resources that confer manhood and about how each of these groups then develops their own modifications to preserve and claim their manhood. It is about the power of these definitions themselves to serve to maintain the real-life power that men have over women and that some men have over other men.

This definition of manhood has been summarized cleverly by psychologist Robert Brannon (1976) into four succinct phrases:

1. "No Sissy Stuff!" One may never do anything that even remotely suggests femininity. Masculinity is the relentless repudiation of the feminine.
2. "Be a Big Wheel." Masculinity is measured by power, success, wealth, and status. As the current saying goes, "He who has the most toys when he dies wins."
3. "Be a Sturdy Oak." Masculinity depends on remaining calm and reliable in a crisis, holding emotions in check. In fact, proving you're a man depends on never showing your emotions at all. Boys don't cry.
4. "Give 'em Hell." Exude an aura of manly daring and aggression. Go for it. Take risks.

These rules contain the elements of the definition against which virtually all American men are measured. Failure to embody these rules, to affirm the power of the rules and one's achievement of them is a source of men's confusion and pain. Such a model is, of course, unrealizable for any man. But we keep trying, valiantly and vainly, to measure up. American masculinity is a relentless test.[2] The chief test is contained in the first rule. Whatever the variations by race, class, age, ethnicity, or sexual orientation, being a man means "not being like women." This notion of antifemininity lies at the heart of contemporary and historical conceptions of manhood, so that masculinity is defined more by what one is not rather than who one is.

Masculinity as the Flight from the Feminine

Historically and developmentally, masculinity has been defined as the flight from women, the repudiation of femininity. . . .

The drive to repudiate the mother as the indication of the acquisition of masculine gender identity has three consequences for the young boy. First, he pushes away his real mother, and with her the traits of nurturance, compassion, and tenderness she may have embodied. Second, he suppresses those traits in himself, because they will reveal his incomplete separation from mother. His life becomes a lifelong project to demonstrate that he possesses none of his mother's traits. Masculine identity is born in the renunciation of the feminine, not in the direct affirmation of the masculine, which leaves masculine gender identity tenuous and fragile.

Third, as if to demonstrate the accomplishment of these first two tasks, the boy also learns to devalue all women in his society, as the living embodiments of those traits in himself he has learned to despise. Whether or not he was aware of it, Freud also described the origins of sexism—the systematic devaluation of women—in the desperate efforts of the boy to separate from mother. We may *want* "a girl just like the girl that married dear old Dad," as the popular song had it, but we certainly don't want to *be like* her.

This chronic uncertainty about gender identity helps us understand several obsessive behaviors. Take, for example, the continuing problem of the school-yard bully. Parents remind us that the bully is the *least* secure about his manhood, and so he is constantly trying to prove it. But he "proves" it by choosing opponents he is absolutely certain he can defeat; thus the standard taunt to a bully is to "pick on someone your own size." He can't, though, and after defeating a smaller and weaker opponent, which he was sure would prove his manhood, he is left with the empty gnawing feeling that he has not proved it after all, and he must find another opponent, again one smaller and weaker, that he can again defeat to prove it to himself.[3] . . .

When does it end? Never. To admit weakness, to admit frailty or fragility, is to be seen as a wimp, a sissy, not a real man. But seen by whom?

Masculinity as a Homosocial Enactment

Other men: We are under the constant careful scrutiny of other men. Other men watch us, rank us, grant our acceptance into the realm of manhood. Manhood is demonstrated for other men's approval. It is other men who evaluate the performance. Literary critic David Leverenz (1991) argues that "ideologies of manhood have functioned primarily in relation to the gaze of male peers and male authority" (p. 769). Think of how men boast to one another of their accomplishments—from their latest sexual conquest to the size of the fish they caught—and how we constantly parade the markers of manhood—wealth, power, status, sexy women—in front of other men, desperate for their approval.

That men prove their manhood in the eyes of other men is both a consequence of sexism and one of its chief props. "Women have, in men's minds, such a low place on the social ladder of this country that it's useless to define yourself in terms of a woman," noted playwright David Mamet. "What men need is men's approval." Women become a kind of currency that men use to improve their ranking on the masculine social scale. (Even those moments of heroic conquest of women carry, I believe, a current of homosocial evaluation.) Masculinity is a *homosocial* enactment. We test ourselves, perform heroic feats, take enormous risks, all because we want other men to grant us our manhood. . . .

Masculinity as Homophobia

. . . That nightmare from which we never seem to awaken is that those other men will see that sense of inadequacy, they will see that in our own eyes we are not who we are pretending to be. What we call masculinity is often a hedge against being revealed as a fraud, an exaggerated set of activities that keep others from seeing through us, and a frenzied effort to keep at bay those fears within ourselves. Our real fear "is not fear of women but of being ashamed or humiliated in front of other men, or being dominated by stronger men" (Leverenz, 1986, p. 451).

This, then, is the great secret of American manhood: *We are afraid of other men.* Homophobia is a central organizing principle of our cultural definition of manhood. Homophobia is more than the irrational fear of gay men, more than the fear that we might be perceived as gay. "The word 'faggot' has nothing to do with homosexual experience or even with fears of homosexuals," writes David Leverenz (1986). "It comes out of the depths of manhood: a label of ultimate contempt for anyone who seems sissy, untough, uncool" (p. 455). Homophobia is the fear that other men will unmask us, emasculate us, reveal to us and the world that we do not measure up, that we are not real men. We are afraid to let other men see that fear. Fear makes us ashamed, because the recognition of fear in ourselves is proof to ourselves that we are not as manly as we pretend, that we are, like the young man in a poem by Yeats, "one that ruffles in a manly pose for all his timid heart." Our fear is the fear of humiliation. We are ashamed to be afraid.

Shame leads to silence—the silences that keep other people believing that we actually approve of the things that are done to women, to minorities, to gays and lesbians in our culture. The frightened silence as we scurry past a woman being hassled by men on the street. That furtive silence when men make sexist or racist jokes in a bar. That clammy-handed silence when guys in the office make gay-bashing jokes. Our fears are the sources of our silences, and men's silence is what keeps the system running. This might help to explain why women often complain that their male friends or partners are often so understanding when they are alone and yet laugh at sexist jokes or even make those jokes themselves when they are out with a group.

The fear of being seen as a sissy dominates the cultural definitions of manhood. It starts so early. "Boys among boys are ashamed to be unmanly," wrote one educator in 1871 (cited in Rotundo, 1993, p. 264). I have a standing bet with a friend that I can walk onto any playground in America where 6-year-old boys are happily playing and by asking one question, I can provoke a fight. That question is simple: "Who's a sissy around here?" Once posed, the challenge is made. One of two things is likely to happen. One boy will accuse another of being a sissy, to which that boy will respond that he is not a sissy, that the first boy is. They may have to fight it out to see who's lying. Or a whole group of boys will surround one boy and all shout "He is! He is!" That boy will either burst into tears and run home crying, disgraced, or he will have to take on several boys at once, to prove that he's not a sissy. (And what will his father or older brothers tell him if he chooses to run home crying?) It will be some time before he regains any sense of self-respect.

Violence is often the single most evident marker of manhood. Rather it is the willingness to fight, the desire to fight. The origin of our expression that one has a chip on one's shoulder lies in the practice of an adolescent boy in the country or small town at the turn of the century, who would literally walk around with a chip of wood balanced on his shoulder—a signal of his readiness to fight with anyone who would take the initiative of knocking the chip off (see Gorer, 1964, p. 38; Mead, 1965).

As adolescents, we learn that our peers are a kind of gender police, constantly threatening to unmask us as feminine, as sissies. One of the favorite tricks when I was an adolescent was to ask a boy to look at his fingernails. If he held his palm toward his face and curled his fingers back to see them, he passed the test. He'd look at his nails "like a man." But if he held the back of his hand away from his face, and looked at his fingernails with arm outstretched, he was immediately ridiculed as sissy.

As young men we are constantly riding those gender boundaries, checking the fences we have constructed on the perimeter, making sure that nothing even remotely feminine might show through. The possibilities of being unmasked are everywhere. Even the most seemingly insignificant thing can pose a threat or activate that haunting terror. On the day the students in my course "Sociology of Men and Masculinities" were scheduled to discuss homophobia and male-male friendships, one student provided a touching illustration. Noting that it was a beautiful day, the first day of spring after a brutal northeast winter, he decided to wear shorts to class. "I had this really nice pair of new Madras shorts," he commented. "But then I thought to myself, these shorts have lavender and pink in them. Today's class topic is homophobia. Maybe today is not the best day to wear these shorts."

Our efforts to maintain a manly front cover everything we do. What we wear. How we talk. How we walk. What we eat. Every mannerism, every movement contains a coded gender language. Think, for example, of how you would answer the question: How do you "know" if a man is homosexual? When I ask this question in classes or workshops, respondents invariably provide a pretty standard list of stereotypically effeminate behaviors. He walks a certain way, talks a certain way, acts a certain way. He's very emotional; he shows his feelings. One woman commented that she "knows" a man is gay if he really cares about her; another said she knows he's gay if he shows no interest in her, if he leaves her alone.

Now alter the question and imagine what heterosexual men do to make sure no one could possibly get the "wrong idea" about them. Responses typically refer to the original stereotypes, this time as a set of negative rules about behavior. Never dress that way. Never talk or walk that way. Never show your feelings or get emotional. Always be prepared to demonstrate sexual interest in women that you meet, so it is impossible for any woman to get the wrong idea about you. In this sense, homophobia, the fear of being perceived as gay, as not a real man, keeps men exaggerating all the traditional rules of masculinity, including sexual predation with women. Homophobia and sexism go hand in hand. . . .

Homophobia as a Cause of Sexism, Heterosexism, and Racism

Homophobia is intimately interwoven with both sexism and racism. The fear—sometimes conscious, sometimes not—that others might perceive us as homosexual propels men to enact all manner of exaggerated masculine behaviors and attitudes to make sure that no one could possibly get the wrong idea about us. One of the centerpieces of that exaggerated masculinity is putting women down, both by excluding them from the public sphere and by the quotidian put-downs in speech and behaviors that organize the daily life of the American man. Women and gay men become the "other" against which heterosexual men project their identities, against whom they stack the decks so as to compete in a situation in which they will always win, so that by suppressing them, men can stake a claim for their own manhood. Women threaten emasculation by representing the home, workplace, and familial responsibility, the negation of fun. Gay men have historically played the role of the consummate sissy in the American popular mind because homosexuality is seen as an inversion of normal gender development. There have been other "others." Through American history, various groups have represented the sissy, the non-men against whom American men played out their definitions of manhood, often with vicious results. In fact, these changing groups provide an interesting lesson in American historical development.

At the turn of the 19th century, it was Europeans and children who provided the contrast for American men. The "true American was vigorous, manly, and direct, not effete and corrupt like the supposed Europeans," writes Rupert Wilkinson (1986). "He was plain rather than ornamented, rugged rather than luxury seeking, a liberty loving common man or natural gentleman rather than an aristocratic oppressor or servile minion" (p. 96). The "real man" of the early 19th century was neither noble nor serf. By the middle of the century, black slaves had replaced the effete nobleman. Slaves were seen as dependent, helpless men, incapable of defending their women and children, and therefore less than manly. Native Americans were cast as foolish and naive children, so they could be infantilized as the "Red Children of the Great White Father" and therefore excluded from full manhood.

By the end of the century, new European immigrants were also added to the list of the unreal men, especially the Irish and Italians, who were seen as too passionate and emotionally volatile to remain controlled sturdy oaks, and Jews, who were seen as too bookishly effete and too physically puny to truly measure up. In the mid-20th century, it was also Asians—first the Japanese during the Second World War, and more recently, the Vietnamese during the Vietnam War—who have served as unmanly templates against which American men have hurled their gendered rage. Asian men were seen as small, soft, and effeminate—hardly men at all.

Such a list of "hyphenated" Americans—Italian-, Jewish-, Irish-, African-, Native-, Asian-, gay—composes the majority of American men. So manhood is only possible for a distinct minority, and the definition has been constructed to prevent the others from achieving it. Interestingly, this emasculation of one's enemies has a flip side— and one that is equally gendered. These very groups that have historically been cast as less than manly were also, often simultaneously, cast as hypermasculine, as sexu- ally aggressive, violent rapacious beasts, against whom "civilized" men must take a decisive stand and thereby rescue civilization. Thus black men were depicted as rampaging sexual beasts, women as carnivorously carnal, gay men as sexually insa- tiable, southern European men as sexually predatory and voracious, and Asian men as vicious and cruel torturers who were immorally disinterested in life itself, willing to sacrifice their entire people for their whims. But whether one saw these groups as effeminate sissies or as brutal savages, the terms with which they were perceived were gendered. These groups become the "others," the screens against which traditional conceptions of manhood were developed. . . .

Power and Powerlessness in the Lives of Men

I have argued that homophobia, men's fear of other men, is the animating condi- tion of the dominant definition of masculinity in America, that the reigning defini- tion of masculinity is a defensive effort to prevent being emasculated. In our efforts to suppress or overcome those fears, the dominant culture exacts a tremendous price from those deemed less than fully manly: women, gay men, nonnative-born men, men of color. This perspective may help clarify a paradox in men's lives, a paradox in which men have virtually all the power and yet do not feel powerful (see Kaufman, 1993).

Manhood is equated with power—over women, over other men. Everywhere we look, we see the institutional expression of that power—in state and national legisla- tures, on the boards of directors of every major U.S. corporation or law firm, and in every school and hospital administration. . . .

When confronted with the analysis that men have all the power, many men react incredulously. "What do you mean, men have all the power?" they ask. "What are you talking about? My wife bosses me around. My kids boss me around. My boss bosses me around. I have no power at all! I'm completely powerless!"

Men's feelings are not the feelings of the powerful, but of those who see themselves as powerless. These are the feelings that come inevitably from the discontinuity between the social and the psychological, between the aggregate analysis that reveals how men are in power as a group and the psychological fact that they do not feel powerful as individuals. They are the feelings of men who were raised to believe themselves entitled to feel that power, but do not feel it. No wonder many men are frustrated and angry. . . .

Why, then, do American men feel so powerless? Part of the answer is because we've constructed the rules of manhood so that only the tiniest fraction of men come to believe that they are the biggest of wheels, the sturdiest of oaks, the most virulent repudiators of femininity, the most daring and aggressive. We've managed to disempower the overwhelming majority of American men by other means—such as discriminating on the basis of race, class, ethnicity, age, or sexual preference. . .

Others still rehearse the politics of exclusion, as if by clearing away the playing field of secure gender identity of any that we deem less than manly—women, gay men, nonnative-born men, men of color—middle-class, straight, white men can re-ground their sense of themselves without those haunting fears and that deep shame that they are unmanly and will be exposed by other men. This is the manhood of racism, of sexism, of homophobia. It is the manhood that is so chronically insecure that it trembles at the idea of lifting the ban on gays in the military, that is so threatened by women in the workplace that women become the targets of sexual harassment, that is so deeply frightened of equality that it must ensure that the playing field of male competition remains stacked against all newcomers to the game.

Exclusion and escape have been the dominant methods American men have used to keep their fears of humiliation at bay. The fear of emasculation by other men, of being humiliated, of being seen as a sissy, is the leitmotif in my reading of the history of American manhood. Masculinity has become a relentless test by which we prove to other men, to women, and ultimately to ourselves, that we have successfully mastered the part. The restlessness that men feel today is nothing new in American history; we have been anxious and restless for almost two centuries. Neither exclusion nor escape has ever brought us the relief we've sought, and there is no reason to think that either will solve our problems now. Peace of mind, relief from gender struggle, will come only from a politics of inclusion, not exclusion, from standing up for equality and justice, and not by running away.

NOTES

1. Much of this work is elaborated in *Manhood: The American Quest* (in press).

2. Although I am here discussing only American masculinity, I am aware that others have located this chronic instability and efforts to prove manhood in the particular cultural and economic arrangements of Western society. Calvin, after all, inveighed against the disgrace "for men to become effeminate," and countless other theorists have described the mechanics of manly proof (see, for example, Seidler, 1994).

3. Such observations also led journalist Heywood Broun to argue that most of the attacks against feminism came from men who were shorter than 5 ft. 7 in. "The man who, whatever his physical size, feels secure in his own masculinity and in his own relation to life is rarely resentful of the opposite sex" (cited in Symes, 1930, p. 139).

REFERENCES

Brannon, R. (1976). The male sex role—and what it's done for us lately. In R. Brannon & D. David (Eds.), *The forty-nine percent majority* (pp. 1–40). Reading, MA: Addison-Wesley.

Connell, R. W. (1987). *Gender and power.* Stanford, CA: Stanford University Press.

Freud, S. (1933/1966). *New introductory lectures on psychoanalysis* (L. Strachey, Ed.). New York: Norton.

Goffman, E. (1963). *Stigma*. Englewood Cliffs, NJ: Prentice Hall.

Gorer, G. (1964). *The American people: A study in national character*. New York: Norton.

Kaufman, M. (1993). *Cracking the armour: Power and pain in the lives of men*. Toronto: Viking Canada.

Leverenz, D. (1986). Manhood, humiliation and public life: Some stories. *Southwest Review, 71,* Fall.

Leverenz, D. (1991). The last real man in America: From Natty Bumppo to Batman. *American Literary Review, 3.*

Marx, K., & F. Engels. (1848/1964). The communist manifesto. In R. Tucker (Ed.), *The Marx-Engels reader*. New York: Norton.

Mead, M. (1965). *And keep your powder dry*. New York: William Morrow.

Rotundo, E. A. (1993). *American manhood: Transformations in masculinity from the revolution to the modern era*. New York: Basic Books.

Seidler, V. J. (1994). *Unreasonable men: Masculinity and social theory*. New York: Routledge.

Symes, L. (1930). The new masculinism. *Harper's Monthly, 161,* January.

Tocqueville, A. de. (1835/1967). *Democracy in America*. New York: Anchor.

Weber, M. (1905/1966). *The Protestant ethic and the spirit of capitalism*. New York: Charles Scribner's.

Wilkinson, R. (1986). *American tough: The tough-guy tradition and American character*. New York: Harper & Row.

7 Transgender Feminism
Queering the Woman Question
Susan Stryker

Many years ago, I paid a visit to my son's kindergarten room for parent-teacher night. Among the treats in store for us parents that evening was a chance to look at the *My Favorite Things* book that each child had prepared over the first few weeks of classes. Each page was blank except for a pre-printed line that said 'My favorite color is (blank)' or 'My favorite food is (blank)', or 'My favorite story is (blank)'; students were supposed to fill in the blanks with their favorite things and draw an accompanying picture. My son had filled the blanks and empty spaces of his book with many such things as 'green', 'pizza' and '*Goodnight Moon*', but I was unprepared for his response to 'My favorite animal is (blank)'. His favorite animal was 'yeast'. I looked up at the teacher, who had been watching me in anticipation of this moment. 'Yeast?' I said, and she, barely suppressing her glee, said, 'Yeah. And when I asked why yeast was his favorite animal, he said, "It just makes the category animal seem more interesting."'

At the risk of suggesting that the category 'woman' is somehow not interesting *enough* without a transgender supplement, which is certainly not my intent, I have to confess that there is a sense in which 'woman', as a category of human personhood, is indeed, for me, *more* interesting when we include transgender phenomena within its rubric. The work required to encompass transgender within the bounds of womanhood takes women's studies, and queer feminist theorising, in important and necessary directions. It takes us directly into the basic questions of the sex/gender distinction, and of the concept of a sex/gender system, that lie at the heart of Anglophone feminism. Once there, transgender phenomena ask us to follow basic feminist insights to their logical conclusion (biology is not destiny, and one is not born a woman, right?). And yet, transgender phenomena simultaneously threaten to refigure the basic conceptual and representational framework within which the category 'woman' has been conventionally understood, deployed, embraced and resisted.

Perhaps 'gender', transgender tells us, is not related to 'sex' in quite the same way that an apple is related to the reflection of a red fruit in the mirror; it is not a mimetic relationship. Perhaps 'sex' is a category that, like citizenship, can be attained by the non-native residents of a particular location by following certain procedures. Perhaps gender has a more complex genealogy, at the level of individual psychobiography as well as collective socio-historical process, than can be grasped or accounted for by the currently dominant binary sex/gender model of Eurocentric modernity. And perhaps what is to be learned by grappling with transgender concerns is relevant to a great

Edited by Stacy Gillis, Gillian Howie, and Rebecca Munford, *Third Wave Feminism,* published 2004. Reproduced with permission of Palgrave Macmillan.

many people, including nontransgendered women and men. Perhaps transgender discourses help us think in terms of embodied specificities, as *women's* studies has traditionally tried to do, while also giving us a way to think about gender as a system with multiple nodes and positions, as *gender* studies increasingly requires us to do. Perhaps transgender studies, which emerged in the academy at the intersection of feminism and queer theory over the course of the last decade or so, can be thought of as one productive way to 'queer the woman question'.[1] If we define 'transgender phenomena' broadly as anything that disrupts or denaturalises normative gender, and which calls our attention to the processes through which normativity is produced and atypicality achieves visibility, 'transgender' becomes an incredibly useful analytical concept. What might 'transgender feminism'—a feminism that focuses on marginalised gender expressions as well as normative ones—look like?

As an historian of the United States, my training encourages me to approach currently salient questions by looking at the past through new eyes. Questions that matter now, historians are taught to think, are always framed by enabling conditions that precede them. Thus, when I want to know what transgender feminism might be, I try to learn what it has already been. When I learned, for example, that the first publication of the post-WWII transgender movement, a short-lived early 1950s magazine called *Transvestia*, was produced by a group calling itself The Society for Equality in Dress (Meyerowitz 2002, 179), I not only saw that a group of male transvestites in Southern California had embraced the rhetoric of first wave feminism and applied the concept of gender equality to the marginalised topic of cross-dressing; I also came to think differently about Amelia Bloomer and the antebellum clothing reform movement. To the extent that breaking out of the conventional constructions of womanhood is both a feminist and transgender practice, what we might conceivably call transgender feminism arguably has been around since the first half of the nineteenth century.

Looking back, it is increasingly obvious that transgender phenomena are not limited to individuals who have 'transgendered' personal identities. Rather, they are signposts that point to many different kinds of bodies and subjects, and they can help us see how gender can function as part of a more extensive apparatus of social domination and control. Gender as a form of social control is not limited to the control of bodies defined as 'women's bodies', or the control of female reproductive capacities. Because genders are categories through which we recognise the personhood of others (as well as ourselves), because they are categories without which we have great difficulty in recognising personhood at all, gender also functions as a mechanism of control when some loss of gender status is threatened, or when claims of membership in a gender are denied. Why is it considered a heterosexist put-down to call some lesbians mannish? Why, if a working-class woman does certain kinds of physically demanding labour, or if a middle-class woman surpasses a certain level of professional accomplishment, is their feminine respectability called into question? Stripping away gender, and misattributing gender, are practices of social domination, regulation and control that threaten social abjection; they operate by attaching transgender stigma to various unruly bodies and subject positions, not just to 'transgendered' ones.[2] . . .

Transgender issues also engage many of the foundational questions in the social sciences and life sciences as they pertain to feminist inquiry. The biological body, which is typically assumed to be a single organically unified natural object characterised by one and only one of two available sex statuses, is demonstrably no such thing. The so-called 'sex of the body' is an interpretive fiction that narrates a complex amalgamation of gland secretions and reproductive organs, chromosomes and genes, morphological characteristics and physiognomic features. There are far more than two viable aggregations of sexed bodily being. At what cost, for what purposes, and through what means do we collapse this diversity of embodiment into the social categories 'woman' and 'man'? How does the psychical subject who forms in this material context become aware of itself, of its embodied situation, of its position in language, family or society? How does it learn to answer to one or the other of the two personal pronouns 'he' or 'she', and to recognise 'it' as a disavowed option that forecloses personhood? How do these processes vary from individual to individual, from place to place, and from time to time? These are questions of importance to feminism, usually relegated to the domains of biology and psychology, that transgender phenomena can help us think through. Transgender feminism gives us another axis, along with critical race studies or disability studies, to learn more about the ways in which bodily difference becomes the basis for socially constructed hierarchies, and helps us see in new ways how we are all inextricably situated, through the inescapable necessity of our own bodies, in terms of race, sex, gender or ability.

For all the reasons I have suggested, transgender phenomena are *interesting* for feminism, women's studies, gender studies, sexuality studies, and so forth. But *interesting*, by itself, is not enough, when hard decisions about budgets and staffing have to be made in academic departments, priorities and commitments actualised through classroom allocations and affirmative action hiring. *Interesting* also has to be *important*, and transgender is rarely considered important. All too often transgender is thought to name only a largely irrelevant class of phenomena that occupy the marginal fringe of the hegemonic gender categories man and woman, or else it is seen as one of the later, minor accretions to the gay and lesbian movement, along with bisexual and intersexed. At best, transgender is considered a portent of a future that seems to await us, for good or ill. But it remains a canary in the cultural coal mine, not an analytical workhorse for pulling down the patriarchy and other associated social ills. As long as transgender is conceived as the fraction of a fraction of a fraction of a movement, as long as it is thought to represent only some inconsequential outliers in a bigger and more important set of data, there is very little reason to support transgender concerns at the institutional level. Transgender will always lose by the numbers. The transgender community is tiny. In (so-called) liberal democracies that measure political strength by the number of votes or the number of dollars, transgender does not count for much, or add up to a lot. But there is another way to think about the importance of transgender concerns at this moment in our history.

One measure of an issue's potential is not how many people directly identify with it but, rather, how many other issues it can be linked with in a productive fashion. How, in other words, can an issue be *articulated*, in the double sense of 'articulation,' meaning both 'to bring into language', and 'the act of flexibly conjoining.[3] Articulating a transgender politics is part of the specialised work that I do as an activist transgender intellectual. How many issues can I link together through my experience of the category transgender?

To the extent that I am perceived as a woman (which is most of the time), I experience the same misogyny as other women, and to the extent that I am perceived as a man (which happens every now and then), I experience the homophobia directed toward gay men – both forms of oppression, in my experience, being rooted in a cultural devaluation of the feminine. My transgender status, to the extent that it is apparent to others, manifests itself through the appearance of my bodily surface and my shape, in much the same way that race is constructed, in part, through visuality and skin, and in much the same way that the beauty system operates by privileging certain modes of appearance. My transsexual body is different from most other bodies, and while this difference does not impair me, it has been medicalised, and I am sometimes disabled by the social oppression that takes aim at the specific form of my difference. Because I am formally classified as a person with a psychopathology known as Gender Identity Disorder, I am subject to the social stigma attached to mental illness, and I am more vulnerable to unwanted medical-psychiatric interventions. Because changing personal identification documents is an expensive and drawn-out affair, I have spent part of my life as an undocumented worker. Because identification documents such as drivers licenses and passports are coded with multiple levels of information, including previous names and 'AKAs', my privacy, and perhaps my personal safety, is at risk every time I drive too fast or cross a border. When I travel I always have to ask myself whether some aspect of my appearance, some bit of data buried in the magnetic strip on some piece of plastic with my picture on it, will create suspicion and result in my detention? In this era of terror and security, we are all surveyed, we are all profiled, but some of us have more to fear from the state than others. Staying home, however, does not make me safer. If I risk arrest by engaging in non-violent demonstrations, or violent political protest, the incarceration complex would not readily accommodate my needs; even though I am a post-operative male-to-female transsexual, I could wind up in a men's prison where I would be at extreme risk of rape and sexual assault. Because I am transgendered, I am more likely to experience discrimination in housing, employment and access to health care, and more likely to experience violence. These are not abstract issues: I have lost jobs, and not been offered jobs, because I am transgendered. I have had doctors walk out of exam rooms in disgust; I have had more trouble finding and retaining housing because I am transgendered; I have had my home burglarised and my property vandalised, and I have been assaulted, because I am transgendered.

Let me recapitulate what I can personally articulate through transgender: misogyny, homophobia, racism, looksism, disability, medical colonisation, coercive psychiatrisation, undocumented labour, border control, state surveillance, population profiling, the prison-industrial complex, employment discrimination, housing discrimination, lack of health care, denial of access to social services, and violent hate crimes. These issues are my issues, not because I think it is chic to be politically progressive. These issues are my issues, not because I feel guilty about being white, highly educated or a citizen of the United States. These issues are my issues, not because my bodily being lives the space where these issues intersect. I articulate these issues when my mouth speaks the words that my mind puts together from what my body knows. It is by winning the struggles over these issues that my body as it is lived for me survives – or by losing them, that it will die. If these issues are your issues as well, then transgender needs to be part of your intellectual and political agenda. It is one of your issues.

I conclude now with some thoughts on yet another aspect of transgender articulation, the one mentioned in my title, which is how transgender issues articulate, or join together, feminist and queer projects. 'Trans-' is troublesome for both LGBT communities and feminism, but the kind of knowledge that emerges from this linkage is precisely the kind of knowledge that we desperately need in the larger social arena.

Trans is not a 'sexual identity', and therefore fits awkwardly in the LGBT rubric. That is, 'transgender' does not describe a sexual orientation (like homosexual, bisexual, heterosexual or asexual), nor are transgender people typically attracted to other transgender people in the same way that lesbians are attracted to other lesbians, or gay men to other gay men. Transgender status is more like race or class, in that it cuts across the categories of sexual identity.[4] Neither is transgender (at least currently, in Eurocentric modernity) an identity term like 'woman' or 'man' that names a gender category within a social system. It is a way of being a man or a woman, or a way of marking resistance to those terms. Transgender analyses of gender oppression and hierarchy, unlike more normative feminist analyses, are not primarily concerned with the differential operations of power upon particular identity categories that create inequalities within gender systems, but rather with how the system itself produces a multitude of possible positions that it then works to centre or to marginalise.

Transgender practices and identities are a form of gender trouble, in that they call attention to contradictions in how we tend to think about gender, sex and sexuality. But the transgender knowledges that emerge from these troubling contradictions, I want to argue, can yoke together queer and feminist projects in a way that helps break the impasse of identity politics that has so crippled progressive movements in the United States. Since the early 1970s, progressive politics have fragmented along identity lines practically to the point of absurdity. While it undoubtedly has been vital over the past few decades of movement history to enunciate the particularities of all our manifold forms of bodily being in the world, it is equally important that we now find new ways of articulating our commonalities without falling into the equally dead-end logic of totalising philosophies and programmes.

Transgender studies offers us one critical methodology for thinking through the diverse particularities of our embodied lives, as well for thinking through the commonalities we share through our mutual enmeshment in more global systems. Reactionary political movements have been very effective in telling stories about shared values – family, religion, tradition. We who work at the intersection of queer and feminist movements, we who have a different vision of our collective future, need to become equally adept in telling stories that link us in ways that advance the cause of justice, and that hold forth the promise of happy endings for all our strivings. Bringing transgender issues into women's studies, and into feminist movement building, is one concrete way to be engaged in that important work.

While it is politically necessary to include transgender issues in feminist theorising and organising, it is not intellectually responsible, nor ethically defensible, to teach transgender studies in academic women's studies without being engaged in peer-to-peer conversations with various sorts of trans- and genderqueer people. Something crucial is lost when academically based feminists fail to support transgender inclusion in the academic workplace. Genderqueer youth who have come of age after the 'queer' 90s' are now passing through the higher education system, and they increasingly fail to recognise the applicability of prevailing modes of feminist discourse for their own lives and experiences. How we each live our bodies in the world is a vital source of knowledge for us all, and to teach trans studies without being in dialogue with trans people is akin to teaching race studies only from a position of whiteness, or gender studies only from a position of masculinity. Why is transgender not a category targeted for affirmative action in hiring, and valued the same way that racial diversity is valued? It is past time for feminists who have imagined that transgender issues have not been part of their own concerns to take a long, hard look in the mirror. What in their own constructions of self, their own experiences of gender, prevents their recognition of transgender people as being somehow like themselves – as people engaged in parallel, intersecting, and overlapping struggles, who are not fundamentally Other?

Transgender phenomena now present queer figures on the horizon of feminist visibility. Their calls for attention are too often received, however, as an uncomfortable solicitation from an alien and unthinkable monstrosity best left somewhere outside the village gates. But justice, when we first feel its claims upon us, typically points us toward a future we can scarcely imagine. At the historical moment when racial slavery in the United States at long last became morally indefensible, and the nation plunged into civil war, what did the future of the nation look like? When greenhouse gas emissions finally become equally morally indefensible, what shape will a post-oil world take? Transgender issues make similar claims of justice upon us all, and promise equally unthinkable transformations.[5] Recognising the legitimacy of these claims will change the world, and feminism along with it, in ways we can now hardly fathom. It is about time.

NOTES

1. This essay was first delivered as a keynote address at the *Third Wave Feminism* conference at the University of Exeter, UK (25 July 2002); and in revised form at the Presidential Session plenary on 'Transgender Theory' at the *National Women's Studies Association* Annual Meeting, Oakland, California (17 June 2006). Many of the ideas I present here have been worked out in greater detail elsewhere in my work (see Stryker 1994, 1998, 2004, and 2006); see also my conversation with Marysia Zalewski. For another account of the relationship between recent feminist scholarship and transgender issues see Cressida Heyes.

2. My thoughts on the role of transgender phenomena for understanding US history in general are significantly indebted to Joanne Meyerowitz (2006).

3. The concept of 'articulation' is taken from Ernesto Laclau and Chantal Mouffe (93–194).

4. See Joshua Gamson on the trouble transgender presents to identity movements.

5. On monstrosity and justice see Nikki Sullivan.

WORKS CITED

Billings, Dwight B., and Thomas Urban. 'The Sociomedical Construction of Transsexualism: An Interpretation and Critique.' *Social Problems* 29 (1981): 266–82.

Blackwood, Evelyn, and Saskia Wieringa, eds. *Female Desires: Same Sex Relations and Transgender Practices Across Cultures.* New York: Columbia University Press, 1999.

Butler, Judith. 'Contingent Foundations: Feminism and the Question of "Postmodernism".' *Feminists Theorize the Political.* Ed. Judith Butler and Joan W. Scott. New York: Routledge, 1992. 3–21.

Gamson, Joshua. 'Must Identity Movements Self-Destruct? A Queer Dilemma.' *Social Problems* 42.3 (1995): 390–406.

Hausman, Bernice. *Changing Sex: Transsexualism, Technology, and the Idea of Gender.* Durham: Duke University Press, 1995.

Heyes, Cressida. 'Feminist Solidarity after Queer Theory: The Case of Transgender.' *Signs* 28.4 (2003): 1093–120.

Laclau, Ernesto, and Chantal Mouffe. *Hegemony and Socialist Strategy: Towards a Radical Democratic Politics.* 2nd ed. London: Verso, 2001.

Members of the Gay and Lesbian Historical Society. 'MTF Transgender Activism in San Francisco's Tenderloin: Commentary and Interview with Elliot Blackstone.' *GLQ: A Journal of Lesbian and Gay Studies* 4.2 (1998): 349–72.

Meyerowitz, Joanne. *How Sex Changed: A History of Transsexuality in the United States.* Cambridge: Harvard University Press, 2002.

——. 'A New History of Gender.' *Trans/Forming Knowledge: The Implications of Transgender Studies for Women's, Gender, and Sexuality Studies.* University of Chicago, 17 Feb. 2006. Accessed: 27 June 2006. <http:// humanities.uchicago.edu/orgs/cgs/Trans%20Conference%20Audio%20Files/Session%202_Intro_Meyerowitz.mp3>.

8 Debunking the Pathology of Poverty

Susan Greenbaum

The House Budget Committee's March 3, 2014 report, *The War on Poverty: 50 Years Later*,[1] states that "the single most important determinant of poverty is family structure," closely followed by a disinclination to work. The sponsor of the report, Rep. Paul Ryan, R-Wisc., claims the problem is single-parent households raising children with neither the desire nor capacity to acquire skills to support themselves as adults—creating a vicious cycle of dependency persisting across generations. He blames government-sponsored social programs for permitting the lazy among us to avoid taking responsibility for themselves and their children, and he believes the cure for this self-inflicted condition is tough love: Poor people need stronger incentives to get off the couch and find a job. . . .

Ryan traces his ideas about family structure to the 1965 Moynihan Report, written by Daniel Patrick Moynihan, then an assistant secretary in the Department of Labor and later a U.S. Senator from New York. Moynihan argued that poverty is perpetuated by defective cultural values, an idea more generally known as the culture of poverty. That term was coined in 1959 by Oscar Lewis, an anthropologist, and was used repeatedly by Michael Harrington, a popular journalist who wrote about American poverty, but as a theory it was heavily disputed by most social scientists until the mid-1980s. With the rise of conservative politics and periodic declines in the economy, this allegedly scientific concept has repeatedly served as a convenient explanation for persistent inequality, a state of affairs that benefits the wealthy and the politicians who serve their interests. Instead of plumbing the pathologies of elite culture, recently labeled "affluenza," a sociopathic disorder based on too much privilege, most poverty research has focused on the decisions and values of single mothers in poor neighborhoods and their allegedly errant menfolk and delinquent sons.

A Cultural Plague

In his report, officially titled *The Negro Family: The Case for National Action,* Moynihan claimed that African-American family values produced too many fatherless households and nurtured what he called a "tangle of pathology," a self-perpetuating, self-defeating cultural flaw responsible for persistently high rates of poverty and violent crime. Conservative columnists and politicians seized on the report, promulgated by a liberal in Lyndon B. Johnson's administration, as official evidence that African-American culture was dangerously pathological. Civil rights leaders saw it as an

Greenbaum, Susan. "Debunking the Pathology of Poverty." *Al Jazeera America*, March 26, 2014. Reprinted courtesy of *Al Jazeera America*. http://america.aljazeera.com/opinions/2014/3/culture -of-povertysocialwelfarepaulryanaffluenza.html attempt to blame the black community for systemic problems of racial discrimination. A wide spectrum of academic researchers criticized the report, finding errors and mistaken statistical logic; it was a hasty analysis wrapped in provocative rhetoric. Over the next decade, more evidence was brought forth that challenged Moynihan's data and assumptions (and Lewis'). By the late 1970s, the premise that poor people have a distinctive culture that causes them to fail seemed to have been rejected.

Reagan's election in 1980, however, rehabilitated the culture of poverty concept by invoking images of welfare queens and the supposed dangers of a dependent underclass. In 1984, Charles Murray, a fellow at the American Enterprise Institute, wrote a popular book called *Losing Ground*, which claimed harmful social programs and bad behavior by the poor were the main causes of the growing poverty of the era. Liberal academics countered that unemployment in deindustrialized urban areas was the main cause of poverty, though some of their cohort also conceded Moynihan's original premise, arguing that economic failure partly resulted from ineffective parenting within the underclass. Once again, cause and effect were up for grabs, and conservatives (then, as now) opted for the appealing explanation that poor people cause their own problems.

. . . Murray is a co-author of *The Bell Curve*, published in 1994, which controversially posited a genetic link between race and IQ. His 2008 book, *Coming Apart*, argued that the white lower classes were largely abandoning marriage and family fidelity, that they too have been infected with the tangle of pathology. The steep rise in single-parent households among whites and Latinos is decried as a spreading cultural plague of bad family values, but what these trends actually confirm is the connection between a lagging economy and the ability of poor people to afford marriage.

Charting the poverty rate against other historical data shows that recessions bring steep rises in poverty and recoveries bring declines. The current rate is just over 15 percent (up from 11 percent in 2000), which is where it has been since 2009. It was also that high in 1983 and 1993, both periods of economic decline. Poverty has not returned to the extreme rates of the early 1960s (when it was over 20 percent), before the federal government enacted anti-poverty programs, which played an important role in reducing poverty in the recessions that followed. Earlier peaks were short-lived. Today, though, poverty has remained at 15 percent for nearly five years. We are warned that this is the new normal, and, disturbingly, so it seems to be.

Bad Behavior from the Top

So what causes poverty? What precipitates recessions that throw people out of work and curtail vital services in cash-strapped municipalities and states? The last one, which began in 2008, resulted from bad behavior, though not by poor people. Rather, we saw fraudulent and predatory practices by the captains of finance, corrupt behavior by regulators and elected officials and an ethos condoning exploitation at all levels of the economy, especially against the most vulnerable. These practices are also cultural — driven by the rationalized prerogatives of people with too much wealth and power — and they wreak much more havoc than the shortcomings of poor parents.

For example, the decision of many employers to short workers' wages by not pay-ing for overtime or by altering records of time and tips is a costly cultural choice. The Economic Policy Institute determined[2] that wage theft in 2008 amounted to almost $200 million, nearly four times the haul from all types of robberies in 2009 (about $57 million). The Wall Street–caused collapse of 2008 saw 3.6 million jobs lost and up to 4 million home foreclosures, including a great many black and Latino victims of fraudulent, predatory mortgages. The wealthy perpetrators of this bad behavior have been perversely rewarded. Meanwhile, the racial wealth gap has grown enormously since 2008. Wealth inequality in the U.S. is greater now than at any time since 1928, and the share funneled to the top 1 percent continues to grow. . . .

It is time to put an end to this canard once and for all. Until we stop blaming the wrong people and accept the fact that government can help, we will perpetuate the current dystopic state as the new normal. We need to lift the fog induced by the so-called culture of poverty and recognize that we really could wage an effective war against poverty.

NOTES

1. House Budget Committee Majority Staff (2014, March 3). *The War on Poverty: 50 Years Later.* U.S. House of Representatives Committee on the Budget.

2. Lafter, G. (2013, October 13). *The Legislative Attack on American Wages and Labor Standards, 2011–2012.* Economic Policy Institute.

9 Disability and the Justification of Inequality in American History

Douglas C. Baynton

Since the social and political revolutions of the eighteenth century, the trend in western political thought has been to refuse to take for granted inequalities between persons or groups. Differential and unequal treatment has continued, of course, but it has been considered incumbent on modern societies to produce a rational explanation for such treatment. In recent decades, historians and other scholars in the humanities have studied intensely and often challenged the ostensibly rational explanations for inequalities based on identity—in particular, gender, race, and ethnicity. Disability, however, one of the most prevalent justifications for inequality, has rarely been the subject of historical inquiry.

Disability has functioned historically to justify inequality for disabled people themselves, but it has also done so for women and minority groups. That is, not only has it been considered justifiable to treat disabled people unequally, but the *concept* of disability has been used to justify discrimination against other groups by attributing disability to them. Disability was a significant factor in the three great citizenship debates of the nineteenth and early twentieth centuries: women's suffrage, African American freedom and civil rights, and the restriction of immigration. When categories of citizenship were questioned, challenged, and disrupted, disability was called on to clarify and define who deserved, and who was deservedly excluded from, citizenship. Opponents of political and social equality for women cited their supposed physical, intellectual, and psychological flaws, deficits, and deviations from the male norm. These flaws—irrationality, excessive emotionality, physical weakness—are in essence mental, emotional, and physical disabilities, although they are rarely discussed or examined as such. Arguments for racial inequality and immigration restrictions invoked supposed tendencies to feeble-mindedness, mental illness, deafness, blindness, and other disabilities in particular races and ethnic groups. Furthermore, disability figured prominently not just in arguments *for* the inequality of women and minorities but also in arguments *against* those inequalities. Such arguments took the form of vigorous denials that the groups in question actually had these disabilities; they were not disabled, the argument went, and therefore were not proper subjects for discrimination. Rarely have oppressed groups denied that disability is an adequate justification for social and political inequality. Thus, while disabled people can be considered one of the minority groups historically assigned inferior status and subjected to discrimination, disability has functioned for all such groups as a sign of and justification for inferiority. . . .

From *The New Disability History*, Paul K. Longmore and Lauri Umansky, eds. Copyright © 2000 New York University Press. Reprinted by permission of the publisher.

The metaphor of the natural versus the monstrous was a fundamental way of constructing social reality in Edmund Burke's time. By the late nineteenth and early twentieth centuries, however, the concept of the natural was to a great extent displaced or subsumed by the concept of normality.[1] Since then, normality has been deployed in all aspects of modern life as a means of measuring, categorizing, and managing populations (and resisting such management). Normality is a complex concept, with an etiology that includes the rise of the social sciences, the science of statistics, and industrialization with its need for interchangeable parts and interchangeable workers. It has been used in a remarkable range of contexts and with a bewildering variety of connotations. The natural and the normal both are ways of establishing the universal, unquestionable good and right. Both are also ways of establishing social hierarchies that justify the denial of legitimacy and certain rights to individuals or groups. Both are constituted in large part by being set in opposition to culturally variable notions of disability—just as the natural was meaningful in relation to the monstrous and the deformed, so are the cultural meanings of the normal produced in tandem with disability[2]. . . .

As an evolutionary concept, normality was intimately connected to the western notion of progress. By the mid-nineteenth century, nonwhite races were routinely connected to people with disabilities, both of whom were depicted as evolutionary laggards or throwbacks. As a consequence, the concept of disability, intertwined with the concept of race, was also caught up in ideas of evolutionary progress. Physical or mental abnormalities were commonly depicted as instances of atavism, reversions to earlier stages of evolutionary development. Down's syndrome, for example, was called Mongolism by the doctor who first identified it in 1866 because he believed the syndrome to be the result of a biological reversion by Caucasians to the Mongol racial type. Teachers of the deaf at the end of the century spoke of making deaf children more like "normal" people and less like savages by forbidding them the use of sign language, and they opposed deaf marriages with a rhetoric of evolutionary progress and decline. . . .

Disability arguments were prominent in justifications of slavery in the early to mid-nineteenth century and of other forms of unequal relations between white and black Americans after slavery's demise. The most common disability argument for slavery was simply that African Americans lacked sufficient intelligence to participate or compete on an equal basis in society with white Americans. This alleged deficit was sometimes attributed to physical causes, as when an article on the "diseases and physical peculiarities of the negro race" in the *New Orleans Medical and Surgical Journal* helpfully explained, "It is the defective hematosis, or atmospherization of the blood, conjoined with a deficiency of cerebral matter in the cranium, and an excess of nervous matter distributed to the organs of sensation and assimilation, that is the true cause of that debasement of mind, which has rendered the people of Africa unable to take care of themselves." Diseases of blacks were commonly attributed to "inferior organisms and constitutional weaknesses," which were claimed to be among "the most pronounced race characteristics of the American negro." While the supposedly higher intelligence of "mulattos" compared to "pure" blacks was offered as evidence for the superiority of whites, those who argued against "miscegenation" claimed to the contrary that the products of "race-mixing" were themselves less intelligent and less healthy than members of either race in "pure" form.[3] A medical doctor, John Van Evrie of New York, avowed that the "disease and disorganization" in the "abnormal," "blotched, deformed" offspring of this "monstrous" act "could no more exist beyond a given period than any other physical degeneration, no more than tumors, cancers, or other abnormal growths or physical disease can become permanent." Some claimed greater "corporeal vigor" for "mixed offspring" but a deterioration in "moral and intellectual endowments," while still others saw greater intelligence but "frailty," "less stamina," and "inherent physical weakness."[4]

A second line of disability argument was that African Americans, because of their inherent physical and mental weaknesses, were prone to become disabled under conditions of freedom and equality. A New York medical journal reported that deafness was three times more common and blindness twice as common among free blacks in the North compared to slaves in the South. John C. Calhoun, senator from South Carolina and one of the most influential spokesmen for the slave states, thought it a powerful argument in defense of slavery that the "number of deaf and dumb, blind, idiots, and insane, of the negroes in the States that have changed the ancient relation between the races" was seven times higher than in the slave states.[5]

While much has been written about the justification of slavery by religious leaders in the South, more needs to be said about similar justifications by medical doctors. Dr. Samuel Cartwright, in 1851, for example, described two types of mental illness to which African Americans were especially subject. The first, Drapetomania, a condition that caused slaves to run away—"as much a disease of the mind as any other species of mental alienation"—was common among slaves whose masters had "made themselves too familiar with them, treating them as equals." The need to submit to a master was built into the very bodies of African Americans, in whom "we see '*genu flexit*' written in the physical structure of his knees, being more flexed or bent, than any other kind of man." The second mental disease peculiar to African Americans, Dysaesthesia Aethiopis—a unique ailment differing "from every other species of mental disease, as it is accompanied with physical signs or lesions of the body"—resulted in a desire to avoid work and generally to cause mischief. It was commonly known to overseers as "rascality." Its cause, similar to that of Drapetomania, was a lack of firm governance, and it was therefore far more common among free blacks than among slaves—indeed, nearly universal among them—although it was a "common occurrence on badly-governed plantations" as well.[6]

Dr. Van Evrie also contributed to this line of thought when he wrote in the 1860s that education of African Americans came "at the expense of the body, shortening the existence" and resulted in bodies "dwarfed or destroyed" by the unnatural exertion. "An 'educated negro,' like a 'free negro,' is a social monstrosity, even more unnatural and repulsive than the latter." He argued further that, since they belonged to a race inferior by nature, *all* blacks were necessarily inferior to (nearly) *all* whites. It occasionally happened that a particular white person might not be superior to all black people because of a condition that "deforms or blights individuals; they may be idiotic, insane, or otherwise incapable." But these unnatural exceptions to the rule were "the result of human vices, crimes, or ignorance, immediate or remote." Only disability might lower a white person in the scale of life to the level of being of a marked race.[7] . . .

Daryl Michael Scott has described how both conservatives and liberals have long used an extensive repertory of "damage imagery" to describe African Americans. Conservatives "operated primarily from within a biological framework and argued for the innate inferiority of people of African descent" in order to justify social and political exclusion. Liberals maintained that social conditions were responsible for black inferiority and used damage imagery to argue for inclusion and rehabilitation; but regardless of their intentions, Scott argues, liberal damage imagery "reinforced the belief system that made whites feel superior in the first place." Both the "contempt and pity" of conservatives and liberals—a phrase that equally well describes historically prevalent attitudes toward disabled people—framed Americans of African descent as defective. Scott cites the example of Charles S. Johnson, chair of the social science department and later president of Fisk University, who told students in a 1928 speech that "the sociologists classify Negroes with cripples, persons with recognized physical handicaps." Like Johnson, Scott is critical of the fact that "African Americans were often lumped with the 'defective,' 'delinquent,' and dependent classes." This is obviously a bad place to be "lumped." Scott does not ask, however, why that might be the case.[8] The attribution of disease or disability to racial minorities has a long history. Yet, while many have pointed out the injustice and perniciousness of attributing these qualities to a racial or ethnic group, little has been written about why these attributions are such powerful weapons for inequality, why they were so furiously denied and condemned by their targets, and what this tells us about our attitudes toward disability.

During the long-running debate over women's suffrage in the nineteenth and early twentieth centuries, one of the rhetorical tactics of suffrage opponents was to point to the physical, intellectual, and psychological flaws of women, their frailty, irrationality, and emotional excesses. By the late nineteenth century, these claims were sometimes expressed in terms of evolutionary progress; like racial and ethnic minorities, women were said to be less evolved than white men, their disabilities a result of lesser evolutionary development. Cynthia Eagle Russett has noted that "women and savages, together with idiots, criminals, and pathological monstrosities [those with congenital disabilities] were a constant source of anxiety to male intellectuals in the late nineteenth century."[9] What all shared was an evolutionary inferiority, the result of arrested development or atavism.

Paralleling the arguments made in defense of slavery, two types of disability argument were used in opposition to women's suffrage: that women had disabilities that made them incapable of using the franchise responsibly, and that because of their frailty women would become disabled if exposed to the rigors of political participation. The American anti-suffragist Grace Goodwin, for example, pointed to the "great temperamental disabilities" with which women had to contend: "woman lacks endurance in things mental. . . . She lacks nervous stability. The suffragists who dismay England are nervesick women." The second line of argument, which was not incompatible with the first and often accompanied it, went beyond the claim that women's flaws made them incapable of exercising equal political and social rights with men to warn that if women were given those rights, disability would surely follow. This argument is most closely identified with Edward Clarke, author of *Sex in Education; or, A Fair Chance for Girls*. Clarke's argument chiefly concerned education for women, though it was often applied to suffrage as well. Clarke maintained that overuse of the brain among young women was in large part responsible for the "numberless pale, weak, neuralgic, dyspeptic, hysterical, menorraghic, dysmenorrhoeic girls and women" of America. The result of excessive education in this country was "bloodless female faces, that suggest consumption, scrofula, anemia, and neuralgia." An appropriate education designed for their frail constitutions would ensure "a future secure from neuralgia, uterine disease, hysteria, and other derangements of the nervous system."[10]

Similarly, Dr. William Warren Potter, addressing the Medical Society of New York in 1891, suggested that many a mother was made invalid by inappropriate education: "her reproductive organs were dwarfed, deformed, weakened, and diseased, by artificial causes imposed upon her during their development."[11] Dr. A. Lapthorn Smith asserted in *Popular Science Monthly* that educated women were increasingly "sick and suffering before marriage and are physically disabled from performing physiological functions in a normal manner." Antisuffragists likewise warned that female participation in politics invariably led to "nervous prostration" and "hysteria," while Dr. Almroth E. Wright noted the "fact that there is mixed up with the woman's movement much mental disorder." A prominent late nineteenth-century neurophysiologist, Charles L. Dana, estimated that enfranchising women would result in a 25 percent increase in insanity among them and "throw into the electorate a mass of voters of delicate nervous stability . . . which might do injury to itself without promoting the community's good." The answer for Clarke, Potter, and others of like mind was special education suited to women's special needs. As with disabled people today, women's social position was treated as a medical problem that necessitated separate and special care. Those who wrote with acknowledged authority on the "woman question" were doctors. As Clarke wrote, the answer to the "problem of woman's sphere . . . must be obtained from physiology, not from ethics or metaphysics."[12] . . .

Disability figured not just in arguments *for* the inequality of women and minorities but also in arguments *against* those inequalities. Suffragists rarely challenged the notion that disability justified political inequality and instead disputed the claim that women suffered from these disabilities. Their arguments took three forms: one, women were not disabled and therefore deserved the vote; two, women were being erroneously and slanderously classed with disabled people, with those who were legitimately denied suffrage; and three, women were not naturally or inherently disabled but were *made* disabled by inequality— suffrage would ameliorate or cure these disabilities. . . .

Ethnicity also has been defined by disability. One of the fundamental imperatives in the initial formation of American immigration policy at the end of the nineteenth century was the exclusion of disabled people. Beyond the targeting of disabled people, the concept of disability was instrumental in crafting the image of the undesirable immigrant. The first major federal immigration law, the Act of 1882, prohibited entry to any "lunatic, idiot, or any person unable to take care of himself or herself without becoming a public charge." Those placed in the categories "lunatic" and "idiot" were automatically excluded. The "public charge" provision was intended to encompass people with disabilities more generally and was left to the examining officer's discretion. The criteria for excluding disabled people were steadily tightened as the eugenics movement and popular fears about the decline of the national stock gathered strength. The Act of 1891 replaced the phrase "*unable* to take care of himself or herself without becoming a public charge," with "*likely* to become a public charge." The 1907 law then denied entry to anyone judged "mentally or physically defective, such mental or physical defect being of a nature which *may affect* the ability of such alien to earn a living." These changes considerably lowered the threshold for exclusion and expanded the latitude of immigration officials to deny entry.[13]

The category of persons *automatically* excluded was also steadily expanded. In 1903, people with epilepsy were added and, in addition to those judged insane, "persons who have been insane within five years previous [or] who have had two or more attacks of insanity at any time previously." This was reduced to one "attack" in the 1917 law; the classification of "constitutional psychopathic inferiority" was also added, which inspection regulations described as including "various unstable individuals on the border line between sanity and insanity . . . and persons with abnormal sex instincts."[14] This was the regulation under which, until recently, gays and lesbians were excluded. One of the significant factors in lifting this ban, along with other forms of discrimination against gays and lesbians, was the decision by the American Psychiatric Association in 1973 to remove homosexuality from its list of mental illnesses. That is, once gays and lesbians were declared not to be disabled, discrimination became less justifiable.

Legislation in 1907 added "imbeciles" and "feeble-minded persons" to the list, in addition to "idiots," and regulations for inspectors directed them to exclude persons with "any mental abnormality whatever . . . which justifies the statement that the alien is mentally defective." These changes encompassed a much larger number of people and again granted officials considerably more discretion to judge the fitness of immigrants for American life. Fiorello H. LaGuardia, who worked his way through law school as an interpreter at Ellis Island, later wrote that "over fifty percent of the deportations for alleged mental disease were unjustified," based as they often were on "ignorance on the part of the immigrants or the doctors and the inability of the doctors to understand the particular immigrant's norm, or standard."[15]

The detection of physical disabilities was a major aspect of the immigration inspector's work. The Regulations for the medical inspection of immigrants in 1917 included a long list of diseases and disabilities that could be cause for exclusion, among them arthritis, asthma, bunions, deafness, deformities, flat feet, heart disease, hernia, hysteria, poor eyesight, poor physical development, spinal curvature, vascular disease of the heart, and varicose veins. . . .

In short, the exclusion of disabled people was central to the laws and the work of the immigration service. As the Commissioner General of Immigration reported in 1907, "The exclusion from this country of the morally, mentally, and physically deficient is the principal object to be accomplished by the immigration laws." Once the laws and procedures limiting the entry of disabled people were firmly established and functioning well, attention turned to limiting the entry of undesirable ethnic groups. Discussion on this topic often began by pointing to the general public agreement that the laws excluding disabled people had been a positive, if insufficient, step. In 1896, for example, Francis Walker noted in the *Atlantic Monthly* that the necessity of "straining out" immigrants who were "deaf, dumb, blind, idiotic, insane, pauper, or criminal" was "now conceded by men of all shades of opinion"; indeed there was a widespread "resentment at the attempt of such persons to impose themselves upon us." As one restrictionist wrote, the need to exclude the disabled was "self evident."[16]

For the more controversial business of defining and excluding undesirable ethnic groups, however, restrictionists found the *concept* of disability to be a powerful tool. That is, while people with disabilities constituted a distinct category of persons unwelcome in the United States, the charge that certain ethnic groups were mentally and physically deficient was instrumental in arguing for *their* exclusion. The belief that discriminating on the basis of disability was justifiable in turn helped justify the creation of immigration quotas based on ethnic origin. The 1924 Immigration Act instituted a national quota system that severely limited the numbers of immigrants from southern and eastern Europe, but long before that, disabilities stood in for nationality. Superintendents of institutions, philanthropists, immigration reformers, and politicians had been warning for decades before 1924 that immigrants were disproportionately prone to be mentally defective—up to half the immigrants from southern and eastern Europe were feebleminded, according to expert opinion.[17] Rhetoric about "the slow-witted Slav," the "neurotic condition of our Jewish immigrants," and, in general, the "degenerate and psychopathic types, which are so conspicuous and numerous among the immigrants," was pervasive in the debate over restriction.[18] The laws forbidding entry to the feebleminded were motivated in part by the desire to limit immigration from inferior nations, and conversely, it was assumed that the 1924 act would reduce the number of feebleminded immigrants. The issues of ethnicity and disability were so intertwined in the immigration debate as to be inseparable. . . .

Historians have scrutinized the attribution of mental and physical inferiority based on race and ethnicity, but only to condemn the slander. With their attention confined to ethnic stereotypes, they have largely ignored what the attribution of disability might also tell us about attitudes toward disabled people. Racial and ethnic prejudice is exposed while prejudice against people with disabilities is passed over as insignificant and understandable. As a prominent advocate of restriction wrote in 1930, "The necessity of the exclusion of the crippled, the blind, those who are likely to become public charges, and, of course, those with a criminal record is self evident."[19] The necessity has been treated as self-evident by historians as well, so much so that even the possibility of discrimination against people with disabilities in immigration law has gone unrecognized. In historical accounts, disability is present but rendered invisible or insignificant. While it is certain that immigration restriction rests in good part on a fear of "strangers in the land," in John Higham's phrase, American immigration restriction at the turn of the century was also clearly fueled by a fear of *defectives* in the land.

Still today, women and other groups who face discrimination on the basis of identity respond angrily to accusations that they might be characterized by physical, mental, or emotional disabilities. Rather than challenging the basic assumptions behind the hierarchy, they instead work to remove themselves from the negatively marked categories—that is, to disassociate themselves from those people who "really are" disabled—knowing that such categorization invites discrimination. For example, a recent proposal in Louisiana to permit pregnant women to use parking spaces reserved for people with mobility impairments was opposed by women's organizations. A lobbyist for the Women's Health Foundation said, "We've spent a long time trying to dispel the myth that pregnancy is a disability, for obvious reasons of discrimination." She added, "I have no problem with it being a courtesy, but not when a legislative mandate provides for pregnancy in the same way as for disabled persons."[20] To be associated with disabled people or with the accommodations accorded disabled people is stigmatizing. . . .

This common strategy for attaining equal rights, which seeks to distance one's own group from imputations of disability and therefore tacitly accepts the idea that disability is a legitimate reason for inequality, is perhaps one of the factors responsible for making discrimination against people with disabilities so persistent and the struggle for disability rights so difficult. . . .

Disability is everywhere in history, once you begin looking for it, but conspicuously absent in the histories we write. When historians do take note of disability, they usually treat it merely as personal tragedy or an insult to be deplored and a label to be denied, rather than as a cultural construct to be questioned and explored. Those of us who specialize in the history of disability, like the early historians of other minority groups, have concentrated on writing histories of disabled people and the institutions and laws associated with disability. This is necessary and exciting work. It is through this work that we are building the case that disability is culturally constructed rather than natural and timeless—that disabled people have a history, and a history worth studying. Disability, however, more than an identity, is a fundamental element in cultural signification and indispensable for *any* historian seeking to make sense of the past. It may well be that all social hierarchies have drawn on culturally constructed and socially sanctioned notions of disability. If this is so, then there is much work to do. It is time to bring disability from the margins to the center of historical inquiry.

NOTES

1. Ian Hacking, *The Taming of Chance* (Cambridge and New York: Cambridge University Press, 1990), 160–66. See also Georges Canguilhem, *The Normal and the Pathological* (New York: Zone Books, 1989); Douglas C. Baynton, *Forbidden Signs: American Culture and the Campaign against Sign Language* (Chicago: University of Chicago Press, 1996), chaps. 5–6.

2. Francois Ewald, "Norms Discipline, and the Law," *Representations* 30 (Spring 1990): 146, 149–150, 154; Lennard Davis, *Enforcing Normalcy: Disability, Deafness, and the Body* (London: Verso, 1995); Baynton, *Forbidden Signs,* chaps. 5 and 6.

3. Samuel A. Cartwright, "Report on the Diseases and Physical Peculiarities of the Negro Race," *New Orleans Medical and Surgical Journal* 7 (May 1851): 693; George M. Fredrickson, *The Black Image in the White Mind* (New York: Harper and Row, 1971), 250–51; J. C. Nott, "The Mulatto a Hybrid," *American Journal of Medical Sciences* (July 1843), quoted in Samuel Forry, "Vital Statistics Furnished by the Sixth Census of the United States," *New York Journal of Medicine and the Collateral Sciences* 1 (September 1843): 151–53.

4. John H. Van Evrie, *White Supremacy and Negro Subordination, or Negroes a Subordinate Race* (New York: Van Evrie, Horton, & Co., 1868), 153–55; Forry, "Vital Statistics," 159; Paul B. Barringer, *The American Negro: His Past and Future* (Raleigh: Edwards & Broughton, 1900), 10.

5. Cited in Forry, "Vital Statistics," 162–63. John C. Calhoun, "Mr. Calhoun to Mr. Pakenham," in Richard K. Cralle, ed., *The works of John C. Calhoun* (New York: D. Appleton, 1888), 5:337.

6. Cartwright, "Report," 707–10. See also Thomas S. Szasz, "The Sane Slave: A Historical Note on the use of Medical Diagnosis as Justificatory Rhetoric," *American Journal of Psychotherapy* 25 (1971): 228–39.

7. Van Evrie, *White Supremacy,* 121, 181, 221. Van Evrie notes in his preface that the book was completed "about the time of Mr. Lincoln's election" and was therefore originally an argument in favor of the continuation of slavery but presently constituted an argument for its restoration.

8. Daryl Michael Scott, *Contempt and Pity: Social Policy and the Image of the Damaged Black Soul, 1880–1996* (Chapel Hill: University of North Carolina Press, 1997), xi–xvii; 12, 208 n. 52.

9. Cynthia Eagle Russett, *Sexual Science: The Victorian Construction of Womanhood* (Cambridge, Mass.: Harvard University Press, 1989), 63. See also Lois N. Magner, "Darwinism and the Woman Question: The Evolving Views of Charlotte Perkins Gilman," in Joanne Karpinski, ed., *Critical Essays on Charlotte Perkins Gilman* (New York: G. K. Hall, 1992), 119–20.

10. Grace Duffield Goodwin, *Anti-Suffrage: Ten Good Reasons* (New York: Duffield and Co., 1913), 91–92 (in Smithsonian Institution Archives, Collection 60—Warshaw Collection, "Women," Box 3). Edward Clarke, *Sex in Education; or, A Fair Chance for Girls* (1873; reprint, New York: Arno Press, 1972), 18, 22, 62.

11. William Warren Potter, "How Should Girls Be Educated? A Public Health Problem for Mothers, Educators, and Physicians," *Transactions of the Medical Society of the State of New York* (1891): 48, quoted in Martha H. Verbrugge, *Able Bodied Womanhood: Personal Health and Social Change in Nineteenth-Century Boston* (Oxford and New York: Oxford University Press, 1988), 121.

12. A. Lapthorn Smith, "Higher Education of Women and Race Suicide," *Popular Science Monthly* (March 1905), reprinted in Louise Michele Newman, ed., *Men's Ideas/Women's Realities: Popular Science, 1870–1915* (New York: Pergamon Press, 1985), 149; Almroth E. Wright quoted in Mara Mayor, "Fears and Fantasies of the Anti-Suffragists," *Connecticut Review* 7 (April 1974): 67; Charles L. Dana quoted in Jane Jerome Camhi, *Women against Women: American Anti-Suffragism, 1880–1920* (New York: Carlson Publishing Co., 1994), 18; Clarke, *Sex in Education,* 12.

13. *United States Statutes at Large* (Washington, D.C.: Government Printing Office, 1883), 22:214. *United States Statutes at Large* (Washington, D.C.: Government Printing Office, 1891),

26:1084; *United States Statutes at Large* (Washington, D.C.: Government Printing Office, 1907), 34:899. Emphases added.

14. *United States Statutes at Large* (Washington, D.C.: Government Printing Office, 1903), 32:1213; United States Public Health Service, *Regulations Governing the Medical Inspection of Aliens* (Washington, D.C.: Government Printing Office, 1917), 28–29.

15. *Statutes* (1907), 34:899; United States Public Health Service, *Regulations,* 30–31; Fiorello H. LaGuardia, *The Making of an Insurgent: An Autobiography, 1882–1919* (1948; reprint, New York: Capricorn, 1961), 65.

16. U.S. Bureau of Immigration, *Annual Report of the Commissioner of Immigration* (Washington, D.C.: Government Printing Office, 1907), 62; Francis A. Walker, "Restriction of Immigration," *Atlantic Monthly* 77 (June 1896): 822; Ellsworth Eliot, Jr., M.D., "Immigration," in Madison Grant and Charles Steward Davison, eds., *The Alien in Our Midst, or Selling Our Birthright for a Mess of Industrial Pottage* (New York: Galton Publishing Co., 1930), 101.

17. See James W. Trent, Jr., *Inventing the Feeble Mind: A History of Mental Retardation in the United States* (Berkeley: University of California Press, 1994), 166–69.

18. Thomas Wray Grayson, "The Effect of the Modern Immigrant on Our Industrial Centers" in *Medical Problems of Immigration* (Easton, Penn.: American Academy of Medicine, 1913), 103, 107–9.

19. Ellsworth Eliot, Jr., M.D., "Immigration," in Grant and Davison, *Alien in Our Midst,* 101.

20. Heather Salerno, "Mother's Little Dividend: Parking," *Washington Post* (September 16, 1997): A1.

10 Domination and Subordination
Jean Baker Miller

What do people do to people who are different from them and why? On the individual level, the child grows only via engagement with people very different from her/himself. Thus, the most significant difference is between the adult and the child. At the level of humanity in general, we have seen massive problems around a great variety of differences. But the most basic difference is the one between women and men.

On both levels it is appropriate to pose two questions. When does the engagement of difference stimulate the development and the enhancement of both parties to the engagement? And, conversely, when does such a confrontation with difference have negative effects: When does it lead to great difficulty, deterioration, and distortion and to some of the worst forms of degradation, terror, and violence—both for individuals and for groups—that human beings can experience? It is clear that "mankind" in general, especially in our Western tradition but in some others as well, does not have a very glorious record in this regard.

It is not always clear that in most instances of difference there is also a factor of inequality—inequality of many kinds of resources, but fundamentally of status and power. One useful way to examine the often confusing results of these confrontations with difference is to ask: What happens in situations of inequality? What forces are set in motion? While we will be using the terms "dominant" and "subordinate" in the discussion, it is useful to remember that flesh and blood women and men are involved. Speaking in abstractions sometimes permits us to accept what we might not admit to on a personal level.

Temporary Inequality

Two types of inequality are pertinent for present purposes. The first might be called temporary inequality. Here, the lesser party is *socially* defined as unequal. Major examples are the relationships between parents and children, teachers and students, and, possibly, therapists and clients. There are certain assumptions in these relationships which are often not made explicit, nor, in fact, are they carried through. But they are the social structuring of the relationship.

The "superior" party presumably has more of some ability or valuable quality, which she/he is supposed to impart to the "lesser" person. While these abilities vary with the particular relationship, they include emotional maturity, experience in the world, physical skills, a body of knowledge, or the techniques for acquiring certain kinds of knowledge. The superior person is supposed to engage with the lesser in such a way as to bring the lesser member up to full parity; that is, the child is to be

From *Toward a New Psychology of Women*. © 1976, 1986 by Jean Baker Miller. Reprinted by permission of the author.

helped to become the adult. Such is the overall task of this relationship. The lesser, the child, is to be given to, by the person who presumably has more to give. Although the lesser party often also gives much to the superior, these relationships are *based in service* to the lesser party. That is their *raison d'être*.

It is clear, then, that the paramount goal is to end the relationship; that is, to end the relationship of inequality. The period of disparity is meant to be temporary. People may continue their association as friends, colleagues, or even competitors, but not as "superior" and "lesser." At least this is the goal.

The reality is that we have trouble enough with this sort of relationship. Parents or professional institutions often tip toward serving the needs of the donor instead of those of the lesser party (for example, schools can come to serve teachers or administrators, rather than students). Or the lesser person learns how to be a good "lesser" rather than how to make the journey from lesser to full stature. Overall, we have not found very good ways to carry out the central task: to foster the movement from unequal to equal. In childrearing and education we do not have an adequate theory and practice. Nor do we have concepts that work well in such other unequal so-called "helping" relationships as healing, penology, and rehabilitation. Officially, we say we want to do these things, but we often fail.

We have a great deal of trouble deciding on how many rights "to allow" to the lesser party. We agonize about how much power the lesser party shall have. How much can the lesser person express or act on her or his perceptions when these definitely differ from those of the superior? Above all, there is great difficulty in maintaining the conception of the lesser person *as a person of as much intrinsic worth as the superior.*

A crucial point is that power is a major factor in all of these relationships. But power alone will not suffice. Power exists and it has to be taken into account, not denied. The superiors hold all the real power, but power will not accomplish *the task.* It will not bring the unequal party up to equality.

Our troubles with these relationships may stem from the fact that they exist within the context of a second type of inequality that tends to overwhelm the ways we learn to operate in the first kind. The second type molds the very ways we perceive and conceptualize what we are doing in the first, most basic kind of relationships.

The second type of inequality teaches us how to enforce inequality, but not how to make the journey from unequal to equal. Most importantly, its consequences are kept amazingly obscure—in fact they are usually denied. . . . However, the underlying notion is that this second type has determined, and still determines, the only ways we can think and feel in the first type.

Permanent Inequality

In these relationships, some people or groups of people are defined as unequal by means of what sociologists call ascription; that is, your birth defines you. Criteria may be race, sex, class, nationality, religion, or other characteristics ascribed at birth. Here, the terms of the relationships are very different from those of temporary inequality. There is, for example, no notion that superiors are present primarily to help inferiors, to impart to them their advantages and "desirable" characteristics. There is no assumption that the goal of the unequal relationship is to end the inequality; in fact, quite the reverse. A series of other governing tendencies are in force, and occur with great regularity. . . . While some of these elements may appear obvious, in fact there is a great deal of disagreement and confusion about psychological characteristics brought about by conditions as obvious as these.

Dominants

Once a group is defined as inferior, the superiors tend to label it as defective or sub-standard in various ways. These labels accrete rapidly. Thus, blacks are described as less intelligent than whites, women are supposed to be ruled by emotion, and so on. In addition, the actions and words of the dominant group tend to be destructive of the subordinates. All historical evidence confirms this tendency. And, although they are much less obvious, there are destructive effects on the dominants as well. The latter are of a different order and are much more difficult to recognize.

Dominant groups usually define one or more acceptable roles for the subordinate. Acceptable roles typically involve providing services that no dominant group wants to perform for itself (for example, cleaning up the dominant's waste products). Functions that a dominant group prefers to perform, on the other hand, are carefully guarded and closed to subordinates. Out of the total range of human possibilities, the activities most highly valued in any particular culture will tend to be enclosed within the domain of the dominant group; less valued functions are relegated to the subordinates.

Subordinates are usually said to be unable to perform the preferred roles. Their incapacities are ascribed to innate defects or deficiencies of mind or body, therefore immutable and impossible of change or development. It becomes difficult for dominants even to imagine that subordinates are capable of performing the preferred activities. More importantly, subordinates themselves can come to find it difficult to believe in their own ability. The myth of their inability to fulfill wider or more valued roles is challenged only when a drastic event disrupts the usual arrangements. Such disruptions usually arise from outside the relationship itself. For instance, in the emergency situation of World War II, "incompetent" women suddenly "manned" the factories with great skill.

It follows that subordinates are described in terms of, and encouraged to develop, personal psychological characteristics that are pleasing to the dominant group. These characteristics form a certain familiar cluster: submissiveness, passivity, docility, dependency, lack of initiative, inability to act, to decide, to think, and the like. In general, this cluster includes qualities more characteristic of children than adults—immaturity, weakness, and helplessness. If subordinates adopt these characteristics they are considered well-adjusted.

However, when subordinates show the potential for, or even more danger-ously have developed other characteristics—let us say intelligence, initiative, assertiveness—there is usually no room available within the dominant framework for acknowledgement of these characteristics. Such people will be defined as at least unusual, if not definitely abnormal. There will be no opportunities for the direct application of their abilities within the social arrangements. (How many women have pretended to be dumb!)

Dominant groups usually impede the development of subordinates and block their freedom of expression and action. They also tend to militate against stirrings of greater rationality or greater humanity in their own members. It was not too long ago that "nigger lover" was a common appellation, and even now men who "allow their women" more than the usual scope are subject to ridicule in many circles.

A dominant group, inevitably, has the greatest influence in determining a culture's overall outlook—its philosophy, morality, social theory, and even its science. The dominant group, thus, legitimizes the unequal relationship and incorporates it into society's guiding concepts. The social outlook, then, obscures the true nature of this relationship—that is, the very existence of inequality. The culture explains the events that take place in terms of other premises, premises that are inevitably false, such as racial or sexual inferiority. While in recent years we have learned about many such falsities on the larger social level, a full analysis of the psychological implications still remains to be developed. In the case of women, for example, despite overwhelming evidence to the contrary, the notion persists that women are meant to be passive, submissive, docile, secondary. From this premise, the outcome of therapy and encounters with psychology and other "sciences" are often determined.

Inevitably, the dominant group is the model for "normal human relationships." It then becomes "normal" to treat others destructively and to derogate them, to obscure the truth of what you are doing, by creating false explanations, and to oppose actions toward equality. In short, if one's identification is with the dominant group, it is "normal" to continue in this pattern. Even though most of us do not like to think of ourselves as either believing in, or engaging in, such dominations, it is, in fact, difficult for a member of a dominant group to do otherwise. But to keep on doing these things, one need only behave "normally."

It follows from this that dominant groups generally do not like to be told about or even quietly reminded of the existence of inequality. "Normally" they can avoid awareness because their explanation of the relationship becomes so well integrated *in other terms;* they can even believe that both they and the subordinate group share the same interests and, to some extent, a common experience. If pressed a bit, the familiar rationalizations are offered: the home is "women's natural place," and we know "what's best for them anyhow."

Dominants prefer to avoid conflict—open conflict that might call into question the whole situation. This is particularly and tragically so, when many members of the dominant group are not having an easy time of it themselves. Members of a dominant group, or at least some segments of it, such as white working-class men (who are themselves also subordinates), often feel unsure of their own narrow toehold on the material and psychological bounties they believe they desperately need. What dominant groups usually cannot act on, or even see, is that the situation of inequality in fact deprives them, particularly on the psychological level.

Clearly, inequality has created a state of conflict. Yet dominant groups will tend to suppress conflict. They will see any questioning of the "normal" situation as threatening; activities by subordinates in this direction will be perceived with alarm. Dominants are usually convinced that the way things are is right and good, not only for them but especially for the subordinates. All morality confirms this view, and all social structure sustains it.

It is perhaps unnecessary to add that the dominant group usually holds all of the open power and authority and determines the ways in which power may be acceptably used.

Subordinates

What of the subordinates' part in this? Since dominants determine what is normal for a culture, it is much more difficult to understand subordinates. Initial expressions of dissatisfaction and early actions by subordinates always come as a surprise; they are usually rejected as atypical. After all, dominants *knew* that all women needed and wanted was a man around whom to organize their lives. Members of the dominant group do not understand why "they"—the first to speak out—are so upset and angry.

The characteristics that typify the subordinates are even more complex. A subordinate group has to concentrate on basic survival. Accordingly, direct, honest reaction to destructive treatment is avoided. Open, self-initiated action in its own self-interest must also be avoided. Such actions can, and still do, literally result in death for some subordinate groups. In our own society, a woman's direct action can result in a combination of economic hardship, social ostracism, and psychological isolation—and even the diagnosis of a personality disorder. Any one of these consequences is bad enough. . . .

It is not surprising then that a subordinate group resorts to disguised and indirect ways of acting and reacting. While these actions are designed to accommodate and please the dominant group, they often, in fact, contain hidden defiance and "put ons." Folk tales, black jokes, and women stories are often based on how the wily peasant or sharecropper outwitted the rich landowner, boss, or husband. The essence of the story rests on the fact that the overlord does not even know that he has been made a fool of.

One important result of this indirect mode of operation is that members of the dominant group are denied an essential part of life—the opportunity to acquire self-understanding through knowing their impact on others. They are thus deprived of "consensual validation," feedback, and a chance to correct their actions and expressions. Put simply, subordinates won't tell. For the same reasons, the dominant group is deprived also of valid knowledge about the subordinates. (It is particularly ironic that the societal "experts" in knowledge about subordinates are usually members of the dominant group.)

Subordinates, then, know much more about the dominants than vice versa. They have to. They become highly attuned to the dominants, able to predict their reactions of pleasure and displeasure. Here, I think, is where the long story of "feminine intuition" and "feminine wiles" begins. It seems clear that these "mysterious" gifts are in fact skills, developed through long practice, in reading many small signals, both verbal and nonverbal.

Another important result is that subordinates often know more about the dominants than they know about themselves. If a large part of your fate depends on accommodating to and pleasing the dominants, you concentrate on them. Indeed, there is little purpose in knowing yourself. Why should you when your knowledge of the dominants determines your life? This tendency is reinforced by many other restrictions. One can know oneself only through action and interaction. To the extent that their range of action or interaction is limited, subordinates will lack a realistic evaluation of their capacities and problems. Unfortunately, this difficulty in gaining self-knowledge is even further compounded.

Tragic confusion arises because subordinates absorb a large part of the untruths created by the dominants; there are a great many blacks who feel inferior to whites, and women who still believe they are less important than men. This internalization of dominant beliefs is more likely to occur if there are few alternative concepts at hand. On the other hand, it is also true that members of the subordinate group have certain experiences and perceptions that accurately reflect the truth about themselves and the injustice of their position. Their own more truthful concepts are bound to come into opposition with the mythology they have absorbed from the dominant group. An inner tension between the two sets of concepts and their derivations is almost inevitable.

From a historical perspective, despite the obstacles, subordinate groups have tended to move toward greater freedom of expression and action, although this progress varies greatly from one circumstance to another. There were always some slaves who revolted; there were some women who sought greater development or self-determination. Most records of these actions are not preserved by the dominant culture, making it difficult for the subordinate group to find a supporting tradition and history.

Within each subordinate group, there are tendencies for some members to imitate the dominants. This imitation can take various forms. Some may try to treat their fellow subordinates as destructively as the dominants treat them. A few may develop enough of the qualities valued by the dominants to be partially accepted into their fellowship. Usually they are not wholly accepted, and even then only if they are willing to forsake their own identification with fellow subordinates. "Uncle Toms" and certain professional women have often been in this position. (There are always a few women who have won the praise presumably embodied in the phrase "she thinks like a man.")

To the extent that subordinates move toward freer expression and action, they will expose the inequality and throw into question the basis for its existence. And they will make the inherent conflict an open conflict. They will then have to bear the burden and take the risks that go with being defined as "troublemakers." Since this role flies in the face of their conditioning, subordinates, especially women, do not come to it with ease.

What is immediately apparent from studying the characteristics of the two groups is that mutually enhancing interaction is not probable between unequals. Indeed, conflict is inevitable. The important questions, then, become: Who defines the conflict? Who sets the terms? When is conflict overt or covert? On what issues is the conflict fought? Can anyone win? Is conflict "bad," by definition? If not, what makes for productive or destructive conflict?

Suggestions for Further Reading

Alba, Richard D. *Ethnic Identity: The Transformation of White American Identity.* New Haven, CT: Yale University Press, 1990.

Blazina, Chris. *Cultural Myth of Masculinity.* Westport, CT: Praeger Publishers, 2003.

Butler, Judith. *Undoing Gender.* New York: Routledge, 2004.

Connell, R. W. *Masculinities,* 2nd ed. Berkeley: University of California Press, 2005.

De Beauvoir, Simone. *The Second Sex.* New York: Alfred A. Knopf, 1952.

Dunbar-Ortiz, Roxanne. *An Indigenous Peoples' History of the United States.* Boston: Beacon Press, 2015.

Fausto-Sterling, Anne. *Sexing the Body: Gender Politics and the Construction of Sexuality.* New York: Basic Books, 2000.

Feinberg, Leslie. *Transgender Warriors: Making History from Joan of Arc to Dennis Rodman.* Boston: Beacon Press, 1997.

Feinberg, Leslie. *Trans Liberation: Beyond Pink or Blue.* Boston: Beacon Press, 1999.

Frankenberg, Ruth. *White Women, Race Matters.* Minneapolis: University of Minnesota Press, 1993.

Gould, Stephen. *The Mismeasure of Man.* New York: W. W. Norton, 1984.

Greenbaum, Susan. *Blaming the Poor: The Long Shadow of the Moynihan Report on Cruel Images of Poverty.* New Brunswick, NJ: Rutgers University Press, 2015.

Gregory, Steven, and Roger Sanjek, eds. *Race.* New Brunswick, NJ: Rutgers University Press, 1994.

Hubbard, Ruth. *The Politics of Women's Biology.* New Brunswick, NJ: Rutgers University Press, 1990.

Katz, Jonathan Ned. *The Invention of Heterosexuality.* Chicago: University of Chicago Press, 2007.

Kimmel, Michael. *Manhood in America,* 3rd ed. New York: Oxford University Press, 2011.

———. *Misframing Men: The Politics of Contemporary Masculinities.* New Brunswick, NJ: Rutgers University Press, 2010.

Kleinman, Sherryl, Martha Copp, and Kent Sandstrom. "Making Sexism Visible: Birdcages, Martians, and Pregnant Men." *Teaching Sociology, 35,* pp. 126–142.

Lopez, Ian F. Haney. *White by Law: The Legal Construction of Race.* New York: New York University Press, 1996.

Lorber, Judith. *Paradoxes of Gender.* New Haven, CT: Yale University Press, 1995.

Lowe, Marion, and Ruth Hubbard, eds. *Women's Nature: Rationalizations of Inequality.* New York: Pergamon Press, 1984.

Memmi, Albert. *Dominated Man.* Boston: Beacon Press, 1969.

Omi, Michael, and Howard Winant. *Racial Formations in the United States,* 2nd ed. New York: Routledge & Kegan Paul, 1994.

Roberts, Dorothy. *Fatal Invention: How Science, Politics, and Big Business Re-Create Race in the Twenty-First Century.* New York: The New Press, 2012.

Roediger, David. *Colored White: Transcending the Racial Past.* Berkeley: University of California Press, 2003.

———. *The Wages of Whiteness: Race and the Making of the American Working Class.* New York: Verso, 2007.

Sanday, Peggy R. *Female Power and Male Dominance: On the Origins of Sexual Inequality.* New York: Cambridge University Press, 1981.

Stryker, Susan. *Transgender History.* Berkeley: Seal Press, 2008.

Williams, Gregory Howard. *Life on the Color Line.* New York: Dutton, 1995.

PART II

Understanding Racism, Sexism, Heterosexism, and Class Privilege

In Part II, we spend some time analyzing systems of oppression and examining the relations of dominance and subordination they incorporate almost seamlessly into daily life. Racism, sexism, heterosexism, and class privilege are systems of advantage that provide those with the "right" race, sex, sexual orientation, and class (or some intersection of these) with opportunities and rewards that are unavailable to other individuals and groups in society. Sometimes they work in isolation from each other, but most often they operate in combination to create a system of advantage and disadvantage that enhances the life chances of some while limiting the life chances of others.

The construction of difference as deviance or deficiency underlies the systems of oppression that determine how power, privilege, wealth, and opportunity are distributed. We are surrounded by differences every day, but our society places a value on only some of them. By valuing the characteristics and lifestyles of certain individuals or groups and devaluing those of others, society constructs some of its members as "other." These "others" are understood to be less deserving, less intelligent, even less human. Once this happens, it is possible to distribute wealth, opportunity, and justice unequally without appearing to be unfair. The social construction of race, class, gender, and sexuality as difference—where being white, male, cisgender, European, heterosexual, and prosperous confers the highest forms of status and privilege while everyone else is considered less able and less worthy—lies at the heart of racism, sexism, heterosexism, and classism.

Some people are uncomfortable with words like "racism," "sexism," and "oppression," which seem to them highly charged and unnecessarily accusatory. They prefer to talk about "discrimination" and "prejudice." However, those who wish to emphasize the complex, pervasive, and self-perpetuating nature of the system of beliefs, policies, practices, and attitudes that enforce the relations of subordination and domination in our society find the term "discrimination" too narrow and too limited to make the point effectively. Words like "racism," "sexism," and "oppression" are more appropriate because they capture the comprehensive nature of the systems being studied. In Selection 4, Marilyn Frye does a good job of explaining the meaning of "oppression" in the course of using that concept to convey the pervasive nature of sexism. Frye uses the metaphor of a birdcage to illustrate how a system of oppression, in this case sexism, imprisons its victims through a set of interlocking impediments to motion. Taken alone, none of the barriers seems very powerful or threatening; taken together, they are unyielding.

Racism and sexism are systems of advantage. In the United States, racism perpetuates an interlocking system of institutions, attitudes, privileges, and rewards that work to the benefit of white people just as sexism works to the advantage of men. In Selection 1, Beverly Daniel Tatum elaborates on this definition of racism (originally offered by David Wellman in his book *Portraits of White Racism*), and discusses the resistance that some of us feel about acknowledging both the existence of racism and the advantages it bestows on people with white privilege. Once racism is defined as a system of advantages based on race, it is no longer possible to attribute racism to people of color because clearly they do not systematically benefit from racism; only white people do. This of course does not deny that people of all colors are capable of hateful and hurtful behavior, nor does it prevent us from taking them to task for their prejudice. But it does mean that we will reserve the term "racism" to refer specifically to the comprehensive system of advantages that work to the benefit of white people in the United States. For more on this important and provocative distinction, you will want to turn directly to the essay by Tatum.

In Selection 2, Eduardo Bonilla-Silva examines the claim made by many white people in the United States today that racism is a thing of the past and that they personally do not see race or skin color (or, by extension, sex, class, disability, etc.); they just see "human beings." Bonilla-Silva and other sociologists have coined the term "color-blind racism" to refer to this new version of racial ideology. In this essay (a written version of a speech he gave at Texas A&M), Bonilla-Silva argues that, contrary to what many would like to believe, it is not racists or bigots who perpetuate the system of racial inequality in this country, but the ordinary behavior of well-meaning whites as they simply follow "the racial script of America." In this way, Bonilla-Silva directs our attention to the ways in which white supremacy and white privilege are institutionalized by the ordinary operations of society. He spends most of his essay examining the central frames of color-blind racism that allow many who benefit from white privilege to perpetuate the racial status quo without ever having to take responsibility for society's ongoing racism. In contrast to the older and cruder version of racism, Bonilla-Silva warns us, "[t]oday there is a sanitized, color-blind way of calling minorities 'niggers,' 'spics,' or 'chinks.'" Today, most whites justify keeping minorities out of the good things in life with the language of liberalism . . . ."

Angelo Ancheta (Selection 3) asks us to consider racial relations beyond the binary of black and white, and argues that because legal paradigms, or models, depend on this dichotomous thinking, they are unable to encompass the complexity of the racialization of Asian Americans. Ancheta offers a discussion of anti-Asian violence as illustrative of the racial subordination that Asian Americans experience, emphasizing that dynamics of immigration and nativism are essential to how race is configured in the United States.

The term "sexism" refers to the oppression of women by men in a society that is largely patriarchal. As we discussed, Marilyn Frye provides a powerful analysis of the sexism that persists in American culture. "Heterosexism" parallels "racism" and "sexism," and, according to Suzanne Pharr in Selection 5, involves the assumption that the world is and must be heterosexual at the same time that it rationalizes the existing distribution of power and privilege that flows from this assumption. In her essay, Pharr argues that economics, violence, and homophobia are the most effective weapons of sexism, and thus homophobia and heterosexism are oppressive of all women, regardless of their sexual orientation. For more current statistics on economic inequality (which continue to support Pharr's claims), take a look at the material in Part V of this book.

Finally, "class privilege" refers to the system of advantages that continues to ensure that wealth, power, opportunity, and privilege go hand in hand. In Selection 6, Gregory Mantsios explores some of the myths about class that mislead people about their real-life chances and documents the impact of class position on daily life. Many in the United States are unaware of the full force of class privilege; the statistics in this article suggest that the class position of one's family, not hard work, intelligence, or determination, is probably the single most significant determinant of future success. This gap between people's beliefs about what it takes to succeed and the tremendous role that class privilege plays in determining who is successful provides a dramatic illustration of the effectiveness of systems of oppression both in perpetuating the current systems of advantage and in rendering their continuing operation invisible to so many. This point will be taken up again in Part VIII.

In Selection 7, Annette Lareau looks at the ways in which class affects parenting practices and documents how middle class children regardless of race are reared to interact with institutions much differently than their poor and working class peers. She further explores how these different parenting styles affect how children will deal with the educational system and other institutional settings throughout their lives, thus demonstrating how class intersects with their futures from the moment they set foot in their elementary school classrooms.

In Section 8, Kimberlé Crenshaw, a critical-race theorist, discusses the concept of intersectionality with journalist/blogger Bim Adewunmi. Intersectionality is a framework that examines how racism, sexism, and classism interact to form multiple and compounding layers of oppression. Intersectionality is greater than the sum of its parts. For example, the experience of racism and sexism that black women experience can't be understood by looking at how sexism affects white women and racism affects black men. Intersectionality calls for an understanding of the specific and simultaneous ways that different forms of oppression operate.

These are powerful and disturbing claims, and they are likely to provoke equally strong reactions from readers. Some will feel angry, others will feel depressed and discouraged, some will feel uncomfortable, others will be skeptical, and some will simply feel confused. This is understandable. If some people, as these definitions suggest, have more than their share, then others have less than they deserve, and each of us must wonder where we will stand in the final computation. Further, many readers who are white and working class or middle class will be hard pressed to imagine what kind of privilege they exercise. They look at their own lives and the lives of their parents and friends and see people who have worked very hard for everything they have achieved. The idea that they are privileged may seem very foreign to them.

These ideas won't be easy to reconcile. "Heterosexism, class privilege, male privilege—what have these abstract and politically charged terms got to do with me?" many will ask. "I work hard, try to get ahead, wish others well, and feel more like a victim myself than a victimizer." Yet this understandable response illustrates how effectively systems of oppression function in contemporary society to rationalize the hierarchy they create, often making its operation invisible both to those who benefit from it and to those who are shortchanged by it. In addition, it points to the complicated and ambiguous nature of privilege, in which a single individual can be privileged in some respects at the very same time that he or she is disadvantaged in other respects. Let us examine these two points in more detail.

Many people who are privileged fail to realize that they are in fact privileged because the systems of oppression so effectively make the current distribution of privilege and power appear almost "natural." In many cases, people with privileges have enjoyed them for so long that they have simply come to take them for granted. Instead of recognizing them as special benefits that come with, for example, white skin, they just assume that these privileges are things to which they have a right. For more on this topic, see Peggy McIntosh's essay, Selection 9, which does an excellent job of examining how white privilege works.

In other cases, privilege may be difficult to identify and acknowledge because the individual is privileged in some respects but not in others. For example, those who are privileged by virtue of their sex or sexual orientation may be disadvantaged in other respects—say, by virtue of their race/ethnicity or their class position or both. The disadvantages they experience in some areas may seem so unfair and so egregious that they prevent them from recognizing the privileges they nonetheless enjoy. For example, a poor, white, single mother who receives public assistance and who feels very much at the mercy of an unfair and inhumane system might still be able to call upon her white skin privilege or her heterosexual privilege in certain situations and be oblivious to that privilege because she feels so disadvantaged in other respects. A working class or lower middle class white male who has trouble stretching his paycheck to cover all his expenses may be so preoccupied with his financial situation that he doesn't recognize the male privilege and white skin privilege from which he nonetheless benefits—privileges which may not feel at all like privileges to him because he takes them for granted and regards them as "natural" and "normal." And finally, since most people are basically decent and fair, those who are privileged are often simply reluctant to acknowledge that they have unfair advantages over others because that would require that they reevaluate their sense of who they are and what they have accomplished in their lives. Robin DiAngelo's piece, Selection 10, examines these very issues. Her essay is a reflection of her own experience as a white woman who comes from a working class background to demonstrate how racial privilege interacts with class oppression.

As should by now be clear, all of the thinkers whose work is included in Part II share the belief that the various systems of oppression operate in relation to one another, forming an interlocking system of advantages and disadvantages that rationalize and preserve the prevailing distribution of power and privilege in society. As you read these articles, try to keep an open mind about this claim. If these thinkers are correct, they have something important to tell us about our society and the forces that will be in place as each of us goes about creating our own future.

1 Defining Racism

"Can We Talk?"

Beverly Daniel Tatum

Early in my teaching career, a White student I knew asked me what I would be teaching the following semester. I mentioned that I would be teaching a course on racism. She replied, with some surprise in her voice, "Oh, is there still racism?" I assured her that indeed there was and suggested that she sign up for my course. Fifteen years later, after exhaustive media coverage of events such as the Rodney King beating, the Charles Stuart and Susan Smith cases, the O. J. Simpson trial, the appeal to racial prejudices in electoral politics, and the bitter debates about affirmative action and welfare reform, it seems hard to imagine that anyone would still be unaware of the reality of racism in our society. But in fact, in almost every audience I address, there is someone who will suggest that racism is a thing of the past. There is always someone who hasn't noticed the stereotypical images of people of color in the media, who hasn't observed the housing discrimination in their community, who hasn't read the newspaper articles about documented racial bias in lending practices among well-known banks, who isn't aware of the racial tracking pattern at the local school, who hasn't seen the reports of rising incidents of racially motivated hate crimes in America—in short, someone who hasn't been paying attention to issues of race. But if you are paying attention, the legacy of racism is not hard to see, and we are all affected by it.

The impact of racism begins early. Even in our preschool years, we are exposed to misinformation about people different from ourselves. Many of us grew up in neighborhoods where we had limited opportunities to interact with people different from our own families. When I ask my college students, "How many of you grew up in neighborhoods where most of the people were from the same racial group as your own?" almost every hand goes up. There is still a great deal of social segregation in our communities. Consequently, most of the early information we receive about "others"—people racially, religiously, or socioeconomically different from ourselves—does not come as the result of firsthand experience. The secondhand information we do receive has often been distorted, shaped by cultural stereotypes, and left incomplete.

Some examples will highlight this process. Several years ago one of my students conducted a research project investigating preschoolers' conceptions of Native Americans.[1] Using children at a local day care center as her participants, she asked these three- and four-year-olds to draw a picture of a Native American. Most children were stumped by her request. They didn't know what a Native American was. But when she rephrased the question and asked them to draw a picture of an

From "Why Are All the Black Kids Sitting Together in the Cafeteria?" and Other Conversations about Race, pp. 3–13. Copyright © 1997 by Beverly Daniel Tatum. Reprinted by permission of Perseus Books, LLC.

Indian, they readily complied. Almost every picture included one central feature: feathers. In fact, many of them also included a weapon—a knife or tomahawk—and depicted the person in violent or aggressive terms. Though this group of children, almost all of whom were White, did not live near a large Native American population and probably had had little if any personal interaction with American Indians, they all had internalized an image of what Indians were like. How did they know? Cartoon images, in particular the Disney movie *Peter Pan,* were cited by the children as their number-one source of information. At the age of three, these children already had a set of stereotypes in place. Though I would not describe three-year-olds as prejudiced, the stereotypes to which they have been exposed become the foundation for the adult prejudices so many of us have.

Sometimes the assumptions we make about others come not from what we have been told or what we have seen on television or in books, but rather from what we have *not* been told. The distortion of historical information about people of color leads young people (and older people, too) to make assumptions that may go unchallenged for a long time. Consider this conversation between two White students following a discussion about the cultural transmission of racism:

"Yeah, I just found out that Cleopatra was actually a Black woman."

"What?"

The first student went on to explain her newly learned information. The second student exclaimed in disbelief, "That can't be true. Cleopatra was beautiful!"

What had this young woman learned about who in our society is considered beautiful and who is not? Had she conjured up images of Elizabeth Taylor when she thought of Cleopatra? The new information her classmate had shared and her own deeply ingrained assumptions about who is beautiful and who is not were too incongruous to allow her to assimilate the information at that moment.

Omitted information can have similar effects. For example, another young woman, preparing to be a high school English teacher, expressed her dismay that she had never learned about any Black authors in any of her English courses. How was she to teach about them to her future students when she hadn't learned about them herself? A White male student in the class responded to this discussion with frustration in his response journal, writing "It's not my fault that Blacks don't write books." Had one of his elementary, high school, or college teachers ever told him that there were no Black writers? Probably not. Yet because he had never been exposed to Black authors, he had drawn his own conclusion that there were none.

Stereotypes, omissions, and distortions all contribute to the development of prejudice. *Prejudice* is a preconceived judgment or opinion, usually based on limited information. I assume that we all have prejudices, not because we want them, but simply because we are so continually exposed to misinformation about others. Though I have often heard students or workshop participants describe someone as not having "a prejudiced bone in his body," I usually suggest that they look again. Prejudice is one of the inescapable consequences of living in a racist society. Cultural racism—the cultural images and messages that affirm the assumed superiority of Whites and the assumed inferiority of people of color—is like smog in the air. Sometimes it is so thick it is visible, other times it is less apparent, but always, day in and day out, we are breathing it in. None of us would introduce ourselves as "smog-breathers" (and most of us don't want to be described as prejudiced), but if we live in a smoggy place, how can we avoid breathing the air? If we live in an environment in which we are bombarded with stereotypical images in the media, are frequently exposed to the ethnic jokes of friends and family members, and are rarely informed of the accomplishments of oppressed groups, we will develop the negative categorizations of those groups that form the basis of prejudice.

People of color as well as Whites develop these categorizations. Even a member of the stereotyped group may internalize the stereotypical categories about his or her own group to some degree. In fact, this process happens so frequently that it has a name, *internalized oppression.* Some of the consequences of believing the distorted messages about one's own group will be discussed in subsequent chapters.

Certainly some people are more prejudiced than others, actively embracing and perpetuating negative and hateful images of those who are different from themselves. When we claim to be free of prejudice, perhaps what we are really saying is that we are not hatemongers. But none of us is completely innocent. Prejudice is an integral part of our socialization, and it is not our fault. Just as the preschoolers my student interviewed are not to blame for the negative messages they internalized, we are not at fault for the stereotypes, distortions, and omissions that shaped our thinking as we grew up.

To say that it is not our fault does not relieve us of responsibility, however. We may not have polluted the air, but we need to take responsibility, along with others, for cleaning it up. Each of us needs to look at our own behavior. Am I perpetuating and reinforcing the negative messages so pervasive in our culture, or am I seeking to challenge them? If I have not been exposed to positive images of marginalized groups, am I seeking them out, expanding my own knowledge base for myself and my children? Am I acknowledging and examining my own prejudices, my own rigid categorizations of others, thereby minimizing the adverse impact they might have on my interactions with those I have categorized? Unless we engage in these and other conscious acts of reflection and reeducation, we easily repeat the process with our children. We teach what we were taught. The unexamined prejudices of the parents are passed on to the children. It is not our fault, but it is our responsibility to interrupt this cycle.

Racism: A System of Advantage Based on Race

Many people use the terms *prejudice* and *racism* interchangeably. I do not, and I think it is important to make a distinction. In his book *Portraits of White Racism,* David Wellman argues convincingly that limiting our understanding of racism to prejudice does not offer a sufficient explanation for the persistence of racism. He defines racism as a "system of advantage based on race."[2] In illustrating this definition, he provides example after example of how Whites defend their racial advantage—access to better schools, housing, jobs—even when they do not embrace overtly prejudicial thinking. Racism cannot be fully explained as an expression of prejudice alone.

This definition of racism is useful because it allows us to see that racism, like other forms of oppression, is not only a personal ideology based on racial prejudice, but a *system* involving cultural messages and institutional policies and practices as well as the beliefs and actions of individuals. In the context of the United States, this system clearly operates to the advantage of Whites and to the disadvantage of people of color. Another related definition of racism, commonly used by antiracist educators and consultants, is "prejudice plus power." Racial prejudice when combined with social power—access to social, cultural, and economic resources and decision-making—leads to the institutionalization of racist policies and practices. While I think this definition also captures the idea that racism is more than individual beliefs and attitudes, I prefer Wellman's definition because the idea of systematic advantage and disadvantage is critical to an understanding of how racism operates in American society.

In addition, I find that many of my White students and workshop participants do not feel powerful. Defining racism as prejudice plus power has little personal relevance. For some, their response to this definition is the following: "I'm not really prejudiced, and I have no power, so racism has nothing to do with me." However, most White people, if they are really being honest with themselves, can see that there are advantages to being White in the United States. Despite the current rhetoric about affirmative action and "reverse racism," every social indicator, from salary to life expectancy, reveals the advantages of being White.[3]

The systematic advantages of being White are often referred to as White privilege. In a now well-known article, "White Privilege: Unpacking the Invisible Knapsack," Peggy McIntosh, a White feminist scholar, identified a long list of societal privileges that she received simply because she was White.[4] She did not ask for them, and it is important to note that she hadn't always noticed that she was receiving them. They included major and minor advantages. Of course she enjoyed greater access to jobs and housing. But she also was able to shop in department stores without being followed by suspicious salespeople and could always find appropriate hair care products and makeup in any drugstore. She could send her child to school confident that the teacher would not discriminate against him on the basis of race. She could also be late for meetings, and talk with her mouth full, fairly confident that these behaviors would not be attributed to the fact that she was White. She could express an opinion in a meeting or in print and not have it labeled the "White" viewpoint. In other words, she was more often than not viewed as an individual, rather than as a member of a racial group.

This article rings true for most White readers, many of whom may have never considered the benefits of being White. It's one thing to have enough awareness of racism to describe the ways that people of color are disadvantaged by it. But this new understanding of racism is more elusive. In very concrete terms, it means that if a person of color is the victim of housing discrimination, the apartment that would otherwise have been rented to that person of color is still available for a White person. The White tenant is, knowingly or unknowingly, the beneficiary of racism, a system of advantage based on race. The unsuspecting tenant is not to blame for the prior discrimination, but she benefits from it anyway.

For many Whites, this new awareness of the benefits of a racist system elicits considerable pain, often accompanied by feelings of anger and guilt. These uncomfortable emotions can hinder further discussion. We all like to think that we deserve the good things we have received, and that others, too, get what they deserve. Social psychologists call this tendency a "belief in a just world."[5] Racism directly contradicts such notions of justice.

Understanding racism as a system of advantage based on race is antithetical to traditional notions of an American meritocracy. For those who have internalized this myth, this definition generates considerable discomfort. It is more comfortable simply to think of racism as a particular form of prejudice. Notions of power or privilege do not have to be addressed when our understanding of racism is constructed in that way.

The discomfort generated when a systemic definition of racism is introduced is usually quite visible in the workshops I lead. Someone in the group is usually quick to point out that this is not the definition you will find in most dictionaries. I reply, "Who wrote the dictionary?" I am not being facetious with this response. Whose interests are served by a "prejudice only" definition of racism? It is important to understand that the system of advantage is perpetuated when we do not acknowledge its existence.

Racism: For Whites Only?

Frequently someone will say, "You keep talking about White people. People of color can be racist, too." I once asked a White teacher what it would mean to her if a student or parent of color accused her of being racist. She said she would feel as though she had been punched in the stomach or called a "low-life scum." She is not alone in this feeling. The word *racist* holds a lot of emotional power. For many White people, to be called racist is the ultimate insult. The idea that this term might only be applied to Whites becomes highly problematic for after all, can't people of color be "low-life scum" too?

Of course, people of any racial group can hold hateful attitudes and behave in racially discriminatory and bigoted ways. We can all cite examples of horrible hate crimes which have been perpetrated by people of color as well as Whites. Hateful behavior is hateful behavior no matter who does it. But when I am asked, "Can people of color be racist?" I reply, "The answer depends on your definition of racism." If one defines racism as racial prejudice, the answer is yes. People of color can and do have racial prejudices. However, if one defines racism as a system of advantage based on race, the answer is no. People of color are not racist because they do not systematically benefit from racism. And equally important, there is no systematic cultural and institutional support or sanction for the racial bigotry of people of color. In my view, reserving the term *racist* only for behaviors committed by Whites in the context of a White-dominated society is a way of acknowledging the ever-present power differential afforded Whites by the culture and institutions that make up the system of advantage and continue to reinforce notions of White superiority. (Using the same logic, I reserve the word *sexist* for men. Though women can and do have gender-based prejudices, only men systematically benefit from sexism.)

Despite my best efforts to explain my thinking on this point, there are some who will be troubled, perhaps even incensed, by my response. To call the racially motivated acts of a person of color acts of racial bigotry and to describe similar acts committed by Whites as racist will make no sense to some people, including some people of color. To those, I will respectfully say, "We can agree to disagree." At moments like these, it is not agreement that is essential, but clarity. Even if you don't like the definition of racism I am using, hopefully you are now clear about what it is. If I also understand how you are using the term, our conversation can continue—despite our disagreement.

Another provocative question I'm often asked is "Are you saying all Whites are racist?" When asked this question, I again remember that White teacher's response, and I am conscious that perhaps the question I am really being asked is, "Are you saying all Whites are bad people?" The answer to that question is of course not. However, all White people, intentionally or unintentionally, do benefit from racism. A more relevant question is what are White people as individuals doing to interrupt racism? For many White people, the image of a racist is a hood-wearing Klan member or a name-calling Archie Bunker figure. These images represent what might be called *active racism,* blatant, intentional acts of racial bigotry and discrimination. *Passive racism* is more subtle and can be seen in the collusion of laughing when a racist joke is told, of letting exclusionary hiring practices go unchallenged, of accepting as appropriate the omissions of people of color from the curriculum, and of avoiding difficult race-related issues. Because racism is so ingrained in the fabric of American institutions, it is easily self-perpetuating.[6] All that is required to maintain it is business as usual.

I sometimes visualize the ongoing cycle of racism as a moving walkway at the airport. Active racist behavior is equivalent to walking fast on the conveyor belt. The person engaged in active racist behavior has identified with the ideology of White supremacy and is moving with it. Passive racist behavior is equivalent to standing still on the walkway. No overt effort is being made, but the conveyor belt moves the bystanders along to the same destination as those who are actively walking. Some of the bystanders may feel the motion of the conveyor belt, see the active racists ahead of them, and choose to turn around, unwilling to go to the same destination as the White supremacists. But unless they are walking actively in the opposite direction at a speed faster than the conveyor belt—unless they are actively antiracist—they will find themselves carried along with the others.

So, not all Whites are actively racist. Many are passively racist. Some, though not enough, are actively antiracist. The relevant question is not whether all Whites are racist, but how we can move more White people from a position of active or passive racism to one of active antiracism. The task of interrupting racism is obviously not the task of Whites alone. But the fact of White privilege means that Whites have greater access to the societal institutions in need of transformation. To whom much is given, much is required.

It is important to acknowledge that while all Whites benefit from racism, they do not all benefit equally. Other factors, such as socioeconomic status, gender, age, religious affiliation, sexual orientation, mental and physical ability, also play a role in our access to social influence and power. A White woman on welfare is not privileged to the same extent as a wealthy White heterosexual man. In her case, the systematic disadvantages of sexism and classism intersect with her White privilege, but the privilege is still there. This point was brought home to me in a 1994 study conducted by a Mount Holyoke graduate student, Phyllis Wentworth.[7] Wentworth interviewed a group of female college students, who were both older than their peers and were the first members of their families to attend college, about the pathways that led them to college. All of the women interviewed were White, from working-class backgrounds, from families where women were expected to graduate from high school and get married or get a job. Several had experienced abusive relationships and other personal difficulties prior to coming to college. Yet their experiences were punctuated by "good luck" stories of apartments obtained without a deposit, good jobs offered without experience or extensive reference checks, and encouragement provided by willing mentors. While the women acknowledged their good fortune, none of them discussed their Whiteness. They had not considered the possibility that being White had worked in their favor and helped give them the benefit of the doubt at critical junctures. This study clearly showed that even under difficult circumstances, White privilege was still operating.

It is also true that not all people of color are equally targeted by racism. We all have multiple identities that shape our experience. I can describe myself as a light-skinned, well-educated, heterosexual, able-bodied, Christian African American woman raised in a middle-class suburb. As an African American woman, I am systematically disadvantaged by race and by gender, but I systematically receive benefits in the other categories, which then mediate my experience of racism and sexism. When one is targeted by multiple isms—racism, sexism, classism, heterosexism, ableism, anti-Semitism, ageism—in whatever combination, the effect is intensified. The particular combination of racism and classism in many communities of color is life-threatening. Nonetheless, when I, the middle-class Black mother of two sons, read another story about a Black man's unlucky encounter with a White police officer's deadly force, I am reminded that racism by itself can kill.

NOTES

1. C. O'Toole, "The effect of the media and multicultural education on children's perceptions of Native Americans" (senior thesis, Department of Psychology and Education, Mount Holyoke College, South Hadley, MA, May 1990).

2. For an extended discussion of this point, see David Wellman, *Portraits of White racism* (Cambridge: Cambridge University Press, 1977), ch. 1.

3. For specific statistical information, see R. Farley, "The common destiny of Blacks and Whites: Observations about the social and economic status of the races," pp. 197–233 in H. Hill and J. E. Jones, Jr. (Eds.), *Race in America: The struggle for equality* (Madison: University of Wisconsin Press, 1993).

4. P. McIntosh, "White privilege: Unpacking the invisible knapsack," *Peace and Freedom* (July/August 1989): 10–12.

5. For further discussion of the concept of "belief in a just world," see M. J. Lerner, "Social psychology of justice and interpersonal attraction," in T. Huston (Ed.), *Foundations of interpersonal attraction* (New York: Academic Press, 1974).

6. For a brief historical overview of the institutionalization of racism and sexism in our legal system, see "Part V: How it happened: Race and gender issues in U.S. law," in P. S. Rothenberg (Ed.), *Race, class, and gender in the United States: An integrated study,* 3d ed. (New York: St. Martin's Press, 1995).

7. P. A. Wentworth, "The identity development of non-traditionally aged first-generation women college students: An exploratory study" (master's thesis, Department of Psychology and Education, Mount Holyoke College, South Hadley, MA, 1994).

2 Color-Blind Racism

Eduardo Bonilla-Silva

This is an edited version of a talk given on March 7, 2001, at a forum on racism at Texas A&M, sponsored by the Multicultural Leadership Forum and the Department of Multicultural Studies.

For most Americans, talking about racism is talking about white supremacist organizations or Archie Bunkers. I anchor my remarks from a different theoretical shore and one that will make many of you feel quite uncomfortable. I contend that racism is, more than anything else, *a matter of group power; it is about a dominant racial group (whites) striving to maintain its systemic advantages and minorities fighting to subvert the racial status quo.* Hence, although "bigots" are part of America's (and A&M's) racial landscape, they are not the central actors responsible for the reproduction of racial inequality. If bigots are not the cogs propelling America's racial dynamics, who are they? My answer: regular white folks just following the racial script of America. Today most whites assert that they "don't see any color, just people"; that although the ugly face of discrimination is still with us, it is no longer the main factor determining minorities' life chances; and, finally, that they, like Dr. Martin Luther King, aspire to live in a society where "people are judged by the content of their character and not by the color of their skin." More poignantly, and in a curious case of group projection, many whites insist that minorities (especially blacks) are the ones responsible for our "racial problems."

But regardless of whites' "sincere fictions," racial considerations shade almost everything that happens in this country. Blacks—and dark-skinned racial minorities—lag well behind whites in virtually every relevant social indicator. For example, blacks are poorer, earn less, and are significantly less wealthy than whites. They also receive an inferior education than do whites even when they attend integrated settings. Regarding housing, blacks pay more for similar units and, because of discrimination, cannot access the totality of the housing market in any locality. In terms of social interaction, blacks receive impolite and discriminatory treatment in stores, restaurants, attempting to hail taxicabs, driving, and in a host of other commercial and social transactions. In short, blacks are, using the apt metaphor coined by Professor Derrick Bell, "at the bottom of the well."

How is it possible to have this tremendous level of racial inequality in a country where most people (whites) claim that race is no longer a relevant social factor and that "racists" are a species on the brink of extinction? More significantly, how do whites explain the contradiction between their professed color blindness and

From the lecture "The Strange Enigma of Racism in Contemporary America," by Eduardo Bonilla-Silva. Reprinted by permission of the author.

America's color-coded inequality? I will attempt to answer both of these questions. My main argument is that whites have developed a new, powerful ideology that justifies contemporary racial inequality and thus help maintain "systemic white privilege." I label this new ideology "color-blind racism" because this term fits quite well the language used by whites to defend the racial status quo. This ideology emerged in the 1960s concurrently with what I have labeled the "New Racism." "New Racism" practices maintain white privilege, and, unlike those typical of Jim Crow, tend to be slippery, institutional, and apparently nonracial. Post civil rights discrimination, for the most part, operates in a "now you see it, now you don't" fashion. For instance, instead of whites relying on housing covenants or on the Jim Crow signs of the past (e.g., "This is a WHITE neighborhood"), today realtors steer blacks into certain neighborhoods, individual whites use "smiling discrimination" to exclude blacks (e.g., studies by HUD and The Urban Institute), and, in some white neighborhoods, sponsorship is the hidden strategy relied upon to keep them white. Similar practices are at work in universities, banks, restaurants, and other venues.

Because the tactics for maintaining systemic white privilege changed in the 1960s, the rationalizations for explaining racial inequality changed, too. Whereas Jim Crow racism explained blacks' social standing as the product of their imputed biological and moral inferiority, color-blind racism explains it as the product of market dynamics, naturally occurring phenomena, and presumed cultural deficiencies. Below, I will highlight the central frames of color-blind racism with interview data from two projects: the 1997 Survey of College Students and the 1998 Detroit Area Study. The four central frames of color-blind racism are (1) *Abstract Liberalism*, (2) *Naturalization*, (3) *Biologization of Culture*, and (4) *Minimization of Racism*. I discuss each frame separately.

Abstract Liberalism

Whereas the principles of liberalism and humanism were not extended to nonwhites in the past, they have become the main rhetorical weapons to justify contemporary racial inequality. Whites use these principles in an *abstract* way that allows them to support the racial status quo in an apparently "reasonable" fashion. For example, Eric, a corporate auditor in his forties, opposed reparations by relying on an abstract notion of opportunity. He erupted in anger when asked if he thought reparations were due to blacks for the injuries caused by slavery and Jim Crow.

> Oh tell them to shut up, OK! I had nothing to do with the whole situation. The opportunity is there, there is no reparation involved and let's not dwell on it. I'm very opinionated about that!

After suggesting that Jews and Japanese are the only groups worthy of receiving reparations, he added,

> But something that happened three Goddamned generations ago, what do you want us to do about it now? Give them opportunity, give them scholarships, but reparations . . .

Was Eric just a white man with a "principled opposition" to government intervention? This does not seem to be the case since Eric, like most whites, makes a distinction between government spending on behalf of victims of child abuse, the homeless, and battered women (groups whom he deems as legitimate candidates for assistance) and on behalf of blacks (a group whom he deems as unworthy of assistance).

Another tenet of liberalism that whites use to explain racial matters is the Jeffersonian idea of meritocracy—"the cream rises to the top." And whites seem unconcerned by the fact that the color of the "cream" is usually white. For example, Bob, a student at Southern University, explained his opposition to the idea of providing blacks unique educational opportunities in meritocratic fashion:

> No, I would not. I think, um, I believe that you should be judged on your qualifications, your experience, your education, your background, not on your race.

Accordingly, Bob opposed affirmative action as follows:

> I oppose them mainly because, not because I am a racist, but because I think you should have the best person for the job. . . . If I was a business owner, I would want the best person in there to do the job. If I had two people, and had to choose, had to have one black to meet the quota, I think that's ridiculous.

Bob then added the following clincher: "I think (affirmative action) had a good purpose when it was instilled (sic) because it alleviated a lot of anger maybe . . . minorities felt that they were getting a foot back in the door, but I think times have changed." Bob's argumentative reasonableness is bolstered by his belief that "times have changed" and that as far as discrimination in America [is concerned], "the bigger things are already taken care of."

Another tenet of liberalism that whites employ to state their racial views is the notion of individualism. For example, Beverly, a co-owner of a small business and homemaker in her forties, stated her belief that the government has a duty to see that no one is prevented from moving into neighborhoods because of racial considerations. Yet, when asked whether the government should work to guarantee that residential integration becomes a reality, Beverly said the following:

> (Sighs) It, it, it just isn't that important. Where you decide to live is where you decide to live. If you decided to live in and can afford to live in a very upscale house, great! If you're black and you can afford that, fantastic! I mean, people have choices as to where they live. If they have the economic background or money to do this with . . . I can't envision . . . 97 percent of the black people saying, "I'm going to live in a white neighborhood 'cause it will make my life better." And I can't imagine 97 percent of the white people saying, "I'm gonna move to a black neighborhood 'cause it will make me feel better." You know, I, I, where you decide to live is your choice.

Carol, a student at SU, invoked the notion of individual choice to justify her taste for whiteness. While reviewing her romantic life in response to a question, Carol said:

> Um, there really is hardly any (laughs). My romantic life is kinda dry (laughs). I mean, as far as guys go, I mean, I know you're looking for um, white versus minority and. . . . I am interested in white guys, I mean, I don't want it to look like a prejudice thing or anything.

After stating her preference for "white guys," Carol had to do some major rhetorical work to avoid appearing racist. Thus, she interjected the following odd comment to save face: "if a guy comes along and he's black and like I love him, it's not gonna, I mean, I, it's not, I don't think the white–black issue's gonna make a difference, you know what I mean?"

Naturalization

The word "natural" or the phrase "That's the way it is" is often interjected when whites use this frame to normalize events or actions that could otherwise be interpreted as racially motivated (e.g., residential segregation) or even as racist (e.g., preference for whites as friends and partners). For example, Mark, a student at MU, acknowledged that: "most of my close friends don't . . . (I) also don't have that many close black friends." Mark reacted immediately to his potentially problematic confession (no black friends) by saying,

> Um . . . I don't know, I guess that circles are tight. It's not like we exclude, I don't feel like we exclude people. I don't think that we go out of our way to include people either, but it's just kinda like that. It seems like that's just the way it works out almost . . .

Later in the interview, Mark, a business major, revealed that most of the students in the business school are white males. When asked if he thought the way things were set up in the business school was racist, Mark answered the following:

> I don't really think it's racist. I just think . . . I don't know if it's a perfect example, I just think it's an example . . . or just things aren't set up in such a way where I wouldn't say it favors whites. That's just the way that happens um . . . in the business school. That's all.

Ray, another student at MU, naturalized the fact that he had no minority associates while growing up because, "they lived in different neighborhoods, they went to different schools" and "It wasn't like people were trying to exclude them . . . It's just the way things were." Hence, his response to a question about whether blacks self-segregate or are made to feel unwelcome by whites was the following:

> I would say it's a combination of the two factors. Um . . . and I don't think that . . . I don't . . . I think it's fair it's, uh . . . it's not necessarily fair to read prejudice into either half of the bargain. Um . . . I think it's just, 'em . . . I think it's like what I was saying earlier, I think people feel comfortable around people that they feel that they can identify with.

After struggling rhetorically with the implications of his argument, Ray stated that: "Ah um . . . I think, yes, things are somewhat segregated, but I think it's more, I think it's more about just people . . . feeling comfortable around each other than it is about active discrimination."

Detroit whites also used this frame widely. For instance, Bill, a manager in a manufacturing firm, explained the limited level of post 1954 school integration as a natural affair.

Bill: I don't think it's anybody's fault. Because people tend to group with their own people. Whether it's white or black or upper-middle class or lower class or, you know, upper class, you know, Asians. People tend to group with their own. Doesn't mean if a black person moves into your neighborhood, they shouldn't go to your school? They should and you should mix and welcome them and everything else, but you can't force people together. . . . If people want to be together, they should intermix more.

Int: OK. Hmm, so the lack of mixing is really just kind of an individual lack of desire?

Bill: Well, yeah individuals, it's just the way it is. You know, people group together for lots of different reasons: social, religious. Just as animals in the wild, you know. Elephants group together, cheetahs group together. You bus a cheetah into an elephant herd because they should mix? You can't force that [laughs].

The Biologization of Culture

Modern racial ideology no longer relies on the claim that blacks are biologically inferior to whites. Instead, it has biologized their presumed cultural practices (i.e., presented them as *fixed* features) and used that as the *rationale* for explaining racial inequality. For instance, Karen, a student at MU, agreed with the premise that blacks are poor because they lack the drive to succeed.

I think, to some extent, that's true. Just from, like looking at the black people that I've met in my classes and the few that I knew before college that . . . not like they're—I don't want to say waiting for a handout, but to some extent, that's kind of what I'm like hinting at. Like, almost like they feel like they were discriminated against hundreds of years ago, now what are you gonna give me? Ya' know, or maybe even it's just their background, that they've never, like maybe they're first generation to be in college so they feel like just that is enough for them.

Although many white respondents used this frame as crudely as Karen, most used it in a kinder and gentler way. For example, Jay, a student at WU, answered the question on why blacks have a worse overall standing than whites as follows:

Hmm, I think it's due to lack of education. I think because if they didn't grow up in a household that ahhh, afforded them the time to go to school and they had to go out and get jobs right away, I think it is just a cycle (that) perpetuates things, you know. I mean, some people, I mean, I can't say that blacks can't do it because, obviously, there are many, many of them (that) have succeeded in getting good jobs and all that . . .

Although Jay admitted "exceptional blacks," he immediately went back to the cultural frame to explain blacks' status.

So it's possible that the cycle seems to perpetuate itself because it, I mean, let's say go out and get jobs and they start, they settle down much earlier than they would normally if they had gone to school and then they have kids at a young age and they—these kids have to go and get jobs and so (on).

Detroit respondents used this cultural frame too, but, in general, used it in a more crude fashion than students. For instance, Ian, a manager of information security in an automobile company in his late fifties, explained blacks' worse status compared to whites as follows:

> The majority of 'em just don't strive to do anything, to make themselves better. Again, I've seen that all the way through. "I do this today, I'm fine, I'm happy with it, I don't need anything better." Never, never, never striving or giving extra to, to make themselves better.

Minimization of Racism

Although whites and blacks believed that discrimination is still a problem in America, they dispute its salience. In general, whites believe that discrimination has all but disappeared whereas blacks believe that discrimination—old- and new-fashioned—is as American as cherry pie. For instance, Kim, a student at SU, answered a question dealing with blacks' claims of discrimination in the following manner:

> Um, I disagree. I think that um, I think that it even more like . . . it's uh . . . I mean, from what I've heard, you pretty much have to hire, you know, you have to (hire) everyone, you know? They have quotas and stuff . . .

When asked if she believes the reason why blacks lag behind whites is because they are lazy, Kim said:

> Yeah, I totally agree with that, think that um, I mean, again, I don't think, you know, they're all like that, but I mean . . . I mean, I mean . . . it's just that . . . I mean, if it wasn't that way, why would there be so many blacks living in the projects? You know, why would there be so many poor blacks? If, if they worked hard, if, if they just went out and went to college and just worked as hard as they could, they would, I mean, they, they could make it just as high as anyone else.

Detroit whites were even more likely than students to use this frame and to use it in a direct and crude manner. Sandra, a retail salesperson in her early forties, answered the question on discrimination as follows:

> I think if you are looking for discrimination, I think it's there to be found. But if you make the best of any situation, and if you don't use it as an excuse I think sometimes it's an excuse because, ah, people felt they deserved a job, ah whatever! I think if things didn't go their way I know a lot of people have a tendency to use . . . prejudice or racism as—whatever—as an excuse. I think in some ways, yes there is . . . umm . . . people who are prejudiced. It's not only blacks, it's about Spanish, or women. In a lot of ways there (is) a lot of reverse discrimination. It's just what you wanna make of it.

The policy implications of adopting this frame are extremely important. Since whites do not believe that discrimination is a normal part of America, they view race-targeted government programs as illegitimate. Thus, Henrietta, a transsexual school teacher in his fifties, answered a question on reparations as follows:

> As a person who was once reverse discriminated against, I would have to say no. Because the government does not need those programs if they, if people would be

motivated to bring themselves out of the poverty level. Ah, [coughing] when we talk about certain programs, when the Irish came over, when the Italians, the Polish, and the Eastern European Jews, they all were immigrants who lived in terrible conditions too, but they had one thing in common, they all knew that education was the way out of that poverty. And they did it. I'm not saying . . . the blacks were brought over here maybe not willingly, but if they realize education's the key, that's it. And that's based on individuality.

Conclusions

I have illustrated the four central frames of color-blind racism, namely, abstract liberalism, naturalization, biologization of culture, and minimization of racism. These frames are central to *old* and *young* whites alike. They form an impregnable yet elastic ideological wall that *barricades* whites off from America's racial reality. An impregnable wall because they provide whites a safe, color-blind way to state racial views without appearing to be irrational or rabidly racist. And an elastic wall—and, hence, a stronger one—because these frames do not rely on absolutes ("All blacks are . . ." or "Discrimination ended in 1965"). Instead, color-blind racism gives room for exceptions and allows for a variety of ways of using the frames—from crude and direct to kinder and indirect—for whites to state their racial views in an angry tone ("Darned lazy blacks") or as compassionate conservatives ("Poor blacks are trapped in *their* inferior schools in *their* cycle of poverty. What a pity.").

Thus, my answers to the strange enigma of racism without "racists" is the following: America does not depend on Archie Bunkers to defend white supremacy. Modern racial ideology does not thrive on the ugliness of the past, on the language and tropes typical of slavery and Jim Crow. Today there is a sanitized, color-blind way of calling minorities "niggers," "spics," or "chinks." Today most whites justify keeping minorities out of the good things in life with the language of liberalism ("I am all for equal opportunity; that's why I oppose affirmative action!"). And today as yesterday, whites do not feel guilty about minorities' plight. Today they believe that minorities have the opportunities to succeed and that if they don't, it's because they do not try hard. And if minorities dare talk about discrimination, they are rebuked with statements such as "Discrimination ended in the sixties, man" or "You guys are hypersensitive."

3   Neither Black nor White

Angelo N. Ancheta

Race Relations in Black and White

"Are you black or are you white?" For Asian Americans the obvious answer would seem to be "neither." Yet, when questions of race relations arise, a dichotomy between black and white typically predominates. Formed largely through inequities and conflicts between blacks and whites, discourse on race relations provides minimal space to articulate experiences independent of a black–white framework. The representation of Asian Americans is especially elusive and often shifts, depending on context, between black and white.

Popular works on race suggest that expositions of Asian American experiences are peripheral, more often confined to the footnotes than expounded in the primary analyses. Studs Terkel's *Race* frames race relations through a dialogue about blacks and whites, confined almost entirely to the opinions of blacks and whites. Andrew Hacker's *Two Nations: Black and White, Separate, Hostile, Unequal* contains, as its subtitle implies, extensive discussions of inequality between blacks and whites, but only a minimal analysis of inequality among other racial groups.[1] The controversial books *The Bell Curve*, by Charles Murray and Richard Herrnstein, and *The End of Racism*, by Dinesh D'Souza, go to considerable length to expound arguments that blacks as a group are less intelligent than whites and suffer from cultural pathologies that inhibit advancement to the level of whites. When discussed at all, Asian Americans are offered as a "model minority" group, to be contrasted with blacks and likened to whites because of their higher IQ scores and cultural values stressing family, hard work, and educational achievement.

News media portrayals of racial minorities suffer from the same tendency to reduce race relations to a simple black–white equation. Popular television news shows such as ABC's *Nightline* offer recurring programming on race relations, but typically confine their analyses to black–white relations. Public opinion polls on race and civil rights usually exclude Asian Americans as subjects or as participants, or reduce them to the category of "Other." News coverage of racially charged events is most often framed by black versus white antagonisms. . . .

Public policies that reflect and reinforce race relations also approach race in terms of black and white. Historically, the major landmarks denoting both racial subordination and progress in racial rights have been measured through the experiences of

Ancheta, Angelo. "Neither Black Nor White," in *Asian American Studies Now: A Critical Reader*, edited by Jean Yu-Wen Shen Wu and Thomas Chen. Copyright © by Rutgers, the State University of New Jersey. Reprinted by permission of Rutgers University Press.

African Americans. Slavery and its abolition, the black codes and the Reconstruction-era constitutional amendments, Jim Crow laws and the desegregation cases culminating in *Brown v. Board of Education,* the struggles of the civil rights movement and the federal legislation of the 1960s—these are the familiar signs that have dominated the landscape of civil rights in the United States. Debates on affirmative action have occasionally shone the spotlight on Asian Americans, but almost exclusively as unintended victims of affirmative action in higher education. Problems of ongoing racial discrimination and inequality among Asian American communities are largely ignored.

Not that focusing on black experiences is unjustified. African Americans have been the largest racial minority group in the United States since the country's birth, and continue to endure the effects of racial subordination. By any social or economic measure, African Americans suffer extensive inequality because of race. In describing the African American experience, the statement of the Kerner Commission resonates as strongly today as it did in 1968: "Our nation is moving toward two societies, one black, one white—separate but unequal."[2] But to say that our nation is moving toward two separate and unequal societies, however disconcerting, is fundamentally incomplete. Underlying the Kerner Commission's statement is the assumption that our nation's cities are divisible along a single racial axis. Cleavages between black and white persist but American race relations are not an exclusively black–white phenomenon and never have been. . . .

Black and White by Analogy

Dualism is a convenient lens through which to view the world. Black or white, male or female, straight or gay—the categories help us frame reality and make sense of it. In matters of race, a black–white dichotomy has been the dominant model, based primarily on the fact that African Americans have been the largest and most conspicuous nonwhite racial group in the United States. But the legal history of the United States is punctuated by the abridgment of rights among other racial and ethnic groups such as Asian Americans, and the country's changing demographics are mandating new perspectives based on the experiences of immigrants. Still, the black–white model is the regnant paradigm in both social and legal discussions of race.

How can Asian Americans fit within a black–white racial paradigm? Historian Gary Okihiro poses the question this way: "Is yellow black or white?" Okihiro suggests that Asian Americans have been "near-blacks" in the past and "near-whites" in the present, but that "[y]ellow is emphatically neither white nor black."[3] Recognizing the dominance of the black–white paradigm in the law, Frank Wu adopts a similar view proposing that Asian Americans have been forced to fit within race relations discourse through analogy to either whites or blacks. He posits that American society and its legal system have conceived of racial groups as whites, blacks, honorary whites, or constructive (legal jargon for "implied") blacks.[4]

For most of the nation's history, Asian Americans have been treated primarily as constructive blacks. Asian Americans for decades endured many of the same disabilities of racial subordination as African Americans—racial violence, segregation, unequal access to public institutions and discrimination in housing, employment, and education. The courts even classified Asian Americans as if they were black. In the mid-nineteenth century, the California Supreme Court held in *People v. Hall* that Chinese immigrants were barred from testifying in court under a statute prohibiting the testimony of blacks, by reasoning that "black" was a generic term encompassing all nonwhites, including Chinese: "[T]he words 'Black person' . . . must be taken as contradistinguished from White, and necessarily excludes all races other than the Caucasian."[5]

Similarly, in *Gong Lum v. Rice*, decided twenty-seven years before *Brown v. Board of Education*, the United States Supreme Court upheld the constitutionality of sending Asian American students to segregated schools. Comparing its earlier rulings on the "separate but equal" doctrine, the Court stated: "Most of the cases cited arose, it is true, over the establishment of separate schools as between white pupils and black pupils, but we can not think that the question is any different or that any different result can be reached . . . where the issue is as between white pupils and the pupils of the yellow races."[6] In the eyes of the Supreme Court, yellow equaled black, and neither equaled white.

In more recent years, the inclusion of Asian Americans in civil rights laws and race-conscious remedial programs has relied on the historical parallels between the experiences of Asian Americans and African Americans. The civil rights protections available to Asian Americans are most often contingent upon the rights granted to African Americans. Civil rights laws that apply to Asian Americans, as constructive blacks, can usually trace their origins to a legislative intent to protect African Americans from racial discrimination.

The treatment of Asian Americans as "honorary whites" is more unusual. In the Reconstruction-era South, Asian Americans were initially afforded a status above blacks for a period of time during the nineteenth century; Louisiana, for example, counted Chinese as whites for census purposes before 1870.[7] The status was short-lived: the Chinese were soon reduced to constructive black status under systems of racial segregation. More contemporary race relations controversies appear to have elevated Asian Americans to the status of honorary whites, particularly in the minds of those who oppose race-conscious remedies such as affirmative action. Asian Americans are often omitted from protection in affirmative action programs as a matter of course, lumped with whites even in contexts where Asian Americans still face racial discrimination and remain underrepresented.

The rigidity of the legal system's treatment of race as either black or white is evident in civil rights litigation filed by Asian American plaintiffs in the earlier half of this century. . . . Asian Americans sought, quite unsuccessfully, to be classified as white under the law, in recognition of the social and legal stigmas attached to being categorized as black. Gong Lum, for example, argued that his daughter Martha should not have to attend the school for colored children in Mississippi because "'[c]olored' describes only one race, and that is the negro."[8] Because his daughter was "pure Chinese," Gong Lum argued that she ought to have been classified with whites rather than blacks. The Court rejected this reasoning and held that yellow was black when it came to segregation.

During the late nineteenth and early twentieth centuries, Asian Americans sought to be classified as white in attempts to become naturalized citizens.[9] Congress enacted naturalization legislation in 1790 to limit citizenship to "free white persons." After the Civil War, the law was amended to allow persons of "African nativity" or "African descent" to naturalize, but Congress rejected extending naturalization to Asian immigrants. Asian immigrants sought relief through the courts, but had little success arguing that they were white: Burmese, Chinese, Filipino, Hawaiian, Japanese, and Korean plaintiffs were all held to be nonwhite; mixed-race plaintiffs who were half-white and half-Asian were also held to be nonwhite.[10] The United States Supreme Court laid to rest any questions about the racial bar in *Ozawa v. United States,* ruling that Japanese immigrants were not white, and in *United States v. Thind,* ruling that Asian Indian immigrants were not white.[11] Asian immigrants were prohibited by statute from naturalizing through the 1940s, and the racial bar on naturalization was not repealed until 1952.

From today's vantage point, these attempts by Asian immigrants to be classified as white may seem absurd and even subordinative, because they symbolically pushed blacks down the social ladder relative to whites and Asians. But when the legal paradigm limits options to black or white and nothing else, curious and unseemly choices inevitably arise. The solution, of course, is to develop and rely on theories that comprehend the complexity of race relations, which includes discerning that the experiences of Asian Americans are not the same as the experiences of African Americans.

Racism in Context: Anti-Asian Violence

To better understand the experiences of Asian Americans, consider how racial subordination operates within a specific context: anti-Asian violence. Racial violence is not a new phenomenon, and the histories of all racial minorities include extensive violence, whether it is the genocide of Native American tribes during the expansion of the United States, the terrorism against blacks in the South, the military conquest and ongoing border violence against Latinos in the Southwest, or the attacks on Asian immigrant laborers in the West. Incidents of anti-Asian violence reveal unique themes of prejudice and discrimination that illustrate the dynamics of racism against Asian Americans.[12] . . .

The most notorious episode of recent anti-Asian violence was the killing of Vincent Chin in 1982. Chin, a twenty-seven-year-old Chinese American, was celebrating his upcoming wedding at a Detroit bar when he was approached by Ronald Ebens and Michael Nitz, two white automobile factory workers. Ebens and Nitz thought Chin was Japanese and blamed him for the loss of jobs in the automobile industry. After calling Chin a "jap," the two men chased him out of the bar. They eventually caught Chin and proceeded to beat him repeatedly with a baseball bat. Chin died from his injuries a few days later. Ebens and Nitz each pleaded guilty to manslaughter but received only probation and a fine. Ebens was later convicted of federal civil rights violations, but his conviction was overturned on appeal and he was acquitted on retrial. Neither Ebens nor Nitz spent any time in prison for the killing.

A similar incident occurred in 1989 in Raleigh, North Carolina. Jim (Ming Hai) Loo had been playing pool with several friends when he was approached by Robert Piche and his brother Lloyd Piche, who began calling Loo and his friends "chinks" and "gooks" and blaming them for the death of American soldiers in Vietnam. Once outside, Robert Piche pistol-whipped Loo on the back of the head, causing Loo to fall onto a broken bottle that pierced his brain. Loo died from his injuries two days later. Robert Piche was convicted and sentenced to thirty-seven years in prison; Lloyd Piche was sentenced to six months in prison by a state court, and sentenced to four years in prison for federal civil rights violations.

Another tragic illustration of anti-Asian violence is the multiple killings of Asian American children at the Cleveland Elementary School in Stockton, California, in 1989. Patrick Purdy used an AK-47 assault rifle to spray bullets into a crowded schoolyard, killing five children and wounding over twenty others before turning the gun on himself. Although initially labeled the product of a disturbed mind obsessed with guns and the military, the shootings were later proved to be motivated by racial hatred. A report issued by the California attorney general's office found that Purdy targeted the school because it was heavily populated by Southeast Asian children.[13]

Perpetrators who are affiliated with hate groups have been responsible for many anti-Asian crimes. During the early 1980s, when tensions erupted between Vietnamese immigrant fishermen and native-born fishermen in several coastal states, the Ku Klux Klan engaged in extensive harassment and violence against Vietnamese fishermen along the Gulf Coast of Texas. Federal litigation was required to end a pattern of threats, cross burnings, arsons, and shootings.[14] In 1990, Hung Truong, a fifteen-year-old Vietnamese boy living in Houston, was attacked by two men who were later identified as white supremacist "skinheads." After following Truong and his friends as they walked down the street, the two assailants jumped out of their car, one wielding a club, and shouted "White power." They chased Truong and proceeded to kick and beat him, even as he pleaded for his life. The two men admitted at trial that they attacked Truong because he was Vietnamese.

In August 1999, Joseph Ileto, a Filipino American postal worker, was gunned down in California's San Fernando Valley by Buford Furrow, Jr., a white supremacist who earlier the same day had riddled the North Valley Jewish Community Center with over seventy rounds from a semi-automatic weapon and wounded several individuals, including three small children. Linked to anti-Semitic and white supremacist groups, Furrow shot Ileto nine times and admitted that he had targeted Ileto because he was a "chink or spic," terms that were no doubt tied to Furrow's perception that an individual like Ileto was somehow less than fully American. Ironically, Ileto was wearing a clear symbol of membership in American society—the uniform of a U.S. Postal Service mail carrier—at the time he was killed. Pleading guilty to avoid the imposition of a federal death penalty, Furrow was ultimately sentenced to multiple life sentences without possibility of parole.[15]

More common, however, are incidents that do not involve formal hate groups and that occur in day-to-day interactions among people at work, in schools, at home, and on the street. Here are some examples, all of which occurred during 2002:

- A Japanese American man in Rancho Santa Margarita, California was attacked in his front yard by a perpetrator who threw eggs at him and shouted "You dirty Jap!" while leaving the scene.

- While stalled in traffic, a Korean American woman, along with her young son, were approached by a man who slapped the woman, asked her if she was Korean several times, and shouted: "Why don't you go fuck some Japanese bastard?," "What are you doing in this country?," "Go back to your country," and "Go back to where you came from."

- In a supermarket parking lot in Fort Lee, New Jersey, a Korean American woman was verbally assaulted by a couple, one of whom yelled, "Where did you learn to drive? You chink!" After confronting the couple, the woman was threatened by another customer who yelled, "Yeah, go back to your own country!" . . .

- At a business in Los Angeles, a perpetrator brandished a knife and told a South Asian American victim, "I don't like Indians or Pakistanis and if you don't go back to your country, I'll kill you." . . .

- In Beverly Hills, California, a South Asian American man working as a restaurant valet was accosted by an individual who called the man an "Indian mother fucker" and asked "Are you a terrorist?" before attempting to assault the victim.[16] . . .

Racial Themes

Without question, the examples of anti-Asian violence demonstrate that overt racism is still a serious problem for Asian Americans, just as it has been for African Americans and other racial minorities. Some types of anti-Asian violence can thus be explained by treating violence against Asian Americans and other racial minority groups as expressions of white racism. Anti-Asian violence committed by white supremacists targeting anyone who is not white fits within a binary model of race that places all racial minorities in the same category of "nonwhite."

But many incidents of anti-Asian violence suggest that more complex dynamics are at work. Members of one Asian ethnic group are often mistaken for being members of other Asian ethnic groups. Racial and ethnic slurs are interlaced with nativist anti-immigrant rhetoric. Resentment about economic competition, both foreign and domestic, is often implicated. Even hostility rooted in the United States' previous military involvement in Asian countries may be a factor. And a white–nonwhite framework cannot explain racial violence in which members of one nonwhite group victimize members of another nonwhite group. Several basic themes can be gleaned from these and other examples of violence against Asian Americans.

Racialization

One theme is the importance of *racial* categorizing in anti-Asian violence. The killing of Vincent Chin is an example of how anti-Asian violence is racialized: based on his physical appearance, Chin, a Chinese American, was taken to be a Japanese national by his killers, who had made him the focus of their anger and frustration toward Japanese competition in the automobile industry. A perpetrator who makes the race-based generalization that all Asians look alike puts every Asian American at risk, even if the specific antagonisms are targeted against a smaller subset of people.

The attribution of specific ethnic characteristics to anyone falling within the racial category of "Asian" is common in anti-Asian violence. For example, when Luyen Phan Nguyen, a Vietnamese premedical student, was killed in Coral Springs, Florida, in 1992, he was taunted with slurs at a party and later chased down by a group of men who beat and kicked him repeatedly. Among the epithets directed at Nguyen during the beating were "chink," "vietcong," and "sayonara"—three separate and distinct ethnic slurs.

Nativism and Racism

Another theme manifested by anti-Asian violence is the centrality of nativism, which John Higham defines as "intense opposition to an internal minority on the ground of its foreign (i.e., 'un-American') connections."[17] Asian Americans are equated with foreigners, or they are at least presumed to be foreign-born. Race and nativism thus intersect to produce a distinctive form of subordination of Asian Americans—what Robert Chang labels "nativistic racism."[18]

In many incidents, Asian American victims are perceived and categorized as foreigners by their assailants: Vincent Chin was transformed into a Japanese national; Jim Loo became a Vietnamese adversary; immigrant merchants were remade as foreign investors and capitalists. Even Joseph Ileto, wearing the uniform of a U.S. Postal Service mail carrier, was reduced to the position of an outsider. Anti-immigrant epithets such as "Go home!" or "Why don't you go back to your own country?" frequently accompany anti-Asian violence, along with specific racial and ethnic slurs. And under the rubric of foreign outsider, Asian Americans fall into an array of unpopular categories: economic competitor, organized criminal, "illegal alien," or just unwelcome immigrant.

Patriotic racism is a peculiar and especially deep-seated form of nativist racism. American military conflicts against the Japanese during World War II, against Koreans and Chinese during the Korean War, and against the Vietnamese during the Vietnam War have generated intense animosity against Asian Americans. During World War II, the federal government's internment of Japanese Americans, most of whom were United States citizens, reflected patriotic racism at its worst, as a formal governmental policy. Intimidation and violence against Asian Americans is still common on December 7 because of the hostility that arises on the anniversary of the bombing of

Pearl Harbor by Japan. And with the ongoing war against terrorism, South Asians, coupled with Arab Americans and Muslim Americans, have been subjected to extensive harassment, intimidation, and discrimination.

Racial Hierarchies and Interracial Conflict

A related theme made evident by anti-Asian violence revolves around the intermediate position that Asian Americans appear to occupy on a social and economic ladder that places whites on top and blacks at the bottom. Black-on-Asian hate crimes often contain strong elements of cultural conflict and nativism—blacks, like whites, treat Asians as foreigners. But black-on-Asian crimes also have strains traceable to resentment over the economic achievements of Asian Americans, particularly their entrepreneurial success in the inner cities. The destruction of Korean immigrants' businesses in 1992, many located in the historically black residential area of South Central Los Angeles, reflected a growing anger against Asian American prosperity.

In this context, the "model minority" stereotype of Asian Americans becomes a two-edged sword, breeding not only incomplete and inaccurate images of Asian American success but resentment and hostility on the part of other racial groups. Racial differentiation often places Asian Americans in a middle position within the racial hierarchy of the United States—neither black nor white, and somewhere between black and white.

The Limits of Black and White

Hate violence is the most extreme form of racial subordination against Asian Americans, but it sheds light on important differences between the subordination of Asian Americans and African Americans. A binary model of race based on relations between blacks and whites cannot fully describe the complex racial matrix that exists in the U.S. In terms of representation, a black–white model ignores or marginalizes the experiences of Asian Americans, Latinos, Native Americans, Arab Americans, and other groups who have extensive histories of discrimination against them. A black–white model discounts the role of immigration in race relations and confines discussion on the impact race has had on anti-immigrant policies that affect the nation's growing Asian American and Latino populations. A black–white model also limits any analysis of the relations and tensions between racial and ethnic groups, which are increasingly significant in urban areas where racial "minorities" are now becoming majorities.

In essence a black–white model fails to recognize that the basic nature of discrimination can differ among racial and ethnic groups. Theories of racial inferiority have been applied, often with violent force, against Asian Americans, just as they have been applied against blacks and other racial minority groups. But the causes of anti-Asian subordination can be traced to other factors as well, including nativism, differences in language and culture, perceptions of Asians as economic competitors, international relations, and past military involvement in Asian countries. Recent immigration from Asian countries has elevated culture and language to prominent places on the race relations landscape, challenging even the integrity of the racial category "Asian American." And the promotion in recent years of a "model minority" racial stereotype, based on the high education levels and incomes of some Asian Americans, represents a curious and distorted form of racism, denying the existence of Asian American poverty and inequality. All of these considerations point to the need for an analysis of race that is very different from the dominant black–white paradigm. . . .

NOTES

1. Andrew Hacker, *Two Nations: Black and White, Separate, Hostile, Unequal,* rev. ed. (New York: Ballantine Books, 1995). Hacker even suggests that Asian Americans and Latinos, particularly second- and later-generation individuals, are "merging" into the white race, through intermarriage and assimilation (18–19).

2. *Report of the National Advisory Commission on Civil Disorders* (New York: Bantam, 1968), 1.

3. Gary Y. Okihiro, *Margins and Mainstreams: Asians in American History and Culture* (Seattle and London: University of Washington Press, 1994), 34.

4. Frank H. Wu, "Neither Black nor White: Asian Americans and Affirmative Action," *Boston College Third World Law Journal* 15 (Summer 1995): 225, 249–251.

5. 4 Cal. 399, 404 (1854).

6. 275 U.S. 78, 87 (1927).

7. James W. Loewen, *The Mississippi Chinese: Between Black and White* (Cambridge, Mass.: Harvard University Press, 1971).

8. *Gong Lum v. Rice,* 275 U.S. 78, 79 (1927).

9. Ian F. Haney López, *White by Law: The Legal Construction of Race* (New York and London: New York University Press, 1996).

10. Ibid., appendix A. As Haney López notes, a legal strategy arguing for whiteness rather than blackness may have had some tactical advantage at the time, because the 1870 naturalization statute employed a geographic test rather than a racial test of eligibility for blacks: the law referred to persons of "African nativity, or African descent," rather than to "black persons." More likely, though, Asian American plaintiffs sought to distinguish themselves from blacks because of the stigmas attached to being black, and sought the only available alternative—to be classified as white.

11. 260 U.S. 178 (1922); 261 U.S. 204 (1923).

12. Note, "Racial Violence against Asian Americans," *Harvard Law Review* 106 (June 1993): 1926.

13. Nelson Kempsky, *A Report to Attorney General John K. Van de Kemp on Patrick Purdy and the Cleveland School Killings* (Sauamento: California Department of Justice, Office of the Attorney General, 1989).

14. *Vietnamese Fisherman's Association v. Knights of the Ku Klux Klan,* S43 F. Supp. 198 (S.D. Tex. 1982) (permanent injunction); *Vietnamese Fisherman's Association v. Knights of the Ku Klux Klan,* 518 F. Supp. 993 (S.D. Tex. 1981) (preliminary injunction).

15. "Moving Beyond the Past," *AsianWeek,* 25 May 2000; Henry Weinstein, "Furrow Gets 5 Life Terms for Racist Rampage Court: The White Supremacist Wounded Five People at a Valley Jewish Center and Murdered a Filipino American Postal Worker in 1999," *Los Angeles Times,* 27 March 2001, p. B1.

16. National Asian Pacific American Legal Consortium, 2002 *Audit of Violence against Asian Pacific Americans: Tenth Annual Report* (Washington, D.C.: National Asian Pacific American Legal Consortium, 2004), 14–23.

17. John Higham, *Strangers in the Land: Patterns of American Nativism, 1860–1925* (New York: Atheneum, 1970), 4.

18. Robert S. Chang, "Toward an Asian American Legal Scholarship: Critical Race Theory, Post-Structuralism, and Narrative Space," *California Law Review* 81 (October 1993): 1241, 1255.

4 Oppression

Marilyn Frye

It is a fundamental claim of feminism that women are oppressed. The word "oppression" is a strong word. It repels and attracts. It is dangerous and dangerously fashionable and endangered. It is much misused, and sometimes not innocently.

The statement that women are oppressed is frequently met with the claim that men are oppressed too. We hear that oppressing is oppressive to those who oppress as well as to those they oppress. Some men cite as evidence of their oppression their much-advertised inability to cry. It is tough, we are told, to be masculine. When the stresses and frustrations of being a man are cited as evidence that oppressors are oppressed by their oppressing, the word "oppression" is being stretched to meaninglessness; it is treated as though its scope includes any and all human experience of limitation or suffering, no matter the cause, degree or consequence. Once such usage has been put over on us, then if ever we deny that any person or group is oppressed, we seem to imply that we think they never suffer and have no feelings. We are accused of insensitivity, even of bigotry. For women, such accusation is particularly intimidating, since sensitivity is one of the few virtues that has been assigned to us. If we are found insensitive, we may fear we have no redeeming traits at all and perhaps are not real women. Thus are we silenced before we begin: the name of our situation drained of meaning and our guilt mechanisms tripped.

But this is nonsense. Human beings can be miserable without being oppressed, and it is perfectly consistent to deny that a person or group is oppressed without denying that they have feelings or that they suffer.

We need to think clearly about oppression, and there is much that mitigates against this. I do not want to undertake to prove that women are oppressed (or that men are not), but I want to make clear what is being said when we say it. We need this word, this concept, and we need it to be sharp and sure.

The root of the word "oppression" is the element "press." *The press of the crowd; pressed into military service; to press a pair of pants; printing press; press the button.* Presses are used to mold things or flatten them or reduce them in bulk, sometimes to reduce them by squeezing out the gases or liquids in them. Something pressed is something caught between or among forces and barriers which are so related to each other that jointly they restrain, restrict or prevent the thing's motion or mobility. Mold. Immobilize. Reduce.

The mundane experience of the oppressed provides another clue. One of the most characteristic and ubiquitous features of the world as experienced by oppressed people is the double bind—situations in which options are reduced to a very few and

From *The Politics of Reality: Essays in Feminist Theory* by Marilyn Frye. Copyright © 1983. Used by permission of Crossing Press, an imprint of Crown Publishing Group, a division of Penguin Random House LLC. All rights reserved. Any third party use of this material outside of this publication is prohibited. Interested parties must apply directly to Penguin Random House LLC for permission.

all of them expose one to penalty, censure or deprivation. For example, it is often a requirement upon oppressed people that we smile and be cheerful. If we comply, we signal our docility and our acquiescence in our situation. We need not, then, be taken note of. We acquiesce in being made invisible, in our occupying no space. We participate in our own erasure. On the other hand, anything but the sunniest countenance exposes us to being perceived as mean, bitter, angry or dangerous. This means, at the least, that we may be found "difficult" or unpleasant to work with, which is enough to cost one one's livelihood; at worst, being seen as mean, bitter, angry or dangerous has been known to result in rape, arrest, beating and murder. One can only choose to risk one's preferred form and rate of annihilation.

Another example: It is common in the United States that women, especially younger women, are in a bind where neither sexual activity nor sexual inactivity is all right. If she is heterosexually active, a woman is open to censure and punishment for being loose, unprincipled or a whore. The "punishment" comes in the form of criticism, snide and embarrassing remarks, being treated as an easy lay by men, scorn from her more restrained female friends. She may have to lie and hide her behavior from her parents. She must juggle the risks of unwanted pregnancy and dangerous contraceptives. On the other hand, if she refrains from heterosexual activity, she is fairly constantly harassed by men who try to persuade her into it and pressure her to "relax" and "let her hair down"; she is threatened with labels like "frigid," "uptight," "man-hater," "bitch" and "cocktease." The same parents who would be disapproving of her sexual activity may be worried by her inactivity because it suggests she is not or will not be popular, or is not sexually normal. She may be charged with lesbianism. If a woman is raped, then if she has been heterosexually active she is subject to the presumption that she liked it (since her activity is presumed to show that she likes sex), and if she has not been heterosexually active, she is subject to the presumption that she liked it (since she is supposedly "repressed and frustrated"). Both heterosexual activity and heterosexual nonactivity are likely to be taken as proof that you wanted to be raped, and hence, of course, weren't *really* raped at all. You can't win. You are caught in a bind, caught between systematically related pressures.

Women are caught like this, too, by networks of forces and barriers that expose one to penalty, loss or contempt whether one works outside the home or not, is on welfare or not, bears children or not, raises children or not, marries or not, stays married or not, is heterosexual, lesbian, both or neither. Economic necessity; confinement to racial and/or sexual job ghettos; sexual harassment; sex discrimination; pressures of competing expectations and judgments about *women, wives* and *mothers* (in the society at large, in racial and ethnic subcultures and in one's own mind); dependence (full or partial) on husbands, parents or the state; commitment to political ideas; loyalties to racial or ethnic or other "minority" groups; the demands of self-respect and responsibilities to others. Each of these factors exists in complex tension with every other, penalizing or prohibiting all of the apparently available options. And nipping at one's heels, always, is the endless pack of little things. If one dresses one way, one is subject to the assumption that one is advertising one's sexual availability; if one dresses another way, one appears to "not care about oneself" or to be "unfeminine." If one uses "strong language," one invites categorization as a whore or slut; if one does not, one invites categorization as a "lady"—one too delicately constituted to cope with robust speech or the realities to which it presumably refers.

The experience of oppressed people is that the living of one's life is confined and shaped by forces and barriers which are not accidental or occasional and hence avoidable, but are systematically related to each other in such a way as to catch one between and among them and restrict or penalize motion in any direction. It is the experience of being caged in: all avenues, in every direction, are blocked or booby-trapped.

Cages. Consider a birdcage. If you look very closely at just one wire in the cage, you cannot see the other wires. If your conception of what is before you is determined by this myopic focus, you could look at that one wire, up and down the length of it, and be unable to see why a bird would not just fly around the wire any time it wanted to go somewhere. Furthermore, even if, one day at a time, you myopically inspected each wire, you still could not see why a bird would have trouble going past the wires to get anywhere. There is no physical property of any one wire, *nothing* that the closest scrutiny could discover, that will reveal how a bird could be inhibited or harmed by it except in the most accidental way. It is only when you step back, stop looking at the wires one by one, microscopically, and take a macroscopic view of the whole cage, that you can see why the bird does not go anywhere; and then you will see it in a moment. It will require no great subtlety of mental powers. It is perfectly *obvious* that the bird is surrounded by a network of systematically related barriers, no one of which would be the least hindrance to its flight, but which, by their relations to each other, are as confining as the solid walls of a dungeon.

It is now possible to grasp one of the reasons why oppression can be hard to see and recognize: one can study the elements of an oppressive structure with great care and some good will without seeing the structure as a whole, and hence without seeing or being able to understand that one is looking at a cage and that there are people there who are caged, whose motion and mobility are restricted, whose lives are shaped and reduced.

The arresting of vision at a microscopic level yields such common confusion as that about the male door-opening ritual. This ritual, which is remarkably wide-spread across classes and races, puzzles many people, some of whom do and some of whom do not find it offensive. Look at the scene of the two people approaching a door. The male steps slightly ahead and opens the door. The male holds the door open while the female glides through. Then the male goes through. The door closes after them. "Now how," one innocently asks, "can those crazy womenslibbers say that is oppressive? The guy *removed* a barrier to the lady's smooth and unruffled progress." But each repetition of this ritual has a place in a pattern, in fact in several patterns. One has to shift the level of one's perception in order to see the whole picture.

The door-opening pretends to be a helpful service, but the helpfulness is false. This can be seen by noting that it will be done whether or not it makes any practical sense. Infirm men and men burdened with packages will open doors for ablebodied women who are free of physical burdens. Men will impose themselves awkwardly and jostle everyone in order to get to the door first. The act is not determined by convenience or grace. Furthermore, these very numerous acts of unneeded or even noisome "help" occur in counterpoint to a pattern of men not being helpful in many practical ways in which women might welcome help. What *women* experience is a world in which gallant princes charming commonly make a fuss about being helpful and providing small services when help and services are of little or no use, but in which there are rarely ingenious and adroit princes at hand when substantial assistance is really wanted either in mundane affairs or in situations of threat, assault or terror. There is no help with the (his) laundry; no help typing a report at 4:00 A.M.; no help in mediating disputes among relatives or children. There is nothing but advice that women should stay indoors after dark, be chaperoned by a man, or when it comes down to it, "lie back and enjoy it."

The gallant gestures have no practical meaning. Their meaning is symbolic. The door-opening and similar services provided are services which really are needed by people who are for one reason or another incapacitated—unwell, burdened with parcels, etc. So the message is that women are incapable. The detachment of the acts from the concrete realities of what women need and do not need is a vehicle for the message that women's actual needs and interests are unimportant or irrelevant. Finally, these gestures imitate the behavior of servants toward masters and thus mock women, who are in most respects the servants and caretakers of men. The message of the false helpfulness of male gallantry is female dependence, the invisibility or insignificance of women, and contempt for women.

One cannot see the meanings of these rituals if one's focus is riveted upon the individual event in all its particularity, including the particularity of the individual man's present conscious intentions and motives and the individual woman's conscious perception of the event in the moment. It seems sometimes that people take a deliberately myopic view and fill their eyes with things seen microscopically in order not to see macroscopically. At any rate, whether it is deliberate or not, people can and do fail to see the oppression of women because they fail to see macroscopically and hence fail to see the various elements of the situation as systematically related in larger schemes.

As the cageness of the birdcage is a macroscopic phenomenon, the oppressiveness of the situations in which women live our various and different lives is a macroscopic phenomenon. Neither can be *seen* from a microscopic perspective. But when you look macroscopically you can see it—a network of forces and barriers which are systematically related and which conspire to the immobilization, reduction and molding of women and the lives we live.

5 | Homophobia as a Weapon of Sexism

Suzanne Pharr

Patriarchy—an enforced belief in male dominance and control—is the ideology and sexism the system that holds it in place. The catechism goes like this: Who do gender roles serve? Men and the women who seek power from them. Who suffers from gender roles? Women most completely and men in part. How are gender roles maintained? By the weapons of sexism: economics, violence, homophobia.

Why then don't we ardently pursue ways to eliminate gender roles and therefore sexism? It is my profound belief that all people have a spark in them that yearns for freedom, and the history of the world's atrocities—from the Nazi concentration camps to white dominance in South Africa to the battering of women—is the story of attempts to snuff out that spark. When that spark doesn't move forward to full flame, it is because the weapons designed to control and destroy have wrought such intense damage over time that the spark has been all but extinguished.

Sexism, that system by which women are kept subordinate to men, is kept in place by three powerful weapons designed to cause or threaten women with pain and loss. . . .

We have to look at economics not only as the root cause of sexism but also as the underlying, driving force that keeps all the oppressions in place. In the United States, our economic system is shaped like a pyramid, with a few people at the top, primarily white males, being supported by large numbers of unpaid or low-paid workers at the bottom. When we look at this pyramid, we begin to understand the major connection between sexism and racism because those groups at the bottom of the pyramid are women and people of color. We then begin to understand why there is such a fervent effort to keep those oppressive systems (racism and sexism and all the ways they are manifested) in place to maintain the unpaid and low-paid labor.

As in most other countries, in the United States, income is unequally distributed. However, among the industrialized countries of the world, the U.S. has the most unequal distribution of income of all. (See *The State of Working America 2000/2001*, p. 388.) What's more, over the past 30 plus years, income distribution has become even more unequal. In an OpEd piece distributed by Knight/Ridder/Tribune NewsService, Holly Sklar reports that poverty rates in 2001 were higher than in the 1970s and the top 5% of households got richer at the expense of everyone else. According to the U.S. Census bureau, there were 33 million poor in the U.S. in 2001 and median pretax income fell for all households except those

From *Homophobia: A Weapon of Sexism*. Published by Chardon Press, Berkeley, CA. Copyright © 1997 by Suzanne Pharr. Distributed by the Women's Project, 2224 Main St., Little Rock, AR 72206. Reprinted by permission of the author.

in the top 5%. In other words, income inequality increased dramatically. In 1967, the wealthiest 5% of households had 17.5% of the income and by 2001 they had increased their share to 22.4%, while the bottom fifth had to make do with 3.5% of aggregate income, down from 4% in 1967 (September 30, 2002). And wealth is even more unequally distributed than income. According to U.S. government figures for 1997, the wealthiest 10% of U.S. families own more than 72% of the total wealth, with 39% of the total wealth concentrated in the hands of the wealthiest 1%. In contrast, the bottom 40% of the population owns less than 1%.

In order for this top-heavy system of economic inequity to maintain itself, the 90 percent on the bottom must keep supplying cheap labor. A very complex, intricate system of institutionalized oppressions is necessary to maintain the status quo so that the vast majority will not demand its fair share of wealth and resources and bring the system down. Every institution—schools, banks, churches, government, courts, media, etc.—as well as individuals must be enlisted in the campaign to maintain such a system of gross inequity.

What would happen if women gained the earning opportunities and power that men have? What would happen if these opportunities were distributed equitably, no matter what sex one was, no matter what race one was born into, and no matter where one lived? What if educational and training opportunities were equal? Would women spend most of our youth preparing for marriage? Would marriage be based on economic survival for women? What would happen to issues of power and control? Would women stay with our batterers? If a woman had economic independence in a society where women had equal opportunities, would she still be thought of as owned by her father or husband?

Economics is the great controller in both sexism and racism. If a person can't acquire food, shelter, and clothing and provide them for children, then that person can be forced to do many things in order to survive. The major tactic, worldwide, is to provide unrecompensed or inadequately recompensed labor for the benefit of those who control wealth. Hence, we see women performing unpaid labor in the home or filling low-paid jobs, and we see people of color in the lowest-paid jobs available.

The method is complex: limit educational and training opportunities for women and for people of color and then withhold adequate paying jobs with the excuse that people of color and women are incapable of filling them. Blame the economic victim and keep the victim's self-esteem low through invisibility and distortion within the media and education. Allow a few people of color and women to succeed among the profitmakers so that blaming those who don't "make it" can be intensified. Encourage those few who succeed in gaining power now to turn against those who remain behind rather than to use their resources to make change for all. Maintain the myth of scarcity—that there are not enough jobs, resources, etc., to go around—among the middle class so that they will not unite with laborers, immigrants, and the unemployed. The method keeps in place a system of control and profit by a few and a constant source of cheap labor to maintain it.

If anyone steps out of line, take her/his job away. Let homelessness and hunger do their work. The economic weapon works. And we end up saying, "I would do this or that—be openly who I am, speak out against injustice, work for civil rights, join a labor union, go to a political march, etc.—if I didn't have this job. I can't afford to lose it." We stay in an abusive situation because we see no other way to survive. . . .

Violence against women is directly related to the condition of women in a society that refuses us equal pay, equal access to resources, and equal status with males. From this condition comes men's confirmation of their sense of ownership of women, power over women, and assumed right to control women for their own means. Men physically and emotionally abuse women because they *can,* because they live in a world that gives them permission. Male violence is fed by their sense of their *right* to dominate and control, and their sense of superiority over a group of people who, because of gender, they consider inferior to them.

It is not just the violence but the threat of violence that controls our lives. Because the burden of responsibility has been placed so often on the potential victim, as women we have curtailed our freedom in order to protect ourselves from violence. Because of the threat of rapists, we stay on alert, being careful not to walk in isolated places, being careful where we park our cars, adding incredible security measures to our homes—massive locks, lights, alarms, if we can afford them—and we avoid places where we will appear vulnerable or unprotected while the abuser walks with freedom. Fear, often now so commonplace that it is unacknowledged, shapes our lives, reducing our freedom. . . .

Part of the way sexism stays in place is the societal promise of survival, false and unfulfilled as it is, that women will not suffer violence if we attach ourselves to a man to protect us. A woman without a man is told she is vulnerable to external violence and, worse, that there is something wrong with her. When the male abuser calls a woman a lesbian, he is not so much labeling her a woman who loves women as he is warning her that by resisting him, she is choosing to be outside society's protection from male institutions and therefore from wide-ranging, unspecified, ever-present violence. When she seeks assistance from woman friends or a battered women's shelter, he recognizes the power in woman bonding and fears loss of her servitude and loyalty: the potential loss of his control. The concern is not affectional/sexual identity: the concern is disloyalty and the threat is violence.

The threat of violence against women who step out of line or who are disloyal is made all the more powerful by the fact that women do not have to do anything—they may be paragons of virtue and subservience—to receive violence against our lives: the violence still comes. It comes because of the woman-hating that exists throughout society. Chance plays a larger part than virtue in keeping women safe. Hence, with violence always a threat to us, women can never feel completely secure and confident. Our sense of safety is always fragile and tenuous.

Many women say that verbal violence causes more harm than physical violence because it damages self-esteem so deeply. Women have not wanted to hear battered women say that the verbal abuse was as hurtful as the physical abuse: to acknowledge that truth would be tantamount to acknowledging that *virtually every woman is a battered woman.* It is difficult to keep strong against accusations of being a bitch, stupid, inferior, etc., etc. It is especially difficult when these individual assaults are backed up by a society that shows women in textbooks, advertising, TV programs, movies, etc. as debased, silly, inferior, and sexually objectified, and a society that gives tacit approval to pornography. When we internalize these messages, we call the result "low self-esteem," a therapeutic individualized term. It seems to me we should use the more political expression: when we internalize these messages, we experience *internalized sexism,* and we experience it in common with all women living in a sexist world. The violence against us is supported by a society in which woman-hating is deeply imbedded.

In "Eyes on the Prize," a 1987 Public Television documentary about the Civil Rights Movement, an older white woman says about her youth in the South that it was difficult to be anything different from what was around her when there was no vision for another way to be. Our society presents images of women that say it is appropriate to commit violence against us. Violence is committed against women because we are seen as inferior in status and in worth. It has been the work of the women's movement to present a vision of another way to be.

Every time a woman gains the strength to resist and leave her abuser, we are given a model of the importance of stepping out of line, of moving toward freedom. And we all gain strength when she says to violence, "Never again!" Thousands of women in the last fifteen years have resisted their abusers to come to this country's 1100 battered women's shelters. There they have sat down with other women to share their stories, to discover that their stories again and again are the same, to develop an analysis that shows that violence is a statement about power and control, and to understand how sexism creates the climate for male violence. Those brave women are now a part of a movement that gives hope for another way to live in equality and peace.

Homophobia works effectively as a weapon of sexism because it is joined with a powerful arm, heterosexism. Heterosexism creates the climate for homophobia with its assumption that the world is and must be heterosexual and its display of power and privilege as the norm. Heterosexism is the systemic display of homophobia in the institutions of society. Heterosexism and homophobia work together to enforce compulsory heterosexuality and that bastion of patriarchal power, the nuclear family. The central focus of the rightwing attack against women's liberation is that women's equality, women's self-determination, women's control of our own bodies and lives will damage what they see as the crucial societal institution, the nuclear family. The attack has been led by fundamentalist ministers across the country. The two areas they have focused on most consistently are abortion and homosexuality, and their passion has led them to bomb women's clinics and to recommend deprogramming for homosexuals and establishing camps to quarantine people with AIDS. To resist marriage and/or heterosexuality is to risk severe punishment and loss.

It is not by chance that when children approach puberty and increased sexual awareness they begin to taunt each other by calling these names: "queer," "faggot," "pervert." It is at puberty that the full force of society's pressure to conform to heterosexuality and prepare for marriage is brought to bear. Children know what we have taught them, and we have given clear messages that those who deviate from standard expectations are to be made to get back in line. The best controlling tactic at puberty is to be treated as an outsider, to be ostracized at a time when it feels most vital to be accepted. Those who are different must be made to suffer loss. It is also at puberty that misogyny begins to be more apparent, and girls are pressured to conform to societal norms that do not permit them to realize their full potential. It is at this time that their academic achievements begin to decrease as they are coerced into compulsory heterosexuality and trained for dependency upon a man, that is, for economic survival.

There was a time when the two most condemning accusations against a woman meant to ostracize and disempower her were "whore" and "lesbian." The sexual revolution and changing attitudes about heterosexual behavior may have led to some lessening of the power of the word *whore,* though it still has strength as a threat to sexual property and prostitutes are stigmatized and abused. However, the word *lesbian* is still fully charged and carries with it the full threat of loss of power and privilege, the threat of being cut asunder, abandoned, and left outside society's protection.

To be a lesbian is to be *perceived* as someone who has stepped out of line, who has moved out of sexual/economic dependence on a male, who is woman-identified. A lesbian is perceived as someone who can live without a man, and who is therefore (however illogically) against men. A lesbian is perceived as being outside the acceptable, routinized order of things. She is seen as someone who has no societal institutions to protect her and who is not privileged to the protection of individual males. Many heterosexual women see her as someone who stands in contradiction to the sacrifices they have made to conform to compulsory heterosexuality. A lesbian is perceived as a threat to the nuclear family, to male dominance and control, to the very heart of sexism.

Gay men are perceived also as a threat to male dominance and control, and the homophobia expressed against them has the same roots in sexism as does homophobia against lesbians. Visible gay men are the objects of extreme hatred and fear by heterosexual men because their breaking ranks with male heterosexual solidarity is seen as a damaging rent in the very fabric of sexism. They are seen as betrayers, as traitors who must be punished and eliminated. In the beating and killing of gay men we see clear evidence of this hatred. When we see the fierce homophobia expressed toward gay men, we can begin to understand the ways sexism also affects males through imposing rigid, dehumanizing gender roles on them. The two circumstances in which it is legitimate for men to be openly physically affectionate with one another are in competitive sports and in the crisis of war. For many men, these two experiences are the highlights of their lives, and they think of them again and again with nostalgia. War and sports offer a cover of all-male safety and dominance to keep away the notion of affectionate openness being identified with homosexuality. When gay men break ranks with male roles through bonding and affection outside the arenas of war and sports, they are perceived as not being "real men," that is, as being identified with women, the weaker sex that must be dominated and that over the centuries has been the object of male hatred and abuse. Misogyny gets transferred to gay men with a vengeance and is increased by the fear that their sexual identity and behavior will bring down the entire system of male dominance and compulsory heterosexuality.

If lesbians are established as threats to the status quo, as outcasts who must be punished, homophobia can wield its power over all women through lesbian baiting. Lesbian baiting is an attempt to control women by labeling us as lesbians because our behavior is not acceptable, that is, when we are being independent, going our own way, living whole lives, fighting for our rights, demanding equal pay, saying no to violence, being self-assertive, bonding with and loving the company of women, assuming the right to our bodies, insisting upon our own authority, making changes that include us in society's decision-making; lesbian baiting occurs when women are called lesbians because we resist male dominance and control. And it has little or nothing to do with one's sexual identity.

To be named as lesbian threatens all women, not just lesbians, with great loss. And any woman who steps out of role risks being called a lesbian. To understand how this is a threat to all women, one must understand that any woman can be called a lesbian and there is no real way she can defend herself: there is no way to credential one's sexuality. ("The Children's Hour," a Lillian Hellman play, makes this point when a student asserts two teachers are lesbians and they have no way to disprove it.) She may be married or divorced, have children, dress in the most feminine manner, have sex with men, be celibate—but there are lesbians who do all those things. *Lesbians look like all women and all women look like lesbians.* There is no guaranteed method of identification, and as we all know, sexual identity can be kept hidden. (The same is true for men. There is no way to prove their sexual identity, though many go to extremes to prove heterosexuality.) Also, women are not necessarily born lesbian. Some seem to be, but others become lesbians later in life after having lived heterosexual lives. Lesbian baiting of heterosexual women would not work if there were a definitive way to identify lesbians (or heterosexuals).

We have yet to understand clearly how sexual identity develops. And this is disturbing to some people, especially those who are determined to discover how lesbian and gay identity is formed so that they will know where to start in eliminating it. (Isn't it odd that there is so little concern about discovering the causes of heterosexuality?) There are many theories: genetic makeup, hormones, socialization, environment, etc. But there is no conclusive evidence that indicates that heterosexuality comes from one process and homosexuality from another.

We do know, however, that sexual identity can be in flux, and we know that sexual identity means more than just the gender of people one is attracted to and has sex with. To be a lesbian has as many ramifications as for a woman to be heterosexual. It is more than sex, more than just the bedroom issue many would like to make it: it is a woman-centered life with all the social interconnections that entails. Some lesbians are in long-term relationships, some in short-term ones, some date, some are celibate, some are married to men, some remain as separate as possible from men, some have children by men, some by alternative insemination, some seem "feminine" by societal standards, some "masculine," some are doctors, lawyers and ministers, some laborers, housewives and writers: what all share in common is a sexual/affectional identity that focuses on women in its attractions and social relationships.

If lesbians are simply women with a particular sexual identity who look and act like all women, then the major difference in living out a lesbian sexual identity as opposed to a heterosexual identity is that as lesbians we live in a homophobic world that threatens and imposes damaging loss on us *for being who we are,* for choosing to live whole lives. Homophobic people often assert that homosexuals have the choice of not being homosexual; that is, we don't have to act out our sexual identity. In that case, I want to hear heterosexuals talk about their willingness not to act out their sexual identity, including not just sexual activity but heterosexual social interconnections and heterosexual privilege. It is a question of wholeness. It is very difficult for one to be denied the life of a sexual being, whether expressed in sex or in physical affection, and to feel complete, whole. For our loving relationships with humans feed the life of the spirit and enable us to overcome our basic isolation and to be interconnected with humankind.

If, then, any woman can be named a lesbian and be threatened with terrible losses, what is it she fears? Are these fears real? Being vulnerable to a homophobic world can lead to these losses:

- *Employment.* The loss of job leads us right back to the economic conection to sexism. This fear of job loss exists for almost every lesbian except perhaps those who are self-employed or in a business that does not require societal approval. Consider how many businesses or organizations you know that will hire and protect people who are openly gay or lesbian.

- *Family.* Their approval, acceptance, love.

- *Children.* Many lesbians and gay men have children, but very, very few gain custody in court challenges, even if the other parent is a known abuser. Other children may be kept away from us as though gays and lesbians are abusers. There are written and unwritten laws prohibiting lesbians and gays from being foster parents or from adopting children. There is an irrational fear that children in contact with lesbians and gays will become homosexual through influence or that they will be sexually abused. Despite our knowing that 95 percent of those who sexually abuse children are heterosexual men, there are no policies keeping heterosexual men from teaching or working with children, yet in almost every school system in America, visible gay men and lesbians are not hired through either written or unwritten law.

- *Heterosexual privilege and protection.* No institutions, other than those created by lesbians and gays—such as the Metropolitan Community Church, some counseling centers, political organizations such as the National Gay and Lesbian Task Force, the National Coalition of Black Lesbians and Gays, the Lambda Legal Defense and Education Fund, etc.—affirm homosexuality and offer protection. Affirmation and protection cannot be gained from the criminal justice system, mainline churches, educational institutions, the government.

■ *Safety.* There is nowhere to turn for safety from physical and verbal attacks because the norm presently in this country is that it is acceptable to be overtly homophobic. Gay men are beaten on the streets; lesbians are kidnapped and "deprogrammed." The National Gay and Lesbian Task Force, in an extended study, has documented violence against lesbians and gay men and noted the inadequate response of the criminal justice system. One of the major differences between homophobia/heterosexism and racism and sexism is that because of the Civil Rights Movement and the women's movement racism and sexism are expressed more covertly (though with great harm); because there has not been a major, visible lesbian and gay movement, it is permissible to be overtly homophobic in any institution or public forum. Churches spew forth homophobia in the same way they did racism prior to the Civil Rights Movement. Few laws are in place to protect lesbians and gay men, and the criminal justice system is wracked with homophobia.

■ *Mental health.* An overtly homophobic world in which there is full permission to treat lesbians and gay men with cruelty makes it difficult for lesbians and gay men to maintain a strong sense of well-being and self-esteem. Many lesbians and gay men are beaten, raped, killed, subjected to aversion therapy, or put in mental institutions. The impact of such hatred and negativity can lead one to depression and, in some cases, to suicide. The toll on the gay and lesbian community is devastating.

■ *Community.* There is rejection by those who live in homophobic fear, those who are afraid of association with lesbians and gay men. For many in the gay and lesbian community, there is a loss of public acceptance, a loss of allies, a loss of place and belonging.

■ *Credibility.* This fear is large for many people: the fear that they will no longer be respected, listened to, honored, believed. They fear they will be social outcasts.

The list goes on and on. But any one of these essential components of a full life is large enough to make one deeply fear its loss. A black woman once said to me in a workshop, "When I fought for Civil Rights, I always had my family and community to fall back on even when they didn't fully understand or accept what I was doing. I don't know if I could have borne losing them. And you people don't have either with you. It takes my breath away."

What does a woman have to do to get called a lesbian? Almost anything, sometimes nothing at all, but certainly anything that threatens the status quo, anything that steps out of role, anything that asserts the rights of women, anything that doesn't indicate submission and subordination. Assertiveness, standing up for oneself, asking for more pay, better working conditions, training for and accepting a non-traditional (you mean a man's?) job, enjoying the company of women, being financially independent, being in control of one's life, depending first and foremost upon oneself, thinking that one can do whatever needs to be done, but above all, working for the rights and equality of women.

In the backlash to the gains of the women's liberation movement, there has been an increased effort to keep definitions man-centered. Therefore, to work on behalf of women must mean to work against men. To love women must mean that one hates men. A very effective attack has been made against the word *feminist* to make it a derogatory word. In current backlash usage, *feminist* equals *man-hater* which equals *lesbian*. This formula is created in the hope that women will be frightened away from their work on behalf of women. Consequently, we now have women who believe in the rights of women and work for those rights while from fear deny that they are feminists, or refuse to use the word because it is so "abrasive."

So what does one do in an effort to keep from being called a lesbian? She steps back into line, into the role that is demanded of her, tries to behave in such a way that doesn't threaten the status of men, and if she works for women's rights, she begins modifying that work. When women's organizations begin doing significant social change work, they inevitably are lesbian-baited; that is, funders or institutions or community members tell us that they can't work with us because of our "man-hating attitudes" or the presence of lesbians. We are called too strident, told we are making enemies, not doing good. . . .

In my view, homophobia has been one of the major causes of the failure of the women's liberation movement to make deep and lasting change. (The other major block has been racism.) We were fierce when we set out but when threatened with the loss of heterosexual privilege, we began putting on brakes. Our best-known nationally distributed women's magazine was reluctant to print articles about lesbians, began putting a man on the cover several times a year, and writing articles about women who succeeded in a man's world. We worried about our image, our being all right, our being "real women" despite our work. Instead of talking about the elimination of sexual gender roles, we stepped back and talked about "sex role stereotyping" as the issue. Change around the edges for middle-class white women began to be talked about as successes. We accepted tokenism and integration, forgetting that equality for all women, for all people—and not just equality of white middle-class women with white men—was the goal that we could never put behind us.

But despite backlash and retreats, change is growing from within. The women's liberation movement is beginning to gain strength again because there are women who are talking about liberation for all women. We are examining sexism, racism, homophobia, classism, anti-Semitism, ageism, ableism, and imperialism, and we see everything as connected. This change in point of view represents the third wave of the women's liberation movement, a new direction that does not get mass media coverage and recognition. It has been initiated by women of color and lesbians who were marginalized or rendered invisible by the white heterosexual leaders of earlier efforts. The first wave was the 19th and early 20th century campaign for the vote; the second, beginning in the 1960s, focused on the Equal Rights Amendment and abortion rights. Consisting of predominantly white middle-class women, both failed in recognizing issues of equality and empowerment for all women. The third wave of the movement, multi-racial and multi-issued, seeks the transformation of the world for us all. We know that we won't get there until everyone gets there; that we must move forward in a great strong line, hand in hand, not just a few at a time.

We know that the arguments about homophobia originating from mental health and Biblical/religious attitudes can be settled when we look at the sexism that permeates religious and psychiatric history. The women of the third wave of the women's liberation movement know that *without the existence of sexism, there would be no homophobia.*

Finally, we know that as long as the word *lesbian* can strike fear in any woman's heart, then work on behalf of women can be stopped; the only successful work against sexism must include work against homophobia.

6 Class in America

Gregory Mantsios

There wasn't much attention given to America's class divide, at least not until a band of mostly young activists decided to occupy Wall Street in the fall of 2011 and in the process capture the media spotlight, add the word "99 percenters" to our lexicon, and change the national—and in many ways, the international—discourse. While there has been recent interest in the rising level of inequality, the class divide is anything but recent and its consequences remain severely understated in the mass media. Perhaps most importantly, the point that is missed is that inequality is persistent and structural—and it manifests itself in a multitude of cultural and social ways.

Americans, in general, don't like to talk about class. Or so it would seem. We don't speak about class privileges, or class oppression, or the class nature of society. These terms are not part of our everyday vocabulary, and in most circles this language is associated with the language of the rhetorical fringe. Unlike people in most other parts of the world, we shrink from using words that classify along economic lines or that point to class distinctions: Phrases like "working class," "upper class," "capitalist class," and "ruling class" are rarely uttered by Americans.

For the most part, avoidance of class-laden vocabulary crosses class boundaries. There are few among the poor who speak of themselves as lower class; instead, they refer to their race, ethnic group, or geographic location. Workers are more likely to identify with their employer, industry, or occupational group than with other workers, or with the working class. Neither are those at the upper end of the economic spectrum likely to use the word "class[1]." In her study of 38 wealthy and socially prominent women, Susan Ostrander asked participants if they considered themselves members of the upper class. One participant responded, "I hate to use the word 'class.' We are responsible, fortunate people, old families, the people who have something." Another said, "I hate [the term] upper class. It is so non-upper class to use it. I just call it 'all of us—those who are well-born."[2]

It is not that Americans, rich or poor, aren't keenly aware of class differences— those quoted above obviously are; it is that class is usually not in the domain of public conversation. Class is not discussed or debated in public because class identity has been stripped from popular culture. The institutions that shape mass culture and define the parameters of public debate have avoided class issues. In politics, in primary and secondary education, and in the mass media, formulating issues in terms of class has been considered culturally unacceptable, unnecessarily combative, and even un-American. (See my essay "Media Magic: Making Class Invisible," on page 562 of this volume.)

The author wishes to thank Maya Pinto for her assistance in updating this article. Greg Mantsios, "Class in America: Myths and Realities."© by Gregory Mantsios, 2012. Reprinted by permission of the author.

There are, however, two notable exceptions to this phenomenon. First, it is acceptable in the United States to talk about "the middle class." Interestingly enough, the term middle class appears to be acceptable precisely because it mutes class differences. References to the middle class by politicians, for example, are designed to encompass and attract the broadest possible constituency. Not only do references to the middle class gloss over differences, but they also avoid any suggestion of conflict or injustice.

This leads us to a second exception to the class-avoidance phenomenon. We are, on occasion, presented with glimpses of the upper class and the lower class (the language used is "the wealthy" and "the poor"). In the media, these presentations are designed to satisfy some real or imagined voyeuristic need of "the ordinary person." As curiosities, the ground-level view of street life and trailer parks and the inside look at the rich and the famous serve as unique models, one to avoid and one to emulate. In either case, the two sets of lifestyles are presented as though they have no causal relation to each other: There is nothing to suggest that our economic system allows people to grow wealthy *at the expense of* those who are not.

Similarly, when politicians and social commentators draw attention to the plight of the poor, they do so in a manner that obscures the class structure and denies any sense of exploitation. Wealth and poverty are viewed as one of several natural and inevitable states of being: Differences are only differences. One may even say differences are the American way, a reflection of American social diversity.

We are left with one of two possible explanations for why Americans usually don't talk about class: Either class distinctions are not relevant to U.S. society, or we mistakenly hold a set of beliefs that obscure the reality of class differences and their impact on people's lives.

Let's look at four common, albeit contradictory, beliefs about class in America that have persisted over time.

Myth 1: We are a middle-class nation. Despite some variations in economic status, most Americans have achieved relative affluence in what is widely recognized as a consumer society.

Myth 2: Class really doesn't matter in the United States. Whatever differences do exist in economic standing, they are—for the most part—irrelevant. Our democracy provides for all regardless of economic class: Rich or poor, we are all equal in the eyes of the law.

Myth 3: We live in a land of upward mobility. The American public as a whole is steadily moving up the economic ladder and each generation propels itself to greater economic well-being.

Myth 4: Everyone has an equal chance to succeed. Success in the United States requires no more than hard work, sacrifice, and perseverance: "In America, anyone can become a billionaire; it's just a matter of being in the right place at the right time."

In trying to assess the legitimacy of these beliefs, we want to ask several important questions. Are there significant class differences among Americans? If these differences do exist, are they getting bigger or smaller? Do class differences have a significant impact on the way we live? How much upward mobility is there in the

United States? Finally, does everyone in the United States really have an equal opportunity to succeed and an equal voice in our democracy?

The Economic Spectrum

For starters, let's look at difference. An examination of available data reveals that variations in economic well-being are, in fact, dramatic. Consider the following:

- The richest 20 percent of Americans hold nearly 90 percent of the total household wealth in the country. The wealthiest 1 percent of the American population holds 36 percent of the total national wealth. That is, the top 1 percent own over one-third of all the consumer durables (such as houses, cars, televisions, and computers) and financial assets (such as stocks, bonds, property, and bank savings).[3]

- There are 323,067 Americans—approximately 1 percent of the adult population—who earn more than $1 million annually.[4] There are over 1,000 billionaires in the United States today, more than 70 of them worth over $10 billion each.[5] It would take the typical American earning $49,445 (the median income in the United States)—and spending absolutely nothing at all—a total of 202,240 years (or over 2,500 lifetimes) to earn $10 billion.

Affluence and prosperity are clearly alive and well in certain segments of the U.S. population. However, this abundance is in sharp contrast to the poverty that persists in America. At the other end of the spectrum:

- More than 15 percent of the American population—that is, 1 of every 7 people in this country—live below the official poverty line (calculated at $11,139 for an individual and $22,314 for a family of four).[6] In 2010, there were 42 million poor people in the United States—the largest number since the Census Bureau began publishing poverty statistics more than 50 years ago.[7]

- An estimated 3.5 million people—of whom nearly 1.4 million are children—are homeless.[8]

- The 2010 U.S. Census reported that more than 1 out of every 5 children under the age of 18 lives in poverty.[9]

Reality 1: The contrast between rich and poor is sharp, and with one-third of the American population living at one extreme or the other, it is difficult to argue that we live in a classless society.

While those at the bottom of the economic ladder have fared poorly relative to those at the top, so too have those in the middle—and their standing relative to the top has been declining as well.

- The middle fifth of the population holds less than 4 percent of the national wealth.[10]

■ The share of wealth held by the middle fifth 30 years ago was 5.2 percent of the total. Today's share held by the middle sector is 23 percent less than what it was 3 decades ago.[11]

Reality 2: The middle class in the United States holds a very small share of the nation's wealth and that share has declined steadily.

The gap between rich and poor—and between the rich and the middle class—leaves the vast majority of the American population at a distinct disadvantage.

■ Eighty percent of the population—that is, four out of every five Americans, is left sharing a little more than 10 percent of the nation's wealth.[12]

■ The income gap between the very rich (top 1 percent) and everyone else (the 99 percent) more than tripled over the past 3 decades, creating the greatest concentration of income since 1928.[13]

This level of inequality is neither inevitable nor universal. The income gap between rich and poor in a country is generally measured by a statistic called the Gini coefficient, which provides a mathematical ratio and scale that allows comparisons between countries of the world. The U.S. government's own reports using the Gini coefficient show that the United States ranked number 95 out of 134 countries studied—that is, 94 countries (including almost all the industrialized nations of the world) had a more equal distribution of income than the United States.[14]

The numbers and percentages associated with economic inequality are difficult to fully comprehend. To help his students visualize the distribution of income, the well-known economist Paul Samuelson asked them to picture an income pyramid made of children's blocks, with each layer of blocks representing $1,000. If we were to construct Samuelson's pyramid today, the peak of the pyramid would be much higher than the Eiffel Tower, yet almost all of us would be within 6 feet of the ground.[15] In other words, a small minority of families takes the lion's share of the national income, and the remaining income is distributed among the vast majority of middle-income and low-income families. Keep in mind that Samuelson's pyramid represents the distribution of income, not wealth (accumulated resources). The distribution of wealth is skewed even further. Ten billion dollars of wealth would reach more than 1,000 times the height of the Eiffel Tower.[16]

Reality 3: Middle- and lower-income earners—what many in other parts of the world would refer to as the working class—share a miniscule portion of the nation's wealth. For the most part, the real class divide in the United States is between the very wealthy and everyone else—and it is a divide that is staggering.

American Lifestyles

The late political theorist/activist Michael Harrington once commented, "America has the best-dressed poverty the world has ever known."[17] Clothing disguises much of the poverty in the United States, and this may explain, in part, the country's middle-class image. With increased mass marketing of "designer" clothing and with shifts in the nation's economy from blue-collar (and often better-paying) manufacturing jobs to white-collar and pink-collar jobs in the service sector, it is becoming increasingly difficult to distinguish class differences based on appearance.[18] The dress-down environment prevalent in the high-tech industry (what American Studies scholar Andrew Ross refers to as the "no-collar movement") has reduced superficial distinctions even further.[19]

Beneath the surface, there is another reality. Let's look at some "typical" and not-so-typical lifestyles.

American Profile	
Name:	Harold S. Browning
Father:	Manufacturer, industrialist
Mother:	Prominent social figure in the community
Principal child-rearer:	Governess
Primary education:	An exclusive private school on Manhattan's Upper East Side *Note:* A small, well-respected primary school where teachers and administrators have a reputation for nurturing student creativity and for providing the finest educational preparation *Ambition:* "To become President"
Supplemental tutoring:	Tutors in French and mathematics
Summer camp:	Sleep-away camp in northern Connecticut *Note:* Camp provides instruction in the creative arts, athletics, and the natural sciences
Secondary education:	A prestigious preparatory school in Westchester County *Note:* Classmates included the sons of ambassadors, doctors, attorneys, television personalities, and well-known business leaders *Supplemental education:* Private SAT tutor *After-school activities:* Private riding lessons *Ambition:* "To take over my father's business" *High-school graduation gift:* BMW
Family activities:	Theater, recitals, museums, summer vacations in Europe, occasional winter trips to the Caribbean *Note:* As members of and donors to the local art museum, the Brownings and their children attend private receptions and exhibit openings at the invitation of the museum director

Higher education:	An Ivy League liberal arts college in Massachusetts *Major:* Economics and political science *After-class activities:* Debating club, college newspaper, swim team *Ambition:* "To become a leader in business"
First full-time job (age 23):	Assistant manager of operations, Browning Tool and Die, Inc. (family enterprise)
Subsequent employment:	3 years—Executive assistant to the president, Browning Tool and Die *Responsibilities included:* Purchasing (materials and equipment), personnel, and distribution networks 4 years—Advertising manager, Lackheed Manufacturing (home appliances) 3 years—Director of marketing and sales, Comerex, Inc. (business machines)
Current employment (age 38):	Executive vice president, SmithBond and Co. (digital instruments) *Typical daily activities:* Review financial reports and computer printouts, dictate memoranda, lunch with clients, initiate conference calls, meet with assistants, plan business trips, meet with associates *Transportation to and from work:* Chauffeured company limousine *Annual salary:* $324,000 *Ambition:* "To become chief executive officer of the firm, or one like it, within the next five to ten years"
Current residence:	Eighteenth-floor condominium on Manhattan's Upper West Side, eleven rooms, including five spacious bedrooms and terrace overlooking river *Interior:* Professionally decorated and accented with elegant furnishings, valuable antiques, and expensive artwork *Note:* Building management provides doorman and elevator attendant; family employs au pair for children and maid for other domestic chores
Second residence:	Farm in northwestern Connecticut, used for weekend retreats and for horse breeding (investment/hobby)

> *Note:* To maintain the farm and cater to the family when they are there, the Brownings employ a part-time maid, groundskeeper, and horse breeder

Harold Browning was born into a world of nurses, maids, and governesses. His world today is one of airplanes and limousines, five-star restaurants, and luxurious living accommodations. The life and lifestyle of Harold Browning is in sharp contrast to that of Bob Farrell.

American Profile

Name:	Bob Farrell
Father:	Machinist
Mother:	Retail clerk
Principal child-rearer:	Mother and sitter
Primary education:	A medium-size public school in Queens, New York, characterized by large class size, outmoded physical facilities, and an educational philosophy emphasizing basic skills and student discipline
	Ambition: "To become President"
Supplemental tutoring:	None
Summer camp:	YMCA day camp
	Note: Emphasis on team sports, arts and crafts
Secondary education:	Large regional high school in Queens
	Note: Classmates included the sons and daughters of carpenters, postal clerks, teachers, nurses, shopkeepers, mechanics, bus drivers, police officers, salespersons
	Supplemental education: SAT prep course offered by national chain
	After-school activities: Basketball and handball in school park
	Ambition: "To make it through college"
	High-school graduation gift: $500 savings bond
Family activities:	Family gatherings around television set, softball, an occasional trip to the movie theater, summer Sundays at the public beach
Higher education:	A two-year community college with a technical orientation
	Major: Electrical technology
	After-school activities: Employed as a part-time bagger in local supermarket
	Ambition: "To become an electrical engineer"

First full-time job (age 19):	Service-station attendant
	Note: Continued to take college classes in the evening
Subsequent employment:	Mail clerk at large insurance firm; manager trainee, large retail chain
Present employment (age 38):	Assistant sales manager, building supply firm
	Typical daily activities: Demonstrate products, write up product orders, handle customer complaints, check inventory
	Transportation to and from work: City subway
	Annual salary: $45,261
	Additional income: $6,100 in commissions from evening and weekend work as salesman in local men's clothing store
	Ambition: "To open up my own business"
Current residence:	The Farrells own their own home in a working-class neighborhood in Queens, New York

Bob Farrell and Harold Browning live very differently: One is very privileged, the other much less so. The differences are class differences, which have a profound impact on the way they live. They are differences between playing a game of handball in the park and taking riding lessons at a private stable; watching a movie on television and going to the theater; and taking the subway to work and being driven in a limousine. More important, the difference in class determines where they live, who their friends are, how well they are educated, what they do for a living, and what they come to expect from life.

Yet, as dissimilar as their lifestyles are, Harold Browning and Bob Farrell have some things in common: they live in the same city, they work long hours, and they are highly motivated. More importantly, they are both white males.

Let's look at someone else who works long and hard and is highly motivated. This person, however, is black and female.

American Profile	
Name:	Cheryl Mitchell
Father:	Janitor
Mother:	Waitress
Principal child-rearer:	Grandmother
Primary education:	Large public school in Ocean Hill-Brownsville, Brooklyn, New York
	Note: Rote teaching of basic skills and emphasis on conveying the importance of good attendance, good manners, and good work habits; school patrolled by security guards
	Ambition: "To be a teacher"

Supplemental tutoring:	None
Summer camp:	None
Secondary education:	Large public school in Ocean Hill-Brownsville *Note:* Classmates included sons and daughters of hairdressers, groundskeepers, painters, dressmakers, dishwashers, domestics *Supplemental education:* None *After-school activities:* Domestic chores, part-time employment as babysitter and housekeeper *Ambition:* "To be a social worker" *High-school graduation gift:* Corsage
Family activities:	Church-sponsored socials
Higher education:	One semester of local community college *Note:* Dropped out of school for financial reasons
First full-time job (age 17):	Counter clerk, local bakery
Subsequent employment:	File clerk with temporary-service agency, supermarket checker
Current employment (age 38):	Nurse's aide at a municipal hospital *Typical daily activities:* Make up hospital beds, clean out bedpans, weigh patients and assist them to the bathroom, take temperature readings, pass out and collect food trays, feed patients who need help, bathe patients, and change dressings *Annual salary:* $17,850 *Ambition:* "To get out of the ghetto"
Current residence:	Three-room apartment in the South Bronx, needs painting, has poor ventilation, is in a high-crime area *Note:* Cheryl Mitchell lives with her four-year-old son and her elderly mother

When we look at Cheryl Mitchell, Bob Farrell, and Harold Browning, we see three very different lifestyles. We are not looking, however, at economic extremes. Cheryl Mitchell's income as a nurse's aide puts her above the government's official poverty line.[20] Below her on the income pyramid are 42 million poverty-stricken Americans. Far from being poor, Bob Farrell has an annual income ($51,361) as an assistant sales manager that puts him above the median income level—that is, more than 50 percent of the U.S. population earns less money than Bob Farrell.[21] And while Harold Browning's income puts him in a high-income bracket, he stands only a fraction of the way up Samuelson's income pyramid. Well above him are the 323,067 Americans whose annual incomes exceed $1 million. Yet Harold Browning spends more money on his horses than Cheryl Mitchell earns in a year.

Reality 4: Even ignoring the extreme poles of the economic spectrum, we find enormous class differences in the lifestyles among the haves, the have-nots, and the have-littles.

Class affects more than lifestyle and material well-being. It has a significant impact on our physical and mental well-being as well. Researchers have found an inverse relationship between social class and health. Lower-class standing is correlated with higher rates of infant mortality, eye and ear disease, arthritis, physical disability, diabetes, nutritional deficiency, respiratory disease, mental illness, and heart disease.[22] In all areas of health, poor people do not share the same life chances as those in the social class above them. Furthermore, low income correlates with a lower quality of treatment for illness and disease. The results of poor health and poor treatment are borne out in the life expectancy rates within each class. Researchers have found that the higher one's class standing is, the higher one's life expectancy is. Conversely, they have also found that within each age group, the lower one's class standing, the higher the death rate; in some age groups, the figures are as much as two and three times higher.[23]

It's not just physical and mental health that is so largely determined by class. The lower a person's class standing is, the more difficult it is to secure housing; the more time is spent on the routine tasks of everyday life; the greater is the percentage of income that goes to pay for food, health care (which accounts for 23 percent of spending for low-income families)[24] and other basic necessities; and the greater is the likelihood of crime victimization.[25]

Class and Educational Attainment

School performance (grades and test scores) and educational attainment (level of schooling completed) also correlate strongly with economic class. Furthermore, despite some efforts to make testing fairer and schooling more accessible, current data suggest that the level of inequity is staying the same or getting worse.

In his study for the Carnegie Council on Children in 1978, Richard De Lone examined the test scores of over half a million students who took the College Board exams (SATs). His findings were consistent with earlier studies that showed a relationship between class and scores on standardized tests; his conclusion: "the higher the student's social status, the higher the probability that he or she will get higher grades."[26] Today, more than 30 years after the release of the Carnegie report, College Board surveys reveal data that are no different: test scores still correlate with family income.

Average Combined Scores by Income (400 to 1600 scale)[27]	
Family Income	Median Score
More than $200,000	1721
$160,000 to $200,000	1636
$140,000 to $160,000	1619
$120,000 to $140,000	1594
$100,000 to $120,000	1580
$80,000 to $100,000	1545
$60,000 to $80,000	1503
$40,000 to $60,000	1461
$20,000 to $40,000	1398
less than $20,000	1323

These figures are based on the test results of 1,647,123 SAT takers in 2010–2011.

In another study conducted 30 years ago, researcher William Sewell showed a positive correlation between class and overall educational achievement. In comparing the top quartile (25 percent) of his sample to the bottom quartile, he found that students from upper-class families were twice as likely to obtain training beyond high school and four times as likely to attain a postgraduate degree. Sewell concluded: "Socioeconomic background . . . operates independently of academic ability at every stage in the process of educational attainment."[28]

Today, the pattern persists. There are, however, two significant changes. On the one hand, the odds of getting into college have improved for the bottom quartile of the population, although they still remain relatively low compared to the top. On the other hand, the chances of completing a 4-year college degree for those who are poor are extraordinarily low compared to the chances for those who are rich. Researchers estimate college completion is 10 times more likely for the top 25 percent of the population than it is for the bottom 25 percent.[29]

Reality 5: From cradle to grave, class position has a significant impact on our well-being. Class accurately predicts chances for survival, educational achievement, and economic success.

Media-induced excitement over big payoff reality shows, celebrity salaries, and multimillion-dollar lotteries suggests that we in the United States live in a "rags to riches" society. So too does news about dot-com acquisitions and initial public offerings (IPOs) that provide enormous windfalls to young company founders. But rags-to-riches stories notwithstanding, the evidence suggests that "striking it rich" is extremely rare and that class mobility in general is uncommon and becoming increasingly so.

One study showed that 79 percent of families remained in the same quintile (fifth) of income earners or moved up or down only one quintile. (Of this group, most families did not move at all).[30] Another study showed that fewer than one in five men surpass the economic status of their fathers.[31] Several recent studies have shown that there is less class mobility in the United States than in most industrialized democracies in the world. One such study placed the United States in a virtual tie for last place.[32] Why does the United States occupy such a low position on the mobility scale? Several explanations have been offered: The gap between rich and poor in the United States is greater; the poor are poorer in the United States and have farther to go to get out of poverty; and the United States has a lower rate of unionization than other industrialized nations.

The bottom line is that very affluent families transmit their advantages to the next generation and poor families stay trapped.[33] For those whose annual income is in six figures, economic success is due in large part to the wealth and privileges bestowed on them at birth. Over 66 percent of the consumer units with incomes of $100,000 or more have inherited assets. Of these units, over 86 percent reported that inheritances constituted a substantial portion of their total assets.[34]

Economist Harold Wachtel likens inheritance to a series of Monopoly games in which the winner of the first game refuses to relinquish his or her cash and commercial property for the second game. "After all," argues the winner, "I accumulated my wealth and income by my own wits." With such an arrangement, it is not difficult to predict the outcome of subsequent games.[35]

Reality 6: All Americans do not have an equal opportunity to succeed, and class mobility in the United States is lower than that of the rest of the industrialized world. Inheritance laws provide built-in privileges to the offspring of the wealthy and add to the likelihood of their economic success while handicapping the chances for everyone else.

One would think that increases in worker productivity or a booming economy would reduce the level of inequality and increase class mobility. While the wages of workers *may* increase during good times—that is, relative to what they were in the past—the economic advantages of higher productivity and a booming economy go disproportionately to the wealthy, a factor that adds still further to the level of inequality. For example, during the period 2001 to 2007, the U.S. economy expanded and productivity (output per hours worked) increased by more than 15 percent. During that same period, however, the top 1 percent of U.S. households took two-thirds of the nation's income gains, their inflation-adjusted income grew more than ten times faster than the income of the bottom 90 percent, and their share of the national income reached its highest peak. At the same time, the inflation-adjusted weekly salary of the average American during that 6-year economic expansion declined by 2.3 percent.[36] Observing similar patterns in U.S. economic history, one prominent economist described economic growth in the United States as a "spectator sport for the majority of American families."[37] Economic decline, on the other hand, is much more "participatory," with layoffs and cuts in public services hitting middle- and lower-income families hardest—families that rely on public services (e.g., public schools, transportation) and have fewer resources to fall back on during difficult economic times.

Reality 7: Inequality in the United States is persistent in good times and bad.

While most Americans rely on their wages or salaries to make ends meet, the rich derive most of their wealth from such income-producing assets as stocks, bonds, business equity, and non-home real estate. This type of wealth is even more highly concentrated than wealth in general. Over 89 percent of all stocks in the U.S., for example, are owned by the wealthiest 10 percent of Americans.[38] This makes the fortunes of the wealthy (whether they are corporate executives, investment bankers, or not) closely tied to the fortunes of corporate America and the world of finance. While defenders of capitalism and the capitalist class argue that what's good for corporate America is good for all of America, recent economic experience has raised more doubts than ever about this. Putting aside illegal manipulation of the financial system, the drive to maximize corporate profit has led to job destruction (as companies seek cheaper labor in other parts of the world and transfer investments off shore); deregulation (e.g., so environmental protections don't inhibit corporate profit); and changes in tax policy that favor corporations (through loopholes) and those who rely on corporate profit for their wealth (by taxing their capital gains at lower rates).

Reality 8: The privileges that accrue to the wealthy are tied to the worlds of capital and finance—worlds whose good fortune are often the misfortune of the rest of the population.

Government is often portrayed as the spoiler of Wall Street—and at times it is. There are certainly examples of the government imposing fines for environmental violations, establishing regulations that protect consumers and workers, restrict corporate conduct, etc. But government as the "great equalizer" often isn't what it appears to be. In 2010, for example, when the federal government concluded a fraud case against a major investment bank (Goldman Sachs), it touted the case as one of the largest settlements in U.S. history—a whopping $550 million dollars. It turns out that $550 million was less than 4 percent of what the bank paid its executives in bonuses that year.

Similarly, changes in policy that reduce taxes are often touted as vehicles for leveling the playing field and bringing economic relief to the middle class. But at best, these do little or nothing to help middle- and low-income families. More often than not, they increase the level of inequality by providing disproportionate tax benefits to the wealthy while reducing public budgets and increasing the costs of such public services as transportation and college tuition. For example, changes in tax policy over the last five decades—especially those during the 1980s—have favored the wealthy: Federal taxes for the wealthiest 0.1 percent have fallen from 51 to 26 percent over the last 50 years, while the rate for middle income earners has risen from 14 to 16 percent.[39]

It's not just that economic resources are concentrated in the hands of a few; so too are political resources. And it is the connection between wealth and political power that allows economic inequality to persist and grow. Moreover, as the costs of political influence rise, so does the influence of the "monied" class. Running for public office has always been an expensive proposition, but it's become increasingly so: It now costs on average, $1.4 million in campaign funds to win a seat in the House of Representatives and $7 million to win a seat in the U.S. Senate.[40] Most politicians rely on wealthy donors to finance their campaigns. Alternatively, wealthy individuals who want to make public policy often underwrite their own campaigns.* The average wealth of U.S. senators, for example, is $12.6 million.[41]

High-priced lobbyists also ensure that the interests of the wealthy and of corporate America are well represented in the halls of government. Not surprisingly, organizations that track the connection between political contributions and votes cast by public officials find a strong correlation between money and voting.[42] It's not that the power of the economic elite is absolute; it's not. The power of the wealthy is often mitigated by social movements and by grassroots organizations that advocate on behalf of the poor and working class. The Occupy Wall Street movement—like movements that came before it—changed not only the public debate, but led to policy reforms as well. The power of the rich, however, remains so disproportionate that it severely undermines our democracy. Over three-quarters of a century ago, such an assault on democratic principles led Supreme Court Justice Louis Brandeis to observe, "We can have democracy in this country or we can have great wealth concentrated in the hands of a few, but we can't have both." Talking about the power elite or the ruling class may put people off, but there is no doubt that the interests of the wealthy predominate in American politics.

Reality 9: Wealth and power are closely linked. The economic elite have a grossly disproportionate amount of political power—more than enough power to ensure that the system that provides them such extraordinary privileges perpetuates itself.

Spheres of Power and Oppression

When we look at society and try to determine what it is that keeps most people down—what holds them back from realizing their potential as healthy, creative, productive individuals—we find institutional forces that are largely beyond individual control. Class domination is one of these forces. People do not choose to be poor or working class; instead, they are limited and confined by the opportunities afforded or denied them by a social and economic system. The class structure in the United States is a function of its economic system: capitalism, a system that is based on private rather than public ownership and control of commercial enterprises. Under capitalism, these enterprises are governed by the need to produce a profit for the owners, rather than to fulfill societal needs. Class divisions arise from the differences between those who own and control corporate enterprise and those who do not.

---

*Over the course of three elections, Michael Bloomberg spent more than $261 million of his own money to become mayor of New York City. He spent $102 million in his last mayoral election alone—more than $172 per vote.

Racial and gender domination are other forces that hold people down. Although there are significant differences in the way capitalism, racism, and sexism affect our lives, there are also a multitude of parallels. And although class, race, and gender act independently of each other, they are at the same time very much interrelated.

On the one hand, issues of race and gender cut across class lines. Women experience the effects of sexism whether they are well-paid professionals or poorly paid clerks. As women, they are not only subjected to stereotyping and sexual harassment, they face discrimination and are denied opportunities and privileges that men have. Similarly, a wealthy black man faces racial oppression, is subjected to racial slurs, and is denied opportunities because of his color. Regardless of their class standing, women and members of minority races are constantly dealing with institutional forces that hold them down precisely because of their gender, the color of their skin, or both.

On the other hand, the experiences of women and minorities are differentiated along class lines. Although they are in subordinate positions vis-à-vis white men, the particular issues that confront women and people of color may be quite different, depending on their position in the class structure.

Power is incremental and class privileges can accrue to individual women and to individual members of a racial minority. While power is incremental, oppression is cumulative, and those who are poor, black, and female are often subject to all of the forces of class, race, and gender discrimination simultaneously. This cumulative situation is what is sometimes referred to as the double and triple jeopardy of women and people of color.

Chances of Being Poor in America[43]					
White male/ female	White female head*	Hispanic male/ female	Hispanic female head*	Black male/ female	Black female head*
1 in 14	1 in 4	1 in 4	1 in 2	1 in 4	1 in 2

*Persons in families with female householder, no husband present.

Furthermore, oppression in one sphere is related to the likelihood of oppression in another. If you are black and female, for example, you are much more likely to be poor or working class than you would be as a white male. Census figures show that the incidence of poverty varies greatly by race and gender.

In other words, being female and being nonwhite are attributes in our society that increase the chances of poverty and of lower-class standing.

Reality 10: Racism and sexism significantly compound the effects of class in society.

None of this makes for a very pretty picture of our country. Despite what we like to think about ourselves as a nation, the truth is that the qualities of our lives and the opportunities for success are highly circumscribed by our race, our gender, and the class we are born into. As individuals, we feel hurt and angry when someone is treating us unfairly; yet as a society we tolerate unconscionable injustice. A more just society will require a radical redistribution of wealth and power. We can start by reversing the current trends that polarize us as a people and adapt policies and practices that narrow the gaps in income, wealth, power, and privilege. That will only come about with pressure from below: strong organizations and mass movements advocating for a more just and equitable society.

NOTES

1. See Jay MacLead, *Ain't No Makin' It: Aspirations and Attainment in a Lower-Income Neighborhood* (Boulder, CO: Westview Press, 1995); Benjamin DeMott, *The Imperial Middle* (New York: Morrow, 1990); Ira Katznelson, *City Trenches: Urban Politics and Patterning of Class in the United States* (New York: Pantheon Books, 1981); Charles W. Tucker, "A Comparative Analysis of Subjective Social Class: 1945–1963," *Social Forces*, no. 46 (June 1968): 508–514; Robert Nisbet, "The Decline and Fall of Social Class," *Pacific Sociological Review* 2 (Spring 1959): 11–17; and Oscar Glantz, "Class Consciousness and Political Solidarity," *American Sociological Review* 23 (August 1958): 375–382.

2. Susan Ostrander, "Upper-Class Women: Class Consciousness as Conduct and Meaning," in *Power Structure Research*, ed. G. William Domhoff (Beverly Hills, CA: Sage Publications, 1980), 78–79. Also see Stephen Birmingham, *America's Secret Aristocracy* (Boston: Little Brown, 1987).

3. Economic Policy Institute, "Wealth Holdings Remain Unequal in Good and Bad Times," *The State of Working America* (Washington, D.C.: Economic Policy Institute, 2011), accessed September 25, 2011, http://www.stateofworkingamerica.org/files/files/Figure%20B _wealth_dis_byclass.xlsx.

4. The number of individuals filing tax returns that had a gross adjusted income of $1 million or more in 2008 was 323,067 ("Tax Stats at a Glance," Internal Revenue Service, U.S. Treasury Department, available at http://www.irs.gov/pub/irs-soi/10taxstatscard .pdf). The adult population (18 years and over) of the United States in 2008 was 229,945,000, according to U.S. Census figures, U.S. Census Bureau, *Current Population Survey, Annual Social and Economic Supplement 2010*, available at http://www.census.gov /compendia/statab/2012/tables/12s0007.pdf.

5. *Forbes*. "The World's Billionaires List: United States," accessed September 25, 2011, http://www.forbes.com/wealth/billionaires#p_1_s_arank_-1__225.

6. Based on 2010 census figures. Carmen DeNavas-Walt, Bernadette D. Proctor, and Jessica C. Smith, U.S. Census Bureau, Current Population Reports, P60-239, *Income, Poverty, and Health Insurance Coverage in the United States: 2010* (Washington, DC: U.S. Government Printing Office)

7. U.S. Census Bureau, "Poverty," available at http://www.census.gov/hhes/www /poverty/about/overview/index.html.

8. National Coalition for the Homeless, "How Many People Experience Homelessness?" NCH Fact Sheet #2, July 2009, http://www.nationalhomeless.org/factsheets/How _Many.html?.

9. See U.S. Census Bureau, "Poverty," available at http://www.census.gov/hhes/www /poverty/about/overview/index.html.

10. Economic Policy Institute, *The State of Working America*, accessed September 25, 2011, http://www.stateofworkingamerica.org/files/files/Figure%20B_wealth_dis_byclass.xlsx.

11. Edward N. Wolff, "Recent Trends in Household Wealth in the U.S." Levy Economics Institute of Bard College Working Paper no. 502, Levy Economics Institute, Annandale-on-Hudson, NY, March 2010.

12. Economic Policy Institute, "Wealth Holdings Remain Unequal in Good and Bad Times," *The State of Working America* (Washington, DC: Economic Policy Institute, 2001), accessed September 25, 2011, http://www.stateofworkingamerica.org/files/files/Figure%20B_wealth_dis_byclass.xlsx.

13. Arloc Sherman and Chad Stone, "Income Gaps Between Very Rich and Everyone Else More Than Tripled in Last Three Decades, New Data Show," Center for Budget and Policy Studies, June 26, 2010.

14. See the CIA report *The World Factbook*, https://www.cia.gov/library/publications/the-world-factbook/rankorder/2172rank.html.

15. Paul Samuelson, *Economics*, 10th ed. (New York: McGraw-Hill, 1976), 84.

16. Calculated at 1.5 inches per children's block and 1,050 feet for the height of the Eiffel Tower.

17. Michael Harrington, *The Other America* (New York: Macmillan, 1962), 12–13.

18. Stuart Ewen and Elizabeth Ewen, *Channels of Desire: Mass Images and the Shaping of American Consciousness* (New York: McGraw-Hill, 1982).

19. Andrew Ross, *No-Collar: The Humane Workplace and Its Hidden Costs* (New York: Basic Books, 2002).

20. Based on a poverty threshold for a three-person household in 2007 of $16,650 (DeNavas-Walt et al., p. 1).

21. The median income in 2007 was $45,113 for men working full time, year round; $35,102 for women, and $50,233 for households (DeNavas-Walt et. al., p. 6).

22. U.S. Government Accountability Office, *Poverty in America: Economic Research Shows Adverse Impacts on Health Status and Other Social Conditions* (Washington, DC: U.S. Government Accountability Office, 2007), 9–16; see also E. Pamuk, D. Makuc, K. Heck, C. Reuben, and K. Lochner, *Health, United States, 1998: Socioeconomic Status and Health Chartbook* (Hyattsville, MD: National Center for Health Statistics, 1998), 145–159; Vincente Navarro, "Class, Race, and Health Care in the United States," in *Critical Perspectives in Sociology*, 2nd ed., ed. Bersh Berberoglu (Dubuque, IA: Kendall/Hunt, 1993), 148–156; Melvin Krasner, *Poverty and Health in New York City* (New York: United Hospital Fund of New York, 1989). See also U.S. Department of Health and Human Services, "Health Status of Minorities and Low Income Groups, 1985"; and Dan Hughes, Kay Johnson, Sara Rosenbaum, Elizabeth Butler, and Janet Simons, *The Health of America's Children* (The Children's Defense Fund, 1988).

23. Pamuk et al., *Health, United States, 1998*; Kenneth Neubeck and Davita Glassberg, *Sociology: A Critical Approach* (New York: McGraw-Hill, 1996), 436–438; Aaron Antonovsky, "Social Class, Life Expectancy, and Overall Mortality," in *The Impact of Social Class* (New York: Thomas Crowell, 1972), 467–491. See also Harriet Duleep, "Measuring the Effect of Income on Adult Mortality Using Longitudinal Administrative Record Data," *Journal of Human Resources* 21, no. 2 (Spring 1986); and Paul Farmer, *Pathologies of Power: Health, Human Rights, and the New War on the Poor* (Berkeley: University of California Press, 2005).

24. Patricia Ketsche, Sally Wallace, and Kathleen Adams, "Hidden Health Care Costs Hit Low-Income Families the Hardest," Georgia State University, September 21, 2011 http://www.gsu.edu/news/54728.html.

25. Pamuk et al., *Health, United States, 1998*, figure 20; Dennis W. Roncek, "Dangerous Places: Crime and Residential Environment," *Social Forces* 60, no. 1 (September 1981), 74–96. See also Steven D. Levitt, "The Changing Relationship Between Income and Crime Victimization," *Economic Policy Review* 5, no. 3 (September 1999).

26. Richard De Lone, *Small Futures* (New York: Harcourt Brace Jovanovich, 1978), 14–19.

27. College Board, "2011 College-Bound Seniors Total Group Profile Report," available at http://professionals.collegeboard.com/profdownload/cbs2011_total_group_report.pdf.

28. William H. Sewell, "Inequality of Opportunity for Higher Education," *American Sociological Review* 36, no. 5 (1971): 793–809.

29. Thomas G. Mortenson, "Family Income and Educational Attainment, 1970 to 2009," *Postsecondary Education Opportunity*, no. 221 (November 2010).

30. Derived from David Leonhardt, "A Closer Look at Income Mobility," *New York Times*, May 14, 2005; and Katharine Bradbury and Jane Katz, "Trends in U.S. Family Income Mobility 1969–2006," Federal Reserve Bank of Boston, 2009.

31. De Lone, *Small Futures*, 14–19. See also Daniel McMurrer, Mark Condon, and Isabel Sawhill, "Intergenerational Mobility in the United States," (Washington DC: Urban Institute, 1997), http://www.urban.org/publications/406796.html?; and Bhashkar Mazumder, "Earnings Mobility in the U.S.: A New Look at Intergenerational Inequality," Federal Reserve Bank of Chicago Working Paper no. 2001-18, March 21, 2001. doi: 10.2139/ssrn.295559.

32. Miles Corak, "Do Poor Children Become Poor Adults? Lessons from a Cross-Country Comparison of Generational Earnings Mobility" (Bonn, Germany: IZA, 2006). Available at http://repec.iza.org/dp1993.pdf .

33. Jason DeParle, "Harder for Americans to Rise From Lower Rungs," *New York Times*, January 4, 2012.

34. Howard Tuchman, *Economics of the Rich* (New York: Random House, 1973), 15. See also Greg Duncan, Ariel Kalil, Susan Mayer, Robin Tepper, and Monique Payne, "The Apple Does Not Fall Far From the Tree," in *Unequal Chances: Family Background and Economic Success*, ed. Samuel Bowles, Herbert Gintis, and Melissa Groves (Princeton, NJ: Princeton University Press, 2008), 23–79; Bhashkar Mazumder, "The Apple Falls Even Closer to the Tree Than We Thought," in Bowles, et. al., 80–99. For more information on inheritance, see Samuel Bowles and Herbert Gintis, "The Inheritance of Inequality," *Journal of Economic Perspectives* 16, no. 3 (Summer 2002): 2–30; and Tom Hertz, *Understanding Mobility in America*, Center for American Progress, available at http://www.americanprogress.org/wp-content/uploads/kf/hertz_mobility_analysis.pdf?.

35. Howard Wachtel, *Labor and the Economy* (Orlando, FL: Academic Press, 1984), 161–162.

36. See Hannah Shaw and Chad Stone, "Incomes at the Top Rebounded in First Full Year of Recovery, New Analysis of Tax Data Shows," Center on Budget and Policy Priorities, March 7, 2011, http://www.cbpp.org/files/3-7-12inc.pdf. Also see Andrew Fieldhouse and Ethan Pollack, "Tenth Anniversary of the Bush-era Tax Cuts," Economic Policy Institute, June 1, 2011, http://www.epi.org/publication/tenth_anniversary_of_the_bush-era_tax_cuts/.

37. Alan Blinder, quoted by Paul Krugman, in "Disparity and Despair," *U.S. News and World Report*, March 23, 1992, 54.

38. Derived from Edward N. Wolff, "Recent Trends in Household Wealth in the U.S." Levy Economics Institute at Bard College, March 2010, table 9. Available at http://www.levyinstitute.org/pubs/wp_589.pdf.

39. The National Economic Council, "The Buffett Rule: A Basic Principle of Tax Fairness," White House, April 2012, citing Internal Revenue System Statistics of Income 2005 Public Use File, National Bureau of Economic Research TAXISM, and CEA calculations. Available at

http://www.whitehouse.gov/sites/default/files/Buffett_Rule_Report_Final.pdf. Also cited in *The New York Times* editorial "Mr. Obama and the 'Buffett Rule,'" April 10, 2012. Available at http://www.nytimes.com/2012/04/11/opinion/mr-obama-and-the-buffett-rule.html?_r=0.

40. Campaign Finance Institute, "2010 Federal Election," accessed March 22, 2011, http://cfinst.org/federal/election2010.aspx.

41. 2009 figures from the Center for Responsive Politics, "Average Wealth of Members of Congress," available at http://www.opensecrets.org/pfds/averages.php.

42. See Larry Bartels, *Unequal Democracy: The Political Economy of the New Gilded Age* (Princeton, NJ: Princeton University Press, 2008), chapter 9; see also MAPLight.org (MAP-Light tracks political contributions and their impact on the votes of public officials).

43. DeNavas-Walt et al., *Income, Poverty, and Health Insurance Coverage in the United States: 2010.*

7 Unequal Childhoods: Class, Race, and Family Life

Annette Lareau

Laughing and yelling, a white fourth-grader named Garrett Tallinger splashes around in the swimming pool in the backyard of his four-bedroom home in the suburbs on a late spring afternoon. As on most evenings, after a quick dinner his father drives him to soccer practice. This is only one of Garrett's many activities. His brother has a baseball game at a different location. There are evenings when the boys' parents relax, sipping a glass of wine. Tonight is not one of them. As they rush to change out of their work clothes and get the children ready for practice, Mr. and Mrs. Tallinger are harried.

Only ten minutes away, a Black fourth-grader, Alexander Williams, is riding home from a school open house.[1] His mother is driving their beige, leather-upholstered Lexus. It is 9:00 P.M. on a Wednesday evening. Ms. Williams is tired from work and has a long Thursday ahead of her. She will get up at 4:45 A.M. to go out of town on business and will not return before 9:00 P.M. On Saturday morning, she will chauffeur Alexander to a private piano lesson at 8:15 A.M., which will be followed by a choir rehearsal and then a soccer game. As they ride in the dark, Alexander's mother, in a quiet voice, talks with her son, asking him questions and eliciting his opinions.

Discussions between parents and children are a hallmark of middle-class child rearing. Like many middle-class parents, Ms. Williams and her husband see themselves as "developing" Alexander to cultivate his talents in a concerted fashion. Organized activities, established and controlled by mothers and fathers, dominate the lives of middle-class children such as Garrett and Alexander. By making certain their children have these and other experiences, middle-class parents engage in a process of *concerted cultivation*. From this, a robust sense of entitlement takes root in the children. This sense of entitlement plays an especially important role in institutional settings, where middle-class children learn to question adults and address them as relative equals.

Only twenty minutes away, in blue-collar neighborhoods, and slightly farther away, in public housing projects, childhood looks different. Mr. Yanelli, a white working-class father, picks up his son Little Billy, a fourth grader, from an after-school program. They come home and Mr. Yanelli drinks a beer while Little Billy first watches television, then rides his bike and plays in the street. Other nights, he and his Dad sit on the sidewalk outside their house and play cards. At about 5:30 P.M. Billy's mother gets home from her job as a house cleaner. She fixes dinner and the entire family sits down to eat together.

Republished with permission of University of California Press Books, from *Unequal Childhoods: Class, Race, and Family Life* by Annette Lareau, copyright © 2011; permission conveyed through Copyright Clearance Center, Inc.

Extended family are a prominent part of their lives. Ms. Yanelli touches base with her "entire family every day" by phone. Many nights Little Billy's uncle stops by, sometimes bringing Little Billy's youngest cousin. In the spring, Little Billy plays baseball on a local team. Unlike for Garrett and Alexander, who have at least four activities a week, for Little Billy, baseball is his only organized activity outside of school during the entire year. Down the road, a white working-class girl, Wendy Driver, also spends the evening with her female cousins, as they watch a video and eat popcorn, crowded together on the living room floor.

Farther away, a Black fourth-grade boy, Harold McAllister, plays outside on a summer evening in the public housing project in which he lives. His two male cousins are there that night, as they often are. After an afternoon spent unsuccessfully searching for a ball so they could play basketball, the boys had resorted to watching sports on television. Now they head outdoors for a twilight water balloon fight. Harold tries to get his neighbor, Miss Latifa, wet. People sit in white plastic lawn chairs outside the row of apartments. Music and television sounds waft through the open windows and doors.

The adults in the lives of Billy, Wendy, and Harold want the best for them. Formidable economic constraints make it a major life task for these parents to put food on the table, arrange for housing, negotiate unsafe neighborhoods, take children to the doctor (often waiting for city buses that do not come), clean children's clothes, and get children to bed and have them ready for school the next morning. But unlike middle-class parents, these adults do not consider the concerted development of children, particularly through organized leisure activities, an essential aspect of good parenting. Unlike the Tallingers and Williamses, these mothers and fathers do not focus on concerted cultivation. For them, the crucial responsibilities of parenthood do not lie in eliciting their children's feelings, opinions, and thoughts. Rather, they see a clear boundary between adults and children. Parents tend to use directives: they tell their children what to do rather than persuading them with reasoning. Unlike their middle-class counterparts, who have a steady diet of adult organized activities, the working-class and poor children have more control over the character of their leisure activities. Most children are free to go out and play with friends and relatives who typically live close by. Their parents and guardians facilitate the *accomplishment of natural growth*.[2] Yet these children and their parents interact with central institutions in the society, such as schools, which firmly and decisively promote strategies of concerted cultivation in child rearing. For working-class and poor families, the cultural logic of child rearing at home is out of sync with the standards of institutions. As a result, while children whose parents adopt strategies of concerted cultivation appear to gain a sense of entitlement, children such as Billy Yanelli, Wendy Driver, and Harold McAllister appear to gain an emerging sense of distance, distrust, and constraint in their institutional experiences.

America may be the land of opportunity, but it is also a land of inequality. . . . this historical moment, middle-class parents tend to adopt a cultural logic of child rearing that stresses the concerted cultivation of children. Working-class and poor parents, by contrast, tend to undertake the accomplishment of natural growth. In the accomplishment of natural growth, children experience long stretches of leisure time, child-initiated play, clear boundaries between adults and children, and daily interactions with kin. Working-class and poor children, despite tremendous economic strain, often have more "childlike" lives, with autonomy from adults and control over their extended leisure time. Although middle-class children miss out on kin relationships and leisure time, they appear to (at least potentially) gain important institutional advantages. From the experience of concerted cultivation, they acquire skills that could be valuable in the future when they enter the world of work. Middle-class white and Black children in my study did exhibit some key differences; yet the biggest gaps were not within social classes but, as I show, across them. It is these class differences and how they are enacted in family life and child rearing that shape the ways children view themselves in relation to the rest of the world.

Cultural Repertoires

Professionals who work with children, such as teachers, doctors, and counselors, generally agree about how children should be raised. Of course, from time to time they may disagree on the ways standards should be enacted for an individual child or family. For example, teachers may disagree about whether or not parents should stop and correct a child who mispronounces a word while reading. Counselors may disagree over whether a mother is being too protective of her child. Still, there is little dispute among professionals on the broad principles for promoting educational development in children through proper parenting.[3] These standards include the importance of talking with children, developing their educational interests, and playing an active role in their schooling. Similarly, parenting guidelines typically stress the importance of reasoning with children and teaching them to solve problems through negotiation rather than with physical force. Because these guidelines are so generally accepted, and because they focus on a set of practices concerning how parents should raise children, they form a *dominant set of cultural repertoires* about how children should be raised. This widespread agreement among professionals about the broad principles for child rearing permeates our society. A small number of experts thus potentially shape the behavior of a large number of parents.

Professionals' advice regarding the best way to raise children has changed regularly over the last two centuries. From strong opinions about the merits of bottle feeding, being stern with children, and utilizing physical punishment (with dire warnings of problematic outcomes should parents indulge children), there have been shifts to equally strongly worded recommendations about the benefits of breast feeding, displaying emotional warmth toward children, and using reasoning and negotiation as mechanisms of parental control. Middle-class parents appear to shift their behaviors in a variety of spheres more rapidly and more thoroughly than do working-class or poor parents.[4] As professionals have shifted their recommendations from bottle feeding to breast feeding, from stern approaches to warmth and empathy, and from spanking to time-outs, it is middle-class parents who have responded most promptly.[5] Moreover, in recent decades, middle-class children in the United States have had to face the prospect of "declining fortunes."[6] Worried about how their children will get ahead, middle-class parents are increasingly determined to make sure that their children are not excluded from any opportunity that might eventually contribute to their advancement.

Middle-class parents who comply with current professional standards and engage in a pattern of concerted cultivation deliberately try to stimulate their children's development and foster their cognitive and social skills. The commitment among working-class and poor families to provide comfort, food, shelter, and other basic support requires ongoing effort, given economic challenges and the formidable demands of child rearing. But it stops short of the deliberate cultivation of children and their leisure activities that occurs in middle-class families. For working-class and poor families, sustaining children's natural growth is viewed as an accomplishment.[7]

What is the outcome of these different philosophies and approaches to child rearing? Quite simply, they appear to lead to the *transmission of differential advantages* to children. In this study, there was quite a bit more talking in middle-class homes than in working-class and poor homes, leading to the development of greater verbal agility, larger vocabularies, more comfort with authority figures, and more familiarity with abstract concepts. Importantly, children also developed skill differences in interacting with authority figures in institutions and at home. Middle-class children such as Garrett Tallinger and Alexander Williams learn, as young boys, to shake the hands of adults and look them in the eye. In studies of job interviews, investigators have found that potential employees have less than one minute to make a good impression. Researchers stress the importance of eye contact, firm handshakes, and displaying comfort with bosses during the interview. In poor families like Harold McAllister's, however, family members usually do not look each other in the eye when conversing. In addition, as Elijah Anderson points out, they live in neighborhoods where it can be dangerous to look people in the eye too long.[8] The types of social competence transmitted in the McAllister family are valuable, but they are potentially less valuable (in employment interviews, for example) than those learned by Garrett Tallinger and Alexander Williams.

The white and Black middle-class children in this study also exhibited an emergent version of the *sense of entitlement* characteristic of the middle-class. They acted as though they had a right to pursue their own individual preferences and to actively manage interactions in institutional settings. They appeared comfortable in these settings; they were open to sharing information and asking for attention. Although some children were more outgoing than others, it was common practice among middle-class children to shift interactions to suit *their* preferences. Alexander Williams knew how to get the doctor to listen to his concerns (about the bumps under his arm from his new deodorant). His mother explicitly trained and encouraged him to speak up with the doctor. Similarly, a Black middle-class girl, Stacey Marshall, was taught by her mother to expect the gymnastics teacher to accommodate her individual learning style. Thus, middle-class children were trained in "the rules of the game" that govern interactions with institutional representatives.

They were not conversant in other important social skills, however, such as organizing their time for hours on end during weekends and summers, spending long periods of time away from adults, or hanging out with adults in a nonobtrusive, subordinate fashion. Middle-class children also learned (by imitation and by direct training) how to make the rules work in their favor. Here, the enormous stress on reasoning and negotiation in the home also has a potential advantage for future institutional negotiations. Additionally, those in authority responded positively to such interactions. Even in fourth grade, middle-class children appeared to be acting on their own behalf to gain advantages. They made special requests of teachers and doctors to adjust procedures to accommodate their desires.

The working-class and poor children, by contrast, showed an emerging *sense of constraint* in their interactions in institutional settings. They were less likely to try to customize interactions to suit their own preferences. Like their parents, the children accepted the actions of persons in authority (although at times they also covertly resisted them). Working-class and poor parents sometimes were not as aware of their children's school situation (as when their children were not doing homework). Other times, they dismissed the school rules as unreasonable. For example, Wendy Driver's mother told her to "punch" a boy who was pestering her in class; Billy Yanelli's parents were proud of him when he "beat up" another boy on the playground, even though Billy was then suspended from school. Parents also had trouble getting "the school" to respond to their concerns. When Ms. Yanelli complained that she "hates" the school, she gave her son a lesson in powerlessness and frustration in the face of an important institution. Middle-class children such as Stacey Marshall learned to make demands on professionals, and when they succeeded in making the rules work in their favor they augmented their "cultural capital (i.e., skills individuals inherit that can then be translated into different forms of value as they move through various institutions) for the future.[9] When working-class and poor children confronted institutions, however, they generally were unable to make the rules work in their favor nor did they obtain capital for adulthood. Because of these patterns of legitimization, children raised according to the logic of concerted cultivation can gain advantages, in the form of an emerging sense of entitlement, while children raised according to the logic of natural growth tend to develop an emerging sense of constraint.[10]

Social Stratification and Individualism

Public discourse in America typically presents the life accomplishments of a person as the result of her or his individual qualities. Songs like "I Did It My Way," memoirs, television shows, and magazine articles, celebrate the individual. Typically, individual outcomes are connected to individual effort and talent, such as being a "type A" personality, being a hard worker, or showing leadership. These cultural beliefs provide a framework for Americans' views of inequality.

Indeed, Americans are much more comfortable recognizing the power of individual initiative than recognizing the power of social class. Studies show that

Americans generally believe that responsibility for their accomplishments rests on their individual efforts. Less than one-fifth see "race, gender, religion, or class as very important for 'getting ahead' in life.'"[11] Compared to Europeans, individuals in the United States are much more likely to believe they can improve their standard of living. Put differently, Americans believe in the American dream: "The American dream that we were all raised on is a simple but powerful one—if you work hard and play by the rules, you should be given a chance to go as far as your God-given ability will take you."[12] This American ideology that each individual is responsible for his or her life outcomes is the expressed belief of the vast majority of Americans, rich and poor.

Yet there is no question that society is stratified. Highly valued resources such as the possession of wealth; having an interesting, well-paying, and complex job; having a good education; and owning a home, are not evenly distributed throughout the society. Moreover, these resources are transferred across generations: One of the best predictors of whether a child will one day graduate from college is whether his or her parents are college graduates. Of course, relations of this sort are not absolute: Perhaps two-thirds of the members of society ultimately reproduce their parents' level of educational attainment, while about one-third take a different path. Still, there is no question that we live in a society characterized by considerable gaps in resources or, put differently, by substantial *inequality*. As I explain . . . however, reasonable people have disagreed about whether families in different economic positions "share distinct, life-defining experiences."[13] Many insist that there is not a clear, coherent, and sustained experiential pattern. In this book, I demonstrate the existence of a cultural logic of child rearing that tends to differ according to families' social class positions. I see these interweaving practices as coming together in a messy but still recognizable way. In contrast to many, I suggest that social class does have a powerful impact in shaping the daily rhythms of family life. . .

In sum, I see it as a mistake to accept, carte blanche, the views of officials in dominant institutions (e.g., schools or social service agencies) regarding how children should be raised. Indeed, outside of institutional settings there are benefits and costs to both of these logics of child rearing. For example, concerted cultivation places intense labor demands on busy parents, exhausts children, and emphasizes the development of individualism, at times at the expense of the development of the notion of the family group. Middle-class children argue with their parents, complain about their parents' incompetence, and disparage parents' decisions. In other historical moments, a ten-year-old child who gave orders to a doctor would have been chastised for engaging in disrespectful and inappropriate behavior. Nor are the actions of children who display an emerging sense of entitlement intrinsically more valuable or desirable than those of children who display an emerging sense of constraint. In a society less dominated by individualism than the United States, with more of an emphasis on the group, the sense of constraint displayed by working-class and poor children might be interpreted as healthy and appropriate. But in this society, the strategies of the working-class and poor families are generally denigrated and seen as unhelpful or even harmful to children's life chances. The benefits that accrue to middle-class children can be significant, but they are often invisible to them and to others. In popular language, middle-class children can be said to have been "born on third base but believe they hit a triple." . . .

NOTES

1. Choosing words to describe social groups also becomes a source of worry, especially over the possibility of reinforcing negative stereotypes. I found the available terms to describe members of racial and ethnic groups to be problematic in one way or another. The families I visited uniformly described themselves as "Black." Recognizing that some readers have strong views that Black should be capitalized, I have followed that convention, despite the lack of symmetry with the term white. In sum, this book alternates among the terms "Black," "Black American," "African American," and "white," with the understanding that "white" here refers to the subgroup of non-Hispanic whites.

2. Some readers have expressed concern that this phrase, "the accomplishment of natural growth," underemphasizes all the labor that mothers and fathers do to take care of children. They correctly note that working-class and poor parents themselves would be unlikely to use such a term to describe the process of caring for children. These concerns are important. As I stress in the text (especially in the chapter on Katie Brindle, Chapter 5) it does take an enormous amount of work for parents, especially mothers, of all classes to take care of children. But poor and working-class mothers have fewer resources with which to negotiate these demands. Those whose lives the research assistants and I studied approached the task somewhat differently than did middle-class parents. They did not seem to view children's leisure time as their responsibility; nor did they see themselves as responsible for assertively intervening in their children's school experiences. Rather, the working-class and poor parents carried out their chores, drew boundaries and restrictions around their children, and then, within these limits, allowed their children to carry out their lives. It is in this sense that I use the term "the accomplishment of natural growth."

3. For discussions of the role of professionals, see Eliot Freidson, *Professional Powers;* Magali Sarfatti Larson, *The Rise of Professionalism;* and, although quite old, the still valuable collection by Amitai Etzioni, *The Semi-Professionals and Their Organizations.* Of course, professional standards are always contested and are subject to change over time. I do not mean to suggest there are not pockets of resistance and contestation. At the most general level, however, there is virtually uniform support for the idea that parents should talk to children at length, read to children, and take a proactive, assertive role in medical care.

4. Sharon Hays, in her 1996 book *The Cultural Contradictions of Motherhood,* studies the attitudes of middle-class and working-class mothers toward child rearing. She finds a shared commitment to "intensive mothering," although there are some differences among the women in her study in their views of punishment (with middle-class mothers leaning toward reasoning and working-class women toward physical punishment). My study focused much more on behavior than attitudes. If I looked at attitudes, I saw fewer differences; for example, all exhibited the desire to be a good mother and to have their children grow and thrive. The differences I found, however, were significant in how parents *enacted* their visions of what it meant to be a good parent.

5. See Urie Bronfenbrenner's article, "Socialization and Social Class through Time and Space."

6. Katherine Newman, *Declining Fortunes,* as well as Donald Barlett and James B. Steele, *America: What Went Wrong?* See also Michael Hout and Claude Fischer, "A Century of Inequality."

7. Some readers expressed the concern that the contrast to natural would be "unnatural," but this is not the sense in which the term *natural growth* is used here. Rather, the contrast is with words such as cultivated, artificial, artifice, or manufactured. This contrast in the logic of child rearing is a heuristic device that should not be pushed too far since, as sociologists have shown, all social life is constructed in specific social contexts. Indeed, family life has varied dramatically over time. See Philippe Aries, *Centuries of Childhood,* Herbert Gutman, *The Black Family in Slavery and Freedom, 1750–1925,* and Nancy Scheper-Hughes, *Death without Weeping.*

8. Elijah Anderson, *Code of the Street;* see especially Chapter 2.

9. See also David Swartz's excellent book *Culture and Power.*

10. I did not study the full range of families in American society, including elite families of tremendous wealth, nor, at the other end of the spectrum, homeless families. In addition, I have a purposively drawn sample. Thus, I cannot state whether there are other forms of child rearing corresponding to other cultural logics. Still, data from quantitative studies based on nationally representative data support the patterns I observed. For differences by parents' social class position and children's time use, see especially Sandra Hofferth and John Sandberg, "Changes in American Children's Time, 1981–1997." Patterns of language use with children are harder to capture in national surveys, but the work of Melvin Kohn and Carmi Schooler, especially *Work and Personality,* shows differences in parents' child-rearing values. Duane Alwin's studies of parents' desires are generally consistent with the results reported here. See Duane Alwin, "Trends in Parental Socialization Values." For differences in interventions in institutions, there is extensive work showing social class differences in parent involvement in education. See the U.S. Department of Education, *The Condition of Education, 2001,* p. 175.

11. In this book, unless otherwise noted, the statistics reported are from 1993 to 1995, which was when the data were collected. Similarly, unless otherwise noted, all monetary amounts are given in (unadjusted) dollars from 1994 to 1995. The figure reported here is from Everett Ladd, *Thinking about America,* pp. 21–22.

12. This quote is from President Bill Clinton's 1993 speech to the Democratic Leadership Council. It is cited in Jennifer Hochschild, *Facing Up to the American Dream,* p. 18.

13. Paul Kingston, *The Classless Society,* p. 2.

8   Intersectionality: An Everyday Metaphor Anyone Can Use

Kimberlé Crenshaw, interviewed by Bim Adewunmi

Kimberlé Crenshaw is a Civil Rights activist and renowned scholar of gender, race, and the law. Her writing about the intersection of these three socio-political conditions has led to an entirely new way of understanding social oppression and justice, and so been named Intersectionality.

Departing from the conventional approach of viewing social phenomenon from a singular lens, such as through gender or race exclusively, Crenshaw writes about the experience of black women as simultaneously shaped by race and gender, and looks at the legal and political dimensions that produce patterns of oppression, marginalization, and subordination.

Here in her classic article "Mapping the Margins: Intersectionality, Identity Politics, and Violence Against Women of Color," Crenshaw describes the problem an intersectional framework addresses:

> *The problem with identity politics is not that it fails to transcend difference, as some critics charge, but rather the opposite — that it frequently conflates or ignores intra group differences. In the context of violence against women, this elision of difference is problematic, fundamentally because the violence that many women experience is often shaped by other dimensions of their identities, such as race and class. Moreover, ignoring differences within groups frequently contributes to tension among groups, another problem of identity politics that frustrates efforts to politicize violence against women. Feminist efforts to politicize experiences of women and antiracist efforts to politicize experiences of people of color have frequently proceeded as though the issues and experiences they each detail occur on mutually exclusive terrains. Although racism and sexism readily intersect in the lives of real people, they seldom do in feminist and antiracist practices. And so, when the practices expound identity as "woman" or "person of color" as an either/or proposition, they relegate the identity of women of color to a location that resists telling.*

Crenshaw's work on intersectionality has influenced research in sociology, feminist theory, and critical race theory, among others. In the following interview conducted with Crenshaw in 2014, she reflects upon the theory of intersectionality, its origins, and the ways in which it has been utilized over the last few decades.

From the *New Statesman,* http://www.newstatesman.com/lifestyle/2014/04/kimberl-crenshaw-intersectionality-i-wanted-come-everyday-metaphor-anyone-could

• • •

For Crenshaw, a law professor at UCLA and Columbia, intersectionality theory came about specifically to address a particular problem. "It's important to clarify that the term was used to capture the applicability of black feminism to anti-discrimination law," she says. In the lecture she delivered at the LSE (London School of Economics) later that evening, she brought up the case of *Degraffenreid vs General Motors*, in which five black women sued GM on the grounds of race and gender discrimination. "The particular challenge in the law was one that was grounded in the fact that anti-discrimination law looks at race and gender separately," she says. "The consequence of that is when African American women or any other women of colour experience either compound or overlapping discrimination, the law initially just was not there to come to their defence."

The court's thinking was that black women could not prove gender discrimination because not all women were discriminated against, and they couldn't prove race discrimination because not all black people were discriminated against. A compound discrimination suit would, in the courts' eyes, constitute preferential treatment, something nobody else could do. Crenshaw laughs when she adds: "Of course, no one else *had* to do that. Intersectionality was a way of addressing what it was that the courts weren't seeing."

Cases like these informed much of her earlier work on intersectionality – trying to show how these African American plaintiffs' arguments rested on the ability to show that the discrimination they were experiencing was the combination of two different kinds of policies. But there was an additional point to the theory as well: pointing out that the tools being used to remedy the overlapping discrimination – anti-discrimination law – were themselves inadequate. "You've got to show that the kind of discrimination people have conceptualised is limited because they stop their thinking when the discrimination encounters another kind of discrimination," she says. "I wanted to come up with a common everyday metaphor that people could use to say: "it's well and good for me to understand the kind of discriminations that occur along this avenue, along this axis – but what happens when it flows into another axis, another avenue?"

Laid out like this, it may seem baffling that so many have had a problem with the idea of intersectionality. What is it, I asked Crenshaw, that makes it so difficult for people to grasp? She pauses briefly before she answers. "I'm only speculating, but there are lots of different reasons. I mean, intersectionality is not easy," she says. "It's not as though the existing frameworks that we have – from our culture, our politics or our law – automatically lead people to being conversant and literate in intersectionality."

On the charge that intersectionality is not new, she gets philosophical. "Well, a lot of things aren't new," she says. "Class is not new and race is not new. And we still continue to contest and talk about it, so what's so unusual about intersectionality not being new and therefore that's not a reason to talk about it? Intersectionality draws attention to invisibilities that exist in feminism, in anti-racism, in class politics, so obviously it takes a lot of work to consistently challenge ourselves to be attentive to aspects of power that we don't ourselves experience." But, she stresses, this has been the project of black feminism since its very inception: drawing attention to the erasures, to the ways that "women of colour are invisible in plain sight."

"Within any power system," she continues, "there is always a moment – and some-times it lasts a century – of resistance to the implications of that. So we shouldn't really be surprised about it."

There is sometimes a failure to make analogies, she says. Feminists who have answers for the questions of class politics and how it plays out along gender lines sometimes exhibit an unwillingness to apply the same principles around feminism and race. "That ability to be intersectional – even though it's not called that – isn't replicated in [this] conversation," she says. I think that the same kind of openness and fluidity and willingness to interrogate power that we as feminists expect from men in alliance on questions of class should also be the expectation that women of colour can rely upon with our white feminist allies."

I bring up a tweet I recently read, about the "perils of yelling at white women for a living" to ask what form pushback takes when discussing intersectionality in feminism. "At the end of the day, it really is a question of power: who has the power to end the debate? To walk away? To say, 'I'm done talking about it, and I can go on with my rhetoric in a 'business as usual' kind of response?'" She smiles. "Sometimes it feels like those in power frame themselves as being tremendously disempowered by critique. A critique of one's voice isn't taking it away. If the underlying assumption behind the category 'women' or 'feminist' is that we are a coalition then there have to be coalitional practices and some form of accountability."

But she also stresses the importance of black feminists being the originators of dialogues about their own experience. "When I was writing in the late 80s, there was a strain of discourse among women who were not the subjects of traditional femi-nism, to simply make critique a difference," she says. "So just the claim of 'woman' or 'feminist', prompted some women of colour to say, "but that's not me". Well, yeah – that might not be you. But say what difference it makes that it's not you – what difference does it make in what kinds of interventions come out of a feminist frame that doesn't attend to race?" She pauses, spreads her hands. "That is our responsi-bility. It's up to us. Granted, the space has to be open and there has to be a sense of receptivity among the sisterhood, but I really don't want other women to feel that it's their responsibility to theorise what's happening to us. It's up to us to consistently tell those stories, articulate what difference the difference makes, so it's incorporated within feminism and within anti-racism. I think it's important that we do that apart, because we don't want to be susceptible to the idea that this is just about the politics of recognition."

No discussion of Crenshaw's work can be complete without discussing the con-gressional hearings of October 1991, organised to address the claim that Supreme Court nominee Clarence Thomas had sexually harassed a colleague, Anita Hill. In his denial of the allegations, Thomas said it was a "high tech lynching". Crenshaw was part of the legal team that represented Hill – and arguably changed the course of history with regards to the recognition of sexual harassment in the workplace. A documentary film, *Anita*, has been made of the events of the time, a period Crenshaw describes as "life-defining."

"When we were defending Anita Hill, it felt like there was 10 of us against the whole world," she says. "There was overwhelming criticism of Anita Hill from

Clarence Thomas's camp, the Republican camp, from the White House, from the Senate Judiciary Committee. And the Democrats were not defending her." Thomas's 'lynching' comment, she says, communicated to many African Americans this was a race issue – leaving Hill with no base to rally. "Lynching is representative of the quintessential moment of racism – and that in turn centres African American male experiences," she says.

Crenshaw talks about a sort of "collective forgetting" – the fact that black women were not spared from lynching themselves, and the way that racist sexism played out for black women involved sexual violence that was never prosecuted. Rosa Parks, she says, "was a rape crisis advocate before she sat down on that Montgomery bus. The very fact that there are a range of experiences around sexualised racism that's not remembered – and we only remember one experience – is what then replayed itself in the 1990s."

She describes coming out of the Capitol to find it ringed by largely African American women "holding hands singing gospel songs in support of Clarence Thomas. It was like one of these moments where you literally feel that you have been kicked out of your community, all because you are trying to introduce and talk about the way that African American women have experienced sexual harassment and violence. It was a defining moment."

One consequence of this was Anita Hill's claim being taken up by mainstream white feminists – only she was stripped of her race, reinforcing the idea that the case was a race vs. gender issue. "She simply became a colourless woman, and we as African American women feminists were trying to say, "you cannot talk about this just in gender terms – you have to be intersectional – there is a long history you cannot ignore," but they didn't have the skills to be able to talk about it," she says. That led to another big moment: the moment when, as Crenshaw puts it, African American feminists had to "buy their way into the conversation."

Nearly 2,000 African American feminists across the US collectively raised $60,000 and bought ad space in the *New York Times*. The ad, called African American Women in Defense of Ourselves, was signed by 1,600 women, and covered among other things, the historical discrimination against black women, as well as what had been happening in the hearings. "That was a moment where black women came forward. Twenty years later," says Crenshaw, "*that* has been forgotten." The legacy of the Anita Hill case is one that subsequent generations of women in the workplace will benefit from. "Many women who talk about the Anita Hill thing, they celebrate what's happened with women in general: the fact that we have more elected officials now because they were outraged when they saw what the men were doing, Emily's List came in and really helped women get elected, and so on. So sexual harassment is now recognised; what's not doing as well is the recognition of black women's unique experiences with discrimination."

The forgetting is important to note. Crenshaw recalls the strong anti-harassment work of the civil rights movement, and speaks of a "certain ahistoricism" in some of the conversations around feminism and anti-racism work. "Intersectionality was something I wrote in 1986, '87 and there's a whole generation now that has come to the conversation after black feminism and other forms of intersectional work tilled the soil," she says. "And I think sometimes it's hard for people to imagine what the world was like at the point when none of that work had been done. So I think it's useful to tell genealogies that include social histories – so people have a sense that the way we talked about it *then* was as against the constraints of the time. And the way we talk about it *now* has built upon that. There are many things that are forgotten, and many other things that are elevated."

9 White Privilege
Unpacking the Invisible Knapsack
Peggy McIntosh

Through work to bring materials from Women's Studies into the rest of the curriculum, I have often noticed men's unwillingness to grant that they are over-privileged, even though they may grant that women are disadvantaged. They may say they will work to improve women's status, in the society, the university, or the curriculum, but they can't or won't support the idea of lessening men's. Denials which amount to taboos surround the subject of advantages which men gain from women's disadvantages. These denials protect male privilege from being fully acknowledged, lessened or ended.

Thinking through unacknowledged male privilege as a phenomenon, I realized that since hierarchies in our society are interlocking, there was most likely a phenomenon of white privilege which was similarly denied and protected. As a white person, I realized I had been taught about racism as something which puts others at a disadvantage, but had been taught not to see one of its corollary aspects, white privilege, which puts me at an advantage.

I think whites are carefully taught not to recognize white privilege, as males are taught not to recognize male privilege. So I have begun in an untutored way to ask what it is like to have white privilege. I have come to see white privilege as an invisible package of unearned assets which I can count on cashing in each day, but about which I was "meant" to remain oblivious. White privilege is like an invisible weightless knapsack of special provisions, maps, passports, codebooks, visas, clothes, tools and blank checks.

Describing white privilege makes one newly accountable. As we in Women's Studies work to reveal male privilege and ask men to give up some of their power, so one who writes about having white privilege must ask, "Having described it, what will I do to lessen or end it?"

After I realized the extent to which men work from a base of unacknowledged privilege, I understood that much of their oppressiveness was unconscious. Then I remembered the frequent charges from women of color that white women whom they encounter are oppressive. I began to understand why we are justly seen as oppressive, even when we don't see ourselves that way. I began to count the ways in which I enjoy unearned skin privilege and have been conditioned into oblivion about its existence.

© 1989 Peggy McIntosh. "White Privilege: Unpacking the Invisible Knapsack" first appeared in *Peace and Freedom Magazine,* July/August, 1989, pp. 10–12, a publication of the Women's International League for Peace and Freedom, Philadelphia, PA. Reprinted by permission. Anyone who wishes to reproduce more than 35 copies of this article must apply to the author, Dr. Peggy McIntosh, at mmcintosh@wellesley.edu. This article may not be electronically posted except by the National SEED Project.

My schooling gave me no training in seeing myself as an oppressor, as an unfairly advantaged person, or as a participant in a damaged culture. I was taught to see myself as an individual whose moral state depended on her individual moral will. My schooling followed the pattern my colleague Elizabeth Minnich has pointed out: whites are taught to think of their lives as morally neutral, normative, and average, and also ideal, so that when we work to benefit others, this is seen as work which will allow "them" to be more like "us."

I decided to try to work on myself at least by identifying some of the daily effects of white privilege in my life. I have chosen those conditions which I think in my case *attach somewhat more to skin-color privilege* than to class, religion, ethnic status, or geographical location, though of course all these other factors are intricately intertwined. As far as I can see, my African American co-workers, friends and acquaintances with whom I come into daily or frequent contact in this particular time, place, and line of work cannot count on most of these conditions.

1. I can if I wish arrange to be in the company of people of my race most of the time.
2. If I should need to move, I can be pretty sure of renting or purchasing housing in an area which I can afford and in which I would want to live.
3. I can be pretty sure that my neighbors in such a location will be neutral or pleasant to me.
4. I can go shopping alone most of the time, pretty well assured that I will not be followed or harassed.
5. I can turn on the television or open to the front page of the paper and see people of my race widely represented.
6. When I am told about our national heritage or about "civilization," I am shown that people of my color made it what it is.
7. I can be sure that my children will be given curricular materials that testify to the existence of their race.
8. If I want to, I can be pretty sure of finding a publisher for this piece on white privilege.
9. I can go into a music shop and count on finding the music of my race represented, into a supermarket and find the staple foods which fit with my cultural traditions, into a hairdresser's shop and find someone who can cut my hair.
10. Whether I use checks, credit cards, or cash, I can count on my skin color not to work against the appearance of financial reliability.
11. I can arrange to protect my children most of the time from people who might not like them.
12. I can swear, or dress in secondhand clothes, or not answer letters, without having people attribute these choices to the bad morals, the poverty, or the illiteracy of my race.
13. I can speak in public to a powerful male group without putting my race on trial.
14. I can do well in a challenging situation without being called a credit to my race.

15. I am never asked to speak for all the people of my racial group.
16. I can remain oblivious of the language and customs of persons of color who constitute the world's majority without feeling in my culture any penalty for such oblivion.
17. I can criticize our government and talk about how much I fear its policies and behavior without being seen as a cultural outsider.
18. I can be pretty sure that if I ask to talk to "the person in charge," I will be facing a person of my race.
19. If a traffic cop pulls me over or if the IRS audits my tax return, I can be sure I haven't been singled out because of my race.
20. I can easily buy posters, postcards, picture books, greeting cards, dolls, toys, and children's magazines featuring people of my race.
21. I can go home from most meetings of organizations I belong to feeling somewhat tied in, rather than isolated, out-of-place, outnumbered, unheard, held at a distance, or feared.
22. I can take a job with an affirmative action employer without having co-workers on the job suspect that I got it because of my race.
23. I can choose public accommodation without fearing that people of my race cannot get in or will be mistreated in the places I have chosen.
24. I can be sure that if I need legal or medical help, my race will not work against me.
25. If my day, week, or year is going badly, I need not ask of each negative episode or situation whether it has racial overtones.
26. I can choose blemish cover or bandages in "flesh" color and have them more or less match my skin.

I repeatedly forgot each of the realizations on this list until I wrote it down. For me white privilege has turned out to be an elusive and fugitive subject. The pressure to avoid it is great, for in facing it I must give up the myth of meritocracy. If these things are true, this is not such a free country; one's life is not what one makes it; many doors open for certain people through no virtues of their own.

In unpacking this invisible knapsack of white privilege, I have listed conditions of daily experience which I once took for granted. Nor did I think of any of these perquisites as bad for the holder. I now think that we need a more finely differentiated taxonomy of privilege, for some of these varieties are only what one would want for everyone in a just society, and others give license to be ignorant, oblivious, arrogant and destructive.

I see a pattern running through the matrix of white privilege, a pattern of assumptions which were passed on to me as a white person. There was one main piece of cultural turf; it was my own turf, and I was among those who could control the turf. *My skin color was an asset for any move I was educated to want to make.* I could think of myself as belonging in major ways, and of making social systems work for me. I could freely disparage, fear, neglect, or be oblivious to anything outside of the dominant cultural forms. Being of the main culture, I could also criticize it fairly freely.

In proportion as my racial group was being made confident, comfortable, and oblivious, other groups were likely being made inconfident, uncomfortable, and alienated. Whiteness protected me from many kinds of hostility, distress, and violence, which I was being subtly trained to visit in turn upon people of color.

For this reason, the word "privilege" now seems to me misleading. We usually think of privilege as being a favored state, whether earned or conferred by birth or luck. Yet some of the conditions I have described here work to systematically overempower certain groups. Such privilege simply *confers dominance* because of one's race or sex.

I want, then, to distinguish between earned strength and unearned power conferred systemically. Power from unearned privilege can look like strength when it is in fact permission to escape or to dominate. But not all of the privileges on my list are inevitably damaging. Some, like the expectation that neighbors will be decent to you, or that your race will not count against you in court, should be the norm in a just society. Others, like the privilege to ignore less powerful people, distort the humanity of the holders as well as the ignored groups.

We might at least start by distinguishing between positive advantages which we can work to spread, and negative types of advantages which unless rejected will always reinforce our present hierarchies. For example, the feeling that one belongs within the human circle, as Native Americans say, should not be seen as privilege for a few. Ideally it is an *unearned entitlement.* At present, since only a few have it, it is an unearned advantage for them. This paper results from a process of coming to see that some of the power which I originally saw as attendant on being a human being in the U.S. consisted in *unearned advantage* and *conferred dominance.*

I have met very few men who are truly distressed about systemic, unearned male advantage and conferred dominance. And so one question for me and others like me is whether we will be like them, or whether we will get truly distressed, even outraged, about unearned race advantage and conferred dominance and if so, what we will do to lessen them. In any case, we need to do more work in identifying how they actually affect our daily lives. Many, perhaps most, of our white students in the U.S. think that racism doesn't affect them because they are not people of color; they do not see "whiteness" as a racial identity. In addition, since race and sex are not the only advantaging systems at work, we need similarly to examine the daily experience of having age advantage, or ethnic advantage, or physical ability, or advantage related to nationality, religion, or sexual orientation.

Difficulties and dangers surrounding the task of finding parallels are many. Since racism, sexism, and heterosexism are not the same, the advantaging associated with them should not be seen as the same. In addition, it is hard to disentangle aspects of unearned advantage which rest more on social class, economic class, race, religion, sex and ethnic identity than on other factors. Still, all of the oppressions are interlocking, as the Combahee River Collective Statement of 1977 continues to remind us eloquently.

One factor seems clear about all of the interlocking oppressions. They take both active forms which we can see and embedded forms which as a member of the dominant group one is taught not to see. In my class and place, I did not see myself as a racist because I was taught to recognize racism only in individual acts of meanness by members of my group, never in invisible systems conferring unsought racial dominance on my group from birth.

Disapproving of the systems won't be enough to change them. I was taught to think that racism could end if white individuals changed their attitudes. [But] a "white" skin in the United States opens many doors for whites whether or not we approve of the way dominance has been conferred on us. Individual acts can palliate, but cannot end, these problems.

To redesign social systems we need first to acknowledge their colossal unseen dimensions. The silences and denials surrounding privilege are the key political tool here. They keep the thinking about equality or equity incomplete, protecting unearned advantage and conferred dominance by making these taboo subjects. Most talk by whites about equal opportunity seems to me now to be about equal opportunity to try to get into a position of dominance while denying that *systems* of dominance exist.

It seems to me that obliviousness about white advantage, like obliviousness about male advantage, is kept strongly inculturated in the United States so as to maintain the myth of meritocracy, the myth that democratic choice is equally available to all. Keeping most people unaware that freedom of confident action is there for just a small number of people props up those in power, and serves to keep power in the hands of the same groups that have most of it already.

Though systemic change takes many decades, there are pressing questions for me and I imagine for some others like me if we raise our daily consciousness on the perquisites of being light-skinned. What will we do with such knowledge? As we know from watching men, it is an open question whether we will choose to use unearned advantage to weaken hidden systems of advantage, and whether we will use any of our arbitrarily-awarded power to try to reconstruct power systems on a broader base.

10 My Class Didn't Trump My Race: Using Oppression to Face Privilege

Robin J. DiAngelo

I was born to working class parents; my father was a construction worker and my mother was a switchboard operator. When I was 2, my parents divorced and my mother began to raise us on her own; at that point we entered into poverty. I have never understood people who say, "we were poor but we didn't know it because we had lots of love." Poverty hurts. It isn't romantic, or some form of "living simply." Poor people are not innocent and child-like. The lack of medical and dental care, the hunger, and the ostracization, are concrete. The stress of poverty made my household much more chaotic than loving.

We were evicted frequently, and moved four to five times a year. There were periods when oatmeal was the only food in our house. I had no health or dental care during my childhood, and today all of my front teeth are filled because by the time I was 10 they were rotten. If we got sick, my mother would beat us, screaming that we could not get sick because she could not afford to take us to the doctor. We occasionally had to live in our car, and I was left with relatives for 8 months while my mother tried to secure housing for us. My teacher once held my hands up to my fourth-grade class as an example of poor hygiene and with the class as her audience, told me to go home and tell my mother to wash me.

I used to stare at the girls in my class and ache to be like them; to have a father, to wear pretty clothes, to go to camp, to be clean and get to sit with them. I knew we didn't have enough money and that meant that I couldn't join them in school or go to their houses or have the same things they had. But the moment the real meaning of poverty crystallized for me came when we were visiting another family. As we were leaving I heard one of their daughters ask her mother, "What is wrong with them?" I stopped, riveted. I too, wanted to know. Her mother held her finger to her lips and whispered, "Shhh, they're *poor*." This was a revelatory moment for me. The shock came not just in the knowledge that we were poor, but that it was exposed. There was something wrong with us, indeed, and it was something that was obvious to others and that we couldn't hide, something shameful that could be seen but should not be named. It took me many years to gain a structural analysis of class that would help shift this sense of shame.

I begin this narrative with my class background because it so deeply informs my understanding of race. From an early age I had the sense of being an outsider; I was

DiAngelo, Robin. "My Class Didn't Trump My Race: Using Oppression to Face Privilege" from *Multicultural Perspectives* by Robin DiAngelo. © 2006. Reproduced by permission of the National Association for Multicultural Education (www.nameorg.org) and the author.

acutely aware that I was poor, that I was dirty, that I was not normal, and that there was something "wrong" with me. But I also knew that I was *not* Black. We were at the lower rungs of society, but there was always someone on the periphery, just below us. I knew that "colored" people existed and that they should be avoided. I can remember many occasions when I reached for candy or uneaten food laying on the street and was admonished by my grandmother not to touch it because a "colored person" may have touched it. The message was clear to me; if a colored person touched something it became dirty. The irony here is that the marks of poverty were clearly visible on me: poor hygiene, torn clothes, homelessness, hunger. Yet through comments such as my grandmother's, a racial Other was formed in my consciousness, an Other through whom I became clean. Race was the one identity that aligned me with the other girls in my school.

I left home as a teenager and struggled to survive. As I looked at what lay ahead, I could see no path out of poverty other than education. The decision to take that path was frightening for me; I had never gotten the message that I was smart and academia was a completely foreign social context. But once I was in academia, I understood that a college degree is not conferred upon those who are smarter or who try harder than others, it comes through a complex web of intersecting systems of privileges that include internal expectations as well as external resources. In academia, racism, a key system that I benefit from, helped to mediate my class-based disadvantages. . . .

Since those early days, I have led dialogues on race with police officers, social workers, teachers, and in both the private and government sectors. I recently completed my dissertation on how White student teachers reproduce racism in interracial dialogues about race. As I look at the world now, I see racism as ever-present and multidimensional. I realize that poor and working class White people don't necessarily have any less racism than middle or upper class White people, our racism is just conveyed in different ways and we enact it from a different social location than the middle or upper classes.

As I reflect back on the early messages I received about being poor and being White, I now realize that my grandmother and I *needed* people of color to cleanse and realign us with the dominant White culture that our poverty had separated us from. I now ask myself how the classist messages I internalized growing up lead me to collude in racism. For example, as a child who grew up in poverty, I received constant reminders that I was stupid, lazy, dirty, and a drain on the resources of hardworking people. I internalized these messages, and they work to silence me. Unless I work to uproot them, I am less likely to trust my own perceptions or feel like I have a "right" to speak up. I may not attempt to interrupt racism because the social context in which it is occurring intimidates me. My fear on these occasions may be coming from a place of internalized class inferiority, but in practice my silence colludes with racism and ultimately benefits me by protecting my White privilege and maintaining racial solidarity with other White people. This solidarity connects and realigns me with White people across other lines of difference, such as the very class locations that have silenced me in the first place. I am also prone to use others to elevate me, as in the example with my grandmother. So although my specific class background mediated the way I learned racism and how I enact it, in the end it still socialized me to collude with the overall structure.

It is my observation that class dictates proximity between Whites and people of color. Poor Whites are most often in closest proximity to people of color because they tend to share poverty. I hear the term "White trash" frequently. It is not without significance that this is one of the few expressions in which race is named for Whites. I think the proximity of the people labeled as White trash to people of color is why; race becomes marked or "exposed" by virtue of a closeness to people of color. In a racist society, this closeness both highlights and pollutes Whiteness. Owning class people also have people of color near them because people of color are often their domestics and gardeners—their servants. But they do not interact socially with people of color in the same way that poor Whites do. Middle class Whites are generally the furthest away from people of color. They are the most likely to say that, "there were no people of color in my neighborhood or school. I didn't meet a Black person until I went to college" (often adding, "so I was lucky because I didn't learn anything about racism"). Looking specifically at how class shaped my racial identity has been very helpful to me in attempting to unravel the specific way I manifest my internalized racial superiority.

I am no longer poor. Although I still carry the marks of poverty, those marks are now only internal. But these marks limit me in more than what I believe I deserve or where I think I belong; they also interfere with my ability to stand up against injustice, for as long as I believe that I am not as smart or as valuable as other White people, I won't challenge racism. I believe that in order for Whites to unravel our internalized racial dominance, we have two interwoven tasks. One is to work on our own internalized oppression—the ways in which we impose limitations on ourselves based on the societal messages we receive about the inferiority of the lower status groups we belong to. The other task is to face the internalized dominance that results from being socialized in a racist society—the ways in which we consciously or unconsciously believe that we are more important, more valuable, more intelligent, and more deserving than people of color. I cannot address the interwoven complexity of other White people's social locations. However, after years facilitating dialogues on race with thousands of White people from a range of class positions (as well as varied gender, sexual orientation, religious, and ability positions), and bearing witness to countless stories and challenges from people of color about my own racism and that of other Whites, I have come to see some very common patterns of internalized dominance. These patterns are shared across other social positions due to the bottom line nature of racism: Regardless of one's other locations, White people know on some level that being White in this society is "better" than being a person of color, and this, along with the very real doors Whiteness opens, serves to mediate the oppression experienced in those other social locations. In the next section of this article, I will identify several of these patterns of internalized dominance that are generally shared among Whites.

We Live Segregated Lives

Growing up in segregated environments (schools, workplaces, neighborhoods, media images, historical perspectives, etc.), we are given the message that our experiences and perspectives are the only ones that matter. We receive this message day in and day out, and it is not limited to a single moment, it is a *relentless experience*. Virtually all of our teachers, history books, role models, movie and book characters, are White like us. Further, as White people, we are taught not to feel any loss about the absence of people of color in our lives. In fact, the absence of people of color is what defines our schools and neighborhoods as "good." And we get this message regardless of where we are oppressed in other areas of our lives. Because we live primarily segregated lives in a White-dominated society, we receive little or no authentic information about racism and are thus unprepared to think critically or complexly about it. Although segregation is often mediated somewhat for poor urban (and other) Whites who may live near and have friendships with people of color on the microlevel, segregation is still operating on the macrolevel and informing our collective perspectives and what is deemed the most valuable or "official" knowledge.

Whites from the lower classes who may have more integrated lives on the microlevel still receive the message that achievement means moving out of poverty and away from the neighborhoods and schools that define us. Upward mobility is the great class goal in the United States, and the social environment gets tangibly Whiter the higher up one goes, whether it be in academia or management. Whiter environments, in turn, are marked as the most socially and economically valuable. Reaching towards the most valuable places in society thus entails leaving people of color behind. . . .

We Are Raised to Value the Individual and to See Ourselves as Individuals, Rather Than as Part of a Socialized Group

Individuality allows us to present ourselves as having "just arrived on the scene," unique and original, outside of socialization and unaffected by the relentless racial messages we receive. This also allows us to distance ourselves from the actions of our group and demand that we be granted the benefit of the doubt (because we are individuals) in all cases. Thus we get very irate when we are "accused" of racism, because as individuals, we are "different" from other White people and expect to be seen as such. We find intolerable any suggestion that our behavior or perspectives are typical of our group as a whole, and this ensures that we cannot deepen our understanding of racism.

Seeing ourselves as individuals erases our history and hides the way in which wealth has accumulated over generations and benefits us, *as a group*, today. Further, being an individual is a privilege only afforded to White people. By focusing on ourselves as individuals, Whites are able to conceptualize the racist patterns in our behavior as "just our personality" and not connected to intergroup dynamics. For example, I might be an extrovert and cut people off when I am engaged in a discussion. I can say, "that is just my personality, I do that to everyone. That is how we talked at the dinner table in my family." But the moment I cut off a person of color, it becomes racism because the history and the impact of that behavior for both of us is different. The freedom to remain oblivious to that fact, with no sense that this obliviousness has any consequences of importance, is White privilege (racism).

If we use the line of reasoning that we are all individuals and social categories such as race, class, and gender don't matter and are just "labels" that stereotype us, then it follows that we all end up in our own "natural" places. Those at the top are merely a collection of individuals who rose under their own individual merits, and those at the bottom are there due to individual lack. Group membership is thereby rendered inoperative and racial disparities are seen as essential rather than structural. Thus the discourse of individuality is not only connected to the discourse of meritocracy, but also with the Darwinism of the "bell curve." It behooves those of us oppressed in other places to understand group membership, for the discourse of individuality may benefit us in terms of racial privilege but ultimately holds all of our oppressions in place. . . .

We Feel That We Should Be Judged by Our Intentions Rather Than the Effects of Our Behavior

A common White reasoning is that as long as we didn't intend to perpetuate racism, then our actions don't count as racism. We focus on our intentions and discount the impact, thereby invalidating people of color's experiences and communicating that the effects of our behavior on them are unimportant. We then spend great energy explaining to people of color why our behavior is not racism at all. This invalidates their perspectives while enabling us to deny responsibility for making the effort to understand enough about racism to see our behavior's impact in both the immediate interaction and the broader, historical context.

We Believe That if We Can't Feel Our Social Power, Then We Don't Have Any

White social power is so normalized that it is outside of our conscious awareness. Yet we often expect that power is something that one can feel, rather than something one takes for granted. The issue of social power is where a lower class location often becomes confused with a lack of racial privilege. For example, in discussions on race I often hear White working class men protest that they don't have any social power. They work long and grueling hours, often in jobs in which they have no long-term security, and come home feeling beaten and quite disempowered. These men can often not relate to the concept of holding social power. But if being able to feel racial privilege is required before Whites can acknowledge its reality, we will not be able to see (and thus change) it. The key to recognizing power is in recognizing normalcy—what is not attended to or in need of constant navigation. These men are indeed struggling against social and economic barriers, but race is simply not one of them; in fact, race is a major social current running in their direction and not only moving them along, but helping them navigate their other social struggles. Not feeling power is not necessarily aligned with how others perceive or respond to us, or our relationship to social and institutional networks.

We Think It Is Important Not to Notice Race

The underlying assumption of a colorblind discourse is that race is a defect and it is best to pretend that we don't notice it. But if we pretend we don't notice race, we cannot notice racism. If we don't notice racism, we can't understand or interrupt it in ourselves or others. We have to start being honest about the fact that we do notice race (when it isn't White) and then pay attention to what race means in our everyday lives. White people and people of color do not have the same racial experience, and this has profound and tangible consequences that need to be understood if we want to stop colluding with racism. . . .

Racism Has Been Constructed as Belonging to Extremists and Being Very Bad

Racism is a deeply embedded, multidimensional, and internalized system that all members of this society are shaped by. Yet dominant culture constructs racism as primarily in the past and only currently occurring as isolated acts relegated to individual bad people (usually living somewhere in the South, or "old"). Although many White people today sincerely believe that racism is a bad thing, our abhorrence of racism coupled with a superficial conceptualization of it causes us to be highly defensive about any suggestion that we perpetuate it. Many Whites (and liberal Whites in particular) think that we can deal with racism in our heads (and without ever interacting with people of color) by deciding that we have not been affected because we don't want to have been affected.

A superficial understanding of racism coupled with a desire to distance ourselves from being perceived as "bad" is further complicated by resentments we may feel about places in our lives where we suffer from other forms of social injustice. It is often very difficult for Whites who have not been validated for the oppression they experience elsewhere to keep their attention on a form of oppression from which they benefit. But I have found that when I explore how classism and other oppressions I experience set me up to participate in racism, I am more able to interrupt the manifestation of both in my life. By placing racism in the center of my analysis, I have been able to begin to unravel my other group socializations and how they work together to support social hierarchies.

Interrupting Internalized Dominance

I have found that a key to interrupting my internalized racial dominance is to defer to the knowledge of people whom I have been taught, in countless ways, are less knowledgeable and less valuable than I am. I must reach for humility and be willing to *not know*. I may never fully understand the workings of racism, as I have been trained my entire life to perpetuate racism while denying its reality. I do not have to understand racism for it to be real, and my expectation that I could is part of my internalized dominance. Reaching for racial humility as a White person is not the same for me as being mired in class shame.

My class position is only one social location from which I learned to collude with racism. For example, I have also asked myself how I learned to collude with racism as a Catholic and a woman. How did it shape my sense of racial belonging, of racial *correctness*, to be presented with God, the ultimate and universal authority, as White? How did the active erasure of Jesus' race and ethnicity shape my racial consciousness? How did the universalization of Catholicism as the true religion for all peoples of the world engender racial superiority within me when all the authorities within that religion were White like myself? At the same time, how did my conditioning under Catholicism not to question authority lead me to silently collude with the racism of other Whites?

As a White woman, how did I internalize racial superiority through the culture's representation of White women as the embodiment of ultimate beauty? What has it meant for me to have a key signifier of female perfection—Whiteness—available to me? How have images of White women in the careers deemed valuable for woman shaped my goals? How has mainstream feminism's articulation of White women's issues as universal women's issues shaped what I care about? At the same time, what has it meant to live under patriarchy and to be taught that as a woman I am less intelligent, that I should not speak up, that I should defer to others, and at all times be nice and polite? How have all of these messages ultimately set me up to collude in the oppression of people of color? By asking questions such as these I have been able to gain a much deeper and more useful analysis of racism, and rather than finding that centering racism denies my other oppressions, I find that centering racism has been a profound way to address the complexity of all my social locations.

Suggestions for Further Reading

Baird, Robert M., and Stuart E. Rosenbaum, eds. *Bigotry, Prejudice, and Hatred,* 2nd ed. Buffalo, NY: Prometheus Press, 1999.

Bonilla-Silva, Eduardo. *Racism Without Racists: Color-Blind Racism and the Persistence of Racial Inequality in the U.S.* New York: Rowman & Littlefield, 2003.

———. *White Supremacy and Racism in the Post–Civil Rights Era.* Boulder, CO: Rienner, 2001.

Brandt, Eric, ed. *Dangerous Liaisons: Blacks, Gays, and the Struggle for Equality.* New York: New Press, 1999.

Brown, Michael K., et al. *Whitewashing Race in America: The Myth of a Color-Blind Society.* Berkeley: University of California Press, 2005.

Chang, Jeff. *Who We Be: A Cultural History of Race in Post–Civil Rights America.* New York: St. Martin's Press, 2014.

Cose, Ellis. *The Rage of a Privileged Class.* New York: HarperCollins, 1994.

Crenshaw, Kimberlé Williams. "Mapping the Margins: Intersectionality, Identity Politics, and Violence Against Women of Color." In *The Feminist Philosophy Reader*, edited by Alison Bailey and Chris Cuomo, 279–309. New York: McGraw-Hill, 2008.

Currah, Paisley, Richard M. Juang, and Shannon Price Minter, eds. *Transgender Rights.* Minneapolis: University of Minnesota Press, 2006.

DeMott, Benjamin. *The Trouble with Friendship: Why Americans Can't Think Straight About Race.* New York: Atlantic Monthly Press, 1995.

Dusky, Lorraine. *Still Unequal: The Shameful Truth About Women and Justice in America.* New York: Crown Books, 1996.

Dyer, Richard. *White.* London: Routledge, 1997.

Faludi, Susan. *Backlash: The Undeclared War Against American Women,* 15th anniversary ed. New York: Broadway, 2006.

———. *Stiffed: The Betrayal of the American Man.* New York: HarperPerennial, 2000.

Feagin, Joe R. *Racist America: Roots, Realities, and Future Reparations.* New York: Routledge, 2000.

Freedman, Estelle B., ed. *The Essential Feminist Reader.* New York: Modern Library, 2007.

Glenn, Evelyn Nakano. *Unequal Freedom: How Race and Gender Shaped American Citizenship and Labor.* Cambridge, MA: Harvard University Press, 2004.

Harris, Leonard. *Racism.* New York: Humanities Books, 1999.

Ignatiev, Noel. *How the Irish Became White.* New York: Routledge, 2008.

Incite! Women of Color Against Violence, eds. *The Color of Violence: The Incite! Anthology.* Cambridge, MA: South End Press, 2006.

Johnson, Allan G. *Privilege, Power, and Difference,* 2nd ed. New York: McGraw-Hill, 2005.

Kadi, Joanne. *Thinking Class: Sketches from a Cultural Worker.* Boston: South End Press, 1996.

Katznelson, Ira. *When Affirmative Action Was White: An Untold History of Racial Inequality in Twentieth-Century America.* New York: W. W. Norton, 2005.

Kimmel, Michael. *The Gendered Society.* New York: Oxford University Press, 2000.

Lareau, Annette. *Unequal Childhoods: Class, Race, and Family Life,* 2nd ed. Berkeley: University of California Press, 2011.

Lee, Erika. *The Making of Asian America: A History.* New York: Simon and Schuster, 2015.

Lipsitz, George. *The Possessive Investment in Whiteness,* Rev. ed. Philadelphia, PA: Temple University Press, 2006.

Marable, Manning. *Race, Reform, and Rebellion: The Second Reconstruction in Black America, 1945–2006,* 3rd ed. Jackson, MS: University Press of Mississippi, 2007.

Perry, Barbara. *In the Name of Hate: Understanding Hate Crimes.* New York: Routledge, 2001.

Pharr, Suzanne. *Homophobia as a Weapon of Sexism.* Inverness, CA: Chardon Press, 1988.

Rhode, Deborah L. *Speaking of Sex: The Denial of Gender Inequality.* Cambridge, MA: Harvard University Press, 1997.

Ronai, Carol R., et al. *Everyday Sexism in the Third Millennium.* New York: Routledge, 1997.

Shipler, David K. *A Country of Strangers: Blacks and Whites in America.* New York: Knopf, 1997.

Sue, Derald Wing. *Microaggressions in Everyday Life: Race, Gender, and Sexual Orientation.* Hoboken, NJ: John Wiley & Sons, 2010.

Williams, Lena. *It's the Little Things, the Everyday Interactions That Get Under the Skin of Blacks and Whites.* New York: Harcourt, 2000.

PART III

Complicating Questions of Identity: Race, Ethnicity, and Immigration

The United States has always been a nation of diverse immigrants, but recent waves of immigration bringing more than the expected number of Asians and Latinos to these shores are dramatically changing the racial/ethnic mix in this country. According to recent estimates, by the year 2050 whites will no longer be a majority. And in many parts of the country, whites are already the minority population. Selection 2, Mae Ngai provides an overview of U.S. immigration policy and a look at the changing picture of U.S. demographics. What are the implications of these changes for the way we think about the categories of race and ethnicity and how we define "minority"? What kinds of racial/ethnic categories are adequate to capture the identities of such a rich mix of peoples and cultures, a mix that is often embodied in the multiethnic heritage that individuals in the U.S. increasingly want to claim?

As Ngai explores, the United States has a long, complex history with regard to both legal and illegal immigration. Her piece traces the many ways immigration has informed not just the American legal system and the concept of "citizen" but also the very fabric of the United States. As each new wave of immigrants arrives on our shores, the systems we have in place in this country struggle to expand and adapt to account for these new identities.

The difficulty of coming up with adequate categories and paradigms gained national attention in 2000 when the Census Bureau set out to survey the U.S population, as it does every ten years. Until the 2000 census, respondents had been asked to identify with one and only one race when filling out the census questionnaire. Beginning with the 2000 census, respondents were given the option of identifying with up to six different racial groups. Although the new categories and the ways in which the data is now interpreted continue to be met with criticism, the change reflects the indisputably multicultural nature of the U.S. population and gives an indication of how complicated the project of defining racial/ethnic identity adequately and appropriately has become. Evelyn Alsultany grapples with this complexity in Selection 3.

While it is common today for many people to identify themselves as "Hispanic," before that category was created by the U.S. government and appeared in the census in 1980, very few people in the United States thought of themselves as such. This is a good example of the ways in which race/ethnicity is socially constructed. Currently, the census asks respondents to select a race by choosing one or more racial categories from among 15 options (plus the write-in "some other race"), such as American Indian or Alaska Native, Asian Indian, Chinese, Other Asian, Other Pacific Islander, Black, or White. In addition, respondents are given the option of choosing "Hispanic" as their ethnicity. According to this approach to classification, there can be white Hispanics, black Hispanics, and Asian Hispanics. But what is the basis for assigning or choosing this ethnic identity? By common language? Many but not all Hispanics speak Spanish. By physical characteristics? As articles in this part point out, people who identify as Hispanic come in every shade of skin color. By shared culture? There is significant cultural diversity among people in this category. National origin? Some point to ancestry in a Spanish-speaking country as the basis for this categorization, but this too is not without complications. Some Mexican Americans, like authors Sandra Cisneros and Luis Rodriguez, reject the term "Hispanic" and prefer to be identified as Latino/a or Chicano/a. They contend, as do many people from the Americas and the Caribbean, that the term "Hispanic" is associated with predominantly white Spain and Portugal, whereas "Latino" preserves the connection with the darker-skinned indigenous Indian population of the Americas that was conquered by those European nations centuries ago. In Selection 4, Mireya Navarro explores some of the complexities involved in articulating a Latina/o or Hispanic racial/ethnic identity.

Because for the most part it is white people and a largely white power structure that have had the ability to create racial/ethnic categories and apply them, people of color from very different ethnic backgrounds have often been lumped together with a total disregard for the important cultural, social, and economic differences associated with their individual ethnic and class backgrounds and their places of origin. People born in Puerto Rico, Mexico, and Spain may all be grouped together by white people as Latinos or Hispanics even though this categorization ignores important differences among them. In the same way, through white eyes people from Ethiopia, Namibia, and Haiti may all look "black," but this simplistic categorization leaves out vastly different histories and heritages. In Selection 5, Christina M. Greer looks at these distinctions of race and ethnicity in black communities. Greer shows the complexity of racial formation by focusing on the relationships between native-born black Americans and black ethnic immigrants.

In Selection 6, Noy Thrupkaew examines the failure of the U.S. government and of many people in the United States to recognize the unique situations and challenges faced by various populations lumped together as "Asian Americans." She finds the concept of Asians as a "model minority" more than problematic. Quoting Frank Wu, Thrupkaew suggests that the model minority myth is kept alive by political conservatives who use it to rationalize and obscure the unequal distribution of wealth, opportunity, and privilege in this county. By idealizing the success of Asian Americans, conservatives imply that African Americans and Latinos who do not succeed do not work hard enough. Further, although in reality many Southeast Asians in the United States (largely from Cambodia, Laos, and Vietnam) have an extremely high rate of poverty, by grouping them within the broad category of "Asians," the model minority myth is kept alive and the needs of this particular population are largely ignored.

Part III concludes with a selection from Moustafa Bayoumi, who chronicles the experiences of Arab and Muslim Americans in the period immediately following September 11, 2001, when they were deemed threatening and/or suspicious. Bayoumi places this discussion in a historical context, tracing both the ways that Muslim communities have been perceived over time as well as how other racial/ethnic groups have been designated "a problem."

1 Immigration in the United States: New Economic, Social, Political Landscapes with Legislative Reform on the Horizon

Faye Hipsman and Doris Meissner

Immigration has shaped the United States as a nation since the first newcomers arrived over 400 years ago. Beyond being a powerful demographic force responsible for how the country and its population became what they are today, immigration has contributed deeply to many of the economic, social, and political processes that are foundational to the United States as a nation.

Although immigration has occurred throughout American history, large-scale immigration has occurred during just four peak periods: the peopling of the original colonies, westward expansion during the middle of the 19th century, and the rise of cities at the turn of the 20th century. The fourth peak period began in the 1970s and continues today.

These peak immigration periods have coincided with fundamental transformations of the American economy. The first saw the dawn of European settlement in the Americas. The second allowed the young United States to transition from a colonial to an agricultural economy. The industrial revolution gave rise to a manufacturing economy during the third peak period, propelling America's rise to become the leading power in the world. Today's large-scale immigration has coincided with globalization and the last stages of transformation from a manufacturing to a 21st century knowledge-based economy. As before, immigration has been prompted by economic transformation, just as it is helping the United States adapt to new economic realities. . . .

Early History

In the decades prior to 1880, immigration to the United States was primarily European, driven by forces such as industrialization in Western Europe and the Irish potato famine. The expanding frontiers of the American West and the United States' industrial revolution drew immigrants to U.S. shores. Chinese immigrants began to arrive in large numbers for the first time in the 1850s after gold was discovered in California in 1848.

Federal oversight of immigration began in 1882, when Congress passed the Immigration Act. It established the collection of a fee from each noncitizen arriving at a U.S. port to be used by the Treasury Department to regulate immigration. Arriving immigrants were screened for the first time under this act, and entry by anyone

"Immigration in the United States: New Economic, Social, Political Landscapes with Legislative Reform on the Horizon." Originally published by the Migration Policy Institute, an independent, nonpartisan think tank dedicated to the study of the movement of people worldwide.

deemed a "convict, lunatic, idiot, or person unable to take care of himself or herself without becoming a public charge" was prohibited.

As the mining boom in the West began to subside, animosity toward the large populations of Chinese laborers and other foreigners surged, and so began a series of legislative measures to restrict immigration of certain racial groups, beginning with nationals of China. The Chinese Exclusion Act of 1882 was the first such law. It halted immigration of Chinese laborers for ten years, barred Chinese naturalization, and provided for the deportation of Chinese in the country illegally. In a follow-on bill, Congress passed the 1888 Scott Act and banned the return of Chinese nationals with lawful status in the United States if they departed the country. In 1892, the Geary Act extended the ten-year ban on Chinese labor immigration, and established restrictive policies toward Chinese immigrants with and without legal status.

Between 1880 and 1930, over 27 million new immigrants arrived, mainly from Italy, Germany, Eastern Europe, Russia, Britain, Canada, Ireland, and Sweden. This peak immigration period—the last large-scale immigration wave prior to the current period—also led to new restrictions.

In an expansion of racial exclusion, and by overriding a presidential veto, Congress passed the 1917 Immigration Act which prohibited immigration from a newly drawn "Asiatic barred zone" covering British India, most of Southeast Asia, and nearly all of the Middle East. It also expanded inadmissibility grounds to include anarchists, persons previously deported within the past year, and illiterate individuals over the age of 16.

Nativist and restrictionist sentiment continued through the 1920s, prompting the United States to introduce numerical limitations on immigration for the first time. The Immigration and Naturalization Act of 1924 established the national-origins quota system, which set a ceiling on the number of immigrants that could be admitted to the United States from each country. It strongly favored northern and western European immigration. The 1952 Immigration and Nationality Act continued the national-origins quota system but for the first time allocated an immigration quota for Asian countries.

The Post-1965 Era

Although the discriminatory nature of the national-origins quota system had become increasingly discredited, it took until the Kennedy era and the ripple effects of the nation's civil-rights movement for a new philosophy guiding immigration to take hold. The resulting Immigration and Nationality Act Amendments of 1965 repealed the national-origins quota system and replaced it with a seven-category preference system based primarily on family unification. Overall, the legislation set in motion powerful forces that are still shaping the United States today.

The year before the 1965 Act, Congress terminated the Bracero program, which it had authorized during World War II to recruit agricultural workers from Mexico to fill farm-labor shortages in the United States. In the wake of these and other sweeping changes in the global economy, immigration flows that had been European-dominated for most of the nation's history gave way to predominantly Latin American and Asian immigration.

Today's large-scale immigration began in the 1970s, and has been made up of both legal and illegal flows. Prior periods of large-scale immigration occurred before visas were subject to numerical ceilings, so the phenomenon of "illegal immigration" is a relatively recent element of immigration policy history and debates.

The largest source country of legal admissions, Mexico, has also accounted for the largest share of illegal immigrants who cross the southwest land border with the United States to seek the comparatively higher wages available from U.S. jobs.

By the mid-1980s, an estimated 3 to 5 million noncitizens were living unlawfully in the country. To address illegal immigration, Congress passed the Immigration Reform and Control Act of 1986 (IRCA), which was intended to act as a "three-legged stool." . . .

Four years later, Congress passed the Immigration Act of 1990 to revamp the legal immigration system and admit a greater share of highly-skilled and educated immigrants. . . .

Overall, IRCA and its enforcement mechanisms were no match for the powerful forces that drive illegal migration. Both IRCA and the 1990 Act failed to adequately foresee and incorporate measures to provide and manage continued flows of temporary and permanent immigrants to meet the country's labor market needs, especially during the economic boom years of the 1990s.

As a result, illegal immigration grew dramatically and began to be experienced not only in the six traditional immigration destination states of New York, New Jersey, Florida, Texas, Illinois, and California, but also in many other areas across the southeast, midwest, and mountain states that had not had experience with large-scale immigration for up to a century. Although immigration served as a source of economic productivity and younger workers in areas where the population and workforces were aging, a large share of the immigration was comprised of illegal immigration flows. Thus, the challenge to deeply-held rule-of-law principles and the social change represented by this immigration generated progressively negative public sentiment about immigration that prompted Congress to pass a set of strict new laws in 1996, as follows:

- The Personal Responsibility and Work Opportunity Reconciliation Act (PR-WORA), commonly known as the Welfare Reform Act, denied access to federal public benefits, such as Medicaid, Supplemental Security Income (SSI), and food stamps to categories of authorized and unauthorized immigrants. Some states later chose to reinstate some of these benefits for authorized immigrants who lost eligibility under PRWORA.

- The Illegal Immigration Reform and Immigrant Responsibility Act (IIRIRA) bolstered immigration enforcement, increased penalties for immigration-related crimes, provided for expedited removal of inadmissible noncitizens, barred unlawfully present immigrants from re-entry for long periods of time, and set income requirements for immigrants' family sponsors at 125 percent of the federal poverty level. IIRIRA also required the government to track foreign visitors' entries and exits, which became a key element in the government's security strategy after the 9/11 terrorist attacks.

- The Anti-Terrorism and Effective Death Penalty Act (AEDPA) made it easier to arrest, detain, and deport noncitizens.

Subsequently, Congress returned to shoring up legal immigration measures in 2000 by enacting the American Competitiveness in the Twenty-First Century Act to meet demand for skilled immigrants—especially in science, math, and engineering specialties—and enable employers to fill technology jobs that are a critical dimension of the post-industrial, information age economy. . . .

The Lasting Impact of 9/11 on Immigration Policy

No recent event has influenced the thinking and actions of the American public and its leaders as much as the terrorist attacks of September 11, 2001. . . .

Because the 9/11 hijackers obtained valid visas to travel to the United States, despite some being known by U.S. intelligence and having been encountered by law enforcement agencies, the immigration system came under particular scrutiny. The Immigration and Naturalization Service (INS), which had been part of the Department of Justice since 1941, was dissolved and its functions were transferred to three newly created agencies within DHS, as follows:

- Customs and Border Protection (CBP) oversees the entry of all people and goods at all ports of entry and enforces laws against illegal entry between the ports.
- Immigration and Customs Enforcement (ICE) is responsible for enforcement of immigration and customs requirements in the interior of the United States, including employer requirements, detention, and removals.
- U.S. Citizenship and Immigration Services (USCIS) adjudicates immigrant benefit applications, such as visa petitions, naturalization applications, and asylum and refugee requests, and administers the E-Verify program.

An additional new post-9/11 immigration entity has been US-VISIT, which is housed in the National Protection and Programs Directorate (NPPD) of DHS. It manages the IDENT biometric fingerprint information system used by all immigration agencies—including consulates abroad in visa screening—to confirm the identity of noncitizens entering the country. . . .

In June 2002, the U.S. Attorney General began the National Security Entry-Exit Registration System (NSEERS), a program that placed extra travel screening requirements on nationals from a list of 25 countries associated with an Al Qaeda presence (and North Korea). Additionally, males over the age of 16 who were nationals of designated NSEERS countries and already living in the United States were required to register with the federal government and appear for "special registration" interviews with immigration officials. The program was discontinued in 2011.

In 2005, the REAL ID Act prohibited states from issuing driver's licenses to unauthorized individuals, and expanded terrorism-related grounds of inadmissibility, removal, and ineligibility for asylum. One year later, the Secure Fence Act of 2006 authorized the completion of 700 miles of fencing along the southwest border with Mexico. . . .

One immediate result of tightened screening procedures was a dramatic drop in the number of visas the government issued to individuals wishing to visit, work, and live in the United States. Between 2001 and 2002, the number of nonimmigrant visas fell by 24 percent. Present visa issuances have returned to pre-9/11 levels, but it has taken ten years to rebound.

A Profile of Today's Immigrant Population

The U.S. foreign-born population (legal and illegal) is 40.4 million, or 13 percent of the total U.S. population of 311.6 million, according to 2011 American Community Survey estimates. Although this is a numerical high historically, the foreign born make up a smaller percentage of the population today than in 1890 and 1910 when the immigrant share of the population peaked at 15 percent. The foreign-born share fell to a low of 5 percent (9.6 million) in 1970. About 20 percent of all international migrants reside in the United States, which, as a country, accounts for less than 5 percent of the world's population.

The foreign-born population is comprised of approximately 42 percent naturalized citizens, 31 percent permanent residents (green card holders), and 27 percent unauthorized immigrants. Roughly 11.7 million, or 29 percent of the immigrant population is from Mexico, the largest immigration source country. Chinese and Indian immigrants make up the second and third largest immigrant groups, with 1.9 million or 5 percent of the foreign-born population each. In 2010, India replaced the Philippines as the third largest source country (see Table 1). The top three regions of origin of the foreign-born population are Latin America, Asia, and Europe (see Figure 1).

TABLE 1 Immigrant Population by Country of Birth Residing in the United States, 1960 to 2011

Sending Country	Estimate	Percentage
Mexico	11.7 million	29
China (inc. Hong Kong)	1.9 million	5
India	1.9 million	5
Philippines	1.8 million	4
El Salvador	1.3 million	3
Vietnam	1.3 million	3
Cuba	1.1 million	3
Korea	1.1 million	3
Dominican Republic	900,000	2
Guatemala	851,000	2

Source: MPI Data Hub, available online.

Figure 1: Foreign Born Population by Region of Origin, 2011

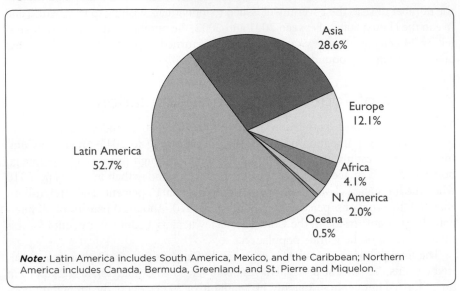

Note: Latin America includes South America, Mexico, and the Caribbean; Northern America includes Canada, Bermuda, Greenland, and St. Pierre and Miquelon.

The foreign-born population is geographically concentrated, with 65 percent residing in the six states that have long been the country's main immigrant destinations—about 25 percent in California alone (in 2011). The other immigrant-heavy states are New York (11 percent of all foreign born), Texas (10 percent), Florida (9 percent), Illinois (4 percent), and New Jersey (5 percent). The proximity of several of these states to Mexico and longstanding, continuous immigration to traditional metropolitan destinations in New York, New Jersey, and Illinois created strong networks that have grown over time.

While these states continue to draw and represent the bulk of the foreign-born population, newcomers—particularly unauthorized immigrants from Mexico—began to settle in many additional destinations during the 1990s. Employment opportunities—particularly in agriculture, food manufacturing and construction—mainly fueled the new settlement patterns. They combined with lower costs of living and "hollowing out", i.e. depopulation of certain areas of the country due to aging and internal migration. As a result, states like Georgia, Nevada, and many others have become known as the "new growth" or "new destination" immigration states.

Ten states, mostly in the south and west, have experienced over 270 percent immigrant population growth since 1990. They are North Carolina, Georgia, Tennessee, Arkansas, Nevada, South Carolina, Kentucky, Nebraska, Utah, and Alabama. These changes and patterns help to explain why immigration has become an issue of national political concern and debate. . . .

Over the past 150 years, the levels of legal immigration have varied, from over 1 million people per year during the early 20th century to a trickle during the Great Depression and World War II (see Figure 2). Immigrants legalized under IRCA caused

Figure 2: Legal Immigration to the United States, FY 1820 to 2011

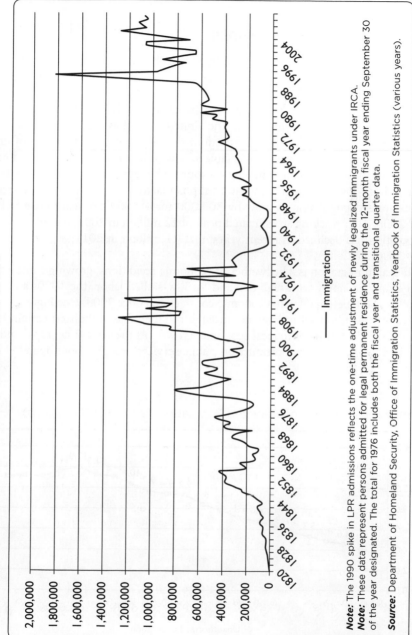

Note: The 1990 spike in LPR admissions reflects the one-time adjustment of newly legalized immigrants under IRCA.

Note: These data represent persons admitted for legal permanent residence during the 12-month fiscal year ending September 30 of the year designated. The total for 1976 includes both the fiscal year and transitional quarter data.

Source: Department of Homeland Security, Office of Immigration Statistics, Yearbook of Immigration Statistics (various years).

the number of authorized immigrants to peak in the late 1980s. The 1990s and 2000s, until the recession, have registered historic highs in overall immigration levels. . . .

Unauthorized Immigrants

Unauthorized immigrants enter the United States by crossing the land border clandestinely between formal ports of entry, using documents fraudulently for admission at a port of entry, or overstaying a valid temporary visa.

Illegal immigration began to build and reach relatively high levels in the early 1970s. Immigration policymaking in the United States has been preoccupied with the issues it represents for much of the four decades since. The numbers of unauthorized immigrants who were not eligible for IRCA's legalization but remained in the United States, in addition to immigration spurred by rapid job creation in the 1990s and early 2000s, combined with powerful push factors in Mexico, have caused the unauthorized population to grow by 300,000 to 500,000 per year between 1990 and 2006. After reaching an estimated peak of 12 million in 2007, the unauthorized population has declined in recent years, to 11.1 million in 2011, according to the Pew Hispanic Center.

Illegal immigration is a bellwether of economic conditions, growing substantially in a strong economy with high demand for low-skilled labor (the 1990s and early 2000s), and tapering off with economic contraction (since 2008) (see Figure 3). The arrival of unauthorized immigrants in large numbers has revitalized certain communities and contributes to local economic growth. At the same time, rapid and unchecked social change and pressure on public services brought about by individuals

Figure 3: Estimated Unauthorized Population, 1990 to 2011 (millions)

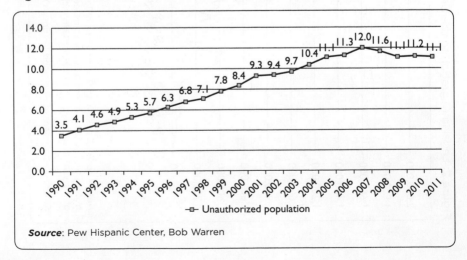

Source: Pew Hispanic Center, Bob Warren

here illegally has sparked anger and resentment, making immigration a hotly contested issue of national concern.

DHS estimates that 59 percent of unauthorized residents are Mexican born; with El Salvador accounting for 6 percent, Guatemala 5 percent, Honduras 3 percent, and China 2 percent. The ten leading countries of origin also include the Philippines, India, Korea, Ecuador, and Vietnam, which represented 85 percent of the unauthorized immigrant population in 2011.

Roughly 46 percent of unauthorized adult immigrants are parents of young children. As of 2010, there were 5.5 million minors with at least one unauthorized parent. While 1 million of these minors are also unauthorized, the vast majority—4.5 million—are U.S.-born, and are, therefore, American citizens.

Immigrant Integration

While the public debate tends to focus disproportionately on questions of who, how many, and what kind of noncitizens should be admitted to the United States, many see immigrant integration as the true test of a successful immigration system. Unlike other traditional immigration countries, such as Canada and Australia, for example, the United States does not have a federally-driven immigrant integration policy or an agency responsible for making sure immigrants effectively become part of U.S. society. Instead, integration policies are limited, underfunded, largely ad hoc, and often target narrow immigrant groups, such as refugees or migrant workers.

Historically, schools, churches, employers, and community-based groups have taken the lead at the local level to spearhead immigrant integration efforts that include English classes, job training, and health care clinics. In recent years, several states and cities have launched integration initiatives aimed at improving opportunities and services available to immigrants.

Federal policies that affect immigrant integration outcomes include the No Child Left Behind Act passed in 2001 that required schools and funding for states to ensure that limited English proficient (LEP) children become proficient in English. In 2009, the Children's Health Insurance Program (CHIP) was expanded to cover authorized immigrant children. Additionally, the federal Adult Education program funds English education and GED preparation.

Access to basic rights and mainstream institutions in American society like most jobs in the labor market, public education, community and emergency health care systems, and citizenship have been the pillars of successful integration, despite that fact that they do not represent explicit, formal policy efforts. Integration is commonly measured by comparing indicators such as income, education, health, and living standards for foreign and native-born populations. Despite the absence of broad immigrant integration policies, the foreign born have historically become well integrated in the United States. At the same time, today's large numbers of foreign born, especially the sizable unauthorized population who may gain legal status if CIR is enacted, pose substantial immigrant integration challenges for all levels of government and society—as well as for the individuals themselves—in the years ahead.

Immigration Enforcement

As illegal immigration intensified during recent decades, immigration enforcement has been the dominant focus of the federal government's response to immigration for at least 25 years. Enforcement involves visa screening; land border enforcement between ports of entry; land, air, and sea ports of entry admissions, employer enforcement, detention and removal of criminals and others who have violated immigration laws, and immigration administrative courts. Nonetheless, the dominant focus of immigration enforcement has been the southwest land border enforcement.

The U.S.-Mexico border is a diverse area that spans more than 1,900 miles. For most of the period since the Border Patrol was created in 1924, chronic lack of funding and adequate resources prevented it from carrying out its mission of preventing illegal border crossings. That began to change with stepped up border enforcement during the 1990s.

Since then, the federal government has invested billions of dollars into personnel, infrastructure, and technology on the border. The Border Patrol now has more than 21,000 agents, having doubled in size since just 2005; 651 miles of border fencing has been built (mandated in the 2006 Secure Fence Act); and a vast array of cameras, ground sensors, aircraft, and drones are in place. More than $11 billion was spent on border enforcement in FY 2011.

As a result, crossing points that were traditionally used by people entering illegally into the country have been largely closed off, making it difficult, dangerous, and expensive to cross. The number of apprehensions the Border Patrol makes has decreased from nearly 1.7 million in 2000 to 365,000 in 2012.

Immigration enforcement capabilities in the country's interior have also been significantly strengthened. Deportations, federal partnerships with state and local law enforcement agencies, and efforts to discourage hiring of unauthorized immigrants are all parts of the equation.

Since 1986, the government has carried out more than 4 million deportations (or removals). Almost half have occurred since 2007. Annual removals have climbed steeply for the last 15 years, from roughly 30,000 in 1990 to 188,500 in 2000, to over 400,000 in 2012. Deportation levels are largely governed by Congress, which provides the enforcement agencies with levels of funding that specify the numbers to be detained and removed each year. . . .

A New Era of Lower Levels of Immigration?

Despite the large numbers of unauthorized immigrants residing in the United States, numerous indicators suggest that changing migration dynamics have set in that will reduce levels of illegal immigration in the future, even as the U.S. economy rebounds. After growing annually for several decades, the size of the unauthorized population has begun to decline since 2007. Furthermore, the number of migrants arrested while attempting to cross the border has fallen dramatically during the last decade, especially since 2008. The Pew Hispanic Center estimates that immigration from Mexico has reached net zero and has possibly reversed, meaning that inflows and outflows are approximately equal or outflows are greater.

A combination of factors is responsible for the new trends. First, sectors that typically employ unauthorized immigrants—including construction, hospitality, and tourism—experienced deep job loss in the recession, so job demand for lower-skilled workers has diminished. Second, the buildup of immigration enforcement at the border and in the U.S. interior has raised the costs, risks, and difficulty of migrating illegally. Finally, structural changes in Mexico—sustained economic growth, improved rates of high school graduation, falling fertility rates, a decline in the size and growth of the prime working-age population, and the emergence of a strong middle class—have slowed emigration.

Taken together, these changes represent significant, lasting new developments that are likely to remain in place during the near-term future.

SOURCES

Bergeron, Claire. 2013. Going to the Back of the Line. Washington, DC: Migration Policy Institute.

Britz, Emma and Jeanne Batalova. 2013. Frequently Requested Statistics on Immigrants and Immigration in the United States. *Migration Information Source*, January 2013.

Customs and Border Protection. 2013. *U.S. Border Patrol Statistics*.

Fix, Michael, ed. 2007. *Securing the Future: U.S. Immigrant Integration Policy*. Washington, DC: Migration Policy Institute.

Gzesh, Susan. 2006. Central Americans and Asylum Policy in the Reagan Era. *Migration Information Source*, April 2006.

Hoefer, Michael, Nancy Rytina, and Bryan Baker. 2012. Estimates of the Unauthorized Immigrant Population Residing in the United States: January 2011. Washington, DC: Department of Homeland Security, Office of Immigration Statistics.

Immigration and Customs Enforcement. 2013. *Removal Statistics*.

Ji, Qingqing and Jeanne Batalova. 2012. Temporary Admissions of Nonimmigrants to the United States. *Migration Information Source*, November 2012.

Office of Immigration Statistics. Various Years. Yearbook of Immigration Statistics. Washington, DC: Department of Homeland Security.

McCabe, Kristen and Doris Meissner. 2010. Immigration and the United States: Recession Affects Flows, Prospects for Reform. *Migration Information Source*, January 2010.

Meissner, Doris, Deborah W. Meyers, Demetrios G. Papademetriou, and Michael Fix. 2006. *Immigration and America's Future: A New Chapter*. Washington, DC: Migration Policy Institute.

Meissner, Doris, Kerwin, Donald M., Chishti, Muzaffar, and Claire Bergeron. 2013. *Immigration Enforcement in the United States: The Rise of a Formidable Machinery*. Washington, DC: Migration Policy Institute.

Migration Policy Institute. 2011. American Community Survey and Census Data on the Foreign Born by State.

Migration Policy Institute. U.S. Historical Immigration Trends.

Motel , Seth and Eileen Patten. 2013. Statistical Portrait of the Foreign-Born Population in the United States, 2011. Washington, DC: Pew Hispanic Center.

Passel, Jeffrey, D'Vera Cohn, and Ana Gonzalez-Barrera. 2013. Net Migration from Mexico Falls to Zero—and Perhaps Less. Washington, DC: Pew Hispanic Center.

Passel, Jeffrey and D'Vera Cohn. 2012. Unauthorized Immigrants: 11.1 Million in 2011. Washington, DC: Pew Hispanic Center.

Rytina, Nancy. 2012. Estimates of the Legal Permanent Resident Population in 2011. Washington, DC: DHS, Office of Immigration Statistics.

Russell, Joseph and Jeanne Batalova. 2012. Green Card Holders and Legal Immigration to the United States. *Migration Information Source*, October 2012.

Russell, Joseph and Jeanne Batalova. 2012. *Refugees and Asylees in the United States*.

2 Impossible Subjects: Illegal Aliens and the Making of America

Mae Ngai

In 2001 the United States Immigration and Naturalization Service ordered Rosario Hernandez of Garland, Texas, deported to his native Mexico. Hernandez, a 39-year-old construction worker, had immigrated to Texas from Guadalajara, Mexico, when he was a teenager. His removal was ordered on grounds that he had been convicted three times for driving while intoxicated—twice nearly twenty years ago and once ten years later. After the third conviction Hernandez served five weekends in jail, joined Alcoholics Anonymous, and gave up drinking. However, according to laws passed by Congress in 1996 the multiple convictions amounted to an "aggravated felony" and made his removal mandatory, not subject to review by a judge. Hernandez considered the deportation unfair: "I already paid for my mistakes," he said. "How can they punish somebody two times for the same thing?"

Hernandez is married to a U.S. citizen and has two children, who are also American citizens. His wife Renee said, "I respect him for admitting to his mistakes and changing his life. What people don't realize is that this was a surprise attack on my life, as well. We have a baby here whose whole person is forming. He changes every day, and you want both parents to be a part of that." Hernandez's older son, Adrian, asks, "Where is my daddy going to be?"[1]

When I read Hernandez's story I was struck by its resemblance to another story. . . . In the early 1930s the INS ordered Mrs. Lillian Joann Flake, a longtime resident of Chicago, deported to her native Canada. Like Hernandez, Flake was married to an American citizen and had a daughter, also a citizen. She had a record of theft and shoplifting, which the INS considered "crimes of moral turpitude." Flake's deportation was canceled by an act of grace by Secretary of Labor Frances Perkins. The 1996 laws, however, explicitly deny administrative relief in cases like Hernandez's.[2]

Then, as now, legal reformers and immigrant advocates publicized deportation stories like these in order to call attention to what they believed was a problem in American immigration policy. Reformers argued that the nation's sovereign right to determine the conditions under which foreigners enter and remain in the country runs into trouble when the government expels people who have acquired families and property in the United States. They found cases like Hernandez's and Flake's

Republished with permission of Princeton University Press from *Impossible Subjects,* Mae Ngai, Copyright © 2014; permission conveyed through Copyright Clearance Center, Inc.

compelling because embedded in their narratives were normative judgments that esteem the immigrant's integration into society and the sanctity of the family. Deportation, which devalues assimilation—indeed cancels it—and separates families, seemed draconian punishment for crimes of drunk driving and petty theft. In Flake's time, reformers wrote almost exclusively about deportation cases involving Europeans and paid scant attention, if any, to the deportation of Mexican or Chinese criminal aliens. Nowadays, however, non-European cases like Hernandez's also receive public sympathy, especially when they involve rehabilitated criminals who are longtime permanent residents with families. This shift reflects the increase in the number of immigrants from the third world over the last quarter century and contemporary multicultural sensibilities.

We ought not rush to the conclusion, however, that race no longer operates in either the practice or representation of deportation. Then, as now, few reformers advocated for those aliens who entered the country by crossing the border without authorization. That preoccupation has focused on the United States–Mexico border and therefore on illegal immigrants from Mexico and Central America, suggesting that race and illegal status remain closely related.

But we might ask, first, what it is about the violation of the nation's sovereign space that produces a different kind of illegal alien and a different valuation of the claims that he or she can make on society? Unauthorized entry, the most common form of illegal immigration since the 1920s, remains vexing for both state and society. Undocumented immigrants are at once welcome and unwelcome: they are woven into the economic fabric of the nation, but as labor that is cheap and disposable. Employed in western and southwestern agriculture during the middle decades of the twentieth century, today illegal immigrants work in every region of the United States, and not only as farmworkers. They also work in poultry factories, in the kitchens of restaurants, on urban and suburban construction crews, and in the homes of middle-class Americans. Marginalized by their position in the lower strata of the workforce and even more so by their exclusion from the polity, illegal aliens might be understood as a caste, unambiguously situated outside the boundaries of formal membership and social legitimacy.

At the same time, illegal immigrants are also members of ethno-racial communities; they often inhabit the same social spaces as their co-ethnics and, in many cases, are members of "mixed status" families. Their accretion engenders paradoxical effects. On the one hand, the presence of large illegal populations in Asian and Latino communities has historically contributed to the construction of those communities as illegitimate, criminal, and unassimilable. Indeed, the association of these minority groups as unassimilable foreigners has led to the creation of "alien citizens"—persons who are American citizens by virtue of their birth in the United States but who are presumed to be foreign by the mainstream of American culture and, at times, by the state.

On the other hand, ethno-racial minority groups pursue social inclusion, making claims of belonging and engaging with society, irrespective of formal status. Latino studies scholars Williams Flores and Rena Benmayor, for example, argue that the mobilization of "cultural citizenship" by subordinate ethnic groups is "redressive" and contributes to a multicultural society. From another angle, a nonjuridical concept of membership suggests the production of collectivities that are not national but trans-national, sited in borderlands or in diaspora.[3] The liabilities of illegal alienage and alien citizenship may thus be at least partially offset through individual and collective agency, within and across nation-state boundaries. . . .

I focus on the years 1924 to 1965, which mark the tenure of the national origins quota system put into place by the Johnson–Reed Immigration Act of 1924.[4] The Johnson–Reed Act was certainly not the nation's first restrictive immigration law. The exclusion of Chinese, other Asians, and various classes of undesirable aliens (paupers, criminals, anarchists, and the like) in the late nineteenth and early twentieth centu-ries signaled the beginnings of a legal edifice of restriction. But the 1924 act was the nation's first *comprehensive* restriction law. It established for the first time *numerical limits* on immigration and a *global* racial and national hierarchy that favored some immigrants over others. The regime of immigration restriction remapped the nation in two important ways. First, it drew a new ethnic and racial map based on new cat-egories and hierarchies of difference. Second, and in a different register, it articulated a new sense of territoriality, which was marked by unprecedented awareness and state surveillance of the nation's contiguous land borders.

Most of the scholarship about immigration to the United States focuses on the period before 1924, the era of open immigration from Europe, and the period since 1965, when the national origins quota system was abolished and immigration from the third world increased. Thus, at one level, this study is an attempt to address a gap in the historiography of American immigration. Although Americans long ago con-cluded that the national origins quota system was an illiberal policy that blighted the nation's democratic tradition, we still know little about *how* that restriction actually worked, how the nation was racially and spatially reimagined. To be sure, historians have studied the consequence of the *absence* of immigration during these decades. Most important, the cutoff of European immigration created conditions for the second generation of those immigrants who had come to the United States from the 1890s to World War I to more readily assimilate into American society. The loosen-ing of these ethnic groups' ties to their homelands facilitated that process, as did the spread of American popular culture and consumerism, industrial-class formation and organization, and the nationally unifying experience of World War II.[5]

But restriction meant much more than fewer people entering the country; it also invariably generated illegal immigration and introduced that problem into the internal spaces of the nation. Immigration restriction produced the illegal alien as a *new legal and political subject*, whose inclusion within the nation was simultane-ously a social reality and a legal impossibility—a subject barred from citizenship and without rights. Moreover, the need of state authorities to identify and distin-guish between citizens, lawfully resident immigrants, and illegal aliens posed en-forcement, political, and constitutional problems for the modern state. The illegal alien is thus an "impossible subject," a person who cannot be and a problem that cannot be solved.

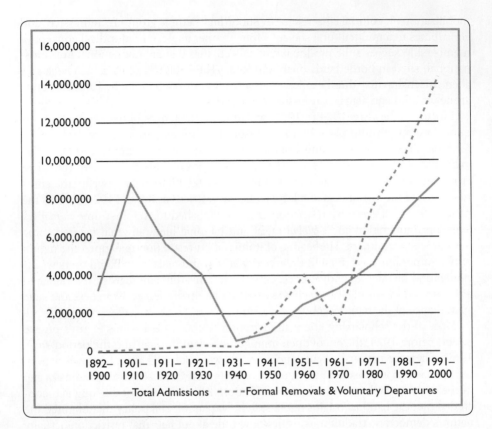

Even as Congress abolished quotas based on national origin in 1965, it preserved the principle of numerically limiting immigration and, in fact, extended it to cover the entire globe. Americans remain committed to the principle of numerical restriction to the present day. The controversies over immigration policy taking place at the beginning of the twenty-first century center on whether immigrants contribute positively or deleteriously to the nation's economy and culture, but there is virtually no political support for open or numerically unrestricted immigration. If the principle of immigration restriction has become an unquestioned assumption of contemporary politics, we need to ask how it got to be that way and to consider its place in the historical construction of the nation.

Immigration and Citizenship

Immigration policy is constitutive of Americans' understanding of national membership and citizenship, drawing lines of inclusion and exclusion that articulate a desired composition—imagined if not necessarily realized—of the nation. The concept is manifest in the titles of books on U.S. immigration policy: *The Face of the Nation,*

Making Americans, A Nation by Design.[6] In the United States immigration has always been understood as a path that leads to citizenship, as sociologist Rogers Brubaker has noted: "Admission to citizenship is viewed as the normal sequel to admission for settlement." Chinese exclusion, the exception that proves the rule, was another means by which the nation defined itself.[7]

The telos of immigrant settlement, assimilation, and citizenship has been an enduring narrative of American history, but it has not always been the reality of migrants' desires or their experiences and interactions with American society and state. The myth of "immigrant America" derives its power in large part from the labor that it performs for American exceptionalism. As political theorist Bonnie Honig argues, the myth "shores up the national narrative of liberal consensual citizenship, allowing a disaffected citizenry to experience its regime as choiceworthy, to see it through the eyes of still-enchanted newcomers whose choice to come here . . . reenact[s] liberalism's . . . fictive foundation in individual acts of uncoerced consent."[8]

Yet if the iconic immigrant serves exceptionalist political culture, that narrative is legally grounded in a relatively easy process of naturalization (five years residence with no criminal record) and in the principle of *jus soli*, which confers citizenship upon all those born on U.S. soil and, therefore, to the American-born children of immigrants. Moreover, in matters other than the admission and expulsion of aliens, the Constitution protects all persons, not just citizens. Aliens do not enjoy all the privileges of citizenship—notably the franchise—but outside the immigration domain, and in civil society generally, they have the same rights as citizens to equal protection under the Fourteenth Amendment.[9] The capaciousness of the Constitution in this regard is not unproblematic: critics have argued that aliens' lack of substantive rights in matters of immigration compromises their rights while they are present. Legal and political theorists also dispute the implications of the Constitution's protection of aliens. While some cite it as evidence of the nation's inclusive traditions, others worry that the extension of so many rights to aliens diminishes the value of citizenship.[10]

Nevertheless, the line between alien and citizen is soft. At least in principle, access to naturalization ensures that the condition of alienage, with its limited rights, is temporary. This principle is important because it recognizes the moral and political imperative of equality that is central to liberal democracy.[11] Yet the promise of citizenship applies only to the *legal* alien, the lawfully present immigrant. The *illegal* immigrant has no right to be present, let alone embark on the path to citizenship. The illegal alien crosses a territorial boundary, but, once inside the nation, he or she stands at another juridical boundary. It is here, I suggest, that we might paradoxically locate the outermost point of exclusion from national membership.

Some readers might find this unproblematic, for, after all, the nation is bounded and exclusion from citizenship would seem a logical consequence of illegal immigration. But, as this [work] aims to show, illegal alienage is not a natural or fixed condition but the product of positive law; it is contingent and at times it is unstable. The line between legal and illegal status can be crossed in both directions. An illegal alien can, under certain conditions, adjust his or her status and become legal and hence eligible for citizenship. And legal aliens who violate certain laws can become illegal and hence expelled and, in some cases, forever barred from reentry and the possibility of citizenship. I suggest that shifts in the boundary between legal and illegal status might tell us a lot about how the nation has imagined and constructed itself over time.

This line of inquiry intervenes in a burgeoning field of citizenship studies. Legal scholar Linda Bosniak has observed that recent scholarship largely concerns not citizenship as formal membership in the nation-state but issues of substantive citizenship, such as civic virtue and group identities in a multicultural society. Many scholars presume that as a formal status category, universal liberal citizenship in the United States has been achieved, that its historical exclusions based on race and gender have been overcome, and that the challenge, now, is to go beyond passive citizenship to normative definitions of active citizenship.[12] However, the presence of aliens within the national community suggests that "citizenship's threshold and its substantive character are, in fact, deeply interwoven." Illegal aliens, who comprise a caste that lives and works outside of citizenship, pose an even greater predicament and challenge for liberal democratic society.[13]

Immigration Policy and the Production of Racial Knowledge

A second, related theme of this [work] concerns how restrictive immigration laws produced new categories of racial difference. The construction of racial hierarchies has been, of course, an ongoing project in American history since the colonial period. If we understand that race is not a biological fact but a socially constructed category of difference, it should also be emphasized that, as Paul Gilroy states, "there is no racism in general."[14] Race is always historically specific. At times, a confluence of economic, social, cultural, and political factors has impelled major shifts in society's understanding (and construction) of race and its constitutive role in national identity formation. The Civil War was obviously one of those times; the present multicultural moment is another. I argue that the 1920s was also an extraordinary time when immigration policy realigned and hardened racial categories in the law.

The national origins quota system classified Europeans as nationalities and assigned quotas in a hierarchy of desirability, but at the same time the law deemed all Europeans to be part of a white race, distinct from those considered to be not white. Euro-American identities turned both on ethnicity—that is, a nationality-based cultural identity that is defined as capable of transformation and assimilation—and on a racial identity defined by whiteness.

The 1924 Johnson–Reed Act also excluded from immigration Chinese, Japanese, Indians, and other Asians on grounds that they were racially ineligible for naturalized citizenship, a condition that was declared by the Supreme Court in the 1920s.[15] These developments resolved the legal ambiguities and conflicts over the racial status of Asians that had vexed the law since their arrival in the mid-nineteenth century. They also simultaneously solidified the legal boundaries of the "white race."[16]

The immigration laws during the 1920s did not assign numerical quotas to Mexicans, but the enforcement provisions of restriction—notably visa requirements and border-control policies—profoundly affected Mexicans, making them the single largest group of illegal aliens by the late 1920s. The actual and imagined association of Mexicans with illegal immigration was part of an emergent Mexican "race problem," which also witnessed the application of Jim Crow segregation laws to Mexicans in the Southwest, especially in Texas, and, at the federal level, the creation of "Mexican" as a separate racial category in the census.[17]

Thus, unlike Euro-Americans, whose ethnic and racial identities became uncoupled during the 1920s, Asians' and Mexicans' ethnic and racial identities remained conjoined. The legal racialization of these ethnic groups' national origin cast them as permanently foreign and unassimilable to the nation. I argue that these racial formations produced "alien citizens"—Asian Americans and Mexican Americans born in the United States with formal U.S. citizenship but who remained alien in the eyes of the nation.

Alien citizenship was not a new phenomenon, nor was it just the consequence of immigration legislation. Indeed, alien citizenship flowed directly from the histories of conquest, colonialism, and semicolonialism that constituted the United States' relations with Mexico and in Asia. Those histories indelibly stamped the social experiences and subordination of Mexicans and Asians with racisms that were, as cultural critic Lisa Lowe described, the "material trace of history." For Chinese and other Asians, alien citizenship was the invariable consequence of racial exclusion from immigration and naturalized citizenship. For Mexicans, the concept of alien citizenship captured the condition of being a foreigner in one's former native land. The immigration experiences and racial formations of Asians and Mexicans in twentieth-century America cannot be understood apart from these legacies of conquest and colonialism.[18]

In one sense alien citizenship spoke to a condition of racial otherness, a badge of foreignness that could not be shed. But alien citizenship was not only a racial metaphor. While not strictly a legal term, the concept underwrote both formal and informal structures of racial discrimination and was at the core of major, official race policies, notably the repatriation of 400,000 persons of Mexican descent during the Great Depression (of which half were estimated to be U.S. citizens) and the internment of 120,000 persons of Japanese ancestry during World War II (two-thirds of them citizens).[19]

The racial formations of Asians and Mexicans in the 1920s were particularly significant because they modified a racial map of the nation that had been marked principally by the contours of white and black and that had denoted race as a sectional problem. But that changed with the Great Migration of African Americans, and to a lesser extent, Mexicans, to northern cities during the World War I era. Immigration law was part of an emergent race policy that was broader, more comprehensive, and national in scope. In addition to immigration law, that policy involved the legal justification for de facto segregation in the North and the completion of the legal process of forced assimilation of American Indians.[20]

In this period the concept of race itself also changed, from late-nineteenth-century race science, which centered on physiognomic difference and hierarchy, to twentieth-century racial ideas that linked race to both physiognomy and nationality. Modern racial ideology depended increasingly on the idea of complex cultural, national, and physical *difference* more than on simple biological hierarchy.[21]

The system of racial classification and regulation that emerged in the 1920s should be seen in the context of a longer historical process of legal configuring within the national state, which had struggled since the late nineteenth century to find a racial logic capable of circumventing the imperative of equality established by the Fourteenth Amendment. That process involved a double move. On the one hand the law separated public and private spheres, prohibiting racial discrimination by the state but permitting it in private relations. On the other hand Congress and the courts sneaked racial distinctions into public policy through doctrinal rationalizations like "separate but equal."[22] During the 1920s the legal traditions that had justified racial discrimination against African Americans were extended to other ethnoracial groups in immigration law through the use of euphemism ("aliens ineligible to citizenship") and the invention of new categories of identity ("national origins"). . . .

The interactions, conflicts, and negotiations between migrants, the state, and society that animate the history in this [work], I argue, are integral to the historical processes that define and redefine the nation. I do not believe that immigrants are external to the nation but that, as Homi Bhabha wrote, "the migrants, the minorities, the diasporic come to change the history of the nation."[23]

NOTES

1. "Immigrant Ex-Cons Fight Deportation," *Houston Chronicle,* May 6, 2001, sec. A, 1. Illegal Immigration Reform and Immigrant Responsibility Act of 1996 (Division C of Public Law 104-208, 110 Stat. 3009); Antiterrorism and Effective Death Penalty Act of 1996 (Public Law 104-132, 110 Stat. 1214). Since 1996, immigration law no longer refers to deportation but calls the procedure removal . I use deportation for purposes of historical continuity. In June 2001 the U.S. Supreme Court overturned the IIRIRA's provisions that applied deportation retroactively to crimes that were not deportable offenses when they were committed. *INS v. St. Cyr,* 121 S. Ct. 2271 (2001).

2. Letter, James Houghterling to Sen. James Lewis, April 20, 1938, file 55819/402B, box 75, accession 58A734, U.S. Immigration and Naturalization Service, RG (Record Group) 85, National Archives, Washington, DC.

3. William Flores and Rina Benmayor, eds., *Latino Cultural Citizenship: Claiming Identity, Space, and Rights* (Boston: Beacon Press, 1996), 267. For other perspectives on cultural citizenship, see Aihwa Ong, "Cultural Citizenship as Subject Making: Immigrants Negotiate Racial and Cultural Boundaries in the United States," *Current Anthropology* 35 (1996): 737–62; Aihwa Ong and Donald Nonini, eds., *Undergrounded Empires: The Cultural Politics of Modern Transnationalism* (New York: Routledge, 1997); Lok Siu, "Diasporic Cultural Citizenship: Chineseness and Belonging in Panama and Central America," *Social Text* 69, no. 19 (Winter 2001): 7–28. On transnational communities, see, for example, Linda Basch, Nina Glick Schiller, and Christina Blanc, *Nations Unbound: Transnational Projects, Postcolonial Predicaments and Deterritorialized Nation-States* (Langhorne, PA: Gordon and

Breach, 1993); Robert C. Smith, "Transnational Localities: Community, Technology and the Politics of Membership within the Context of Mexico and U.S. Migration," in *Transnationalism from Below,* ed. Michael Peter Smith and Luis Eduardo Guarnizo (New Brunswick, NJ: Transaction, 1998).

4. Act of May 25, 1924 (43 Stat. 153); named for its sponsors, Rep. Albert Johnson (R-Wash.) and Sen. David Reed (R-Penn.).

5. Thomas Archdeacon, *Becoming American: An Ethnic History* (New York: Free Press, 1988); Philip Gleason, "American Identity and Americanization," in *Harvard Encyclopedia of American Ethnic Groups,* ed. Stephen Therstrom (Cambridge, MA: Harvard University Press, 1980), 31–58; Kathleen Neils Conzen, et al., "The Invention of Ethnicity: A Perspective from the USA," *Journal of American Ethnic History* 12 (Fall 1992): 3–41; Russell Kazal, "Revisiting Assimilation: The Rise, Fall and Reappraisal of a Concept in American History," *American Historical Review* 100, no. 2 (April 1995): 437–71; Gary Gerstle, *Working-Class Americanism: The Politics of Labor in a Textile City, 1914–1960* (Princeton: Princeton University Press, 2002 [1989]); James Barrett, "Americanization from the Bottom Up: Immigration and the Remaking of the Working Class in the U.S., 1880–1930," *Journal of American History* 79, no. 3 (December 1992): 996–1020; Lizabeth Cohen, *Making a New Deal: Industrial Workers in Chicago, 1919–1930* (New York: Cambridge University Press, 1990).

6. Keith Fitzgerald, *The Face of the Nation: Immigration, the State, and National Identity* (Stanford: Stanford University Press, 1996); Desmond King, Making Americans: Immigration, Race, and the Origins of Diverse Democracy (Cambridge, MA: Harvard University Press, 2000); Aristide Zolberg, A Nation by Design? Immigration Policy in the Fashioning of America (Cambridge, MA: Harvard University Press and Russell Sage Foundation, 2004).

7. Rogers Brubaker, "Citizenship and Naturalization: Politics and Policies," in *Immigration and the Politics of Citizenship in Liberal Democratic Societies,* ed. Rogers Brubaker (Lanham, MD: University Press of America, 1989), 121; Lisa Lowe, *Immigrant Acts: On Asian American Cultural Politics* (Durham: Duke University Press, 1996), 6–7, 13–14.

8. Bonnie Honig, *Democracy and the Foreigner* (Princeton: Princeton University Press, 2001), 75.

9. The residency requirements for naturalization varied during the first years of the republic; the five-year period was set by the Naturalization Act of 1802. See James Kettner, *The Development of American Citizenship, 1608–1870* (Chapel Hill: University of North Carolina Press, 1978), 245–46. However, eligibility for citizenship was limited to "free white persons" (Nationality Act of 1790) and to "persons of African nativity and descent" (Nationality Act of 1870) until the McCarran-Walter Immigration and Naturalization Act of 1952 repealed all racial requirements for citizenship. National citizenship to all those born in the United States was granted by the Fourteenth Amendment and upheld in *United States v. Wonk Kim Ark,* 169 U.S. 649 (1898); equal protection for all persons was upheld in *Yick Wo v. Hopkins,* 118 U.S. 356 (1886).

10. Hiroshi Motomura, "The Curious Evolution of Immigration Law: Procedural Surrogates for Substantive Constitutional Rights," *Columbia Law Review* 92 (1992): 1625–1704; Linda Bosniak, "Membership, Equality, and the Difference That Alienage Makes," *New York University Law Review* 69 (1994):1047–1149; Alexander Bickel, *The Morality of Consent* (New Haven: Yale University Press, 1975), 54; Peter Schuck, "Membership in the Liberal Polity: The Devaluation of American Citizenship," in Brubaker, *Immigration and the Politics of Citizenship in Liberal Democratic Societies,* 62–63.

11. Brubaker, "Citizenship and Naturalization," 99, 109.

12. Linda Bosniak, "Universal Citizenship and the Problem of Alienage," *Northwestern University Law Review* 94, (2000): 963–1147. On citizenship scholarship, see, for example, Michael Walzer, *Spheres of Justice: A Defense of Pluralism and Equality* (New York: Basic Books, 1983); Iris Marion Young, *Justice and the Politics of Difference* (Princeton: Princeton University Press, 1990); Will Kymlicka, *Multicultural Citizenship: A Liberal Theory of Minority Rights* (New York: Oxford University Press, 1995); Nancy Fraser and Linda Gordon, "Civil Citizenship against Social Citizenship?: On the Ideology of Contract-versus-Charity," in *The Condition of Citizenship,* ed. Bart van Steenbergen (London: Sage, 1994), 90–107; David Hollinger, *Postethnic America: Beyond Multiculturalism* (New York: Basic Books, 1995); Lauren Berlant, *The Queen of America Goes to Washington City: Essays on Sex and Citizenship* (Durham: Duke University Press, 1997); Yasemin Soysal, *Limits of Citizenship: Migrants and Post-national Membership in Europe* (Chicago: University of Chicago Press, 1994). See also Will Kymlicka and Wayne Norman, "Return of the Citizen: A Survey of Recent Work on Citizenship Theory," *Ethics* 104 (1994): 352–81. On achievement of universal citizenship, see Judith Shklar, *American Citizenship: The Quest for Inclusion* (Cambridge, MA: Harvard University Press, 1991); Rogers M. Smith, *Civic Ideals: Conflicting Visions of Citizenship in U.S. History* (New Haven: Yale University Press, 1997); Charles Kesler, "The Promise of American Citizenship," in *Immigration and Citizenship in the Twenty-First Century,* ed. Noah M. J. Pickus (Lanham, MD: University Press of America, 1998), 3–39.

13. Bosniak, "Universal Citizenship," 965.

14. Paul Gilroy, "One Nation under a Groove: The Cultural Politics of 'Race' and Racism in Britain," in *The Anatomy of Racism,* ed. David Theo Goldberg (New York: Routledge, 1990), 265.

15. *Ozawa v. United States,* 260 U.S. 178 (1922), and *United States v. Thind,* 261 U.S. 204 (1923). Related cases in 1923 upheld state laws proscribing agricultural land ownership by aliens ineligible to citizenship (*Terrance v. Thompson,* 263 U.S. 197; 263 U.S. 326); also in this period *Gong Lum v. Rice,* 275 U.S. 78 (1927) upheld a Mississippi law that deemed Chinese ineligible to attend white schools.

16. Ian Haney-López, *White by Law: The Legal Construction of Race* (New York: New York University Press, 1995).

17. David Montenajo, *Anglos and Mexicans in the Making of Texas, 1836–1986* (Austin: University of Texas Press, 1987); David Gutíerrez, Walls and Mirrors: Mexican Americans, Mexican Immigrants, and the Politics of Ethnicity (Berkeley: University of California Press, 1995). The "Mexican" race category in the census was short lived.

18. Lowe, *Immigrant Acts,* 26; George Sánchez, "Race, Nation and Culture in Recent Immigration Studies," *Journal of American Ethnic History* (Summer 1999); 66–83. U.S. relations with Japan were not colonial but, rather, relations of competing colonialisms.

19. For discussion on racialization of Asian Americans in law, see also Neil T. Gotanda, "Citizenship Nullification and the Impossibility of Asian American Politics," in *Asian Americans and Politics: Perspectives, Experiences, Prospects,* ed. Gordon H. Chang (Washington, DC: Woodrow Wilson Center Press, and Stanford: Stanford University Press, 2001); Robert S. Chang, *Disoriented* (New York: New York University Press, 1999).

20. Michael Omi and Howard Winant, *Racial Formation in the United States from the 1960s to the 1990s* (New York: Routledge, 1994), 55. The United States Supreme Court would not sanction de jure segregation in the North, but it did legitimate de facto segregation based on free market principles in *Corrigan v. Buckley,* which upheld the use of racial covenants in real property. *Buchanan v. Warley,* 245 U.S. 60 (1917), *Corrigan v. Buckley,*

271 U.S. 323 (1926). See Gilbert Orofsky, *Harlem, the Making of a Ghetto: Negro New York, 1890–1930* (New York, 1968); Donald Massey and Nancy Denton, *American Apartheid: Segregation and the Making of the Underclass* (Cambridge, MA: Harvard University Press, 1993). The Indian Citizenship Act of 1924, which declared all Native American Indians to be American citizens, completed the process of "assimilation" that stripped Native American Indians of their sovereignty. Citizenship in the case of Indians, however, was circumscribed by their continued status as wards, a legal status that codified their presumed racial backwardness. Act of June 2, 1924 (43 Stat. 253). See Frederick Hoxie, *A Final Promise: The Campaign to Assimilate the Indians, 1880–1920* (Cambridge: Cambridge University Press, 1995 [1984]), 236–37.

21. Paul Gilroy, *The Black Atlantic* (Cambridge, MA: Harvard University Press, 1992), 9–11. See also John Haller, *Outcasts from Evolution: Scientific Attitudes towards Racial Inferiority, 1859–1900* (Urbana: University of Illinois Press, 1971).

22. *Civil Rights Cases,* 109 U.S. 3 (1883); *Plessy v. Ferguson,* 163 U.S. 537 (1896); Neil Gotanda, "A Critique of 'Our Constitution Is Color-Blind,'" *Stanford Law Review* 44 (1991): 1–68.

23. Homi Bhabha, *The Location of Culture* (New York: Routledge, 1994), 169–70.

3 Los Intersticios: Recasting Moving Selves

Evelyn Alsultany

> Ethnicity in such a world needs to be recast so that our moving selves can be
> acknowledged. . . . Who am I? When am I? The questions that are asked in the street,
> of my identity, mold me. Appearing in the flesh, I am cast afresh, a female of color—
> skin color, hair texture, clothing, speech, all marking me in ways that I could scarcely
> have conceived of.
>
> —MEENA ALEXANDER

I'm in a graduate class at the New School in New York City. A white female sits next
to me and we begin "friendly" conversation. She asks me where I'm from. I reply that
I was born and raised in New York City and return the question. She tells me she is
from Ohio and has lived in New York for several years. She continues her inquiry:
"Oh . . . well, how about your parents?" (I feel her trying to map me onto her narrow cartography; New York is not a sufficient answer. She analyzes me according to
binary axes of sameness and difference. She detects only difference at first glance, and
seeks to pigeonhole me. In her framework, my body is marked, excluded, not from
this country. A seemingly "friendly" question turns into a claim to land and belonging.) "My father is Iraqi and my mother Cuban," I answer. "How interesting. Are you
a U.S. citizen?"

I am waiting for the NYC subway. A man also waiting asks me if I too am Pakistani.
I reply that I'm part Iraqi and part Cuban. He asks if I am Muslim, and I reply that I
am Muslim. He asks me if I am married, and I tell him I'm not. In cultural camaraderie he leans over and says that he has cousins in Pakistan available for an arranged
marriage if my family so desires. (My Cubanness, as well as my own relationship to
my cultural identity, evaporates as he assumes that Arab plus Muslim equals arranged
marriage. I can identify: he reminds me of my Iraqi relatives and I know he means
well.) I tell him that I'm not interested in marriage but thank him for his kindness.
(I accept his framework and respond accordingly, avoiding an awkward situation in
which he realizes that I am not who he assumes I am, offering him recognition and
validation for his [mis]identification.)

I am in a New York City deli waiting for my bagel to toast. The man behind the
counter asks if I'm an Arab Muslim (he too is Arab and Muslim). I reply that yes, I am
by part of my father. He asks my name, and I say, "Evelyn." In utter disdain, he tells
me that I could not possibly be Muslim; if I were truly Muslim I would have a Muslim
name. What was I doing with such a name? I reply (after taking a deep breath and

Copyright © 2002. From *This Bridge We Call Home*, Gloria E. Anzaldúa and AnaLouise Keating, eds.
Reproduced by permission of Taylor and Francis Group, LLC, a division of Informa plc.

telling myself that it's not worth getting upset over) that my Cuban mother named me and that I honor my mother. He points to the fact that I'm wearing lipstick and have not changed my name, which he finds to be completely inappropriate and despicable, and says that I am a reflection of the decay of the Arab Muslim in America.

I'm on an airplane flying from Miami to New York. I'm sitting next to an Ecuadorian man. He asks me where I'm from. I tell him. He asks me if I'm more Arab, Latina, or American, and I state that I'm all of the above. He says that's impossible. I must be more of one ethnicity than another. He determines that I am not really Arab, that I'm more Latina because of the camaraderie he feels in our speaking Spanish.

I am in Costa Rica. I walk the streets and my brown skin and dark hair blend in with the multiple shades of brown around me. I love this first-time experience of blending in! I walk into a coffee shop for some café con leche, and my fantasy of belonging is shattered when the woman preparing the coffee asks me where I'm from. I tell her that I was born and raised in New York City by a Cuban mother and an Arab father. She replies, "Que eres una gringa."

I am shocked by the contextuality of identity: that my body is marked as gringa in Costa Rica, as Latina in some U.S. contexts, Arab in others, in some times and spaces not adequately Arab, or Latina, or "American," and in other contexts simply as *other.*

My body becomes marked with meaning as I enter public space. My identity fractures as I experience differing dislocations in multiple contexts. Sometimes people otherize me, sometimes they identify with me. Both situations can be equally problematic. Those who otherize me fail to see a shared humanity and those who identify with me fail to see difference; my Arab or Muslim identity negates my Cuban heritage. Identification signifies belonging or home, and I pretend to be that home for the mistaken person. It's my good deed for the day (I know how precious it can be to find a moment of familiarity with a stranger). The bridge becomes my back as I feign belonging, and I become that vehicle for others, which I desire for myself. Although it is illusory, I do identify with the humanity of the situation—the desire to belong in this world, to be understood. But the frameworks used to (mis)read my body, to disconnect me, wear on me. I try to develop a new identity. What should I try to pass for next time? Perhaps I'll just say I'm Cuban to those who appear to be Arab or South Asian. A friend suggests I say I'm an Italian from Brooklyn. I wonder if I could successfully pass for that. Ethnicity needs to be recast so that our moving selves can be acknowledged.

NOTES

I would like to thank Marisol Negrón, Alexandra Lang, María Helena Rueda, Ericka Beckman, Karina Hodoyan, Sara Rondinel, Jessi Aaron, and Cynthia María Paccacerqua for their feedback in our writing seminar at Stanford University with Mary Pratt. I would especially like to thank Mary Pratt for her invaluable feedback, and AnaLouise Keating and Gloria Anzaldúa for their thoughtful editing.

4 For Many Latinos, Racial Identity Is More Culture than Color

Mireya Navarro

Every decade, the Census Bureau spends billions of dollars and deploys hundreds of thousands of workers to get an accurate portrait of the American population. Among the questions on the census form is one about race, with 15 choices, including "some other race."

More than 18 million Latinos checked this "other" box in the 2010 census, up from 14.9 million in 2000. It was an indicator of the sharp disconnect between how Latinos view themselves and how the government wants to count them. Many Latinos argue that the country's race categories—indeed, the government's very conception of identity—do not fit them.

The main reason for the split is that the census categorizes people by race, which typically refers to a set of common physical traits. But Latinos, as a group in this country, tend to identify themselves more by their ethnicity, meaning a shared set of cultural traits, like language or customs.

So when they encounter the census, they see one question that asks them whether they identify themselves as having Hispanic ethnic origins and many answer it as their main identifier. But then there is another question, asking them about their race, because, as the census guide notes, "people of Hispanic, Latino or Spanish origin may be of any race," and more than a third of Latinos check "other."

This argument over identity has gained momentum with the growth of the Latino population, which in 2010 stood at more than 50 million. Census Bureau officials have acknowledged that the questionnaire has a problem and say they are wrestling with how to get more Latinos to pick a race. In 2010, they tested different wording in questions and last year they held focus groups, with a report on the research scheduled to be released by this summer.

Some experts say officials are right to go back to the drawing table. "Whenever you have people who can't find themselves in the question, it's a bad question," said Mary C. Waters, a sociology professor at Harvard who specializes in the challenges of measuring race and ethnicity.

The problem is more than academic—the census data on race serves many purposes, including determining the makeup of voting districts, and monitoring discriminatory practices in hiring and racial disparities in education and health. When respondents do not choose a race, the Census Bureau assigns them one, based on factors like the racial makeup of their neighborhood, inevitably leading to a less accurate count.

From *The New York Times,* January 14, 2012. Copyright © 2012 The New York Times. All rights reserved. Used by permission and protected by the Copyright Laws of the United States. The printing, copying, redistribution, or retransmission of this Content without express written permission is prohibited.

Latinos, who make up close to 20 percent of the American population, generally hold a fundamentally different view of race. Many Latinos say they are too racially mixed to settle on one of the government-sanctioned standard races—white, black, American Indian, Alaska native, native Hawaiian, and a collection of Asian and Pacific Island backgrounds.

Some regard white or black as separate demographic groups from Latino. Still others say Latinos are already the equivalent of another race in this country, defined by a shared set of challenges.

"The issues within the Latino community—language, immigration status—do not take into account race," said Peter L. Cedeño, 43, a lawyer and native New Yorker born to Dominican immigrants. "We share the same hurdles."

At a time when many multiracial Americans are proudly asserting their mixed-race identity, many Latinos, an overwhelmingly blended population with Indian, European, African and other roots, are sidestepping or ignoring questions of race.

Erica Lubliner, who has fair skin and green eyes—legacies of her Jewish father and her Mexican mother—said she was so "conflicted" about the race question on the census form that she left it blank.

Ms. Lubliner, a recent graduate of the medical school at the University of California, Los Angeles, in her mid-30s, was only 9 when her father died, and she grew up steeped in the language and culture of her mother. She said she has never identified with "the dominant culture of white." She believes her mother is a mix of white and Indian. "Believe me, I am not a confused person," she said. "I know who I am, but I don't necessarily fit the categories well."

Alejandro Farias, 23, from Brownsville, Tex., a supervisor for a freight company, sees himself simply as Latino. His ancestors came from the United States, Mexico and Portugal. When pressed, he checked "some other race."

"Race to me gets very confusing because we have so many people from so many races that make up our genealogical tree," he said.

Yet race matters. How Latinos identify themselves—and how the census counts them—affects the political clout of Latinos and other minority groups. Some studies have found that African-Latinos tend to be significantly more supportive of government-sponsored health care and much less supportive of the death penalty than Latinos who identify as white, a rift that is also found in the broader white and black populations.

This racial effect "weakens the political effectiveness of Latinos as a group," said Gary M. Segura, a political science professor at Stanford who has conducted some of the research.

A majority of Latinos identify themselves as white. Among them is Fiordaliza A. Rodriguez, 40, a New York lawyer who says she considers herself white because "I am light-skinned" and that is how she is viewed in her native Dominican Republic.

But she says there is no question that she is seen as different from the white majority in this country. Ms. Rodriguez recalled an occasion in a courtroom when a white lawyer assumed she was the court interpreter. She surmised the confusion had to do with ethnic stereotyping, "no matter how well you're dressed."

Some of the latest research, however, shows that many Latinos—like Irish and Italian immigrants before them—drop the Latino label to call themselves simply "white." A study published last year in the *Journal of Labor Economics* found that the parents of more than a quarter of third-generation children with Mexican ancestry do not identify their children as Latino on census forms.

Most of this ethnic attrition occurs among the offspring of parents or grandparents married to non-Mexicans, usually non-Hispanic whites. These Latinos tend to have high education, high earnings and high levels of English fluency. That means that many successful Latinos are no longer present in statistics tracking Latino economic and social progress across generations, hence many studies show little or no progress for third-generation Mexican immigrants, said Stephen J. Trejo, an economist at the University of Texas at Austin and co-author of the study.

And a more recent study by University of Southern California researchers found that more than two million people, or 6 percent of those who claimed any type of Latin American ancestry on census surveys, did not ultimately identify as Latino or Hispanic. The trend was more prevalent among those of mixed parentage, who spoke only English and who identified as white, black or Asian when asked their race.

James Paine, whose father is half Mexican-American, said it never occurred to him to claim a Latino identity. Mr. Paine, 25, the owner of a real estate investment management company in La Jolla, Calif., spent summers with his Mexican-American aunt and attends his father's big family reunions every year (his mother is white of Irish and French descent). But he says he does not speak Spanish or live in a Latino neighborhood.

"If the question is 'What's your heritage?' I'd say Irish-Mexican," he said. "But the question is 'What are you?' and the answer is I'm white."

On the other side of the spectrum are black Latinos, who say they feel the sting of racism much the same as other blacks. A sense of racial pride has been emerging among many black Latinos who are now coming together in conferences and organizations.

Miriam Jimenez Roman, 60, a scholar on race and ethnicity in New York, says that issues like racial profiling of indigenous-looking and dark-skinned Latinos led her to appear in a 30-second public service announcement before the 2010 census encouraging Latinos of African descent to "check both: Latino and black." "When you sit on the subway, you just see a black person, and that's really what determines the treatment," she said. The 2010 census showed 1.2 million Latinos who identified as black, or 2.5 percent of the Hispanic population.

Over the decades, the Census Bureau has repeatedly altered how it asks the race question, and on the 2010 form, it added a sentence spelling out that "Hispanic origins are not races." The change helped steer 5 percent more Latinos away from "some other race," with the vast majority of those choosing the white category.

Still, critics of the census questionnaire say the government must move on from racial distinctions based on 18th-century binary thinking and adapt to Americans' sense of self.

But Latino political leaders say the risk in changing the questions could create confusion and lead some Latinos not to mark their ethnicity, shrinking the overall Hispanic numbers.

Ultimately, said Angelo Falcon, president of the National Institute for Latino Policy and chairman of the Census Advisory Committee on the Hispanic Population, this is not just a tussle over identity, it is a political battle, too.

"It comes down to what yields the largest numbers for which group," he said.

5 Black Ethnics
Race, Immigration, and the Pursuit of the American Dream
Christina M. Greer

A Theory of Black Elevated Minority Status

Before Barack Obama exploded onto the national political scene in 2004, the Republicans, as some may remember, were giddy with excitement over their own special potential candidate for the presidency. In 1992, Colin Powell's name was being thrown around as a possible running mate for then president George H. W. Bush, and in 1995, his name was mentioned as a possible GOP presidential candidate. Powell seemed to have stepped out of a GOP's dream. He was a general in the US Army, and for many whites, he transcended race. Not only had he been quoted on the record as saying, "I ain't that black" (Gates 1997: 84), but he seemed to be the antithesis of Jesse Jackson, the most recent serious black candidate for a party's nomination. Jackson had run for the Democratic nomination for presidency in 1984 and 1988 and was what many in white America viewed as a quintessential African American: descendant of US slavery and the South, a student of the Baptist preaching tradition, a product of a broken home, and a social agitator.[1] General Powell, for many, was a product of arguably one of the most established institutions of American patriotism. He was fair skinned, "articulate," a product of the US military, and a leader in what many viewed as a successful Gulf War. But Powell possessed something else that made him *special*: In the eyes of some of his supporters, he was not African American. For many, it was his Jamaican heritage that made him different, that explained his discipline, professional excellence, and supreme intellect.

Fast forward to 2008, when Barack Obama, the son of a man from Kenya and a woman from Kansas, captivated the hearts of so many Americans. Many of the same conversations began linking Obama and Powell as an ideal presidential candidate, despite not being *really* African American—that is, not a descendant of US slavery and therefore possessing a different relationship with America. I wondered if Obama would have been as attractive to American voters, white voters in particular, if his background were that of a man from Detroit and a woman from Duluth, or a man from Newark and a woman from Nebraska, or a man from Oakland and a woman from Omaha. You see where I am going with this line of thought. The subtle but significant message of his non–African American heritage was a variable both black

Black Ethnics: Race, Immigration, and the Pursuit of the American Dream by Christina M. Greer (2013): pp. 11–12, 20–21, 21–22, 22–23, 24–25, 25–26. © Oxford University Press 2013.

and white voters initially discussed, debated, and ultimately digested. Many voters saw Obama as black, whether his dad was from Kenya or Kentucky. For some voters, when presented with ethnic diversity, Obama's lack of "authenticity" complicated their sense of racial attachment. For others, though, the comparisons to Jesse Jackson were endless. Whereas Jackson was portrayed as obsessed with race and racial politics, specifically black politics, Obama was presented as a "postracial" candidate. Obama had a racial identity that linked him to the black population, but he was different. For many, he did not have the same "racial baggage" as ninth-generation African Americans—the Jesse Jacksons of the world—thus begging the question, what does racial identity and ethnic distinction mean for blacks living in America? . . .

The Blurred Color Line

. . . Over one hundred years ago, caste systems were recognized as "natural" ways of organizing individuals in American society. Rigid castelike systems no longer exist in the United States, but a new type of caste system threatens the country today. It is not one imposed by overt white power subjugating people of color into slave and indentured servant positions; rather, the new caste system that now threatens American democracy comes from within the deeply seated mind-sets of those who were once held in subservient positions. This mind-set is even shared by newly arriving immigrants who possess a knowledge of America's past practices and who strive to position themselves as far from the "bottom" caste as possible. The modern-day caste struggle is most poignantly played out in some of the interactions between native-born black Americans and their black ethnic counterparts who understand the continued burden of the color line and the weight of race in the United States. . . .

At the core, all discussions of race and ethnicity for blacks in America must emphasize the duality that exists for these diverse groups of blacks. Afro-Caribbean and African immigrants living in America have experienced forms of oppression, racism, and subjugation as blacks, even by blacks. For example, residential segregation of blacks has often swiftly introduced black immigrant ethnic groups to the inequities still faced by blacks in the United States. However, this forced integration of native-born blacks and foreign-born blacks, due to segregation, has also produced tensions, mistrust, and competition among black groups (Kasinitz, Battle, and Miyares 2001; Massey and Denton 1988). The historically racist black-white paradigm has extended to black immigrants in many ways. However, this black-white paradigm has also manifested itself in more positive ways for foreign-born blacks. The historical racism and oppression in the United States seems to have either placed Afro-Caribbean and African populations with black Americans, both literally and symbolically, or have treated Afro-Caribbean and African immigrants as different, that is, harder working, smarter, and/or "better" than native-born blacks, what Rogers (2006) defines as "good blacks."

The understanding of race for black newcomers is that racial formation and construction is a largely unique phenomenon applicable to the United States. New immigrants may not easily or readily accept or adhere to the racial categories ascribed to them upon their arrival in the country and therefore cannot (or should not) be expected to automatically accept or identify with the larger black American racial category or group as a whole. Studies have documented Afro-Caribbean populations expressing disillusionment with assimilation in the United States and thereby becoming "black Americans" as opposed to just "Americans," like their white immigrant counterparts (Rogers 2000; Waters 1994; Foner 1987).[2] . . . Once black immigrants arrive in the United States, they become black American, not just American. The concepts of race, identity, and national origin have created a complex set of issues for the individual and for the larger group. . . .

Many immigrant groups share similar obstacles when arriving in the United States. Some scholars have argued that African and Caribbean immigrants may have more in common with other immigrants from across the globe than with native-born black Americans (Portes and Rumbaut 2001). First-generation black immigrants in the United States have faced overwhelming pressures to identify only as "blacks" (Kasinitz 1992; Foner 1987). In fact, they have been described as "invisible immigrants" (Bryce-Laporte 1972), because rather than being contrasted with other immigrants (for example, evaluating Jamaican successes as compared with Chinese), they have been compared most often to black Americans.[3] Because racial phenotype seems to link black ethnics into one racial group, can and will substantive coalitions form? Black groups are clearly grouped together in the United States. However, whether their fates are ultimately linked is part of a larger and constantly changing black ethnic puzzle.

Linked Fates and Coalition Building

Over the past several decades, significant strides have been made by blacks achieving educational success, attaining occupational advancements, and being incorporated into the middle class. However, dark skin is still correlated with poverty in the United States and throughout the globe (Segura and Rodrigues 2006); therefore, class position, societal status, and opportunities for political and economic advancement are in many ways racially assigned in the United States. Race is obviously a physical characteristic that has been used in this country to distinguish a certain group of people with similar phenotypes. This color distinction has led to widespread discrimination and inequities, as Rogers (2006) analyzed, thus lumping phenotypically similar individuals together based on outward identity, without accounting for the existence of differing self-identifications and belief systems.

The racial socialization of people of African descent living in the United States has had distinguishing effects on black populations, one of a "blended" cultural heritage (Larkey, Hecht, and Martin 1993) that emphasizes and connects to African ancestry and representation, as well as subjugation in American culture (Anglin and Whaley 2006). Due to shared skin color with native-born populations, foreign-born black phenotype serves as a basis for discrimination in America (Deaux et al. 2007).

New black immigrants also discover the inequities present in America and the subsequent negotiations with race and identity that directly affect their pursuits of becoming "American" without the mandatory modifier "black." For foreign-born blacks, their American status has a permanent "black" modifier attached to it. The permanent prefix aids in preventing native-born and foreign-born populations from attaining the same American incorporation experienced by other nonblack immigrants. Black racial classification has affected first and second-generation black ethnics in that they did not experience the same processes of assimilation as previous white immigrant populations (Waters 1998; Kinder and Sanders 1996). . . . Thus, black immigrants seek ways to reduce and possibly diminish the negative effects of the minority status imposed on their American status. It is because of this linking of black immigrants to native-born blacks that in-group fighting and competition decreases opportunities for substantive coalition building. As Afro-Caribbean and African black populations are occasionally promoted to elevated minority status over native-born black populations by whites, coalitional efforts are severely jeopardized and undermined within the larger black group. In that, one group is promoted and their interests are advanced at the expense and exclusion of others.[4] . . .

All of the Blacks Are American. All of the Immigrants Are Latino. But Some of Us Are . . . ?

Black Americans have largely been categorized in comparison to whites, based on region, political affiliation, class, and education levels. Segura and Rodrigues (2006: 376) argued that the "historical construction of a racial dynamic that is almost exclusively binary, i.e., black and white . . . [and] racial and ethnic interactions between Anglos and other minority groups are assumed to mimic—to some degree—the black-white experience." Simply put, Segura and Rodrigues argued that the "black-white paradigm is no longer sufficient to provide genuine understanding of the political circumstances and experiences of all nonwhite groups" (ibid.: 391). . . .

Several nonblack and nonwhite immigrant groups have expressed feelings of an "in-between" status in which they are "not Black but not White" (Perlmann and Waldinger 1997: 905) or "native born, and not black" (Cordero-Guzman, Smith, and Grosfoguel 2001: 6; Smith 1996). This in-between status for nonblack and non-white immigrants extends to black immigrants as well, thereby creating a complex duality in defining race, place, and status in American society.[5] Relationships pertaining to electoral behaviors, partisanship, group mobilization, and other group politics cannot necessarily easily translate into similar black immigrant experiences and relationships with whites and other nonblack populations (Leighley and Vedlitz 1999). According to the US census, the face of black America now includes over 1.5 million immigrants from African nations and over 3.5 million black immigrants from the Caribbean, representing close to 10 percent of the total black population (US Census Bureau 2010).

How blacks in America imagine and create black ethnic coalitions directly relates to how scholars can apply these multifaceted relationships to numerous other ethnic communities. The physical characteristics that seem to link native-born and immigrant blacks and the inequities of resources that continue to affect black peoples in America have led to what Bobo and Hutchings (1996) label as in-group superiorities, elements of ethnocentrism, and overall group hostilities. The limited access to larger political and economic goals creates intraracial tensions and resentments between native-born and newcomer populations. However, the competition among black groups jockeying for anything but last place in the social order has also created a link, bond, or even an understanding of the role of blackness in American society. Descriptive representation—that is, shared characteristics along racial and ethnic (and gender) lines—helps promote feelings of "solidarity, familiarity, and self-esteem among members of that respective group" (Junn and Masuoka 2008: 731; see also Dovi 2002; Mansbridge 2003; Pitkin 1967). The jockeying for economic and political placement in civil society is intraracial (between black ethnic groups) as well as extraracial (between other minority, immigrant, and ethnic groups). It is because of the systemic racism that has occurred, and (to the surprise of many black immigrants) still occurs, that a sense of black racial alliance can be measured. . . .

NOTES

1. This label was applied to Jackson for his many protests pertaining to civil rights, equal rights, corporate divestment from South Africa, housing equity, etc.

2. There is a host of literature that outlines how Jewish, Italian, Irish, and other white ethnic populations became "white." However, although their paths to incorporation may have begun with an identification with blacks during the early stages of assimilation, these immigrant groups were able to transcend ethnicity and identify racially, thus shedding light on the fluidity of ethnicity and the permanence of race. Whites are grouped into a homogeneous category. Sipress (1997: 181) comments: "The 'whitening' of Irish-Americans provides an example of a marginal social group that embraced a racial identity to advance its own interests." The "whitening" of the Irish race is discussed by Ignatiev (1995: 1), who notes that "whites" are "those who partake of the privileges of the white skin in this society. Its most wretched members share a status higher, in certain respects, than that of the most exalted persons excluded from it." Similar assimilation tactics were used by Italian and Jewish immigrants in the nineteenth and twentieth centuries as well (Fears 2003). These ethnic groups often used party politics and coalition building to bridge the cultural divide (Logan 2003). However, the political inclusion, participation, and ultimate assimilation of Irish, Italian, and Jewish immigrants has also been largely due to the color line in America. Whereas these immigrants were not considered white at some point in time, the color line shifted, and inclusion followed suit.

3. Multiracial coalitions primarily focus on the issues of racial and ethnic equality (Hochschild and Rogers 2000). However, this emphasis on equality in the face of diverse histories and negotiations with assimilation and incorporation, often leading to groups fragmenting into competitive factions. Thus, biracial and multiracial coalitions are thought to be unattainable due to past political disagreements, individual attitudes about other groups, and fears among minority groups within the larger group (Tedin and Murray 1994). Intraracial distrust exists among black ethnic populations and has thus contributed to ethnic factions and decreased rates of collective actions (Okamoto 2003). However, possibilities for coalition building will still be greater among groups with a shared racial classification even if

cross-racial migratory narratives may appear more similar. See also Hochschild, Weaver, and Burch 2012.

4. Betancur and Gills (2000) also argue that coalitional efforts are undermined when influential leaders advance only the interests of one group to the exclusion of others. This is most clearly demonstrated in Miami when observing the NAACP and the loss of significant numbers of members of Haitian descent. The defection of Haitian members from the NAACP as well as the National Urban League signaled a disconnect between the black American leadership and predominantly black American membership within these two organizations, and a small but growing population who felt their needs and wants (i.e., increased attention to international issues, specifically issues affecting Haitians both in Haiti and in Florida) were not being addressed by the organization elite.

5. Okamoto (2003) argued that the construction of pan-ethnic boundaries and a pan-ethnic identity affect collective action efforts. Similarly, Padilla (1985) stated that differences in language, culture, and immigration histories also affect organizing capabilities and understandings of a common fate.

6 The Myth of the Model Minority

Noy Thrupkaew

Mali Keo fled Cambodia with her husband and four children in 1992. Several years later, she was still haunted by searing memories of "the killing fields," the forced-labor camps where millions of Cambodians died, victims of Communist despot Pol Pot's quest for a perfect agrarian society. Because of the brutal beatings she suffered at the hands of Pol Pot's Khmer Rouge, she was still wracked with physical pain as well. Traumatized and ailing, uneducated, unskilled, and speaking very little English, Mali Keo (a pseudonym assigned by researchers) could barely support her children after her husband abandoned the family.

And now she may not even have public assistance to fall back on, because the 1996 welfare-reform act cut off most federal benefits to immigrants and subsequent amendments have not entirely restored them. In what was supposed to be the land of her salvation, Mali Keo today is severely impoverished. Living in a hard-pressed neighborhood of Philadelphia, she struggles with only mixed success to keep her children out of trouble and in school.

The Southeast Asia Resource Action Center (SEARAC), an advocacy group in Washington, estimates that more than 2.2 million Southeast Asians now live in the United States. They are the largest group of refugees in the country and the fastest-growing minority. Yet for most policy makers, the plight of the many Mali Keos has been overshadowed by the well-known success of the Asian immigrants who came before and engendered the myth of the "model minority." Indeed, conservatives have exploited this racial stereotype—arguing that Asians fare well in the United States because of their strong "family values" and work ethic. These values, they say, and not government assistance, are what all minorities need in order to get ahead.

Paradoxically, Southeast Asians—supposedly part of the model minority—may be suffering most from the resulting public policies. They have been left in the hands of underfunded community-assistance programs and government agencies that, in one example of well-intentioned incompetence, churn out forms in Khmer and Lao for often illiterate populations. But fueled by outrage over bad services and a fraying social safety-net, Southeast Asian immigrants have started to embrace that most American of activities, political protest—by pushing for research on their communities, advocating for their rights, and harnessing their political power.

The model-minority myth has persisted in large part because political conservatives are so attached to it. "Asian Americans have become the darlings of the right," said Frank Wu, a law professor at Howard University and the author of *Yellow: Race beyond Black and White.* "The model-minority myth and its depiction of Asian-American success tells a reassuring story about our society working."

Reprinted with permission from *The American Prospect*, vol. 13, no. 7, April 8, 2002. The American Prospect, 11 Beacon Street, Suite 1120, Boston, MA 02108. All rights reserved.

The flip side is also appealing to the right. Because Asian Americans' success stems from their strong families and their dedication to education and hard work, conservatives say, then the poverty of Latinos and African Americans must be explained by their own "values": They are poor because of their nonmarrying, school-skipping, and generally lazy and irresponsible behavior, which government handouts only encourage.

The model-minority myth's "racist love," as author Frank Chin terms it, took hold at a sensitive point in U.S. history: after the 1965 Watts riots and the immigration reforms of that year, which selectively allowed large numbers of educated immigrants into the United States. Highly skilled South and East Asian nurses, doctors, and engineers from countries like India and China began pouring into the United States just as racial tensions were at a fever pitch.

Shortly thereafter, articles like "Success Story of One Minority in the U.S.," published by *U.S. News & World Report* in 1966, trumpeted: "At a time when it is being proposed that hundreds of billions be spent to uplift Negroes and other minorities, the nation's 300,000 Chinese Americans are moving ahead on their own, with no help from anyone else." *Newsweek* in 1971 had Asian Americans "outwhiting the whites." And *Fortune* in 1986 dubbed them a "superminority." As Wu caricatures the model-minority myth in his book:

> Asian Americans vindicate the American Dream. . . . They are living proof of the power of the free market and the absence of racial discrimination. Their good fortune flows from individual self-reliance and community self-sufficiency, not civil-rights activism or government welfare benefits.

A closer look at the data paints another picture, however. If Asian-American households earn more than whites, statistics suggest, it's not because their individual earnings are higher but because Asian Americans live in larger households, with more working adults. In fact, a recent University of Hawaii study found that "most Asian Americans are overeducated compared to whites for the incomes they earn"—evidence that suggests not "family values" but market discrimination.

What most dramatically skews the data, though, is the fact that about half the population of Asian (or, more precisely, Asian-Pacific Islander) Americans is made up of the highly educated immigrants who began arriving with their families in the 1960s. The plight of refugees from Cambodia, Laos, and Vietnam, who make up less than 14 percent of Asian Americans, gets lost in the averaging. Yet these refugees, who started arriving in the United States after 1975, differ markedly from the professional-class Chinese and Indian immigrants who started coming 10 years earlier. The Southeast Asians were fleeing wartime persecution and had few resources. And those disadvantages have had devastating effects on their lives in the United States. The most recent census data available show that 47 percent of Cambodians, 66 percent of Hmong (an ethnic group that lived in the mountains of Laos), 67 percent of Laotians, and 34 percent of Vietnamese were impoverished in 1990—compared with 10 percent of all Americans and 14 percent of all Asian Americans. Significantly, poverty rates among Southeast Asian Americans were much higher than those of even the "nonmodel" minorities: 21 percent of African Americans and 23 percent of Latinos were poor.

Yet despite the clear inaccuracies created by lumping population together, the federal government still groups Southeast Asian refugees under the overbroad category of "Asian" for research and funding purposes. "We've labored under the shadow of this model myth for so long," said Ka Ying Yang, SEARAC's executive director. "There's so little research on us, or we're lumped in with all other Asians, so people don't know the specific needs and contributions of our communities."

To get a sense of those needs, one has to go back to the beginning of the Southeast Asian refugees' story and the circumstances that forced their migration. In 1975, the fall of Saigon sent shock waves throughout Southeast Asia, as communist insurgents toppled U.S.-supported governments in Vietnam and Cambodia. In Laos, where the CIA had trained and funded the Hmong to fight Laotian and Vietnamese communists as U.S. proxies, the communists who took over vowed to purge the country of ethnic Hmong and punish all others who had worked with the U.S. government.

The first refugees to leave Southeast Asia tended to be the most educated and urban, English-speakers with close connections to the U.S. government. One of them was a man who wishes to be identified by the pseudonym John Askulraskul. He spent two years in a Laotian re-education camp—punishment for his ability to speak English, his having been educated, and, most of all, his status as a former employee of the United States Agency for International Development (USAID).

"They tried to brainwash you, to subdue you psychologically, to work you to death on two bowls of rice a day," Askulraskul told me recently.

After being released, he decided to flee the country. He, his sister, and his eldest daughter, five and a half years old, slipped into the Mekong River with a few others. Clinging to an inflated garbage bag, Askulraskul swam alongside their boat out of fear that his weight would sink it.

After they arrived on the shores of Thailand, Askulraskul and his daughter were placed in a refugee camp, where they waited to be reunited with his wife and his two other daughters.

It was not to be.

"My wife tried to escape with two small children. But my daughters couldn't make it"—he paused, drawing a ragged breath—"because the boat sank."

Askulraskul's wife was swept back to Laos, where she was arrested and placed in jail for a month. She succeeded in her next escape attempt, rejoining her suddenly diminished family.

Eventually, with the help of his former boss at USAID, they moved to Connecticut, where Askulraskul found work helping to resettle other refugees. His wife, who had been an elementary-school teacher, took up teaching English as a second language (ESL) to Laotian refugee children. His daughter adjusted quickly and went to school without incident.

Askulraskul now manages a project that provides services for at-risk Southeast Asian children and their families. "The job I am doing now is not only a job," he said. "It is part of my life and my sacrifice. My daughter is 29 now, and I know raising kids in America is not easy. I cannot save everybody, but there is still something I can do."

Like others among the first wave of refugees, Askulraskul considers himself one of the lucky ones. His education, U.S. ties, and English-language ability—everything that set off the tragic chain of events that culminated in his daughters' deaths—proved enormously helpful once he was in the United States.

But the majority of refugees from Southeast Asia had no such advantages. Subsequent waves frequently hailed from rural areas and lacked both financial resources and formal schooling. Their psychological scars were even deeper than the first group's, from their longer years in squalid refugee camps or the killing fields. The ethnic Chinese who began arriving from Vietnam had faced harsh discrimination as well, and the Amerasians—the children of Vietnamese women and U.S. soldiers—had lived for years as pariahs.

Once here, these refugees often found themselves trapped in poverty, providing low-cost labor, and receiving no health or other benefits, while their lack of schooling made decent jobs almost impossible to come by. In 1990, two-thirds of Cambodian, Laotian, and Hmong adults in America had less than a high-school education—compared with 14 percent of whites, 25 percent of African Americans, 45 percent of Latinos, and 15 percent of the general Asian-American population. Before the welfare-reform law cut many of them off, nearly 30 percent of Southeast Asian Americans were on welfare—the highest participation rate of any ethnic group. And having such meager incomes, they usually lived in the worst neighborhoods, with the attendant crime, gang problems, and poor schools.

But shouldn't the touted Asian dedication to schooling have overcome these disadvantages, lifting the refugees' children out of poverty and keeping them off the streets? Unfortunately, it didn't. "There is still a high number of dropouts for Southeast Asians," Yang said. "And if they do graduate, there is a low number going on to higher education."

Their parents' difficulty in navigating American school systems may contribute to the problem. "The parents' lack of education leads to a lack of role models and guidance. Without those things, youth can turn to delinquent behavior and in some very extreme cases, gangs, instead of devoting themselves to education," said Narin Sihavong, director of SEARAC's Successful New Americans Project, which interviewed Mali Keo. "This underscores the need for Southeast Asian school administrators or counselors who can be role models, ease the cultural barrier, and serve as a bridge to their parents."

"Sometimes families have to choose between education and employment, especially when money is tight," said Porthira Chimm, a former SEARAC project director. "And unfortunately, immediate money concerns often win out."

The picture that emerges—of high welfare participation and dropout rates, low levels of education and income—is startlingly similar to the situation of the poorest members of "nonmodel" minority groups. Southeast Asians, Latinos, and African Americans also have in common significant numbers of single-parent families. Largely as a result of the killing fields, nearly a quarter of Cambodian households are headed by single women. Other Southeast Asian families have similar stories. Sihavong's mother, for example, raised him and his five siblings on her own while his father was imprisoned in a Laotian re-education camp.

No matter how "traditional" Southeast Asians may be, they share the fate of other people of color when they are denied access to good education, safe neighborhoods, and jobs that provide a living wage and benefits. But for the sake of preserving the model-minority myth, conservative policy makers have largely ignored the needs of Southeast Asian communities.

One such need is for psychological care. Wartime trauma and "lack of English proficiency, acculturative stress, prejudice, discrimination, and racial hate crimes" place Southeast Asians "at risk for emotional and behavioral problems," according to the U.S. surgeon general's 2001 report on race and mental health. One random sample of Cambodian adults found that 45 percent had post-traumatic stress disorder and 51 percent suffered from depression.

John Askulraskul's past reflects trauma as well, but his education, English-language ability, and U.S. connections helped level the playing field. Less fortunate refugees need literacy training and language assistance. They also need social supports like welfare and strong community-assistance groups. But misled by the model-minority myth, many government agencies seem to be unaware that Southeast Asians require their services, and officials have done little to find these needy refugees or accommodate them. Considering that nearly two-thirds of Southeast Asians say they do not speak English very well and more than 50 percent live in linguistically isolated ethnic enclaves, the lack of outreach and translators effectively denies them many public services.

The problem extends beyond antipoverty programs, as Mali Keo's story illustrates. After her husband left her, she formed a relationship with another man and had two more children. But he beat the family for years, until she asked an organization that served Cambodian refugees to help her file a restraining order. If she had known that a shelter was available, she told her interviewer, even one without Khmer-speaking counselors, she would have escaped much earlier.

Where the government hasn't turned a blind eye, it has often wielded an iron fist. The welfare-reform law of 1996, which cut off welfare, SSI, and food-stamp benefits for most noncitizens—even those who are legal permanent residents—sent Southeast Asian communities into an uproar. Several elderly Hmong in California committed suicide, fearing that they would become burdens to their families. Meanwhile, the lack of literacy programs prevented (and still does prevent) many refugees from passing the written test that would gain them citizenship and the right to public assistance.

"We achieved welfare reform on the backs of newcomers," Frank Wu said. "People said that 'outsiders' don't have a claim to the body politic, and even liberals say we should care for 'our own' first." Few seemed to ask the question posed by sociologist Donald Hernandez: "What responsibility do we have to ensure a basic standard of living for immigrants who have fled their countries as a result of the American government's economic, military, and political involvement there?"

But welfare reform also had a second effect. "It was such a shocking event, it completely galvanized the Southeast Asian community," said Karen Narasaki, executive director of the National Asian Pacific American Legal Consortium. "In different Asian cultures, you have 'the crab who crawls out of the bucket gets pulled back' [and] 'the nail that sticks out gets pounded down.' But in the United States, 'the squeaky wheel gets the grease,' and people had to learn that."

The learning process has been a difficult one. At first, because of their past negative experiences with the United States and their homeland governments, many Southeast Asians feared political involvement. Many saw themselves as non-citizens and second-class "outsiders" with a precarious standing in the United States. But as they have grown more familiar with this country, even noncitizens have started to think of themselves less as refugees in a temporary home and more as "new Americans" who are entitled to shape their destinies through political engagement.

The energy for this new activism grew out of the mutual-assistance associations (MAAs) that have taken root in various Southeast Asian communities. Primarily staffed by people like Askulraskul—the more successful members of the ethnic groups they serve—MAAs form the backbone of support for Southeast Asians, providing, among many other things, child care, job training, school liaisons, and assistance with navigating government bureaucracies.

But the MAAs are facing problems of their own. The funding they used to get from the federal Office of Refugee Resettlement is dwindling. In 1996 new federal guidelines mandated that these funds go exclusively to organizations serving the most recent refugees. (In response, several Southeast Asian MAAs have tried to stay afloat by offering their services to newer refugees from places like Ethiopia and Iraq.) As for outside funding, only 0.3 percent of all philanthropic aid goes to groups that work specifically with Asian-American populations, according to the 1998 edition of *Foundation Giving*. "A lot of people in philanthropy think [that Asians] are doing so well, they don't need help," Narasaki said.

Despite these problems, MAAs and national advocacy organizations like SEARAC have won limited restorations of benefits and food stamps for immigrants. And a significant victory came in 2000, when legislation sponsored by Minnesota Senator Paul Wellstone was adopted: It will allow Hmong veterans—or their widows—from America's "secret war" in Laos to take the U.S. citizenship test in Hmong, with a translator.

One key to the MAAs' success is their networking with other minority-advocacy groups, says Sandy Dang, executive director of Asian American LEAD, an organization based in Washington, that provides a range of services for Vietnamese Americans, including ESL classes, youth mentoring, and parent-support groups.

When Dang founded the organization, she didn't know how to write grant proposals, so she asked the director of a nearby youth center for Latin Americans to provide guidance. "The Latino organizations have a lot of empathy for people starting out," she said. "They understand the refugee-immigrant experience.

"Disadvantaged people share a lot in common," Dang continued, "and we have to help each other. People who are empowered in this country like to play us off each other, like with the model-minority myth. They need the poor and disadvantaged to fight each other. Because if we unite, we can make it difficult for them."

Southeast Asians are disproving the model-minority myth not just with their difficult lives but with their growing insistence that it takes more than "traditional values" and "personal responsibility" to survive in this country. It takes social supports and participation in the legacy of civil rights activism as well.

The refugees and their children are forging their identities as new Americans and are starting to emerge as a political force. At first, Yang said, "we had no time to think about anything else but our communities—and no one was thinking about us. But now we know that what we were grappling with [affects both] me and my neighbor, who might be poor black, Latino, or Asian. We are no longer refugees, we are Americans. And we know what being 'successful' is: It's being someone who is truly aware of the meaning of freedom to speak out."

7 How Does It Feel to Be a Problem?

Moustafa Bayoumi

How does it feel to be a problem? Just over a century ago, W. E. B. Du Bois asked that very question in his American classic *The Souls of Black Folk*, and he offered an answer. "Being a problem is a strange experience," he wrote, "peculiar even," no doubt evoking the "peculiar institution" of slavery. Du Bois composed his text during Jim Crow, a time of official racial segregation that deliberately obscured to the wider world the human details of African-American life. Determined to pull back "the veil" separating populations, he showed his readers a fuller picture of the black experience, including "the meaning of its religion, the passion of its human sorrow, and the struggle of its greater souls."

A century later, Arabs and Muslim Americans are the new "problem" of American society, but there have of course been others. Native Americans, labeled "merciless Indian savages" by the Declaration of Independence, were said to be beyond civilization and able to comprehend only the brute language of force. With the rise of Catholic immigration to the country in the nineteenth century, Irish and Italian Americans were attacked for their religion. They suffered mob violence and frequent accusations of holding papal loyalties above republican values. During World War I, German Americans were loathed and reviled, sauerkraut was redubbed "liberty cabbage," and several states banned the teaching of German, convinced that the language itself promoted un-American values. Between the world wars, anti-Semitism drove Jewish Americans out of universities and jobs and fueled wild and pernicious conspiracy theories concerning warfare and world domination. Japanese Americans were herded like cattle into internment camps during World War II (as were smaller numbers of German, Italian, Hungarian, and Romanian Americans). Chinese Americans were commonly suspected of harboring Communist sympathies during the McCarthy era, frequently losing careers and livelihoods. And Hispanic Americans have long been seen as outsider threats to American culture, even though their presence here predates the formation of the present-day United States.

But since the terrorist attacks of September 11 and the wars in Afghanistan and Iraq, Arabs and Muslims, two groups virtually unknown to most Americans prior to 2001, now hold the dubious distinction of being the first new communities of suspicion after the hard-won victories of the civil-rights era. . . .

In this rocky terrain, young Arab and Muslim Americans are forging their lives as the newest minorities in the American imagination. In their circumstances and out

"Preface," "Afterword," from *How Does It Feel to Be a Problem?* by Moustafa Bayoumi, copyright © 2008 by Moustafa Bayoumi. Used by permission of Penguin Press, an imprint of Penguin Publishing Group, a division of Penguin Random House LLC.

of their actions, they are also shaping the contours of a future American society. And though they don't always succeed in their efforts, the human drama of their predicament has now become a part of what it means to be an American.

The burning question really is whether American society will treat them as equals. The answer is not entirely clear. Simply put, the general public seems divided about the Arabs and Muslims in our midst. On the one hand, the last few years have seen a spirit of inclusion and desire for mutual cooperation spread across the country. Arab and Muslim organizations have matured in this environment, as they engage the general public more openly and fully than before, and the results are evident. Islam is increasingly understood as an American religion—in 2006 the first American Muslim, Keith Ellison, was elected to Congress—and Arab Americans are now frequently acknowledged to be an integral part of the United States. Despite an unwarranted controversy, the first dual-language Arabic-English New York City public high school opened its doors in Brooklyn in 2007. Arabs and Muslims are successfully integrating themselves into the institutional framework of American society.

Yet too many people continue to see Arabs and Muslims in America—particularly the young generation—through narrowed eyes, as enemies living among us. Key members of the political class, an often shrill news media, and a law-enforcement establishment that succumbs to ethnic and religious profiling lead the charge, and Muslims and Arabs are scrutinized for sedition at every turn. Even the most mundane facts of their lives, such as visiting mosques and *shisha* cafés, are now interpreted as something sinister and malevolent. On any given day, popular feelings seem to swing wildly between these poles of fear and acceptance, illustrating what the sociologist Louise Cainkar has called "the apparent paradox of this historical moment: [where] repression and inclusion may be happening at the same time."

It's a strange place to inhabit, and it reveals not only the bifurcated nature of contemporary American society but also the somewhat precarious condition of Arab and Muslim Americans. Because their situation here is ultimately dependent less on what happens on the home front and more on what happens in the Middle East, Muslim and Arab Americans know that their own domestic security and their ability to live full American lives turn on the winds of global conflicts and on America's posture in the world and its policies abroad.

In *The Souls of Black Folk*, W. E. B. Du Bois observed that the treatment of African Americans stands as "a concrete test of the underlying principles of the great republic." In fact, the same can be said about Arabs and Muslims today. However, the principles currently at stake revolve not only around issues of full equality and inclusion, but fundamentally around the consequences that American foreign policy has on domestic civil rights. This condition is not new, and the history is important to remember.

● ● ●

Islam was practiced in this land centuries ago. As far back as the colonial era, many West African Muslims were sold into slavery, making Muslim-American history older than the republic itself. Mustapha, historians tell us, was actually a fairly common name among slaves in colonial South Carolina. For their part, Arabs have been arriving on these shores since the latter part of the nineteenth century, when mostly Christian Arabs from Mount Lebanon packed up their belongings and landed on Ellis Island with an average of $31.85 in their pockets, more than the $12.26 that Polish immigrants carried or the $21.32 of the Greeks. The migrations of both Arabs and Muslims have ebbed and flowed over the years for many reasons, primarily because of the vicissitudes of American immigration law.

In the late nineteenth century, a few years after they began arriving in the United States, Arab Americans established themselves on Washington Street in Lower Manhattan (dubbed "Little Syria"), where they opened stores, published lots of newspapers, lived closely, fought among themselves, and worried about being too different from other Americans or about becoming too American. (The move to Brooklyn happened mostly in the 1940s, with the construction of the Brooklyn Battery Tunnel, which razed much of Little Syria.) The early community thrived mostly as pack peddlers who, after stocking up on jewelry and notions from the stores on Washington Street, would then set off to sell their Holy Land wares, criss-crossing the country, often on foot.

The Washington Street shops spawned a certain amount of nineteenth-century exotic curiosity. An 1892 *New York Tribune* article noted that in them were boxes piled high with gossamer silks, olivewood trinkets, and luxurious satins. "In the midst of all this riot of the beautiful and odd," the article says, "stands the dealer, the natural gravity of his features relaxed into a smile of satisfaction at the wonder and delight expressed by his American visitor. But the vision ends, and with many parting 'salaams' one goes back to the dust and dirt, the noise and bustle" of Washington Street.

The early Arab-American community also encountered ethnic bigotry typical of the period. An 1890 *New York Times* article, for example, manages to illustrate this in a few words, while insulting a few others along the way. "The foreign population in the lower part of this city has of late years been increased by the Arabic-speaking element from the Lebanon, in Syria," it begins. "In clannishness and outlandish manners these people resemble the Chinese and what are called the Diego Italians. Nearly all of them are Maronite [Christians], and in many respects they are inferior to the Chinese and Italians, who do possess a certain amount of self-respect and are willing to work honestly and work hard for a living." The comments seem antiquarian today ("Diego Italians"?), but what we find here, between exoticism and chauvinism, is precisely the nation's early-twentieth-century spirit, which welcomed and reviled foreigners simultaneously. (Like any ethnic story, really, Arab-American history reveals as much or more about *American* culture as it does about immigrant ethnic mores.)

The second phase of Arab-American history dates from around 1909 until 1944. During this period the main issue plaguing the Arab-American community, beside the growing unrest in Palestine, was whether Arabs could naturalize as American citizens. According to the citizenship laws of the period (and until 1952), only "free white persons" could qualify for naturalization, and laws were passed explicitly to bar "Asiatics" from American citizenship. Confronted with this reality, the Arab-American community from across the nation mobilized to prove that they were indeed "free white people," and a series of court rulings eventually affirmed that position. A close examination of these years similarly reveals much less about the genetic makeup of Arabs and much more about America's domestic racial politics between the wars.

When an immigration judge ruled in 1942 that the Yemeni Ahmed Hassan—perhaps the first Arab Muslim to face the court (the others had been Arab Christians)—could not petition for citizenship, the community faced a setback. "Arabs are not white persons within the meaning of the [Immigration] Act," wrote Judge Arthur Tuttle, who heard Hassan's petition, citing Hassan's Muslim background as proof of his racial difference. "Apart from the dark skin of the Arabs," he explained, "it is well known that they are a part of the Mohammedan world and that a wide gulf separates their culture from that of the predominately [sic] Christian peoples of Europe."

Yet less than a year and a half later, the court changed its mind. In 1944, Mohamed Mohriez, "an Arab born in Sanhy, Badan, Arabia," who had been in the United States since 1921, succeeded in his case. Why the change? District Judge Charles E. Wyzanski explained. The "vital interest [of the United States] as a world power" required granting Mohriez's petition, wrote the judge, because it was now necessary "to promote friendlier relations between the United States and other nations and so as to fulfill the promise that we shall treat all men as created equal." Part of these warmer ties included a controversial aid package made in February 1943 under the Lend-Lease Act to Saudi Arabia, as the United States was now eager to secure access to kingdom's massive oil reserves. In other words, as the United States assumed its leadership role on the world stage, the domestic understandings of America's racial-classification system and where Arabs fit within it altered alongside. The exigencies of international politics changed the supposedly immutable facts of the Arab "race," all within the span of seventeen months.

The decision was significant, but it had little effect on the Arab-American community, since immigration was still mostly a closed door until 1965. But when the immigration laws changed again in that year, abandoning the quota system that had favored European immigrants, the community grew substantially with new arrivals. . . . This is also a period when two other important things were happening in the United States: the civil-rights movement and, after 1967, the deepening role of the United States in the Middle East in the wake of the 1967 Arab-Israeli War. Now, unlike in the earlier periods of Arab-American history, it will be American foreign policy and its designs on the Middle East—and not America's domestic ethnic or racial hierarchies—that define the parameters of Arab American life. . . .

• • •

At least since the Second World War and especially since 1967, the United States has become progressively intertwined in the affairs of the Middle East. ("Whoever controls the Middle East controls access to three continents," counseled British ambassador Sir Oliver Franks to American officials in 1950.) But that involvement has been far from benign. For several long decades and through a series of security pacts, arms sales, military engagements, covert actions, and overt wars, the United States has followed a course that supported one dictatorial regime after another, sought control of the natural resources of the region, attempted to forge client states amenable to U.S. interests, and, with the cooperation of native elites, engaged in a policy of neorealist stability at the expense of the aspirations of the vast majority of people who live in the region. . . .

One can debate whether this history since 1967 constitutes an "imperial" or "hegemonic" posture of the United States concerning the Middle East. . . . But since the terrorist attacks of 2001, things have taken a decidedly imperial turn, culminating now in the direct military occupation of a major Arab country, an adventure labeled a "colonial war in the postcolonial age," by former national security adviser Zbigniew Brzezinski. And the political theorists of empire have repeatedly cautioned that the consequences of imperialism can reach far beyond the colony.

In the middle book of *The Origins of Totalitarianism*, titled *Imperialism*, Hannah Arendt explores the political history and implications of imperial rule, noting its bases of authority and actions in the world. She draws attention precisely to many of those pursuits and tactics of imperialism that confront us today: the establishment of penal colonies, the horrors of conquest, wild profiteering, colonial lawlessness, arbitrary and exceptional exercises of power, and the growth of racism along with its political exploitation. Arendt and others also have warned that in the long run imperialism tends not to be exercised solely in some blank, foreign space "out there" but has the dangerous capacity to return home and undermine the nation. She borrows this observation in part from the historian of the British Empire J. A. Hobson, who observed long ago that imperialism corrodes a nation's psyche and endangers its republican institutions. Arendt labels her caution the "boomerang effects" of imperialism.

The current erosion of domestic civil rights in the age of terror ought to be viewed through this lens. This is not only about the ways that torture has been normalized into American culture or how the moral questions raised by maintaining the penal colony at Guantánamo Bay cost the Republic's soul dearly. It is also about the specific ways that imperialism is boomeranging back directly to the home front. With the passage of the Military Commissions Act, for example, the concept of indefinite detentions—even of United States citizens—has now been enshrined into law. The government claims a national security exception in key legal cases and further employs the use of "secret evidence." Warrantless wiretapping is now legal and pervasive. The government's use of all these instruments of law has been detailed by others, most notably by the *Boston Globe's* Charlie Savage in his book *Takeover: The Return of the Imperial Presidency and the Subversion of American Democracy*. But each of them has been used before the "war on terror" on certain members of the Arab-American community, as the United States sought to impose its will over the Arab region. What we are currently living through is the slow creep of imperial high-handedness into the rest of American society, performed in the name of national security and facilitated through the growth of racist policies. This fact alone menaces the foundations of American society far beyond what has happened to Arab- and Muslim-American communities. "It is indeed a nemesis of Imperialism," writes Hobson, "that the arts and crafts of tyranny, acquired and exercised in our unfree Empire, should be turned against our liberties at home." . . .

Suggestions for Further Reading

Ancheta, Angelo N. *Race, Rights, and the Asian American Experience*. Piscataway, NJ: Rutgers University Press, 2006.

Foner, Nancy. *New Immigrants in New York*. New York: Columbia University Press, 2001.

Fox, Geoffrey F. *Hispanic Nation: Culture, Politics, and the Constructing of Identity*. Tucson: University of Arizona Press, 1997.

Glenn, Evelyn Nakano. *Unequal Freedom: How Race and Gender Shaped American Citizenship*. Cambridge, MA: Harvard University Press, 2014.

Greer, Christina. *Black Ethnics: Race, Immigration, and the Pursuit of the American Dream*. New York: Oxford University Press, 2013.

Lee, Jennifer, and Min Zhou. *The Asian American Achievement Paradox*. New York: Russell Sage Foundation, 2015.

Lee, Stacey J. *Unraveling the "Model Minority" Stereotype: Listening to Asian American Youth*, 2nd ed. New York: Teachers College Press, 2009.

Morales, Ed. *Living in Spanglish: The Search for Latino Identity in America*. New York: St. Martin's Press, 2003.

Ngai, Mae M. *Impossible Subjects: Illegal Aliens and the Making of Modern America*. Princeton, NJ: Princeton University Press, 2005.

Pedraza, Silvia, and Rubén G. Rumbaut. *Origins and Destinies: Immigration, Race, and Ethnicity in America*. Florence, KY: Wadsworth, 1995.

Pinder, Sherrow O. *The Politics of Race and Ethnicity in the United States: Americanization, De-Americanization, and Racialized Ethnic Groups*. New York: Palgrave Macmillan, 2010.

Portes, Alejandro, and Rubén G. Rumbaut. *Legacies: The Story of the Immigrant Second Generation*. Berkeley: University of California Press, 2001.

Prashad, Vijay. *The Karma of Brown Folk*. Minneapolis: University of Minnesota Press, 2001.

Prashad, Vijay. *Uncle Swami: South Asians in America Today*. New York: The New Press, 2012.

Roediger, David R. *Working Toward Whiteness: How America's Immigrants Became White: The Strange Journey from Ellis Island to the Suburbs*. New York: Basic Books, 2005.

Schmid, Carol L. *The Politics of Language: Conflict, Identity, and Cultural Pluralism in Comparative Perspective*. New York: Oxford University Press, 2001.

Schmidt, Ronald, Sr. *Language Policy and Identity Politics in the United States*. Philadelphia: Temple University Press, 2000.

Smith, Andrea. *Conquest: Sexual Violence and American Indian Genocide*. Cambridge: South End Press, 2005.

Sniderman, Paul M., and Thomas Piazza. *Black Pride, Black Prejudice*. Princeton, NJ: Princeton University Press, 2002.

Suárez-Orozco, Marcelo M., and Mariela M. Páez, eds. *Latinos: Remaking America*. Berkeley: University of California Press, 2008.

Treitler, Vilna Bashi. *The Ethnic Project: Transforming Racial Fiction into Ethnic Factions*. Palo Alto, CA: Stanford University Press, 2013.

Tuan, Mia. *Forever Foreigners or Honorary Whites? The Asian Ethnic Experience Today*. New Brunswick, NJ: Rutgers University Press, 1999.

Waldinger, Roger. *Strangers at the Gates*. Berkeley: University of California Press, 2001.

PART IV

Discrimination in Everyday Life

The systems of oppression we have been studying—racism, sexism, heterosexism, and class privilege—express themselves in everyday life in a variety of ways. Sometimes they are reflected in the prejudiced attitudes that people carry with them into the workplace or the community. Sometimes they erupt in racist, sexist, or homophobic utterances that reach us across the playground or through our car radio. Sometimes they are in evidence in the discriminatory policies and practices of government and business. In this part, we will have an opportunity to read news articles and other materials that describe discrimination against individuals or groups because of their race/ethnicity, gender, gender identity, sexual orientation, class position, or some combination of these.

Refusing to hire a qualified person because of his or her race/ethnicity, gender, gender identity, and/or sexual orientation, or refusing to rent an apartment or sell a home to that person, are fairly straightforward examples of discrimination. Most people would agree that such behavior is unfair or unjust. But once we move beyond these clear-cut cases, it becomes difficult to reach agreement. Is a joke told by a popular radio personality that portrays women or gays in a derogatory way sexist, racist, and homophobic, or is it merely a joke? Does the fact that most major U.S. corporations have few if any women in senior management positions indicate discriminatory hiring policies? Is the underrepresentation of women of all colors and men of color in the U.S. Congress de facto evidence of racism and sexism in society, or does it merely reflect a shortage of qualified individuals? Who determines what it means to be qualified? How do we arrive at the criteria by which students are admitted to colleges or senior management is hired? Is it possible that the very criteria employed reflect a subtle but pervasive discriminatory bias? Can individuals and institutions be racist, sexist, and homophobic in their normal, everyday operations, quite apart from—even without—their conscious or explicit intent? These are just some of the questions that are raised by the articles that appear in Part IV.

Selection 1 is an excerpt from a 1981 report issued by the U.S. Commission on Civil Rights. It provides a historical overview of the kinds of discrimination against women and "minorities" that is part of our shared history. In addition, it offers some categories and distinctions that will prove useful as we read about the cases in the articles that follow. According to this report, discrimination can take many forms. It can exist at the level of individual attitudes and behavior, as when a doctor refuses to treat a patient because of the patient's sexual orientation; or it can be carried out through the routine application of the rules, policies, and practices of organizations when they unfairly prevent members of certain groups from receiving a promotion or being given a highly valued work assignment; and it can be carried out by the day-to-day, unexamined practices of schools, government agencies, and other institutions so that it is pervasive enough within the social structure as to constitute structural discrimination. "Structural discrimination" refers to an interlocking cycle of discrimination in which discrimination in one area—for example, education—leads to discrimination in other areas, such as employment and housing, creating a cycle of discrimination and disadvantage from which it is difficult to emerge.

As the articles in Part IV make clear, discrimination of every type is a fact of life in every area of contemporary society. Why then do so many people, in particular so many young people, seem to believe that racism and sexism are largely things of the past? Perhaps because many people mistakenly believe that whether an act is discriminatory or racist can be determined by examining the motives of the person involved rather than by looking at the consequences of the act itself. (If you haven't already looked at the Tatum and Bonilla-Silva articles in Part II, you might want to do so now.) In fact, racism and sexism can be unintentional as well as intentional, and good people who mean well can inadvertently do and say things that are racist, sexist, and homophobic. For example, the recruiter who fails to hire a woman because of an assumption that women will be uncomfortable functioning within the prevailing company culture may indeed have meant well, but if we put the recruiter's intentions aside, we can see that this is a clear example of discrimination because it effectively denies women access to certain jobs. If the company culture is not welcoming to women, the right thing to do is to change that culture, not deny women employment.

As the members of the U.S. Civil Rights Commission point out, even superficially "color-blind" or "gender-neutral" organizational practices can end up placing men of color and all women at a disadvantage. Seemingly innocuous height requirements for a particular job may discriminate disproportionately against members of certain ethnic groups and women; "standard" ways of posting job openings may exclude those who are not part of the "old boys' network," and even those of us who mean no harm can end up reinforcing heterosexism, racism, sexism, or class privilege through our unexamined and seemingly innocent choices. As the articles in this part make clear, racism, sexism, heterosexism, and class privilege are part of both our past and our present, part of our history and part of everyday life. Learning to recognize discrimination is an essential prerequisite for acting to end it.

1 The Problem: Discrimination
U.S. Commission on Civil Rights

Making choices is an essential part of everyday life for individuals and organizations. These choices are shaped in part by social structures that set standards and influence conduct in such areas as education, employment, housing, and government. When these choices limit the opportunities available to people because of their race, sex, or national origin, the problem of discrimination arises.

Historically, discrimination against minorities and women was not only accepted but it was also governmentally required. The doctrine of white supremacy used to support the institution of slavery was so much a part of American custom and policy that the Supreme Court in 1857 approvingly concluded that both the North and the South regarded slaves "as beings of an inferior order, and altogether unfit to associate with the white race, either in social or political relations; and so far inferior, that they had no rights which the white man was bound to respect."[1] White supremacy survived the passage of the Civil War amendments to the Constitution and continued to dominate legal and social institutions in the North as well as the South to disadvantage not only blacks,[2] but other racial and ethnic groups as well—American Indians, Alaskan Natives, Asian and Pacific Islanders and Hispanics.[3]

While minorities were suffering from white supremacy, women were suffering from male supremacy. Mr. Justice Brennan has summed up the legal disabilities imposed on women this way:

> [T]hroughout much of the 19th century the position of women in our society was, in many respects, comparable to that of blacks under the pre–Civil War slave codes. Neither slaves nor women could hold office, serve on juries, or bring suit in their own names, and married women traditionally were denied the legal capacity to hold or convey property or to serve as legal guardians of their own children.[4]

In 1873 a member of the Supreme Court proclaimed, "Man is, or should be, woman's protector and defender. The natural and proper timidity and delicacy which belongs to the female sex evidently unfits it for many of the occupations of civil life."[5] Such romantic paternalism has alternated with fixed notions of male superiority to deny women in law and in practice the most fundamental of rights, including the right to vote, which was not granted until 1920;[6] the Equal Rights Amendment has yet to be ratified.[7]

White and male supremacy are no longer popularly accepted American values. The blatant racial and sexual discrimination that originated in our conveniently forgotten past, however, continues to manifest itself today in a complex interaction of

From *Affirmative Action in the 1980s*. U.S. Commission on Civil Rights 65 (January 1981): 9–15.

attitudes and actions of individuals, organizations, and the network of social structures that make up our society.

Individual Discrimination

The most common understanding of discrimination rests at the level of prejudiced individual attitudes and behavior. Although open and intentional prejudice persists, individual discriminatory conduct is often hidden and sometimes unintentional.[8] Some of the following are examples of deliberately discriminatory actions by consciously prejudiced individuals. Some are examples of unintentionally discriminatory actions taken by persons who may not believe themselves to be prejudiced but whose decisions continue to be guided by deeply ingrained discriminatory customs.

- Personnel officers whose stereotyped beliefs about women and minorities justify hiring them for low level and low paying jobs exclusively, regardless of their potential experience or qualifications for higher level jobs.[9]
- Administrators, historically white males, who rely on "word-of-mouth" recruiting among their friends and colleagues, so that only their friends and protégés of the same race and sex learn of potential job openings.[10]
- Employers who hire women for their sexual attractiveness or potential sexual availability rather than their competence, and employers who engage in sexual harassment of their female employees.[11]
- Teachers who interpret linguistic and cultural differences as indications of low potential or lack of academic interest on the part of minority students.[12]
- Guidance counselors and teachers whose low expectations lead them to steer female and minority students away from "hard" subjects, such as mathematics and science, toward subjects that do not prepare them for higher paying jobs.[13]
- Real estate agents who show fewer homes to minority buyers and steer them to minority or mixed neighborhoods because they believe white residents would oppose the presence of black neighbors.[14]
- Families who assume that property values inevitably decrease when minorities move in and therefore move out of their neighborhoods if minorities do move in.[15]
- Parole boards that assume minority offenders to be more dangerous or more unreliable than white offenders and consequently more frequently deny parole to minorities than to whites convicted of equally serious crimes.[16]

These contemporary examples of discrimination may not be motivated by conscious prejudice. The personnel manager is likely to deny believing that minorities and women can only perform satisfactorily in low level jobs and at the same time allege that other executives and decision makers would not consider them for higher level positions. In some cases, the minority or female applicants may not be aware that they have been discriminated against—the personnel manager may inform them that they are deficient in experience while rejecting their applications because of prejudice; the white male administrator who recruits by word-of-mouth from his friends or white male work force excludes minorities and women who never learn of the available positions. The discriminatory results these activities cause may not even be desired. The guidance counselor may honestly believe there are no other realistic alternatives for minority and female students.

Whether conscious or not, open or hidden, desired or undesired, these acts build on and support prejudicial stereotypes, deny their victims opportunities provided to others, and perpetuate discrimination, regardless of intent.

Organizational Discrimination

Discrimination, though practiced by individuals, is often reinforced by the well-established rules, policies, and practices of organizations. These actions are often regarded simply as part of the organization's way of doing business and are carried out by individuals as just part of their day's work.

Discrimination at the organizational level takes forms that are similar to those on the individual level. For example:

- Height and weight requirements that are unnecessarily geared to the physical proportions of white males and, therefore, exclude females and some minorities from certain jobs.[17]

- Seniority rules, when applied to jobs historically held only by white males, make more recently hired minorities and females more subject to layoff—the "last hired, first fired" employee—and less eligible for advancement.[18]

- Nepotistic membership policies of some referral unions that exclude those who are not relatives of members who, because of past employment practices, are usually white.[19]

- Restrictive employment leave policies, coupled with prohibitions on part-time work or denials of fringe benefits to part-time workers, that make it difficult for the heads of single parent families, most of whom are women, to get and keep jobs and meet the needs of their families.[20]

- The use of standardized academic tests or criteria, geared to the cultural and educational norms of the middle-class or white males, that are not relevant indicators of successful job performance.[21]

- Preferences shown by many law and medical schools in the admission of children of wealthy and influential alumni, nearly all of whom are white.[22]

- Credit policies of banks and lending institutions that prevent the granting of mortgage monies and loans in minority neighborhoods, or prevent the granting of credit to married women and others who have previously been denied the opportunity to build good credit histories in their own names.[23]

Superficially "color-blind" or "gender-neutral," these organizational practices have an adverse effect on minorities and women. As with individual actions, these organizational actions favor white males, even when taken with no conscious intent to affect minorities and women adversely, by protecting and promoting the status quo arising from the racism and sexism of the past. If, for example, the jobs now protected by "last hired, first fired" provisions had always been integrated, seniority would not operate to disadvantage minorities and women. If educational systems from kindergarten through college had not historically favored white males, many more minorities and women would hold advanced degrees and thereby be included among those involved in deciding what academic tests should test for. If minorities had lived in the same neighborhoods as whites, there would be no minority neighborhoods to which mortgage money could be denied on the basis of their being minority neighborhoods.

In addition, these barriers to minorities and women too often do not fulfill legitimate needs of the organization, or these needs can be met through other means that adequately maintain the organization without discriminating. Instead of excluding all women on the assumption that they are too weak or should be protected from strenuous work, the organization can implement a reasonable test that measures the strength actually needed to perform the job or, where possible, develop ways of doing the work that require less physical effort. Admissions to academic and professional schools can be decided not only on the basis of grades, standardized test scores, and the prestige of the high school or college from which the applicant graduated, but also on the basis of community service, work experience, and letters of recommendation. Lending institutions can look at the individual and his or her financial ability rather than the neighborhood or marital status of the prospective borrower.

Some practices that disadvantage minorities and women are readily accepted aspects of everyday behavior. Consider the "old boy" network in business and education built on years of friendship and social contact among white males, or the exchanges of information and corporate strategies by business acquaintances in racially or sexually exclusive country clubs and locker rooms paid for by the employer.[24] These actions, all of which have a discriminatory impact on minorities and women, are not necessarily acts of conscious prejudice. Because such actions are so often considered part of the "normal" way of doing things, people have difficulty recognizing that they are discriminating and therefore resist abandoning these practices despite the clearly discriminatory results. Consequently, many decision makers have difficulty considering, much less accepting, nondiscriminatory alternatives that may work just as well or better to advance legitimate organizational interests but without systematically disadvantaging minorities and women.

This is not to suggest that all such discriminatory organizational actions are spurious or arbitrary. Many may serve the actual needs of the organization. Physical size or strength at times may be a legitimate job requirement; sick leave and insurance policies must be reasonably restricted; educational qualifications are needed for many jobs; lending institutions cannot lend to people who cannot reasonably demonstrate an ability to repay loans. Unless carefully examined and then modified or eliminated, however, these apparently neutral rules, policies, and practices will continue to perpetuate age-old discriminatory patterns into the structure of today's society.

Whatever the motivation behind such organizational acts, a process is occurring, the common denominator of which is unequal results on a very large scale. When unequal outcomes are repeated over time and in numerous societal and geographical areas, it is a clear signal that a discriminatory process is at work.

Such discrimination is not a static, one-time phenomenon that has a clearly limited effect. Discrimination can feed on discrimination in self-perpetuating cycles.[25]

- The employer who recruits job applicants by word-of-mouth within a predominantly white male work force reduces the chances of receiving applications from minorities and females for open positions. Since they do not apply, they are not hired. Since they are not hired, they are not present when new jobs become available. Since they are not aware of new jobs, they cannot recruit other minority or female applicants. Because there are no minority or female employees to recruit others, the employer is left to recruit on his own from among his predominantly white and male work force.[26]

- The teacher who expects poor academic performance from minority and female students may not become greatly concerned when their grades are low. The acceptance of their low grades removes incentives to improve. Without incentives to improve, their grades remain low. Their low grades reduce their expectations, and the teacher has no basis for expecting more of them.[27]

- The realtor who assumes that white home owners do not want minority neighbors "steers" minorities to minority neighborhoods. Those steered to minority neighborhoods tend to live in minority neighborhoods. White neighborhoods then remain white, and realtors tend to assume that whites do not want minority neighbors.[28]

- Elected officials appoint voting registrars who impose linguistic, geographic, and other barriers to minority voter registration. Lack of minority registration leads to low voting rates. Lower minority voting rates lead to the election of fewer minorities. Fewer elected minorities leads to the appointment of voting registrars who maintain the same barriers.[29]

Structural Discrimination

Such self-sustaining discriminatory processes occur not only within the fields of employment, education, housing, and government but also between these structural areas. There is a classic cycle of structural discrimination that reproduces itself. Discrimination in education denies the credentials to get good jobs. Discrimination in employment denies the economic resources to buy good housing. Discrimination in housing confines minorities to school districts providing inferior education, closing the cycle in a classic form.[30]

With regard to white women, the cycle is not as tightly closed. To the extent they are raised in families headed by white males, and are married to or live with white males, white women will enjoy the advantages in housing and other areas that such relationships to white men can confer. White women lacking the sponsorship of white men, however, will be unable to avoid gender-based discrimination in housing, education, and employment. White women can thus be the victims of discrimination produced by social structures that is comparable in form to that experienced by minorities.

This perspective is not intended to imply that either the dynamics of discrimination or its nature and degree are identical for women and minorities. But when a woman of any background seeks to compete with men of any group, she finds herself the victim of a discriminatory process. Regarding the similarities and differences between the discrimination experienced by women and minorities, one author has aptly stated:

> [W]hen two groups exist in a situation of inequality, it may be self-defeating to become embroiled in a quarrel over which is more unequal or the victim of greater oppression. The more salient question is how a condition of inequality for both is maintained and perpetuated—through what means is it reinforced?[31]

The following are additional examples of the interaction between social structures that affect minorities and women:

- The absence of minorities and women from executive, writing, directing, news reporting, and acting positions in television contributes to unfavorable stereotyping on the screen, which in turn reinforces existing stereotypes among the public and creates psychological roadblocks to progress in employment, education, and housing.[32]

- Living in inner-city high crime areas in disproportionate numbers, minorities, particularly minority youth, are more likely to be arrested and are more likely to go to jail than whites accused of similar offenses, and their arrest and conviction records are then often used as bars to employment.[33]

- Because of past discrimination against minorities and women, female and minority-headed businesses are often small and relatively new. Further disadvantaged by contemporary credit and lending practices, they are more likely than white male–owned businesses to remain small and be less able to employ full-time specialists in applying for government contracts. Because they cannot monitor the availability of government contracts, they do not receive such contracts. Because they cannot demonstrate success with government contracts, contracting officers tend to favor other firms that have more experience with government contracts.[34]

Discriminatory actions by individuals and organizations are not only pervasive, occurring in every sector of society, but also cumulative with effects limited neither to the time nor the particular structural area in which they occur. This process of discrimination, therefore, extends across generations, across organizations, and across social structures in self-reinforcing cycles, passing the disadvantages incurred by one generation in one area to future generations in many related areas.[35]

These interrelated components of the discriminatory process share one basic result: the persistent gaps seen in the status of women and minorities relative to that of white males. These unequal results themselves have real consequences. The employer who wishes to hire more minorities and women may be bewildered by charges of racism and sexism when confronted by what appears to be a genuine shortage of qualified minority and female applicants. The guidance counselor who sees one promising minority student after another drop out of school or give up in despair may be resentful of allegations of racism when there is little he or she alone can do for the student. The banker who denies a loan to a female single parent may wish to do differently, but believes that prudent fiscal judgment requires taking into account her lack of financial history and inability to prove that she is a good credit risk. These and other decision makers see the results of a discriminatory process repeated over and over again, and those results provide a basis for rationalizing their own actions, which then feed into that same process.

When seen outside the context of the interlocking and intertwined effects of discrimination, complaints that many women and minorities are absent from the ranks of qualified job applicants, academically inferior and unmotivated, poor credit risks, and so forth, may appear to be justified. Decision makers like those described above are reacting to real social problems stemming from the process of discrimination. But many too easily fall prey to stereotyping and consequently disregard those minorities and women who have the necessary skills or qualifications. And they erroneously "blame the victims" of discrimination,[36] instead of examining the past and present context in which their own actions are taken and the multiple consequences of these actions on the lives of minorities and women.

The Process of Discrimination

Although discrimination is maintained through individual actions, neither individual prejudices nor random chance can fully explain the persistent national patterns of inequality and underrepresentation. Nor can these patterns be blamed on the persons who are at the bottom of our economic, political, and social order. Overt racism and sexism as embodied in popular notions of white and male supremacy have been widely repudiated, but our history of discrimination based on race, sex, and national origin has not been readily put aside. Past discrimination continues to have present effects. The task today is to identify those effects and the forms and dynamics of the discrimination that produced them.

Discrimination against minorities and women must now be viewed as an interlocking process involving the attitudes and actions of individuals and the organizations and social structures that guide individual behavior. That process, started by past events, now routinely bestows privileges, favors, and advantages on white males and imposes disadvantages and penalties on minorities and women. This process is also self-perpetuating. Many normal, seemingly neutral, operations of our society create stereotyped expectations that justify unequal results; unequal results in one area foster inequalities in opportunity and accomplishment in others; the lack of opportunity and accomplishment confirms the original prejudices or engenders new ones that fuel the normal operations generating unequal results.

As we have shown, the process of discrimination involves many aspects of our society. No single factor sufficiently explains it, and no single means will suffice to eliminate it. Such elements of our society as our history of *de jure* discrimination, deeply ingrained prejudices,[37] inequities based on economic and social class,[38] and the structure and function of all our economic, social, and political institutions[39] must be continually examined in order to understand their part in shaping today's decisions that will either maintain or counter the current process of discrimination.

It may be difficult to identify precisely all aspects of the discriminatory process and assign those parts their appropriate importance. But understanding discrimination starts with an awareness that such a process exists and that to avoid perpetuating it, we must carefully assess the context and consequences of our everyday actions. . . .

NOTES

1. Dred Scott v. Sandford, 60 U.S. (19 How.) 393, 408 (1857).

2. For a concise summary of this history, see U.S. Commission on Civil Rights, *Twenty Years After Brown*, pp. 4–29 (1975); *Freedom to the Free: 1863, Century of Emancipation* (1963).

3. The discriminatory conditions experienced by these minority groups have been documented in the following publications by the U.S. Commission on Civil Rights: *The Navajo Nation: An American Colony* (1975); *The Southwest Indian Report* (1973); *The Forgotten Minority: Asian Americans in New York City* (State Advisory Committee Report 1977); *Success of Asian Americans: Fact or Fiction?* (1980); *Stranger in One's Land* (1970); *Toward Quality Education for Mexican Americans* (1974); *Puerto Ricans in the Continental United States: An Uncertain Future* (1976).

4. Frontiero v. Richardson, 411 U.S. 677, 684–86 (1973), citing L. Kanowitz, *Women and the Law: The Unfinished Revolution,* pp. 5–6 (1970), and G. Myrdal, *An American Dilemma* 1073 (20th Anniversary Ed., 1962). Justice Brennan wrote the opinion of the Court, joined by Justices Douglas, White, and Marshall. Justice Stewart concurred in the judgment. Justice Powell, joined by Chief Justice Burger and Justice Blackmun, wrote a separate concurring opinion. Justice Rehnquist dissented. See also H. M. Hacker, "Women as a Minority Group," *Social Forces,* vol. 30 (1951), pp. 60–69; W. Chafe, *Women and Equality: Changing Patterns in American Culture* (New York: Oxford University Press, 1977).

5. Bradwell v. State, 83 U.S. (16 Wall) 130, 141 (1873) (Bradley, J., concurring), quoted in *Frontiero, supra* note 4.

6. U.S. Const. amend. XIX.

7. See U.S. Commission on Civil Rights, *Statement on the Equal Rights Amendment* (December 1978).

8. See, e.g., R. K. Merton, "Discrimination and the American Creed," in R. K. Merton, *Sociological Ambivalence and Other Essays* (New York: The Free Press, 1976), pp. 189–216. In this essay on racism, published for the first time more than 30 years ago, Merton presented a

typology which introduced the notion that discriminatory actions are not always directly related to individual attitudes of prejudice. Merton's typology consisted of the following: Type I—the unprejudiced nondiscriminator; Type II—the unprejudiced discriminator; Type III—the prejudiced nondiscriminator; Type IV—the prejudiced discriminator. In the present context, Type II is crucial in its observation that discrimination is often practiced by persons who are not themselves prejudiced, but who respond to, or do not oppose, the actions of those who discriminate because of prejudiced attitudes (Type IV). See also D. C. Reitzes, "Prejudice and Discrimination: A Study in Contradictions," in *Racial and Ethnic Relations,* ed. H. M. Hughes (Boston: Allyn and Bacon, 1970), pp. 56–65.

9. See R. M. Kanter and B. A. Stein, "Making a Life at the Bottom," in *Life in Organizations, Workplaces as People Experience Them,* ed. Kanter and Stein (New York: Basic Books, 1976), pp. 176–90; also L. K. Howe, "Retail Sales Worker," ibid., pp. 248–51; also R. M. Kanter, *Men and Women of the Corporation* (New York: Basic Books, 1977).

10. See M. S. Granovetter, *Getting a Job: A Study of Contract and Careers* (Cambridge: Harvard University Press, 1974), pp. 6–11; also A. W. Blumrosen, *Black Employment and the Law* (New Brunswick, N.J.: Rutgers University Press, 1971), p. 232.

11. See U.S. Equal Employment Opportunity Commission, "Guidelines on Discrimination Because of Sex," 29 C.F.R. §1604.4 (1979); L. Farley, *Sexual Shakedown: The Sexual Harassment of Women on the Job* (New York: McGraw-Hill, 1978), pp. 92–96, 176–79; C. A. Mackinnon, *Sexual Harassment of Working Women* (New Haven: Yale University Press, 1979), pp. 25–55.

12. See R. Rosenthal and L. F. Jacobson, "Teacher Expectations for the Disadvantaged," *Scientific American,* 1968 (b) 218, 219–23; also D. Bar Tal, "Interactions of Teachers and Pupils," in *New Approaches to Social Problems,* ed. I. H. Frieze, D. Bar Tal, and J. S. Carrol (San Francisco: Jossey Bass, 1979), pp. 337–58; also U.S. Commission on Civil Rights, *Teachers and Students, Report V: Mexican American Education Study. Differences in Teacher Interaction with Mexican American and Anglo Students* (1973), pp. 22–23.

13. Ibid.

14. U.S. Department of Housing and Urban Development, "Measuring Racial Discrimination in American Housing Markets: The Housing Market Practices Survey" (1979); D. M. Pearce, "Gatekeepers and Home Seekers: Institutional Patterns in Racial Steering," *Social Problems,* vol. 26 (1979), pp. 325–42; "Benign Steering and Benign Quotas: The Validity of Race Conscious Government Policies to Promote Residential Integration," 93 *Harv. L. Rev.* 938, 944 (1980).

15. See M. N. Danielson, *The Politics of Exclusion* (New York: Columbia University Press, 1976), pp. 11–12; U.S. Commission on Civil Rights, *Equal Opportunity in Suburbia* (1974).

16. See L. L. Knowles and K. Prewitt, eds., *Institutional Racism in America* (Englewood Cliffs, N.J.: Prentice Hall, 1969), pp. 58–77, and E. D. Wright, *The Politics of Punishment* (New York: Harper and Row, 1973). Also, S. V. Brown, "Race and Parole Hearing Outcomes," in *Discrimination in Organizations,* ed. R. Alvarez and K. G. Lutterman (San Francisco: Jossey Bass, 1979), pp. 355–74.

17. Height and weight minimums that disproportionately exclude women without a showing of legitimate job requirement constitute unlawful sex discrimination. *See* Dothard v. Rawlinson, 433 U.S. 321 (1977); Bowe v. Colgate Palmolive Co., 416 F.2d 711 (7th Cir. 1969). Minimum height requirements used in screening applicants for employment have also been held to be unlawful where such a requirement excludes a significantly higher percentage of Hispanics than other national origin groups in the labor market and no job relatedness is shown. See Smith v. City of East Cleveland, 520 F.2d 492 (6th Cir. 1975).

18. U.S. Commission on Civil Rights, *Last Hired, First Fired* (1976); Tangren v. Wackenhut Servs., Inc., 480 F. Supp. 539 (D. Nev. 1979).

19. U.S. Commission on Civil Rights, *The Challenge Ahead, Equal Opportunity in Referral Unions* (1977), pp. 84–89.

20. A. Pifer, "Women Working: Toward a New Society," pp. 13–34, and D. Pearce, "Women, Work and Welfare: The Feminization of Poverty," pp. 103–24, both in K. A. Fernstein, ed., *Working Women and Families* (Beverly Hills: Sage Publications, 1979). Disproportionate numbers of single-parent families are minorities.

21. See Griggs v. Duke Power Company, 401 U.S. 424 (1971); U.S. Commission on Civil Rights, *Toward Equal Educational Opportunity: Affirmative Admissions Programs at Law and Medical Schools* (1978), pp. 10–12; I. Berg, *Education and Jobs: The Great Training Robbery* (Boston: Beacon Press, 1971), pp. 58–60.

22. See U.S. Commission on Civil Rights, *Toward Equal Educational Opportunity: Affirmative Admissions Programs at Law and Medical Schools* (1978), pp. 14–15.

23. See U.S. Commission on Civil Rights, *Mortgage Money: Who Gets It? A Case Study in Mortgage Lending Discrimination in Hartford, Conn.* (1974); J. Feagin and C. B. Feagin, *Discrimination American Style, Institutional Racism and Sexism* (Englewood Cliffs, N.J.: Prentice Hall, 1976), pp. 78–79.

24. See *Club Membership Practices by Financial Institutions: Hearing before the Comm. on Banking, Housing and Urban Affairs, United States Senate*, 96th Cong., 1st Sess. (1979). The Office of Federal Contract Compliance Programs of the Department of Labor has proposed a rule that would make the payment or reimbursement of membership fees in a private club that accepts or rejects persons on the basis of race, color, sex, religion, or national origin a prohibited discriminatory practice. 45 Fed. Reg. 4954 (1980) (to be codified in 41 C.F.R. §60–1.11).

25. See U.S. Commission on Civil Rights, *For All the People . . . By All the People* (1969), pp. 122–23.

26. See note 10.

27. See note 12.

28. See notes 14 and 15.

29. See Statement of Arthur S. Flemming, Chairman, U.S. Commission on Civil Rights, before the Subcommittee on Constitutional Rights of the Committee on the Judiciary of the U.S. Senate on S.407, S.903, and S.1279, Apr. 9, 1975, pp. 15–18, based on U.S. Commission on Civil Rights, *The Voting Rights Act: Ten Years After* (January 1975).

30. See, e.g., U.S. Commission on Civil Rights, *Equal Opportunity in Suburbia* (1974).

31. Chafe, *Women and Equality*, p. 78.

32. U.S. Commission on Civil Rights, *Window Dressing on the Set* (1977).

33. See note 16; Gregory v. Litton Systems, Inc., 472 F.2d 631 (9th Cir. 1972); Green v. Mo.-Pac. R.R., 523 F.2d 1290 (8th Cir. 1975).

34. See U.S. Commission on Civil Rights, *Minorities and Women as Government Contractors*, pp. 20, 27, 125 (1975).

35. See, e.g., A. Downs, *Racism in America and How to Combat It* (U.S. Commission on Civil Rights, 1970); "The Web of Urban Racism," in *Institutional Racism in America*, ed. Knowles and Prewitt (Englewood Cliffs, N.J.: Prentice Hall, 1969), pp. 134–76. Other factors in addition to race, sex, and national origin may contribute to these interlocking institutional patterns. In *Equal Opportunity in Suburbia* (1974), this Commission documented what it termed "the cycle of urban poverty" that confines minorities in central cities with declining tax bases, soaring educational and other public needs, and dwindling employment opportunities,

surrounded by largely white, affluent suburbs. This cycle of poverty, however, started with and is fueled by discrimination against minorities. *See also* W. Taylor, *Hanging Together, Equality in an Urban Nation* (New York: Simon & Schuster, 1971).

36. The "self-fulfilling prophecy" is a well-known phenomenon. "Blaming the victim" occurs when responses to discrimination are treated as though they were the causes rather than the results of discrimination. *See* Chafe, *Women and Equality,* pp. 76–78; W. Ryan, *Blaming the Victim* (New York: Pantheon Books, 1971).

37. See, e.g., J. E. Simpson and J. M. Yinger, *Racial and Cultural Minorities* (New York: Harper and Row, 1965), pp. 49–79; J. M. Jones, *Prejudice and Racism* (Reading, Mass.: Addison Wesley, 1972), pp. 60–111; M. M. Tumin, "Who Is Against Desegregation?" in *Racial and Ethnic Relations,* ed. H. Hughes (Boston: Allyn and Bacon, 1970), pp. 76–85; D. M. Wellman, *Portraits of White Racism* (Cambridge: Cambridge University Press, 1977).

38. See, e.g., D. C. Cox, *Caste, Class and Race: A Study in Social Dynamics* (Garden City, N.Y.: Doubleday, 1948); W. J. Wilson, *Power, Racism and Privilege* (New York: Macmillan, 1973).

39. H. Hacker, "Women as a Minority Group," *Social Forces,* vol. 30 (1951), pp. 60–69; J. Feagin and C. B. Feagin, *Discrimination American Style;* Chafe, *Women and Equality;* J. Feagin, "Indirect Institutionalized Discrimination," *American Politics Quarterly,* vol. 5 (1977), pp. 177–200; M. A. Chesler, "Contemporary Sociological Theories of Racism," in *Towards the Elimination of Racism,* ed. P. Katz (New York: Pergamon Press, 1976); P. Van den Berghe, *Race and Racism: A Comparative Perspective* (New York: Wiley, 1967); S. Carmichael and C. Hamilton, *Black Power* (New York: Random House, 1967); Knowles and Prewitt, *Institutional Racism in America;* Downs, *Racism in America and How to Combat It.*

2 The New Jim Crow
Mass Incarceration in the Age of Colorblindness
Michelle Alexander

It was no ordinary Sunday morning when presidential candidate Barack Obama stepped to the podium at the Apostolic Church of God in Chicago. It was Father's Day. Hundreds of enthusiastic congregants packed the pews at the overwhelmingly black church eager to hear what the first black Democratic nominee for president of the United States had to say.

The message was a familiar one: black men should be better fathers. Too many are absent from their homes. For those in the audience, Obama's speech was an old tune sung by an exciting new performer. His message of personal responsibility, particularly as it relates to fatherhood, was anything but new; it had been delivered countless times by black ministers in churches across America. The message had also been delivered on a national stage by celebrities such as Bill Cosby and Sidney Poitier. And the message had been delivered with great passion by Louis Farrakhan, who more than a decade earlier summoned one million black men to Washington, D.C., for a day of "atonement" and recommitment to their families and communities.

The mainstream media, however, treated the event as big news, and many pundits seemed surprised that the black congregants actually applauded the message. For them, it was remarkable that black people nodded in approval when Obama said: "If we are honest with ourselves, we'll admit that too many fathers are missing—missing from too many lives and too many homes. Too many fathers are MIA. Too many fathers are AWOL. They have abandoned their responsibilities. They're acting like boys instead of men. And the foundations of our families are weaker because of it. You and I know this is true everywhere, but nowhere is this more true than in the African American community."

The media did not ask—and Obama did not tell—where the missing fathers might be found.

The following day, social critic and sociologist Michael Eric Dyson published a critique of Obama's speech in *Time* magazine. He pointed out that the stereotype of black men being poor fathers may well be false. Research by Boston College social psychologist Rebekah Levine Coley found that black fathers not living at home are more likely to keep in contact with their children than fathers of any other ethnic or racial group. Dyson chided Obama for evoking a black stereotype for political gain, pointing out that "Obama's words may have been spoken to black folk, but they were aimed at those whites still on the fence about whom to send to the White House."[1] Dyson's critique

Excerpt from *The New Jim Crow*. Copyright © 2010 by Michelle Alexander. Reprinted by permission of The New Press, www.thenewpress.com.

was a fair one, but like other media commentators, he remained silent about where all the absent black fathers could be found. He identified numerous social problems plaguing black families, such as high levels of unemployment, discriminatory mortgage practices, and the gutting of early-childhood learning programs. Not a word was said about prisons.

The public discourse regarding "missing black fathers" closely parallels the debate about the lack of eligible black men for marriage. The majority of black women are unmarried today, including 70 percent of professional black women.[2] "Where have all the black men gone?" is a common refrain heard among black women frustrated in their efforts to find life partners.

The sense that black men have disappeared is rooted in reality. The U.S. Census Bureau reported in 2002 that there are nearly 3 million more black adult women than men in black communities across the United States, a gender gap of 26 percent.[3] In many urban areas, the gap is far worse, rising to more than 37 percent in places like New York City. The comparable disparity for whites in the United States is 8 percent.[4] Although a million black men can be found in prisons and jails, public acknowledgment of the role of the criminal justice system in "disappearing" black men is surprisingly rare. Even in the black media—which is generally more willing to raise and tackle issues related to criminal justice—an eerie silence can often be found.[5]

Ebony magazine, for example, ran an article in December 2006 entitled "Where Have the Black Men Gone?" The author posed the popular question but never answered it.[6] He suggested we will find our black men when we rediscover God, family, and self-respect. A more cynical approach was taken by Tyra Banks, the popular talk show host, who devoted a show in May 2008 to the recurring question, "Where Have All the Good Black Men Gone?" She wondered aloud whether black women are unable to find "good black men" because too many of them are gay or dating white women. No mention was made of the War on Drugs or mass incarceration.

The fact that Barack Obama can give a speech on Father's Day dedicated to the subject of fathers who are "AWOL" without ever acknowledging that the majority of young black men in many large urban areas are currently under the control of the criminal justice system is disturbing, to say the least. What is more problematic, though, is that hardly anyone in the mainstream media noticed the oversight. One might not expect serious analysis from Tyra Banks, but shouldn't we expect a bit more from the *New York Times* and CNN? Hundreds of thousands of black men are unable to be good fathers for their children, not because of a lack of commitment or desire but because they are warehoused in prisons, locked in cages. They did not walk out on their families voluntarily; they were taken away in handcuffs, often due to a massive federal program known as the War on Drugs.

More African American adults are under correctional control today—in prison or jail, on probation or parole—than were enslaved in 1850, a decade before the Civil War began.[7] The mass incarceration of people of color is a big part of the reason that a black child born today is less likely to be raised by both parents than a black child born during slavery.[8] The absence of black fathers from families across America is not simply a function of laziness, immaturity, or too much time watching Sports Center.

Thousands of black men have disappeared into prisons and jails, locked away for drug crimes that are largely ignored when committed by whites.

The clock has been turned back on racial progress in America, though scarcely anyone seems to notice. All eyes are fixed on people like Barack Obama and Oprah Winfrey, who have defied the odds and risen to power, fame, and fortune. For those left behind, especially those within prison walls, the celebration of racial triumph in America must seem a tad premature. More black men are imprisoned today than at any other moment in our nation's history. More are disenfranchised today than in 1870, the year the Fifteenth Amendment was ratified prohibiting laws that explicitly deny the right to vote on the basis of race.[9] Young black men today may be just as likely to suffer discrimination in employment, housing, public benefits, and jury service as a black man in the Jim Crow era—discrimination that is perfectly legal, because it is based on one's criminal record.

This is the new normal, the new racial equilibrium.

The launching of the War on Drugs and the initial construction of the new system required the expenditure of tremendous political initiative and resources. Media campaigns were waged; politicians blasted "soft" judges and enacted harsh sentencing laws; poor people of color were vilified. The system now, however, requires very little maintenance or justification. In fact, if you are white and middle class, you might not even realize the drug war is still going on. Most high school and college students today have no recollection of the political and media frenzy surrounding the drug war in the early years. They were young children when the war was declared, or not even born yet. Crack is out; terrorism is in.

Today, the political fanfare and the vehement, racialized rhetoric regarding crime and drugs are no longer necessary. Mass incarceration has been normalized, and all of the racial stereotypes and assumptions that gave rise to the system are now embraced (or at least internalized) by people of all colors, from all walks of life, and in every major political party. We may wonder aloud "where have the black men gone?" but deep down we already know. It is simply taken for granted that, in cities like Baltimore and Chicago, the vast majority of young black men are currently under the control of the criminal justice system or branded criminals for life. This extraordinary circumstance—unheard of in the rest of the world—is treated here in America as a basic fact of life, as normal as separate water fountains were just a half century ago . . . .

How It Works

Precisely how the system of mass incarceration works to trap African Americans in a virtual (and literal) cage can best be understood by viewing the system as a whole . . . . Only when we view the cage from a distance can we disengage from the maze of rationalizations that are offered for each wire and see how the entire apparatus operates to keep African Americans perpetually trapped.

This, in brief, is how the system works: The War on Drugs is the vehicle through which extraordinary numbers of black men are forced into the cage. The entrapment occurs in three distinct phases . . . . The first stage is the roundup. Vast numbers of people are swept into the criminal justice system by the police, who conduct drug operations primarily in poor communities of color. They are rewarded in cash—through drug forfeiture laws and federal grant programs—for rounding up as many people as possible, and they operate unconstrained by constitutional rules of procedure that once were considered inviolate. Police can stop, interrogate, and search anyone they choose for drug investigations, provided they get "consent." Because there is no meaningful check on the exercise of police discretion, racial biases are granted free rein. In fact, police are allowed to rely on race as a factor in selecting whom to stop and search (even though people of color are no more likely to be guilty of drug crimes than whites)—effectively guaranteeing that those who are swept into the system are primarily black and brown.

The conviction marks the beginning of the second phase: the period of formal control. Once arrested, defendants are generally denied meaningful legal representation and pressured to plead guilty whether they are or not. Prosecutors are free to "load up" defendants with extra charges, and their decisions cannot be challenged for racial bias. Once convicted, due to the drug war's harsh sentencing laws, drug offenders in the United States spend more time under the criminal justice system's formal control—in jail or prison, on probation or parole—than drug offenders anywhere else in the world. While under formal control, virtually every aspect of one's life is regulated and monitored by the system, and any form of resistance or disobedience is subject to swift sanction. This period of control may last a lifetime, even for those convicted of extremely minor, nonviolent offenses, but the vast majority of those swept into the system are eventually released. They are transferred from their prison cells to a much larger, invisible cage.

The final stage has been dubbed by some advocates as the period of invisible punishment.[10] This term, first coined by Jeremy Travis, is meant to describe the unique set of criminal sanctions that are imposed on individuals after they step outside the prison gates, a form of punishment that operates largely outside of public view and takes effect outside the traditional sentencing framework. These sanctions are imposed by operation of law rather than decisions of a sentencing judge, yet they often have a greater impact on one's life course than the months or years one actually spends behind bars. These laws operate collectively to ensure that the vast majority of convicted offenders will never integrate into mainstream, white society. They will be discriminated against, legally, for the rest of their lives—denied employment, housing, education, and public benefits. Unable to surmount these obstacles, most will eventually return to prison and then be released again, caught in a closed circuit of perpetual marginality.

In recent years, advocates and politicians have called for greater resources devoted to the problem of "prisoner re-entry," in view of the unprecedented numbers of people who are released from prison and returned to their communities every year. While the terminology is well intentioned, it utterly fails to convey the gravity of the situation facing prisoners upon their release. People who have been convicted of felonies almost never truly reenter the society they inhabited prior to their conviction. Instead, they enter a separate society, a world hidden from public view, governed by a set of oppressive and discriminatory rules and laws that do not apply to everyone else. They become members of an undercaste—an enormous population of predominately black and brown people who, because of the drug war, are denied basic rights and privileges of American citizenship and are permanently relegated to an inferior status. This is the final phase, and there is no going back.

Nothing New?

Some might argue that as disturbing as this system appears to be, there is nothing particularly new about mass incarceration; it is merely a continuation of past drug wars and biased law enforcement practices. Racial bias in our criminal justice system is simply an old problem that has gotten worse, and the social excommunication of "criminals" has a long history; it is not a recent invention. There is some merit to this argument.

Race has always influenced the administration of justice in the United States. Since the day the first prison opened, people of color have been disproportionately represented behind bars. In fact, the very first person admitted to a U.S. penitentiary was a "light skinned Negro in excellent health," described by an observer as "one who was born of a degraded and depressed race, and had never experienced anything but indifference and harshness."[11] Biased police practices are also nothing new, a recurring theme of African American experience since blacks were targeted by the police as suspected runaway slaves. And every drug war that has ever been waged in the United States—including alcohol prohibition—has been tainted or driven by racial bias.[12] Even postconviction penalties have a long history. The American colonies passed laws barring criminal offenders from a wide variety of jobs and benefits, automatically dissolving their marriages and denying them the right to enter contracts. These legislatures were following a long tradition, dating back to ancient Greece, of treating criminals as less than full citizens. Although many collateral sanctions were repealed by the late 1970s, arguably the drug war simply revived and expanded a tradition that has ancient roots, a tradition independent of the legacy of American slavery.

In view of this history and considering the lack of originality in many of the tactics and practices employed in the era of mass incarceration, there is good reason to believe that the latest drug war is just another drug war corrupted by racial and ethnic bias. But this view is correct only to a point.

In the past, the criminal justice system, as punitive as it may have been during various wars on crime and drugs, affected only a relatively small percentage of the population. Because civil penalties and sanctions imposed on ex-offenders applied only to a few, they never operated as a comprehensive system of control over any racially or ethnically defined population. Racial minorities were always overrepresented among current and ex-offenders, but as sociologists have noted, until the mid-1980s, the criminal justice system was marginal to communities of color. While young minority men with little schooling have always had relatively high rates of incarceration, "before the 1980s the penal system was not a dominant presence in the disadvantaged neighborhoods."[13]

Today, the War on Drugs has given birth to a system of mass incarceration that governs not just a small fraction of a racial or ethnic minority but entire communities of color. In ghetto communities, nearly everyone is either directly or indirectly subject to the new caste system. The system serves to redefine the terms of the relationship of poor people of color and their communities to mainstream, white society, ensuring their subordinate and marginal status. The criminal and civil sanctions that were once reserved for a tiny minority are now used to control and oppress a racially defined majority in many communities, and the systematic manner in which the control is achieved reflects not just a difference in scale. The nature of the criminal justice system has changed. It is no longer concerned primarily with the prevention and punishment of crime, but rather with the management and control of the dispossessed. Prior drug wars were ancillary to the prevailing caste system. This time the drug war *is* the system of control.

If you doubt that this is the case, consider the effect of the war on the ground, in specific locales. Take Chicago, Illinois, for example. Chicago is widely considered to be one of America's most diverse and vibrant cities. It has boasted black mayors, black police chiefs, black legislators, and is home to the nation's first black president. It has a thriving economy, a growing Latino community, and a substantial black middle class. Yet as the Chicago Urban League reported in 2002, there is another story to be told.[14]

If Martin Luther King Jr. were to return miraculously to Chicago, some forty years after bringing his Freedom Movement to the city, he would be saddened to discover that the same issues on which he originally focused still produce stark patterns of racial inequality, segregation, and poverty. He would also be struck by the dramatically elevated significance of one particular institutional force in the perpetuation and deepening of those patterns: the criminal justice system. In the few short decades since King's death, a new regime of racially disparate mass incarceration has emerged in Chicago and become the primary mechanism for racial oppression and the denial of equal opportunity.

In Chicago, like the rest of the country, the War on Drugs is the engine of mass incarceration, as well as the primary cause of gross racial disparities in the criminal justice system and in the ex-offender population. About 90 percent of those sentenced to prison for a drug offense in Illinois are African American.[15] White drug offenders are rarely arrested, and when they are, they are treated more favorably at every stage of the criminal justice process, including plea bargaining and sentencing.[16] Whites are consistently more likely to avoid prison and felony charges, even when they are repeat offenders.[17] Black offenders, by contrast, are routinely labeled felons and released into a permanent racial undercaste.

The total population of black males in Chicago with a felony record (including both current and ex-felons) is equivalent to 55 percent of the black adult male population and an astonishing 80 percent of the adult black male workforce in the Chicago area.[18] This stunning development reflects the dramatic increase in the number and race of those sent to prison for drug crimes. From the Chicago region alone, the number of those annually sent to prison for drug crimes increased almost 2,000 percent, from 469 in 1985 to 8,755 in 2005.[19] That figure, of course, does not include the thousands who avoid prison but are arrested, convicted, and sentenced to jail or probation. They, too, have criminal records that will follow them for life. More than 70 percent of all criminal cases in the Chicago area involve a class D felony drug possession charge, the lowest-level felony charge.[20] Those who do go to prison find little freedom upon release.

When people are released from Illinois prisons, they are given as little as $10 in "gate money" and a bus ticket to anywhere in the United States. Most return to impoverished neighborhoods in the Chicago area, bringing few resources and bearing the stigma of their prison record.[21] In Chicago, as in most cities across the country, ex-offenders are banned or severely restricted from employment in a large number of professions, job categories, and fields by professional licensing statutes, rules, and practices that discriminate against potential employees with felony records. According to a study conducted by the DePaul University College of Law in 2000, of the then ninety-eight occupations requiring licenses in Illinois, fifty-seven placed stipulations and/or restrictions on applicants with a criminal record.[22] Even when not barred by law from holding specific jobs, ex-offenders in Chicago find it extraordinarily difficult to find employers who will hire them, regardless of the nature of their conviction. They are also routinely denied public housing and welfare benefits, and they find it increasingly difficult to obtain education, especially now that funding for public education has been hard hit, due to exploding prison budgets.

The impact of the new caste system is most tragically felt among the young. In Chicago (as in other cities across the United States), young black men are more likely to go to prison than to college.[23] As of June 2001, there were nearly 20,000 more black men in the Illinois state prison system than enrolled in the state's public universities.[24] In fact, there were more black men in the state's correctional facilities that year *just on drug charges* than the total number of black men enrolled in undergraduate degree programs in state universities.[25] To put the crisis in even sharper focus, consider this: just 992 black men received a bachelor's degree from Illinois state universities in 1999, while roughly 7,000 black men were released from the state prison system the following year just for drug offenses.[26] The young men who go to prison rather than college face a lifetime of closed doors, discrimination, and ostracism. Their plight is not what we hear about on the evening news, however. Sadly, like the racial caste systems that preceded it, the system of mass incarceration now seems normal and natural to most, a regrettable necessity. . . .

NOTES

1. Michael Eric Dyson, "Obama's Rebuke of Absentee Black Fathers," *Time*, June 19, 2008.

2. Sam Roberts, "51% of Women Now Living with a Spouse, *New York Times*, Jan 16, 2007.

3. See Jonathan Tilove, "Where Have All the Men Gone? Black Gender Gap Is Widening," *Seattle Times*, May 5, 2005; and Jonathan Tilove, "Where Have All the Black Men Gone?" *Star-Ledger* (Newark), May 8, 2005.

4. Ibid.

5. Cf. Salim Muwakkil, "Black Men: Missing," *In These Times*, June 16, 2005.

6. G. Garvin, "Where Have the Black Men Gone?" *Ebony*, Dec. 2006.

7. One in eleven black adults was under correctional supervision at year end 2007, or approximately 2.4 million people. See Pew Center on the States, *One in 31: The Long Reach of American Corrections* (Washington, DC: Pew Charitable Trusts, 2009). According to the 1850 Census, approximately 1.7 million adults (ages 15 and older) were slaves.

8. See Andrew J. Cherlin, *Marriage, Divorce, Remarriage*, rev. ed. (Cambridge, MA: Harvard University Press, 1992), 110.

9. See Glenn C. Loury, *Race, Incarceration, and American Values* (Cambridge, MA: MIT Press, 2008), commentary by Pam Karlan.

10. See Marc Mauer and Meda Chesney-Lind, eds., *Invisible Punishment: The Collateral Consequences of Mass Imprisonment* (New York: The New Press, 2002); and Jeremy Travis, *But They All Come Back: Facing the Challenges of Prisoner Reentry* (Washington, DC: Urban Institute Press, 2005).

11. Negley K. Teeters and John D. Shearer, *The Prison at Philadelphia, Cherry Hill: The Separate System of Prison Discipline, 1829–1913* (New York: Columbia University Press, 1957), 84.

12. See David Musto, *The American Disease: Origins of Narcotics Control*, 3rd ed. (New York: Oxford University Press, 1999), 4, 7, 43–44, 219–20, describing the role of racial bias in earlier drug wars; and Doris Marie Provine, *Unequal Under Law: Race in the War on Drugs* (Chicago: University of Chicago Press, 2007), 37–90, describing racial bias in alcohol prohibition, as well as other drug wars.

13. Mary Pattillo, David F. Weiman, and Bruce Western, *Imprisoning America: The Social Effect of Mass Incarceration* (New York: Russell Sage Foundation, 2004), 2.

14. Paul Street, *The Vicious Circle. Race, Prison, Jobs, and Community in Chicago, Illinois, and the Nation* (Chicago: Chicago Urban League, Department of Research and Planning, 2002).

15. Street, *Vicious Circle*, 3.

16. Alden Loury, "Black Offenders Face Stiffest Drug Sentences," *Chicago Reporter*, Sept. 12, 2007.

17. Ibid.

18. Street, *Vicious Circle*, 15.

19. Donald G. Lubin et al., *Chicago Metropolis 2020: 2006 Crime and Justice Index*, (Washington, DC: Pew Center on the States, 2006), 5, www.pewcenteronthestates.org/report_detail.aspx?id=33022.

20. Report of the Illinois Disproportionate Justice Impact Study Commission, Dec. 2010, available at www.centerforhealthandjustice.org/DJIS_ExecSumm_FINAL.pdf.

21. Lubin et al., *Chicago Metropolis 2020*, 37.

22. Ibid., 35.

23. Ibid., 3; see also Bruce Western, *Punishment and Inequality in America* (New York: Russell Sage Foundation, 2006), 12.

24. Street, *Vicious Circle*, 3.

25. Ibid.

26. Ibid.

3 Deportations Are Down, But Fear Persists Among Undocumented Immigrants

Tim Henderson

BALTIMORE—A young father of three, an unauthorized immigrant, is haunted by the story of a close friend he says was falsely accused of rape and deported to Central America.

"He was at the store waiting and somebody came up and said he had been charged, and they took him away," said the man, a member of a weekly support group for unauthorized immigrants of inner-city Baltimore. Some are so stressed out by their status they suffer from blurred vision, weakness and dizziness, their caregivers say.

"Now he's back in the home country and there's a black mark against him if he ever comes back," said the man, who, like others in the group, did not want to be identified by name out of fear of deportation. "If you don't have money for lawyers and bail, and you didn't do the crime, they deport you."

The fear of deportation persists in immigrant enclaves across the country, despite a new federal policy in effect since last November that has dramatically reduced the number of noncriminal deportations. Cities like Baltimore and states like California and Nevada that want to provide more services to unauthorized immigrants are finding that it takes a lot of reassurance to get such people out of the shadows.

Advocates say immigrants' fear can prevent them from cooperating with police and derail attempts to ensure that all drivers are licensed. Their fear can also endanger growth in areas that are looking to immigrants to help reverse population losses.

California, which this year rolled out alternative driver's licenses for unauthorized immigrants and others unqualified for regular licenses, emphasized that police don't want to use the distinctive licenses to identify drivers for deportation, said Erika Contreras, chief of staff for state Sen. Ricardo Lara, a Democrat.

The state organized 200 presentations and workshops to introduce the new licenses in hopes of bringing immigrants out of the shadows. "A law enforcement officer was right there saying, 'Come out, don't be afraid, we want you to have a driver's license and we want you to get insurance. Everybody will be safer,' " Contreras said recently at an event sponsored by The Pew Charitable Trusts (Pew funds *Stateline*).

Fear persists even in places that, like Baltimore, have made a point of welcoming unauthorized immigrants. Mayor Stephanie Rawlings-Blake, a Democrat, has been outspoken[1] about the importance of immigrants to the city's growth as other groups decline.

Baltimore joined Atlanta, Detroit and Nashville in a campaign[2] last year, National Welcoming Week, to promote immigrant-friendly policies. Baltimore police, for example, are trained to accept foreign forms of ID without questioning immigration status.

Reprinted from Stateline, a project of The Pew Charitable Trusts, © 2015.

Catalina Rodriguez, director of the Mayor's Office of Immigrant and Multicultural Affairs in Baltimore, said many of the changes aimed to improve immigrants' access to city services.

"It's part of building a relationship with the community, part of breaking the barriers down," Rodriguez said. "We want to let them know it's OK for them to call the police and tell them what's happening in the neighborhood."

'He Would Have Killed Me'

One support group member, who works in construction, said he feels a duty to report crimes, partly because he was treated well by police when he was assaulted recently.

The police stopped an attacker who had slammed the man's head with a car door and tried to take his car keys, but didn't ask about his immigration status, the man said.

"Thank goodness. If they hadn't done that, he would have killed me," he said. "It was a dark day for me, but I was treated well. I am afraid of deportation because I have a family and that family depends on me."

But others in the group said they find any interaction with police worrisome, and weren't so sure they would report a crime.

"It is a risk, so I might not call unless it's something serious—maybe if it was two or three against one, something really unfair," another man said.

The Police Executive Research Forum, which studies best practices for police, found in a study last year that police can often be caught between enforcing immigration laws and forging ties to the community.

Alabama, for instance, passed a law in 2011 requiring police to check immigration status during traffic stops if there is reasonable suspicion that the individual is in the country illegally, one of the nation's most far-reaching laws aimed at unauthorized immigrants. But local farmers complained that the law frightened migrant workers into leaving the state until local sheriffs stopped enforcing it.

When Prince William County, Virginia, passed a similar law in 2007, then Chief of Police Charlie Deane publicly expressed many reservations, saying it would cause anger at his officers and limit cooperation. "You cannot keep the community safe unless the majority of the community has trust in the police and will call, will bear witness when they need to," Deane said.

A University of Texas study[3] this year found that crimes, especially violent crimes, are reported less often in cities with many immigrants. The study, which analyzed the National Crime Victimization Survey, said fear of deportation played a role.

Immigrants may "rationally decide not to report crime to the police because of their citizenship status," the study concluded.

Much Less Risk

The Migration Policy Institute (MPI) estimates[4] that only 13 percent of unauthorized immigrants are at high risk of deportation under federal priorities announced last year, down from 27 percent before then.

The new policy stresses deportation of serious criminals, although some misdemeanors can still be deportable. And, because the government reserves the right to deport anyone it deems a national security threat, and some immigration crimes like recent border crossings or returning after deportation remain deportable, the new rules don't guarantee safety for immigrants.

Stories of questionable deportations can spread fast and cause continued tension, according to Marc Rosenblum, a deputy director at MPI. He cited the case of Max Villatoro, a pastor and married father of four, who was deported[5] to Honduras this year over a drunken driving conviction.

U.S. Immigration and Customs Enforcement considers the crime a "significant misdemeanor," which is still deportable. But the new rules give ICE discretion[6] in handling such cases if the person is not a threat to national security, border security or public safety.

"We still don't know how strictly ICE is going to interpret these new priorities," Rosenblum said.

Preliminary numbers support the idea that the new policies are cutting down on deportations. A recent report[7] obtained by The Associated Press shows deportations down more than 40 percent from 2012.

Detainers, or holds placed on local prisoners for possible deportation, have also dropped, but many are still being held who have not yet been convicted of any crime, according to an April report[8] from the Transactional Records Access Clearinghouse at Syracuse University.

That's one reason why states and cities that want to minimize deportations still need to limit cooperation with ICE detainers, said Jose Magana-Salgado, an attorney for the Immigrant Legal Resource Center.

"ICE is going to send more detainers to localities that cooperate more," Magana-Salgado said, adding that many immigrants are sometimes painted as criminals merely because of immigration charges like returning after deportation or repeated border crossings.

Single Mothers Feel Vulnerable

In Baltimore, unauthorized immigrants who are single mothers say they feel especially vulnerable.

"It's worse for a single mom," said one woman who came from Mexico 10 years ago and works as a housecleaner, asking that her full name not be used. "When I leave to go to work in the morning I don't know what's going to happen if I don't come back. What would happen to my daughters?"

San Juanita García, who studies female immigrants at the University of North Carolina, said the specter of deportation is especially hard on women.

"Mexican immigrant women experience a deportation threat directly taking a toll on their mental health, indicative of their more precarious status," she said.

Baltimore support group members said they knew people who felt pressured by court-appointed attorneys into signing guilty pleas for felony crimes they did not commit. They are in prison awaiting deportation.

"They're locked up, desperate, and they sign something and boom, 10 years and then they get deported," especially those who can't afford lawyers, said a woman who works at a bakery.

Several also told stories about seeing ICE cars waiting and watching at workplaces, bus stops, even playgrounds where mothers pick up their children.

The amount of vigilance seems unfair, another woman said: "It seems totally unjust because you see people who are working honestly, who don't rob anybody, don't commit any kind of crime, and especially a single mother is afraid they're going to take her away."

NOTES

1. "The Role of Immigrants in Growing Baltimore." Created by The Baltimore Mayor's Office, The New Americans Task Force, and the Abell Foundation, September 2014. Available at: http://mayor.baltimorecity.gov/sites/default/files/RoleOfImmigrantsInGrowing Baltimore20140917.pdf

2. "From the Halls of Government to the Heart of Communities, National Welcoming Week Celebrates and Uplifts Immigrants." *Welcoming America*. N.p., 02 Oct. 2014.

3. Gutierrez, C. M., and D. S. Kirk. "Silence Speaks: The Relationship between Immigration and the Underreporting of Crime." *Crime & Delinquency* (2015).

4. Rosenblum, Marc. "Understanding the Potential Impact of Executive Action on Immigration Enforcement." *Migrationpolicy.org*. N.p., 13 July 2015.

5. Hines, Holly. "Attorney: Pastor Max Villatoro Deported; 'no Easy Way' to Get US Visa." *Iowa City Press Citizen*. N.p., 20 Mar. 2015.

6. "Policies for the Apprehension, Detention, and Removal of Undocumented Immigrants." U.S. Department of Homeland Security Memorandum, November 20, 2014. Available at: http://www.dhs.gov/sites/default/files/publications/14_1120_memo _prosecutorial_discretion.pdf

7. Caldwell, Alicia. "US Government Deports Fewest Immigrants in Nearly a Decade." The Big Story. N.p., 6 Oct. 2015. Web.

8. Trac Immigration. "Further Decrease in ICE Detainer Use: Still Not Targeting Serious Criminals." August 28, 2015. Available at: http://trac.syr.edu/immigration/reports/402/

4 The Ghosts of Stonewall
Policing Gender, Policing Sex
Joey L. Mogul, Andrea J. Ritchie, and Kay Whitlock

Our entire movement started from fighting police violence, and we're still fighting police violence. In many ways, it's gotten worse.
— Imani Henry, founder of TransJustice[1]

On a hot August night in 1966, "drag queens" and gay "hustlers" at the Compton Cafeteria in the Tenderloin District of San Francisco rose up and fought back when police tried to arrest them for doing nothing more than being out.[2] The late 1960s saw frequent police raids, often accompanied by brutality, on gay establishments across the country, which were meeting with increasing resistance. The previous five years had also seen uprisings in Watts, Detroit, Chicago, and Newark and dozens of other cities, in many cases sparked by incidents of widespread racial profiling and abuse of people of color by police.[3]

It was against this backdrop that, in the early morning hours of Saturday, June 28, 1969, police raided the Stonewall Inn in New York City. Claiming to be enforcing liquor laws, they began arresting employees and patrons of the private lesbian and gay establishment. Police action, which included striking patrons with billy clubs while spewing homophobic abuse, sparked outrage among those present. Led by people described by many as drag queens and butch lesbians, bar patrons, joined by street people, began yelling "Gay Power!" and throwing shoes, coins, and bricks at the officers. Over the next several nights, police and queers clashed repeatedly in the streets of the West Village. One report described the impacts of the police response to the uprising as follows:

> At one point, Seventh Avenue . . . looked like a battlefield in Vietnam. Young people, many of them queens, were lying on the sidewalk bleeding from the head, face, mouth, and even the eyes. Others were nursing bruised and often bleeding arms, legs, backs, and necks.[4]

The Stonewall Uprising, as the rebellion against the raids came to be known, has been mythically cast as the "birthplace" of the modern LGBT rights movement in the United States, although in reality it was but one of its primary catalysts. In the weeks that followed, the Gay Liberation Front, inspired by contemporaneous movements such as the women's liberation movement, the Black Panthers, and the Young Lords, was formed.[5] Spontaneous resistance to police raids on gay bars and bathhouses blossomed in the ensuing decade. The 1970 protest march commemorating the one-year

Republished with permission of Beacon Press, from *Queer (In)Justice: The Criminalization of LGBT People in the United States*, Mogul, J. L., Ritchie, A. J., & Whitlock, K. Copyright © 2011; permission conveyed through Copyright Clearance Center, Inc.

anniversary of the raid on the Stonewall Inn grew into an annual worldwide celebration of gay pride.

Fast forward three decades to March 2003, when the Power Plant, a private club in the Highland Park area of Detroit, frequented primarily by African American gay men, lesbians, and transgender women, was filled to capacity. Around 3:00 a.m., between 50 and 100 officers from the Wayne County Sheriff's Department dressed in black clothing, with guns drawn and laser sights on, suddenly cut the lights and stormed the premises, shouting orders for everyone to "hit the floor." Over 350 people in the club at that time were handcuffed, forced to lie face down on the floor, and detained for up to twelve hours, left to "sit in their own and others' urine and waste." Some were kicked in the head and back, slammed into walls, and verbally abused. Officers on the scene were heard saying things like "it's a bunch of fags" and "those fags in here make me sick." As at Stonewall, the officers claimed to be enforcing building and liquor codes. The sheriff's department said they were responding to complaints from neighbors and concerns for public safety. They had obtained a warrant to search the premises, but rather than execute it during the daytime against only the owner of the establishment, they chose to wait until the club was full, and then unjustifiably arrested over 300 people, citing them for "loitering inside a building," an offense carrying a maximum fine of $500. Vehicles within a three-block radius of the club were also ticketed and towed, despite the fact that some of the car owners had never even entered the club that night.[6]

The policing of queer sexualities has been arguably the most visible and recognized point of contact between LGBT people and the criminal legal system. From the images that form the opening sequence of *Milk*—the 2008 biopic about gay San Francisco supervisor Harvey Milk—of groups of white gay men hiding from cameras as they are rounded up by police in the 1950s, to the historic clashes with police of the late 1960s and early 1970s, police repression and resistance to it are central themes of gay life in the United States. Groundbreaking gay rights organizations such as the Mattachine Society and the Daughters of Bilitis have expressed strong concern about bar raids and police harassment.[7] A study conducted by the National Gay Task Force (now the NGLTF) in the mid-eighties found that 23 percent of gay men and 13 percent of lesbians reported having been harassed, threatened with violence, or physically attacked by police because of their sexual orientation.[8] It remains a daily occurrence for large numbers of LGBT people. According to reports made to the National Coalition of Anti-Violence Programs (NCAVP) in 2008, law enforcement officers were the third-largest category of perpetrators of anti-LGBT violence.[9] Incidences of reported police violence against LGBT people increased by 150 percent between 2007 and 2008, and the number of law enforcement officers reported to have engaged in abusive treatment of LGBT people increased by 11 percent.[10] In 2000, the NCAVP stated that 50 percent of bias-related violence reported by transgender women in San Francisco was committed by police and private security officers.[11]

As demonstrated by the Power Plant incident, in many ways, policing of queers has not changed significantly since the days when it sparked outrage and resistance from LGBT communities, although its focus has narrowed to some degree. According to the New York City Anti-Violence Project, "Young queer people of color, transgender youth, homeless and street involved youth are more vulnerable to police violence . . . AVP's data analysis also reveals that transgender individuals are at a greater risk of experiencing police violence and misconduct than non trans people."[12] The National Center for Lesbian Rights (NCLR) and Transgender Law Center reported in 2003 that one in four transgender people in San Francisco had been harassed or abused by the police.[13] Far from fading into the annals of LGBT history, police violence against queers is alive and well.

Yet with the exception of sodomy law enforcement, since the mid 1970s resistance to abusive policing of LGBT people has largely been absent from the agendas of national mainstream LGBT organizations, particularly as police have increasingly narrowed their focus to segments of LGBT communities with little power or voice inside and outside such groups. Similarly, while mainstream police accountability and civil rights organizations have called for accountability in a limited number of cases involving LGBT individuals, policing of gender and queer sexualities has not been central to their analysis of the issue. It is essential to bring the persistent police violence experienced by LGBT people to the fore of these movements to ensure the ghosts of Stonewall do not continue to haunt for years to come. . . .

Policing Gender

Queer encounters with police are not limited to those driven by efforts to punish deviant sexualities. Sylvia Rivera, one of the veterans of the Stonewall Uprising, described the treatment of transgender women at the time: "When drag queens were arrested, what degradation there was! . . . We always felt that the police were the real enemy . . . . We were disrespected. A lot of us were beaten up and raped."[14]

Law enforcement officers have fairly consistently and explicitly policed the borders of the gender binary. Historically and up until the 1980s, such policing took the form of enforcement of sumptuary laws, which required individuals to wear at least three articles of clothing conventionally associated with the gender they were assigned at birth, and subjected people to arrest for impersonating another gender.[15] . . .

Currently, gender is often directly policed through arbitrary and violent arrests of transgender and gender-nonconforming people for using the "wrong" restroom—even though there is generally no law requiring individuals who use bathrooms designated as for men or women to have any particular set of characteristics. As Franke notes, sumptuary laws and bathroom signs serve similar functions, creating and reinforcing an "official symbolic language of gendered identity that rightfully belongs to either sex. 'Real women' and 'real men' conform to the norms; the rest of us are deviants. Curiously, in life and in law, bathrooms seem to be the site where one's sexual authenticity is tested."[16] . . .

Beyond bathrooms, gender policing takes place through routine harassment. Verbal abuse of transgender and gender-nonconforming people is commonplace. According to a Los Angeles study of 244 transgender women, 37 percent of respondents reported experiencing verbal abuse from a police officer on at least one occasion.[17] It also takes place through arrests of individuals who carry identification reflecting the "wrong" gender. Such policing draws on and reinforces the criminalizing archetype of transgender and gender-nonconforming people as intrinsically dishonest and deceptive. It often extends to routinely subjecting transgender and gender-nonconforming people to inappropriate, invasive, and unlawful searches conducted for the purpose of viewing or touching individuals' genitals, either to satisfy law enforcement officers' curiosity, or to determine a person's "real" gender. Jeremy Burke, a white transgender man arrested in San Francisco in 2002, was kicked and beaten, and forcibly strip-searched by several female officers, then placed naked and handcuffed in a holding tank. A dress was later thrown into the cell, which Burke refused to wear. An officer subsequently forced Burke to display his genitalia, justifying police actions by saying, "The boss doesn't know where to put you," and then taunting him further, stating, "That's the biggest clit I ever saw."[18]

Gender nonconformity is also often punished in and of itself, through physical violence, drawing on a toxic amalgam of queer criminalizing archetypes. Controlling narratives framing women of African descent as masculine and women of color as sexually degraded are also at play, dictating punishment for failure to conform to racialized gender norms. For instance, Black lesbians frequently report being punched in the chest by officers who justify their violence by saying something along the lines of, "You want to act like a man, I'll treat you like a man."[19] A Latina lesbian arrested at a demonstration in New York City in 2003 reported that an officer walked her by cells holding men and told her, "You think you're a man, we'll put you in there and see what happens." A Black lesbian in Atlanta reported being raped by a police officer who told her the world needed "one less dyke."[20]

At other times, gender policing is subtler. Gender nonconformity in appearance or expression gives rise to police presumptions of disorder, violence, and mental instability, among other qualities. Such presumptions are heightened when synergistically reinforced by equally powerful stereotypes based on race, class, or both. In routine daily interactions, police can be described as succumbing to "classification anxiety."[21] When officers feel challenged in engaging in the rigid classification of individuals as male and female, gay and straight, an individual's mere presence in public spaces is experienced as a disruption of the social order. Queer, transgender, and gender-nonconforming people are threatening because they place in question "identities previously conceived as stable, unchallengeable, grounded and 'known,'" which serve as critical tools of heterosexist culture.[22] As a transgender woman said, "If people can't put a label on you they get confused . . . people have to know who you are. You categorize in your mind. One of the first things you do is determine sex—if you can't do that, it blows the whole system up."[23] Where law enforcement officers experience classification anxiety, the consequences are widespread harassment, abuse, and arbitrary arrest.

• • •

In Feinberg's words, "Even where the laws are not written down, police are empowered to carry out merciless punishment for sex and gender difference."[24] Beyond the daily violence and humiliation law enforcement officers mete out on the streets, police also serve as a first point of contact with the criminal legal system, thereby playing a critical role in shaping how queers will be treated within it. Alternately determining whether queers will be seen as victims or suspects, fueling archetype-driven prosecutions, and driving incarceration and punishment, policing of queers continues to warrant concerted attention on the part of LGBT, police accountability, and civil rights movements.

NOTES

1. Imani Henry, founder of TransJustice, an organizing initiative of the Audre Lorde Project, www.alp.org.

2. For more information, see www.comptonscafeteriariot.org/main.html.

3. Urvashi Vaid, *Virtual Equality: The Mainstreaming of Gay & Lesbian Liberation,* (New York: Anchor Books, 1995), 55–56; and Michael Bronski, "Stonewall Was a Riot," *ZNet,* June 10, 2009, www.zmag.org/znet/viewArticle/21666 (accessed July 14, 2009).

4. Leigh W. Rutledge, *The Gay Decades: From Stonewall to the Present: The People and Events That Shaped Gay Lives* (New York: Penguin, 1992), 3.

5. Bronski, "Stonewall Was a Riot."

6. Amnesty International, *Stonewalled: Police Abuse and Misconduct against Lesbian, Gay, Bisexual and Transgender People in the U.S.* (New York: Amnesty International USA, 2005), 30; and Jeff Montgomery, executive director, Triangle Foundation, to Don Cox, chief of staff, Wayne County Sheriff's Department, March 11, 2003 (on file with coauthor Ritchie).

7. Bronski, "Stonewall Was a Riot."

8. Kevin Berrill, "Criminal Justice Subcommittee: Hearing on Police Practices—Testimony Submitted by Kevin Berrill, Violence Project Director of the National Gay Task Force," November 28, 1983 (on file with coauthors).

9. National Coalition of Anti-Violence Programs, *Anti-Lesbian, Gay, Bisexual and Transgender Violence in 2008* (2009), 13, 15.

10. National Coalition of Anti-Violence Programs, *Anti-Lesbian, Gay, Bisexual and Transgender Violence in 2007* (2008), 3. See also NCAVP, *Anti-LGBT Violence in 2008,* 5. It should be noted that these figures likely fall far short of reflecting the totality of police violence against LGBT people. NCAVP's member organizations' primary focus is on collecting data on anti-LGBT violence broadly defined, rather than specifically on police misconduct against queers. It should also be noted that in 2007 the NCAVP reported a 133 percent increase in reported cases of false arrest or "entrapment" of queers by police.

11. National Coalition of Anti-Violence Programs, *Anti-Lesbian, Gay, Bisexual and Transgender Violence in 2000* (2001), 47.

12. NCAVP, *Anti-LGBT Violence in 2007,* 40.

13. Shannon Minter and Christopher Daley, *Trans Realities: A Legal Needs Assessment of San Francisco's Transgender Communities,* National Center for Lesbian Rights, Transgender Law Center (2003).

14. Leslie Feinberg, " 'I'm glad I was in the Stonewall Riot': Leslie Feinberg Interviews Sylvia Rivera," *Workers' World,* July 2, 1998.

15. Gwen Smith, "Transsexual Terrorism," *Washington Blade,* October 3, 2003. See also Elaine Craig, "Transphobia and the Relational Production of Gender," *Hastings Women's Law Journal* 18 (2007): 162.

16. Franke, "Central Mistake," 69, 57. See also Amnesty, *Stonewalled,* 20.

17. Reback et al., *The Los Angeles Transgender Health Study: Community Report* (Los Angeles: University of California at Los Angeles, 2001). See also Amnesty, *Stonewalled*, 48–52.

18. R. Gierach, "Transgender Sues San Francisco Law Enforcement for Brutality," *Lesbian News* 28, no. 2 (September 2002): 16.

19. Andrea Ritchie, "Law Enforcement Violence against Women of Color," in *The Color of Violence: The INCITE! Anthology* (Cambridge, MA: South End, 2006).

20. Amnesty, *Stonewalled*, 41.

21. See Leslie Pearlman, "Transsexualism as Metaphor: The Collision of Sex and Gender," *Buffalo Law Review* 43 (1995): 835, 844.

22. Marjorie Garber, *Vested Interests: Cross-Dressing and Cultural Anxiety* (New York: Harper Perennial, 1992).

23. Annie Woodhouse, *Fantastic Women: Sex, Gender and Transvestism* (Rutgers, NJ: Rutgers University Press, 1989), xiii.

24. Feinberg, *Trans Liberation*, 11.

5 The Transgender Crucible

Sabrina Rubin Erdely

This article contains accounts of different forms of violence and assault, including transphobic, racist, and sexual violence.

A dozen eggs, bacon, maybe some biscuits: CeCe McDonald had a modest shopping list in mind, just a few things for breakfast the next day. It was midnight, the ideal time for a supermarket run. Wearing a lavender My Little Pony T-shirt and denim cutoffs, CeCe grabbed her purse for the short walk to the 24-hour Cub Foods. She preferred shopping at night, when the darkened streets provided some relief from the stares, whispers and insults she encountered daily as a transgender woman. CeCe, 23, had grown accustomed to snickers and double takes – and was practiced in talking back to strangers who'd announce, "That's a man!" But such encounters were tiring; some days a lady just wanted to buy her groceries in peace.

And so it was that on a warm Saturday night in June 2011, CeCe and four friends, all African-Americans in their twenties, found themselves strolling the tree-lined streets of her quiet working-class Longfellow neighborhood in Minneapolis, toward a commercial strip. Leading the way was CeCe's roommate Latavia Taylor and two purse-carrying gay men – CeCe's makeshift family, whom she called "cousin" and "brothers" – with CeCe, a fashion student at a local community college, and her lanky boyfriend trailing behind. They were passing the Schooner Tavern when they heard the jeering.

"Faggots."

Gathered outside the dive bar were a handful of cigarette-smoking white people, looking like an aging biker gang in their T-shirts, jeans and bandannas, motorcycles parked nearby. Hurling the insults were 47-year-old Dean Schmitz, in a white button-down and thick silver chain, and his 40-year-old ex-girlfriend Molly Flaherty, clad in black, drink in hand. "Look at that boy dressed as a girl, tucking his dick in!" hooted Schmitz, clutching two beer bottles freshly fetched from his Blazer, as CeCe and her friends slowed to a stop. "You niggers need to go back to Africa!"

Chrishaun "CeCe" McDonald stepped in front of her friends, a familiar autopilot kicking in, shunting fury and fear to a distant place while her mouth went into motion. "Excuse me. We are people, and you need to respect us," CeCe began in her lisping delivery, one acrylic-nailed finger in the air, her curtain of orange microbraids swaying. With her caramel skin, angled jaw and square chin, friends called her "CeCe" for her resemblance to the singer Ciara; even her antagonist Flaherty would later describe CeCe as "really pretty." "We're just trying to walk to the store," CeCe continued, raising her voice over the blare of Schmitz and Flaherty's free-associating invective: "bitches with dicks," "faggot-lovers," "niggers," "rapists." The commotion was drawing more patrons out of the bar – including a six-foot-eight, 310-pound

Copyright © Rolling Stone LLC 2014. All Rights Reserved. Used by permission.

biker in leather chaps – and CeCe's boyfriend, Larry Thomas, nervously called to Schmitz, "Enjoy your night, man – just leave us alone." CeCe and her friends turned to go. Then Flaherty glanced at Schmitz and laughed.

"I'll take all of you bitches on!" Flaherty hollered, and smashed CeCe in the side of her face with a glass tumbler.

Just like that, a mundane walk to the store turned into a street brawl, in a near-farcical clash of stereotypes. Pandemonium erupted as CeCe and Flaherty seized each other by the hair; the bikers swung fists and hurled beer bottles, hollering "beat that faggot ass!"; and CeCe's friends flailed purses and cracked their studded belts as whips. When the two sides separated, panting and disoriented, Flaherty was curled up amid the broken glass screaming, mistakenly, that she'd been knifed, and CeCe stood over her, her T-shirt drenched with her own blood. Touching her cheek, CeCe felt a shock of pain as her finger entered the open wound where Flaherty's glass had punctured her salivary gland. Purse still over her shoulder, CeCe fast-walked from the scene. She'd made it more than a half-block away when she heard her friends calling, "Watch your back!"

CeCe whirled around to see Schmitz heading toward her: walking, then running, his face a twist of wild, unrestrained hatred. CeCe felt terror burst out from that remote place where she normally locked it away. She didn't know that Schmitz's veins were pounding with cocaine and meth. She didn't know of his lengthy rap sheet, including convictions for assault. Nor did she know that under Schmitz's shirt, inked across his solar plexus, was a four-inch swastika tattoo. All CeCe needed to see was the look on his face to know her worst fears were coming true: Her young life was about to end as a grim statistic, the victim of a hate crime.

"Come here, bitch!" Schmitz roared as he closed in. CeCe pedaled backward, blood dripping from her slashed face.

"Didn't y'all get enough?" CeCe asked, defiant and afraid, while her hand fished into her large handbag for anything to protect herself. Her fingers closed on a pair of black-handled fabric scissors she used for school. She held them up high as a warning, their five-inch blades glinting in the parking-lot floodlights. Schmitz stopped an arm's length away, raising clenched fists and shuffling his feet in a boxing stance. His eyes were terrible with rage.

"Bitch, you gonna stab me?" he shouted. They squared off for a tense moment: the furious white guy, amped up on meth, Nazi tattoo across his belly; the terrified black trans woman with a cartoon pony on her T-shirt; the scissors between them. CeCe saw Schmitz lunge toward her and braced herself for impact. Their bodies collided, then separated. He was still looking at her.

"Bitch – you stabbed me!"

"Yes, I did," CeCe announced, even as she wondered if that could possibly be true; in the adrenaline of the moment, she'd felt nothing. Scanning Schmitz over, she saw no sign of injury – though in fact he'd sustained a wound so grisly that CeCe would later recall to police that the button-down shirt Schmitz wore that night was not white but "mainly red. Like one of them Hawaiian shirts." CeCe waited until he turned to rejoin his crowd. Then she and Thomas ran arm in arm down the block toward the nearly empty Cub Foods parking lot, where they waited for police to arrive.

They didn't see the scene unfolding behind them: how Schmitz took a few faltering steps, uttered, "I'm bleeding," then lifted his shirt to unleash a geyser of blood. CeCe had stabbed him in the chest, burying the blade almost three and a half inches deep, slicing his heart. Blood sprayed the road as Schmitz staggered, collapsed and, amid his friends' screams, died. When CeCe and Thomas waved down a police car minutes later, she was promptly handcuffed and arrested.

• • •

Given the swift political advances of the transgender movement, paired with its new pop-culture visibility, you'd be forgiven for believing that to be gender-nonconforming today is to be accepted, celebrated, even trendy – what with trans models in ads for American Apparel and Barneys; Facebook's more than 50 gender options for users to choose from; and Eurovision song-contest winner Conchita Wurst, who accepted the trophy in an evening gown and a full beard. When this spring Secretary of Defense Chuck Hagel recommended a review of the military's ban on allowing trans people to serve openly—by one estimate, trans people are as much as twice as likely as the general U.S. population to serve in the armed forces—his announcement seemed to herald a new era of recognition. But the appearance of tolerance belies the most basic day-to-day reality: No community living in America today is as openly terrorized as transgender women, especially trans women of color . . . .

. . . Living with a gender identity different from one's birth anatomy (a phenomenon thought to affect as many as one in 10,000 people) means that trans women live with constant anxiety of being recognized as trans – "getting spooked" or "getting clocked" – because reactions can be harsh to the extreme. Though transgender people make up perhaps 10 percent of the LGBT community, they account for a shocking proportion of its hate-crime statistics, with trans people nearly twice as likely to be threatened as their LGB peers. And trans people all too often meet with violent deaths: Of the 25 reported anti-LGBT homicides in 2012, according to the National Coalition of Anti-Violence Programs, transgender people accounted for more than half of the victims. All of those trans homicide victims were trans women of color.

Highlighting the danger, transgender murders tend to be gruesome, often involving torture and mutilation, as in the 2012 California murder of 37-year-old Brandy Martell, who was shot in the genitals; or the brutal hatchet slaying last July in Philadelphia of 31-year-old Diamond Williams, whose body was hacked to pieces and strewn in an overgrown lot. After Williams' alleged killer reportedly confessed that he'd killed Williams, a prostitute he'd solicited, when he'd realized she was trans – commonly known as the "trans panic defense" – online commenters were quick to agree "the cross-dresser had it coming": that Williams' transgender status was an act of duplicity whose logical punishment was death. "It's socially sanctioned to say that," says Cox. "If a guy is even attracted to her, then she has to die. What is that?" And when these cases go unresolved, as they often do – like last summer's vicious Harlem beating death of 21-year-old Islan Nettles, reportedly after a catcalling admirer turned vengeful – the lack of resolution seems a further reminder to trans women of their own disposability. It's telling that the closest thing the trans community has to a long-running Pride event is Transgender Day of Remembrance, a day of mourning for victims of violence.

"It takes a toll. This life is not an easy life," says trans woman Anya Stacy Neal. "Trust me, if this was a choice, I would have packed it up a long time ago."

As the sisterhood is picked off one by one, each gets a chilling vision of her own fate. "You rarely hear of a trans woman just living a long life and then dying of old age," says CeCe today, seated at a friend's Minneapolis dining-room table with her legs crossed ladylike at the knee. Wearing a striped cardigan that she opens to reveal, laughing, a T-shirt reading it's all about me, CeCe's an animated run-on talker with a lip ring and a warm, open nature, whose cadences recall the church days of her youth, mouth opening wide to flash a tongue stud. "You never hear, 'She passed on her own, natural causes, old age,' no, no, no," she continues, ticking off on her fingers. "She's either raped and killed, she's jumped and killed, stalked and killed – or just killed." Which is why, amid all the death and sorrow, CeCe, whose jagged life experience embodies the archetypal trans woman's in so many ways, has become an LGBT folk hero for her story of survival – and for the price she paid for fighting back . . . .

From earliest childhood CeCe had felt at odds with her boy's body, boyish clothes and boy's name (a name that she still can't discuss without anguish). She'd always felt such an irrepressible girlishness. In grade school she walked with graceful wrists and swishing hips, to the consternation of her family. CeCe was the oldest of seven, raised on Chicago's gritty South Side by a single mother; a dozen family members crammed under one roof, where no one could fail to notice young CeCe sashaying in her mother's heels. "You need to pray that out of you," her religious family instructed, and at night, CeCe tearfully pleaded with God to take away her sinful attraction to boys. Better yet, she prayed to awaken a girl, in the body He had surely meant for her.

She redoubled her prayers as other kids began to mock her femininity, and their taunts turned violent. CeCe was chased through the neighborhood, beaten up and, around seventh grade, attacked by five high schoolers yelling "kill that faggot," who kicked her in the mouth so savagely that her incisor tore through the skin above her lip. Such bullying is the norm for transgender kids, nearly nine out of 10 of whom are harassed by peers, and 44 percent of whom are physically assaulted. But no number of beatings could change CeCe. In school she'd dash into the girls' bathroom when the coast was clear, frightened of being seen in the boys' room sitting down to pee. She joined the cheerleading squad – gleefully doing splits at basketball games – coming to class in her mom's blouse or platform shoes, though she'd change back into boy clothes before returning home, fearful of her family's wrath, and of losing the love of her mother, who was trying to persuade CeCe onto a more traditional path.

"It kind of scared me," says mom Christi McDonald of CeCe's femininity. "I know it's a cruel world, and if you're different it's hard for people to accept you." Christi bought CeCe baggy jeans and dropped hints about cute girls, just as when CeCe was smaller Christi had urged her to draw pictures of Superman instead of sketching dresses. "I kept questioning him, 'Why are you doing this?'" Christi says, adjusting her pronouns to add, "I just wanted a peaceful life for her."

CeCe had always tried staying in her mom's good graces by being a responsible, diligent child, constantly neatening the house, making the beds and whipping up recipes inspired by cooking shows, but nonetheless she felt her mother grow distant. CeCe was unable to find sanctuary with her family, and tensions grew in the crowded three-bedroom house. One day, an uncle found an undelivered love note she'd written to a boy and, CeCe says, knocked her to the kitchen floor and choked her. She ran away from home, never to return. She was 14.

She crashed with friends before taking up residence in a glorified drug den where other runaways congregated. CeCe tried to see the bright side of her family's rejection: She was finally free to be herself. The first time she tried on a bra and panties, she felt a shiver of recognition that she was headed in the right direction. Instead, she fell right through a trapdoor. She'd reached a crucial point in the too-typical trans woman's narrative, in which, cut loose at a young age from family, she falls directly into harm's way. Up to 40 percent of U.S. homeless youth are LGBT. Adrift without money, shelter, education or a support system, they're exposed to myriad dangers. According to one study, 58 percent of LGBT homeless youth are sexually assaulted (compared with 33 percent of their hetero peers). Drug and alcohol use is rampant. CeCe grew up fast. "Honey, I think there's not too much in this world that I haven't heard or seen or done," she tells me. "And a lot of that is sad."

She learned to sell crack and marijuana. Out in the streets, her appearance in girls' clothing was met with outbursts of violence, as when a man once threw an empty 40-ounce bottle at her head, knocking her unconscious; another time, a stranger pulled a knife. Even more traumatic, a handsome man lured CeCe into his home with an invitation to smoke weed – "I was like, 'Oh, my goodness, this is so cool.' Very naive, thinking everybody is good" – then pushed her face-forward onto his bed and anally raped her. The assault changed CeCe profoundly, crystallizing how expendable she was in the eyes of the world. Never had she felt so degraded, and so certain no one would care. Living in poverty and unpredictability so extreme that she sometimes found herself sleeping on park benches and eating grass to fill her belly, CeCe decided to offer herself in the one last arena where she felt she had worth.

At 15, CeCe was a child prostitute working the strip off Belmont Avenue in Boystown, climbing into men's cars to earn up to $1,000 on a Saturday night. In choosing the sex trade, CeCe was heading down a well-worn path. Studies of urban transgender women have found that upward of 50 percent had engaged in sex work. It's a risky job, in which the threat of violence is only one hazard. Transgender women are considered the fastest-growing HIV-positive population in the country, with a meta-analysis showing that nearly 28 percent of trans women in America have the virus. Bearing the highest risk are trans women in sex work, who are four times more likely to be living with HIV than other female sex workers . . . .

"I became this soulless drone," says CeCe. She entertained a dim hope she'd get AIDS and die. She was tired of internalizing hostility and worthlessness, mentally exhausted from constantly scanning for danger. Such daily burdens take a heavy toll: Though the suicide-attempt rate in the general population is estimated to be 4.6 percent, the National Transgender Discrimination Survey found that an extraordinary

41 percent of trans respondents had attempted suicide, with the rate soaring to 64 percent for sexual-assault victims. The first time CeCe attempted suicide, it was with pills washed down with a bottle of NyQuil. The second time, she crushed up a pile of pills and drank it down with juice. Asked how many times she tried to kill herself, CeCe has to think for a long moment; it's hard to sort out, since her late teens were basically an extended death wish. So much so that when one night a man on a street corner pointed a gun at her, shouting, "Faggot, I'll kill you," CeCe just looked at him and said, "Shoot me."

Surely it would have been far easier for CeCe if she'd given up, renounced her womanhood and opted to live life as a gay man. And yet even in her darkest despair, CeCe never considered retreat an option. If she was going to continue living, it was going to be as a lady. For her there was no decision-making; she felt she couldn't "choose" to be a man, because she'd never been male to begin with . . . .

[In 2006, CeCe took a Greyhound bus to the Twin Cities,] hoping to escape her Chicago misery and start anew. Instead she'd been floundering, in and out of shelters, flirting with coke and meth addictions, jailed for shoplifting and other misdemeanors, and hospitalized for suicidal ideation. But she'd also started visiting a drop-in youth center, where she learned how to regain control of her life bit by bit. "CeCe caught my attention right away," says her case manager Abby Beasley. "Her energy, she's just so bubbly, laughing constantly, just a real loving person. I put more work into her than I did anybody else, trying to help her stabilize her life."

Education was a first step: CeCe earned her GED, then enrolled in Minneapolis Community and Technical College, focusing on fashion design. Estrogen came next. A doctor diagnosed CeCe with gender dysphoria – determining that there was an incongruity between her biological sex and her gender identity – after which she started wearing a hormone patch on her hip, the cost covered by state medical assistance. CeCe watched with amazement as over the following months she developed smooth skin, fuller hips and, most fulfilling of all, breasts. Finally seeing her outer self match her inner self "was definitely something like a relief," she remembers. In an important move for CeCe, she called her mother to re-establish ties after years of separation. "Are those real?" Christi exclaimed when she finally got her first glimpse of CeCe post-hormones, and CeCe laughed in reply.

A legal name change tied a ribbon on CeCe's transition, a bureaucratic process that yielded a government ID identifying her by her carefully chosen new name: Chrishaun Reed Mai'luv McDonald. It was a name she liked for its mystique and personality; Chrishaun was also her aunt's name, keeping her tethered just a little bit to her past.

Secure in her identity at last, CeCe felt something free up within herself. And with confidence also came a new ability to stand up to street harassment; for perhaps the first time, she felt herself truly worth defending. "It's not OK that you called me a tranny," she'd lecture a surprised heckler. "You're gonna apologize, and then you're gonna go home and think about why you turned my pretty smile into an ugly mug." Satisfied, she'd coolly walk on, her self-respect growing with each small triumph.

"She looked like someone who knew where she was heading in life," says Larry Thomas, who caught sight of CeCe at a corner store and, knowing full well she was trans, gave her his phone number – thus beginning, in fits and starts, that thing that eludes so many trans women: an actual in-the-daylight relationship. Thomas was a straight man who usually kept his "flings" with trans women on the down-low. But CeCe began occupying much of his time, and she started to wonder if she wasn't doomed to live a lonely life after all.

Then came more good fortune, when in May 2011, after a decade of couch-surfing homelessness, CeCe moved into the very first apartment of her own. It was a two-bedroom oasis she shared with a roommate. Though still unemployed – CeCe paid her rent with general assistance and SSI – she was certain now that she was a college student with a permanent address, that remaining piece of the puzzle would be forthcoming.

"I was feeling really accomplished," remembers CeCe wistfully as she stands on the sidewalk looking up at the weather-beaten three-story brick apartment building on an early spring day. She tries flashing her patented wide smile, but it evaporates. We're taking a tour through her old neighborhood, and in skinny jeans, cropped jacket and a colorful head scarf, CeCe points at the second-floor window where she once lived, so full of potential and promise—a period that lasted for a single, shining month . . . .

• • •

In a police interrogation room hours after the stabbing, CeCe had given a full confession. "I was only trying to defend myself," CeCe sobbed. Police interviews with nearly a dozen witnesses would paint a consistent picture of the events of that night: Dean Schmitz and Molly Flaherty started the confrontation, Flaherty had triggered the fight by breaking a glass on CeCe's face, and Schmitz had pursued CeCe when she'd tried to escape—all precisely the way CeCe recounted in her confession. But no witness had seen exactly how the stabbing had transpired. "I didn't jab him; I didn't force the scissors into him; he was coming after me," CeCe insisted to detectives. "He ran into the scissors." And yet in Hennepin County Jail, CeCe was shocked to learn she was charged with second-degree murder. She faced up to 40 years in prison.

Dressed in orange scrubs, CeCe would cry and stare at the white brick walls of her cell for hours on end, her thoughts a tangle. There was the horrific knowledge that someone had died by her hand. And there was the agony that the life she'd been trying so hard to build had been decimated in an instant. "There wasn't a moment when I wasn't in pain mentally and spiritually, and even beating myself up for defending myself," CeCe says. She had nothing but time to obsess because she was locked alone in her cell for 23 hours a day. The jail had determined that for her own safety, she be held in solitary confinement.

Trans women have a difficult time behind bars, where they show up in disproportionate numbers; one survey found 16 percent of trans women had been to jail, compared to 2.7 percent of the general population. Once in prison they pose a dilemma, because, as a study of seven California prisons revealed, 59 percent of transgender inmates reported being sexually abused, compared to 4.4 percent of the general inmate population. A common solution, then, is to put them in solitary. For CeCe, who'd previously spent short stints in men's jails, the brain-racking isolation was a form of confinement she'd never known before. "There's no room for sanity," she says of her subsequent mental collapse. When her former caseworker Abby Beasley visited, Beasley was shocked at the sight of CeCe on the other side of the glass, scared and shaken, her left cheek swollen to the size of a golf ball.

"Whatever you can do to help me, please," CeCe begged.

Beasley notified the Trans Youth Support Network, a Minneapolis organization, which secured CeCe a pro bono lawyer. The case immediately galvanized the local trans and queer community, who saw CeCe's attack as something that could easily have happened to any of them, and hailed her as a hero. "CeCe was attacked in a racist, transphobic incident that could have killed her," says Billy Navarro Jr. of the Minnesota Transgender Health Coalition, who helped found the Free CeCe campaign. "And then how is she treated? She is prosecuted for having the audacity to survive."

Her support base grew after the Florida shooting death of Trayvon Martin, which stoked a national debate over race, self-defense and justice. CeCe's supporters argued that unlike George Zimmerman, who would be acquitted of all charges, CeCe had been faced with an actual threat, against which she had stood her ground. But they feared the justice system would view CeCe, as a black trans woman, unkindly. A petition advocating for CeCe's release gathered more than 18,000 signatures from across the country. As supporters in FREE CECE T-shirts held rallies outside the jail and packed the courthouse for each hearing, defense lawyer Hersch Izek set about building a case . . . .

The months leading to trial saw the judge's rulings laying waste to CeCe's defense case. Evidence of Schmitz's swastika tattoo was deemed inadmissible, since CeCe never saw the tattoo—it had no bearing on her mindset at the time of the killing—and because, Judge Daniel Moreno wrote, "the tattoo does not establish that [Schmitz] intended to threaten, fight or kill anyone." Schmitz's prior assault convictions were deemed irrelevant, and the judge would allow only limited testimony about the toxicology report showing Schmitz was high on meth, feeding his aggression. The defense's bid to include expert testimony about the lives of transgender women also failed. "The idea was to show the violence transgender individuals face, to bolster the self-defense claim," says Izek. "We'd have to be educating the jury about what it meant to be transgender. That would be difficult. Most wouldn't even know what that meant."

Seated at the defense table with a headache on the morning of the trial, May 2nd, 2012, CeCe looked at the mostly white jury staring back at her. She knew those expressions all too well. She'd been intent on seeing her case through, but glancing at those tasked with deciding her fate, she gave up. "These people weren't going to let me win," she says. She accepted a deal and pleaded guilty to second-degree manslaughter. Her supporters in the courtroom cried as the judge led her through her admission of guilt. CeCe tried her best to choke back tears as she was led from the courtroom, overwhelmed by what was next for her: A 41-month sentence in a state men's prison . . . .

• • •

CeCe was released from the Minnesota Correctional Facility in St. Cloud in January after 19 months, her sentence reduced for good behavior and for the 275 days she'd served prior to trial. While in prison she'd been intent on staying positive and grateful for having continued access to her hormones, and having her own cell with a TV, where she'd escape the hypermasculinity of her fellow inmates for Sex and the City marathons on E!. She says she never encountered violence, kept mostly to herself and even made a couple of friends. Mostly, she tried to work on recovering, and on remaining sane. When she was notified that Molly Flaherty was being prosecuted for attacking her, CeCe declined to testify, viewing it as a pointless act of vengeance potentially bad for her own mental health. (Flaherty pleaded guilty to third-degree assault and was sentenced to six months in jail.) "It's easy, especially for a person who's been through so much, to be a cruel and coldhearted person. But I chose not to be," CeCe says . . . .

"My story wouldn't have been important had I been killed. Because it's like nobody cares," CeCe says forcefully at her dining-room table, as day turns to evening. A shiny, sickle-shaped scar cuts across the jawbone of her left cheek, a permanent reminder of her tragic walk to the supermarket. "But fortunately for me, I'm a survivor. I'm not gonna beat myself up for being a woman, I'm not gonna beat myself up for being trans, I'm not gonna beat myself up for defending myself." She smacks her lips for punctuation. "Cause I am a survivor." . . .

6 Where "English Only" Falls Short

Stacy A. Teicher

Companies Scramble to Cope with Multiple Languages in the Workplace

They were the go-to people when customers needed advice in Spanish about eyeshadow or perfume. But when Hispanic employees wanted to speak Spanish to one another, they say it was forbidden—even on lunch breaks.

Five women who worked for the cosmetics store Sephora in New York filed complaints, and the Equal Employment Opportunity Commission (EEOC) sued last fall on their behalf. They argue the policy is too restrictive and amounts to national-origin discrimination, which is illegal under the Civil Rights Act of 1964.

"All of the [women say] how hurtful it is to be told that you can't speak your own language," says EEOC attorney Raechel Adams. "Language is so closely tied to their culture and their ethnicity. [Ironically,] they were expected to assist Spanish-speaking customers."

As companies hire from an ever more diverse labor pool, they reap the benefits of bilingualism, but they're also running into a Babel of problems. Already, a fifth of the nation's population speaks something other than English as their primary language (in some areas, it's two-fifths). Many of them have limited English proficiency that can lead to costly mistakes or low productivity. Managers worry about compromised safety or the quality of customer service. And if some workers use a foreign language to mock others, morale can break down.

There's no quick fix. Some employers go to the expense of offering classes to improve workers' English. Others turn the tables and train supervisors in languages most often spoken by workers in their industry. What seems the simplest answer to some—an English-only policy—is tricky because conflicts between court rulings and EEOC guidelines leave a lot of gray areas.

In the case of the five New York Hispanics, Sephora denied that it had an English-only rule or discriminated in any way. The court is awaiting the store's answer to the complaint.

English-only policies generate few official grievances. In 2002, the EEOC received 228 such complaints out of about 9,000 claims of national-origin discrimination. But observers say that many more workers who feel silenced don't take action for fear of losing their jobs.

Often what determines fairness is how a policy is implemented and whether there's an atmosphere of ethnic tension. In a case settled recently for $1.5 million, Hispanic

From *The Christian Science Monitor,* January 6, 2004. © 2004 The Christian Science Monitor. All rights reserved. Used by permission and protected by the Copyright Laws of the United States. The printing, copying, redistribution, or retransmission of this Content without express written permission is prohibited.

housekeepers at a casino were not allowed to speak Spanish. A janitor reported that he had to hide in closets to train new employees who understood only Spanish. Others told of harassment by supervisors who called them "wetbacks," accused them of stealing, and fired them for objecting to the English policy. The Colorado Central Station Casino in Black Hawk did not return calls seeking comment. In the settlement, it denied wrongdoing but agreed to remedies such as posting notices declaring there is no English-only rule.

For bilingual people, suppressing the tendency to talk in both languages can be difficult. They may know enough English to get by in their jobs, but to talk about family or other topics with friends, their primary language offers them a much richer vocabulary.

"It's called code-switching," says Nina Perales, regional counsel of the Mexican American Legal Defense Fund (MALDEF), which joined the EEOC in the suit against the casino. "You might switch languages for reason of emphasis or because you're more comfortable explaining certain things in one language versus the other." And sometimes it's even done unconsciously, linguists say.

But when conversations are restricted, "there's almost an issue of dehumanization," says Karl Krahnke, a linguistics professor at Colorado State University. "They are not being viewed as humans with the same social needs as anybody else."

Some insist those complexities shouldn't keep employers from creating a language policy if they think it's good for business. "I speak four languages . . . but a business has the right to establish rules for whatever reason—it could be safety, it could be social . . . so other [workers] won't feel insulted," says Mauro E. Mujica, chairman of U.S. English in Washington, D.C. His organization promotes official-English policies, which exist in 27 states and apply only to government, not the private sector. But workplace policies, he says, should not extend to people's personal time.

No Navajo

Another case takes the debate out of the immigration context. At R.D.'s Drive-In in Page, Ariz., it wasn't a "foreign" language that the boss restricted, but a native one: Navajo.

The town borders the Navajo Nation reservation, and nearly 90 percent of the restaurant's employees are Navajo, though the owners, the Kidman family, are not.

Speaking on the Kidman's behalf, Joe Becker of the Mountain States Legal Foundation in Denver says the family asked employees to sign a language policy in the summer of 2000. Their reason: There were complaints from customers and staff about rude comments being made in Navajo.

The agreement read: "The owner of this business can speak and understand only English. While the owner is paying you as an employee, you are required to use English at all times . . . [except] when the customer cannot understand English. If you feel unable to comply with this requirement, you may find another job."

Elva Josley and three others took exception to the rule. Ms. Josley had worked for the Kidmans for nearly three years and their families were close friends. But this, she says, was hurtful. She says the Kidmans never told her there had been complaints about things being said in Navajo.

Legacy of Suppression

"A lot of Native American people were sent to boarding schools and told not to speak their own language . . . and they were trying to make Christians out of these 'savages,'" she says. "I [said to the Kidmans]: 'It's not fair, because you people are the ones who came to our land and you can't tell us not to be who we are.'" Without native languages, she says, the US wouldn't have had the help of the code talkers during World War II.

The EEOC sued the diner, and Josley hopes the case will be settled soon and will send a message to employers: "Everyone's human and deserves to be respected . . . and next time people will think twice before doing something like this."

7 My Black Skin Makes My White Coat Vanish

Mana Lumumba-Kasongo

The first time it happened I was a brand-spanking-new M.D., filled with an intern's enthusiasm. Proudly wearing my pristine white coat and feeling sure that I was going to save the world, I walked into my patient's room.

"Hello, I'm Dr. Kasongo. How can I help you?" I asked cheerfully. The patient was a pleasant African-American woman whose chief complaint was abdominal pain. I spent the next 10 minutes taking her history, examining her thoroughly and doing a rectal exam to spot signs of internal bleeding. I explained that I'd treat her pain, check her blood work and urine samples, and go from there. "That's great," she said with a smile. "When is the doctor going to see me?"

I frowned. Hadn't she heard me? Hadn't I just administered an invasive exam on her posterior? "I *am* the doctor," I told her, making myself smile again. Did she sense my newness? Was it my lack of confidence that made it hard for her to believe I had a medical degree? I decided that even though I was a 30-year-old intern, it must be the youthful appearance I inherited from my ageless mother that was confusing her.

That was four years ago. There have been many such incidents since then, ranging from the irritating to the comical, and I no longer have much doubt that what baffled my patient was the color of my skin. Several months later, I was having dinner at an upscale hotel in Las Vegas with a friend, when she started choking on a piece of food. As she flailed her arms in obvious distress, frantic cries of "Is there a doctor in the room?" rang out from nearby tables. I assured everyone that I was a doctor and administered the Heimlich maneuver successfully. Even as my friend regained her bearings, people at the surrounding tables kept screaming for a physician. Once the "real doctors"—two white males—came to the table and saw that her airway was clear, they told the staff that it appeared that I was in fact a doctor and that my friend was going to be fine. Yet, far from comforting them, this information produced only quizzical looks.

Over the years, the inability of patients and others to believe that I am a doctor has left me utterly demoralized. Their incredulity persists even now that I am a senior resident, working in one of the world's busiest hospital emergency rooms. How can it be that with all the years of experience I have, all the procedures I've performed and all the people I've interacted with in emergency situations, I still get what I call "the look"? It's too predictable. I walk in the room and introduce myself, then wait for the

From *Newsweek*, April 3, 2006. © 2006 IBT Media. All rights reserved. Used by permission and protected by the Copyright Laws of the United States. The printing, copying, redistribution, or retransmission of this Content without express written permission is prohibited.

patient—whether he or she is black, white or Asian—to steal glances at the ID card that is attached to my scrubs or white coat. (I've thought of having it changed to read something like: *It's true. I'm a real doctor. Perhaps you've seen a black one on TV?*)

I remember talking to one of the white, male attending physicians in my training program after he witnessed one such encounter. "Listen," he said, trying to comfort me, "I can walk in wearing a T shirt and jeans and I'll always be seen as the doctor, even without an introduction. You will not." My heart sank as I thought of Malcolm X's words, "Do you know what white racists call black Ph.D.'s? N- - - -r!"

Only a small portion of the growing number of female doctors—not quite 4 percent—look like me. Perhaps that's why, for most people, "doctor" still doesn't fit the stereotypical image of a black woman in this country. Unfortunately, black children may be even more adversely affected by this than white ones. That point was driven home to me months ago, when a 6-year-old black girl refused to let me treat her when her mother brought her to the emergency room and left us alone. She insisted on being seen by a white doctor, leaving me feeling both embarrassed and humiliated.

Throughout the years, I've spoken to other female doctors about their experiences. While my white, female colleagues sometimes get "the look," it doesn't happen nearly as often as it does for black, female doctors. My African-American peers have their own ways of dealing with it; some even preempt suspicious patients by saying, "Yes, I am a doctor, and you can check online when you get home."

I've decided to try not to be bothered by my patients' attitudes. Like all doctors, I've worked hard to get to where I am. And occasionally I see that there is hope for humanity. A few months ago I treated a white, eighty-something man who had pneumonia. As I set up his IV line, I noticed that he was staring at me. Finally he said, "It must have been very hard for you to make it." After a pause, he added, "A woman—and black." We both laughed. Someone understood.

8 Women in the State Police: Trouble in the Ranks

Jonathan Schuppe

For Victoria Grant, it was the deer testicles in her locker.

For Kimberly Zollitsch, it was the nails in her tires.

For Amy Johnson, it was the name-calling and obscene Valentine signed by a commanding officer.

At a time when the New Jersey State Police is trying to eliminate racial profiling, the agency finds itself grappling with another issue of discrimination. Female troopers say they are harassed by fellow troopers, and the State Police record for hiring women is one of the worst in the nation.

Grant, Zollitsch and Johnson are veteran state troopers who left the force in the last four years and sued, citing years of relentless harassment by male troopers.

Yet other female troopers, such as Capt. Gayle Cameron and Lt. Col. Lori Hennon-Bell, who have been on patrol now for 23 years, say they have had rewarding careers, and that the agency is a better place for women than when they signed on.

But there is general agreement that there are troubling trends.

Today the agency includes 100 women, or 3.7 percent of its 2,708-member force. The female/male ratio ranks 11th from the bottom among state law enforcement agencies, according to 2001 FBI figures. A recent survey of 247 large police forces placed the New Jersey State Police at 235.

There are other numbers that raise concern.

In 2001, a report commissioned by the State Police but never made public found that 80 percent of women troopers—as well as a majority of men—had experienced "sexually harassing behavior" ranging from dirty jokes to unwanted sexual advances.

Attorney General Peter Harvey says the solution lies in recruiting.

"We know discrimination is an aspect of American life that permeates many institutions," said Harvey. "I submit that the real problem is we have to be more consistent in our recruitment efforts, and then promoting consistently talented women up the line."

The troopers union has a harsher view.

"It is shameful and embarrassing that we're not doing a better job in our recruiting of women," said Kenneth McClelland, president of the State Troopers Fraternal Association.

From *The Star-Ledger,* September 28, 2003. © 2003 The Star-Ledger. All rights reserved. Used by permission and protected by the Copyright Laws of the United States. The printing, copying, redistribution, or retransmission of this Content without express written permission is prohibited.

Stress Leave

Kimberly Zollitsch is one of nine female troopers who have sued the State Police in the last five years.

After 15 years on the force, she ended an extended stress leave this summer by retiring with a psychological disability. She says her troubles were prompted by nearly nonstop sexual harassment. As a rookie, she attributed the behavior to hazing. She figured she could roll with it.

"The State Police was known as the best of the best, and to be one of the few females, to add to the number, was inspiring," she said.

But the harassment didn't stop, she said.

In a lawsuit filed in December 2001, Zollitsch recounted how women in the academy were brutalized in boxing matches by bigger men, and forced to go on training runs in white shorts while menstruating. Instructors jogging behind jeered at their female colleagues. While on road patrol, Zollitsch said in her lawsuit, she regularly saw male troopers watching pornographic movies in the barracks.

One colleague took a picture of her buttocks, copied it and posted it around her station in Bridgeton. At Port Norris, her locker and gear were vandalized the night before an inspection. Nails were driven through the tires of her personal car.

One night in December 1999, Zollitsch finished her shift and never returned. Neither the attorney general nor the State Police would comment on the specifics of her case.

But, in a February 2000 letter to her, the Attorney General's Office told Zollitsch that it had substantiated several of her allegations, including her contention she was called derogatory names, that her equipment was smashed and her tires flattened. The letter, reviewed by *The Star-Ledger,* also says two commanders failed to stop troopers from harassing her. But by that time, some of those responsible had retired and were beyond discipline. She doesn't know whether anyone was punished.

"For a long time I guess I just told myself they'll get tired of this and I'll get seniority and it will stop," Zollitsch recalled. "I tried to get through it with the attitude that they're not going to win and I liked doing my job. But a lot of little things built upon themselves to the point where I couldn't take it anymore."

A Success

Gayle Cameron is one of the success stories. She joined the State Police in 1980 when there were only two female troopers.

That year, the State Police announced with great fanfare the nation's first all-female trooper class, a one-shot attempt to boost the number of women. Cameron and 103 other women signed up for five months of intense training at the State Police training academy in Sea Girt. Only 30 made it to graduation day.

Eighteen members of that class, the 96th in State Police history, remain on the force. They include 10 sergeants, four lieutenants, two captains and a lieutenant colonel.

"We were groundbreakers," said Cameron, now a captain in the State Police's Records and Identification Section. "People thought women wouldn't be able to do the job."

Cameron remembers the 96th class graduating to a triumphant sendoff—national media attention and a crowd of supporters that included the state's top law enforcement officials. Attorney General John Degnan told the graduates they would "serve as shining examples for coming generations of women who blaze similar paths and continue to break down the barriers of sexism."

The women soon discovered that the male troopers saw them as second-class troopers or "trooperettes." There were no women's bathrooms or locker rooms. They had to wear uniforms tailored for men.

To the male troopers, the modified push-ups and chin-ups, female-only self-defense drills and other changes in the academy meant the women hadn't earned their dues.

In the stations, some male troopers refused to speak to the women, or called them vulgar nicknames. Others refused to join them on patrols.

Cameron, who was a 23-year-old former teacher from Massachusetts when she enlisted, said discrimination didn't overshadow what she called "a rewarding, worthwhile experience" in the State Police.

Cameron excelled. She became a detective, investigating casinos and organized crime, before winning a coveted assignment on Gov. Christie Whitman's security detail. She investigated discrimination complaints in the Equal Employment Opportunity/Affirmative Action Office and helped the force develop recruiting strategies.

Cameron said today's State Police is a much better place to work than when she joined.

"I think for a number of years we did not do what we could have done to make this a welcoming environment for men, women and minorities who wouldn't have been the typical trooper," Cameron said. "We could have done things better. But I think we are doing it better now and taking the issue seriously."

No Choice

Amy Johnson, also of the 1980 class, says the workplace was so hard on women, many faced this choice: Take a stand or quit. Eventually, she says, she had to do both.

Johnson says she made the mistake of complaining about what she saw as unfair criticism of her patrol reports. Her locker was trashed and lingerie catalogues were left in her mailbox. Supervisors belittled her in front of subordinates and locked her out of a station exercise room.

One commander sent her a Valentine's Day card. "Ah, Valentine's Day! Seems like a good time to use a man, then toss him aside like an old candy wrapper," the card read. The commander wrote, "This card fits you," adding a four-letter slur.

"I was a physical and mental wreck," she recalled.

Johnson says she created some of her own problems, namely by shooting her gun into the air one night while off duty. She was fired, but says her male colleagues who pulled similar stunts didn't lose their jobs. She appealed her dismissal and was reinstated.

Johnson eventually made sergeant, but she says the promotion came with a cost: several stress leaves and three sexual harassment complaints. She retired in 1999 and sued for discrimination a year later.

"I think we've helped the women of the future by saying, 'Enough is enough.'"

In an April 2000 letter to Johnson, a copy of which was reviewed by *The Star-Ledger*, Attorney General John Farmer said an investigation had substantiated several of her complaints, including the vulgar Valentine.

For Victoria Grant, who also joined in 1980, "enough" came four years ago. In 1999, she filed a lawsuit in which she alleged that troopers put dead birds and deer testicles in her locker and mailbox, and dressed a mannequin in her uniform along with pages from pornographic magazines. Grant, who retired this year, declined to be interviewed for this story.

9 Muslim-American Running Back Off the Team at New Mexico State

Matthew Rothschild

This was supposed to be Muammar Ali's year at New Mexico State. "Muammar Ali, who led the team with 561 yards rushing, will get even more opportunities," predicted SI.com in its NCAA football preview.

But he has no opportunities now. He's off the team.

On October 9, he "received a message on his phone answering machine at his home that his jersey was being pulled and that he was released," says a letter from his attorney, George Bach, of the ACLU of New Mexico, to the university.

That letter, dated October 25, alleges that Head Coach Hal Mumme engaged in religious discrimination.

"Coach Mumme questioned Mr. Ali repeatedly about Islam and specifically its ties to Al-Qaeda," the letter states. This made Mr. Ali uncomfortable, it says.

And then, after the team's first game, "despite being the star tailback for several years, Mr. Ali was relegated to fifth string and not even permitted to travel with the team," the letter says.

There were only two other Muslim players on the team, and they were also released, it says. The letter adds that the coach "regularly has players recite the Lord's Prayer after each practice and before each game."

Ali's father, Mustafa Ali, says the trouble started at a practice over the summer when the coach told the players to pray.

"My son and two other players who were Muslim, they were praying in a different manner, and the coach asked them, 'What are you doing?' They said, 'We're Muslims. This is how we pray.' That had a lot to do with how things went south."

Mustafa Ali says things escalated after his son had a personal meeting with Coach Mumme where the coach "questioned him about Al-Islam and Al-Qaeda." His son talked to him about the conversation.

"He told me it was very weird," Mustafa Ali recalls. "It disturbed him quite a bit. He didn't understand why it had anything to do with football."

After that meeting, the coach "never spoke to my son again," Mustafa Ali says.

"And as they moved into summer camp football, my son noticed that he wasn't getting the ball as much and wasn't playing as big a role," he says.

This surprised Mustafa Ali.

"In 2004, he was honorable mention All American in his sophomore year," he says. "He was the fastest, strongest, quickest person on the team."

From *The Progressive*, November 18, 2005. Reprinted by permission of The Progressive, Inc., www.progressive.org.

His son "just knew there was something wrong," Mustafa Ali says.

When his son got cut, "he was upset, he was upset. The coach never gave a reason. None."

I asked to speak to his son, but Mustafa Ali said that would not be possible. "He's not talking to the media at this time," he said. "He's a very shy person."

New Mexico State isn't talking, either.

"The university has received the grievance," says Jerry Nevarez, specialist at the Office of Institutional Equity at New Mexico State.

"It is investigating the grievance, and it will have no further comment until the investigation is done."

Bruce Kite, the school's general counsel, did not return a phone call for comment.

Tyler Dunkel, director of athletic media relations for New Mexico State, said: "We're not commenting on that because there's an investigation going on and to ensure the integrity of the investigation we're not commenting on it until the investigation is finished."

Dunkel expects that to be "in the next couple of weeks."

I asked whether I could talk to Coach Mumme.

Said Dunkel: "No way."

10 Race, Disability and the School-to-Prison Pipeline

Julianne Hing

Enikia Ford-Morthel speaks of Amo (a pseudonym) with the fondness of an auntie talking about a beloved nephew. She recalls watching Amo at his fifth-grade graduation from Cox Academy in Oakland two years ago. The memory of him walking across the stage still fills her with emotion. "He looked so cute in his little white suit, with his jewelry on," Ford-Morthel says of his graduation. "I just cried."

Ford-Morthel and Amo are not actually each other's family. Ford-Morthel was Amo's principal at Cox Academy, a charter school in a particularly rough section of East Oakland. Nor did they always share such closeness. Amo, an African-American boy, arrived at Cox as a fourth-grade terror. "He was hell on wheels," Ford-Morthel says of those early days. On his very first day Amo was in class for just 10 minutes before he got sent to Ford-Morthel's office for starting some kind of trouble, and for the month after that he was never in class for longer than half an hour before he started swearing at his teacher or otherwise interrupting instruction.

He was headed for the discipline track, Ford-Morthel says, and even as a fourth grader, he would easily have been suspended for his behavior in many other schools. "But we sat with him and we had to figure out how to learn him," she says. It turned out that Amo's parents had split up and his dad had a new girlfriend with whom Amo's mom didn't get along. "Most of his experience with adults was them not working together, so he didn't respect very many adults," Ford-Morthel says. "He had huge trust issues, and his academics were horrible—which of course they were, because he was never in class."

So the school assigned Amo a behavior intervention specialist, a coach who stayed nearby, in class all day long. The specialist helped him identify stressors and showed him alternative responses to his violent outbursts, and then helped Amo learn to tap into those more productive stress responses whenever he felt threatened or frustrated. The school bridged these behavioral and emotional interventions with academic ones, and reached out to Amo's parents to get them on the same page about his schooling. There were multiple home visits involved, and lots of time spent earning his parents' trust. Ford-Morthel speaks with particular pride about bringing Amo into a meeting one day with ten adults in the room—including his mom and dad—showing a united dedication to Amo and his education that he'd never seen before.

Without this huge effort, says Ford-Morthel, Amo was on track to land in special education, suspension or both. Amo was exhibiting the kind of disruptive behavior that, for black boys in particular is often confused for a disability in school settings. Many people believe this diagnostic progression—from frustrated, difficult kid to

From "Race, Disability and the School to Prison Pipeline" by Julianne Hing. Copyright © 2015 by Race Forward/Colorlines. Reprinted by permission of Race Forward.

disabled, segregated student—is a primary entry point into what's been called the school-to-prison pipeline.

That phrase has come to represent the nebulous mix of forces that join with harsh school discipline policies to drive striking numbers of students of color away from school and into the criminal justice system. In recent years, migration out of classrooms has been increasingly understood as a defining challenge to racial justice in our nation's schools. "Too many students are unnecessarily removed from class each year due to suspensions, expulsions and other exclusionary discipline practices," U.S. Secretary of Education Arne Duncan said earlier this year, when the Education and Justice departments released a joint guidance warning schools about the school-to-prison pipeline.

Researchers have clearly established the contours of the pipeline. During the 2011 school year, more than 3 million public school students were suspended and over 100,000 expelled. These students were overwhelmingly black. According to the Department of Education, black students are suspended and expelled at three times the rate of white students. Save for American Indians, no other racial group experiences such outsized racial disproportionality in exclusionary discipline. Indeed, the federal government has said that the racial disparity in punishment levels can't be explained by differences in kids' behavior alone. Importantly, just one of those suspensions can double the likelihood that students will drop out of school, and increase the likelihood that students end up in prison. A disproportionate number of students of color are even arrested[1] at school as a form of punishment.

But while the racial disparity is clear, the reasons for it are not. What institutional forces set a child down this path? At least part of the answer seems to be the inadvertent, perverse incentives of the special education system. Frustrated educators—desperate for help in schools that don't have the kinds of interventions Ford-Morthel had available at Cox—are instead using inherently subjective and fuzzy disability classifications to gain access to sorely needed resources. Special education classifications open the door to new tools for engaging the most challenging students, but in the process, they may also be putting those children on a path to prison.

Disability and Discipline

Ford-Morthel, now the chief of schools at Education for Change, the charter network which runs Cox Academy, says she's seen educators' desperation up close. Before she became principal at Cox, she was a teacher and principal in the Hayward Unified School District. She saw firsthand how, absent other classroom supports, teachers turned to the special education system to help fill the gap for their most challenging students. At Cox, she was able to interrupt that process because the school was the testing ground for a federally recognized pilot program designed to reimagine how schools treat challenging students.

Dubbed "All In," the Cox pilot is a partnership spearheaded by Seneca Center, a statewide family services and child welfare organization in California. Seneca won a $3 million grant from the Department of Education in December 2013 to expand its work at Cox to six other schools in the Bay Area. It's a local plan that's garnered national attention for taking a novel approach to meeting the needs of its most vulnerable students. Seneca's pitch: by taking a holistic, community-wide approach to dealing with the trauma kids confront outside of school, educators can better meet the academic challenges students face once they step inside the classroom. And by disentangling the threads of race, disability and school discipline, educators hope to keep kids on track and out of the school-to-prison pipeline.

"The goal is to understand the difference between disability and disadvantage," says Lihi Rosenthal, Division Director for Seneca Center.

There are over a dozen ways to be classified as a special education student under the federal Individuals with Disabilities Education Act, or IDEA. Enacted by Congress in 1974, IDEA spelled out for the first time that students with disabilities had a right to a "free, appropriate public education." Nearly 50 years later it's easy to take such protections for granted, but prior to 1975 states and school districts were under no obligation to provide an education for students with disabilities. By some estimates[2] nearly half of the roughly four million students with disabilities at the time were not served by public schools and when students did receive an education, it was one often isolated from their peers and subpar in academic rigor. Advocates fought for the development of special education programs to meet the needs of students with disabilities that general education clearly wasn't.

If that sounds analogous to desegregation efforts for African-American children, that's because IDEA was made possible by the Supreme Court's landmark 1954 desegregation ruling in Brown v. Board of Education, which marks its 60th anniversary this month. Brown v. Board of Education paved the way for IDEA by providing a legal basis to challenge the de-facto segregation of children with disabilities from their peers. If "separate but equal" was no longer sufficient justification for the educational segregation of African-American children from their white peers, advocates argued, it wasn't going to work for children based on disability status either.

Today, 6.4 million students in the U.S. are classified as needing special education. They make up 13 percent of the nation's K-12 enrollment.[3] For many children with disabilities, classification as an IDEA-eligible student opens up access to extra services and supports that can make the difference between graduating and dropping out. But because of strict IDEA funding streams, acquiring a special education label also becomes the vehicle for students and educators to get help for challenging classroom situations, help that may ironically be worsening those challenges for the students.

Among the myriad special education classifications are disabilities that can be medically diagnosed—like hearing and visual impairments, or traumatic brain injury. Racial disproportionality in these categories is just about nonexistent. With many of these disabilities, parents are already aware of them when they enroll their children in school.

Other designations, like "emotional and behavioral disturbance" or "specific learning disabilities," tend not to come until students arrive in the classroom. These so-called "soft disabilities" are catchalls for broad classes of learning challenges and anti-social behaviors, and the assessment and labeling process for them is open to much more subjectivity. Perhaps not surprisingly, they have come to be defined by deep racial disparities.

For example, white students are more likely to be labeled "autistic" than are students of color, while African-American students are at the highest risk of all races for being labeled with the broad term "specific learning disabilities." In the 2011-2012 school year, black students were twice as likely as Latinos, four times as likely as Asians and 1.4 times as likely as whites to receive special education services for emotional disturbance, according to federal data.[4]

Emotional and behavioral disturbance, according to federal law, is marked by an "inability to learn which cannot be explained by intellectual, sensory, or health factors." The law defines some of the warning signs as anti-social behavior, a child's inability to build positive relationships with teachers and students, inappropriate behavior or even "a general, pervasive mood of unhappiness or depression." Experts, parents and advocates have been sounding the alarm about racial disproportionality in these highly subjective classifications for decades. Documented evidence of the disparities date back to the 1960s. In the 2004 reauthorization of IDEA, Congress acknowledged the deep racial disproportionality that has come to characterize disability categories like "emotional disturbance" and "specific learning disabilities" or "intellectual disability," the new name for what used to be known as "mental retardation." Still, the disparities persist.

While the disproportionality in identification is well-documented—black students have been overrepresented in special education programs since the U.S. Office of Civil Rights started keeping data on the topic in 1968—there isn't one clean answer to explain its causes. Experts have identified a host of possible explanations, ranging from unchecked implicit bias on the part of inadequately prepared teachers to explicit racial bias on the part of educators who want to circumvent federal mandates to integrate schools.

The U.S. public school teaching force is overwhelmingly white and female, and may have less understanding about black students and boys, some have offered. Cultural stereotypes about African Americans being inherently criminal or suspect can condition a teacher to react more harshly to a student who's acting out. And while the use of IQ tests is controversial and waning, they are still deployed in some states as part of special education assessments, even though critics have long said IQ tests are biased against kids of color.

In the wake of Brown v. Board of Education, some states, particularly Southern ones, also used special education classifications as a way to give the illusion of compliance with the law. By slapping black children with special education designations, schools could move them to classrooms separate from their white, general education classmates and still technically be running integrated schools. Roslyn Mickelson, a professor of sociology at the University of North Carolina at Charlotte, has called this kind of academic tracking "second-generation segregation." What is clear, says UCLA's Civil Rights Project Director Dan Losen, is that disproportionality in special education highlights the many places where "bias can seep in."

Once students are labeled as special education, they're placed on an accelerated path toward the school-to-prison pipeline. Students designated as having disabilities are two times as likely as their peers to be punished with suspension and expulsion, and researchers have found that even one suspension in ninth grade doubles[5] the likelihood that students will drop out eventually. In essence, a disability classification heightens the risk that a student will drop out eventually.

The pipeline works most ruthlessly if that student who's been labeled as disabled happens to also be an African-American boy. More than one in every four black boys identified as having disabilities was suspended in the 2011–2012 school year, according to the Department of Education's Office of Civil Rights.[6] The same can be said for American Indian, Pacific Islander and multiracial boys classified with disabilities. Meanwhile, 12 percent of white boys classified with disabilities and 10 percent of Asian boys were suspended.

Having been over-identified as disabled and far disproportionately suspended from school, black students are also subjected to some of the highest rates of school-based arrests. This is the final step along the school-to-prison pipeline. Students of color who are already vulnerable academically and emotionally, and who are most likely to go to under resourced schools, are also met with the highest levels of punishment. Ultimately, they are pushed out of the classroom and too often into the back of a police car. Black students are 16 percent of the nation's student population but 31 percent of those who are arrested at school, while white students are 51 percent of the student population and 39 percent of those arrested at school.

The basic inefficiency of all of this, particularly of suspensions as a sanction for bad behavior, is part of what informs Seneca's alternative approach. "When was the last time you heard, 'Well, this kid got suspended and all of a sudden his behavior just turned around?'" Seneca's CEO Ken Berrick says. "If I thought suspensions worked as an intervention, I'm not sure I'd be against it, but they just don't." In Lihi Rosenthal's experience, exclusionary discipline doesn't get at the root problem. A kid's bad behavior, she says, often masks other troubles. "When you're a fifth grader, it's always better to look bad than to look stupid," she says. Being disruptive can be a great coping skill to get out of doing something you're afraid to do, especially if a teacher's standard response is to send you out of the room. "Of course you're going to flip over a desk every time math work comes," Rosenthal says. "It's actually a brilliant intervention."

The End of Segregation

Cox Academy is located in a particularly rough part of East Oakland. "If you know anything about East Oakland you know there's a lot of crime, and there's a lot of poverty," says Ford-Morthel. Lockdowns triggered by shootings near the school are a regular occurrence. Three days before Thanksgiving last year, seven men were shot across the street from Cox Academy, in what the Contra Costa Times reported[7] as "a hail of gunfire." Five months earlier, two 14-year-olds were shot[8] within a one-block radius of Cox. In 2011, 16-year-old Najon Jackson was shot and killed[9] on the front steps of his grandmother's home one block north of the school. It's not uncommon for a student at Cox Academy to be directly affected by all of this community and police violence just outside the schoolhouse doors, says Ford-Morthel.

Elmhurst Park, where Cox is located, is one of the poorest neighborhoods in Oakland. More than 90 percent of the students at Education for Change schools qualify for free or reduced lunch, according to Ford-Morthel. Students come to school hungry because they haven't eaten breakfast, or even hungrier because they didn't eat dinner the night before. Some students move around from night to night, with no fixed place that they call home. "All-In" was informed by research which has found that dealing with sustained trauma affects kids' ability to form positive relationships, adjust their emotions and tell the difference between threatening and non-threatening relationships, all of which affects how well they're able to do in school. "If you're worried about your mom and whether she's safe at home while you're in math class and you're fidgety and not getting your math work done, that makes sense," says Rosenthal. "That's basic survival."

Given the racial disparities in special education identification and school discipline, it's easy to assume that it's the adults who are failing students facing these kinds of challenges. And yet, Seneca's insistence on reimagining an entire school ecosystem suggests that it's broader than that—that the school-to-prison pipeline stems from fundamental flaws in the structural design of schools. It's not simply that adults are failing kids. It's that the system is failing everyone.

Amo's teacher was far from an easy caricature of a clueless, prejudiced educator intent on shoving black kids out of her classroom. She was a young Latina with a social justice background who Ford-Morthel praised as one of the school's best-performing teachers. Still, she felt defeated dealing with Amo every day. She sent Amo out of the classroom not out of spite but out of desperation. "Teachers, our job is to get results," Ford-Morthel says. "We're experts in instruction. Most teachers just don't have the tools."

"All-In" pairs a general education teacher with a special education teacher, and places two additional counselors in the classroom to provide behavioral support for students for a full year. In a second-grade classroom I visited, that meant there were four adults in a classroom of 24 students. The team works in tandem for the entire year, during which the counselors and special education teacher are helping to build the capacity of the general education teacher to better identify and intervene when students are having difficulties in class. And then the team of counselors and special ed teacher moves on to work in another teacher's classroom. A team of psychologists, counselors, social workers, special education teachers and learning specialists are also on hand at the school to support teachers and students in smaller settings. Instead of merely asking, "What do we need to do to fix these kids?" "All-In" provides school-wide training and support for teachers and other educators to rethink their roles as well.

This is the opposite of what happens in a typical school. There, a teacher's classroom is their kingdom, but it can also be an isolating island, says Seneca's Rosenthal. Typically, a general education teacher is best equipped to handle their general education students, and special education interventions are handled away from the general education environment. The more serious the need, the further special education students are pulled away from the general education setting. School districts end up paying large sums of money to educate children outside of school, which means general education teachers never get training they need to identify and help future students with disabilities. Additionally, a student must gain an Individualized Education Plan (an IEP) that comes with a special education designation in order to be eligible for extra academic and behavioral support. So a special education designation becomes a student's ticket to more supports and services, even though special education is an educational ghetto that's extremely difficult to leave.

The difference with "All-In" is that the model doesn't concern itself so deeply with the line between students with disabilities and students without. Ninety-seven percent of Cox students are MediCal-eligible, which means that they're also entitled to mental health services at their school. So, by pulling together special education and mental health funds, the school can make its broadest level of services available to just about every single student, while saving its most intense interventions for those with the most serious needs. "It's an extraordinarily artificial distinction," Berrick says. "Special education is a continuum. It's not, 'I have no disability, I have no disability, I have no disability. Oh, I have a disability.'" This is especially true for the kinds of emotional and behavioral disabilities which most disproportionately affect the population of students "All-In" is aimed at. Amo, for example, did not have an IEP. "Left unchecked though," says Ford-Morthel, "I can very easily see him being [labeled emotionally disturbed]."

The pilot program allowed the adults in the school to interrupt that journey. "There was violence and separation in his life that he was working out," she says. "And so him talking back wasn't him being like, 'I'm being disrespectful as an African-American boy.' It was about: this is what my life has taught me I need to do."

The obvious question, though, is how replicable is All-In's approach? Placing four adults in one classroom and providing a phalanx of social workers and counselors on-site sounds like extremely expensive, posh schooling. But Seneca CEO Berrick turns the question around on itself: How sustainable is the current approach? Eighty-one percent of Oakland Unified School District's $64.2 million special education budget goes to educating kids in separate classes and in off-site, non-public schools. It costs a district $75,000 per child to educate a kid in a specialized school for students with behavioral and learning disabilities. At that rate, says Rosenthal, "you could get that one student their very own teacher." Oakland Unified School District spends an average of $1,794 per special education student, and the "All-In" model costs $1,052 per student. The funds are there to sustain a reimagined school community.

Oakland Unified's Associate Superintendent Sheilagh Andujar calls All-In "very timely." The racial disparities in special education identification and school discipline are not lost on Andujar, who was appointed to lead the district's special education services last summer. "We're looking into possibilities with this new model," Andujar said, with an emphasis on taking a "system-wide" approach. The ultimate hope is to intervene as soon as possible so "we see a decline in the number of students who are referred for special ed, and those who are labeled in that 'emotionally disturbed' category."

Today, Amo is in seventh grade, and Ford-Morthel still checks in on him. He's hanging on, attending class every day and keeping up decent grades. "He's a stronger kid," says Ford-Morthel, but she knows it'll be all too easy for Amo to fall apart in a system that isn't prepared to acknowledge everything that's going on in his life outside of school. "This is only a start."

NOTES

1. Hing, J. (2012, November 26). The Shocking Details of a Mississippi School-to-Prison Pipeline. Colorlines.

2. Losen, D. (2002). Racial inequity in special education. Cambridge, MA: Civil Rights Project at Harvard University, Harvard Education Press.

3. U.S. Department of Education, National Center for Education Statistics. (2015). Digest of Education Statistics, 2013 (NCES 2015-011), Table 204.30.

4. U.S. Department of Education, Office of Special Education Programs, Individuals with Disabilities Education Act (IDEA) database. Retrieved June 10, 2013, from http://tadnet.public.tadnet.org/pages/712; and National Center for Education Statistics, Common Core of Data (CCD), "State Nonfiscal Survey of Public Elementary/Secondary Education," 2010–11 and 2011–12. (This table was prepared June 2013.)

5. Losen, D., Martinez, T., & California, L. (2013). Out of school & off track: The overuse of suspensions in American middle and high schools. The UCLA Civil Rights Project.

6. U.S. Department of Education for Civil Rights. (2014). Civil Rights Data Collection—Data Snapshot: School Discipline. Issue Brief No.1 (March 2014). Available at: http://www2.ed.gov/about/offices/list/ocr/docs/crdc-discipline-snapshot.pdf

7. Salonga, R., & Ivie, E. (2013, November 26). Seven men shot near East Oakland park Monday evening. *Contra Costa Times*.

8. Artz, M., Alund, N., & Mejia, B. (2013, July 18). Oakland 8-year-old shot dead at sleepover. *San Jose Mercury News*.

9. Lee, H. (2011, August 1). Oakland homicide victim is slain teen's brother. SFGate.

11 The Segregated Classrooms of a Proudly Diverse School

Jeffrey Gettleman

Columbia High School seems to have it all—great sports teams, great academics, famous alumni and an impressive campus with Gothic buildings. But no one boasts about one aspect of this blue-ribbon school, that its classrooms are largely segregated.

Though the school is majority black, white students make up the bulk of the advanced classes, while black students far outnumber whites in lower-level classes, statistics show.

"It's kind of sad," said Ugochi Opara, a senior who is president of the student council. "You can tell right away, just by looking into a classroom, what level it is."

This is a reality at many high schools coast to coast and one of the side effects of aggressive leveling, the increasingly popular practice of dividing students into ability groups.

But at Columbia High, the students nearly revolted. Two weeks ago, a black organization on campus planned a walkout to protest the leveling system. Word soon spread to the principal, who pleaded with the students not to go. The student leaders decided to hold an assembly instead, in which they lashed out at the racial gap.

The student uproar is now forcing district officials to take a hard look at the leveling system and decide how to strike a balance between their two main goals— celebrating diversity and pushing academic achievement.

Educators say that leveling allows smarter students to be challenged while giving struggling ones the special instruction they need. But many students, especially those in the lower levels, which often carry a stigma, say such stratification makes the rocky adolescent years only harder. And at Columbia High, there is no dispute that it is precisely the leveling system that has led to racial segregation.

Anthony Paolini, a senior at Columbia, is one of the few white students in a lower-level math class. The fact that most of his classmates are black does not bother him, he said. But the low expectations do.

"It makes you feel like you're in a hole," he said.

The school, about 15 minutes from downtown Newark, draws from the cosmopolitan towns of Maplewood and South Orange. Some students live in million-dollar homes. Others rely on government lunches. Of 2,024 students, 58 percent are black, 35 percent white, 4 percent Hispanic and 3 percent Asian. The public school sends more than 90 percent of graduates to college, has a dropout rate of less than half a

From *The New York Times*, April 3, 2005. © 2005 The New York Times. All rights reserved. Used by permission and protected by the Copyright Laws of the United States. The printing, copying, redistribution, or retransmission of this Content without express written permission is prohibited.

percent and won a national Blue Ribbon award from the federal government for its academic excellence during the 1992–93 school year. Notable alumni include the actor Zach Braff and the singer Lauryn Hill, and the fact that the two stars, one white, one black, graduated in the same class is seen as a symbol of the diversity Columbia strives to project.

But racial tension is becoming more of an issue. In recent years, the number of black students in the school district has eclipsed the number of white students even though Maplewood and South Orange still are majority white. In the past year, the district has been sued twice for discrimination: once by two former black students who said they were mistreated by teachers after a food-fight in the cafeteria, and also by a group of teachers, mostly black, who accused the principal, who is white, of racial bias.

The superintendent of the district, Peter P. Horoschak, acknowledged that there were, in a sense, two Columbias. The de facto segregation is most visible at the extremes. Statistics for this year show that while a Level 5 math class, the highest, had 79 percent white students, a Level 2 math class, the lowest, had 88 percent black students. Levels 3 and 4 tend to be more mixed, though a school board member, Mila M. Jasey, said, "Some white parents tell me that they know their kid belongs in a Level 3 class but they don't want them to be the only white kid in the class."

Though parents and students are granted some input, students are supposed to be placed in levels primarily based on grades and test scores. Many black students complain that they are unfairly relegated to the lower levels and unable to move up.

Quentin Williams, the 17-year-old leader of the Martin Luther King Association at the school, calls it "contemporary segregation." He said that his organization, one of the largest on campus, had tried to meet with the administration over the issue several times but "got the runaround."

So in mid-March his group planned to walk out of school. They even had the backing of several parents, who volunteered to help. As the date approached, Quentin, a senior, said he felt "a lot of pressure coming in from a lot of different angles."

Student leaders eventually decided that holding an assembly would give them a better opportunity to publicly confront administrators, especially the principal, Renee Pollack. At the assembly, which was mandatory for all students, she stood in front of the student body and apologized for saying anything that might have been construed as insensitive.

Ms. Pollack said later that complaints about her were being spread by teachers on her own staff.

"They were trying to manipulate the kids in order to get at me," said Ms. Pollack, who has been the principal for three years and is up for tenure this month.

The flashpoint of the assembly came when Nathan Winkler, a skinny, intense senior who says he wants to be governor some day, grabbed the microphone and announced that he had no sympathy for people in lower levels because all it took was hard work to move up.

His short outburst was like a cleaver, splitting the student body in two. Many blacks booed him. Many whites cheered. He was then accused of using the term "you people" in his speech—though he did not, according to a videotape of the assembly. After the assembly, he said, he was stalked in the hallways.

He now admits that he spoke out of fear.

"I felt extremely isolated during that assembly," he said. "For the first time I was aware of being part of the minority. White kids are outnumbered at Columbia. I knew that, but I hadn't really felt it before."

Student leaders and administrators are now discussing ways to narrow the so-called achievement gap, like granting students more say in which level they are in; better identifying which level students belong in; expanding a summer school program for students who want to take upper-level classes. Administrators say they had been working on all this before the walkout threat.

"But the students forced the issue," Ms. Pollack acknowledged.

Ms. Pollack also pointed out that this year, more students of color from Columbia have been accepted into Ivy League universities than white students, with two Hispanic, three black and two white students gaining early admission.

The debate over leveling here boils down to fairness. Is it fair just to ensure equal access to upper-level classes? Or does fairness go farther than that and require administrators to truly level the playing field so that the racial makeup of upper classes better resembles the racial makeup of the school?

Stewart Hendricks, a senior whose father is from Guyana and whose mother is Swiss, said that some teachers do seem to have lower expectations for black students but that he did not let them get him down.

"The purpose of high school is to prepare you for the real world," he said. "And in the real world, you can't listen to other peoples' expectations, because in the real world, people are just waiting for you to fail."

Because of his mixed racial heritage, he said, "I guess you can say I'm in the middle of all this."

And in a way, that is why he sympathizes with the principal.

"She's got an entire black population that wants to get rid of the leveling system and an entire white population who would leave this town if they did that," he said. "What's she supposed to do?"

12 Race and Family Income of Students Influence Guidance Counselors' Advice, Study Finds

Eric Hoover

The race and family income of prospective college applicants influence the advice that high-school guidance counselors give them, according to a study released on Monday.

Counselors were more likely to recommend community colleges to middle-class black students with sub-par academic records than to middle-class white students with similar records, the study found. Among wealthier students with poor academic records, however, counselors were more likely to urge white students than black students to attend community colleges.

The study also found that counselors were more likely to recommend community colleges to middle-class students than to wealthier ones, and they recommended four-year colleges more strongly to upper-class students than to middle-class students.

The findings are based on the results of a three-year study sponsored by the National Commission for Cooperative Education, which sent surveys to 20,000 high-school counselors throughout the nation. Respondents received one of 16 profiles of fictional students specifying race, gender, family income, and academic performance. The counselors were asked to indicate how strongly they would recommend that the student seek more information about, visit, and apply to a four-year college and a community college. The results were based on a sample of approximately 1,700 responses.

The study, "High School Guidance Counselors: Facilitators or Pre-Emptors of Social Stratification in Education," was conducted by Frank Linnehan, an associate professor of management at Drexel University; Christy Weer, a Ph.D. candidate at Drexel; and Paul J. Stonely, the commission's president. The researchers plan to present their findings at a meeting of the Academy of Management in August.

Used with permission of *The Chronicle of Higher Education*. Copyright © 2015. All rights reserved.

13 By the Numbers: Sex Crimes on Campus

Dave Gustafson

College is supposed to be a time for personal and intellectual growth, but for too many students, it's also a place where they will be sexually assaulted.

This week, America Tonight will air a series of reports investigating campus assault, culminating in a live town hall program on Friday, Nov. 1.

To better understand the prevalence of sexual assault on college campuses, its perpetrators and the key factors involved, we drew from existing research, studies and polls to see how the data on campus assault breaks down. Bear in mind, as you look at these numbers, that sexual assault remains one of the most underreported crimes in America.[1]

20 to 25 percent of college women experience rape or attempted rape

In a given calendar year, nearly one in 20 U.S. college women will be the victim of a completed or attempted rape, according to "The Sexual Victimization of College Women," a 2000 Justice Department report. During the course of a typical five-year college career, that means as many as 20 to 25 percent can become rape victims.[2]

About one in three gay men, one in five bisexual men and one in 10 heterosexual men reported experiencing unwanted sexual contact during their lifetime, according to the 2010 National Intimate Partner and Sexual Violence released by the Centers for Disease Control and Prevention.[3]

"There is also far less research done surrounding sexual violence within male and LGBTQ-identified communities," this toolkit from the Chicago Taskforce on Violence Against Girls & Young Women explains. "Lack of research paired with cultural stigmas create a culture that does not support survivors to report their assault and in turn, does not provide adequate resources to them."[4]

Students who are gay, lesbian, bisexual, transgender and queer, or who are women of color, immigrants, international students or have a disability may also face a higher risk of sexual abuse[5]—but just how much more risk is tough to say.

9.6 percent of women in a survey of black colleges reported being sexually assaulted

Nearly 10 percent of women at historically black colleges and universities (HBCU) reported in the fall 2008 Historically Black College and University Campus Sexual

Reprinted courtesy of Al Jazeera America. http://america.aljazeera.com/watch/shows/america
-tonight/america-tonight-blog/2013/10/28/by-the-numbers-sexcrimesoncampus.html

Assault Study of 3,951 undergraduates being the victim of a completed sexual assault since entering college.[6]

"Incapacitated sexual assault (6.2%) was slightly more prevalent than physically forced sexual assault (4.8%)," the survey results noted. "[I]t seems that the rates of sexual assault are slightly lower among HBCU women than among their non-HBCU counterparts: a previous study using the same methodology found that 13.7% of non-HBCU undergraduate women experience a completed sexual assault after entering college." Why the difference? It "seems to be driven entirely by a difference in the rate of incapacitated sexual assault, which is likely explained by the fact that HBCU women drink alcohol much less frequently than non-HBCU women."

Beyond the scope of the HBCU college women survey, a 2009 Justice Department report notes that black females ages 12 and older were raped or sexually assaulted at a rate of 2.9 per 1,000 in 2008, compared to 1.2 for females who are white and 0.9 for females of another race. The rates were similar for Hispanic (1.1) and non-Hispanic women (1.5).[7]

Between 80 and 90% of sexual assaults at colleges involve acquaintances, not strangers

The 2005 report "Sexual Assault on Campus: What Colleges and Universities Are Doing About It"[8] sums up the scope of the acquaintance rape problem:

> Counter to widespread stranger rape myths, in the vast majority of these crimes—between 80 and 90 percent—victim and assailant know each other. In fact, the more intimate the relationship, the more likely it is for rape to be completed rather than attempted. Half of all student victims do not label the incident 'rape.' This is particularly true when no weapon was used, no sign of physical injury is evident, and alcohol was involved—factors commonly associated with campus acquaintance rape. Given the extent of non-stranger rape on campus, it is no surprise that the majority of victimized women do not define their experience as a rape.
>
> These reasons help explain why campus sexual assault is not well reported.

9 in 10 rapes on college campuses are perpetrated by serial rapists

This is according to a 20-year study of "undetected" rapists by psychologist David Lisak.[9] One in 16 college men that he interviewed said that they had used physical force to have sexual intercourse or had sex with someone who was too incapacitated by alcohol or drugs to resist.

Only 10 to 25 percent of male college rapists were expelled

According to a database from about 130 colleges and universities[10] that was highlighted in reporting by the Center for Public Integrity and NPR News, men who are responsible for sexual assault are rarely expelled.

Students who live in sorority houses are more likely to be raped than off-campus students

Women who live in a sorority house are three times as likely to be raped compared to students who live off campus, according to a 2004 report in the *Journal of Studies on Alcohol*.[11] The report also found that students who live in dorms on campus are 1.4 times more likely to be raped than off-campus students.

Freshmen and sophomores face the most sexual assault

Of college women who reported a sexually coercive experience, 84 percent said it occurred when they were a freshman or sophomore, according to the 2006 report "An Examination of Sexual Violence Against College Women."[12]

Nearly three-quarters of college female rape victims were intoxicated

A 2004 report in the *Journal of Studies on Alcohol*[13] found that 72 percent of college rape victims were so intoxicated that they could not consent to sex. The study found that students who were under 21, white, used illegal drugs, drank heavily in high school and went to colleges with high rates of heavy episodic drinking also faced higher risk of rape while intoxicated.

More than a third of college rapes happen on campus

A 2002 Justice Department report "Acquaintance Rape of College Students"[14] found that 34 percent of completed rapes and 45 percent of attempted rapes occur on campus.

Nearly 3 in 5 completed campus rapes happen where the victim lives

The "Acquaintance Rape of College Students" study also found that around 31 percent of rapes happen in a residence other than the victim's. Ten percent occur in a fraternity house.

Fewer than 1 in 20 completed and attempted rapes against college women are reported

Less than 5 percent of completed and attempted rapes are reported to law enforcement or campus officials, according to 2000 "Sexual Victimization of College Women"[15] study. In the DOJ acquaintance rape study, more than 40 percent of rape victims who didn't report their attack said they feared reprisal by the attacker or other people. Underreporting sexual assault is a problem at U.S. military academies[16] as well.

Of the two-thirds of rape incidents in which a victim does tell another person, it's usually a friend – not a college official or family member, according to the "Sexual Victimization of College Women" study.

And as this toolkit from the Chicago Taskforce on Violence Against Girls and Young Women explains, there can be many reasons why the crime is so underreported: a survivor may not want to share details with a researcher he or she just met, he or she may be in a long-term abusive relationship or may not have a stable home and so on.

NOTES

1. National Institute of Justice. "Reporting of Sexual Violence Incidents." October 26, 2010. Available at: /www.nij.gov/topics/crime/rape-sexual-violence/pages/rape-notification .aspx

2. Fisher, B. et al. (2000). *The sexual victimization of college women*. Washington, DC: U.S. Dept. of Justice, Office of Justice Programs, National Institute of Justice.

3. Walters, M. L., Chen J., & Breiding, M. J. (2013). *The National Intimate Partner and Sexual Violence Survey (NISVS): 2010 Findings on Victimization by Sexual Orientation*. Atlanta, GA: National Center for Injury Prevention and Control, Centers for Disease Control and Prevention.

4. Chicago Taskforce on Violence Against Girls & Young Women. (2012). "Reporting on Rape and Sexual Violence: A Media Toolkit for Local and National Journalists to Better Media Coverage." Edited by Claudia Garcia-Rojas and designed by Kat Clark. Available at: http://www.chitaskforce.org/wp/wp-content/uploads/2012/10/Chicago-Taskforce-Media-Toolkit.pdf

5. Futures Without Violence. (2012). "Beyond Title IX: Guidelines for Preventing and Responding to Gender-based Violence in Higher Education." Written by Ann Fleck-Henderson, with contributions by Peggy Costello, Maya Raghu, Jennifer Solidum Rose, and Diane Rosenfeld. Available at: www.futureswithoutviolence.org/beyond-title-ix-guidelines-for-preventing-and-responding-to-gender-based-violence-in-higher-education/

6. Krebs, C., Lindquist, C., & Barrick, K. (2013). The Historically Black College and University Campus Sexual Assault (HBCU-CSA) Study, 2008. ICPSR Data Holdings.

7. Catalano, S., Smith, E., Snyder, H., & Rand, M. (2009). Female victims of violence. U.S. Department of Justice Office of Justice Programs.

8. Karjane, H. M., Fisher, B., Cullen, F. T., & National Institute of Justice (U.S.). (2005). Sexual assault on campus: What colleges and universities are doing about it. Washington, DC: U.S. Dept. of Justice, Office of Justice Programs, National Institute of Justice

9. Shapiro, J. (2010, March 4). Myths That Make It Hard To Stop Campus Rape. NPR.

10. Ibid.

11. Dowdall, George W., Meichum Mohler-Kuo, Mary P. Koss, and Henry Wechsler. "Correlates of Rape While Intoxicated in a National Sample of College Women." *Journal of Studies on Alcohol* 65.1 (2004): 37–45. Print.

12. Gross A. M., Winslett A., Roberts M., et al. An examination of sexual violence against college women. Violence Against Women. 2006;12:288–300.

13. Dowdall, George W., Meichum Mohler-Kuo, Mary P. Koss, and Henry Wechsler. "Correlates of Rape While Intoxicated in a National Sample of College Women." *Journal of Studies on Alcohol* 65.1 (2004): 37–45. Print.

14. Sampson, R. (2002). "Acquaintance Rape of College Students." U.S. Department of Justice Problem-Oriented Guides for Police, Problem-Specific Guides Series, Guide No. 17.

15. Fisher, B. et al. (2000). *The sexual victimization of college women.* Washington, DC: U.S. Dept. of Justice, Office of Justice Programs, National Institute of Justice.

16. Shaughnessy, L., & Starr, B. (2012, December 19). Sex assault at military academies underreported, survey finds. CNN.

14 More Blacks Live with Pollution

The Associated Press

An Associated Press analysis of a little-known government research project shows that black Americans are 79 percent more likely than whites to live in neighborhoods where industrial pollution is suspected of posing the greatest health danger.

Residents in neighborhoods with the highest pollution scores also tend to be poorer, less educated and more often unemployed than those elsewhere in the country, AP found.

"Poor communities, frequently communities of color but not exclusively, suffer disproportionately," said Carol Browner, who headed the Environmental Protection Agency during the Clinton administration when the scoring system was developed. "If you look at where our industrialized facilities tend to be located, they're not in the upper middle class neighborhoods."

With help from government scientists, AP mapped the risk scores for every neighborhood counted by the Census Bureau in 2000. The scores were then used to compare risks between neighborhoods and to study the racial and economic status of those who breathe America's most unhealthy air.

President Clinton ordered the government in 1993 to ensure equality in protecting Americans from pollution, but more than a decade later, factory emissions still disproportionately place minorities and the poor at risk, AP found.

In 19 states, blacks were more than twice as likely as whites to live in neighborhoods where air pollution seems to pose the greatest health danger, the analysis showed.

More than half the blacks in Kansas and nearly half of Missouri's black population, for example, live in the 10 percent of their states' neighborhoods with the highest risk scores. Similarly, more than four out of every 10 blacks in Kentucky, Minnesota, Oregon and Wisconsin live in high-risk neighborhoods.

And while Hispanics and Asians aren't overrepresented in high-risk neighborhoods nationally, in certain states they are. In Michigan, for example, 8.3 percent of the people living in high-risk areas are Hispanic, though Hispanics make up 3.3 percent of the statewide population.

All told, there are 12 states where Hispanics are more than twice as likely as non-Hispanics to live in neighborhoods with the highest risk scores. There are seven states where Asians are more than twice as likely as whites to live in the most polluted areas.

The average income in the highest risk neighborhoods was $18,806 when the Census last measured it, more than $3,000 less than the nationwide average.

One of every six people in the high-risk areas lived in poverty, compared with one of eight elsewhere, AP found.

Used with permission of The Associated Press. Copyright © 2016. All rights reserved.

Unemployment was nearly 20 percent higher than the national average in the neighborhoods with the highest risk scores, and residents there were far less likely to have college degrees.

Research over the past two decades has shown that short-term exposure to common air pollution worsens existing lung and heart disease and is linked to diseases like asthma, bronchitis and cancer. Long-term exposure increases the risks.

• • •

The Associated Press analyzed the health risk posed by industrial air pollution using data from the U.S. Environmental Protection Agency and the Census Bureau.

EPA uses toxic chemical air releases reported by factories to calculate a health risk score for each square kilometer of the United States. The scores can be used to compare risks from long-term exposure to factory pollution from one area to another. The scores are based on:

- The amount of toxic pollution released by each factory.
- The path the pollution takes as it spreads through the air.
- The level of danger to humans posed by each different chemical released.
- The number of males and females of different ages who live in the exposure paths.

The scores aren't meant to measure the actual risks of getting sick or the actual exposure to toxic chemicals. Instead, they are designed to help screen for polluted areas that may need additional study of potential health problems, EPA said.

The AP mapped the health risk scores to the census blocks used during the 2000 population count, using a method developed in consultation with EPA. The news service then compared racial and socioeconomic makeup with risk scores in the top 5 percent to the population elsewhere.

Similar analyses were done in each state, comparing the 10 percent of neighborhoods with the highest risk scores to the rest in the state.

To match the 2000 Census data, the AP used health risk scores calculated from industrial pollution reports that companies filed for EPA's 2000 Toxic Release Inventory. It often takes several years for EPA to learn of and correct inaccurate reports from factories, and the 2000 data were more complete than data from more recent reports that were still being corrected.

The AP adjusted the 2000 health risk scores in Census blocks around some plants that filed incorrect air release reports in 2000, after plant officials provided corrected data.

Counties that had the highest potential health risk from industrial air pollution in 2000, according to an AP analysis of government records. The health risk varies from year to year based on the level of factory emissions, the opening of new plants and the closing of older plants.

1. Washington County, Ohio
2. Wood County, W.Va.

3. Muscatine County, Iowa
4. Leflore County, Miss.
5. Cowlitz County, Wash.
6. Henry County, Ind.
7. Tooele County, Utah
8. Scott County, Iowa
9. Gila County, Ariz.
10. Whiteside County, Ill.

Factories whose emissions created the most potential health risk for residents in surrounding communities in 2000, according to an AP analysis of government records.

1. Eramet Marietta Inc., Marietta, Ohio
2. Titan Wheel Corp., Walcott, Iowa (closed in 2003)
3. Eastman Kodak Co., Rochester, N.Y.
4. American Minerals Inc., El Paso, Texas
5. F.W. Winter Inc., Camden, N.J.
6. Meridian Rail Corp., Cicero, Ill.
7. Carpenter Tech. Corp., Reading, Pa.
8. Longview Aluminum LLC, Longview, Wash. (closed in 2001)
9. DDE Louisville, Louisville, Ky.
10. Lincoln Electric Co., Cleveland

15 Pollution, Poverty and People of Color: A Michigan Tribe Battles a Global Corporation

Brian Bienkowski

Head in any direction on Michigan's Upper Peninsula and you will reach gushing rivers, placid ponds and lakes—both Great and small.

An abundant resource, this water has nourished a small Native American community for hundreds of years. So 10 years ago, when an international mining company arrived near the shores of Lake Superior to burrow a mile under the Earth and pull metals out of ore, the Keweenaw Bay Indian Community of the Lake Superior Band of Chippewa had to stand for its rights and its water.

And now, as bulldozers raze the land and the tunnel creeps deeper, the tribe still hasn't backed down.

"The indigenous view on water is that it is a sacred and spiritual entity," said Jessica Koski, mining technical assistant for the Keweenaw Bay community. "Water gives us and everything on Earth life."

The Keweenaw Bay Indians are fighting for their clean water, sacred sites and traditional way of life as Kennecott Eagle Minerals inches towards copper and nickel extraction, scheduled to begin in 2014.

Tribal leaders worry the mine will pollute ground water, the Salmon Trout River and Lake Superior, and strip the spiritual ambiance from their historical sites. Meandering through the Huron Mountains before spilling into Lake Superior, the river is home to endangered coaster trout as well as other fish that the tribe depends on for food.

The Keweenaw Bay community's L'Anse Reservation, home to 1,030 people, is both the oldest and the largest reservation in Michigan and sits about 30 miles west of the river. The struggle of this small community in remote, sleepy northernmost Michigan mirrors that of its native ancestors.

Tribal Injustice

According to the U.S. Bureau of Indian Affairs, there are 565 recognized Native American tribes. About 5.2 million people identified themselves as Native American or Alaska Native in the 2010 U.S. Census. But that sliver of the country's population— 1.7 percent—historically has faced an unfair burden of environmental justice issues.

Since early European immigration there have been palpable culture clashes with Native Americans—with the indigenous people often on the losing end. Infectious diseases, forced assimilation and land grabs marred early relations.

"Pollution, Poverty and People of Color: A Michigan Tribe Battles a Global Corporation" by Brian Bienkowski, Environmental Health News. Reprinted with permission from Brian Bienkowski.

But as the nation grew larger, the environmental justice issues did, too. Native American reservations have been targeted as places to dump industrial waste, and to mine both uranium and coal, leading to polluted rivers, lakes and tribal lands across the country. Some tribes have turned to waste storage or mining as revenue generators.

Native Americans continue to battle poverty, joblessness and low incomes. About 28.4 percent of American Indians and Alaska Natives—nearly twice the national rate—lived in poverty in 2010. Their unemployment hovers around 49 percent, according to the Bureau of Indian Affairs' most recent labor force report[1] in 2005.

Low income and environmental threats often go hand-in-hand, said Kyle Whyte, an assistant professor of philosophy at Michigan State University who studies Native American environmental justice issues.

Native Americans are even more vulnerable than other disadvantaged groups because of their reliance on natural resources for survival, he said. The top environmental justice issues still plaguing their communities are lack of healthy foods and water, and protection of sacred sites—all at play in northern Michigan.

For the 3,552 members of the Keweenaw Bay tribe, it's more than just water at stake. "It is a living thing that provides for us—physically and spiritually," Koski said.

Whyte said this view of water and the surrounding area is unique to tribes and should guide governance. "Part of it is admitting that some groups have a different conception of sacredness than we do," he said.

"Almost more pure than rainfall"

The newest controversy is over the Eagle Project, an underground nickel and copper mine just west of Marquette, Mich., a few miles inland from the shores of Lake Superior. Mine development began in 2010. It is now 75 percent complete and is scheduled to operate in 2014, according to Kennecott Eagle Minerals, owner, developer and future operator of the mine. The tribe, however, hopes to derail it with pending lawsuits.

The concerns about water contamination stem from the method, sulfide mining, which extracts metals from sulfide ores. When the sulfide ores are crushed, the sulfides are exposed to air and water, which catalyzes a chemical reaction that produces highly toxic sulfuric acid. The acid can then drain into nearby rivers, lakes and ground water sources—a phenomenon called acid mine drainage.

"Water is the top environmental concern," Koski said. "In addition to ourselves, all of the plants and wildlife rely on that water, and we have treaty rights for hunting, fishing and gathering."

Company officials say they have addressed environmental concerns.

Any water, including rain and snow, that comes in contact with mining activities is sent to a $10-million water treatment plant that will use a cleansing technology called reverse osmosis, said Daniel Blondeau, communications and media relations advisor at Rio Tinto, the London-based mining company that owns Kennecott.

The water is then either recycled into the mining process or returned into the ground. Blondeau said mining effluent will be tested every day and results will be sent to the state monthly.

Those tasked with keeping Michigan's water clean say they are confident that this treatment method, already used in many places to purify drinking supplies, will work.

"We actually really don't expect a lot of water in the mine . . . I mean there will be some," said Hal Fitch, director of the office of oil, gas and minerals for the Michigan Department of Environmental Quality. "Once that water goes through reverse osmosis treatment, it comes out almost more pure than rainfall . . . In fact, they have to have a roof over treatment plants so the treated water isn't contaminated by rainwater."

Experts tout the reverse osmosis and reuse as an example of technology overcoming environmental obstacles.

"The way Eagle will process the material, there will be no smelting onsite, so there's very little likelihood for contamination," said Klaus Schulz, a senior research geologist with the U.S. Geological Survey. "As long as they aren't putting tailings (leftover mining material) into the streams there should be no problems."

Tailings will be stored in an offsite temporary holding area double-lined with leak detection and collection systems, according to Kennecott officials. The tailings will also be mixed with limestone to neutralize the acid potential.

Schulz said historically mishandled tailings have been to blame for contamination.

"The reverse osmosis is leaps and bounds over what used to happen, which was water being dumped in lakes and rivers," Schulz said. "Plus they'll be recycling and reutilizing the water in the process, which lessens the withdrawal."

Western states have seen the most sulfide mine contamination, Schulz said. Two of the most well-known examples are the Summitville and Gilt Edge mines.

In the 1980s, the Summitville Mine in southwestern Colorado contaminated the Wrightman Fork tributary and the Alamosa River. The acid drainage stemmed from poor holding areas and tailing leakage. Ground water in that area is not used for drinking. But the Alamosa River below the site still cannot support aquatic life.

The Gilt Edge Mine in South Dakota was a gold mine that an insolvent company abandoned in the late 1990s, leaving behind 150 million gallons of acidic heavy-metal-laden water, as well as millions of cubic yards of acid-generating tailings. The Strawberry and Bear Butte creeks have been contaminated.

"Sure, historically there have been issues, but there are techniques today to deal with all of that," Schulz said.

Now-shuttered Wisconsin mine

Under the Treaty of 1842,[2] the Chippewa gave the U.S. government land bordering Lake Superior in what is now the western half of Michigan's Upper Peninsula and northeast Wisconsin. The tribes were paid and allowed to continue hunting, fishing and gathering on the ceded land.

Kennecott now owns about 1,600 acres, including the mine site, within that territory given to the government 170 years ago. Over its seven- to eight-year lifespan, the mine will produce 300 million pounds of nickel and 250 million pounds of copper, and directly employ about 300 people, according to Kennecott estimates.

In recent years, the land surrounding Lake Superior has been a hotspot for companies seeking to mine, process and sell metals. A similar copper and nickel sulfide mine proposal in St. Louis County, Minn., by Polymet Mining, has come under similar attacks by residents concerned about the water supply.

The Eagle mine will be the first to use sulfide extraction in Michigan. The state has had copper mines in the past but it was native copper, not copper tied up in sulfide, Schulz said.

"There are no examples they can point to of sulfide mines that haven't caused pollution," Koski said.

But Kennecott points to its now closed Flambeau Mine that operated in Rusk County, Wis., from 1993 to 1997. Reclamation of the copper and gold mine was completed in 1999, when it was filled back in.

"We have not found any violations of mining permits or state law, have not issued any violations at the Flambeau in compliance," said Phil Fauble, mining coordinator with the Wisconsin Department of Natural Resources.

Kennecott is responsible for the Flambeau site in perpetuity. During mine backfill and site cleanup, the company found a few areas where there was copper contamination. The company took care of the contamination right away, Fauble said. His department hasn't yet completed studies to see if these areas could harm wildlife or people.

Emily Whittaker, executive director of the Yellow Dog Watershed Preserve, an environmental group that is also fighting the Eagle mine, said Flambeau is a reason not to trust Kennecott. She pointed to an ongoing lawsuit brought by the Wisconsin Resource Protection Council that charges Kennecott under the Clean Water Act.

Whittaker said the preparation for mining has already altered the environment in Michigan. Road widening for trucks is probably to blame for increased sedimentation of the Salmon Trout River, she said. Portions of the mine will be drilled directly below the river.

"Our main concern is the condition of the environment. Our secondary concern is the communities that depend on this environment," Whittaker said. "Water is the lifeblood of this area."

Hunting, fishing and blueberry gathering have already been hampered because development has gobbled up prime land, Koski said.

"Right now it's an access issue, with the complete bulldozing," Koski said. "If and when the mine opens, it will be pollution impacting wildlife and treaty-protected resources."

"It is still very sacred to us."

One company compromise—providing access to Eagle Rock—hasn't mollified tensions. Eagle Rock is a spiritual gathering place.

"We went there early afternoon on a Saturday, had to show our ID's . . . show our tribal cards," Koski said. "We had to put on bright green and red vests, wear safety goggles . . . there were cranes everywhere . . . we were escorted by two company officials."

Blondeau said the state requires the company to protect the rock's surface and prohibits any mining activities on the rock. But to the Keweenaw Bay community, these requirements haven't protected the rock's essence.

"We used to drive up freely without permission or being escorted, now there is a high berm and a barbed wire fence," Koski said. "We aren't able to stay the night or do any traditional fasting. The whole integrity of the site is disturbed. But it is still very sacred to us."

Fitch said that Kennecott has provided adequate access. He referred to the site as "the so-called Eagle Rock."

"It never had that name before the project, but I guess there's an oral tradition," Fitch said.

It's these kinds of communication breakdowns that are at the heart of persistent Native American environmental justice issues across the country, Whyte said.

"When a tribe expresses its own knowledge and conceptions of things like the environment to companies or officials, and it is respected, justice issues like being able to protect sacred sites and clean water are often handled in a fair way," Whyte said.

He said the state and federal government has a mixed record on handling Native American issues, and he wasn't so sure that this open communication was happening in the upper reaches of Michigan—especially over Eagle Rock.

"I think it's fair to question whether the company, federal and state governments are truly respecting the unique caretaking practices of the tribe for that space," Whyte said.

Littered with litigation

The only federal regulatory hurdle Kennecott faced was approval of the Environmental Protection Agency's underground injection control program. After reviewing the treatment plans, the EPA determined a federal permit wasn't necessary.

The Keweenaw community initially reached out to the EPA but did not get very far, Koski said. The EPA acknowledges that environmental justice issues persist in Native American communities, even accepting some blame.

"The environmental justice issues facing Native American communities range from direct environmental, public health, cultural and sacred sites impacts, to lack of meaningful involvement and fair treatment in the governmental decision-making processes," according to an emailed response by the EPA's press office.

The EPA did not comment on relations with the Keweenaw Bay Indian Community.

Fitch said the state has included the tribe every step of the way.

"They were there when we went over the rules and didn't say much. We had meetings at the governor's office with them and they didn't say much," Fitch said. "Now they come out and they're critical, and that bothers me."

Koski said the tribe has opposed the mine since talks began. Failing to make much progress at the state or federal level, the Keweenaw Bay community has reached out to the United Nations, meeting with James Anaya, the UN's special rapporteur on the rights of indigenous peoples.

As the project pushes on, it remains littered with litigation.

Currently, the Keweenaw Bay Indian Community and three organizations—the National Wildlife Federation, Huron Mountain Club and Yellow Dog Watershed Preserve—are waiting to hear whether Michigan's Court of Appeals will hear their challenge of a 2006 state permit to build the mine.

In addition, the Huron Mountain Club, a private landowners club, filed a lawsuit in April contending Kennecott didn't get permits from the U.S. Army Corps of Engineers. The lawsuit claims that the permits are necessary since the project could harm the Salmon Trout River, wetlands, endangered species and sacred Native American sites.

So far lawsuits and knocking on government doors have proven fruitless and costly, Koski said. But the tribe will continue its steady drumbeat of opposition, pushing industry and government to respect their land, their water, their beliefs and their rights.

"An elder recently gave me a bracelet symbolizing a rainbow," Koski said. "She said she saw that things were going to be changing.

"There is still a lot of hope."

NOTES

1. U.S. Department of the Interior, Bureau of Indian Affairs. (2005). "American Indian Population and Labor Force Report." Available at: http://www.bia.gov/cs/groups/public /documents/text/idc-001719.pdf

2. Treaty with Chippewa. (1842). Oct. 4, 1842. | 7 Stat., 591. | Proclamation, Mar. 23, 1843. Available at: http://digital.library.okstate.edu/kappler/vol2/treaties/chi0542.htm

16 Testimony

Sonny Singh

Once the term terrorist attack was all over the headlines on September 11, 2001, something inside my 21-year-old, fresh-out-of-college self was dreadfully certain of what was coming next. Before I even had a chance to begin processing and mourning the horrific loss of thousands of lives in New York City, I was getting calls from even the most apolitical of my extended family members, urging me to be careful and "keep a low profile," to not leave my house unless I absolutely had to. No one in my family talked much about racism when I was growing up, but suddenly it was clear that while many in my Sikh family might not share my anti-oppression, leftist politics on paper, they sure as hell knew what it meant to be a target.

For those in the U.S. Sikh community who weren't already dreading the racist backlash immediately after 9/11, the murder of Balbir Singh Sodhi on September 15, 2001, in Phoenix, Arizona (my hometown), surely shook them to the core. Quickly U.S. flags were being distributed at gurdwaras throughout the country, stickers with slogans like "Sikhs love America" in red, white, and blue emerged on car bumpers. Suddenly we became "Sikh Americans," a term seldom used before 9/11.

It's almost ten years later, and I still walk the streets and ride the subway with a hypervigilance built up through a lifetime of being targeted because of my brown skin, turban, and beard. In my daily life in New York City, where I have lived since 2003, I experience some form of explicit harassment from strangers at least once a week, on average. Sometimes several separate incidents in one day. Yes, in New York City, the most diverse city on the planet.

Most commonly, someone will call me a terrorist or "Osama" either directly to my face or to someone they are with, with the intention of me hearing it. And it doesn't stop there.

A few months ago on my first day teaching in a high school in the Bronx, a student walking by me said to his friends, "Look, an Iraqi! He's gonna blow up the school!" and they all burst into laughter.

Last month at the laundromat across the street from my Brooklyn apartment, I found my wet clothes thrown out of the dryers I was using and scattered on the grimy floor.

In 2007, four police cars surrounded me while I was putting up flyers for my band's concert in Williamsburg, Brooklyn (a neighborhood where every street pole is covered with concert flyers). I was handcuffed and arrested and spent 16 hours in jail, where the white cop who arrested me forced me to take off my turban "for my own safety."

"Healing the trauma of post-9/11 racism one story (and melody) at a time" by Sonny Singh. Originally published in *Asian American Literary Review*, September 11, 2011. Reprinted by permission of the author.

In 2006, a stranger ripped off my turban (dastar) while I was riding the subway, which had also happened to me in the fifth grade. I wrote these words after the incident:

> I get off at Smith and 9th Street with my dirty dastar in my hands, not knowing what to do. My eyes fill with tears immediately. I feel naked and exposed, so small, so humiliated, and so, so alone. Why did he do that? Why? Was it fun for him? Did he impress his friends? Does it make him feel like he has more power than someone else—someone who looks like an immigrant, a foreigner, bin Laden?
>
> I get to a corner of the platform and break down in despair, remembering fifth grade vividly, feeling so angry and exhausted from living in this country. The twenty-something years of this shit is going through me at once—the slurs, the obnoxious stares, the go-back-to-your-countries, the threats, the towel/rag/tomato/condom/tumor heads, all of it. But somehow pulling off my turban hurts more than anything. Maybe it's the symbolism of my identity wrapped up in this one piece of cloth that, like my brown skin, I wear everyday.

I am an activist, an educator, and a musician. I dedicate my life to raising consciousness about oppression and injustice in the world and helping people see that change is possible. The music I make is often joyful and celebratory, embodying a hopeful spirit that is so needed in these times.

Yet simultaneously, as I cope with the trauma of bigotry, I struggle in a very personal way to remain hopeful. This is actually the first time I am using that word, trauma, in writing to refer to my experience. Being stared at with contempt and called derogatory names as I walk down the street is my status quo. It is an exhausting status quo. As I get older, it is becoming harder to avoid the emotional toll that a few decades of racist harassment has taken on me. In this post-9/11 climate, there is no "post-" in sight to the trauma of racism.

The reality seems especially bleak in the last year with the right-wing rage that has taken the U.S. by storm with a very clear enemy: Muslims. The hateful fear-mongering perpetuated by pundits and politicians on the evening news has real life consequences indicated by a rise in hate crimes as well as bullying in schools. From Quran Burning days to Stop Islamization of America rallies, Muslim-bashing is becoming an increasingly mainstream phenomenon. As always, the outward appearance of Sikhs makes us especially vulnerable. Just last week, two elderly Sikh men were shot, one of them killed, while going on an afternoon walk in their suburban Sacramento neighborhood.

Trauma upon trauma.

A decade of fear.

How will I, and we, heal?

Every time I step onto a stage and perform, wearing my turban proudly, I am breaking down the barriers and insecurities and anxieties that the trauma of racism has caused me. As my air creates melody through my trumpet and my voice, I am no longer afraid. As a crowd of a hundred or a thousand bursts into joyous dance and celebration the moment I play my first note, everything and anything feels possible.

As an educator, when I share my own experiences of being bullied and harassed with students, I witness transformation happening. When I refuse to separate myself and my experiences from the content I am teaching, I feel empowered and confident in who I am. I witness students coming to a deeper understanding of their own prejudices and working to change them.

After my turban was pulled off on the subway several years ago, the only thing I could do was write. I went home, devastated, and wrote furiously. I emailed what I wrote to some of my closest friends and then eventually cleaned it up and had it published on a racial justice blog. By documenting what happened to me and sharing it, I began my healing process.

In all of these cases, I am sharing my story, whether through a melody, in a classroom, or on a blog. And as I share my post-9/11/01 story here in 2011 with these words, I feel a profound sense of hope that may not be rooted in a logical, physical reality, but perhaps in a deeper reality that connects us all and is a foundation for our belief in liberation and justice. Even in the worst of circumstances, remaining hopeful is a necessity to our survival as people traumatized by oppression. We Sikhs call this chardi kala—a spirit of revolutionary eternal optimism. Our collective struggles for dignity and social justice are not only necessary to tear down systemic inequalities, but also to heal our own personal wounds as oppressed people, always remaining in the chardi kala spirit.

Suggestions for Further Reading

See articles from online news sources, daily newspapers, and weekly and monthly national magazines for accounts of discrimination and harassment as well as responses that address and aim to change these forms of violence.

PART V

The Economics of Race, Class, and Gender

Although in the United States we tend to obscure the distinction between rich and poor, instead proclaiming ourselves all "middle class," economic divisions are real, and the gap between rich and poor in the United States is growing at an alarming rate. In fact it's wider now than at any time since World War II. How does this affect the lives of people living in the United States today? What kind of economic realities do we face as we seek to feed, clothe, house, and educate ourselves and our families? As we have already seen, being born into a particular class, racial/ethnic group, and sex has repercussions that touch upon every aspect of a person's life. In Part V we attempt to further understand these impacts by turning our attention to statistics that reveal the economic realities faced by most ordinary people in their daily lives. Holly Sklar provides a dramatic and thought-provoking introduction to this part in Selection 1.

The 1990s were an incredible decade for economic growth, but the start of the twenty-first century saw workers' pensions, 401K plans, and dot-com millionaires vanish overnight, while the proportion of Americans living in poverty rose significantly. The "Great Recession," which officially began around 2008, only worsened these trends, and the repercussions are still being felt today. The story of the twenty-first century continues to be a persistent increase in the gap between rich and poor, a gap that has been widening slowly but steadily since 1973. Selections 2 through 5 report on the most recent rise in this gap and paint a bleak picture of how ordinary families are faring in this economy. Taking us behind the broad generalizations frequently offered by the media, Selections 4 and 5 examine the unique situations of various Asian American and Latino ethnic groups and explore the specific history of discrimination and the social, cultural, and economic factors that lie behind the racial wealth gap in this country.

In Selection 6, Linda Burnham examines the wage gap through the lens of gender. She offers an intersectional discussion of how the gender gap and the racial gap in wages affect African American women who are both unemployed at higher rates than other women and overrepresented among low-wage workers. The material in this selection documents a persistent wage gap over many years based on sex and suggests that racism and sexism, not ability or qualifications, have determined which jobs women and men do and how much worth is attached to their work. In Selection 7, Ai-jen Poo shows this gap in her piece about domestic workers, who perform one of the oldest forms of labor that has been devalued in our economic system, as well as describing organizing strategies that build from this platform of "women's work" as a way to move toward more equitable distribution of worth and compensation.

In sharp contrast to the reality that the articles and statistics in this section describe, the mythology of the American Dream continues to assure us that hard work and ability, not family background or connections, are the key to success. As we have already seen, the spectacular increase in American inequality has made the gap between the rich and the middle class wider, and hence more difficult to cross, than it was in the past. And this unequal treatment starts well before a student ever thinks of seeking to enroll in higher education. Selection 8, by Bob Feldman, reports on the "savage inequalities" of school funding across the country, which continues to see wealthy, white school districts receiving significantly more funding than poor districts and districts with large numbers of students of color. You may find it interesting to jump back to Part II's "Unequal Childhoods: Class, Race, and Family Life" by Annette Lareau or ahead to Part VIII and the article titled "Still Separate, Still Unequal: America's Educational Apartheid" by Jonathan Kozol.

In Selection 9, Tracie McMillan looks at hunger inequality and finds that "in the United States more than half of hungry households are white, and two-thirds of those with children have at least one working adult—typically in a full-time job." Declining wages help to explain why one-sixth of Americans do not have enough to eat. In Selection 10, Ed Pilkington shows us a different angle on the question of economic inequality through a discussion of how gender expression and self-determination can be shaped by material realities and access to resources.

The relationship between poverty or income inequality and poor health is explored in a sobering article by Alejandro Reuss titled "Cause of Death: Inequality" (Selection 11). According to the findings Reuss presents, there is a high correlation between life expectancy, chronic disease, death by injury, and generally poor health on the one hand and low income or low status on the other. Perhaps most surprising is Reuss's assertion that those of us who are worse off in the United States are not well off by comparison with people in other countries. While we may be better off with respect to consumer goods, he reports, we are decidedly not with respect to health and heath care. His conclusion: Inequality can kill.

Part V concludes with an essay by Eduardo Porter that looks at the alarming ways inequality limits what is held most dear to Americans: democracy. As the gaps grow bigger between the haves and have nots, the U.S. government will find it harder and harder to address inequality, and democratic institutions will in turn be destabilized.

1 Imagine a Country

Holly Sklar

Imagine a country living history in reverse.

The average worker's wage buys less today than it did in the 1970s.

The minimum wage buys less than it did in the 1950s.

Income inequality has roared back to the 1920s.

It's not Ireland.

Imagine a country where the richest family derives its fortune from the nation's largest employer—a company famous for paying poverty wages.

Imagine a country where one out of four children is born into poverty, and wealth is being redistributed upward. Since the 1970s, the richest 1 percent of households has nearly doubled its share of the nation's wealth. The top 1 percent has more wealth than the bottom 90 percent of households combined.

It's not Mexico.

Imagine a country where none of the nation's income growth goes to the bottom 90 percent of people.

Between 1973 and 2010, all of the nation's income growth went to the top 10 percent. Income for the bottom 90 percent declined, adjusted for inflation.

It wasn't always like that. Between 1947 and 1973, the richest 10 percent got 32 percent of the nation's growth. The bottom 90 percent shared 68 percent of the nation's income growth.

Imagine a country where, by 2007, the richest 1 percent had increased their share of the nation's income to the second-highest level on record, nearly tying the record set in 1928—on the eve of a great depression.

Not coincidentally, the nation experienced its worst economic downturn since the great depression—from December 2007 until June 2009, when the economy began growing again but unemployment, underemployment and foreclosures remained high.

Imagine a country where in 2010—the first year of economic recovery after a "great recession"—93 percent of all the nation's income growth went to the richest 1 percent.

Imagine a country where more and more jobs are keeping people in poverty instead of out of poverty.

Imagine a country where healthcare aides can't afford to take sick days. Where farm workers and security guards turn to overwhelmed food banks to help feed their families, and homelessness is rising among working families.

Imagine a country where some are paid so little their children go without necessities—while others are paid so much their grandchildren could live in luxury without having to work at all.

Revised and updated July 22, 2012. © 2012 by Holly Sklar. Permission granted by the author.

Imagine a country ranked number 42—between Uruguay and Cameroon—in the list of nations from greatest to least inequality in family income distribution. More than ninety countries are less unequal.

It's not Argentina.

Imagine a country where taxes were cut so much that the nation's richest bosses pay lower effective rates than workers. The nation's 400 richest taxpayers paid an average federal tax rate of 19.9 percent in 2009—down from 29.9 percent in 1995.

As a *Reuters* columnist observed, "The top 400 paid an average income tax rate of 19.9 percent, the same rate paid by a single worker who made $110,000 in 2009. The top 400 earned five times that much every day."

Imagine a country that gave tax breaks to millionaires while millions of people went without health insurance and the infrastructure built by earlier generations of taxpayers fell apart.

Imagine a country giving nearly a trillion dollars in tax breaks to millionaires and billionaires since 2001 while going into massive debt with other countries.

It's not Greece.

Imagine a country where worker productivity went up, but workers' wages went down.

In the words of the national labor department, "As the productivity of workers increases, one would expect worker compensation [wages and benefits] to experience similar gains." That's what happened between 1947 and 1973. But between 1973 and 2011, productivity grew 80 percent and the average worker wage fell 7 percent adjusted for inflation.

Imagine a country where minimum wage raises have been so little, so late that minimum wage workers earned less in 2012, adjusted for inflation, than they did in 1956.

The national minimum wage reached its peak value back in 1968, when it was $10.55 an hour, adjusted for inflation in 2012 dollars. At the $7.25 minimum wage in effect since 2009, today's full-time minimum wage retail worker, security guard, child care worker or health aide makes just $15,080 a year. Last century's 1968 minimum wage worker made $21,944 a year, adjusted for inflation.

Imagine a country where the minimum wage has become a poverty wage instead of an anti-poverty wage. The minimum wage has lagged so far behind necessities that keeping a roof overhead is a constant struggle and family health coverage would cost nearly all the annual income of a full-time worker at minimum wage.

Imagine a country with poverty rates higher than they were in the 1970s. Imagine a country that sets the official poverty line well below the actual cost of minimally adequate housing, healthcare, food and other necessities. On average, households need more than double the official poverty threshold to meet basic needs.

Imagine a country where some of the worst CEOs make millions more in a year than the best CEOs of earlier generations made in their lifetimes.

In 1980, CEOs of major corporations made an average 45 times the pay of average full-time workers. In 1991, when CEOs made 140 times as much as workers, a prominent pay expert said the CEO "is paid so much more than ordinary workers that he hasn't got the slightest clue as to how the rest of the country lives."

In 2003, a leading business magazine put a pig in a pinstriped suit on the cover and headlined its CEO pay roundup, "Have they no shame? Their performance stank last year, yet most CEOs got paid more than ever." The story began with a quote from George Orwell's *Animal Farm*: "But the pigs were so clever that they could think of a way round every difficulty." In 2011, CEOs at major corporations made 259 times the pay of average full-time workers.

Imagine a country where corporate profits are high and workers' wages are low. The nation's biggest bank explained it this way in 2011: "Reductions in wages and benefits explain the majority of the net improvement in [profit] margins . . . US labor compensation is now at a 50-year low relative to both company sales and US GDP."

It's not England.

Imagine a country where wages have fallen despite greatly increased education. Since 1973, the share of workers without a high school degree has plummeted and the percentage with at least four years of college has more than doubled.

Imagine a country where wages have fallen way behind the costs of major expenses like housing, health and college. Between 1970 and 2009, adjusted for inflation, rent and utilities rose 41 percent, health expenditures rose 50 percent, public college rose 80 percent and private college rose 113 percent.

Imagine a country where the wages of young college graduates (age 21–24) fell 5.4 percent between 2000 and 2011. But, as the College Board reports, "Over the decade from 2000–01 to 2010–11, total borrowing per full-time equivalent student for undergraduate and graduate students combined increased by 57% in inflation-adjusted dollars. Undergraduate borrowing increased by 56% per FTE student."

Students from lower-income families receive smaller grants from colleges and universities than students from upper-income families.

Imagine a country where households headed by persons under age 55 had much lower median net worth (assets minus debt) in 2010 than in 1989, adjusted for inflation.

Imagine a country where more and more two-paycheck households are struggling to afford a home, college, healthcare and retirement once normal for middle-class households with one paycheck. Middle-class households are a medical crisis, out-sourced job or busted pension away from bankruptcy.

Households tried to prop themselves up in the face of falling real wages by maxing out work hours, credit cards and home equity loans. Consumer spending makes up about 70 percent of the economy. An economy fueled by rising debt rather than rising wages is a house of cards.

Imagine a country where underpaid workers are bailing out banks and corporations run by overpaid, undertaxed bosses who milked their companies and country like cash cows and crashed the world economy.

Imagine a country where "too big to fail" banks are bigger than before the financial meltdown. The assets of the five biggest banks were equal to 56 percent of the nation's economy in 2011. That's up from 43 percent in 2006.

It's not Germany.

Imagine a country where more workers are going back to the future of sweat-shops and day labor. Corporations are replacing full-time jobs with disposable "contingent workers." They include temporary employees, on-call workers, contract workers, freelancers and "leased" employees—some of them fired and then "rented" back at a large discount by the same company—and involuntary part-time workers, who want permanent full-time work.

How do workers increasingly forced to migrate from job to job, at low and variable wage rates, without health insurance or paid vacation, much less a pension, care for themselves and their families, pay for college, save for retirement, plan a future, build strong communities?

Imagine a country, which negotiated "free trade" agreements, helping corporations trade freely on cheap labor at home and abroad.

Imagine a country becoming a nation of Scrooge-Marts and outsourcers—with an increasingly low-wage, underemployed workforce instead of a growing middle class.

It's not Canada.

Imagine a country where polls show most workers would join a union if they could, but for decades, employers have routinely violated workers' rights to organize.

A leading business magazine observed in 2004, "While labor unions were largely responsible for creating the broad middle class after World War II . . . that's not the case today. Most . . . employers fiercely resist unionization, which, along with other factors, has helped slash union membership to just 13% of the workforce, vs. a mid-century peak of more than 35%."

By 2011, the union membership rate was just 11.8 percent. Full-time workers who were union members had median 2011 weekly earnings of $938 compared with just $729 for workers not represented by unions.

It's not South Korea.

Imagine a country where nearly two-thirds of women with children under age 6 and more than three-fourths of women with children ages 6–17 are in the labor force, but paid family leave and affordable childcare and after-school programs are scarce. Apparently, kids are expected to have three parents: Two parents with jobs to pay the bills, and another parent to be home in mid-afternoon when school lets out—as well as all summer.

Imagine a country where women working full time earn 77 cents for every dollar men earn. Women don't pay 77 cents on a man's dollar for their education, rent, food or healthcare. The gender wage gap has closed just 13 cents since 1955, when women earned 64 cents for every dollar earned by men. There's still another 23 cents to go.

The average female high school graduate who works full time, year round from ages 25 to 64 will earn about $383,000 less than the average male high school graduate. The gap widens to $654,000 for full-time workers with Bachelor's degrees and $824,000 for workers with Master's degrees. The gap shrinks to $609,000 for those with PhDs. But it balloons for full-time workers with professional degrees: women will earn $1,023,000 less than men in the course of their careers.

Imagine a country where childcare workers, mostly women, typically make less than baggage porters and bellhops and much less than animal trainers and pest control workers. Out of nearly 800 occupations surveyed by the labor department, only 20 have lower median hourly wages than childcare workers.

Imagine a country where women are 47 percent of the nation's labor force but just 4 percent of the CEOs and 14 percent of the executive officers at the largest 500 companies. Never mind that companies with a higher share of women in their senior management teams financially outperform companies with lower representation.

Imagine a country where discrimination against women is pervasive from the bottom to the top of the pay scale, and it's not because women are on the "mommy track." The words of a leading business magazine still ring true, "At the same level of management, the typical woman's pay is lower than her male colleague's—even when she has the exact same qualifications, works just as many years, relocates just as often, provides the main financial support for her family, takes no time off for personal reasons, and wins the same number of promotions to comparable jobs."

Imagine a country where instead of rooting out discrimination, many policy makers blame women for their disproportionate poverty. If women earned as much as similarly qualified men, poverty in single-mother households would be cut in half.

It's not Japan.

Imagine a country where violence against women remains common. "Females made up 70% of victims killed by an intimate partner in 2007, a proportion that has changed very little since 1993," the department of justice reports. In 2007, 24 percent of female homicide victims were killed by a spouse or ex-spouse; 21 percent were killed by a boyfriend or girlfriend; and 19 percent were killed by another family member. Researchers say, "Men commonly kill their female partners in response to the woman's attempt to leave an abusive relationship."

The country has no equal rights amendment.

It's not Pakistan.

Imagine a country whose school system is rigged in favor of the already privileged, with lower caste children tracked by race and income into the most deficient and demoralizing schools and classrooms. Public school budgets are heavily determined by private property taxes, allowing higher income districts to spend more than poorer ones.

In rich districts, kids take modern libraries, laboratories and computers for granted. In poor districts, they are rationing out-of-date textbooks and toilet paper. Rich schools often look like country clubs—with manicured sports fields and swimming pools. In poor districts, schools often look more like jails—with concrete grounds and grated windows. College prep courses, art, music, physical education, field trips and foreign languages are often considered necessities for the affluent, luxuries for the poor.

It's not India.

Imagine a country whose constitution once counted black slaves as worth three-fifths of whites. Today, black per capita income is about three-fifths of whites'.

Imagine a country where racial disparities take their toll from birth to death. The black infant mortality rate is more than double that of whites. Black life expectancy is more than four years less. The official black unemployment rate is about twice that of whites and the black poverty rate is about triple that of whites.

Imagine a country where the government subsidized decades of segregated suburbanization for whites while the inner cities left to people of color were treated as outsider cities—separate, unequal and disposable. Studies have documented continuing discrimination in housing, education, employment, banking, insurance, healthcare and criminal justice.

Imagine a country where the typical white household has more than six times the net worth of the typical household of color. In 2010, median household net worth—including home equity—was $130,600 for white households and just $20,400 for households of color.

It's not South Africa.

Imagine a country that doesn't count you as unemployed just because you're unemployed. To be counted in the official unemployment rate you must be actively searching for work. The government doesn't count people as "unemployed" if they are so discouraged from long and fruitless job searches they have given up looking. It doesn't count as "unemployed" those who couldn't look for work in the past month because they had no childcare, for example. If you need a full-time job, but you're working part-time—whether 1 hour or 34 hours weekly—because that's all you can find, you're counted as employed.

A leading business magazine observed, "Increasingly the labor market is filled with surplus workers who are not being counted as unemployed."

Imagine a country where there is a shortage of jobs, not a shortage of work. Millions of people need work and urgent work needs people—from staffing schools, libraries, health centers and fire stations, to creating affordable housing, to repairing bridges and building mass transit, to cleaning up pollution and converting to renewable energy.

It's not Spain.

Imagine a country with full prisons instead of full employment. The jail and prison population has more than quadrupled since 1980. In 1980, one in every 453 residents was incarcerated. In 2010, the figure was one in every 137. The figures are even grimmer when it comes to people in prison or jail or on probation or parole: one in every 44 people (including children) is under some form of correctional control.

Imagine a country that is Number One in the world when it comes to locking up its own people. It has less than 5 percent of the world's population, but 23 percent of the world's incarcerated population.

Imagine a country where prison is a growth industry. State governments spend an average $29,000 a year to keep someone in prison, while cutting cost-effective programs of education, job training, employment, community development, and mental illness and addiction treatment to keep them out. In the words of a national center on institutions and alternatives, this nation has "replaced the social safety net with a dragnet."

A leading magazine reported in a piece titled "Incarceration Nation" that state expenditures for prisons rose at six times the rate of spending on higher education in the past 20 years. In 2011, the nation's largest state spent $9.6 billion on prisons and $5.7 billion on state colleges and universities. The article noted that since 1980, the state "built one college campus and 21 prisons. A college student costs the state $8,667 per year; a prisoner costs it $45,006 a year."

It's not China.

Imagine a country that imprisons black people at a rate much higher than South Africa did under apartheid. One out of ten black men ages 30–34 were locked up in prisons or jails compared to one out of 61 white men in the same age group in 2010. The overall incarceration rate for black women is three times higher than for white women.

Meanwhile, one out of seven black men and women were unemployed according to the official count in mid 2012 compared to one out of fourteen white men and women. Remember, to be counted in the official unemployment rate you must be actively looking for a job and not finding one. "Surplus" workers are increasingly being criminalized.

Imagine a country whose justice department observed, "The fact that the legal order not only countenanced but sustained slavery, segregation, and discrimination for most of our Nation's history—and the fact that the police were bound to uphold that order—set a pattern for police behavior and attitudes toward minority communities that has persisted until the present day." Racial profiling and "driving while black" are well-known terms.

Imagine a country where from first arrest to third strikes resulting in lifetime sentences—often for nonviolent petty crimes—blacks and Latinos are arrested and imprisoned in massively disproportionate numbers.

Imagine a country waging a racially biased "War on Drugs." Although blacks and whites engage in drug offenses at comparable rates, a human rights group reports, blacks are ten times more likely than whites to enter prison for drug offenses. Between 1999 and 2007, 80 percent or more of all drug arrests were for possession, not sales.

A study in a prominent medical journal found that drug and alcohol rates were slightly higher for pregnant white women than pregnant black women, but black women were about ten times more likely to be reported to authorities by private doctors and public health clinics—under a mandatory reporting law. Poor women were also more likely to be reported.

It is said that truth is the first casualty in war, and the "War on Drugs" is no exception. Contrary to stereotype, "The typical cocaine user is white, male, a high school graduate employed full time and living in a small metropolitan area or suburb," says the nation's former drug czar. A leading newspaper reported that law officers and judges say, "Although it is clear that whites sell most of the nation's cocaine and account for 80% of its consumers, it is blacks and other minorities who continue to fill up [the] courtrooms and jails, largely because, in a political climate that demands that something be done, they are the easiest people to arrest." They are the easiest to scapegoat.

It's not Australia.

Imagine a country that ranks first in the world in wealth and military power, and just 48th in infant mortality, a little better than Croatia and behind countries such as Cuba and South Korea. If the government were a parent, it would be guilty of child abuse. Thousands of children die preventable deaths.

Imagine a country where healthcare is managed for healthy profit. Between 1999 and 2011, the average cost of insurance premiums more than doubled. Other

336 PART V The Economics of Race, Class, and Gender

industrialized countries have universal health coverage. But in this nation, one out of five people under age 65 had no health insurance, public or private, at any time in 2010.

"The absence of health insurance is hazardous to your health," says the Institute of Medicine. "Uninsured people, children as well as adults, suffer worse health and die sooner than those with insurance."

Lack of health insurance typically means lack of preventive healthcare and delayed or second-rate treatment. The uninsured are at much higher risk for chronic disease and disability, and uninsured adults have a 25 percent greater chance of dying (adjusting for demographic, socioeconomic and health characteristics). Uninsured women with breast cancer have a 30 percent to 50 percent higher risk of dying than insured women, for example. Severely injured car crash victims who are uninsured receive less care in the hospital and have a 39 percent higher mortality rate than privately insured patients.

Imagine a country where healthcare is literally a matter of life and death, but every day more than 2000 babies are born without health insurance. The country's northern neighbor, which has universal healthcare, has a life expectancy that is three years longer.

Imagine a country where many descendants of its first inhabitants live on reservations strip-mined of natural resources and have a higher proportion of people in poverty than any other ethnic group.

Imagine a country where centuries of plunder and lies are masked in expressions like "Indian giver." Where the military still dubs enemy territory, "Indian country." The 2011 military operation that killed the nation's No. 1 enemy was called Operation Geronimo.

Imagine a country that has less than 5 percent of the world's population and less than 3 percent of the world's proven oil reserves, but consumes 25 percent of the world's oil. The nation's federal spending on clean energy—including research, development and usage subsidies—rose sharply to $44 billion in 2009, and then plummeted in the years after to $16 billion in 2012, with more decreases expected.

Imagine a country whose per capita carbon dioxide emissions from the consumption of energy are nearly two times that of manufacturing powerhouse Germany, three times that of China and 12 times that of India. It has long obstructed international action against catastrophic climate change and continues subsidizing fossil fuels such as the oxymoronic "clean coal."

It's not Brazil.

Imagine a country whose senate and house of representatives are not representative of the nation. They are overwhelmingly white and male, and increasingly millionaire. Forty-two percent of house members were millionaires in 2010, according to financial disclosure records that don't even include the value of their homes or other non-income producing property. In the 100-member senate in 2010, there were 67 millionaires and no women of color. If the senate reflected the population, only one senator would be a millionaire.

Imagine a country that's ranked just number 79—between Morocco and Turkmenistan—when it comes to the percentage of women in national legislative bodies. Just 17 percent of its senate and house of representatives were women in 2012.

If the 100-member senate reflected the population it would have 51 women and 49 men—including 64 whites, 16 Latinos, 13 blacks, 5 Asian and Pacific Islanders, and 1 Native American and 1 other. Instead, it has 17 women and 83 men—including 96 whites, 2 Latinos, 2 Asians and no blacks or Native Americans.

Imagine a country that made it easier for billionaires and corporations to pour money into elections while making it harder for people to vote.

Imagine a country whose leaders misused a fight against terrorism as camouflage for trampling the bill of rights and undermining democracy. The most fundamental civil liberties, including the right of citizens not to be thrown into prison indefinitely or assassinated on the secret word of government officials, were tossed aside.

Imagine a country that leads the world in arms exports and accounts for 41 percent of world military spending. The next highest country accounts for 8 percent.

In this same country, a five-star general who became president had warned in 1961, "In the councils of government, we must guard against the acquisition of unwarranted influence, whether sought or unsought, by the military-industrial complex . . . We must never let the weight of this combination endanger our liberties or democratic processes. We should take nothing for granted. Only an alert and knowledgeable citizenry can compel the proper meshing of the huge industrial and military machinery of defense with our peaceful methods and goals, so that security and liberty may prosper together."

It's not Russia.

It's the United States.

The words of Dr. Martin Luther King Jr. call down to us today:

"A true revolution of values will soon cause us to question the fairness and justice of many of our past and present policies. We are called to play the Good Samaritan on life's roadside; but . . . one day the whole Jericho road must be transformed so that men and women will not be beaten and robbed as they make their journey through life. . . .

"A true revolution of values will soon look uneasily on the glaring contrast of poverty and wealth. . . . There is nothing but a lack of social vision to prevent us from paying an adequate wage to every American citizen whether he be a hospital worker, laundry worker, maid or day laborer."

SELECTED SOURCES

Bloomberg Businessweek, "Big Banks: Now Even Too Bigger to Fail," April 19, 2012.

Anthony P. Carnevale, et al., *The College Payoff: Education, Occupations, Lifetime Earnings*, Georgetown University Center on Education and the Workforce, 2011.

Catalyst, New York, reports on women in business.

Center for American Women and Politics, Rutgers University, New Jersey.

Center for Responsive Politics, OpenSecrets.org.

Ira J. Chasnoff, et al., "The Prevalence of Illicit-Drug or Alcohol Use During Pregnancy and Discrepancies in Mandatory Reporting," *New England Journal of Medicine*, April 26, 1990.

Children's Defense Fund, Washington, DC.

CIA World Factbook, Country Comparisons.

Citizens for Tax Justice, Washington, DC.

College Board Advocacy & Policy Center, *Trends in Student Aid 2011*.

Congressional Budget Office.

Michelle Conlin and Aaron Bernstein, "Working . . . and Poor," *Business Week*, May 31, 2004.

Graef S. Crystal, *In Search of Excess: The Overcompensation of American Executives* (New York: Norton, 1992/1991).

Economic Policy Institute, Washington, DC.

President Dwight D. Eisenhower, Farewell Radio and Television Address to the American People, January 17, 1961.

Anne B. Fisher, "When Will Women Get To The Top?" *Fortune*, September 21, 1992.

Forbes, annual reports on CEO compensation.

Human Rights Watch, *Decades of Disparity: Drug Arrests and Race in the United States* (2009) and *Targeting Blacks* (2008).

Institute for Women's Policy Research, *The Gender Wage Gap: 2011*, March 2012.

Institute of Medicine, National Academy of Sciences, *America's Uninsured Crisis* (2009) and other reports on the consequences of lack of health insurance.

International Centre for Prison Studies, King's College, London, UK.

Inter-Parliamentary Union, Women in National Parliaments, May 31, 2012.

David Cay Johnston, "The fortunate 400," *Reuters*, June 6, 2012.

J.P. Morgan, *Eye on the Market*, July 11, 2011.

Henry J. Kaiser Family Foundation reports on health insurance costs.

Martin Luther King Jr. *Where Do We Go From Here: Chaos or Community?* (Harper & Row, 1967).

Jonathan Kozol, *The Shame of the Nation: The Restoration of Apartheid Schooling in America* (New York: Crown, 2005) and *Savage Inequalities: Children in America's Schools* (Crown, 1991).

Peter Medoff and Holly Sklar, *Streets of Hope: The Fall and Rise of an Urban Neighborhood* (Boston: South End Press, 1994).

National Center for Public Policy and Higher Education, *Measuring Up 2008: The National Report Card on Higher Education*.

National Center on Institutions and Alternatives.

Emmanuel Saez, "Striking it Richer: The Evolution of Top Incomes in the United States," updated March 2012, and updated data tables for 1913-2010.

Sentencing Project, Washington, DC, reports on incarceration trends and racial disparity in criminal justice.

Holly Sklar, Laryssa Mykyta and Susan Wefald, *Raise The Floor: Wages and Policies That Work For All Of Us* (Boston: South End Press, 2002).

Stockholm International Peace Research Institute, data on world military expenditures and arms transfers.

Jerry Useem, "Have They No Shame?" *Fortune*, April 28, 2003 on CEO pay.

U.S. Census Bureau.

U.S. Centers for Disease Control and Prevention, National Center for Health Statistics.

U.S. Department of Education.

U.S. Department of Justice, Bureau of Justice Statistics.

U.S. Department of Justice, *Female Victims of Violence*, revised October 23, 2009.

U.S. Department of Labor, Bureau of Labor Statistics.

U.S. Energy Information Administration, International Energy Statistics.

U.S. Federal Reserve Board, Survey of Consumer Finances.

U.S. Internal Revenue Service, "The 400 Individual Income Tax Returns Reporting the Highest Adjusted Gross Incomes Each Year, 1992–2009," June 2012.

U.S. Senate, Health, Education, Labor and Pensions Committee, *Saving the American Dream*, September 1, 2011.

Hubert Williams and Patrick V. Murphy, "The Evolving Strategy of Police: A Minority View," *Perspectives on Policing*, U.S. Department of Justice, 1990.

Fareed Zakaria, "Incarceration Nation," *Time*, April 2, 2012.

2 Wealth Inequality Has Widened Along Racial, Ethnic Lines Since End of Great Recession

Rakesh Kochhar and Richard Fry

The Great Recession, fueled by the crises in the housing and financial markets, was universally hard on the net worth of American families. But even as the economic recovery has begun to mend asset prices, not all households have benefited alike, and wealth inequality has widened along racial and ethnic lines.

The wealth of white households was 13 times the median wealth of black households in 2013, compared with eight times the wealth in 2010, according to a new Pew Research Center analysis of data from the Federal Reserve's Survey of Consumer Finances.[1] Likewise, the wealth of white households is now more than 10 times the wealth of Hispanic households, compared with nine times the wealth in 2010.

The current gap between blacks and whites has reached its highest point since 1989, when whites had 17 times the wealth of black households. The current white-to-Hispanic wealth ratio has reached a level not seen since 2001. (Asians and other racial groups are not separately identified in the public-use versions of the Fed's survey.)

Leaving aside race and ethnicity, the net worth of American families overall—the difference between the values of their assets and liabilities—held steady during the economic recovery. The typical household had a net worth of $81,400 in 2013, according to the Fed's survey—almost the same as what it was in 2010, when the median net worth of U.S. households was $82,300 (values expressed in 2013 dollars).

The stability in household wealth follows a dramatic drop during the Great Recession. From 2007 to 2010, the median net worth of American families decreased by 39.4%, from $135,700 to $82,300. Rapidly plunging house prices and a stock market crash were the immediate contributors to this shellacking.

Our analysis of Federal Reserve data does reveal a stark divide in the experiences of white, black and Hispanic households during the economic recovery. From 2010 to 2013, the median wealth of non-Hispanic white households increased from $138,600 to $141,900, or by 2.4%.

Meanwhile, the median wealth of non-Hispanic black households fell 33.7%, from $16,600 in 2010 to $11,000 in 2013. Among Hispanics, median wealth decreased

"Wealth inequality has widened along racial, ethnic lines since end of Great Recession," Pew Research Center, Washington, DC (December, 2014). http://www.pewresearch.org/fact-tank/2014/12/12/racial-wealth-gaps-great-recession/

Figure 2.1: Racial, Ethnic Wealth Gaps Have Grown Since Great Recession
Median net worth of households, in 2013 dollars

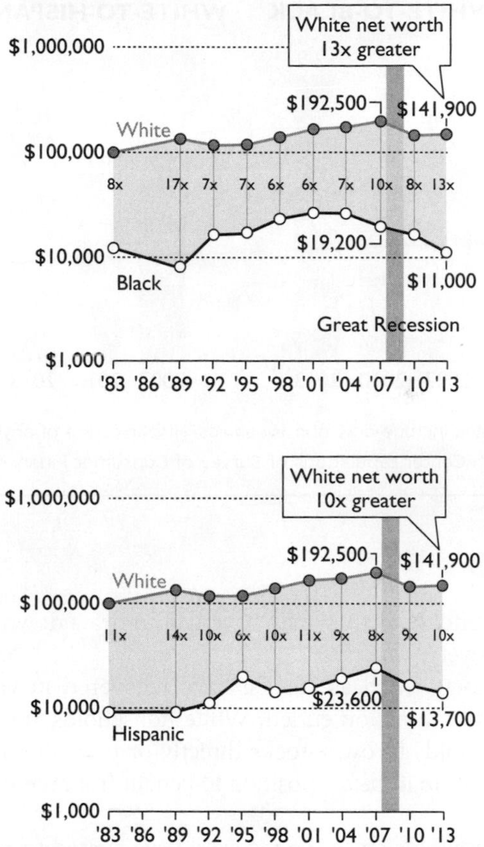

White net worth
13x greater

$192,500⌐ $141,900

White
$1,000,000
$100,000

8x   17x 7x   7x 6x 6x 7x 10x 8x 13x

$10,000

$19,200⌐

Black

$11,000

Great Recession

$1,000
'83 '86 '89 '92 '95 '98 '01 '04 '07 '10 '13

White net worth
10x greater

$192,500⌐ $141,900

White
$1,000,000
$100,000

11x   14x 10x 6x 10x 11x 9x   8x 9x 10x

$10,000

$23,600

Hispanic

$13,700

$1,000
'83 '86 '89 '92 '95 '98 '01 '04 '07 '10 '13

Notes: Blacks and whites include only non-Hispanics. Hispanics are of any race. Chart scale is logarithmic; each gridline is ten times greater than the gridline below it. Great Recession began Dec. '07 and ended June '09.

Source: Pew Research Center tabulations of Survey of Consumer Finances public-use data

by 14.3%, from $16,000 to $13,700. For all families—white, black and Hispanic— median wealth is still less than its pre-recession level.

A number of factors seem responsible for the widening of the wealth gaps during the economic recovery. As the Federal Reserve notes, the median income of minority households (blacks, Hispanics and other non-whites combined) fell 9% from its 2010 to 2013 surveys, compared with a decrease of 1% for non-Hispanic white households.[2] Thus, minority households may not have replenished their savings as

Figure 2.2: Wealth Inequality by Race and Ethnicity Has Grown Since 2007
Median wealth ratios

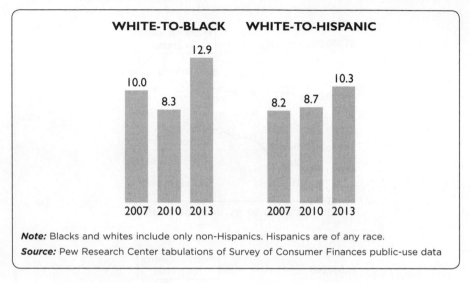

WHITE-TO-BLACK   WHITE-TO-HISPANIC

12.9

10.0   8.3   8.2 8.7   10.3

2007 2010 2013   2007 2010 2013

Note: Blacks and whites include only non-Hispanics. Hispanics are of any race.
Source: Pew Research Center tabulations of Survey of Consumer Finances public-use data

much as white households or they may have had to draw down their savings even more during the recovery.

Also, financial assets, such as stocks, have recovered in value more quickly than housing since the recession ended. White households are much more likely[3] than minority households to own stocks directly or indirectly through retirement accounts. Thus, they were in better position to benefit from the recovery in financial markets.

All American households since the recovery have started to reduce their ownership of key assets, such as homes, stocks and business equity. But the decrease in asset ownership tended to be proportionally greater among minority households. For example, the homeownership rate for non-Hispanic white households fell from 75.3% in 2010 to 73.9% in 2013, a percentage drop of 2%. Meanwhile, the homeownership rate among minority households decreased from 50.6% in 2010 to 47.4% in 2013, a slippage of 6.5%.

While the current wealth gaps are higher than at the beginning of the recession, they are not at their highest levels as recorded by the Fed's survey. Peak values for the wealth ratios were recorded in the 1989 survey—17 for the white-to-black ratio and 14 for the white-to-Hispanic ratio. But those values of the ratios may be anomalies driven by fluctuations in the wealth of the poorest[4]—those with net worth less than $500. Otherwise, the racial and ethnic wealth gaps in 2013 are at or about their highest levels observed in the 30 years for which we have data.

Figure 2.3: Wealth by Race and Ethnicity, 2007–13

Median net worth of households, in 2013 dollars

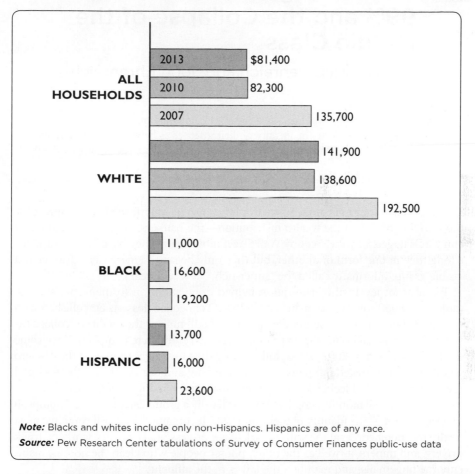

Note: Blacks and whites include only non-Hispanics. Hispanics are of any race.

Source: Pew Research Center tabulations of Survey of Consumer Finances public-use data

NOTES

1. Board of Governors for the Federal Reserve System. *The 2013 Survey of Consumer Finances*. Available at: www.federalreserve.gov/econresdata/scf/scfindex.htm

2. Board of Governors for the Federal Reserve System. *Federal Reserve Bulletin*, September 2014, Vol. 100, No. 4. Available at: www.federalreserve.gov/pubs/bulletin/2014/pdf/scf14.pdf

3. Board of Governors for the Federal Reserve System. *The 2013 Survey of Consumer Finances Chartbook*. Available at: www.federalreserve.gov/econresdata/scf/files/BulletinCharts.pdf

4. "Changes in Family Finances from 1989 to 1992: Evidence from the Survey of Consumer Finances." *The Federal Reserve Bulletin*, October 1994. Prepared by Arthur B. Kennickell and Martha Starr-McCluer of the Federal Reserve Board's Division of Research and Statistics. Available at: www.federalreserve.gov/econresdata/scf/files/1992_bull1094.pdf

3 The Making of the American 99% and the Collapse of the Middle Class

Barbara Ehrenreich and John Ehrenreich

"Class happens when some men, as a result of common experiences (inherited or shared), feel and articulate the identity of their interests as between themselves, and as against other men whose interests are different from (and usually opposed to) theirs."

—E.P. THOMPSON, THE MAKING OF THE ENGLISH WORKING CLASS

The "other men" (and of course women) in the current American class alignment are those in the top 1% of the wealth distribution—the bankers, hedge-fund managers, and CEOs targeted by the Occupy Wall Street movement. They have been around for a long time in one form or another, but they only began to emerge as a distinct and visible group, informally called the "super-rich," in recent years.

Extravagant levels of consumption helped draw attention to them: private jets, multiple 50,000 square-foot mansions, $25,000 chocolate desserts embellished with gold dust. But as long as the middle class could still muster the credit for college tuition and occasional home improvements, it seemed churlish to complain. Then came the financial crash of 2007–2008, followed by the Great Recession, and the 1%—to whom we had entrusted our pensions, our economy, and our political system—stood revealed as a band of feckless, greedy narcissists, and possibly sociopaths.

Still, until a few months ago, the 99% was hardly a group capable of (as Thompson says) articulating "the identity of their interests." It contained, and still contains, most "ordinary" rich people, along with middle-class professionals, factory workers, truck drivers, and miners, as well as the much poorer people who clean the houses, manicure the fingernails, and maintain the lawns of the affluent.

It was divided not only by these class differences, but most visibly by race and ethnicity—a division that has actually deepened since 2008. African-Americans and Latinos of all income levels disproportionately lost their homes to foreclosure in 2007 and 2008, and then disproportionately lost their jobs in the wave of layoffs that followed. On the eve of the Occupy movement, the black middle class had been devastated. In fact, the only political movements to have come out of the 99% before Occupy emerged were the Tea Party movement and, on the other side

From *The Nation,* January 2, 2011. © 2011 The Nation Company, LLC. All rights reserved. Used by permission and protected by the Copyright Laws of the United States. The printing, copying, redistribution, or retransmission of this Content without express written permission is prohibited.

of the political spectrum, the resistance to restrictions on collective bargaining in Wisconsin.

But Occupy could not have happened if large swaths of the 99% had not begun to discover some common interests, or at least to put aside some of the divisions among themselves. For decades, the most stridently promoted division within the 99% was the one between what the right calls the "liberal elite"—composed of academics, journalists, media figures, etc.—and pretty much everyone else.

As *Harper's Magazine* columnist Tom Frank has brilliantly explained, the right earned its spurious claim to populism by targeting that "liberal elite," which supposedly favors reckless government spending that requires oppressive levels of taxes, supports "redistributive" social policies and programs that reduce opportunity for the white middle class, creates ever more regulations (to, for instance, protect the environment) that reduce jobs for the working class, and promotes kinky countercultural innovations like gay marriage. The liberal elite, insisted conservative intellectuals, looked down on "ordinary" middle- and working-class Americans, finding them tasteless and politically incorrect. The "elite" was the enemy, while the super-rich were just like everyone else, only more "focused" and perhaps a bit better connected.

Of course, the "liberal elite" never made any sociological sense. Not all academics or media figures are liberal (Newt Gingrich, George Will, Rupert Murdoch). Many well-educated middle managers and highly trained engineers may favor latte over Red Bull, but they were never targets of the right. And how could trial lawyers be members of the nefarious elite, while their spouses in corporate law firms were not?

A Greased Chute, Not a Safety Net

"Liberal elite" was always a political category masquerading as a sociological one. What gave the idea of a liberal elite some traction, though, at least for a while, was that the great majority of us have never knowingly encountered a member of the actual elite, the 1% who are, for the most part, sealed off in their own bubble of private planes, gated communities, and walled estates.

The authority figures most people are likely to encounter in their daily lives are teachers, doctors, social workers, and professors. These groups (along with middle managers and other white-collar corporate employees) occupy a much lower position in the class hierarchy. They made up what we described in a 1976 essay as the "professional managerial class." As we wrote at the time, on the basis of our experience of the radical movements of the 1960s and 1970s, there have been real, longstanding resentments between the working-class and middle-class professionals. These resentments, which the populist right cleverly deflected toward "liberals," contributed significantly to that previous era of rebellion's failure to build a lasting progressive movement.

As it happened, the idea of the "liberal elite" could not survive the depredations of the 1% in the late 2000s. For one thing, it was summarily eclipsed by the discovery of the actual Wall Street–based elite and their crimes. Compared to them, professionals and managers, no matter how annoying, were pikers. The doctor or school principal might be overbearing, the professor and the social worker might be condescending, but only the 1% took your house away.

There was, as well, another inescapable problem embedded in the right-wing populist strategy: even by 2000, and certainly by 2010, the class of people who might qualify as part of the "liberal elite" was in increasingly bad repair. Public-sector budget cuts and corporate-inspired reorganizations were decimating the ranks of decently paid academics, who were being replaced by adjunct professors working on bare subsistence incomes. Media firms were shrinking their newsrooms and editorial budgets. Law firms had started outsourcing their more routine tasks to India. Hospitals beamed X-rays to cheap foreign radiologists. Funding had dried up for nonprofit ventures in the arts and public service. Hence the iconic figure of the Occupy movement: the college graduate with tens of thousands of dollars in student loan debts and a job paying about $10 a hour, or no job at all.

These trends were in place even before the financial crash hit, but it took the crash and its grim economic aftermath to awaken the 99% to a widespread awareness of shared danger. In 2008, the intention of "Joe the Plumber" to earn a quarter-million dollars a year still had some faint sense of plausibility. A couple of years into the recession, however, sudden downward mobility had become the mainstream American experience, and even some of the most reliably neoliberal media pundits were beginning to announce that something had gone awry with the American dream.

Once-affluent people lost their nest eggs as housing prices dropped off cliffs. Laid-off middle-aged managers and professionals were staggered to find that their age made them repulsive to potential employers. Medical debts plunged middle-class households into bankruptcy. The old conservative dictum—that it was unwise to criticize (or tax) the rich because you might yourself be one of them someday—gave way to a new realization that the class you were most likely to migrate into wasn't the rich, but the poor.

And here was another thing many in the middle class were discovering: the downward plunge into poverty could occur with dizzying speed. One reason the concept of an economic 99% first took root in America rather than, say, Ireland or Spain is that Americans are particularly vulnerable to economic dislocation. We have little in the way of a welfare state to stop a family or an individual in free-fall. Unemployment benefits do not last more than six months or a year, though in a recession they are sometimes extended by Congress. At present, even with such an extension, they reach only about half the jobless. Welfare was all but abolished 15 years ago, and health insurance has traditionally been linked to employment.

In fact, once an American starts to slip downward, a variety of forces kick in to help accelerate the slide. An estimated 60% of American firms now check applicants' credit ratings, and discrimination against the unemployed is widespread enough to have begun to warrant Congressional concern. Even bankruptcy is a prohibitively expensive, often crushingly difficult status to achieve. Failure to pay government-imposed fines or fees can even lead, through a concatenation of unlucky breaks, to an arrest warrant or a criminal record. Where other once-wealthy nations have a safety net, America offers a greased chute, leading down to destitution with alarming speed.

Making Sense of the 99%

The Occupation encampments that enlivened approximately 1,400 cities this fall provided a vivid template for the 99%'s growing sense of unity. Here were thousands of people—we may never know the exact numbers—from all walks of life, living outdoors in the streets and parks, very much as the poorest of the poor have always lived: without electricity, heat, water, or toilets. In the process, they managed to create self-governing communities.

General assembly meetings brought together an unprecedented mix of recent college graduates, young professionals, elderly people, laid-off blue-collar workers, and plenty of the chronically homeless for what were, for the most part, constructive and civil exchanges. What started as a diffuse protest against economic injustice became a vast experiment in class building. The 99%, which might have seemed to be a purely aspirational category just a few months ago, began to will itself into existence.

Can the unity cultivated in the encampments survive as the Occupy movement evolves into a more decentralized phase? All sorts of class, racial, and cultural divisions persist within that 99%, including distrust between members of the former "liberal elite" and those less privileged. It would be surprising if they didn't. The life experience of a young lawyer or a social worker is very different from that of a blue-collar worker whose work may rarely allow for biological necessities like meal or bathroom breaks. Drum circles, consensus decision-making, and masks remain exotic to at least the 90%. "Middle class" prejudice against the homeless, fanned by decades of right-wing demonization of the poor, retains much of its grip.

Sometimes these differences led to conflict in Occupy encampments—for example, over the role of the chronically homeless in Portland or the use of marijuana in Los Angeles—but amazingly, despite all the official warnings about health and safety threats, there was no "Altamont moment": no major fires and hardly any violence. In fact, the encampments engendered almost unthinkable convergences: people from comfortable backgrounds learning about street survival from the homeless, a distinguished professor of political science discussing horizontal versus vertical decision making with a postal worker, military men in dress uniforms showing up to defend the occupiers from the police.

Class happens, as Thompson said, but it happens most decisively when people are prepared to nourish and build it. If the "99%" is to become more than a stylish meme, if it's to become a force to change the world, eventually we will undoubtedly have to confront some of the class and racial divisions that lie within it. But we need to do so patiently, respectfully, and always with an eye to the next big action—the next march, or building occupation, or foreclosure fight, as the situation demands.

4 Immigration Enforcement as a Race-Making Institution

Douglas S. Massey

With 50.5 million persons in 2010, Latinos constitute the largest minority group in the United States, representing 16.3% of the population compared with just 12.6% for African Americans. Mexicans alone numbered 31.8 million persons in 2010 and made up 10.3% of the U.S. population (Ennis, Ríos-Vargas, and Albert 2011). Although fertility will play a large role in population growth moving forward, through 2008 the main source of Latino increase was immigration (Pew Hispanic Center 2011). . . .

. . . Whereas Latino immigrants from the Caribbean are overwhelmingly legal residents or U.S. citizens, 58% of all Mexican immigrants present in the United States in 2010 were unauthorized, compared with 57% of those born in El Salvador, 71% of those from Guatemala, and 77% of those from Honduras. Even considering *all* persons of Mexican, Salvadoran, Guatemalan, and Honduran origin, the shares unauthorized stood 21%, 38%, 50%, and 51%, respectively, in 2010 (Massey and Pren 2012a). Illegality has thus become a fundamental condition of life for sizeable shares of Mexicans and Central Americans living in the United States. . . .

Although the racialization of Latinos goes back to 1848, when the Treaty of Guadalupe Hidalgo brought some 50,000 Mexicans into the United States, the contemporary era of racial formation can be traced back to the 1960s, when the United States adopted a new set of immigration policies that made it difficult for Mexicans and other Latin Americans to enter the country legally (Massey and Pren 2012a). Although the number of Latino arrivals changed little in subsequent years, after 1965 their composition shifted dramatically from documented to undocumented (Massey, Durand, and Pren 2009). . . .

Between 1965 and 2000 a new "Latino threat narrative" came to dominate public debate and media coverage of Latinos in the United States (Chavez 2001, 2008) and U.S. policy makers responded by launching a what Rosen has called a "war on immigrants" (Rosen 1995). This "war" involved an unprecedented militarization of the Mexico-U.S. border, a massive expansion of the immigrant detention system, and a return to mass deportations for the first time since the 1930s (Massey and Sánchez 2010). Government repression accelerated markedly after September 11, 2001 as the war on immigrants was increasingly conflated with the war on terror (Massey and Sánchez 2010; Massey and Pren 2012b). By 2010, America's immigration enforcement apparatus had become a central race-making institution for Latinos, on a par with the criminal justice system for African Americans. . . .

Massey, Douglas. Chapter 9. "Immigration Enforcement as a Race-Making Institution" in *Immigration, Poverty, and Socioeconomic Inequality.* Card, David, and Steven Raphael, eds. © 2013 Russell Sage Foundation, 112 East 64th Street, New York, NY 10065. Reprinted with permission.

Prior to 1965, it was relatively easy for Latin Americans to enter the United States in legal status, as there were no numerical limits placed on immigrants from the Western Hemisphere. Mexico, in particular, also benefitted from a generous bilateral guest worker agreement known as the Bracero Program that in its 22 year history brought nearly five million Mexican workers into the United States on temporary work visas (Massey, Durand, and Malone 2002; Calavita 1992). . . .

During the late 1950s and early 1960s the total annual inflow of migrants from Mexico alone fluctuated around half a million persons per year, all in legal status. At the end of 1964, however, the United States unilaterally terminated the Bracero Program over Mexican protests; and in 1965 congress passed amendments to the Immigration and Nationality Act that placed a first-ever cap of 120,000 total immigrants from the Western Hemisphere. Additional amendments enacted in 1976 put each country in the hemisphere under an annual quota of just 20,000 immigrant visas (Zolberg 2006).

. . . Despite the curtailment of avenues for legal entry, however, the demand for Mexican workers did not change and Mexicans continued to flow to the jobs they had traditionally held (Massey, Durand, and Malone 2002; Massey and Pren 2012a).

The inevitable result of curtailing opportunities for legal entry from Mexico was a sharp rise in undocumented migration. . . .

Figure 4.1: Mexican Migration to the United States 1940–2008

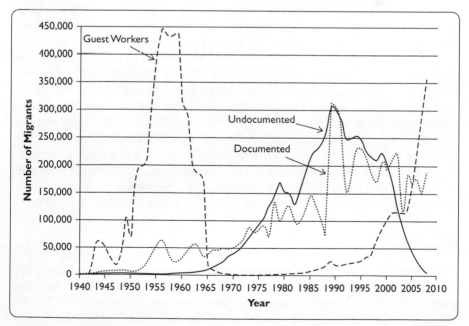

Owing to U.S. policy shifts between the early 1960s and the early 1980s, therefore, Mexican immigration was transformed from an overwhelmingly legal flow to one that was substantially illegal. . . .

The other major surge in undocumented migration from Latin America came during the 1980s, with the U.S. Contra Intervention in Nicaragua and the broader prosecution of the Cold War within Central America. Research clearly indicates that outflows from Central America during the 1980s were driven by the U.S.-sponsored Contra intervention (Lundquist and Massey 2005) as well as the violence and the economic dislocations it produced (Stanley 1987; Jones 1989; Funkhouser 1992; Morrison and May 1994; Alvarado and Massey 2010). Owing to the restrictions imposed in 1965, however, there were few avenues by which refugees from Central America could enter the United States in legal status and, not surprisingly, most ended up coming as undocumented migrants, either moving through Mexico to cross the border without authorization of entering as tourists and overstaying their visas.

. . . Whereas the Nicaraguan Adjustment and Central American Relief Act offered an easy pathway to legal status for Nicaraguans, it grudgingly offered only temporary protected status to other Central Americans. Whereas Nicaraguans had the good fortune of fleeing a left-wing regime at odds with the United States, those from Guatemala, El Salvador, and Honduras had the bad luck to come from nations dominated by right-wing regimes allied with the United States. As a result, although most Central Americans were at some point undocumented, Nicaraguans were able to adjust to documented status whereas other Central Americans ended up languishing in temporary protected status until it was finally revoked with the end of the Cold War, pushing them into undocumented status.

Once again, U.S. policies had manufactured a large population of undocumented migrants. After Mexico, which accounted for an estimated 62% of undocumented migrants present in the United States as of January 1, 2010, the next largest contributors were El Salvador (6%), Guatemala (5%), and Honduras (3%) (Hoefer, Rytina, and Baker 2010). All told, three-quarters of all undocumented migrants come from Mexico or Central America, and no other nation makes up more than 2% of the total. When most Americans visualize an "illegal immigrant," they see a Mexican and, if not a Mexican in particular, certainly a Latino (Lee and Fiske 2006). Adding in Latino migrants from the Caribbean, South America, and Panama, we find that Latin Americans comprise more than 80% of the total unauthorized population. It is doubtful, of course, whether the average Anglo-American can distinguish between a Mexican, Salvadoran, a Dominican, or a Colombian and many simply get categorized as "Mexican," which has become the default Latino identity in the American mind (Lee and Fiske 2006).

Rise of the Latino Threat Narrative

Throughout U.S. history, immigrants have periodically served as scapegoats for America's problems, being blamed for joblessness, low wages, and high social spending while being framed as threats to national security owing to their supposed moral deficits, suspect ideologies, and subversive intentions (Higham 1955; Zolberg 2006;

Schrag 2010). Anti-immigrant hostility rises during periods of economic disloca-tion, ideological conflict, and political uncertainty (Massey 1999; Meyers 2004). The 1970s and 1980s were such a period, as the long postwar economic boom faltered, the New Deal Coalition unraveled, and the Cold War reached its apex. After a brief respite during the 1990s, when the economy rebounded and the Cold War receded, the conditions for popular xenophobia returned with a vengeance with the bursting of the stock market bubble in 2000, the terrorist attacks in 2001, and the collapse of the economy in 2008 (Massey and Sánchez 2010).

Under these circumstances, anti-immigrant hostility is only to be expected; but since 1965 portrayals of Latin American immigrants as a threat to American society have been greatly facilitated by the fact that a rising share of Latino immigrants are present in the country illegally and thus readily framed as lawbreakers, criminals, and terrorists. The growing predominance of undocumented migrants among Latin Americans has contributed to the rise of what Chavez (2008) has called the "Latino threat narrative." . . .

Immigrants clearly perceive the rising hostility against them. By 2006, 70% of Latino immigrants had come to view anti-Hispanic discrimination as a major problem in the United States, 68% worried about being deported themselves, and 35% knew someone who had been deported (Kohut and Suru 2006). Half of all Latino immi-grants interviewed in 2010 felt that Americans were less accepting of immigrants than they had been five years earlier (Lopez, Morin, and Taylor 2010). Whereas only 47% of Latinos saw discrimination against them as a major problem in American society in 2002, by 2010 the share had risen to 61%, and another 24% viewed it as at least a minor problem, bringing the total seeing discrimination as problematic to 85% (Lopez, Morin, and Taylor 2010). . . .

Prosecuting the War on Immigrants

In sum, over the past several decades the repressive power of the state has increasingly been directed against immigrants, documented as well as undocumented. Although the escalation of anti-immigrant repression is apparent at the state and local levels, it is most clearly reflected in federal statistics. Figure 2 shows trends in the budget of the U.S. Border Patrol, the number of Border Patrol Agents, and the number of deportations from the United States (U.S. Office of Immigration Statistics 2012). Each series has been divided by its value in 1986 to indicate the factor by which the enforcement effort has increased since then. . . .

Building a New Underclass

Paradoxically, the effect of increased immigration enforcement was actually to *increase* the net inflow of undocumented migrants and to spread them more widely through-out the nation (Massey, Durand, and Malone 2002; Massey 2008; Massey, Rugh, and Pren 2010). Once they had experienced the costs and risks of undocumented border

Figure 4.2: Indicators of Immigration Enforcement Relative to Levels in 1986

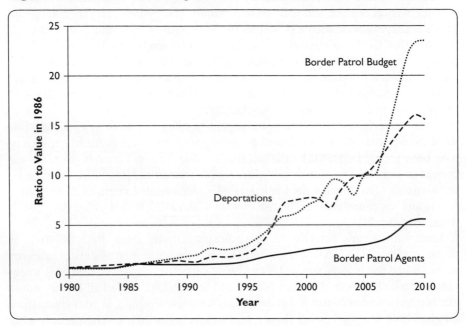

crossing, migrants declined to repeat the experience and remained north of the border rather than returning home, bringing about a pronounced decline in levels of out-migration (Redburn, Reuter, and Majmundar 2011). With the full-scale militarization of the border in San Diego and the erection of a steel wall from the Pacific Ocean to the peaks of the Sierra Madre, in-migrants were diverted away from California toward new crossing points along the border with Arizona and to new destinations throughout the United States (see the chapter by Ellis, Wright, and Townley in this volume). Mexican migration was thus transformed from a largely circular movement of male workers going to three states into a settled population of families living in 50 states (Massey, Durand, and Pren 2009). By 2010, more Latinos were living in undocumented status in more places than at any point in American history (Massey 2011; Massey and Pren 2012a).

As a result of U.S. actions over the past several decades, never before have so many U.S. residents lacked basic legal protections. Undocumented migrants currently constitute a third of all foreigners present in the United States, more than 40% of those from Latin America, and large majorities of those from Mexico and Central America; and because undocumented migrants generally inhabit households containing family members who are not undocumented, the share of people touched by illegal migration is actually much larger. According to estimates by Passel (2006), about a quarter of all persons living in households that contain undocumented migrants are themselves U.S. citizens. . . .

Net undocumented migration appears now to have dropped to zero not because of U.S. enforcement efforts, but owing to a collapsed U.S. economy, declining population growth in Mexico, and generally favorable economic conditions throughout Latin America (Wasem 2011; Redburn, Reuter, and Majmundar 2011). In the past decade, however, the falling number of undocumented migrants has been offset by a rising number of temporary workers. With little fanfare or public awareness, mass guest worker recruitment has returned to the United States, bringing annual entries up to levels last seen in the 1950s (Massey and Pren 2012b). Although only a tiny fraction of Mexicans who entered the United States in 2010 were unauthorized, most of those who entered with documents nonetheless did not possess full labor rights. . . .

. . . With more people occupying ever more vulnerable and exploitable positions in the U.S. labor market, the socioeconomic status of Latinos generally declined over the past several decades. After occupying an intermediate position between blacks and whites in the American status hierarchy, after 1990 Latinos increasingly joined African Americans at the bottom of the socioeconomic distribution to comprise a new American underclass (Massey 2007). In the absence of meaningful immigration reform and a curtailment of repression against immigrants, this population can only be expected to see its problems proliferate and multiply.

Figure 3 illustrates the decline in Latino socioeconomic status by showing trends in median personal income earned by white, black, and Latino males from 1972 through 2010 (in constant dollars). . . .

Figure 4.3: Median Personal Income for White, Black, and Latino Males

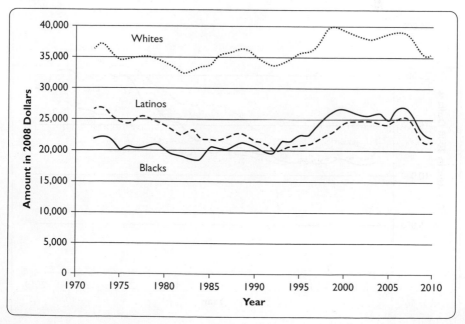

The foregoing figures, of course, do not control for human capital and other characteristics of white, black, and Latino workers, and some have argued that the deterioration in the relative economic standing of Latinos reflects the declining quality of successive immigrant cohorts, especially for Mexicans (Borjas 1995, 1999—see also the chapter by Lewis in this volume). . . . According to Massey and Gelatt (2010), what changed over time was not so much the characteristics of immigrants, as how various forms of human capital were rewarded in the U.S. labor market. . . .

In the early 1970s, all women earned relatively low incomes—both absolutely and compared with men; but things began to change in 1980, when the incomes of white women began to rise steadily, going from a little over $12,000 in that year to peak at almost $23,000 in 2007. Although the upturn for black women lagged behind that of white women, beginning around 1985 their incomes also began to rise and this increase accelerated during the 1990s to narrow the black-white gap substantially, with black female income peaking at almost $21,000 in 2007. In contrast, the income of Latinas remained flat until 1993 and then rose at a slower rate than either white or black women, so that by 2010 the Latina-white gap was wider than it had ever been. Whereas white and Latina women earned roughly the same incomes in 1972, by 2010 Latinas earned a quarter less than whites.

The shifting fortunes of Latinos and African Americans in U.S. labor markets are clearly reflected in U.S. poverty statistics. Figure 5 shows trends in the poverty rate

Figure 4.4: Median Personal Income for White, Black, and Latino Females

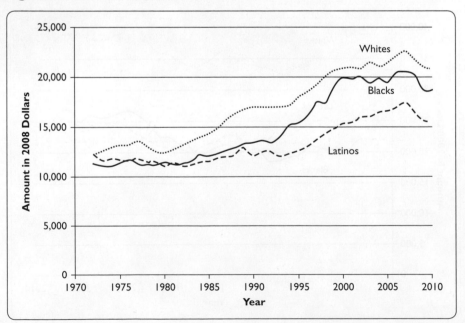

for white, black, and Latino families from 1972 to 2010. Once again Latinos occupied a middle position in the distribution of poverty until 1994, when black and Latino poverty rates converged to identical levels. From then until 2000 black and Latino families shared the same poverty trajectory, but then black poverty rates rose above those of Latinos until 2008 when the onset of the Great Recession brought them back together at around 24% in 2010, some 3.4 times greater than the rate of 7% among white families.

In sum, the foreign data clearly suggest that something happened over the course of the 1990s to undermine earnings among Latinos living in the United States. . . .

The deterioration in the labor market position of Hispanics relative to blacks was accompanied by a similar reversal of fortune in U.S. housing markets. Whereas in 1989 Hispanics were 19% *less likely* than blacks to experience adverse treatment in America's rental housing markets, in 2000 they were 8% *more likely* to suffer discrimination. In addition, although the incidence of discriminatory treatment fell for both groups in the sales market, the decline for Hispanics was much smaller. As a result, whereas blacks in 1989 were twice as likely as Hispanics to experience discrimination in home sales, by 2000 Hispanics were were 18% *more likely* than blacks to experience it (Turner et al. 2002). Consistent with these data, in their audit of rental housing in the San Francisco Bay area, Purnell, Isardi, and Baugh (1999) documented extensive "linguistic profiling" that excluded speakers of Chicano English from access to housing. In addition, several state and local initiatives

Figure 4.5: Poverty Rate for Black, White, and Latino Families

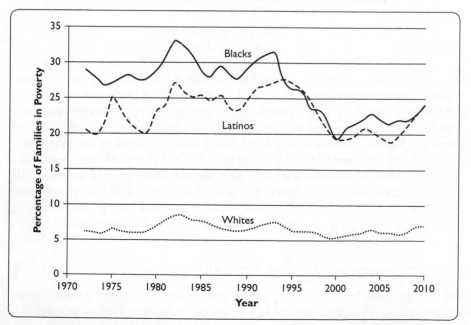

Figure 4.6: Median Net Wealth of Black and Latino Households

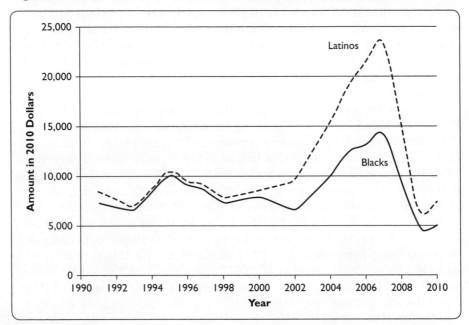

have sought to mandate discrimination on the basis of legal status by forbidding real estate agents from renting or selling homes to those present without authorization (Hopkins 2010). . . .

The effect of the [housing] crisis on Latino wealth is indicated in Figure 6, which shows trends in median net wealth for black and Latino households. Historically both groups have been characterized by low levels of wealth, which prior to 2000 averaged between just $6,000 and $10,000 compared with a range of $70,000 and $80,000 for white households (not shown). Beginning in 2001 the net wealth of Latino and black households began to rise as the housing boom began to reach into neighborhoods where they were located and both groups were targeted for extensive subprime mortgage lending. Given that Latinos were disproportionately living in states affected by the boom, their net wealth rose faster and higher than blacks to peak at $24,000 in 2007 compared with just $14,000 for African Americans. With the collapse of housing prices, however, both groups ended up much at the same place, with a net worth of just $6,000 for the former and $5,000 for the latter by 2009. Latinos, however, experience the greatest decline in net wealth of any major group, with a drop of 73% between peak and trough.

Immigration Reform as Social Justice

Over the past four decades, the immigration enforcement system of the United States has become increasingly important as a major race-making institution in much the same way that the criminal justice system did for African Americans over the same period. In both cases, there were massive increases in arrests, incarcerations, and in the case of immigrants, apprehensions and deportations, combined with huge increases in the relevant agency budgets. The immigrant detention system is now the fastest growing component of America's prison industrial complex. In 2011, for example, some 429,000 immigrants were incarcerated and awaiting trial or deportation, 397,000 were expelled from the United States, and 328,000 were apprehended at the Mexico-U.S. border (American Civil Liberties Union 2012; U.S. Office of Immigration Statistics 2012). As a result, . . . the number incarcerated among Latinos is rapidly rising relative to African Americans. Whereas the ratio of Latino to black prisoners in state and federal penal institutions averaged between 0.34 and 0.39, after 2001 it rose steadily to peak at around 0.59 in 2010. At this rate of change, Latinos will surpass African Americans as the largest prison population around two decades from now.

Whereas among African Americans, the prison industrial complex created a large population of current and ex-felons who suffer a variety of forms of exclusion and discrimination (Pager 2007; Pettit 2012), among Latinos it has generated a population not simply of current and ex-felons, but a larger population of marginalized, repressed, and eminently exploitable undocumented migrants. Despite all their well-documented disadvantages, however, black felons at least retain basic social and economic rights as American citizens, whereas undocumented migrants under current circumstances have virtually no rights at all and are subject to arrest, incarceration without representation, and summary deportation without trial or benefit of counsel. Even documented migrants may now be arrested, detailed, and deported on the say-so of low level Justice Department officials and they have been declared by congress to be deportable ex post facto for crimes they earlier committed (see Legomsky 2000).

The situation is especially dire in the case of Mexicans, the nation's largest immigrant group and the second largest minority after African Americans. At present, nearly 60% of all persons born in Mexico are illegally present; and among those who do hold legal residence papers, two-thirds first entered the United States without documents, thus rendering them legally deportable under current law (Massey and Malone 2003). These figures imply that nearly a quarter (23%) of all persons of Mexican origin living in the United States are currently undocumented, while another 8% are formerly undocumented, putting roughly a third of all Mexican Americans at serious risk of deportation. . . .

REFERENCES

Alvarado, Steven E., and Douglas S. Massey. 2010. "In Search of Peace: Structural Adjustment, Violence, and International Migration." *Annals of the American Academy of Political and Social Science* 630(1): 294-321.

American Civil Liberties Union. 2012. *Immigration Detention.* Retrieved from ACLU Wesbsite November 22, 2012 at http://www.aclu.org/immigrants-rights/detention.

Andreas, Peter. 2000. *Border Games: Policing the US-Mexico Divide.* Ithaca: Cornell University Press.

Borjas, George J. 1995. "Assimilation and Changes in Cohort Quality Revisited: What Happened to Immigrant Earnings in the 1980s?" *Journal of Labor Economics* 13:201-245.

———. 1999. *Heaven's Door: Immigration Policy and the American Economy.* Princeton, NJ: Princeton University Press.

Calavita, Kitty. 1992. *Inside the State: The Bracero Program, Immigration, and the INS.* New York: Routledge.

Chavez, Leo R. 2001. *Covering Immigration: Population Images and the Politics of the Nation.* Berkeley: University of California Press.

———. 2008. *The Latino Threat: Constructing Immigrants, Citizens, and the Nation.* Stanford, CA: Stanford University Press.

Ennis, Sharon R., Merarys Ríos-Vargas, and Nora G. Albert. 2011. *The Hispanic Population: 2010.* 2010 Census Briefs, U.S. Bureau of the Census, Washington, DC.

Funkhouser, Edward. 1992. "Migration from Nicaragua: Some Recent Evidence." *World Development* 20: 1209-18.

Higham, John. 1955. *Strangers in the Land: Patterns of American Nativism, 1860-1925.* New Brunswick, NJ, Rutgers University Press, 1955.

Hopkins, Daniel J. 2010. "Politicized Places: Explaining Where and When Immigrants Provoke Local Opposition." *American Political Science Review* 104:40-60.

Huntington, Samuel P. 2004. *Who Are We? The Challenges to America's National Identity.* New York: Simon and Schuster.

Jones, Richard C. 1989. "Causes of Salvadoran migration to the United States." *The Geographical Review* 79:183-94.

Kohut, Andrew, and Roberto Suro. 2006. *America's Immigration Quandary: No Consensus on Immigration Problem or Proposed Fixes.* Washington, DC. Pew Research Center for the People and the Press and Pew Hispanic Center.

Lee, Tiane L., and Susan T. Fiske. 2006. "Not an Outgroup, Not Yet an Ingroup: Immigrants in the Stereotype Content Model." *International Journal of Intercultural Relations* 30:751-68.

Legomsky, Stephen H. 2000. "Fear and Loathing in Congress and the Courts: Immigration and Judicial Review." *Texas Law Review* 78:1612-20.

Lopez, Mark Hugo, Rich Morin, and Paul Taylor. 2010. *Illegal Immigration Backlash Worries, Divides Latinos.* Washington, DC: Pew Hispanic Center.

Lundquist, Jennifer H., and Douglas S. Massey. 2005. "The Contra War and Nicaraguan Migration to the United States." *Journal of Latin American Studies* 37:29-53.

Massey, Douglas S. 1999. "International Migration at the Dawn of the Twenty-First Century: The Role of the State." *Population and Development Review* 25:303-23.

———. 2007. *Categorically Unequal: The American Stratification System.* New York: Russell Sage Foundation.

———. 2008. *New Faces in New Places: The Changing Geography of American Immigration.* New York: Russell Sage Foundation.

———. 2011. "Epilogue: The Past and Future of Mexico-U.S. Migration." Pp. 241-265 in *Beyond la Frontera: The History of Mexico-U.S. Migration,* edited by Mark Overmyer-Velázquez. New York: Oxford University Press.

———. 2012. "The Racialization of Latinos in the United States." Forthcoming in Michael Tonry and Sandra Bucerius, eds., *The Oxford Handbook on Ethnicity, Crime, and Immigration.* New York: Oxford University Press.

Massey, Douglas S., Jorge Durand, and Nolan J. Malone. 2002. *Beyond Smoke and Mirrors: Mexican Immigration in an Age of Economic Integration.* New York: Russell Sage Foundation.

Massey, Douglas S., Jorge Durand, and Karen A. Pren. 2009. "Nuevos Escenarios de la Migración México-Estados Unidos: Las Consecuencias de la Guerra Antiinmigrante." *Papeles de Población* 61:101-28.

Massey, Douglas S., and Julia Gelatt. 2010. "What Happened to the Wages of Mexican Immigrants? Trends and Interpretations." *Latino Studies* 8:328-54.

Massey, Douglas S., and Nolan J. Malone. 2003. "Pathways to Legalization." *Population Research and Policy Review* 21:473-504.

Massey, Douglas S., and Karen A. Pren. 2012a. "Unintended Consequences of US Immigration Policy: Explaining the Post-1965 Surge from Latin America." *Population and Development Review* 38:1-29.

——. 2012b. "Origins of the New Latino Underclass." *Race and Social Problems* 4(1): 5-17.

Massey, Douglas S., Jacob S. Rugh, and Karen A. Pren. 2010. "The Geography of Undocumented Mexican Migration." *Mexican Studies/Estudios Mexicanos* 26:120-52.

Massey, Douglas S., and Magaly Sánchez R. 2010. *Brokered Boundaries: Creating Immigrant Identity in Anti-Immigrant Times.* New York: Russell Sage Foundation.

Meyers, Eytan. 2004. *International Immigration Policy: A Theoretical and Comparative Analysis.* London: Palgrave Macmillan.

Morrison, Andrew R., and Rachel A. May. 1994. "Escape from Terror: Violence and Migration in Post-Revolutionary Guatemala." *Latin American Research Review* 29:111-32.

National Council of State Legislatures. 2009. *Immigrant Policy Project: 2009 Immigration-Related Bills and Resolutions.* Washington, DC: National Council of State Legislatures, April 22, 2009. Accessed on June 24, 2009 at: http://www.ncsl.org/documents/immig/2009ImmigFinalApril222009.pdf

Pager, Devah. 2007. *Marked: Race, Crime, and Finding Work in an Era of Mass Incarceration.* Chicago, IL: University of Chicago Press.

Passel, Jeffrey. 2006. *The Size and Characteristics of the Unauthorized Migrant Population in the U.S.: Estimates Based on the March 2005 Current Population Survey.* Washington, DC: Pew Hispanic Center.

Pettit, Becky. 2012. *Invisible Men: Mass Incarceration and the Myth of Black Progress.* New York: Russell Sage Foundation.

Pew Hispanic Center. 2011. *The Mexican-American Boom: Births Overtake Immigration.* Washington, DC: Pew Hispanic Center.

Purnell, Thomas, William Idsardi, and John Baugh. 1999. "Perceptual and Phonetic Experiments on American English Dialect Identification." *Journal of Language and Social Psychology* 18:10-30.

Redburn, Steve, Peter Reuter, and Malay Majmundar. 2011. *Budgeting for Immigration Enforcement: A Path to Better Performance.* Washington, DC: National Academies Press.

Rosen, Jeffrey. 1995. "The War on Immigrants: Why the Courts Can't Save Us." *The New Republic,* January 30. Accessed on June 8, 2011 at http://www.tnr.com/article/politics/the-war-immigrants.

Schrag, Peter. 2010. *Not Fit for Our Society: Immigration and Nativism in America.* Berkeley: University of California Press.

Stanley, William D. 1987. "Economic Migrants or Refugees from Violence? A Time-Series Analysis of Salvadoran Migration to the United States." *Latin American Research Review* 22:132-154.

Turner, Margery A., Stephen L. Ross, George C. Galster, and John Yinger. 2002. *Discrimination in Metropolitan Housing Markets: National Results from Phase I.* Washington, DC: U.S. Department of Housing and Urban Development.

U.S. Office of Immigration Statistics. 2012. *The 2011 Yearbook of Immigration Statistics.* Washington, DC: U.S. Office of Immigration Statistics. http://www.dhs.gov/files/statis tics/publications/yearbook.shtm

Wasem, Ruth E. 2011. *Unauthorized Aliens Residing in the United States: Estimates Since 1986.* Washington, DC: Congressional Research Service.

Zolberg, Aristide R. 2006. *A Nation by Design: Immigration Policy in the Fashioning of America.* New York: Russell Sage Foundation.

5 For Asian Americans, Wealth Stereotypes Don't Fit Reality

Seth Freed Wessler

When Rosa Chen first heard one of her college classmates ask her if she was rich, she says she didn't quite understand where the idea was coming from. "Everyone I grew up around was struggling economically like us," she said.

Chen, 19, grew up in San Francisco's Chinatown, one of three daughters of immigrants. Her father is a restaurant cook and her mother does not work because of a disability.

"I was surprised that people would see me as rich," said Chen, who is also a community activist in her hometown. "There was a stereotype about Asians being rich because they live here in San Francisco; like we must be made of money."

Chen is studying communications at the University of San Francisco, a school she says she could only afford to attend because of the sizable financial aid package she was offered. It was there, in college, where she was first confronted with the durable and simplistic cultural notion about Asian-American class status—an idea, opinion researchers say, has taken firm hold in popular opinion.

"There's an assumption that white Americans make about Asian-American social class status based on racial identity. It's the idea of the model minority; that Asian Americans are successful, high income, studious, hard working, quiet," said C.N. Le, PhD., a University of Massachusetts sociologist. "That's the prevailing image that white Americans have and it's of course a set of stereotypes."

On the one hand, based on the most common metrics of class position—income and education—Asian Americans as a whole are doing better than any other single racial group, earning more on average than whites,[1] and more likely to graduate from college.

But like the rest of the country, income inequality among Asian Americans and Pacific Islanders—a diverse grouping of more than 48 ethnic groups[2]—is vast. According to analysis of census data[3] released this week by Karthick Ramakrishnan, PhD, a political scientist at the UC Riverside, about half of all Asian-American income goes to the top 20 percent of Asian-American earners. The bottom 40 percent of Asian-American earners, meanwhile, take home just 13 percent of the income pot.

"The Asian-American community has both of these sides: rich and poor," Ramakrishnan said. "There is some significant class advantage in the Asian-American community, but at the same time, in those communities where there is poverty, the aggregate numbers mask the disparities."

For Asian Americans, Wealth Stereotypes Don't Fit Reality by Seth Freed Wessler. Reprinted with permission of NBC Universal Archives © 2015.

"People coming from the bottom fifth, or even the bottom 40 percent, their lives are very different from what the top 20 percent looks," he said.

Chen grew up in a family at the bottom of the economic ladder. Since her father's arrival from China in the 1980s, he has worked as a cook at a Chinese restaurant. It was on that single income that the family paid below market rent for the tight two-bedroom apartment where Chen, her two older sisters, her mother and father all lived.

"I didn't realize how little we really earned until recently, when I had to pay for college, and apply for financial aid; I realized that we are not that well off at all," Chen said. "I would say that we're financially struggling."

Aggregate figures of Asian-American income do little to reflect Chen's childhood. The national figures are pulled upward by particular communities with high incomes. In the 1970s and 1980s, for example, many South Asian immigrants came to the United States with high levels of education or to study in graduate programs and were able to enter into middle class professions that provided the basis for upward mobility. But others, including Cambodian, Laotian and other Southeast Asian communities, often migrated as refugees, arriving in the US with little in the way of financial resources or skills immediately transferrable to high paying jobs.

"Our analysis of Asian communities often stops at the broad data points," said Farah Ahmed, an analyst with the Center for American Progress who studies racial demographics. "Families who are newer immigrants, who don't speak English as a first language, or those in certain communities are more likely to face poverty. We talk about data in an aggregated way and that misses many realities."

Chen says her reality is more complicated than it appears to many.

"I go to a private college and when people see Chinese people, they assume I have a lot of money going to this school and that fits with the stereotype that Chinese people are rich," she said.

Chen's family economic struggles stem not just from her father's low income, but also from living in San Francisco, one of the most expensive cities in the country.

"It's a hard city to live in," said Chen, who is a volunteer with the Chinatown Community Development Center, a group advocating for low-income housing protections. "I've done a lot of work around affordable housing, to try to stop people with money from kicking people out of the city. For a lot of the low-income families who are here, it's hard to find somewhere to live."

Asian communities in America are concentrated in expensive urban hubs—one in three Asians lives in New York, Los Angeles and San Francisco. When local costs of living are included in analyses of poverty rates, Asian poverty rises by over two percentage points, to more than 16 percent, while white poverty rates fall slightly to 10.4 percent.

Researchers also note that Asian households tend to include more people,[4] which means that even families with larger incomes have to spread those dollars more thinly.

When class is evaluated in terms of wealth—savings and assets minus debts—rather than income, Asian-American status begins to fall. Asian families hold 70 cents to every white dollar of wealth, according to recent research[5] by the Federal Reserve Bank of St. Louis. That's one of the reasons that Asian elders are more likely than the general population to be poor.[6]

"My parents don't have much in the way of retirement savings," Chen said. She and her sisters, she says, "want our parents to live with us and live a good life as they get older. We see it as our job to pay our parents back."

Chen is facing more immediate concerns about her family's economic wellbeing than her parents' old age. The owner of the building where she lives with her parents and one of her older sisters has been threatening recently to evict her family, Chen says. Evictions have been on the rise[7] in her city, due to a California law that allows landlords to oust tenants[8] in order to stop renting units and sell.

"My parents don't want to leave Chinatown, and if we have to leave this apartment, we'd have to leave the city because it's expensive here," Chen said. The family pays $680 for the apartment, about a quarter of the average rent for a two-bedroom apartment in the San Francisco Bay area. "They are really worried about the stability of their lives in San Francisco."

In many ways, Chen says the hidden poverty data among Asian Americans only confirms what she saw and heard around her growing up.

"There's this stereotype about Asians being rich," she said. "These stereotypes are shocking and interesting—how people perceive who you are, and their stereotypes about social class."

NOTES

1. Kai-Hwa Wang, F. (2015, February 27). "Asian Americans Set to Surpass Whites in Median Family Wealth." NBC News.

2. Kai-Hwa Wang, F. (2014, July 23). "A Campaign to Disaggregate Data and Ensure All Students Count." NBC News.

3. Infographic: Income Inequality. (2015, March 17).

4. Hua, V. (2014, August 25). "Asian Americans More Likely to Have Multigenerational Households." NBC News.

5. Boshara, R. et al. (2015). "The Demographics of Wealth: How Age, Education and Race Separate Thrivers from Strugglers in Today's Economy." Federal Reserve Bank of St. Louis.

6. Guillermo, E. (2014, December 11). "Report: Asian-American Elderly in Poor Economic Health." NBC News.

7. City and County of San Francisco. (2014, March 11). "Residential Rent Stabilization and Arbitration Board." *Annual Report on Eviction Notices.* Available at: http://www.sfrb.org/modules/showdocument.aspx?documentid=2700

8. Nawaz, A. (2014, June 18). "Tech Boom Fuels Elderly Evictions in San Francisco." NBC News.

6 Gender and the Black Jobs Crisis
Linda Burnham

Introduction

Ten million African American women wake up and go to work every day.[1] They prepare and serve food at the fast-food chains. They staff the registers at the big-box stores. They tend to the needs of patients in nursing facilities or provide homecare to elders. Often enough, when they're done with one job for the day, they hop a bus and go on to a second. The moms among them start their long days extra early, getting the kids ready for school or dropping them off at daycare. They worry incessantly whether patched-together childcare arrangements will hold up. Yet, at the end of the week, their paychecks are so meager that even the most frugal are desperate to make ends meet. Instead of supporting the lives and aspirations of African American women who are part of the low-wage workforce, the U.S. economy is brutalizing them.

The core of the jobs crisis facing African American women is low wages. African American women are working, and working hard. They participate in the workforce at slightly higher rates than women of every other race or ethnicity, but, in too many cases, their hard work goes unrewarded. Low wages trap black women, together with their families and communities, in cycles of economic distress, with reverberant and widespread social consequences.

There are five key elements of the jobs crisis facing African American women:

1. African American women are overrepresented among low-wage workers, including those workers earning at or below minimum wage.
2. African American women are impacted by both the gender gap and the racial gap in wages.
3. African American women are unemployed at higher rates and for longer periods than other women.
4. African American women were especially hard hit by the most recent recession and have lagged behind in the recovery.
5. African American women in the labor force are far more likely to be single heads of household than are women of other races and ethnicities.

Overrepresentation Among Low-Wage Workers[2]

Women are significantly overrepresented in low-wage occupations and sectors of the economy, contributing to the gender gap in wages. Even within low-wage occupations, women's wages are lower than those of men in the same job categories. African Americans are also significantly overrepresented in low-wage occupations and sectors

Republished with permission of The Discount Foundation.

of the economy, contributing to the racial gap in wages. African American women's economic profile is fundamentally shaped by the confluence of these two persistent trends.

Key sectors of the economy in which both women and African Americans are highly concentrated include service and sales. Occupations for which both women and African Americans form a disproportionately high segment of the workforce include health support occupations, fast food, and retail sales.

For example, African Americans constitute 11.4 percent of the employed civilian labor force, but 16.2 percent of those employed in service occupations. Women make up 46.9 percent of the labor force but are 56.7 percent of those employed in the service sector.[3] The service sector, with median weekly earnings of $508 ($470 for women; $588 for men), compensates workers at a lower rate than any other sector of the economy.[4]

The workforce in some cleaning and caretaking jobs, stereotypically considered women's work, is over 80 percent female. Black workers are concentrated in some of these jobs at double, or even triple, the rate of their share of the employed. Those occupations in which both women and African Americans are significantly overrepresented are especially likely to confer low wages.

Women and African Americans are highly concentrated in healthcare support occupations, with a workforce that is 87.6 percent female and 25.7 percent black. Wages within this group of occupations vary but are particularly low for jobs with higher proportions of African Americans. For example, nursing, psychiatric, and home health aides, taken together as a group, earn $11.87 per hour, bringing full-time, year-round workers just over the poverty threshold for a family of four, while home health aides, considered alone, earn just $10.60 an hour.[5]

Home health aides and personal care aides are among the fastest growing occupations, responsive to the aging of the boomer generation. These occupations are projected to grow by nearly 50 percent between 2012 and 2022, and we can expect that they will be major areas of job growth for black women.[6] Only 40 percent of home health aides and personal care aides are employed full-time year-round, and wages hover around ten dollars an hour. As a result, more than half of homecare workers rely on some form of public assistance: Medicaid, food stamps, or housing assistance.[7] Black women working as nannies, housecleaners, and elder caregivers in the private-pay market are paid just as poorly, are rarely paid for overtime, and are frequently required to take on tasks well beyond the scope of the work they were originally hired to perform.[8] Raising the level of compensation for healthcare support occupations and domestic work is critical to improving the job picture for black women.

Jobs that combine food preparation and serving, including fast food jobs, have the distinction of being both the lowest paid of major U.S. occupations, with median hourly wages of $9.08, and among the largest, accounting for more than three million workers. African Americans are overrepresented at the low end of the food service sector, making up nearly double their share of the employed among fast-food workers (20.5 percent) and an even higher proportion of non-restaurant food servers (23.5 percent), occupations in which the workforce is 62 percent female.[9]

TABLE 6.1 Concentration of Women and African Americans in Low-Wage Occupations

Occupation	Women as % of Total Employed	Black as % of Total Employed	Mean Hourly Wage (2013)	Mean Annual Wage (2013)
Employed persons 16 years or over	46.9	11.4		
Food preparation and serving workers, including fast food	61.9	20.5	9.08	18,880
Cashiers	72.2	18.3	9.82	20,420
Personal care aides	83.9	23.0	10.09	20,990
Childcare workers	95.5	15.9	10.33	21,490
Home health aides			10.60	22,050
Maids & housekeeping	88.6	16.8	10.64	22,130
Food servers, non-restaurant	61.9	23.5	10.77	22,400
Nursing, psychiatric & home health aides	88.5	35.9	11.87	24,700

Wage data from Bureau of Labor Statistics, "Occupational Employment and Wages, May 2013."

Data for women and black workers as percentage of occupation from Bureau of Labor Statistics, "Employed persons by detailed occupation, sex, race and Hispanic or Latino ethnicity."

At $9.82 an hour, cashiers are the lowest paid workers in sales. Here again, in a low-wage occupation that employs more than three million workers, we find a high concentration of female workers (72.2 percent) and a substantial overrepresentation of African Americans (18.3 percent). [In contrast, at the other end of the sales spectrum, wholesale and manufacturing sales representatives earn over $33 an hour; 30 percent of them are women, and 5 percent are African American.][10] Within retail sales, documented racial discrimination in hiring, promotions, and scheduling puts African American women at a further disadvantage.[11]

Not only are these occupations low-wage, many of them pay at or below minimum wage. Nearly two-thirds of workers paid at or below minimum wage are in service occupations (63.6 percent) and nearly half (46.7 percent) are in jobs related to food preparation and serving.[12] African American women's overrepresentation among minimum wage workers is tied to their disproportionate presence in these occupations. Black women are 7.4 percent of wage and salary workers earning hourly wages, but 10.1 percent of those earning minimum wage.[13]

In light of the concentration of black women in low-wage jobs, it comes as no surprise that their earnings trail those of every other demographic group, with the exception of Hispanic women. In the fourth quarter of 2014, the median weekly earnings of black women who were full-time wage and salary workers amounted to 90 percent of those earned by black men but only 82 percent and 66 percent of the earnings of white women and white men respectively. Further, black women are the only group whose median weekly fourth-quarter earnings dropped from 2013 to 2014, sliding from $621 to $602.[14]

While the jobs crisis for black women is, first and foremost, a crisis of wages, low-wage jobs are also characterized by a near-complete absence of benefits, unpredictable or on-demand scheduling, and extremely limited avenues for advancement.

High Rates of Unemployment

High unemployment rates compound the wage crisis for African American women, a long established and persistent problem made worse by the Great Recession. During the recession, jobs were stripped from black men and women and their rates of unemployment ratcheted up alarmingly. Moreover, the vaunted recovery has not been experienced equally across racial groups. The unemployment rate for blacks, already considerably higher than the rates for other racial groups, increased disproportionately, was slower to fall, and has yet to return to the pre-recession rate.

In December 2009, six months into the recovery, black women were unemployed at a rate nearly five percentage points higher than before the recession began, and the rate was still climbing. It peaked at 14.8 percent in July 2011, two years into what was, for some, the recovery before beginning to descend. At the end of 2014, it was still three points higher than it was pre-recession. The unemployment rate for black men peaked at just over 20 percent in March 2010, far higher than the peak rate for any other group. To put this in some perspective, white women's unemployment rate, at its recessionary height of 7.7 percent, never reached the 2007 pre-recession low for black men.[15] In the purportedly recovered economy of 2011, black unemployment stood at 15.8 percent, double the rate for whites (7.9 percent) and significantly higher than the rate for Hispanics (11.5 percent). Blacks remained unemployed, on average,

TABLE 6.2 Unemployment in the Recession and Recovery

Unemployment Rate	Dec. 2007	Dec. 2009	Dec. 2011	Dec. 2014
Black Women	6.8	11.5	13.2	9.8
Black Men	8.4	16.7	15.2	11
White Women	3.6	6.8	6.3	4.1
White Men	4.1	9.6	7.3	4.4

BLS Data Series from Current Population Survey, Unemployment Rate 20 years and over, 2005-2015.

TABLE 6.3 Single Householder, No Spouse Present, as Percentage of Household Types

Race/Ethnicity	Women	Women with Children	Men
Black	30.1	17.4	6.3
American Indian/Alaska Native	21.4	12.3	8.9
Hispanic	19.2	12.1	9.1
Native Hawaiian/Pacific Islander	17	9.8	8.7
Asian	9.5	4.1	4.7
Non-Hispanic White	9.2	4.7	4.0

U.S. Census Bureau, *Households and Families: 2010*, Table 3: "Household Types by Race and Hispanic Origin: 2010."

for seven weeks longer than whites, and black women made up a larger share of the black unemployed (46.9 percent) than white and Hispanic women did in their racial or ethnic groups.[16] Racially disparate patterns in the rates and duration of unemployment attest to the persistence of racial bias in hiring and retention, lending credibility to the conventional wisdom that black workers are the last hired and first fired.

Race, Household Type, and Poverty

African American women are far more likely than the women of every other race or ethnicity to be single-earner heads of household. These households are vulnerable to poverty, especially when children are present. Black women are three to four times as likely as white and Asian women to be the heads of household with children under the age of 18. Seventeen percent of black households are headed by women with children, as compared to 4.7 percent of white and 4.1 percent of Asian households.[17]

TABLE 6.4 Single Female Householders Living in Poverty

Race/Ethnicity	% of Single Female Householders in Poverty
Black	42.5
Hispanic	41.6
White	22.9
Asian	13.7

U.S. Census Bureau, Current Population Reports, September 2014. *Income and Poverty in the United States*, 2013.

TABLE 6.5 Median Income of Same-Sex Couples by Gender and Race	
Same-Sex Couples	**Median Annual Household Income**
Black Female	$39,000
Black Male	44,000
White Female	60,000
White Male	67,000

Black Same-Sex Households in the United States: A Report from the 2000 Census.

Black women are not only far more likely than other women to be single heads of household, but, within this household type, they experience poverty at nearly twice the rate of white women and three times that of Asian women. More than 40 percent of black single female householders live in poverty.[18] Dual-earner families have more spending power than single-earner families, as well as the cushion of a partner's income in times of unemployment. Given that female-headed households are a more common household type among African Americans than are wife-husband households, that safety net is unavailable to black women. As economic fortunes have polarized, so too has marriage stability. People earning little are far less likely to marry than those higher up the income ladder, and the marriages of those who do are less stable.[19]

The combination of low wages, high levels of unemployment, high likelihood of living in single-earner households, and minimal accumulation of wealth and assets has a devastating impact on the economic wellbeing of African American women, their families, and their communities. A focus on the gender gap undifferentiated by race obscures the realities black women face, as does a focus on racial disparities undifferentiated by gender.

Black LGBTQ Workers

LGBTQ workers who are black face added dimensions of gender bias and disadvantage in the labor force. Reliable data about black workers who are LGBTQ is scarce, but studies confirm both high levels of employment discrimination based on race, gender identity, and sexual orientation and high levels of poverty, particularly among black lesbians and transgender individuals. Unprotected from job discrimination in many states and lacking access to the multiple benefits that accrue to married couples and state-recognized family forms, LGBTQ workers in general face particular challenges in the labor force. At the same time, both the gender gap and the racial gap in wages and income are salient within the LGBTQ community.

Black lesbian couples earn about $5000 less per year than black male couples, but white lesbian couples out-earn their black counterparts by $21,000 and white male

TABLE 6.6 Poverty Rates for Heterosexual and Same-Sex Couples by Race and Ethnicity

	Married Heterosexual	Male Same-Sex Couples	Female Same-Sex Couples
African American	9.3	14.4	21.1
American Indian/Alaska Native	12.9	19.1	13.7
Hispanic	16.7	9.2	19.1
White	4.1	2.7	4.3
Asian/Pacific Islander	9.1	4.5	11.8

Albelda, *Poverty in the Lesbian, Gay and Bisexual Community.*

couples out-earn black male couples by $23,000.[20] Poverty rates are also far higher for black lesbian and gay couples than they are for either heterosexual couples or for white same-sex couples. At 21.1 percent, the poverty rate for black lesbian couples is more than five times the rate for white heterosexual couples and close to eight times higher than the rate for white male couples.[21]

Transgender people report exceedingly high rates of gender discrimination in hiring, gender harassment at work, high unemployment, and low wages. In a national survey, black transgender people reported an unemployment rate of 26 percent, high rates of job loss or no-hires due to gender bias, and extremely high incidence of harassment on the job. Not surprisingly, earnings suffer for transgender individuals who are black. Thirty-four percent reported annual incomes of under $10,000, which is twice the rate of extreme poverty among transgender people in general and four times the rate for black people.[22]

Conclusion

To impact the lives of African American women and LGBTQ individuals who work for low wages—along with the fortunes of the families and communities that depend on their income—we need a multi-pronged short-term and long-term advocacy and organizing strategy that raises wages and provides benefits for the occupations in which African American women are highly concentrated, targets gender and race bias in hiring, promotion, and firing, and begins to close the gender and race wage gaps. In short, we need a labor compact that rewards rather than punishes black women for their contributions to the U.S. economy.

NOTES

1. 9.4 million black female workers were in the civilian labor force in 2010. 10.7 million are projected to be part of the workforce in 2018. *Civilian Labor Force and Participation Rates with Projections 1980–2018,* Statistical Abstract of the United States 2012, U.S. Census Bureau, 2012.

2. Low-wage workers are those workers whose hourly wage rates are so low that, even if they worked full-time, year-round, their annual earnings would fall below the poverty threshold for a family of four. Poverty threshold for family of four: $24,250—2015, $23,850—2014, $23,550—2013. http://www.census.gov/hhes/www/poverty/data/threshld/, http://aspe.hhs.gov/poverty/15poverty.cfm#thresholds, accessed March 18, 2015.

3. U.S. Bureau of Labor Statistics, "Employed Persons by Detailed Occupation, Sex, Race, and Hispanic or Latino Ethnicity," Current Population Survey Data 2014, U.S. Department of Labor, http://www.bls.gov/cps/cpsaat11.htm, accessed March 18, 2015.

4. U.S. Bureau of Labor Statistics, "Usual Weekly Earnings of Wage and Salary Workers, Fourth Quarter 2014," U.S. Department of Labor, http://www.bls.gov/news.release/pdf /wkyeng.pdf, accessed March 18, 2015.

5. U.S. Bureau of Labor Statistics, "Occupational Employment and Wages—May 2013," http://www.bls.gov/news.release/pdf/ocwage.pdf, accessed March 3, 2015.

6. U.S. Bureau of Labor Statistics, *Occupational Outlook Handbook,* U.S. Department of Labor, http://www.bls.gov/ooh/fastest-growing.htm, accessed March 18, 2015.

7. Paraprofessional Healthcare Institute (PHI), *Paying the Price: How Poverty Wages Undermine Home Care in America,* February 2015, http://phinational.org/research-reports/paying-price-how-poverty-wages-undermine-home-care-america, accessed March 18, 2015.

8. Linda Burnham and Nick Theodore, *Home Economics: The invisible and unregulated world of domestic work,* National Domestic Workers Alliance, November 2010.

9. U.S. Bureau of Labor Statistics, "Occupational Employment and Wages—May 2013."

10. U.S. Bureau of Labor Statistics, "Occupational Employment and Wages—May 2013."

11. Stephanie Luce and Naoki Fujita, *Discounted Jobs: How Retailers Sell Workers Short,* Murphy Institute at City University of New York and Retail Action Project, 2012.

12. U.S. Bureau of Labor Statistics, *Characteristics of Minimum Wage Workers, 2013,* Table 4, BLS Report 1048, U.S. Department of Labor, March 2014.

13. U.S. Bureau of Labor Statistics, *Characteristics of Minimum Wage Workers, 2013,* Table 1.

14. U.S. Bureau of Labor Statistics, "Usual Weekly Earnings of Wage and Salary Workers," Table 2.

15. Author's analysis of labor force statistics from the Current Population Survey, 2005–2015.

16. U.S. Department of Labor, *The African American Labor Force in the Recovery,* February 29, 2012.

17. Daphne Lofquist, Terry Lugaila, Martin O'Connell, and Sarah Feliz, *Households and Families: 2010,* Table 3, U.S. Census Bureau, April 2012.

18. Carmen DeNavas-Walt and Bernadette D. Proctor, *Income and Poverty in the U.S.: 2013,* U.S. Census Bureau, September 2014.

19. Stephanie Coontz, "The New Instability," *New York Times,* July 26, 2014, http://www.nytimes.com/2014/07/27/opinion/sunday/the-new-instability.html, accessed April 1, 2015.

20. Alain Dang and Somjen Frazer, *Black Same-Sex Households in the United States: A Report from the 2000 Census,* National Gay and Lesbian Task Force and National Black Justice Coalition, Second Edition: December 2005.

21. Randy Albelda, M.V. Lee Badgett, Alyssa Schneebaum, and Gary J. Gates, *Poverty in the Lesbian, Gay and Bisexual Community,* Center for Social Policy Publications, Paper 4, The Williams Institute, 2009.

22. National Justice Coalition, National Center for Transgender Equality, and National Gay and Lesbian Task Force, *Injustice at Every Turn: A Look at Black Responses to the National Transgender Discrimination Survey,* http://nbjc.org/sites/default/files/trans-adjustment -web.pdf, accessed April 1, 2015.

7 Domestic Workers Bill of Rights: A Feminist Approach for a New Economy

Ai-jen Poo

Several years ago, my grandfather had a stroke that left him paralyzed on the left side of his body. My grandmother, while in good health, was over 70 and unable to help him move around, bathe or meet many of his basic needs. So like thousands of other families, they hired a home attendant. The first time I met Ms. Li was a couple of years after she was hired. A second stroke had put my grandfather back in the hospital in critical condition. I remember entering the hospital room to visit him. Ms. Li sat at the side of his bed with a small plastic comb in her hand, slowly combing back his thin grey hair. His eyes were closed, and his expression peaceful and light. I turned to greet my grandmother, who said quietly, "He asks for her to comb his hair. It puts him at ease." Apparently, every morning at home for the last two years, she patiently combed his hair after bathing him. At that moment, it was clear to me that there are few greater gifts than being cared for by another person. It is rooted in the interconnectedness of humanity; we rely on one another, particularly when we face the uncertainty of life.

We live in an economic system that requires us to disconnect from each other despite the fact that we are ultimately interconnected. In fact, many forms of necessary labor are erased and devalued in our current system, particularly work that has historically been associated with women and women of color. The domestic work industry provides a clear window into this reality. Domestic worker organizing not only seeks to address the systemic problems facing the workforce, but also points to ways we can reshape the economy, toward a more sustainable system that adequately supports our basic human needs.

A World of Work in the Home

The estimated 2.5 million women who labor as domestic workers in the United States make it possible for their employers to go to work every day by caring for the most precious elements of their employers' lives: their families and homes. Essentially, domestic workers produce the labor power of the families they work for. Those families go to work knowing that they can return to a clean home, to clean clothes to wear, and to elderly parents and children who will have their basic needs met. In fact, domestic workers have to play the role of nurses, art teachers, counselors, tutors, assistants, and

S&F Online: The Scholar and Feminist Online. Published by The Barnard Center for Research on Women, Issue 8.1: Fall 2009. Republished with permission of the author.

nutritionists. Yet, because this work has historically been associated with the unpaid work of women in the home or with the poorly paid work of Black and immigrant women, it remains undervalued and virtually invisible to public consciousness.

In New York, over 200,000 women of color leave their homes several hours before everyone else, often in the dark, in order to arrive at their employers' homes before they leave for work. Many arrive early to prepare children for school and walk them to their buses. Some even live in their employers' homes, prepare breakfast and pack lunches for the entire household. Because women's work in the home has never been factored into national labor statistics, it is difficult to quantify the economic contributions of this workforce. However, if domestic workers across the city went on strike, almost every industry would be impacted. Doctors, lawyers, bankers, professors, small business owners, civil sector employees and media executives would all be affected. The urban economy would be paralyzed.

Most domestic workers are immigrant women of color from the global South who bear enormous pressure to support families both in the U.S. and abroad. In a recent survey conducted by DataCenter and Domestic Workers United, researchers found that 98% of domestic workers are foreign born and that 59% are the primary income earners for their families. Domestic work remains one of the few professions available to immigrant women in major cities. For this reason, it tends to draw in migrants from poor countries in search of work in our cities' growing informal service sectors. Many urban immigrant communities rely on the income of domestic workers for their economic survival.

The pressure to support their families economically is compounded by domestic workers' responsibilities to provide care for their own families and homes. The more hours they work, the fewer hours they have to spend with their own children: making nutritious meals, helping them with homework, or reading them a bedtime story. If you are working as a domestic worker in the United States, your own family will often be left without the care they need and deserve.

Long hours are just the beginning. While some employers treat their employees with dignity and respect, others use their power to compel their employees to work as many hours as possible for as little as possible. The power imbalance between domestic workers and employers is severe. The employers are commonly of a privileged class, race, and immigration status with respect to the women they hire to care for their homes and families. Most workplaces have one lone worker. The workplace is their employers' private homes—often seen as a "man's castle"—a place where the government has no business or authority. Advocates often compare the industry to the "Wild West" because it seems to function above the law. Employers can utilize sexual and gender-based harassment to instill fear, as well as exploit workers' immigration status to establish control in the workplace. Considering the prevalence of domestic violence, despite generations of organizing and advocacy on the part of the women's movement, one can imagine what is possible behind closed doors.

"Maria" worked as a caregiver for a child with a disability. A Central American woman in her mid-sixties, she came to the United States to support her family, including her diabetic son whose insulin she could not afford. In addition to constant care for a child with a disability, she was responsible for doing the cooking, cleaning, and ironing for the entire household. Maria worked 18 hours per day, six days per week for under $3 per hour. She lived in the basement of her employer's home where a broken sewage system flooded the floor by her bed. She had to collect cardboard and wood from the street during the day so she could use them as stepping stones to her bed at night. After three years working under these terrible conditions, Maria was fired without notice or severance pay. Working as a domestic worker in the United States often means working in unhealthy conditions, facing constant fear of firing, of deportation, of harassment and of abuse.

Domestic work is one our nation's oldest professions, so one should be able to assume that labor laws and other measures would protect the basic rights of the workforce. Instead, domestic workers have been explicitly excluded from labor laws since the New Deal. The exclusion of domestic workers—most of whom were African American women in the South at the time those labor laws were passed—is rooted in the legacy of slavery. It reminds us that Jim Crow is alive and well in the labor laws. In many states, domestic workers are excluded from the definition of "employee." Eight decades after the passage of this nation's foundational labor protections, domestic workers are still struggling to assert basic worker rights like time off and overtime pay.

Organizing for Dignified Work

Since 2000, Domestic Workers United (DWU) has organized Caribbean, Latina and African nannies, housekeepers, and elderly caregivers in New York. They are fighting for power, respect and fair labor standards, and their work helps to build a broader movement for social change. DWU helped organize public pressure for justice for workers like Maria who have been mistreated by their employers. DWU organized demonstrations at Maria's employer's businesses and worked with the CUNY Immigrant and Refugee Rights Clinic to file a successful lawsuit against her employer for unpaid wages. Using this combination of legal pressure and direct action, DWU has helped to recover over $450,000 in stolen wages for workers like Maria.

For the past 5 years, DWU has been waging a campaign to pass the "Domestic Workers Bill of Rights," statewide legislation that would establish basic labor standards for more than 200,000 domestic workers in New York State. These standards would include: notice of termination, a minimum of one day off per week, paid holidays, vacation and sick days and protection from discrimination. The coalition of domestic workers organizations led by DWU has gained tremendous support from labor unions, progressive employers, clergy, academics, student, community and women's organizations. The effort has raised the profile of the workforce considerably. However, the challenges to legislative change are great.

Some legislators have argued, in order to achieve days off and benefits domestic workers must form a union and collectively bargain "like other workers have to do." A few legislators have claimed that they cannot enact a law with these types of provisions because it would provide "special protections" for domestic workers that other workers do not receive by law. However, DWU has argued that the decentralized nature of this industry "wires" it for abuse, and makes it impossible to engage in collective bargaining. There is no collective workforce because workers are isolated as individuals in scattered, unmarked separate homes; and there isn't a central employer with whom to bargain. When one worker bargains with her employer, termination is the standard result. Employers simply seek to hire someone else. In the context of such intensified inequality and the nature of the industry itself, the National Labor Relations Act (the New Deal policy that provides the current framework for collective bargaining in the U.S.) would fail domestic workers, even if they were not excluded. These dynamics make every domestic worker vulnerable to conditions of indentured servitude.

But the Domestic Workers Bill of Rights is not just a campaign to address the impracticality of collective bargaining for the domestic work labor force. The Bill of Rights exposes our moral responsibility to value their work because it makes all other work possible, and it calls for an expansion of the practical role of the government in establishing and enforcing labor standards for all workers. Domestic workers have always been treated as a "special class" of workers; they have been "specially" excluded and undervalued as workers. What does it say about this nation that this workforce— that provides such a crucial type of care—is the least valued and most invisible?

In fact, the work that has historically been associated with women has made it possible for us to be where we are today. Challenging the government to account for this work and to provide appropriate protections points to the necessity for a feminist lens. It is only with this lens that we adequately account for the full reality of our economic system. Everyone needs the care of others at one point or another in their lives. We rely on others to care for us when we are children, in times of need and when we age. Even while institutional sexism devalues this work and tries to render these workers invisible, we all have a relationship to this kind of care-giving labor.

Our common experiences—in giving and receiving care—gives us an opportunity to take action in our common interest towards institutional change. As we emerge from one of the greatest economic crises of our time, we will need models that help us redefine the role of government, and its relationship to the economy. The Bill of Rights points to a new relationship between government and this industry—a relationship that is more proactive and reflective of the economic realities and needs we all face.

Lessons for a New Economy

Organizing with a feminist approach, DWU organizers have utilized everyone's connection to and reliance upon "women's work" as the basis for organizing. They have made the stories of domestic workers central. They tell the story of the work they do and the pride they feel for the work. They also tell the stories of the profound vulnerability and abuses they face. DWU has brought children who were raised by domestic workers and employers who rely on domestic workers together with domestic workers and their own children. The power of their collective stories—as workers and as people who have been the beneficiaries of their caring labor—demonstrate the power and significance of domestic work. The campaign has created the space for everyone to take action from this place of interdependence. They model a world where, in the words of DWU, "all work is valued equally."

Domestic Workers United is a part of a growing national movement of domestic worker resistance. They helped to organize the first national meeting of domestic workers organizations in 2007. After an historic exchange about organizing strategies, domestic worker organizations from around the country decided to form the National Domestic Workers Alliance as a vehicle for domestic workers to build power and raise their voice as a national force for change. Two years later, the Alliance has doubled in size. The Alliance has established a National Training Institute for domestic workers. It is leading campaigns at the state, national and international levels to enforce existing labor laws and to establish new labor standards for domestic workers. In 2010, California domestic worker organizations will be launching their campaign for the California Domestic Workers Bill of Rights. State by state, workers are asserting their rights as workers, and they are challenging the government to take responsibility for mediating their vulnerability to exploitation.

Understanding the power of Ms. Li and Maria's work can help us to structurally recalibrate to what is important in life. Some people will pay more for a pair of shoes than they pay their domestic workers for a week of work. The historic exclusions of domestic workers reinforce this system of values. Similarly, the legislature has waited five years to pass basic legislation to improve the lives of over 200,000 women. There is no organized opposition to the bill, nor is there a significant cost to the State of New York, but the bill has not yet become a legislative priority. The legislature has not yet understood that what seems like a measure that's specific to domestic workers, actually touches all of us. A recalibration is needed, and it must be institutionalized in the form of policy.

The upside-down concentration of the world's resources and wealth in the hands of a small minority at the expense of the vast majority is in fact unsustainable for everyone. Domestic worker policy demands that we recognize and value the basic care that we all require to live and provides a model for reshaping our economy to serve our collective human needs. We will need this kind of balance and systemic equity if we are going to sustain ourselves through the changes and uncertainty to come.

8 "Savage Inequalities" Revisited

Bob Feldman

Richer, Whiter School Districts Are Still Getting More Public Funds, While the Federal Government Looks the Other Way

In the late 1980s, I taught health and social studies in a New York City public school. My students came largely from African-American and Caribbean families, and the school was located in a high-poverty district. Because funding was so tight, we had no textbooks for a required eighth-grade health class, no classroom maps for seventh- and eighth-grade history classes, and no photocopying machines that teachers or students could use for free. There was also no school newspaper or yearbook, and the school band had fewer than twenty instruments.

The conditions in this school illustrated a crisis of funding inequality in the U.S. public school system. In his 1991 book *Savage Inequalities,* Jonathan Kozol, a long-time critic of unequal education, famously exposed this crisis. He noted, for instance, that schools in the rich suburbs of New York City spent more than $11,000 per pupil in 1987, while those in the city itself spent only $5,500. The story was the same throughout the country: per-capita spending for poor students and students of color in urban areas was a fraction of that in richer, whiter suburbs just miles away.

Over ten years after *Savage Inequalities* was first published, how close has the U.S. public school system come to providing equitable funding for all students— funding that is at least equal between districts, or better yet, higher in poorer areas that have greater needs?

Not very far, according to a new report by the Washington, D.C.-based Education Trust. Entitled "The Funding Gap: Low-Income and Minority Students Receive Fewer Dollars," the report examines state and local expenditures in 15,000 school districts during 1999–2000. Since federal funds account for only 7% of public school resources, this study of state and local spending zeroes in on the source of funding inequality.

According to the Education Trust study, the poorest 25% of school districts in each state receive an average of $966 less in state and local funds per pupil than the richest 25%. This gap has narrowed by $173 since 1997, but it does not reflect uniform progress: in nine of 47 states examined, the gap widened by at least $100. In states like New York and Illinois, spending differences remain staggering, totaling $2,152 and $2,060 per student, respectively. These figures, like all those in the study, are

From *Dollars & Sense*, Jan/Feb 2003. Reprinted by permission of *Dollars & Sense*, a progressive economics magazine, www.dollarsandsense.org.

Chart 1: Poor Students Get Less: States with Largest Per-Student Funding Gaps, and U.S. Average

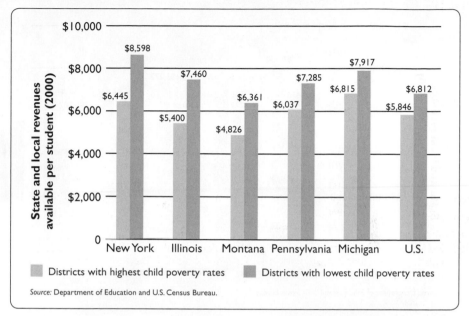

Source: Department of Education and U.S. Census Bureau.

adjusted to account for the greater expense of educating students in poor districts and areas with a high cost of living. (See Chart 1)

Funding inequality puts students of color at a special disadvantage. In two-thirds of states in the Education Trust study, the quarter of school districts with the highest percentage of students of color received at least $100 less in state and local funding than the quarter of districts with the lowest percentage of students of color. New York topped the charts for racial inequality: the quarter of districts with the highest percentage of students of color received $2,034 less in state and local funds per student than the quarter of districts enrolling the smallest percentage. (See Chart 2)

Between 1997 and 2000, 30 of the 47 states studied did move toward providing equal or greater funding for students in poorer districts—and some states made significant progress. Why did this happen? According to Michael Rebell, executive director of the Campaign for Fiscal Equity, lawsuits have produced some changes. New Jersey, for instance, began channeling funds to its poorest districts after a court challenge; as of 2000, the state government provided roughly three times as much per-capita funding to the poorest quarter of districts as it did to the richest quarter. While the state government's targeted funds are counterbalanced by wildly unequal local resources, students in the poorest quarter of districts now receive a net of $324 more per capita than those in the richest quarter. States like Oregon have achieved similar results not by targeting poorer districts, but by assuming a greater share of responsibility for school funding state-wide.

Chart 2: Students of Color Get Less: States with Largest Per-Student Funding Gaps, and U.S. Average

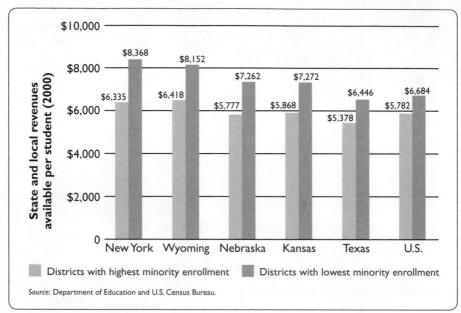

Source: Department of Education and U.S. Census Bureau.

Strategies like New Jersey's and Oregon's help explain the narrowing funding gap, and could be models for other states.

Rebell notes, however, that state-level remedies are fundamentally limited: among states, they are "complex and uneven," and nationally, they leave millions of students unaffected. A more powerful solution might be for the federal government to fund the public school system directly, as governments do in Canada, Japan, and most social democratic countries of Western Europe. Today, the U.S. government does channel money to poor districts through Title I, the largest single federal investment in education. But Title I funds are not intended to equalize funding within states: the federal government leaves that responsibility to state and local authorities, who plainly do not comply.

The needs of students would be justly served by federally guaranteed funding, but current state and federal policies guarantee something very different. As Jonathan Kozol explained a decade ago, "The present system guarantees that those who can buy a $1 million home in an affluent suburb will also be able to provide their children with superior schools." The U.S. public school system is still rigged in favor of students from richer, whiter districts; and as Rebell remarks, the United States remains "the only major developed country in the world that exhibits this shameful pattern of educational inequity."

RESOURCES

Jonathan Kozol, *Savage Inequalities*: *Children in America's Schools* (Crown Publishers, 1991).
Educational Leadership, December 1, 1993 interview with Jonathan Kozol.
Available at: www.ACCESSednetwork.org
"The Funding Gap: Low-Income and Minority Students Receive Fewer Dollars," The
Education Trust, Inc. Available at: www.edtrust.org

9 The New Face of Hunger

Tracie McMillan

On a gold-gray morning in Mitchell County, Iowa, Christina Dreier sends her son, Keagan, to school without breakfast. He is three years old, barrel-chested, and stubborn, and usually refuses to eat the free meal he qualifies for at preschool. Faced with a dwindling pantry, Dreier has decided to try some tough love: If she sends Keagan to school hungry, maybe he'll eat the free breakfast, which will leave more food at home for lunch.

Dreier knows her gambit might backfire, and it does. Keagan ignores the school breakfast on offer and is so hungry by lunchtime that Dreier picks through the dregs of her freezer in hopes of filling him and his little sister up. She shakes the last seven chicken nuggets onto a battered baking sheet, adds the remnants of a bag of Tater Tots and a couple of hot dogs from the fridge, and slides it all into the oven. She's gone through most of the food she got last week from a local food pantry; her own lunch will be the bits of potato left on the kids' plates. "I eat lunch if there's enough," she says. "But the kids are the most important. They have to eat first."

The fear of being unable to feed her children hangs over Dreier's days. She and her husband, Jim, pit one bill against the next—the phone against the rent against the heat against the gas—trying always to set aside money to make up for what they can't get from the food pantry or with their food stamps, issued by the Supplemental Nutrition Assistance Program (SNAP). Congressional cuts to SNAP last fall of $5 billion pared her benefits from $205 to $172 a month.

On this particular afternoon Dreier is worried about the family van, which is on the brink of repossession. She and Jim need to open a new bank account so they can make automatic payments instead of scrambling to pay in cash. But that will happen only if Jim finishes work early. It's peak harvest time, and he often works until eight at night, applying pesticides on commercial farms for $14 an hour. Running the errand would mean forgoing overtime pay that could go for groceries.

It's the same every month, Dreier says. Bills go unpaid because, when push comes to shove, food wins out. "We have to eat, you know," she says, only the slightest hint of resignation in her voice. "We can't starve."

• • •

Chances are good that if you picture what hunger looks like, you don't summon an image of someone like Christina Dreier: white, married, clothed, and housed, even a bit overweight. The image of hunger in America today differs markedly from Depression-era images of the gaunt-faced unemployed scavenging for food on urban streets. "This is not your grandmother's hunger," says Janet Poppendieck, a sociologist at the City University of New York. "Today more working people and their families are hungry because wages have declined."

McMillan, Tracie/National Geographic Creative

In the United States more than half of hungry households are white, and two-thirds of those with children have at least one working adult—typically in a full-time job. With this new image comes a new lexicon: In 2006 the U.S. government replaced "hunger" with the term "food insecure" to describe any household where, sometime during the previous year, people didn't have enough food to eat. By whatever name, the number of people going hungry has grown dramatically in the U.S., increasing to 48 million by 2012—a fivefold jump since the late 1960s, including an increase of 57 percent since the late 1990s. Privately run programs like food pantries and soup kitchens have mushroomed too. In 1980 there were a few hundred emergency food programs across the country; today there are 50,000. Finding food has become a central worry for millions of Americans. One in six reports running out of food at least once a year. In many European countries, by contrast, the number is closer to one in 20.

To witness hunger in America today is to enter a twilight zone where refrigerators are so frequently bare of all but mustard and ketchup that it provokes no remark, in-spires no embarrassment. Here dinners are cooked using macaroni-and-cheese mixes and other processed ingredients from food pantries, and fresh fruits and vegetables are eaten only in the first days after the SNAP payment arrives. Here you'll meet hun-gry farmhands and retired schoolteachers, hungry families who are in the U.S. with-out papers and hungry families whose histories stretch back to the *Mayflower.* Here pocketing food from work and skipping meals to make food stretch are so common that such practices barely register as a way of coping with hunger and are simply a way of life.

It can be tempting to ask families receiving food assistance, If you're really hungry, then how can you be—as many of them are—overweight? The answer is "this par-adox that hunger and obesity are two sides of the same coin," says Melissa Boteach, vice president of the Poverty and Prosperity Program of the Center for American Progress, "people making trade-offs between food that's filling but not nutritious and may actually contribute to obesity." For many of the hungry in America, the extra pounds that result from a poor diet are collateral damage—an unintended side effect of hunger itself.

• • •

As the face of hunger has changed, so has its address. The town of Spring, Texas, is where ranchland meets Houston's sprawl, a suburb of curving streets and shade trees and privacy fences. The suburbs are the home of the American dream, but they are also a place where poverty is on the rise. As urban housing has gotten more expensive, the working poor have been pushed out. Today hunger in the suburbs is growing faster than in cities, having more than doubled since 2007.

Yet in the suburbs America's hungry don't look the part either. They drive cars, which are a necessity, not a luxury, here. Cheap clothes and toys can be found at yard sales and thrift shops, making a middle-class appearance affordable. Consumer electronics can be bought on installment plans, so the hungry rarely lack phones or televisions. Of all the suburbs in the country, northwest Houston is one of the best places to see how people live on what might be called a minimum-wage diet: It has one of the highest percentages of households receiving SNAP assistance where at least one family member holds down a job. The Jefferson sisters, Meme and Kai, live here in a four-bedroom, two-car-garage, two-bath home with Kai's boyfriend, Frank, and an extended family that includes their invalid mother, their five sons, a daughter-in-law, and five grandchildren. The house has a rickety desktop computer in the living room and a television in most rooms, but only two actual beds; nearly everyone sleeps on mattresses or piles of blankets spread out on the floor.

Though all three adults work full-time, their income is not enough to keep the family consistently fed without assistance. The root problem is the lack of jobs that pay wages a family can live on, so food assistance has become the government's—and society's—way to supplement low wages. The Jeffersons receive $125 in food stamps each month, and a charity brings in meals for their bedridden matriarch.

Like most of the new American hungry, the Jeffersons face not a total absence of food but the gnawing fear that the next meal can't be counted on. When Meme shows me the family's food supply, the refrigerator holds takeout boxes and beverages but little fresh food. Two cupboards are stocked with a smattering of canned beans and sauces. A pair of freezers in the garage each contain a single layer of food, enough to fill bellies for just a few days. Meme says she took the children aside a few months earlier to tell them they were eating too much and wasting food besides. "I told them if they keep wasting, we have to go live on the corner, beg for money, or something."

Jacqueline Christian is another Houston mother who has a full-time job, drives a comfortable sedan, and wears flattering clothes. Her older son, 15-year-old Ja'Zarrian, sports bright orange Air Jordans. There's little clue to the family's hardship until you learn that their clothes come mostly from discount stores, that Ja'Zarrian mowed lawns for a summer to get the sneakers, that they're living in a homeless shelter, and that despite receiving $325 in monthly food stamps, Christian worries about not having enough food "about half of the year."

Christian works as a home health aide, earning $7.75 an hour at a job that requires her to crisscross Houston's sprawl to see her clients. Her schedule, as much as her wages, influences what she eats. To save time she often relies on premade food from grocery stores. "You can't go all the way home and cook," she says.

On a day that includes running a dozen errands and charming her payday loan officer into giving her an extra day, Christian picks up Ja'Zarrian and her seven-year-old, Jerimiah, after school. As the sun drops in the sky, Jerimiah begins complaining that he's hungry. The neon glow of a Hartz Chicken Buffet appears up the road, and he starts in: Can't we just get some gizzards, please?

Christian pulls into the drive-through and orders a combo of fried gizzards and okra for $8.11. It takes three declined credit cards and an emergency loan from her mother, who lives nearby, before she can pay for it. When the food finally arrives, filling the car with the smell of hot grease, there's a collective sense of relief. On the drive back to the shelter the boys eat until the gizzards are gone, and then drift off to sleep.

Christian says she knows she can't afford to eat out and that fast food isn't a healthy meal. But she'd felt too stressed—by time, by Jerimiah's insistence, by how little money she has—not to give in. "Maybe I can't justify that to someone who wasn't here to see, you know?" she says. "But I couldn't let them down and not get the food."

• • •

Of course it is possible to eat well cheaply in America, but it takes resources and know-how that many low-income Americans don't have. Kyera Reams of Osage, Iowa, puts an incredible amount of energy into feeding her family of six a healthy diet, with the help of staples from food banks and $650 in monthly SNAP benefits. A stay-at-home mom with a high school education, Reams has taught herself how to can fresh produce and forage for wild ginger and cranberries. When she learned that SNAP benefits could be used to buy vegetable plants, she dug two gardens in her yard. She has learned about wild mushrooms so she can safely pick ones that aren't poisonous and has lobbied the local library to stock field guides to edible wild plants.

"We wouldn't eat healthy at all if we lived off the food-bank food," Reams says. Many foods commonly donated to—or bought by—food pantries are high in salt, sugar, and fat. She estimates her family could live for three months on the nutritious foods she's saved up. The Reamses have food security, in other words, because Kyera makes procuring food her full-time job, along with caring for her husband, whose disability payments provide their only income.

But most of the working poor don't have the time or know-how required to eat well on little. Often working multiple jobs and night shifts, they tend to eat on the run. Healthful food can be hard to find in so-called food deserts—communities with few or no full-service groceries. Jackie Christian didn't resort to feeding her sons fried gizzards because it was affordable but because it was easy. Given the dramatic increase in cheap fast foods and processed foods, when the hungry have money to eat, they often go for what's convenient, just as better-off families do.

• • •

It's a cruel irony that people in rural Iowa can be malnourished amid forests of cornstalks running to the horizon. Iowa dirt is some of the richest in the nation, even bringing out the poet in agronomists, who describe it as "black gold." In 2007 Iowa's fields produced roughly one-sixth of all corn and soybeans grown in the U.S., churning out billions of bushels.

These are the very crops that end up on Christina Dreier's kitchen table in the form of hot dogs made of corn-raised beef, Mountain Dew sweetened with corn syrup, and chicken nuggets fried in soybean oil. They're also the foods that the U.S. government supports the most. In 2012 it spent roughly $11 billion to subsidize and insure commodity crops like corn and soy, with Iowa among the states receiving the highest subsidies. The government spends much less to bolster the production of the fruits and vegetables its own nutrition guidelines say should make up half the food on our plates. In 2011 it spent only $1.6 billion to subsidize and insure "specialty crops"—the bureaucratic term for fruits and vegetables.

Those priorities are reflected at the grocery store, where the price of fresh food has risen steadily while the cost of sugary treats like soda has dropped. Since the early 1980s the real cost of fruits and vegetables has increased by 24 percent. Meanwhile the cost of nonalcoholic beverages—primarily sodas, most sweetened with corn syrup—has dropped by 27 percent.

"We've created a system that's geared toward keeping overall food prices low but does little to support healthy, high-quality food," says global food expert Raj Patel. "The problem can't be fixed by merely telling people to eat their fruits and vegetables, because at heart this is a problem about wages, about poverty."

When Christina Dreier's cupboards start to get bare, she tries to persuade her kids to skip snack time. "But sometimes they eat saltine crackers, because we get that from the food bank," she said, sighing. "It ain't healthy for them, but I'm not going to tell them they can't eat if they're hungry."

The Dreiers have not given up on trying to eat well. Like the Reamses, they've sown patches of vegetables and a stretch of sweet corn in the large green yard carved out of the cornfields behind their house. But when the garden is done for the year, Christina fights a battle every time she goes to the supermarket or the food bank. In both places healthy foods are nearly out of reach. When the food stamps come in, she splurges on her monthly supply of produce, including a bag of organic grapes and a bag of apples. "They love fruit," she says with obvious pride. But most of her food dollars go to the meat, eggs, and milk that the food bank doesn't provide; with noodles and sauce from the food pantry, a spaghetti dinner costs her only the $3.88 required to buy hamburger for the sauce.

What she has, Christina says, is a kitchen with nearly enough food most of the time. It's just those dicey moments, after a new bill arrives or she needs gas to drive the kids to town, that make it hard. "We're not starved around here," she says one morning as she mixes up powdered milk for her daughter. "But some days, we do go a little hungry."

10 "I am Alena": Life as a Trans Woman Where Survival Means Living as Christopher

Ed Pilkington

At 8pm on Sunday, Alena Bradford will settle down like millions of other Americans in front of her TV set for the start of *I Am Cait,* the reality show following the gender transition[1] of Olympic gold medalist Caitlyn Jenner. The eight-part series on the E! channel will tell a story, as Jenner puts it, "about getting to be who you really are."

It promises to be a gripping viewing experience, given the controversial and deeply personal nature of its subject matter. But there will be few people across the country who will be watching quite as intensely as Alena.

If Jenner has become today's figurehead for an elite gender transition, in her case from sporting male hero to female pin-up on the cover of *Vanity Fair,*[2] Alena represents those who have been left behind. To her family and associates in her south Georgia town she is Christopher, an African American man with a round face, pronounced cheekbones and short black hair.

But that isn't who she is at all.

"I am Alena," she says in an unconscious echo of the title of Jenner's TV series. "I may not be externally, but I am Alena. Unfortunately, I live as Christopher."

Alena is one of tens of thousands of trans people across the United States still forced to live in the gender they were assigned at birth, stuck in a half-life in mid-transition. It's a lonely and dangerous place to be, as Caitlyn Jenner pointed out[3] in her ESPY awards speech[4] last week. "They're getting bullied, they're getting beaten up, they're getting murdered and they're committing suicide. The numbers are staggering, but they are the reality of what it's like to be trans today."

Alena's reality is that through a combination of her mother's disapproval, the threat of violence in her deep south community, joblessness and an almost complete lack of medical care, she finds herself at the age of 21 still living in a male body that she considers nothing but a "shell."

"Nothing in me feels like Christopher," she says. Yet she dresses as a man, answers to the name of Christopher and plays a role that feels—day by day, hour by hour—to be existentially wrong. "It's hard trying to be something you're not in order to please people around you. I'm trapped," she says.

She lives in Albany, Georgia,[5] a town of about 70,000 in the far south of the state where every street corner appears to boast an evangelical church, with prevailing social attitudes to match. "This is a Bible belt city," Alena says. "People are supposed to live by the Bible here, so it's different."

Copyright Guardian News & Media Ltd, 2015

Until six months ago, Alena lived in Atlanta, Georgia's capital. She moved there when she was 18 after her mother kicked her out of the house having discovered that Alena—Christopher to her—was transgender. She came across a vial of hormone pills that Alena was taking at the start of transition, and the realization dawned on her.

Alena had known she was sexually attracted to men from a young age, about six years old she thinks. But it wasn't until high school where she made friends with a trans girl named Coco that she made the connection.

"I'm curious, so I asked Coco what being transgender was and she explained, and that was the moment I realized I wasn't a gay male, I was trans. I finally had a word for it. I knew what I'd always been feeling."

After her mother cast her out, Alena made a journey familiar to many trans people in the deep south—to the north. Eighteen months in the big city put Alena well on the road to achieving Caitlyn Jenner's challenge: getting to be who she really is. In Atlanta's more permissive environment she began to build a life as a woman. She had a job working in a call center, rented her own small apartment, and acquired a small circle of trans friends who encouraged her to present herself outwardly as Alena.

They did her makeup, told her to be strong, to be true to herself. She was amazed by her own transformation in Atlanta. "I didn't realize how whole living as a woman made me feel, dressing up and going out that way. I may not have been the cutest thing, but I felt at peace. I felt this is me."

Then last year she lost her job as a result of company cutbacks, and the whole edifice instantly crumbled. No job meant no apartment. Desperate to cling to her new life, she began sleeping in her car, but there was only so long she could go without a regular meal or shower. A month into her nomadic lifestyle, she realized she had to decide: continue living in a car as Alena, or go home to Albany as Christopher.

"I was saying I would never go back home, never, but God has a funny way of making you eat your words and swallow your pride. Here I am back at my mom's— one of the conditions of staying here is that she will not allow me to live as Alena. I want somewhere to stay? Then I live as Christopher."

And that's how it is. When we meet she is dressed in a pair of army-style camouflage pants and a tank top, a black headscarf covering up her hair that she finds distressingly male.

"It has broken my heart," she says about her return to Albany. "I feel defeated."

Two Names, Two Lives

In the small apartment she shares with her mother and younger brother, Alena keeps only male clothes. When she first started buying women's clothes her mother got mad and threw them in the trash can. Alena bought replacements, only to have her mother throw those away too. "We went back and forth for a bit until I got sick of arguing about it," she says.

The irony is that Alena sees her mother as her role model, as the woman she wants to become. "Though we have a very up and down relationship, she's my biggest inspiration, she is the person I aspire to be. My mother raised two boys on her own without ever complaining. I want to be strong like her."

Alena has told this to her mother. "She's flattered, and she isn't. She's flattered that I want to be like her, but isn't that I want to be her."

Alena's mother declined to be interviewed by *The Guardian*.

Alena has no illusions now: she won't persuade her mother to change. So to avoid another fight she keeps her women's clothes at the house of the person she calls her "gay mom", a drag queen called Nakia who acts as her mentor and guide. She has a couple of dresses and wigs and some high-heeled shoes stashed away in Nakia's cupboard.

Most of the time, Alena has to make do with knowing who she is inside while everyone else around her thinks she is the opposite. She runs two separate Facebook pages, one sanitized version as Christopher for her non-accepting family, the second as Alena where she posts her more personal thoughts.

Even when she's with Nakia she won't go out in public dressed as a woman. She knows that having only partially completed hormone treatment, she still looks like a man, or as she puts it: "My shoulders are too broad, my breasts aren't big enough for the size I am. The way I am now, I look like a football player walking down the road in a dress, and that's not a great idea in Albany."

Her mother's disapproval—in part inspired by her religious upbringing—is not unusual in these parts. It's the norm, Alena suggests. "It's how pretty much everybody thinks in south Georgia. If you're born a man you should stay a man, if you're a woman you should stay a woman."

The few times she did venture out on to the street as a woman it ended badly. "I got cat-called. They hollered as I walked down the street: 'Faggot! You're a faggot! [If] I had my gun I would shoot you.' It made me not want to come out dressed like that any more."

Living as Themselves, and Living in Fear

The name-calling Alena can cope with. But it's more than that. It's life-threatening.

At least 10 trans women,[6] most of them black,[7] have been murdered this year and transgender rights groups describe the epidemic of violence and sexual assault as a national crisis. Caitlyn Jenner raised the issue at the ESPYs, talking about Mercedes William, a 17-year-old trans girl whose body was found riddled with stab marks in a field in Mississippi last month. This week, India Clarke, a trans woman in Tampa, Florida, was found dead with signs of blunt force trauma[8] on her torso; police have launched a murder investigation.

Dee Dee Chamblee, a member of the Transgender Law Center's Positively Trans project who lives in Atlanta, said: "In the country towns of south Georgia there are a lot of trans women whose lives are in danger every day. They are having to hide their identity, knowing that if their community finds out they become the target."

Alena herself knows from experience how dangerous it is in Albany to be visibly transgender. She is scared that if she gets discovered when she is out in the street she will find herself in a near-death or fatal situation. A few years ago she made a rare foray out into the town as Alena and was set upon by a group of men.

"I put on a dress and wig and some heels and accessories, and went out. A guy tried to talk to me in a bar. As soon as he started hitting on me I told him, I'm not what you're looking for. But he got mad, and he and his friends jumped on me."

She says the experience has left her wary of appearing in public. "You don't know how far these people are going to go. At that moment I truly understood why trans women are so scared—I didn't trick him and he jumped on me because he hated the fact that he was attracted to me. That's terrifying."

The attack has also made her determined to become "passable"—that is, to come across so convincingly as a woman that no stranger would be able to tell she is transgender. That's the only way she will ever be able to live as Alena, she believes, without forever looking over her shoulder.

But to be able to pass, she requires a steady, affordable supply of prescription hormones—something impossible to come by in Albany.

Alena finds herself in a double-bind that makes securing affordable prescription hormones for transition virtually impossible. She is one of 600,000 Georgians who have been left uninsured for healthcare[9] as a result of the Republican state's refusal to expand Medicaid under Barack Obama's Affordable Care Act[10]—a hardship that she shares with low-income citizens in 19 other states mainly across the deep south.

Even if she were entitled to Medicaid, Georgia—along with 15 other states—specifically excludes health coverage for transition-related treatment, so she wouldn't get anything anyway. A further 26 states have no policies at all regarding transgender health, rendering the system a minefield to negotiate, while only eight states plus Washington DC have reformed the rules to ensure that services are provided.

The state of play is little better with private insurance schemes—10 states plus DC require private policies to cover treatment for transition, the remaining 40 are mute on the subject.

Kellan Baker, a senior fellow at the Center for American Progress, pointed out that "many states exempt Medicaid from treatment for gender dysphoria, ignoring the overwhelming evidence of the medical needs and the psychological impact. That sets up an insurmountable barrier for low-income trans people—and trans people have a very low average income, with surveys showing[11] they suffer twice the unemployment rate of the general population with one in six living on an annual income of $10,000 or less—to finding help from the medical system."

'There's nothing here for me in Albany. Nothing'

Alena is theoretically able to obtain prescription hormones on her mother's insurance. But having scoured Albany and surrounding towns over many months, she has been unable to find a doctor willing to take her on as a patient. She does have a physician in Atlanta, but without Medicaid to pay for the bus, and having traded in her car, she can't afford the 200-mile journey.

"This is a messed-up situation," Alena says with understatement. "I know that resources are out there, that people are willing to help me, but I just can't get to them. There's nothing here for me in Albany. Nothing."

And so, like many transgender individuals, Alena gets her hormones rough-and-ready through the internet. She buys bottles of estradiol, a female sex hormone, for $30 once a month, supplemented when she has the money with Perlutal, a female contraceptive in liquid form that she injects into her muscles.

Sometimes when she needs the drugs quickly she will buy them from other trans women prepared to sell them on the buzzing black market for hormones. No figures exist to indicate the scale of black market hormones in the US, but to those like Dee Dee Chamblee who are active in the community, evidence of the trade is not hard to find.

"It's rampant. Trans women are taking half their hormones and selling the rest on. They are getting all kinds of stuff, taking just about anything to transition their bodies to match up with their minds."

Alena is aware how perilous such do-it-yourself treatment can be, administered entirely in the absence of medical supervision, with scant knowledge of the origins and strengths of the drugs, and with at best intermittent supply.

"I know I don't take hormones like I should. I take a shot when I can get it, and when I have it I take it in double doses, and when I run out I stop taking it. I know that's unhealthy."

Recently, she was present when a trans friend fell sick having injected herself with oestrogen from Mexico. "I was with her when she took the shot. The next day she was in the hospital. I knew then I wasn't taking any more of those shots. How do we know those are human hormones? We don't."

The dangers of bad drugs or medicating yourself at the wrong doses are self-evident. But foregoing the drugs can also carry mortal risks. In addition to the threat of being assaulted on the street because you are not "passable", there is also the danger of self-harm.

A study last year[12] by the National Transgender Discrimination Survey found that the stress and depression associated with failure to transition fully has a terrible cost—the prevalence of suicide attempts is 41% within the trans community, vastly more than the 4.6% of the US population as a whole.

One of the 41% is Alena, who tried to kill herself when she was 15. "It was around the time that I realized I was trans. I felt that my parents would never accept me, that I would never get to live like a woman, and at that point I would rather end my life than have to live like this."

Shedding Her Skin

Today, Alena is arguably no further towards her goal of transition than she was six years ago. What has changed, though, is the clarity of her thinking and her iron-clad determination to transition. She sees it as just a question of time.

On the second day we spend with her, we take Alena clothes shopping so that she can be fully herself just for an hour or two. She buys a $20 red-and-white chiffon dress and a $30 black wig, courtesy of *The Guardian*.

Back at the hotel she puts on her new wardrobe, adding a little lip gloss and mascara. Alena-as-Christopher transforms in front of our eyes into Alena-as-Alena.

"I haven't felt like this in a long time," she says standing in front of the mirror, stroking her long black hair like an adored cat. "I really feel like Alena now. I really do."

She pauses, and then says: "I feel beautiful."

Before she climbs back into her Christopher uniform and we drop her back at her mother's, we ask Alena if she'd be OK taking a walk in her new female clothes, to give us a more intimate sense of the challenges she faces in public.

No, she says gently. She couldn't do that. "I'm not brave enough to endure what would be thrown at me. Not now."

Alena is not there yet. She hasn't got to be who she really is.

But she will. She will get there, she's certain of that. She has it all planned out. First she'll get a job. Then she'll start saving for a security deposit on a home of her own. Finally, when she's ready, she'll leave her mother and shed her male skin.

"As soon as I have the money, I'm gone," she says. "And the minute I'm gone, Christopher is gone."

NOTES

1. Holpuch, A. (2015, June 3). "I Am Cait: Caitlyn Jenner's reality series set to premiere in July." *The Guardian*.

2. Bissinger, B. (2015, July 1). "Caitlyn Jenner: The Full Story." *Vanity Fair*.

3. Gambino, L. (2015, July 16). "Caitlyn Jenner: transgender people 'shouldn't have to take' bullying." *The Guardian*.

4. Daily News Staff. (2015, July 16). "Transcript: Caitlyn Jenner's ESPYs acceptance speech." *Daily News*.

5. The Associated Press, Gainesville, GA. (2015, September 5). "Black couple turns to fair housing law to sue neighbor and city over racial slurs." *The Guardian*.

6. Pilkington, E. (2015, July 4). "LGBT activists call for new focus on violence against transgender community." *The Guardian*.

7. Pilkington, E. (2014, August 1). "Fear and violence in transgender Baltimore: 'It's scary trusting anyone.'" *The Guardian*.

8. Stafford, Z. (2015, July 22). "Florida transgender woman beaten to death is 10th US trans murder in 2015." *The Guardian*.

9. Families U.S.A. (2015, July). "A 50-State Look at Medicaid Expansion." Available at: familiesusa.org/product/50-state-look-medicaid-expansion

10. Siddiqui, S. (2015, July 1). "Barack Obama to Republican states: 'open your hearts' and expand Medicaid." *The Guardian*.

11. The National Center for Transgender Equality and the National Gay and Lesbian Task Force. (2009, November). "National Transgender Discrimination Survey." Available at: www.thetaskforce.org/static_html/downloads/reports/fact_sheets/transsurvey_prelim_findings.pdf

12. Haas, A. P., Rodgers, P. L., and Herman, J. L. (2014, January). "Suicide Attempts among Transgender and Gender Non-Conforming Adults." The Williams Institute. Available at: williamsinstitute.law.ucla.edu/wp-content/uploads/AFSP-Williams-Suicide-Report-Final.pdf

11 Cause of Death: Inequality

Alejandro Reuss

Inequality Kills

You won't see inequality on a medical chart or a coroner's report under "cause of death." You won't see it listed among the top killers in the United States each year. All too often, however, it is social inequality that lurks behind a more immediate cause of death, be it heart disease or diabetes, accidental injury or homicide. Few of the top causes of death are "equal opportunity killers." Instead, they tend to strike poor people more than rich people, the less educated more than the highly educated, people lower on the occupational ladder more than those higher up, or people of color more than white people.

Statistics on mortality and life expectancy do not provide a perfect map of social inequality. For example, in 2002, the life expectancy for women in the United States was about five years longer than the life expectancy for men, despite the many ways in which women are subordinated to men. Take most indicators of socioeconomic status, however, and most causes of death, and it's a strong bet that you'll find illness and injury (or "morbidity") and mortality increasing as status decreases.

Among people between the ages of 25 and 64, those with less than a high school diploma (or equivalent) had an age-adjusted mortality rate more than three times that of people with at least some college, as of 2003. Those without a high school diploma had more than triple the death rate from chronic noncommunicable diseases (e.g., heart disease), more than 3½ times the death rate from injury, and nearly six times the death rate from HIV/AIDS, compared to those with at least some college. People with incomes below the poverty line were nearly twice as likely to have had an asthma attack in the previous year (among those previously diagnosed with asthma) as people with incomes at least twice the poverty line. Poor people were over 2½ times as likely to suffer from a chronic condition that limited their activity and over three times as likely to characterize their own health as "fair" or "poor" (rather than "good" or "very good"), compared to those with incomes over double the poverty line. African Americans have higher death rates than whites from cancer (¼ higher), heart disease (⅓ higher), stroke (½ higher), diabetes (twice as high), homicide (more than 5 times as high), and AIDS (more than 8 times as high). The infant mortality rate for African Americans was, in 2002–2003, over twice as high as for whites. In all, the lower you are in a social hierarchy, the worse your health and the shorter your life are likely to be.

From *Dollars & Sense*, May/June 2001. Reprinted by permission of *Dollars & Sense*, a progressive economics magazine, www.dollarsandsense.org.

The Worse Off in the United States Are Not Well Off by World Standards

You often hear it said that even poor people in rich countries like the United States are rich compared to ordinary people in poor countries. While that may be true when it comes to consumer goods like televisions or telephones, which are widely available even to poor people in the United States, it's completely wrong when it comes to health.

In a 1996 study published in the *New England Journal of Medicine,* University of Michigan researchers found that African-American females living to age 15 in Harlem had a 65% chance of surviving to age 65. That is less than the probability at birth of surviving to age 65 for women in India, according to 2000–2005 data. Meanwhile, Harlem's African-American males reaching age 15 had only a 37% chance of surviving to age 65. That is less than the probability at birth of surviving to age 65 for men in Haiti. Among both African-American men and women, diseases of the circulatory system and cancers were the leading causes of death.

It takes more income to achieve a given life expectancy in a rich country like the United States than it does to achieve the same life expectancy in a less affluent country. So the higher money income of a low-income person in the United States, compared to a middle-income person in a poor country, does not necessarily translate into a longer life span. The average income per person in African-American households ($15,200), for example, is about three times the per capita income of Peru. As of 2002, however, the life expectancy for African-American men in the United States was about 69 years, less than the average life expectancy in Peru. The infant mortality rate for African Americans, 13.5 per 1000 live births, is between that of Uruguay and Bulgaria, both of which have per capita incomes around $8,000.

Health Inequalities in the United States Are Not Just About Access to Health Care

Nearly one sixth of the U.S. population below age 65 lacks health insurance of any kind, private or Medicaid. Among those with incomes below 1½ times the poverty line, over 30% lack health coverage of any kind, compared to 10% for those with incomes more than twice the poverty line. African Americans under age 65 were about 1½ times as likely as whites to lack health insurance; Latinos, nearly three times as likely. Among those aged 55 to 64, uninsured people were about ⅔ as likely as insured people to have seen a primary-care doctor in the last year, and less than half as likely to have seen a specialist, as of 2002–2003. Among women over 40, about 55% of those with incomes below the poverty line had gotten a mammogram in the last two years, compared to 75% of those with incomes over twice the poverty line, as of 2003. Obviously, disparities in access to health care are a major health problem.

But so are environmental hazards; communicable diseases; homicide and accidental death; and smoking, lack of exercise, and other risk factors. These dangers all tend to affect lower-income people more than higher-income, less-educated people more than more-educated, and people of color more than whites. African-American children between the ages of 3 and 10 were nearly twice as likely to have had an asthma attack in the last year as white children, among those previously diagnosed with asthma. The frequency of attacks is linked to air pollution. Among people between ages 25 and 64, those without a high school diploma had over five times the death rate from communicable diseases, compared to those with at least some college. African-American men were, as of 2003, more than seven times as likely to fall victim to homicide as white men; African-American women, more than four times as likely as white women. People without a high school diploma (or equivalent) were nearly three times as likely to smoke as those with at least a bachelor's degree, as of 2003. People with incomes below the poverty line were nearly twice as likely to get no exercise as people with incomes over double the poverty line.

Michael Marmot, a pioneer in the study of social inequality and health, notes that so-called diseases of affluence—disorders, like heart disease or diabetes, associated with high-calorie and high-fat diets, lack of physical activity, etc. increasingly typical in rich societies—are most prevalent among the *least* affluent people in these societies. While recognizing the role of such "behavioral" risk factors as smoking in producing poor health, he argues, "It is not sufficient . . . to ask what contribution smoking makes to generating the social gradient in ill health, but we must ask, why is there a social gradient in smoking?" What appear to be individual "lifestyle" decisions often reflect a broader social epidemiology.

Greater Income Inequality Goes Hand in Hand with Poorer Health

Numerous studies suggest that the more unequal the income distribution in a country, state, or city, the lower the life expectancies for people at all income levels. A 1996 study published in the *American Journal of Public Health,* for example, shows that U.S. metropolitan areas with low per capita incomes and low levels of income inequality have lower mortality rates than areas with high median incomes and high levels of income inequality. Meanwhile, for a given per capita income range, mortality rates always decline as inequality declines.

R.G. Wilkinson, perhaps the researcher most responsible for relating health outcomes to overall levels of inequality (rather than individual income levels), argues that greater income inequality causes worse health outcomes independent of its effects on poverty. Wilkinson and his associates suggest several explanations for this relationship. First, the bigger the income gap between rich and poor, the less inclined the well-off are to pay taxes for public services they either do not use or use in low proportion to the taxes they pay. Lower spending on public hospitals, schools, and other basic services does not affect wealthy people's life expectancies very much, but it affects poor people's life expectancies a great deal. Second, the bigger the income gap between rich and poor, the lower the overall level of social cohesion. High levels of social cohesion are associated with good health outcomes for several reasons. For example, people in highly cohesive societies are more likely to be active in their communities, reducing social isolation, a known health risk factor.

Numerous researchers have criticized Wilkinson's conclusions, arguing that the real reason income inequality tends to be associated with worse health outcomes is that it is associated with higher rates of poverty. But even if they are right and income inequality causes worse health simply by bringing about greater poverty, that hardly makes for a defense of inequality. Poverty and inequality are like partners in crime. "Whether public policy focuses primarily on the elimination of poverty or on reduction in income disparity," argue Wilkinson critics Kevin Fiscella and Peter Franks, "neither goal is likely to be achieved in the absence of the other."

Differences in Status May Be Just as Important as Income Levels

Even after accounting for differences in income, education, and other factors, the life expectancy for African Americans is less than that for whites, U.S. researchers are beginning to explore the relationship between high blood pressure among African Americans and the racism of the surrounding society. African Americans tend to suffer from high blood pressure, a risk factor for circulatory disease, more often than whites. Moreover, studies have found that, when confronted with racism, African Americans suffer larger and longer-lasting increases in blood pressure than when faced with other stressful situations. Broader surveys relating blood pressure in African Americans to perceived instances of racial discrimination have yielded complex results, depending on social class, gender, and other factors.

Stresses cascade down social hierarchies and accumulate among the least empowered. Even researchers focusing on social inequality and health, however, have been surprised by the large effects on mortality. Over 30 years ago, Michael Marmot and his associates undertook a landmark study, known as Whitehall I, of health among British civil servants. Since the civil servants shared many characteristics regardless of job classification—an office work environment, a high degree of job security, etc.—the researchers expected to find only modest health differences among them. To their surprise, the study revealed a sharp increase in mortality with each step down the job hierarchy—even from the highest grade to the second highest. Over ten years, employees in the lowest grade were three times as likely to die as those in the highest grade. One factor was that people in lower grades showed a higher incidence of many "lifestyle" risk factors, like smoking, poor diet, and lack of exercise. Even when the researchers controlled for such factors, however, more than half the mortality gap remained.

Marmot noted that people in the lower job grades were less likely to describe themselves as having "control over their working lives" or being "satisfied with their work situation," compared to those higher up. While people in higher job grades were more likely to report "having to work at a fast pace," lower-level civil servants were more likely to report feelings of hostility, the main stress-related risk factor for heart disease. Marmot concluded that "psycho-social" factors—the psychological costs of being lower in the hierarchy—played an important role in the unexplained mortality gap. Many of us have probably said to ourselves, after a trying day on the job, "They're killing me." Turns out it's not just a figure of speech. Inequality kills—and it starts at the bottom.

RESOURCES

Health, United States, 2005, with Chartbook on Trends in the Health of Americans, National Center for Health Statistics, www.cdc.gov/nchs.

Health, United States, 1998, with Socioeconomic Status and Health Chartbook, National Center for Health Statistics, www.cdc.gov/nchs.

Human Development Report 2005, UN Development Programme, hdr.undp.org.

Human Development Report 2000, UN Development Programme, hdr.undp.org.

World Development Indicators 2000, World Bank.

Lisa Berkman, "Social Inequalities and Health: Five Key Points for Policy-Makers to Know," February 5, 2001, Kennedy School of Government, Harvard University.

Ichiro Kawachi, Bruce P. Kennedy, and Richard G. Wilkinson, eds., *The Society and Population Health Reader, Volume I: Income Inequality and Health.* New York: The New Press, 1999.

Michael Marmot, "Social Differences in Mortality: The Whitehall Studies," in Alan D. Lopez, Graziella Caselli, and Tapani Valkonen, eds., *Adult Mortality in Developed Countries: From Description to Explanation.* New York: Oxford University Press, 1995.

Michael Marmot, "The Social Pattern of Health and Disease," in David Blane, Eric Brunner, and Richard Wilkinson, eds., *Health and Social Organization: Towards a Health Policy for the Twenty-First Century.* New York: Routledge, 1996.

Arline T. Geronimus et al., "Excess Mortality Among Blacks and Whites in the United States, *The New England Journal of Medicine,* 335(21), November 21, 1996.

Nancy Krieger, Ph.D., and Stephen Sidney, M.D., "Racial Discrimination and Blood Pressure: The CARDIA Study of Young Black and White Adults," *American Journal of Public Health,* 86(10), October 1996.

12 Inequality Undermines Democracy

Eduardo Porter

Americans have never been too worried about the income gap. The gap between the rich and the rest has been much wider in the United States than in other developed nations for decades. Still, polls show we are much less concerned about it than people in those other nations are.

Policy makers haven't cared much either. The United States does less than other rich countries to transfer income from the affluent to the less fortunate. Even as the income gap has grown enormously over the last 30 years, government has done little to curb the trend.

Our tolerance for a widening income gap may be ebbing, however. Since Occupy Wall Street and kindred movements highlighted the issue, the chasm between the rich and ordinary workers has become a crucial talking point in the Democratic Party's arsenal. In a speech in Osawatomie, Kansas, last December, President Obama underscored how "the rungs of the ladder of opportunity had grown farther and farther apart, and the middle class has shrunk."

There are signs that the political strategy has traction. Inequality isn't quite the top priority of voters: only 17 percent of Americans think it is extremely important for the government to try to reduce income and wealth inequality, according to a Gallup survey last November. That is about half the share that said reigniting economic growth was crucial.

But a slightly different question indicates views have changed: 29 percent said it was extremely important for the government to increase equality of opportunity. More significant, 41 percent said that there was not much opportunity in America, up from 17 percent in 1998.

Americans have been less willing to take from the rich and give to the poor in part because of a belief that each of us has a decent shot at prosperity. In 1952, 87 percent of Americans thought there was plenty of opportunity for progress; only 8 percent disagreed. As income inequality has grown, though, many have changed their minds.

From 1993 to 2010, the incomes of the richest 1 percent of Americans grew 58 percent while the rest had a 6.4 percent bump. There is little reason to think the trend will go into reverse any time soon, given globalization and technological change, which have weighed heavily on the wages of less educated workers who compete against machines and cheap foreign labor while increasing the returns of top executives and financiers.

From *The New York Times*, March 21, 2012. © 2012 The New York Times. All rights reserved. Used by permission and protected by the Copyright Laws of the United States. The printing, copying, redistribution, or retransmission of this Content without express written permission is prohibited.

The income gap narrowed briefly during the Great Recession, as plummeting stock prices shrunk the portfolios of the rich. But in 2010, the first year of recovery, the top 1 percent of Americans captured 93 percent of the income gains.

Under these conditions, perhaps it is unsurprising that a growing share of Americans have lost faith in their ability to get ahead.

We have accepted income inequality in the past partly because of the belief that capitalism can't work without it. If entrepreneurs invest and workers improve their skills to improve their lot in life, a government that heavily taxed the rich to give to the poor could destroy that incentive and stymie economic growth that benefits everybody.

The nation's relatively fast growth over the last three decades appeared to support this view. The United States grew faster than advanced economies with a more egalitarian distribution of income, like the European Union and Japan, so keeping redistribution to a minimum while allowing markets to function unimpeded was considered the best fuel.

Meanwhile, skeptics of income redistribution pointed out that inequality doesn't look so dire when it is viewed over a lifetime rather than at a single point in time. One study found that about half the households in the poorest fifth of the population moved to a higher quintile within a decade.

Even though the wealthy reaped most of growth's rewards, critics of redistribution noted that incomes grew over the last 30 years for all but the poorest American families. And in the 1990s, a decade of soaring inequality, even families in the bottom fifth saw their incomes rise.

Some economists have argued that inequality is not the right social ill to focus on. "What matters is how the poor and middle class are doing and how much opportunity they have," said Scott Winship, an economist at the Brookings Institution. "Until there is stronger evidence that inequality has a negative effect on the life of the average person, I'm inclined to accept it."

Perhaps Americans' newfound concerns about their lack of opportunity are a reaction to our economic doldrums, with high unemployment and stagnant incomes, and have little to do with inequality. Perhaps these concerns will dissipate when jobs become more plentiful.

Perhaps. Evidence is mounting, however, that inequality itself is obstructing Americans' shot at a better life.

Alan Krueger, Mr. Obama's top economic adviser, offers a telling illustration of the changing views on income inequality. In the 1990s he preferred to call it "dispersion," which stripped it of a negative connotation.

In 2003, in an essay called "Inequality, Too Much of a Good Thing" Mr. Krueger proposed that "societies must strike a balance between the beneficial incentive effects of inequality and the harmful welfare-decreasing effects of inequality." Last January he took another step: "the rise in income dispersion—along so many dimensions—has gotten to be so high, that I now think that inequality is a more appropriate term."

Progress still happens, but there is less of it. Two-thirds of American families— including four of five in the poorest fifth of the population—earn more than their parents did 30 years earlier. But they don't advance much. Four out of 10 children whose family is in the bottom fifth will end up there as adults. Only 6 percent of them will rise to the top fifth.

It is difficult to measure changes in income mobility over time. But some studies suggest it is declining: the share of families that manage to rise out of the bottom fifth of earnings has fallen since the early 1980s. So has the share of people that fall from the top.

And on this count too, the United States seems to be trailing other developed nations. Comparisons across countries suggest a fairly strong, negative link between the level of inequality and the odds of advancement across the generations. And the United States appears at extreme ends along both of these dimensions—with some of the highest inequality and lowest mobility in the industrial world.

The link makes sense: a big income gap is likely to open up other social breaches that make it tougher for those lower down the rungs to get ahead. And that is exactly what appears to be happening in the United States, where a narrow elite is peeling off from the rest of society by a chasm of wealth, power and experience.

The sharp rise in the cost of college is making it harder for lower-income and middle-class families to progress, feeding education inequality.

Inequality is also fueling geographical segregation—pushing the homes of the rich and poor further apart. Brides and grooms increasingly seek out mates with similar levels of income and education. Marriages among less-educated people have become much more likely to fail.

And a growing income gap has bred a gap in political clout that could entrench inequality for a very long time. One study found that public spending on education was lower in countries like Britain and the United States where the rich participate more in the political process than the poor, and higher in countries like Sweden and Denmark, where levels of political participation are approximately similar across the income scale. If the very rich can use the political system to slow or stop the ascent of the rest, the United States could become a hereditary plutocracy under the trappings of liberal democracy.

One doesn't have to believe in equality to be concerned about these trends. Once inequality becomes very acute, it breeds resentment and political instability, eroding the legitimacy of democratic institutions. It can produce political polarization and gridlock, splitting the political system between haves and have-nots, making it more difficult for governments to address imbalances and respond to brewing crises. That too can undermine economic growth, let alone democracy.

Suggestions for Further Reading

Albelda, Randy, et al. *Unlevel Playing Fields: Understanding Wage Inequality and Discrimination,* 2nd ed. Boston: Economic Affairs Bureau, 2004.

Amott, Theresa L., and Julie Atthaei. *Race, Gender, and Work: A Multi-Cultural History of Women in the United States,* rev. ed. Boston: South End Press, 1999.

Aronowitz, Stanley. *How Class Works.* New Haven, CT : Yale University Press, 2004.

Bergmann, Barbara R. *The Economic Emergence of Women,* 2nd ed. New York: Palgrave Macmillan, 2005.

Cashin, Sheryll. *The Failures of Integration: How Race and Class Are Undermining the American Dream.* New York: PublicAffairs, 2005.

Chang, Grace. *Disposable Domestics: Immigrant Women Workers in the Global Economy,* 2nd ed. Chicago: Haymarket Books, 2016.

Children's Defense Fund. *The State of America's Children.* Washington, DC: Children's Defense Fund. Published annually.

Dantzinger, Sheldon H., and Robert H. Haveman. *Understanding Poverty.* Boston: Harvard University Press, 2002.

DeMott, Benjamin. *The Imperial Middle.* New York: William Morrow, 1990.

Domhoff, G. William. *Who Rules America: Power, Politics, and Social Change.* New York: McGraw-Hill, 2006.

Ehrenreich, Barbara. *Bait and Switch: The (Futile) Pursuit of the American Dream.* New York: Metropolitan Books, 2005.

———. *Nickel and Dimed,* 10th anniversary ed. New York: Picador Books, 2011.

Gans, Herbert J. *The War Against the Poor.* New York: Basic Books, 1995.

Glenn, Evelyn Nakano. *Forced to Care: Coercion and Caregiving in America.* Cambridge, MA: Harvard University Press, 2012.

Goldin, Claudia, and Leonard Katz. *The Race Between Education and Technology.* Cambridge, MA: Belknap Press, 2008.

Hacker, Andrew. *Two Nations: Black and White, Separate, Hostile, Unequal.* New York: Scribner, 2003.

Hays, Sharon. *Flat Broke with Children: Women in the Age of Welfare Reform.* New York: Oxford University Press, 2004.

Keister, Lisa A. *Wealth in America: Trends in Wealth Inequality.* Cambridge, MA: Cambridge University Press, 2000.

Kessler Harris, Alice. *In Pursuit of Equity: Women, Men, and the Quest for Economic Citizenship in Twentieth-Century America.* New York: Oxford University Press, 2001.

Kozol, Jonathan. *Savage Inequalities: Children in America's Schools.* New York: Crown, 1991.

Krugman, Paul. *End This Depression Now!* New York: W. W. Norton, 2012.

MacLean, Nancy. *Freedom Is Not Enough.* Cambridge, MA: Harvard University Press, 2008.

Mishel, Lawrence, et al. *The State of Working America,* 12th ed. Ithaca, NY: ILR Press, 2012.

Newman, Katherine S. *No Shame in My Game: The Working Poor in the Inner City.* New York: Vintage Books, 2000.

New York Times. Class Matters. New York: Times Books, 2005.

Phillips, Kevin. *Wealth in America: A Political History of the American Rich.* New York: Broadway Books, 2002.

Polakrow, Valerie. *Lives on the Edge: Single Women and Their Children in the Other America.* Chicago: University of Chicago Press, 1993.

Poo, Ai-Jen. *The Age of Dignity: Preparing for the Elder Boom in a Changing America.* New York: The New Press, 2015.

Rank, Mark Robert. *One Nation Underprivileged: Why American Poverty Affects Us All.* New York: Oxford University Press, 2005.

Sernau, Scott. *Worlds Apart: Social Inequalities in a New Century.* California: Pine Forge Press, 2001.

Shapiro, Thomas M. *The Hidden Costs of Being African American: How Wealth Perpetuates Inequality.* New York: Oxford University Press, 2003.

Sidel, Ruth. *Unsung Heroines: Single Mothers and the American Dream.* Berkeley: University of California Press, 2006.

Shipler, David K. *The Working Poor: Invisible in America.* New York: Vintage Books, 2005.

Stiglitz, Joseph E. *The Price of Inequality: How Today's Divided Society Endangers Our Future.* New York: W. W. Norton, 2012.

Wolff, Edward N. *Top Heavy: The Increasing Inequality of Wealth in America and What Can Be Done About It,* 2nd ed. New York: New Press, 2002.

In addition to these books, the following organizations are good sources for obtaining current statistics analyzed in terms of race, class, and gender:

Asian Nation: asian-nation.org

The Association on American Indian Affairs: http://www.indian-affairs.org/

Children's Defense Fund: www.childrensdefense.org

United for a Fair Economy: www.faireconomy.org

Institute for Women's Policy Research: www.iwpr.org

Institute for Gay and Lesbian Strategic Studies: www.publicagenda.org/sources/institute-gay-and-lesbian
-strategic-studies

The National Urban League: www.nul.org

The National Committee on Pay Equity: www.pay-equity.org

U.S. Bureau of Labor Statistics: www.bls.gov

PART VI

Many Voices, Many Lives: Issues of Race, Class, Gender, and Sexuality in Everyday Life

Statistics can tell us a lot about life in any given society, yet they paint only part of the picture. They can tell us that more than 110,000 Japanese Americans were herded into relocation camps during World War II, but they tell us nothing of the lives lived in those camps or of the repercussions years later of that experience. They can tell us that every day, four women in this country die as a result of domestic violence, but they cannot convey what it means to live in an abusive relationship. Statistics can tell us a story with numbers, but they cannot translate those numbers into lived experience. For that, we must turn to stories about people's lives.

Who will tell these stories? For many years, and not so long ago, the voices of the majority of people in our society were missing from the books in libraries and on college reading lists. The experiences of women from all racial and ethnic groups, regardless of their class position, were missing, as were the history, culture, and experience of many others. In their place were the writings and teachings of a relatively small group—predominantly privileged, white, and male—who offered their experience and their perspective as if it were universal. Ironically, even books about breast-feeding and childbirth were authored exclusively by male "experts" who defined and described a reality they had never known. White sociologists, psychologists, and anthropologists set themselves up as experts on Native American, Latina/o, Hispanic, black, and Asian American experience and culture, offering elaborate critical accounts of the family structure and lifestyle of each group. Novels chronicling the growth to manhood of young white males from the upper or middle class were routinely assigned in high school and college English courses and examined for "universal themes," while novels about the experiences of men of color, working people, lesbian, gay, bisexual and transgender people, and women of all groups were relegated to "special interest" courses and treated as marginal. In short, serious scholarship, "real" science, and "great" literature were by definition produced by well-to-do white males and often focused exclusively on their experiences; accounts of the lives of other groups, written by members of those groups, were largely omitted from conventional classroom settings.

We are fortunate that more accounts of the lives of ordinary people have become available over the past 20 or 30 years, largely as a result of the establishment of women's studies, ethnic studies, and LGBT studies as academic disciplines. These accounts fill in some of the gaps in the limited experience each of us brings to our study of race, class, gender, and sexuality. The selections in Part VI are offered as a way of putting flesh and blood around the often bare-bones statistics provided in Part V. They provide us with an opportunity to move outside the limits of our particular identity, at least for a few minutes, and find out what the world looks like from someone else's perspective. In Part VI, we get a glimpse of what it was like to be a young Native American girl torn from her family and community and sent to live at a typical Indian boarding school many years ago (Selection 1). We hear about life as a young Japanese American growing up on the West Coast during World War II, as Yuri Kochiyama tells of her experiences first in California and then in a relocation camp in Jerome, Arkansas (Selection 2). We listen in as Ta-Nehisi Coates (Selection 4) reflects on his experience in a young black body learning the violence of racism. E. Tammy Kim (Selection 5) documents the plight of undocumented youth negotiating the constraints produced by restrictive immigration policy and their impact on everyday life. Ziba Kashef (Selection 6) and Claudia Rankine (Selection 7) grapple with the assumptions that are made about race, and the effects on those on the receiving end of those assumptions. And we look in as Tommi Avicolli (Selection 8) and Richard Kim (Selection 9) show us the obstacles we set up for our LGBT kids, those whose gender and sexuality fall outside dominant norms and who are bullied into silence, or worse—suicide—and whose lives would be saved by our accepting and including them as they are.

All of these essays and the others in Part VI provide us with unique opportunities to look at everyday life in the United States through the lenses of race, gender, class, and sexuality to see things we may not have noticed before. The pieces in Part VI also broaden our range of vision to include other factors that can have significant impact on life choices, among them religion, age, physical condition, and geographical location. Sometimes these factors play a major role in shaping the way others treat us, in determining how much we are paid, what kinds of educational opportunities are available to us, and where and how we live. In other contexts, these variables will be less significant, perhaps even irrelevant. Reading about them adds another dimension to our understanding of the complex set of factors that interacts with issues of race, class, gender, and sexuality. Joan L. Griscom (Selection 10) examines the ways that ableism, heterosexism, and sexism shape how the law recognizes relationships and the challenges that emerge in medical crises involving caregiving and decision-making. Eric Rodriguez (Selection 11), Kiese Laymon (Selection 12), and Chase Strangio (Selection 13) each offer a reflective narrative that shows us how the intersections of race, class, gender, and sexuality are not static and can produce contradictions when oppression and privilege are simultaneously embodied.

But even as we acknowledge how much there is to learn from looking at the lives and experiences of many different people, there is also a danger in this project: the danger of overgeneralizing. It is easy to take the particular experience or the particular beliefs of one member of a group and attribute them to all members of that group. Many students who are members of a religious, racial, or ethnic minority have had the uncomfortable experience of being asked to speak for all members of that group at some point in their college experience. On the other hand, for the purposes of studying issues of race, class, gender, and sexuality, it is often necessary to look beyond individual differences and generalize about "Chicanas," "gays," or "men" in order to highlight aspects of their experience that are more typical of that group than of others. As we have already seen, it would be naïve to think that the individual exists in a vacuum, untouched by the racism, sexism, heterosexism, and class bias in society. Unless we understand something about the ways different groups experience life in the United States, we will never adequately understand the particular experiences of individual people.

This part ends with Edwidge Danticat (Selection 14) reminding us to make even wider connections as she discusses the racial violence that occurred in June 2015 at a church in Charleston, South Carolina, and the racist policies implemented against Haitians in the Dominican Republic. Danticat says, ". . . we are witnessing, once again, a sea of black bodies in motion, in transit, and in danger. . . . And we will keep asking ourselves, When will this end? When will it stop?"

The essays in this part have been selected because they give us a sense of the diversity of life experience in the United States at the same time that they reflect some of the consequences of the inequalities documented in Part V. For the most part, these articles and essays need no introduction. They speak for themselves.

1 Civilize Them with a Stick

Mary Brave Bird (Crow Dog)
with Richard Erdoes

Gathered from the cabin, the wickiup, and the tepee,
partly by cajolery and partly by threats,
partly by bribery and partly by force,
they are induced to leave their kindred
to enter these schools and take upon themselves
the outward appearance of civilized life.
—ANNUAL REPORT OF THE DEPARTMENT OF INTERIOR, 1901

It is almost impossible to explain to a sympathetic white person what a typical old Indian boarding school was like; how it affected the Indian child suddenly dumped into it like a small creature from another world, helpless, defenseless, bewildered, trying desperately and instinctively to survive and sometimes not surviving at all. I think such children were like the victims of Nazi concentration camps trying to tell average, middle-class Americans what their experience had been like. Even now, when these schools are much improved, when the buildings are new, all gleaming steel and glass, the food tolerable, the teachers well trained and well-intentioned, even trained in child psychology—unfortunately the psychology of white children, which is different from ours—the shock to the child upon arrival is still tremendous. Some just seem to shrivel up, don't speak for days on end, and have an empty look in their eyes. I know of an eleven-year-old on another reservation who hanged herself, and in our school, while I was there, a girl jumped out of the window, trying to kill herself to escape an unbearable situation. That first shock is always there.

Although the old tiyospaye has been destroyed, in the traditional Sioux families, especially in those where there is no drinking, the child is never left alone. It is always surrounded by relatives, carried around, enveloped in warmth. It is treated with the respect due to any human being, even a small one. It is seldom forced to do anything against its will, seldom screamed at, and never beaten. That much, at least, is left of the old family group among full-bloods. And then suddenly a bus or car arrives, full of strangers, usually white strangers, who yank the child out of the arms of those who love it, taking it screaming to the boarding school. The only word I can think of for what is done to these children is kidnapping.

Even now, in a good school, there is impersonality instead of close human contact; a sterile, cold atmosphere, an unfamiliar routine, language problems, and above all the mazaskan-skin, that damn clock—white man's time as opposed to

Excerpts from *Lakota Woman*, copyright © 1990 by Mary Crow Dog and Richard Erdoes. Used by permission of Grove/Atlantic, Inc. Any third party use of this material outside of this publication is prohibited.

Indian time, which is natural time. Like eating when you are hungry and sleeping when you are tired, not when that damn clock says you must. But I was not taken to one of the better, modern schools. I was taken to the old-fashioned mission school at St. Francis, run by the nuns and Catholic fathers, built sometime around the turn of the century and not improved a bit when I arrived, not improved as far as the buildings, the food, the teachers, or their methods were concerned.

In the old days, nature was our people's only school and they needed no other. Girls had their toy tipis and dolls, boys their toy bows and arrows. Both rode and swam and played the rough Indian games together. Kids watched their peers and elders and naturally grew from children into adults. Life in the tipi circle was harmonious—until the whiskey peddlers arrived with their wagons and barrels of "Injun whiskey." I often wished I could have grown up in the old, before-whiskey days.

Oddly enough, we owed our unspeakable boarding schools to the do-gooders, the white Indian-lovers. The schools were intended as an alternative to the outright extermination seriously advocated by Generals Sherman and Sheridan, as well as by most settlers and prospectors overrunning our land. "You don't have to kill those poor benighted heathen," the do-gooders said, "in order to solve the Indian Problem. Just give us a chance to turn them into useful farmhands, laborers, and chambermaids who will break their backs for you at low wages." In that way the boarding schools were born. The kids were taken away from their villages and pueblos, in their blankets and moccasins, kept completely isolated from their families—sometimes for as long as ten years—suddenly coming back, their short hair slick with pomade, their necks raw from stiff, high collars, their thick jackets always short in the sleeves and pinching under the arms, their tight patent leather shoes giving them corns, the girls in starched white blouses and clumsy, high-buttoned boots—caricatures of white people. When they found out—and they found out quickly—that they were neither wanted by whites nor by Indians, they got good and drunk, many of them staying drunk for the rest of their lives. I still have a poster I found among my grandfather's stuff, given to him by the missionaries to tack up on his wall. It reads:

1. Let Jesus save you.
2. Come out of your blanket, cut your hair, and dress like a white man.
3. Have a Christian family with one wife for life only.
4. Live in a house like your white brother. Work hard and wash often.
5. Learn the value of a hard-earned dollar. Do not waste your money on give-aways. Be punctual.
6. Believe that property and wealth are signs of divine approval.
7. Keep away from saloons and strong spirits.
8. Speak the language of your white brother. Send your children to school to do likewise.
9. Go to church often and regularly.
10. Do not go to Indian dances or to the medicine man.

The people who were stuck upon "solving the Indian Problem" by making us into whites retreated from this position only step by step in the wake of Indian protests.

The mission school at St. Francis was a curse for our family for generations. My grandmother went there, then my mother, then my sisters and I. At one time or other every one of us tried to run away. Grandma told me once about the bad times she had experienced at St. Francis. In those days they let students go home only for one week every year. Two days were used up for transportation, which meant spending just five days out of three hundred and sixty-five with her family. And that was an improvement. Before grandma's time, on many reservations they did not let the students go home at all until they had finished school. Anybody who disobeyed the nuns was severely punished. The building in which my grandmother stayed had three floors, for girls only. Way up in the attic were little cells, about five by five by ten feet. One time she was in church and instead of praying she was playing jacks. As punishment they took her to one of those little cubicles where she stayed in darkness because the windows had been boarded up. They left her there for a whole week with only bread and water for nourishment. After she came out she promptly ran away, together with three other girls. They were found and brought back. The nuns stripped them naked and whipped them. They used a horse buggy whip on my grandmother. Then she was put back into the attic—for two weeks.

My mother had much the same experiences but never wanted to talk about them, and then there I was, in the same place. The school is now run by the BIA—the Bureau of Indian Affairs—but only since about fifteen years ago. When I was there, during the 1960s, it was still run by the Church. The Jesuit fathers ran the boys' wing and the Sisters of the Sacred Heart ran us—with the help of the strap. Nothing had changed since my grandmother's days. I have been told recently that even in the '70s they were still beating children at that school. All I got out of school was being taught how to pray. I learned quickly that I would be beaten if I failed in my devotions or, God forbid, prayed the wrong way, especially prayed in Indian to Wakan Tanka, the Indian Creator.

The girls' wing was built like an F and was run like a penal institution. Every morning at five o'clock the sisters would come into our large dormitory to wake us up, and immediately we had to kneel down at the sides of our beds and recite the prayers. At six o'clock we were herded into the church for more of the same. I did not take kindly to the discipline and to marching by the clock, left-right, left-right. I was never one to like being forced to do something. I do something because I feel like doing it. I felt this way always, as far as I can remember, and my sister Barbara felt the same way. An old medicine man once told me: "Us Lakotas are not like dogs who can be trained, who can be beaten and keep on wagging their tails, licking the hand that whipped them. We are like cats, little cats, big cats, wildcats, bobcats, mountain lions. It doesn't matter what kind, but cats who can't be tamed, who scratch if you step on their tails." But I was only a kitten and my claws were still small.

Barbara was still in the school when I arrived and during my first year or two she could still protect me a little bit. When Barb was a seventh-grader she ran away together with five other girls, early in the morning before sunrise. They brought them back in the evening. The girls had to wait for two hours in front of the mother superior's office. They were hungry and cold, frozen through. It was wintertime and they had been running the whole day without food, trying to make good their escape. The mother superior asked each girl, "Would you do this again?" She told them that as punishment they would not be allowed to visit home for a month and that she'd keep them busy on work details until the skin on their knees and elbows had worn off. At the end of her speech she told each girl, "Get up from this chair and lean over it." She then lifted the girls' skirts and pulled down their underpants. Not little girls either, but teenagers. She had a leather strap about a foot long and four inches wide fastened to a stick, and beat the girls, one after another, until they cried. Barb did not give her that satisfaction but just clenched her teeth. There was one girl, Barb told me, the nun kept on beating and beating until her arm got tired.

I did not escape my share of the strap. Once, when I was thirteen years old, I refused to go to Mass. I did not want to go to church because I did not feel well. A nun grabbed me by the hair, dragged me upstairs, made me stoop over, pulled my dress up (we were not allowed at the time to wear jeans), pulled my panties down, and gave me what they called "swats"—twenty-five swats with a board around which Scotch tape had been wound. She hurt me badly.

My classroom was right next to the principal's office and almost every day I could hear him swatting the boys. Beating was the common punishment for not doing one's homework, or for being late to school. It had such a bad effect upon me that I hated and mistrusted every white person on sight, because I met only one kind. It was not until much later that I met sincere white people I could relate to and be friends with. Racism breeds racism in reverse.

2 Then Came the War

Yuri Kochiyama

I was red, white, and blue when I was growing up. I taught Sunday school, and was very, very American. But I was also very provincial. We were just kids rooting for our high school.

My father owned a fish market. Terminal Island was nearby, and that was where many Japanese families lived. It was a fishing town. My family lived in the city proper. San Pedro was very mixed, predominantly white, but there were blacks also.

I was nineteen at the time of the evacuation. I had just finished junior college. I was looking for a job, and didn't realize how different the school world was from the work world. In the school world, I never felt racism. But when you got into the work world, it was very difficult. This was 1941, just before the war. I finally did get a job at a department store. But for us back then, it was a big thing, because I don't think they had ever hired an Asian in a department store before. I tried, because I saw a Mexican friend who got a job there. Even then they didn't hire me on a regular basis, just on Saturdays, summer vacation, Easter vacation, and Christmas vacation. Other than that, I was working like the others—at a vegetable stand, or doing part-time domestic work. Back then, I only knew of two Japanese American girl friends who got jobs as secretaries—but these were in Japanese companies. But generally you almost never saw a Japanese American working in a white place. It was hard for Asians. Even for Japanese, the best jobs they felt they could get were in Chinatowns, such as in Los Angeles. Most Japanese were either in some aspect of fishing, such as in the canneries, or went right from school to work on the farms. That was what it was like in the town of San Pedro. I loved working in the department store, because it was a small town, and you got to know and see everyone. The town itself was wonderful. People were very friendly. I didn't see my job as work—it was like a community job.

Everything changed for me on the day Pearl Harbor was bombed. On that very day—December 7—the FBI came and they took my father. He had just come home from the hospital the day before. For several days we didn't know where they had taken him. Then we found out that he was taken to the federal prison at Terminal Island. Overnight, things changed for us. They took all men who lived near the Pacific waters, and had nothing to do with fishing. A month later, they took every fisherman from Terminal Island, sixteen and over, to places—not the regular concentration camps—but to detention centers in places like South Dakota, Montana, and New Mexico. They said that all Japanese who had given money

From *Asian American Experiences in the United States: Oral Histories of First to Fourth Generation Americans from China, the Philippines, Japan, India, the Pacific Islands, Vietnam and Cambodia.* Copyright © 1991 by Joann Faung Jean Lee. McFarland & Company, Inc., Box 611, Jefferson, NC 28640. www.mcfarlandpub.com. Reprinted by permission of the author.

to any kind of Japanese organization would have to be taken away. At that time, many people were giving to the Japanese Red Cross. The first group was thirteen hundred Isseis—my parents' generation. They took those who were leaders of the community, or Japanese school teachers, or were teaching martial arts, or who were Buddhist priests. Those categories which would make them very "Japanesey," were picked up. This really made a tremendous impact on our lives. My twin brother was going to the University at Berkeley. He came rushing back. All of our classmates were joining up, so he volunteered to go into the service. And it seemed strange that here they had my father in prison, and there the draft board okayed my brother. He went right into the army. My other brother, who was two years older, was trying to run my father's fish market. But business was already going down, so he had to close it. He had finished college at the University of California a couple of years before.

They took my father on December 7th. The day before, he had just come home from the hospital. He had surgery for an ulcer. We only saw him once, on December 13. On December 20th they said he could come home. By the time they brought him back, he couldn't talk. He made guttural sounds and we didn't know if he could hear. He was home for twelve hours. He was dying. The next morning, when we got up, they told us that he was gone. He was very sick. And I think the interrogation was very rough. My mother kept begging the authorities to let him go to the hospital until he was well, then put him back in the prison. They did finally put him there, a week or so later. But they put him in a hospital where they were bringing back all these American Merchant Marines who were hit on Wake Island. So he was the only Japanese in that hospital, so they hung a sheet around him that said, Prisoner of War. The feeling where he was was very bad.

You could see the hysteria of war. There was a sense that war could actually come to American shores. Everybody was yelling to get the "Japs" out of California. In Congress, people were speaking out. Organizations such as the Sons and Daughters of the Golden West were screaming "Get the 'Japs' out." So were the real estate people, who wanted to get the land from the Japanese farmers. The war had whipped up such a hysteria that if there was anyone for the Japanese, you didn't hear about it. I'm sure they were afraid to speak out, because they would be considered not only just "Jap" lovers, but unpatriotic.

Just the fact that my father was taken made us suspect to people. But on the whole, the neighbors were quite nice, especially the ones adjacent to us. There was already a six AM to six PM curfew and a five mile limit on where we could go from our homes. So they offered to do our shopping for us, if we needed.

Most Japanese Americans had to give up their jobs, whatever they did, and were told they had to leave. The edict for 9066—President Roosevelt's edict* for evacuation—was in February 1942. We were moved to a detention center that April. By then the Japanese on Terminal Island were just helter skelter, looking

---

*Executive Order No. 9066 does not mention detention of Japanese specifically, but was used exclusively against the Japanese. Over 120,000 Japanese were evacuated from the West Coast.

for anywhere they could go. They opened up the Japanese school and Buddhist churches, and families just crowded in. Even farmers brought along their chickens and chicken coops. They just opened up the places for people to stay until they could figure out what to do. Some people left for Colorado and Utah. Those who had relatives could do so. The idea was to evacuate all the Japanese from the coast. But all the money was frozen, so even if you knew where you wanted to go, it wasn't that simple. By then, people knew they would be going into camps, so they were selling what they could, even though they got next to nothing for it.

We were fortunate, in that our neighbors, who were white, were kind enough to look after our house, and they said they would find people to rent it, and look after it till we got back. But these neighbors were very, very unusual.

We were sent to an assembly center in Arcadia, California, in April. It was the largest assembly center on the West Coast, having nearly twenty thousand people. There were some smaller centers with about six hundred people. All along the West Coast—Washington, Oregon, California—there were many, many assembly centers, but ours was the largest. Most of the assembly centers were either fairgrounds, or race tracks. So many of us lived in stables, and they said you could take what you could carry. We were there until October.

Even though we stayed in a horse stable, everything was well organized. Every unit would hold four to six people. So in some cases, families had to split up, or join others. We slept on army cots, and for mattresses they gave us muslin bags, and told us to fill them with straw. And for chairs, everybody scrounged around for carton boxes, because they could serve as chairs. You could put two together and it could be a little table. So it was just makeshift. But I was amazed how, in a few months, some of those units really looked nice. Japanese women fixed them up. Some people had the foresight to bring material and needles and thread. But they didn't let us bring anything that could be used as weapons. They let us have spoons, but no knives. For those who had small children or babies, it was rough. They said you could take what you could carry. Well, they could only take their babies in their arms, and maybe the little children could carry something, but it was pretty limited.

I was so red, white, and blue, I couldn't believe this was happening to us. America would never do a thing like this to us. This is the greatest country in the world. So I thought this is only going to be for a short while, maybe a few weeks or something, and they will let us go back. At the beginning no one realized how long this would go on. I didn't feel the anger that much because I thought maybe this was the way we could show our love for our country, and we should not make too much fuss or noise, we should abide by what they asked of us. I'm a totally different person now than I was back then. I was naïve about so many things. The more I think about it, the more I realize how little you learn about American history. It's just what they want you to know.

At the beginning, we didn't have any idea how temporary or permanent the situation was. We thought we would be able to leave shortly. But after several months they told us this was just temporary quarters, and they were building more permanent quarters elsewhere in the United States. All this was so unbelievable. A year before we would never have thought anything like this could have happened to us—not in this country. As time went by, the sense of frustration grew. Many families were already divided. The fathers, the heads of the households, were taken to other camps. In the beginning, there was no way for the sons to get in touch with their families. Before our group left for the detention camp, we were saying goodbye almost every day to other groups who were going to places like Arizona and Utah. Here we finally had made so many new friends—people who we met, lived with, shared the time, and got to know. So it was even sad on that note and the goodbyes were difficult. Here we had gotten close to these people, and now we had to separate again. I don't think we even thought about where they were going to take us, or how long we would have to stay there. When we got on the trains to leave for the camps, we didn't know where we were going. None of the groups knew. It was later on that we learned so and so ended up in Arizona, or Colorado, or some other place. We were all at these assembly centers for about seven months. Once they started pushing people out, it was done very quickly. By October, our group headed out for Jerome, Arkansas, which is on the Texarkana corner.

We were on the train for five days. The blinds were down, so we couldn't look out, and other people couldn't look in to see who was in the train. We stopped in Nebraska, and everybody pulled the blinds to see what Nebraska looked like. The interesting thing was, there was a troop train stopped at the station too. These American soldiers looked out, and saw all these Asians, and they wondered what we were doing on the train. So the Japanese raised the windows, and so did the soldiers. It wasn't a bad feeling at all. There was none of that "you Japs" kind of thing. The women were about the same age as the soldiers—eighteen to twenty-five, and we had the same thing on our minds. In camps, there wasn't much to do, so the fun thing was to receive letters, so on our train, all the girls who were my age, were yelling to the guys, "Hey, give us your address where you're going, we'll write you." And they said, "Are you sure you're going to write?" We exchanged addresses and for a long time I wrote to some of those soldiers. On the other side of the train, I'll never forget there was this old guy, about sixty, who came to our window and said, "We have some Japanese living here. This is Omaha, Nebraska." This guy was very nice, and didn't seem to have any ill feelings for Japanese. He had calling cards, and he said "Will any of you people write to me?" We said, "Sure," so he threw in a bunch of calling cards, and I got one, and I wrote to him for years. I wrote to him about what camp was like, because he said, "Let me know what it's like wherever you end up." And he wrote back, and told me what was happening in Omaha, Nebraska. There were many, many interesting experiences too. Our mail was generally not censored, but all the mail from the soldiers was. Letters meant everything.

When we got to Jerome, Arkansas, we were shocked because we had never seen an area like it. There was forest all around us. And they told us to wait till the rains hit. This would not only turn into mud, but Arkansas swamp lands. That's where they put us—in swamp lands, surrounded by forests. It was nothing like California.

I'm speaking as a person of twenty who had good health. Up until then, I had lived a fairly comfortable life. But there were many others who didn't see the whole experience the same way. Especially those who were older and in poor health and had experienced racism. One more thing like this could break them. I was at an age where transitions were not hard—the point where anything new could even be considered exciting. But for people in poor health, it was hell.

There were army-type barracks, with two hundred to two hundred and five people to each block and every block had its own mess hall, facility for washing clothes, showering. It was all surrounded by barbed wire, and armed soldiers. I think they said only seven people were killed in total, though thirty were shot, because they went too close to the fence. Where we were, nobody thought of escaping because you'd be more scared of the swamps—the poisonous snakes, the bayous. Climatic conditions were very harsh. Although Arkansas is in the South, the winters were very, very cold. We had a pot bellied stove in every room and we burned wood. Everything was very organized. We got there in October, and were warned to prepare ourselves. So on our block, for instance, males eighteen and over could go out in the forest to chop down trees for wood for the winter. The men would bring back the trees, and the women sawed the trees. Everybody worked. The children would pile up the wood for each unit.

They told us when it rained, it would be very wet, so we would have to build our own drainage system. One of the barracks was to hold meetings, so block heads would call meetings. There was a block council to represent the people from different areas.

When we first arrived, there were some things that weren't completely fixed. For instance, the roofers would come by, and everyone would hunger for information from the outside world. We wanted to know what was happening with the war. We weren't allowed to bring radios; that was contraband. And there were no televisions then. So we would ask the workers to bring us back some papers, and they would give us papers from Texas or Arkansas, so for the first time we would find out about news from the outside.

Just before we went in to the camps, we saw that being a Japanese wasn't such a good thing, because everybody was turning against the Japanese, thinking we were saboteurs, or linking us with Pearl Harbor. But when I saw the kind of work they did at camp, I felt so proud of the Japanese, and proud to be Japanese, and wondered why I was so white, white when I was outside, because I was always with white folks. Many people had brothers or sons who were in the military and Japanese American servicemen would come into the camp to visit the families, and we felt so proud of them when they came in their uniforms. We knew that it would only be a matter of time before they would be shipped overseas. Also what made us feel proud was the forming of the 442 unit.*

---

*American soldiers of Japanese ancestry were assembled in two units: the 442 Regimental Combat Team and the 100th Infantry Battalion. The two groups were sent to battle in Europe. The 100th Battalion had over 900 casualties and was known as the Purple Heart Battalion. Combined, the units received 9,486 purple hearts and 18,143 individual decorations.

I was one of these real American patriots then. I've changed now. But back then, I was all American. Growing up, my mother would say we're Japanese. But I'd say, "No, I'm American." I think a lot of Japanese grew up that way. People would say to them, "You're Japanese," and they would say, "No, we're Americans." I don't even think they used the hyphenated term "Japanese-American" back then. At the time, I was ashamed of being Japanese. I think many Japanese Americans felt the same way. Pearl Harbor was a shameful act, and being Japanese Americans, even though we had nothing to do with it, we still somehow felt we were blamed for it. I hated Japan at that point. So I saw myself at that part of my history as an American, and not as a Japanese or Japanese American. That sort of changed while I was in the camp.

I hated the war, because it wasn't just between the governments. It went down to the people, and it nurtured hate. What was happening during the war were many things I didn't like. I hoped that one day when the war was over there could be a way that people could come together in their relationships.

Now I can relate to Japan in a more mature way, where I see its faults and its very, very negative history. But I also see its potential. Scientifically and technologically it has really gone far. But I'm disappointed that when it comes to human rights she hasn't grown. The Japan of today—I feel there are still things lacking. For instance, I don't think the students have the opportunity to have more leeway in developing their lives.

We always called the camps "relocation centers" while we were there. Now we feel it is apropos to call them concentration camps. It is not the same as the concentration camps of Europe; those we feel were death camps. Concentration camps were a concentration of people placed in an area, and disempowered and disenfranchised. So it is apropos to call what I was in a concentration camp. After two years in the camp, I was released.

Going home wasn't much of a problem for us because our neighbors had looked after our place. But for most of our Japanese friends, starting over again was very difficult after the war.

I returned in October of 1945. It was very hard to find work, at least for me. I wasn't expecting to find anything good, just something to tide me over until my boyfriend came back from New York. The only thing I was looking for was to work in a restaurant as a waitress. But I couldn't find anything. I would walk from one end of the town to the other, and down every main avenue. But as soon as they found out I was Japanese, they would say no. Or they would ask me if I was in the union, and of course I couldn't be in the union because I had just gotten there. Anyway, no Japanese could be in the union, so if the answer was no I'm not in the union, they would say no. So finally what I did was go into the rough area of San Pedro—there's a strip near the wharf—and I went down there. I was determined to keep the jobs as long as I could. But for a while, I could last maybe two hours, and somebody would say "Is that a 'Jap'?" And as soon as someone would ask that, the boss would say, "Sorry, you gotta go. We don't want trouble here." The strip wasn't that big, so after I'd go the whole length of it, I'd have to keep coming back to the same restaurants, and say, "Gee, will you give me another chance?" I figure, all these servicemen were coming back and the restaurants didn't have enough waitresses to come in and take these jobs. And so, they'd say "Okay. But soon as somebody asks who you are, or if you're a 'Jap,' or any problem about being a 'Jap,' you go." So I said, "Okay, sure. How about keeping me until that happens?" So sometimes I'd last a night, sometimes a couple of nights that no one would say anything. Sometimes people threw cups at me or hot coffee. At first they didn't know what I was. They thought I was Chinese. Then someone would say, "I bet she's a 'Jap'." And I wasn't going to say I wasn't. So as soon as I said "Yeah," then it was like an uproar. Rather than have them say, "Get out," I just walked out. I mean, there was no point in fighting it. If you just walked out, there was less chance of getting hurt. But one place I lasted two weeks. These owners didn't want to have to let me go. But they didn't want to have problems with the people.

And so I did this until I left for New York, which was about three months later. I would work the dinner shift, from six at night to three in the morning. When you are young you tend not to take things as strongly. Everything is like an adventure. Looking back, I felt the people who were the kindest to me were those who went out and fought, those who just got back from Japan or the Far East. I think the worst ones were the ones who stayed here and worked in defense plants, who felt they had to be so patriotic. On the West Coast, there wasn't hysteria anymore, but there were hostile feelings towards the Japanese, because they were coming back. It took a while, but my mother said that things were getting back to normal, and that the Japanese were slowly being accepted again. At the time, I didn't go through the bitterness that many others went through, because it's not just what they went through, but it is also what they experienced before that. I mean, I happened to have a much more comfortable life before, so you sort of see things in a different light. You see that there are all kinds of Americans, and that they're not all people who hate Japs. You know too that it was hysteria that had a lot to do with it.

All Japanese, before they left camp, were told not to congregate among Japanese, and not to speak Japanese. They were told by the authorities. There was even a piece of paper that gave you instructions. But then people went on to places like Chicago where there were churches, so they did congregate in churches. But they did ask people not to. I think psychologically the Japanese, having gone through a period where they were so hated by everyone, didn't even want to admit they were Japanese, or accept the fact that they were Japanese. Of course, they would say they were Japanese Americans. But I think the psychological damage of the wartime period, and of racism itself, has left its mark. There is a stigma to being Japanese. I think that is why such a large number of Japanese, in particular Japanese American women, have married out of the race. On the West Coast I've heard people say that sixty to seventy percent of the Japanese women have married, I guess, mostly whites. Japanese men are doing it too, but not to that degree. I guess Japanese Americans just didn't want to have that Japanese identity, or that Japanese part. There is definitely some self-hate, and part of that has to do with the racism that's so deeply a part of this society.

Historically, Americans have always been putting people behind walls. First there were the American Indians who were put on reservations, Africans in slavery, their lives on the plantations, Chicanos doing migratory work, and the kinds of camps they lived in, and even, too, the Chinese when they worked on the railroad camps where they were almost isolated, dispossessed people—disempowered. And I feel those are the things we should fight against so they won't happen again. It wasn't so long ago—in 1979—that the feeling against the Iranians was so strong because of the takeover of the U.S. embassy in Iran, where they wanted to deport Iranian students. And that is when a group called Concerned Japanese Americans organized, and that was the first issue we took up, and then we connected it with what the Japanese had gone through. This whole period of what the Japanese went through is important. If we can see the connections of how often this happens in history, we can stem the tide of these things happening again by speaking out against them.

Most Japanese Americans who worked years and years for redress never thought it would happen the way it did. The papers have been signed, we will be given reparation, and there was an apology from the government. I think the redress movement itself was very good because it was a learning experience for the Japanese people; we could get out into our communities and speak about what happened to us and link it with experiences of other people. In that sense, though, it wasn't done as much as it should have been. Some Japanese Americans didn't even learn that part. They just started the movement as a reaction to the bad experience they had. They don't even see other ethnic groups who have gone through it. It showed us, too, how vulnerable everybody is. It showed us that even though there is a Constitution, that constitutional rights could be taken away very easily.

3 Crossing the Border Without Losing Your Past

Oscar Casares

SAN MIGUEL DE ALLENDE, Mexico   Along with it being diez y seis de septiembre, Mexican Independence Day, today is my father's 89th birthday. Everardo Issasi Casares was born in 1914, a little more than a hundred years after Miguel Hidalgo y Costilla rang the church bells of Dolores, summoning his parishioners to rise up against the Spaniards.

This connection has always been important in my family. Though my father was born in the United States, he considers himself a Mexicano. To him, ancestry is what determines your identity. If you have Mexican blood, you are Mexican, whether you were born in Mexico City or New York City. This is not to say he denies his American citizenship—he votes, pays taxes and served in the Army. But his identity is tied to the past. His family came from Mexico, so like them he is Mexicano, punto, end of discussion.

In my hometown, Brownsville, Tex., almost everyone I know is Mexicano: neighbors, teachers, principals, dropouts, doctors, lawyers, drug dealers, priests. Rich and poor, short and tall, fat and skinny, dark- and light-skinned. Every year our Mexican heritage is celebrated in a four-day festival called Charro Days. Men grow beards; mothers draw moustaches on their little boys and dress their little girls like Mexican peasants; the brave compete in a jalapeño-eating contest. But the celebration also commemorates the connection between two neighboring countries, opening with an exchange of gritos (traditional cowboy calls you might hear in a Mexican movie) between a representative from Matamoros, Mexico, standing on one side of the International Bridge and a Brownsville representative standing on the other.

Like many Americans whose families came to this country from somewhere else, many children of Mexican immigrants struggle with their identity, as our push to fully assimilate is met with an even greater pull to remain anchored to our family's country of origin. This is especially true when that country is less than a quarter of a mile away—the width of the Rio Grande—from the new one. We learn both cultures as effortlessly as we do two languages. We learn quickly that we can exist simultaneously in both worlds, and that our home exists neither here nor there but in the migration between these two forces.

But for Mexican-Americans and other immigrants from Spanish-speaking countries who have been lumped into categories like Latino or Hispanic, this struggle has become even more pronounced over the last few years as we have grown into the largest minority group in the United States. Our culture has been both embraced and exploited by advertisers, politicians and the media. And as we move, individually,

As appeared in *The New York Times*, September 16, 2003. Reprinted by permission of 3 Arts Entertainment on behalf of Oscar Casares.

from our small communities, where our identity is clear, we enter a world that wants to assign us a label of its choosing.

When I left Brownsville in 1985 to start at the University of Texas at Austin one of the first things I was asked was, "What are you?" "I'm Mexican," I told the guy, who was thrown off by my height and light skin. "Really, what part of Mexico are you from?" he asked, which led me to explain I was really from Brownsville, but my parents were Mexican. "Really, what part of Mexico?" Here again I had to admit they weren't really born in Mexico and neither were my grandparents or great-grandparents. "Oh," he said, "you're Mexican-American, is what you are."

Mexican-American. I imagined a 300-mile-long hyphen that connected Brownsville to Austin, a bridge between my old and new world. Not that I hadn't seen this word combination, Mexican-American, on school applications, but I couldn't remember the words being spoken to me directly. In Brownsville, I always thought of myself as being equally Mexican and American.

When I graduated that label was again redefined. One of my first job interviews was at an advertising agency, where I was taken on a tour: the media department, the creative department, the account-service department, the Hispanic department. This last department specialized in marketing products to Spanish-speaking consumers. In the group were men and women from Mexico, Puerto Rico and California, but together they were Hispanic. I was hired to work in another department, but suddenly, everyone was referring to me as Hispanic.

Hispanic? Where was the Mexican in me? Where was the hyphen? I didn't want to be Hispanic. The word reminded me of those Mexican-Americans who preferred to say their families came from Spain, which they felt somehow increased their social status. Just hearing the word Hispanic reminded me, too, of people who used the word Spanish to refer to Mexicans. "The Spanish like to get wild at their fiestas," they would say, or "You Spanish people sure do have a lot of babies."

In this same way, the word Hispanic seemed to want to be more user friendly, especially when someone didn't want to say the M word: Mexican. Except it did slip out occasionally. I remember standing in my supervisor's office as he described calling the police after he saw a car full of "Mexicans" drive through his suburban neighborhood.

Away from the border, the word Mexican had come to mean dirty, shiftless, drunken, lustful, criminal. I still cringe whenever I think someone might say the word. But usually it happens unexpectedly, as though the person has pulled a knife on me. I feel the sharp words up against my gut. Because of my appearance, people often say things in front of me they wouldn't say if they knew my real ethnicity—not Hispanic, Latino or even Mexican-American. I am, like my father, Mexican, and on this day of independence, I say this with particular pride.

4 Between the World and Me
Ta-Nehisi Coates

Son,

Last Sunday the host of a popular news show asked me what it meant to lose my body. The host was broadcasting from Washington, D.C., and I was seated in a remote studio on the far west side of Manhattan. A satellite closed the miles between us, but no machinery could close the gap between her world and the world for which I had been summoned to speak. When the host asked me about my body, her face faded from the screen, and was replaced by a scroll of words, written by me earlier that week.

The host read these words for the audience, and when she finished she turned to the subject of my body, although she did not mention it specifically. But by now I am accustomed to intelligent people asking about the condition of my body without realizing the nature of their request. Specifically, the host wished to know why I felt that white America's progress, or rather the progress of those Americans who believe that they are white, was built on looting and violence. Hearing this, I felt an old and indistinct sadness well up in me. The answer to this question is the record of the believers themselves. The answer is American history.

There is nothing extreme in this statement. Americans deify democracy in a way that allows for a dim awareness that they have, from time to time, stood in defiance of their God. But democracy is a forgiving God and America's heresies—torture, theft, enslavement—are so common among individuals and nations that none can declare themselves immune. In fact, Americans, in a real sense, have never betrayed their God. When Abraham Lincoln declared, in 1863, that the battle of Gettysburg must ensure "that government of the people, by the people, for the people, shall not perish from the earth," he was not merely being aspirational; at the onset of the Civil War, the United States of America had one of the highest rates of suffrage in the world. The question is not whether Lincoln truly meant "government of the people" but what our country has, throughout its history, taken the political term "people" to actually mean. In 1863 it did not mean your mother or your grandmother, and it did not mean you and me. Thus America's problem is not its betrayal of "government of the people," but the means by which "the people" acquired their names.

This leads us to another equally important ideal, one that Americans implicitly accept but to which they make no conscious claim. Americans believe in the reality of "race" as a defined, indubitable feature of the natural world. Racism—the need to ascribe bone-deep features to people and then humiliate, reduce, and destroy them—inevitably follows from this inalterable condition. In this way, racism is rendered as the innocent daughter of Mother Nature, and one is left to deplore the Middle Passage

Excerpt(s) from *Between the World and Me* by Ta-Nehisi Coates, copyright © 2015 by Ta-Nehisi Coates. Used by permission of Spiegel & Grau, an imprint of Random House, a division of Penguin Random House LLC. All rights reserved. Any third party use of this material, outside of this publication, is prohibited. Interested parties must apply directly to Penguin Random House LLC for permission.

or the Trail of Tears the way one deplores an earthquake, a tornado, or any other phenomenon that can be cast as beyond the handiwork of men.

But race is the child of racism, not the father. And the process of naming "the people" has never been a matter of genealogy and physiognomy so much as one of hierarchy. Difference in hue and hair is old. But the belief in the preeminence of hue and hair, the notion that these factors can correctly organize a society and that they signify deeper attributes, which are indelible—this is the new idea at the heart of these new people who have been brought up hopelessly, tragically, deceitfully, to believe that they are white.

These new people are, like us, a modern invention. But unlike us, their new name has no real meaning divorced from the machinery of criminal power. The new people were something else before they were white—Catholic, Corsican, Welsh, Mennonite, Jewish—and if all our national hopes have any fulfillment, then they will have to be something else again. Perhaps they will truly become American and create a nobler basis for their myths. I cannot call it. As for now, it must be said that the process of washing the disparate tribes white, the elevation of the belief in being white, was not achieved through wine tastings and ice cream socials, but rather through the pillaging of life, liberty, labor, and land; through the flaying of backs; the chaining of limbs; the strangling of dissidents; the destruction of families; the rape of mothers; the sale of children; and various other acts meant, first and foremost, to deny you and me the right to secure and govern our own bodies.

The new people are not original in this. Perhaps there has been, at some point in history, some great power whose elevation was exempt from the violent exploitation of other human bodies. If there has been, I have yet to discover it. But this banality of violence can never excuse America, because America makes no claim to the banal. America believes itself exceptional, the greatest and noblest nation ever to exist, a lone champion standing between the white city of democracy and the terrorists, despots, barbarians, and other enemies of civilization. One cannot, at once, claim to be superhuman and then plead mortal error. I propose to take our countrymen's claims of American exceptionalism seriously, which is to say I propose subjecting our country to an exceptional moral standard. This is difficult because there exists, all around us, an apparatus urging us to accept American innocence at face value and not to inquire too much. And it is so easy to look away, to live with the fruits of our history and to ignore the great evil done in all of our names. But you and I have never truly had that luxury. I think you know.

I write you in your fifteenth year. I am writing you because this was the year you saw Eric Garner choked to death for selling cigarettes; because you know now that Renisha McBride was shot for seeking help, that John Crawford was shot down for browsing in a department store. And you have seen men in uniform drive by and murder Tamir Rice, a twelve-year-old child whom they were oath-bound to protect. And you have seen men in the same uniforms pummel Marlene Pinnock, someone's grandmother, on the side of a road. And you know now, if you did not before, that the police departments of your country have been endowed with the authority to destroy your body. It does not matter if the destruction is the result of an unfortunate overreaction. It does not matter if it originates in a misunderstanding. It does not matter if the destruction springs from a foolish policy. Sell cigarettes without the proper authority and your body can be destroyed. Resent the people trying to entrap your body and it can be destroyed. Turn into a dark stairwell and your body can be destroyed. The destroyers will rarely be held accountable. Mostly they will receive pensions. And destruction is merely the superlative form of a dominion whose prerogatives include friskings, detainings, beatings, and humiliations. All of this is common to black people. And all of this is old for black people. No one is held responsible.

There is nothing uniquely evil in these destroyers or even in this moment. The destroyers are merely men enforcing the whims of our country, correctly interpreting its heritage and legacy. It is hard to face this. But all our phrasing—race relations, racial chasm, racial justice, racial profiling, white privilege, even white supremacy—serves to obscure that racism is a visceral experience, that it dislodges brains, blocks airways, rips muscle, extracts organs, cracks bones, breaks teeth. You must never look away from this. You must always remember that the sociology, the history, the economics, the graphs, the charts, the regressions all land, with great violence, upon the body.

That Sunday, with that host, on that news show, I tried to explain this as best I could within the time allotted. But at the end of the segment, the host flashed a widely shared picture of an eleven-year-old black boy tearfully hugging a white police officer. Then she asked me about "hope." And I knew then that I had failed. And I remembered that I had expected to fail. And I wondered again at the indistinct sadness welling up in me. Why exactly was I sad? I came out of the studio and walked for a while. It was a calm December day. Families, believing themselves white, were out on the streets. Infants, raised to be white, were bundled in strollers. And I was sad for these people, much as I was sad for the host and sad for all the people out there watching and reveling in a specious hope. I realized then why I was sad. When the journalist asked me about my body, it was like she was asking me to awaken her from the most gorgeous dream. I have seen that dream all my life. It is perfect houses with nice lawns. It is Memorial Day cookouts, block associations, and driveways. The Dream is treehouses and the Cub Scouts. The Dream smells like peppermint but tastes like strawberry shortcake. And for so long I have wanted to escape into the Dream, to fold my country over my head like a blanket. But this has never been an option because the Dream rests on our backs, the bedding made from our bodies. And knowing this, knowing that the Dream persists by warring with the known world, I was sad for the host, I was sad for all those families, I was sad for my country, but above all, in that moment, I was sad for you.

That was the week you learned that the killers of Michael Brown would go free. The men who had left his body in the street like some awesome declaration of their inviolable power would never be punished. It was not my expectation that anyone would ever be punished. But you were young and still believed. You stayed up till 11 P.M. that night, waiting for the announcement of an indictment, and when instead it was announced that there was none you said, "I've got to go," and you went into your room, and I heard you crying. I came in five minutes after, and I didn't hug you, and

I didn't comfort you, because I thought it would be wrong to comfort you. I did not tell you that it would be okay, because I have never believed it would be okay. What I told you is what your grandparents tried to tell me: that this is your country, that this is your world, that this is your body, and you must find some way to live within the all of it. I tell you now that the question of how one should live within a black body, within a country lost in the Dream, is the question of my life, and the pursuit of this question, I have found, ultimately answers itself.

This must seem strange to you. We live in a "goal-oriented" era. Our media vocabulary is full of hot takes, big ideas, and grand theories of everything. But some time ago I rejected magic in all its forms. This rejection was a gift from your grandparents, who never tried to console me with ideas of an afterlife and were skeptical of preordained American glory. In accepting both the chaos of history and the fact of my total end, I was freed to truly consider how I wished to live—specifically, how do I live free in this black body? It is a profound question because America understands itself as God's handiwork, but the black body is the clearest evidence that America is the work of men. I have asked the question through my reading and writings, through the music of my youth, through arguments with your grandfather, with your mother, your aunt Janai, your uncle Ben. I have searched for answers in nationalist myth, in classrooms, out on the streets, and on other continents. The question is unanswerable, which is not to say futile. The greatest reward of this constant interrogation, of confrontation with the brutality of my country, is that it has freed me from ghosts and girded me against the sheer terror of disembodiment.

5 "I wouldn't have come if I'd known."

E. Tammy Kim

In 2001, the DREAM (Development, Relief and Education for Alien Minors) Act was introduced as a bipartisan Senate bill. The goal of this legislation was to provide undocumented immigrants who arrived in the U.S. as children a way to obtain permanent legal status. The bill failed to pass the Senate. Since 2001, over twenty variations of this bill have been introduced, but none have been made into law.

In 2012, the Obama administration announced the DACA (Deferred Action for Childhood Arrivals) program. This "quasi-DREAM" program temporarily defers deportation for people who came to the U.S. as children and are currently without legal immigration status. Immigrants granted this status are allowed to apply for work authorization and receive a Social Security number. DACA status can be renewed two years at a time.

Eligibility criteria for DACA include: arrival in the U.S. before age 16; being between the ages of 14 and 21 on June 15, 2012; residence in the U.S. for five years; current (or completed) high school enrollment, current position in the armed services, or honorable discharge; and no felony or other serious convictions. Although over 1.4 million people qualify for DACA, meeting the eligibility criteria does not guarantee deferred action. The Department of Homeland Security makes these decisions on a case-by-case basis.

Unlike the original proposal in the DREAM Act, DACA is a temporary form of relief that cannot create a pathway to legal status as a legal permanent resident or U.S. citizen. As it was made possible through an Executive Order enacted by the President and not through a law passed by Congress, DACA is not protected from changes or elimination by future administrations.

• • •

Today, June 25: an anxious morning for Supreme Court watchers and anyone interested in immigration. The decision was announced, key sections of Arizona's notorious law upheld. I texted my friend, an immigration insider:

U ok? It's not too bad, right?

Her response (she's a pragmatist):

Not at all! And very good from a Fourth Amendment perspective.

The Court hadn't, at least, denied immigrants the right not to be unreasonably searched or seized.

It's been a significant few weeks for immigration policy. Even before Obama announced his DREAM decision last week, I'd known something was in the works. But

E. Tammy Kim, *Open City Magazine,* Asian American Writers' Workshop

I was skeptical until I heard the president's bass[1] amidst the avian sopranos of the White House Rose Garden:

Effective immediately, the Department of Homeland Security is taking steps to lift the shadow of deportation from these young people.

It was surprising and mysterious in equal measure, particularly following the administration's nationwide implementation of Secure Communities.[2] Would this stop-gap DREAM policy be safe? Who could benefit? The details soon came in: *under 16, continuous presence, school attendance, military service, no criminal record, under 30.* Millions ticked off the criteria for themselves, for their loved ones.

A few days later, before a crowd of Latino elected officials, President Obama spoke again of his policy and the America of our dreams: "a place where knowledge and opportunity were available to anybody who was willing to work for it, anybody who was willing to seize it . . . 'Come, you're welcome.' This is who we are."

• • •

Lis has never felt welcome.

But during an interview last week, in the apartment she shares with her parents and siblings, she spoke with cautious optimism about Obama's announcement. She, her brother, and her sister meet the president's criteria. They will apply for this quasi-DREAM. But still she prefers anonymity, just "Lis."

Ten years ago, she came with her mother and siblings to join her father, who had come earlier to find work. In Ecuador, he was an administrator for a shrimp company; by 2001, the economy was in tatters. America seemed a better option, and he and his family ended up on the Lower East Side.

Lis's father now works as a maintenance man at St. Teresa's Church, where Mass is held in English, Spanish, Mandarin, and Cantonese. Of her father's shift from white- to blue-collar, she said, "It's difficult, yes, but he's a very humble man."

By any measure, Lis, 24, is herself a model of humility. Skinny and bespectacled, with a high-pitched voice and long, straight hair, she's a faithful Catholic and community servant. She recently graduated with a B.S. in childhood education and psychology from City College.

For Lis, becoming a teacher is still her American dream. "I hope to get a job and get my license, but I can't right now because of the whole issue—I can't work. That's where the Obama thing comes into play."

Like other undocumented youth, she began to worry in high school. College was on the horizon, but she was ineligible for financial aid or public licenses. "Before going to college, I wanted to be a veterinarian, and I wanted to be an intern at the Central Park Zoo. I couldn't do any of those things because you need ID or a social security number. There are so many things that you're restricted with." Even small things, like getting into buildings or going out with friends. Once, she couldn't get into a movie because she didn't have ID. "And one time," she recalled, "I remember also forgetting my school ID and I was trying to get into school and they wouldn't let me in."

Back in Ecuador, Lis and her family would drive their car to a beach house two hours away. In the United States, by contrast, they've led a hemmed-in existence, unable to rent a car and afraid to leave New York City. "We take vacations, but we stay in the city. We cannot get a car because we cannot get a driver's license. We cannot travel because we don't have a passport."

"This is what I would like to say to all those people who are against undocumented kids: if I would have known that this would have happened to me, I wouldn't have decided to come here. Because who would want to live in a country where you cannot work in your field and you always feel like you're hiding?"

The president's deferred-action policy will make a significant, if temporary difference. Lis will be able to work and obtain a teaching license, but, "I'm still afraid of being deported," she said. "Another president could come and he could say, 'I don't want this policy. I don't think immigrants should be welcomed.' You never know."

"In Spanish, you have a saying, 'You see the face but you don't see the heart.' *Cara vemos, corazones no sabemos.*" This is why, Lis said, she can count on one hand the number of people she's told about her status.

She plans to continue fighting for a complete DREAM Act at the state and federal levels, as well as comprehensive immigration reform. She believes that "the next step should be targeted to adults, the people who have been working here and paying their taxes—because even if you are undocumented you can pay taxes."

"How would you feel if you and your brother and sister get work authorization but your parents are still undocumented?" I asked.

"We have talked to them about that and they are like, 'As long as you guys feel you have a place here, that's okay.' They have already made their life, and they feel like this is kind of their fault."

"The Irish and Italians used to be immigrants, and nobody wanted them to be here, but then they ended up being wanted," Lis added. "So maybe the same thing can happen with the Latinos . . . probably. Hopefully. I hope so."

NOTES

1. "Remarks by the President on Immigration." June 12, 2012. Available at: http://www.whitehouse.gov/the-press-office/2012/06/15/remarks-president-immigration

2. Preston, J. (2012, May 12). "Despite Opposition, Immigration Agency to Expand Fingerprint Program." *New York Times*.

6 This Person Doesn't Sound White

Ziba Kashef

Kofi? Mani? Sule? Bijan?

Choosing a name for my future son has turned out to be much more complicated than I thought when I started searching online for possibilities.

Reza? Omar? Darius? Malcolm?

While I entertained the sound and significance of each potential moniker (Kofi is Twi for "born on Friday"—what if he's born on Tuesday?), I started to wonder about the consequences of giving him an obviously "ethnic" name. It would reflect his multiracial heritage (black, Iranian, Irish, Hungarian) and hopefully contribute to his sense of cultural pride. But the name would also likely be misspelled, mispronounced, and misunderstood in a country that is largely still ignorant and suspicious of otherness.

My own name, Ziba (zee-bah), has mainly evoked expressions of admiration (How unusual!) and curiosity (How do you spell that?). But on occasion, the revelation that it is Persian, as is my father, has been met with awkward silence or stares. A Middle Eastern name is not particularly welcome in the U.S., especially in the current anti-Muslim/Arab/Middle East political environment.

So as I contemplate my son's name, I'm torn between the desire to emphasize his ethnicity and the desire to minimize the potential for profiling and discrimination against him. While racial discrimination has been understood historically as a practice based on an individual's skin color, recent research is showing that it is also often based on a person's name or speech, with the same destructive effects.

What's in a Name?

A name—and the racial group associated with it—can make the difference between getting a job interview and remaining unemployed, according to one recent study. Researchers at the University of Chicago Graduate School of Business and the Massachusetts Institute of Technology sent 5,000 fake resumes in response to a variety of ads in two major newspapers—the *Boston Globe* and the *Chicago Tribune*. Names on the resumes were selected to sound either distinctively Anglo (e.g., Brendan Baker) or African American (e.g., Jamal Jones). The study revealed that the fictitious job seekers with white names were 50 percent more likely to get calls for interviews. Those stats translate into the need for blacks to mail 15 resumes for every 10 resumes sent by whites in order to land one interview. Sadly, this pattern of affirmative action for white job hunters emerged even among federal contractors and firms that advertised themselves as "equal opportunity" employers.

This article was first published in *ColorLines* Magazine (now Colorlines.com), Fall 2003. Reprinted by permission.

Besides changing their names, there appears to be little black applicants can do to level the playing field. As part of the study, researchers created two sets of resumes—high quality and low quality—to reflect the actual pool of job seekers looking for work in fields ranging from sales, administrative support, clerical services, and customer services. But even having a higher quality resume with such credentials as volunteer experience, computer skills, and special honors failed to improve the black applicants' chances of getting their foot in the door. "The payback that an African American applicant gets from building these skills is much lower than the payback a white applicant would get," the University of Chicago's associate professor Marianne Bertrand noted in a summary of the study.

African and African American names aren't the only ones singled out for prejudice, of course, and the job sphere isn't the only realm in which such discrimination gets played out. In the American-Arab Anti-Discrimination Committee's (ADC) "Report on Hate Crimes and Discrimination Against Arab Americans: The Post-September 11 Backlash," the authors noted that among the dozens of instances of discrimination by airlines that occurred between September 2001 and October 2002, "the passenger's name or perceived ethnicity" alone was often sufficient cause for unprovoked removal from a flight. Discrimination often took place whether or not the passenger was actually Arab or Muslim, resulting in many South Asians and others falling victim to the ignorance of the pilot or another passenger. According to the ADC, one Indian Canadian woman was removed from a plane because her last name was mispronounced as "Attah" and therefore perceived as Middle Eastern. Other passengers were prevented from traveling because their names were similar to those on the FBI watch list.

This type of profiling quickly spread with Jim-Crow-like effects. "We've found that persons named Osama are being regularly denied services, whether in restaurants, stores, or other areas," says the ADC's media director Laila Al-Qatami. Another example recorded by the ADC describes how an Indian American couple were handcuffed and interrogated after purchasing Broadway tickets and specifying that their seats be located in the middle of the theater. Their crime? The "foreign name and accent" of the ticket buyer had made the ticket agent suspicious enough to call the police.

While the ADC has documented more than 700 violent incidents and 800 cases of employment discrimination against Arab Americans since 9/11, many more go unreported and unchallenged. "It is hard to easily label what happens as discrimination. For example, if a person is denied housing or not offered a position with a company," notes Al-Qatami, "can this be linked to discrimination or is the candidate not truly qualified? It is a fine line."

Linguistic Profiling

Names aren't the only potential cues to a person's racial identity: speech may also reveal—or conceal—ethnicity. While searching for housing in the predominantly white neighborhood of Palo Alto, California, in the mid-1990s, John Baugh made appointment after appointment over the phone only to be turned away at the landlord's door. "I was told that there was nothing available," says the Stanford University professor of education and linguistics, who happens to be African American. It didn't take long for him to realize that prospective owners were mistaking his phone voice for that of a white person and inviting him to view apartments. When he showed up for the appointments, he was repeatedly told that there had been some misunderstanding.

This personal affront piqued Baugh's professional curiosity. While it's established that landlords have long discriminated against prospective tenants on the basis of skin color, Baugh decided to test whether they did so on the basis of brief telephone conversations. Using three distinct dialects he learned while growing up in Los Angeles—African American Vernacular English, Chicano English and Standard American English—he placed calls in response to ads for apartments in five Northern California neighborhoods. During those calls, he used various pseudonyms, such as Juan Ramirez for the Chicano English dialect. What emerged was clearer proof of bias against the black and Chicano dialects in predominantly white locales. "[The] research demonstrates that voice is a surrogate for race in many instances when people choose to discriminate over the telephone or use the telephone as the means of discrimination," he explains. Two University of Pennsylvania sociologists uncovered similar results in a separate study of rental housing discrimination.

With his evidence, Baugh, who wrote the book *Beyond Ebonics: Linguistic Pride and Racial Prejudice* (Oxford University Press), has been able to help bolster the claims of a dozen housing discrimination victims in court. Baugh and his colleagues at Stanford are also currently investigating linguistic profiling in education and employment. He cites examples of elementary and secondary school students being placed on non-academic reading tracks based on their accents. "The linguistic profiling that is taking place does have direct educational consequences for the child," he adds—consequences that can affect their ability to later compete in the job market.

Double-Edged Discrimination Data

Research that verifies the persistence of prejudice against people of color because of names and speech can have both positive and negative consequences. On the one hand, employers and landlords can be challenged in court, and in the best-case scenarios, they can also become more aware of subconscious discriminatory practices in order to change them. Shanna L. Smith of the National Fair Housing Alliance, which documents reports of housing discrimination nationwide, has gone so far as to encourage companies to offer employees sensitivity training so they can avoid discriminating and resulting lawsuits, according to an article in *Legal Affairs*.

But Baugh acknowledges that the validation of racial identification by voice can also have negative effects. Prejudiced property owners who have gotten wind of his research can simply discriminate more carefully by either making some appointments with people of color when they have no intention of renting to them, or claiming that despite the evidence, they personally can't identify a person's race by the sound of his or her voice. "I had hoped that this research would expose and eliminate the discrimination but it's far more complicated than that," he says. "If the result . . . is that landlords grant appointments and then deny someone housing face to face, that, to me, is not a real improvement." On the other hand, he points to instances in which criminal courts have allowed police officers and witnesses to identify a suspect solely by the sound of his voice—i.e., I heard the voice of a black/Latino man. This has happened in rape cases when the victim could not see her attacker and other cases in which police used wiretaps but did not actually see a suspect. Such testimony has succeeded and has rarely been challenged in criminal cases. "This issue of voice identification has cut both ways against minority speakers," he explains. "It cuts against them as defendants and it cuts against them as plaintiffs."

While blacks have long been the victims of such bias, Latinos, Asians, and Arab Americans—not to mention other vulnerable groups such as the elderly and disabled—are similarly profiled, experts note. Evidence of discrimination and laws to prevent it (such as the Fair Housing Act and Civil Rights Act) have failed to eradicate "talking while black" and other examples of linguistic racism. They remain largely invisible acts of bigotry—bloodless crimes that injure people of color while quietly reinforcing and perpetuating segregation and white supremacy. Perhaps by the time my future son is an adult, some 50 years after legal discrimination officially ended, he will grow up in a society where his ethnic name and heritage is truly accepted and not punished.

7 "You are in the dark, in the car . . ."

Claudia Rankine

/

You are in the dark, in the car, watching the black-tarred street being swallowed by speed; he tells you his dean is making him hire a person of color when there are so many great writers out there.

You think maybe this is an experiment and you are being tested or retroactively insulted or you have done something that communicates this is an okay conversation to be having.

Why do you feel okay saying this to me? You wish the light would turn red or a police siren would go off so you could slam on the brakes, slam into the car ahead of you, be propelled forward so quickly both your faces would suddenly be exposed to the wind.

As usual you drive straight through the moment with the expected backing off of what was previously said. It is not only that confrontation is headache producing; it is also that you have a destination that doesn't include acting like this moment isn't inhabitable, hasn't happened before, and the before isn't part of the now as the night darkens and the time shortens between where we are and where we are going.

/

When you arrive in your driveway and turn off the car, you remain behind the wheel another ten minutes. You fear the night is being locked in and coded on a cellular level and want time to function as a power wash. Sitting there staring at the closed garage door you are reminded that a friend once told you there exists a medical term—John Henryism—for people exposed to stresses stemming from racism. They achieve themselves to death trying to dodge the build up of erasure. Sherman James, the researcher who came up with the term, claimed the physiological costs were high. You hope by sitting in silence you are bucking the trend.

Claudia Rankine, ["You are in the dark, in the car"] from *Citizen: An American Lyric*. Originally published in *Poetry*. Copyright © 2014 by Claudia Rankine. Reprinted with the permission of The Permissions Company, Inc., on behalf of Graywolf Press, www.graywolfpress.org.

/

When the stranger asks, Why do you care? you just stand there staring at him. He has just referred to the boisterous teenagers in Starbucks as niggers. Hey, I am standing right here, you responded, not necessarily expecting him to turn to you.

He is holding the lidded paper cup in one hand and a small paper bag in the other. They are just being kids. Come on, no need to get all KKK on them, you say.

Now there you go, he responds.

The people around you have turned away from their screens. The teenagers are on pause. There I go? you ask, feeling irritation begin to rain down. Yes, and something about hearing yourself repeating this stranger's accusation in a voice usually reserved for your partner makes you smile.

/

A man knocked over her son in the subway. You feel your own body wince. He's okay, but the son of a bitch kept walking. She says she grabbed the stranger's arm and told him to apologize: I told him to look at the boy and apologize. And yes, you want it to stop, you want the black child pushed to the ground to be seen, to be helped to his feet and be brushed off, not brushed off by the person that did not see him, has never seen him, has perhaps never seen anyone who is not a reflection of himself.

The beautiful thing is that a group of men began to stand behind me like a fleet of bodyguards, she says, like newly found uncles and brothers.

/

The new therapist specializes in trauma counseling. You have only ever spoken on the phone. Her house has a side gate that leads to a back entrance she uses for patients. You walk down a path bordered on both sides with deer grass and rosemary to the gate, which turns out to be locked.

At the front door the bell is a small round disc that you press firmly. When the door finally opens, the woman standing there yells, at the top of her lungs, Get away from my house. What are you doing in my yard?

It's as if a wounded Doberman pinscher or a German shepherd has gained the power of speech. And though you back up a few steps, you manage to tell her you have an appointment. You have an appointment? she spits back. Then she pauses. Everything pauses. Oh, she says, followed by, oh, yes, that's right. I am sorry.

I am so sorry, so, so sorry.

/

8 He Defies You Still
The Memoirs of a Sissy
Tommi Avicolli

You're just a faggot
No history faces you this morning
A faggot's dreams are scarlet
Bad blood bled from words that scarred[1]

Scene One

A homeroom in a Catholic high school in South Philadelphia. The boy sits quietly in the first aisle, third desk, reading a book. He does not look up, not even for a moment. He is hoping no one will remember he is sitting there. He wishes he were invisible. The teacher is not yet in the classroom so the other boys are talking and laughing loudly.

Suddenly, a voice from beside him:

"Hey, you're a faggot, ain't you?"

The boy does not answer. He goes on reading his book, or rather pretending he is reading his book. It is impossible to actually read the book now.

"Hey, I'm talking to you!"

The boy still does not look up. He is so scared his heart is thumping madly; it feels like it is leaping out of his chest and into his throat. But he can't look up.

"Faggot, I'm talking to you!"

To look up is to meet the eyes of the tormentor.

Suddenly, a sharpened pencil point is thrust into the boy's arm. He jolts, shaking off the pencil, aware that there is blood seeping from the wound.

"What did you do that for?" he asks timidly.

"Cause I hate faggots," the other boy says, laughing. Some other boys begin to laugh, too. A symphony of laughter. The boy feels as if he's going to cry. But he must not cry. Must not cry. So he holds back the tears and tries to read the book again. He must read the book. Read the book.

When the teacher arrives a few minutes later, the class quiets down. The boy does not tell the teacher what has happened. He spits on the wound to clean it, dabbing it with a tissue until the bleeding stops. For weeks he fears some dreadful infection from the lead in the pencil point.

From *Radical Teacher*. Copyright © 1985 by Tommi Avicolli. Reprinted by permission of Center for Critical Education and Tommi Avicolli Mecca.

Scene Two

The boy is walking home from school. A group of boys (two, maybe three, he is not certain) grab him from behind, drag him into an alley and beat him up. When he gets home, he races up to his room, refusing dinner ("I don't feel well," he tells his mother through the locked door) and spends the night alone in the dark wishing he would die. . . .

These are not fictitious accounts—I *was* that boy. Having been branded a sissy by neighborhood children because I preferred jump rope to baseball and dolls to playing soldiers, I was often taunted with "hey sissy" or "hey faggot" or "yoo hoo honey" (in a mocking voice) when I left the house.

To avoid harassment, I spent many summers alone in my room. I went out on rainy days when the street was empty.

I came to like being alone. I didn't need anyone, I told myself over and over again. I was an island. Contact with others meant pain. Alone, I was protected. I began writing poems, then short stories. There was no reason to go outside anymore. I had a world of my own.

In the schoolyard today
they'll single you out
Their laughter will leave your ears ringing
like the church bells
which once awed you.[2] . . .

School was one of the more painful experiences of my youth. The neighborhood bullies could be avoided. The taunts of the children living in those endless repetitive row houses could be evaded by staying in my room. But school was something I had to face day after day for some two hundred mornings a year.

I had few friends in school. I was a pariah. Some kids would talk to me, but few wanted to be known as my close friend. Afraid of labels. If I was a sissy, then he had to be a sissy, too. I was condemned to loneliness.

Fortunately, a new boy moved into our neighborhood and befriended me; he wasn't afraid of the labels. He protected me when the other guys threatened to beat me up. He walked me home from school; he broke through the terrible loneliness. We were in third or fourth grade at the time.

We spent a summer or two together. Then his parents sent him to camp and I was once again confined to my room.

Scene Three

High school lunchroom. The boy sits at a table near the back of the room. Without warning, his lunch bag is grabbed and tossed to another table. Someone opens it and confiscates a package of Tastykakes; another boy takes the sandwich. The empty bag is tossed back to the boy who stares at it, dumbfounded. He should be used to this; it has happened before.

Someone screams, "faggot," laughing. There is always laughter. It does not annoy him anymore.

There is no teacher nearby. There is never a teacher around. And what would he say if there were? Could he report the crime? He would be jumped after school if he did. Besides, it would be his word against theirs. Teachers never noticed anything. They never heard the taunts. Never heard the word, "faggot." They were the great deaf mutes, pillars of indifference; a sissy's pain was not relevant to history and geography and god made me to love honor and obey him, amen.

Scene Four

High school Religion class. Someone has a copy of *Playboy*. Father N. is not in the room yet; he's late, as usual. Someone taps the boy roughly on the shoulder. He turns. A finger points to the centerfold model, pink fleshy body, thin and sleek. Almost painted. Not real. The other asks, mocking voice, "Hey, does she turn you on? Look at those tits!"

The boy smiles, nodding meekly; turns away.

The other jabs him harder on the shoulder, "Hey, whatsamatter, don't you like girls?"

Laughter. Thousands of mouths; unbearable din of laughter. In the Arena: thumbs down. Don't spare the queer.

"Wanna suck my dick? Huh? That turn you on, faggot!"

The laughter seems to go on forever. . . .

Behind you, the sound of their laughter
echoes a million times
in a soundless place
They watch how you walk/sit/stand/breathe.[3] . . .

What did being a sissy really mean? It was a way of walking (from the hips rather than the shoulders); it was a way of talking (often with a lisp or in a high-pitched voice); it was a way of relating to others (gently, not wanting to fight, or hurt anyone's feelings). It was being intelligent ("an egghead" they called it sometimes); getting good grades. It meant not being interested in sports, not playing football in the street after school; not discussing teams and scores and playoffs. And it involved not showing fervent interest in girls, not talking about scoring with tits or *Playboy* centerfolds. Not concealing naked women in your history book; or porno books in your locker.

On the other hand, anyone could be a "faggot." It was a catch-all. If you did something that didn't conform to what was the acceptable behavior of the group, then you risked being called a faggot. If you didn't get along with the "in" crowd, you were a faggot. It was the most commonly used put-down. It kept guys in line. They became angry when somebody called them a faggot. More fights started over someone calling someone else a faggot than anything else. The word had power.

It toppled the male ego, shattered his delicate facade, violated the image he projected. He was tough. Without feeling. Faggot cut through all this. It made him vulnerable. Feminine. And feminine was the worst thing he could possibly be. Girls were fine for fucking, but no boy in his right mind wanted to be like them. A boy was the opposite of girl. He was not feminine. He was not feeling. He was not weak.

Just look at the gym teacher who growled like a dog; or the priest with the black belt who threw kids against the wall in rage when they didn't know their Latin. They were men, they got respect.

But not the physics teacher who preached pacifism during lectures on the nature of atoms. Everybody knew what he was—and why he believed in the anti-war movement.

My parents only knew that the neighborhood kids called me names. They begged me to act more like the other boys. My brothers were ashamed of me. They never said it, but I knew. Just as I knew that my parents were embarrassed by my behavior.

At times, they tried to get me to act differently. Once my father lectured me on how to walk right. I'm still not clear on what that means. Not from the hips, I guess, don't "swish" like faggots do.

A nun in elementary school told my mother at Open House that there was "something wrong with me." I had draped my sweater over my shoulders like a girl, she said. I was a smart kid, but I should know better than to wear my sweater like a girl!

My mother stood there, mute. I wanted her to say something, to chastise the nun; to defend me. But how could she? This was a nun talking—representative of Jesus, protector of all that was good and decent.

An uncle once told me I should start "acting like a boy" instead of like a girl. Everybody seemed ashamed of me. And I guess I was ashamed of myself, too. It was hard not to be.

Scene Five

Priest: Do you like girls, Mark?
Mark: Uh-huh.
Priest: I mean *really* like them?
Mark: Yeah—they're okay.
Priest: There's a role they play in your salvation. Do you understand it, Mark?
Mark: Yeah.
Priest: You've got to like girls. Even if you should decide to enter the seminary, it's important to keep in mind God's plan for a man and a woman.[4] . . .

Catholicism of course condemned homosexuality. Effeminacy was tolerated as long as the effeminate person did not admit to being gay. Thus, priests could be effeminate because they weren't gay.

As a sissy, I could count on no support from the church. A male's sole purpose in life was to father children—souls for the church to save. The only hope a homosexual had of attaining salvation was by remaining totally celibate. Don't even think of touching another boy. To think of a sin was a sin. And to sin was to put a mark upon the soul. Sin—if it was a serious offense against god—led to hell. There was no way around it. If you sinned, you were doomed.

Realizing I was gay was not an easy task. Although I knew I was attracted to boys by the time I was about eleven, I didn't connect this attraction to homosexuality. I was not queer. Not I. I was merely appreciating a boy's good looks, his fine features, his proportions. It didn't seem to matter that I didn't appreciate a girl's looks in the same way. There was no twitching in my thighs when I gazed upon a beautiful girl. But I wasn't queer.

I resisted that label—queer—for the longest time. Even when everything pointed to it, I refused to see it. I was certainly not queer. Not I.

We sat through endless English classes, and History courses about the wars between men who were not allowed to love each other. No gay history was ever taught. No history faces you this morning. You're just a faggot. Homosexuals had never contributed to the human race. God destroyed the queers in Sodom and Gomorrah.

We learned about Michelangelo, Oscar Wilde, Gertrude Stein—but never that they were queer. They were not queer. Walt Whitman, the "father of American poetry," was not queer. No one was queer. I was alone, totally unique. One of a kind. Were there others like me somewhere? Another planet, perhaps?

In school, they never talked of the queers. They did not exist. The only hint we got of this other species was in Religion class. And even then it was clouded in mystery—never spelled out. It was sin. Like masturbation. Like looking at *Playboy* and getting a hard-on. A sin.

Once a progressive priest in senior year Religion class actually mentioned homosexuals—he said the word—but was into Erich Fromm, into homosexuals as pathetic and sick. Fixated at some early stage; penis, anal, whatever. Only heterosexuals passed on to the nirvana of sexual development.

No other images from the halls of the Catholic high school except those the other boys knew: swishy faggot sucking cock in an alley somewhere, grabbing asses in the bathroom. Never mentioning how much straight boys craved blowjobs, it was part of the secret.

It was all a secret. You were not supposed to talk about the queers. Whisper maybe. Laugh about them, yes. But don't be open, honest; don't try to understand. Don't cite their accomplishments. No history faces you this morning. You're just a faggot   faggot   no history   just a faggot

Epilogue

The boy marching down the Parkway. Hundreds of queers. Signs proclaiming gay pride. Speakers. Tables with literature from gay groups. A miracle, he is thinking. Tears are coming loose now. Someone hugs him.

You could not control
the sissy in me
nor could you exorcise him
nor electrocute him
You declared him illegal illegitimate
insane and immature
But he defies you still.[5]

NOTES

1. From the poem "Faggot," by Tommi Avicolli, published in *GPU News*, September 1979.
2. *Ibid.*
3. *Ibid.*
4. From the play *Judgment of the Roaches*, by Tommi Avicolli, produced in Philadelphia at the Gay Community Center, the Painted Bride Arts Center and the University of Pennsylvania; aired over WXPN-FM, in four parts; and presented at the Lesbian/Gay Conference in Norfolk, VA, July 1980.
5. From the poem "Sissy Poem," published in *Magic Doesn't Live Here Anymore* (Philadelphia: Spruce Street Press, 1976).

9 Against "Bullying" or On Loving Queer Kids

Richard Kim

When I read that 18-year-old Rutgers freshman Tyler Clementi had committed suicide by jumping off the George Washington Bridge after two other students posted a video of him having sex with another man online, my heart dropped. Tyler grew up in New Jersey and played the violin, and I did too. I don't know what life was like for Tyler before he chose to end it, but my early high school years were spent improvising survival strategies. I mentally plotted the corridors where the jocks hung out and avoided them. I desperately tried to never go to the bathroom during the school day. I was Asian and gay, stood 5'2", weighed 95 pounds and when I got excited about something—which was often—my voice cracked into a register normally only heard among Hannah Montana fans. If it weren't for the fact that I ran really fast and talked even faster and enjoyed the protection of a few popular kids and a couple of kind-hearted teachers—well, it's not hard to imagine a similar fate.

I say all this not to elicit pity—I'm a bigger boy now, and I bash back—but to make it clear that I'm conditioned to abhor people who bully queer kids. There's nothing—nothing—that raises my hackles more than seeing an effeminate boy being teased. But I also find myself reluctant to join the chorus of voices calling for the law to come down hard on Dharun Ravi and Molly Wei, the Rutgers students who posted the video and who are now facing "invasion of privacy" charges. If convicted they could face up to 5 years in prison; some gay rights groups like Garden State Equality are calling for the two to be prosecuted under New Jersey's hate crimes law, which could double the sentence.

What Ravi and Wei did was immature, prurient, and thoughtless; it undoubtedly played some role in what became an awful, awful tragedy. That they acted with homophobic malice, that they understood what the consequences of their actions might be, or that their prank alone, or even chiefly, triggered Clementi's suicide is far less clear. There's no record of Ravi and Wei discriminating against gays in the past, and there's nothing exceptionally homophobic about the tweet Ravi sent—"I saw him making out with a dude. Yay." One could easily insert "fat chick" or "masturbating to porn" into the scenario, which wouldn't have made it any more acceptable—or legal—for Ravi and Wei to surreptitiously broadcast the incident, but might have provided just as much titillation and inducement anyway. More importantly, we know virtually nothing about Clementi's life prior to his last days, including how he felt about his sexuality or whether or not he found affirmation of it at home, among his friends or on the campus at large.

From *The Nation*, November 1, 2010. © 2010 The Nation Company, LLC. All rights reserved. Used by permission and protected by the Copyright Laws of the United States. The printing, copying, redistribution, or retransmission of this Content without express written permission is prohibited.

But for some gays and liberals shaken by Clementi's suicide, the complexities and unknowns don't seem to matter. It's convenient to make Ravi and Wei into little monsters singularly responsible for his death. In the words of Malcolm Lazin—the director of Equality Forum, a gay rights group that's calling for "murder by manslaughter" charges, a demand echoed on sympathetic blogs and Facebook pages—the duo's conduct was "willful and premeditated," an act so "shocking, malicious and heinous" that Ravi and Wei "had to know" it would be "emotionally explosive." Each and every one of these accusations is entirely speculative at this point, a fact that you'd think Lazin, a former US assistant district attorney, would bear in mind before rounding up the firing squad.

Clementi's is the latest in a rash of suicides by gay teenagers, most of them boys. In September alone the body count includes Billy Lucas, a 15-year-old from Indiana who hanged himself after repeatedly being called a "fag" by his classmates; Asher Brown, a 13-year-old Texan who shot himself after his fellow students performed "mock gay acts" on him during gym class; and 13-year-old Seth Walsh from California who hanged himself from a tree in his backyard after being teased for years for being gay. In each of these cases, news reports focused almost exclusively on the bullies—other kids who were 12, 13, 14, 15 years old—as the perpetrators in what's been dubbed "an epidemic of anti-gay bullying." In each of these cases, liberals and gays expressed dismay that the bullies weren't being charged with crimes. Few of the articles asked what home life was like for these gay teens or looked into what role teachers, schools and the broader community played in creating an environment where the only escape from such routine torment seemed death. And too few (with the exception of Ellen DeGeneres and Sarah Silverman) drew the line to the messages mainstream adult America, including its politicians and preachers, sends every day.

It's not hard to do. Senator Jim DeMint of South Carolina is in the news of late for doubling down on his 2004 statement that out gay people (and unwed mothers) should be banned from teaching in public schools. Both New Hampshire Senate candidate Kelly Ayotte and Nevada Senate candidate Sharron Angle support making gay adoption illegal, as did Florida's Charlie Crist until he flipped his position and tacked to the center in his race against Tea Partier Marco Rubio, who still supports the ban. These right-wing policies would discriminate against gay adults, but what fuels them is the anxiety that having openly gay men and women teaching and raising kids would make it known to children that being gay is a survivable, even joyous, condition. As such the real targets are queer kids, and the message is quite simple: Please, don't exist.

At least the right is relatively honest in its brutality. Oregon has no ban on gay teachers, but that didn't stop the Beaverton school district, which is located just outside lefty Portland and has an anti-discrimination policy that includes sexual orientation, from removing Seth Stambaugh from his fourth grade classroom. A 23-year-old teaching intern, Stambaugh responded to a student's question about why he wasn't married by saying that gay marriage is illegal in Oregon. A spokeswoman for the school board claimed that the action wasn't discriminatory, but rather based on concerns about Stambaugh's "professional judgment and age appropriateness."

And there you have a pithy example of the limits of liberal tolerance; even in communities that would denounce the DeMints of the world, a palpable phobia remains when it comes to *the children*. Gay teachers should teach, until they teach about the plain realities of being gay. (It's this vacuum of education that's inspired Dan Savage's direct-to-teen YouTube campaign *It Gets Better*). Let's just have the kids figure it out themselves and come out when they're all grown up, rather than ask pesky questions we'd rather not try to answer: What does the "closet" mean for a kid who announces she's gay when she's 11, or 5, or wants to marry someone like Mommy and not Daddy? What to make of the fact that your little boy begs to dress exclusively like Taylor Swift? Is he gay or trans or just going through a phase—and oh God, isn't not knowing the worst of it?

Even for liberals who like to think of themselves as pro-gay, this is uncharted territory, little discussed except perhaps in the deepest corners of Park Slope. So when faced with something so painful and complicated as gay teen suicide, it's easier to go down the familiar path, to invoke the wrath of law and order, to create scapegoats out of child bullies who ape the denials and anxieties of adults, to blame it on technology or to pare down homophobia into a social menace called "anti-gay bullying" and then confine it to the borders of the schoolyard.

It's tougher, more uncertain work creating a world that loves queer kids, that wants them to live and thrive. But try—try as if someone's life depended on it. Imagine saying I really wish my son turns out to be gay. Imagine hoping that your 2-year-old daughter grows up to be transgendered. Imagine not assuming the gender of your child's future prom date or spouse; imagine keeping that space blank or occupied by boys and girls of all types. Imagine petitioning your local board of education to hire *more* gay elementary school teachers.

Now imagine a world in which Tyler Clementi climbed up a ledge on the George Washington Bridge—and chose to climb back down instead. It's harder to do than you might think.

10 The Case of Sharon Kowalski and Karen Thompson

Ableism, Heterosexism, and Sexism

Joan L. Griscom

In November, 1983, Sharon Kowalski was in a head-on collision with a drunk driver, suffered a severe brain-stem injury, became paralyzed, and lost the ability to speak. Sharon was in a committed partnership with Karen Thompson. Serious conflict soon developed between Karen and Kowalski's parents, erupting in a series of lawsuits that lasted eight years. Karen fought to secure adequate rehabilitation for Sharon as well as access to friends and family of her choice. In 1985, acting under Minnesota guardianship laws, Sharon's father placed her in a nursing home without adequate rehabilitation services and prohibited Karen and others from visiting her. Karen continued to fight through the courts and the media. In 1989, Sharon was finally transferred to an appropriate rehabilitation facility, reunited with lover and friends, and, in 1991, finally allowed her choice to live with Karen.

In this article I tell the story of Sharon Kowalski and Karen Thompson. While the story shows violations of their human rights, it is more than a story of two individuals. The injustices they encountered were modes of oppression that operate at a social-structural level and affect many other people. These oppressions include ableism, discrimination against disabled persons; heterosexism, the structuring of our institutions to legitimate only heterosexual relationships; and sexism, discrimination against women. Their story shows the power of structural discrimination, the intertwining of both our medical and legal systems in ways that denied both of them the fullest quality of life.

A History of the Events

By November 1983, Sharon and Karen had lived in partnership for almost four years. Karen was thirty-six, teaching physical education at St. Cloud State University, devoutly religious, conservative. Sharon was twenty-seven, a fine athlete who had graduated from St. Cloud in physical education and just accepted a staff coaching position. She had grown up in the Iron Mine area of Minnesota, a conservative world where women are expected to marry young. Defying such expectations, she became first in her family to attend college, earning tuition working part-time in the mines. After she and Karen fell in love, they exchanged rings, bought a house together, and vowed lifetime commitment.

Reprinted by permission of the author. I am indebted to Paula Rothenberg for earlier creative editing that much improved the clarity of this essay.

After the accident Sharon lay in a coma for weeks, and doctors were pessimistic about her recovery. Karen spent hours, daily, talking to her, reading the Bible, massaging and stretching her neck, shoulders, and hands. It is essential to massage and stretch brain-injured persons in comas, for their muscles tend to curl up tightly and incur permanent damage. Early in 1984, Karen saw Sharon moving her right index finger, and found that she could indicate answers to questions by moving it. Later she began to tap her fingers, then slowly learned to write letters and words.

The Kowalski parents became suspicious of the long hours Karen was spending with her, and increasingly Karen feared they would try to exclude her from Sharon's life. After consulting a psychologist, she wrote them a letter explaining their love, in hopes they would understand her importance to Sharon. They reacted with shock, denial, and rage. As the nightmare deepened, Karen consulted a lawyer and learned she had no legal rights, unless she won guardianship. In March, 1984, she therefore filed for guardianship, and Donald Kowalski counterfiled.

Guardianship was awarded to Kowalski, but Karen was granted equal access to medical and financial information and full visitation rights. She continued to participate in both physical and occupational therapy. Sharon improved slowly; Karen made her an alphabet board, and she began to spell out answers to questions. Later she began to communicate by typewriter, and in August spoke a few words. But conflicts continued. The day after the court decision Kowalski incorrectly told Karen she did not have visitation rights, and later tried to cancel her work with Sharon's therapists. When Karen and others took Sharon out on day passes, he objected, subsequently testifying in court that he did not want her out in public. In October, Sharon was moved further away, and Kowalski filed to gain full power as guardian. Karen counterfiled to remove him as guardian.

Months elapsed while the legal battles were fought. Sharon was moved several times, regressed in her skills, and became clinically depressed. The Minnesota Civil Liberties Union (MCLU) entered the case, arguing that under the First Amendment Sharon's rights of free speech and free association were being violated. A tri-county Handicap Services Program submitted testimony of Sharon's capacity to communicate, including a long conversation in which she stated she was gay and Karen was her lover. At Sharon's request, the MCLU asked to represent her and suggested she might testify for herself. The court refused both requests, finding that Sharon lacked understanding to make decisions for herself. In July, 1985, Kowalski was awarded full guardianship. Within a day, he denied visitation to Karen, other friends, the MCLU, and disability rights groups; in two days he transferred her to a nursing home near his home with only minimal rehabilitation facilities. In August, 1985, Karen saw Sharon for what would be the last time for over three years.

As this summary indicates, the medical system failed Sharon in at least three respects. First, it failed to supply rehabilitation in the years when it was vital to her recovery. Stark in the medical record is the fact that this woman who was starting to stand and to feed herself was locked away for over three years with an implanted feeding tube, left insufficiently stretched so that muscles that had been starting to work curled back on themselves again. Second, she was deprived of the bombardment of emotional and physical stimulation needed to regenerate her cognitive faculties. Once in the nursing home, for example, she was forbidden regenerative outside excursions. Third, although medical staff often recognized Sharon's unusual response to Karen, they failed to explain to her parents its importance. Despite an urgent need for counseling to assist the parents, none, except for one court-mandated session, took place.

The failure of the medical system was consistently supported by the legal system. Initially the court ruled that Sharon must have access to a young-adult rehabilitation ward. But once Kowalski won full guardianship, he was able to move her to a nursing home without such a ward. In 1985 the Office of Health Facility Complaints investigated Sharon's right to choose visitors, a right guaranteed by the Minnesota Patient Bill of Rights, and found that indeed her right was being violated. However, the appeals court held that the Patient Bill of Rights was inapplicable, since the healthcare facility was not restricting the right of visitation, the guardian was.

The deficiencies of guardianship law are a central problem in this case. First, a guardian can restrict a person's rights, without legal recourse. As is often said, under present laws a guardian can lock up a person and throw away the key. This is a national problem, affecting the disabled, the elderly, anyone presumed incompetent. Second, guardians are inadequately supervised. Under Minnesota law, a guardian is required to have the ward tested annually for competence. Kowalski never did, and for over three years the courts did not require him to. In 1985, Karen first filed a motion to hold him in contempt for failure to arrange testing and for failure to heed Sharon's wishes for visitation. The courts routinely rejected such motions.

Between 1985 and 1988, Karen and the MCLU pursued repeated appeals to various Minnesota courts, all denied. Karen began to seek help from the media, also disability, gay/lesbian, women's, and church groups. She recognized that the legal precedents could be devastating for others, e.g., gay/lesbian couples or unmarried heterosexual couples. The reserved, closeted, conservative professor was slowly transformed into a passionate public speaker in her quest to secure freedom and rehabilitation for Sharon; and slowly she gained national attention. The alternative press responded; national groups such as the National Organization for Women were supportive; the National Committee to Free Sharon Kowalski formed, with regional chapters. Finally the mainstream media began publishing concerned articles; Karen appeared on national TV programs; state and national politicians, including Jesse Jackson, spoke out. Meanwhile Sharon remained in the nursing home, cut off from friends, physically regressed, psychologically depressed.

The first break in the case came in February, 1988. In response to a new motion from Karen, requesting that Sharon be tested for competence, testing was ordered. In January, 1989, she was moved to the Miller-Dwan Medical Center for a 60-day evaluation. Kowalski unsuccessfully argued in court against both the move and the testing. Sharon immediately expressed her wish to see Karen. On February 2, 1989, Karen visited her for the first time in three and a half years, an event which made banner headlines in the alternative press across the nation. She was, however, highly depressed, with numerous physical problems: for example, her feet had curled up so tightly that she was no longer able to stand. More significant was her cognitive ability; to this day, her short-term memory loss remains considerable.

The competency evaluation nevertheless demonstrated that she could communicate on an adult level and had significant potential for rehabilitation. The report recommended "her return to pre-morbid home environment," and added:

> We believe Sharon has shown areas of potential and ability to make rational choices in many areas of her life. She has consistently indicated a desire to return home . . . to live with Karen Thompson again.

Donald Kowalski subsequently resigned as guardian, for both financial and health reasons, and the parents stopped attending medical conferences. In June, 1989, Sharon was transferred to a long-term rehabilitation center for brain-injured young adults. Here she had extensive occupational, physical, and speech therapy. Again Karen spent hours with her and took her out on trips. She had surgery on her legs, feet, toes, left shoulder and arm to reverse the results of three years of inadequate care. She began to use a speech synthesizer and a motorized wheelchair.

Karen subsequently filed for guardianship. Medical staff testified unanimously that Sharon was capable of deciding for herself what relationships she wanted and where she wished to live. They testified that she was capable of living outside an institution and Karen was best qualified to care for her in a home environment. Witnesses for the Kowalskis opposed the petition. The judge appeared increasingly uncomfortable with the national publicity. While in 1990 he allowed Sharon and Karen to fly out to San Francisco where each received a Woman of Courage Award from the National Organization for Women, he refused Sharon permission to attend the first Disability Pride Day in Boston. He issued a gag order against Karen, which was overturned on appeal. Finally, in April, 1991, he denied Karen guardianship and awarded it to a supposedly "neutral third party," a former classmate of Sharon who lived near the Kowalski parents and had testified against Karen in a 1984 hearing. This decision raised the alarming possibility that Sharon might be returned to the inadequate facility. Karen appealed it.

In December, 1991, the appeals court reversed the judge's ruling and granted guardianship to Karen, on two bases: first, the medical testimony that Sharon was able to make her own choices; and second, the fact that the two women are "a family of affinity" that deserves respect. This is a major decision in U.S. legal history, setting important legal precedents both for disabled people and gay/lesbian families. Sharon and Karen now live together.

The Three Modes of Oppression

Sharon and Karen were denied their rights by three interacting systems of oppression: ableism, heterosexism, and sexism. Originally Karen believed that their difficulties were merely personal problems. All her life she had believed that our social institutions are basically fair, designed to support individual rights. In the book she co-authored with Julie Andrzejewski[1], she documented her growing awareness that widespread social/political forces were involved in their supposedly personal problems and that the oppression they experienced was systemic.

Ableism was rampant throughout. Sharon's inability to speak was often construed as incompetence, and her particular kinds of communication were not recognized. Quite early Karen noticed some did not speak to Sharon, some talked loudly as if she was deaf, others spoke to her as if she were a child. One doctor discussed her in her presence as if she was not there. When Karen later asked how she felt about this, she typed out "Shitty." Probably one reason she responded to Karen more than anyone was that Karen talked extensively and read to her, played music, asked questions, and constantly consulted her wishes. Although the MCLU and the Handicap Services Program submitted transcripts of long conversations with her, the courts did not accept these as evidence of competence, relying instead on testimony from people who had much less interaction with her. A major article in the St. Paul *Pioneer Press* (1987) described the Kowalskis visiting the room "where their eerily silent daughter lies trapped in her twisted body." Eerily silent? This is the person who typed out "columbine" when asked her favorite flower, answered arithmetical questions correctly, and responded to numerous questions about her life, feelings, and wishes. She also communicates nonverbally in many ways: gestures, smiles, tears, and laughter.

Thanks to ableism, Sharon was often stereotyped as helpless. The presumption of helplessness "traps" her far more severely than her "twisted body." Once a person is labeled helpless, there is no need to consult her wishes, consider her written communications, hear her testimony. When Sharon arrived at Miller-Dwan for competency testing, Karen reported with joy that staff was giving her information and allowing her choices, even if her choice was to do nothing. Most seriously, if a person is seen as helpless, then there is no potential for rehabilitation. As Ellen Bilofsky[2] has written, Sharon was presumed "incompetent until proven competent." If Karen's legal motion for competency testing had not been accepted, Sharon might have remained in the nursing home indefinitely, presumed incompetent.

Finally, ableism can lead to keeping disabled persons hidden, literally out of sight. Kowalski argued against day passes, resisted Karen's efforts to take Sharon out, and testified he would not take her to a church or shopping center because he did not wish to put her "on display . . . in her condition." Although medical staff could see that outside trips provided Sharon with pleasure and stimulation, both important for cognitive rehabilitation, they cooperated with the father in denying them. According to an article in the *Washington Post,* he once said, "What the hell difference does it make if she's gay or lesbian or straight or anything because she's laying there in diapers? . . . let the poor kid rest in peace."

Invisible in the nursing home, cut off from lover and friends, Sharon had little chance to demonstrate competence. The wonder is that after three and a half years of loss, loneliness, and lack of care, she was able to emerge from her depression and respond to her competency examiners. To retain her capacity for response, through such an experience, suggests a strong spirit.

The second mode of oppression infusing this case is heterosexism, the structuring of our institutions so as to legitimate heterosexuality only. Glaringly apparent is the failure to recognize gay/lesbian partnerships. When Karen was first to arrive at the hospital after the accident, she was not allowed access to Sharon or even any information, because she was not "family." Seeing her anguish, a Roman Catholic priest interceded, brought information, and arranged for a doctor to speak with her. Although the two women considered themselves married, in law they were not, and therefore lacked any legal rights as a couple. If heterosexual, there would have been no denial of visitation, no long nightmare of the three-and-a-half-year separation. While unmarried heterosexual partners might have trouble securing guardianship, married partners would not.

Because of heterosexism, Sharon's emotional need for her partner and Karen's rehabilitative effect on her were not honored. Because of Sharon's response, Karen was often included in the therapeutic work. Yet, prior to 1989, medical staff often refused to testify to this positive effect. Perhaps they feared condoning the same-sex relationship, perhaps they wished to stay out of the conflict. One neurologist, Dr. Keith Larson, did testify, although stipulating that he spoke as friend of the court, not as witness for Karen.

> The reason I'm here today is . . . to deliver an observation that I have agonized over and thought a great deal about, and prayed a little bit. . . . I cannot help but say that Sharon's friend, Karen, can get out of Sharon physical actions, attempts at vocalization, and longer periods of alertness and attention than can really any of our professional therapists.

Why was it necessary to "agonize" over this testimony? Pray about it? Make such a tremendous effort? Clearly, were one of the partners male, Larson would have had no difficulty. He simply would have reported that the patient responded to her partner. Some medical staff did testify positively, without effort; and after 1989, testimony from medical personnel was strong and unanimous. However, repeatedly, the courts ignored it.

Finally, heterosexism is evident in a consistent tendency to exaggerate the role of sex in same-sex relationships. Many believe that the lives of gay/lesbian people revolve around sex, though evidence from all social-psychological research is that homosexual people are no more sexually active than heterosexual people. Further, gay/lesbian sex is often perceived as sexual exploitation rather than an expression of mutual caring. The final denial of Karen's visitation rights was based on the charge that she might sexually abuse Sharon. A physician hired by the Kowalskis, Dr. William L. Wilson, leveled this charge:

> Karen Thompson has been involved in bathing Sharon Kowalski behind a closed door for a prolonged period of time. . . . Ms. Thompson has [also] alleged a sexual relationship with Sharon Kowalski that existed prior to the accident. Based on this knowledge and my best medical judgment . . . I feel that visits by Karen Thompson at this time would expose Sharon Kowalski to a high risk of sexual abuse.

Accordingly, Wilson directed the nursing home staff not to let Karen visit. Even though under statutes, Karen could have continued to visit while the court decisions were under appeal, the nursing home was obliged to obey the doctor's order.

In this instance, ableism and heterosexism merge. If they were unmarried heterosexual partners, sexual abuse probably would not have been an issue. If married, the issue would not exist. Ableism often denies disabled persons their sexuality, though a person does not lose her sexuality simply because she becomes disabled. Also, a person who loses the capacity to speak has a special need for touching. What were Sharon's sexual rights? When she was starting to emerge from the coma, she once reached out and touched Karen's breast, and later placed Karen's hand on her breast. At the time Karen did not dare ask medical advice for fear of revealing their relationship. Even to raise such questions might have exposed her to more charges of sexual abuse.

While same-sex relationships are often called "anti-family" in our heterosexist society, actually such relationships create family, in that they create stable emotional and economic units. Family, in this sense, may be defined as a kin-like unit of two or more persons related by blood, marriage, adoption, or primary commitment, who usually share the same household. Sharon and Karen considered themselves married. Karen's long pilgrimage over almost nine years testifies to an extraordinary depth of commitment. Sharon consistently said she was gay, Karen was her lover, she wanted to live with her. While marriage has historically occurred between two sexes, history cannot determine its definition. In U.S. history, marriage between black and white persons was forbidden for centuries. In 1967, when the Supreme Court finally declared miscegenation laws unconstitutional, there were still such laws in sixteen states.

Sexism is sufficiently interfused with heterosexism that they are hard to separate. Often sexism enforces a social role on women in which they are subordinated to men. Women in the Minnesota world where Sharon grew up were expected to marry young and submit to their husbands' authority, an intrinsically sexist model. According to this model, her partnership with Karen was illegitimate. Sexism also is apparent in awarding guardianship to the father. Had Sharon been a man rather than a twenty-eight-year-old "girl," such a decision might be less possible; but in a sexist society, it is appropriate to assign an adult woman to her male parent. Finally, our society devalues friendship, especially between women. Once, very early, a doctor advised Karen to forget Sharon. The gist of his remarks was that "Sharon's parents will always be her parents. They have to deal with this, but you don't. Maybe you should go back to leading your own life." Friendship between the two women was unimportant. Ableism as well as sexism is apparent in these remarks.

This case makes clear that the modes of oppression work simultaneously. Like Audre Lorde[3], I argue that "there is no hierarchy of oppression." Disability was not more important than sexuality in curtailing Sharon's freedoms; they worked together seamlessly, in her life as in the legal and medical systems. Admittedly, any individual's perspective on the case may reflect the issue most central to her or his life: e.g., the gay press, reporting the case, emphasized heterosexism, and the disability rights press emphasized ableism. Working in coalition on this case, some women were ill at ease with disability rights activists; and some disability rights groups were anxious about associating with gay/lesbian issues. But there are lesbians and gays in the disabled community, and disabled folks in women's groups. Karen experienced the inseparability of the issues once when invited to speak to a Presbyterian group. They asked her to speak only about ableism since they had already "done" gay/lesbian concerns. She tried, but found it nearly impossible; she had to censor her material, ignore basic facts, leave out crucial connections.

In each mode of oppression, one group of persons takes power over another, and this power is institutionalized. Disabled people, women, gay men and lesbians, and others are all to some degree denied their full personhood by the structures of our society. Their choices can be denied, their sexuality is controlled. On the basis of ableism, heterosexism, and sexism, both Karen Thompson's and Sharon Kowalski's opportunities for the fullest quality of life were taken from them. Sharon lost cognitive ability that might have been saved. As the Minnesota Civil Liberties Union put it, "The convicted criminal loses only his or her liberty; Sharon Kowalski has lost the right to choose whom she may see, who she may like, and who she may love." To change this picture took nearly nine years of struggle by a partner who lived out her vow of lifetime commitment and the work of many committed persons and groups.

Conclusion

Many national groups joined the struggle to provide rehabilitation for Sharon and bring her home, including disability rights activists, gays and lesbians, feminists and male supporters, and civil rights groups. In addition there were thousands of people drawn to this case by simple human rights. After all, any of us could be hit by a drunk driver, become disabled, and in the process lose our legal and medical rights. The Kowalski/Thompson case stands as a warning that in our deeply divided society, freedom is still a privilege and rights are fragile.

People living in nontraditional families need legal protection to secure legal and medical rights. Karen Thompson stresses the importance of making your relationships known to your family of birth, if possible, and informing them of your wishes in case of disability or death. Also, it is essential to execute a durable power of attorney, a document that stipulates a person to make medical and financial decisions for you, in case of need. Copies should be given to your physician. While requirements vary between states and powers of attorney are not always enforceable, they may protect your rights. Information about how to execute them may be found in your public library, in consultation with a competent lawyer, or in Appendix B of the book *Why Can't Sharon Kowalski Come Home?*

NOTES

1. Karen Thompson and Julie Andrzejewski. *Why Can't Sharon Kowalski Come Home?* San Francisco: Spinster/Aunt Lute, 1988. All quotations in text are from this book.

2. Ellen Bilofsky. "The Fragile Rights of Sharon Kowalski." *Health/PAC Bulletin,* 1989, *19,* 4–16.

3. Audre Lorde. "There Is No Hierarchy of Oppressions." *Interracial Books for Children Bulletin,* 1983, *14,* 9.

11 Gentrification Will Drive My Uncle Out of His Neighborhood, and I Will Have Helped

Eric Rodriguez

My *tío* Pedro lives behind a trendy bar on Sunset Boulevard in Los Angeles's Echo Park. The apartment owners told him the other day that the price of rent would be going up—again. He is one of many who will be pushed out by rising prices, and I am one of the very people pushing him out.

Since moving back here in July 2014, I've had one foot in my former community and the other in this new place I call "home"—while slowly robbing my uncle of his own. I don't know what the right thing to do is. I did what he and moms told me to do to avoid the gangs and violence: I got an education, and I earn more money than the rest of my family. I made it out of the neighborhood. Now, moving back feels wrong.

When I was a kid you could buy tacos at the park for a dollar. The vendors upped their prices the moment different people came into the neighborhood and were willing to pay more. Now many of the *mamis* with their thin eyebrows and big hooped earrings can't afford living here, nor can many of the shaved headed homies in white t-shirts and tattoos. They're disappearing. As are those random *tiendas* at the center of commerce on Sunset Boulevard which close every other week, only to be replaced by a new coffee shop.

My *tío* works in construction so money is not, well, flowing. Not in the way it does to the developers who buy up charming bungalows in the neighborhood and then demolish them to build mid-rise monstrosities. It's 'modern' and makes money, the developers say. You don't get it, they tell me, despite having lived in one in New York City and being an alumnus of a Wall Street investment bank. I get it, I just don't agree with it. *Tío* Pedro could not afford to live in one; he actually thinks they're hideous too. And so he laments the former neighborhood, its charm and character and affordability, minus the gangs and violence, of course.

Violence was common back in the 1990s around here. The park was off-limits at night because of the drug dealing and gang fights. It's different now; the park is safer than ever. I took a girl there for a walk around the lake in the evening the other day and saw the bust of José Martí, the Cuban revolutionary whose writings and philosophy led to Cuba's independence from Spain, and smiled at the thought of how Echo Park itself had wrestled its independence from the crime and violence it was once chained to.

But there are bizarre things happening now.

The other day a few friends and I smoked a joint near the boathouse and no one—not even the cops—cared much to stop and check things out. Back in the day it didn't

Copyright Guardian News & Media Ltd, 2015

go down like that at all. Don't take my word for it either; look at Frank Romero's "Arrest of the Paleteros." Even selling ice cream those days was a crime for people of color.

One day my cousin, Echo Park Pete, was walking with me around the lake and he said, referring to the drug use: "Man, I went to jail for this shit and now people do it all the time and the cops don't give a shit." I thought about offering a plausible explanation, you know, invoking my Ivy League education, but it felt forced. It is what it is: discrimination. I kept my stupid mouth shut.

This is the *new* neighborhood. A place where coffee shops and trendy bars are popping up, and drug use at the park goes unchecked because the new people using look different than the ones previously using. One group of people is moving in and another is being moved out. Call it gentrification; call it what you want, but it's happening. I see it happening—because I'm part of it.

12 My Vassar College Faculty ID Makes Everything OK

Kiese Laymon

The fourth time a Poughkeepsie police officer told me that my Vassar College Faculty ID could make everything OK was three years ago. I was driving down Wilbur Avenue. When the white police officer, whose head was way too small for his neck, asked if my truck was stolen, I laughed, said no, and shamefully showed him my license and my ID, just like Lanre Akinsiku.[1] The ID, which ensures that I can spend the rest of my life in a lush state park with fat fearless squirrels, surrounded by enlightened white folks who love talking about Jon Stewart, Obama, and civility,[2] has been washed so many times it doesn't lie flat.

After taking my license and ID back to his car, the police officer came to me with a ticket and two lessons. "Looks like you got a good thing going on over there at Vassar College," he said. "You don't wanna it ruin it by rolling through stop signs, do you?"

I sucked my teeth, shook my head, kept my right hand visibly on my right thigh, rolled my window up, and headed back to campus.

One more ticket.

Two more condescending lessons from a lame armed with white racial supremacy, anti-blackness, a gun, and a badge. But at least I didn't get arrested.

Or shot eight times.

My Vassar College Faculty ID made everything okay. A little over two hours later, I sat in a closed room on Vassar's campus in a place called Main Building.

In the center of my ID, standing dusty orange and partially hidden by shadows of massive trees, is a picture of Vassar College's Main Building. Black women students took the building over in 1969 to demand, among other things, that the administration affirmatively reckon with its investment in anti-blackness and white racial supremacy. A multiracial group of students led by Cleon Edwards occupied Main again in 1990, after Daniel Patrick Moynihan reportedly told a Jamaican Dutchess County official, "If you don't like it in this country, why don't you pack your bags and go back where you came from?"

Reprinted by permission of Kiese Laymon.

453

I sat in a room in Main that day with a senior professor and two high-ranking administrators. We were having one of those meetings you're not supposed to talk about. Near the end of the meeting, this senior professor affirmed his/her commitment to "African Americans" and said I was a "fraud."

I tucked both hands underneath my buttocks, rested my left knuckle beneath my ID as tears pooled in the gutters of both eyes. I'd been hungry before. I'd been beaten. I'd had guns pulled on me. I never felt as pathetic, angry, and terrified as I felt in that room.

I came into that meeting knowing that the illest part of racial terror in this nation is that it's sanctioned by sorry overpaid white bodies that will never be racially terrorized and maintained by a few desperate underpaid black and brown bodies that will. I left that meeting knowing that there are few things more shameful than being treated like a nigger by—and under the gaze of—intellectually and imaginatively average white Americans who are not, and will never have to be, half as good at their jobs as you are at yours.

I sat in that meeting thinking about the first day I got my ID. It was nine years earlier and I remember walking to the gym, maybe 100 yards behind Main Building and being asked by a white boy in yellow flip-flops if I could sell him some weed.

I just looked at his flip-flops.

And he just looked at my black neck. And when I told him that I taught English, he contorted his bushy brow, said "Word," and trotted off.

Later that year, maybe 30 yards to the left of Main Building, security routinely entered my office asking for my ID despite my name on the door and pictures of me, my Mama, and them all over my desk. In that same building, one floor lower, after I got my first book deal, I was told by another senior white member of my department that it was "all right" if I spoke to him "in ebonics." Later that year, a white senior professor walked in at the end of one of my classes and told me, in front of my students, "Don't talk back to me."

I wanted to put my palm through this man's esophagus and burn that building down, but I thought about prison and my Grandmama's health care. So I cussed his ass out and went about the business of eating too much fried cheese and biscuits at a local buffet.

A few summers later, right in front of Main Building, two security guards stopped me for walking past the President's house without identification. They threatened to call the Poughkeepsie police on me. I told the officers, "Fuck you" and "Show me your ID" for a number of reasons, but mostly because I'd sold one of them a car a few years ago, and Vassar's security officers don't carry guns.

Like nearly every black person I know from the deep South who has one of these faculty IDs, I anticipated reckoning daily with white racial supremacy at my job.

But.

I didn't expect to smell the crumbling of a real human heart when I went to the police station to get my student, Mat, who had been missing for days. Mat was a beautiful Southern black boy suffering from bipolar disorder.

I didn't anticipate hearing the hollowed terror and shame in my student Rachel's voice at 2 in the morning after she was arrested by Poughkeepsie police for jaywalking while her white friends just watched. Rachel went to jail that night.

I didn't expect to feel the cold cracked hands of administrators when we pushed the college to allow Jade, a black Phi Beta Kappa student from DC, back into school after they suspended her for a full year for verbally intimidating her roommate.

I didn't expect to taste my own tears when watching three black women seniors tell two heads of security and the Dean of the College that they, and another Asian American woman, deserve to not have security called on them for being black women simply doing their laundry and reading books on a Sunday afternoon. I didn't expect the Dean of the College and the heads of security to do absolutely nothing after this meeting.

I didn't expect to have to wrap my arms around Leo, a Chicano student who stood shivering and sobbing in front of Poughkeepsie police after getting jumped on Raymond Ave. by kids he called "my own people." Didn't expect to take him to the police station and have the questioning officer ask Leo, "Why do you use the term 'Latino'? Can you tell me what country the boys who jumped you were from?" The officer told Leo that his partner was Colombian and could tell where a person was from just by looking at them. Leo told me that he felt "most Chicano, most Latino, and most like a Vassar student" that night.

I didn't expect that.

I didn't expect to see my student Orion, a black boy from Boston, sitting palms down on the sidewalk in front of a police car a few Thursdays ago on my way from the gym. I got in the face of the two interrogating officers telling them, "He didn't do nothing" and "Leave my student the fuck alone," when I found out he was being accused of trying to steal a security golf cart.

I didn't expect the same two security guards who'd stopped me for walking in front of the President's house to tell the officers interrogating Orion that the golf cart was theirs and Orion was "a good kid, a Vassar student" who was just going to get a slice of pizza.

By the time one of the heads of Vassar security, in the presence of the current Dean of the College, told one of my colleagues and me that there was "no racial profiling on campus" and that we were making the black and brown students say there was, I expected almost everything.

I expected that four teenage black boys from Poughkeepsie would have security called on them for making too much noise in the library one Sunday afternoon. I expected security to call Poughkeepsie police on these 15- and 16-year-olds when a few of them couldn't produce an ID. I expected police to drive on the lawn in front of the library, making a spectacle of these black boys' perceived guilt.

A few days after Vassar called police on those children, a police officer visited one of the boys while he was in class and questioned him about some stolen cell phones and iPods at Vassar. When the kid said he didn't know anything about any stolen cell phones, the officer told the 15-year-old black child, who might have applied to Vassar in three years, to never go back to Vassar College again.

I didn't expect that.

Vassar College, the place that issues my faculty ID, a place so committed to access and what they call economic diversity,[3] did its part to ensure that a black Poughkeepsie child, charged with nothing, would forever be a part of the justice system for walking through a library without an ID.

There is no way on earth that a 15-year-old child visited by police officers at his school for walking through a local college library while black is going to be OK.

And neither are we.

But.

My Vassar College Faculty ID affords me free smoothies, free printing paper, paid leave, and access to one of the most beautiful libraries on Earth. It guarantees that I have really good health care and more disposable income than anyone in my Mississippi family. But way more than I want to admit, I'm wondering what price we pay for these kinds of IDs, and what that price has to do with the extrajudicial disciplining and killing of young cis and trans black human beings.

You have a Michigan State Faculty ID, and seven-year old Aiyana Stanley-Jones was killed in a police raid. You have a Wilberforce University Faculty ID and 12-year-old Tamir Rice was shot dead by police for holding a BB gun. I have a Vassar College Faculty ID and NYPD suffocated Shereese Francis while she lay face-down on a mattress. You have a University of Missouri Student ID and Mike Brown's unarmed 18-year-old black body lay dead in the street for four and a half hours.

But.

"We are winning," my mentor, Adisa Ajamu, often tells me. "Improvisation, transcendence, and resilience—the DNA of the Black experience—are just synonyms for fighting preparedness for the long winter of war."

Adisa is right. But to keep winning, to keep our soul and sanity in this terror-filled coliseum, at some point we have to say fuck it. We have to say fuck them. And most importantly, we must say to people and communities that love us, "I love you. Will you please love me? I'm listening."

We say that most profoundly with our work. We say that most profoundly with our lives. The question is, can we mean what we must say with our work and our lives and continue working at institutions like Vassar College.

Listening to our people and producing rigorous, soulful work are not antithetical. My teachers: Noel Didla, Paula Madison, Brittney Cooper, Rosa Clemente, Osagyefo Sekou, Eve Dunbar, Imani Perry, Darnell Moore, Josie Duffy, Kimberle Crenshaw, Mark Anthony Neal, Mychal Denzel Smith, dream hampton, Regina Bradley, Marlon Peterson, Jamilah LeMieux, Luke Harris, Chanda Hsu Prescod-Weinstein, and Carlos Alamo show me this every day.

They also show me that though there's an immense price to pay in and out of so-called elite American educational institutions, the depth of this price differs based on sexuality, gender, race, access to wealth, and the status of one's dependents.

I paid the price of having sorry gatekeepers at Vassar question the validity of my book contracts, question my graduation from undergrad, question my graduation from grad school, question whether or not I was given tenure as opposed to earning it. And like you, when questioned so much, of course I outworked them, but scars accumulated in battles won sometimes hurt more than battles lost.

I gained 129 pounds. I got sick. I kept hurting someone who would have never hurt me. I rarely slept.

I kept fighting. And praying. And I got my work out. And I worked on healing. And I taught my kids. And I served my community. And I got hit again. And I swung at folks who weren't even swinging at me. And my best friend, who was also reckoning with the "Vassar" part of her Vassar Faculty ID, and I took turns lying to each other, sealing off our hearts in favor of arguments and unpaid labor. And when I earned leaves that I should have spent at home in Forest, Mississippi, with the 85-year-old woman who gave me the skills of improvisation, transcendence, and resilience, I stayed at Vassar College and guided tons of independent studies, directed flailing programs, helped incompetent administrators do their jobs, and chaired hollow committees.

My family needed me home. My soul needed to be there. But I was afraid to be somewhere where my Vassar College Faculty ID didn't matter worth a damn. I was afraid to let the Mississippi black folks who really got me oversee all my new stretch marks, afraid they'd hear the isolation and anxiety in my voice, afraid they'd find the crumpled bank receipts from money taken out at casinos. I was afraid to show my Mama, Auntie, and Grandma that I felt alone and so much sadder than the 27-year-old black boy they remember being issued a Vassar College Faculty ID 12 years ago.

OK.

A half an inch below my name on my bent ID is a nine digit identification number, and in the top left corner, hanging in the blue sky, is a 27-year-old black boy wearing an emerald green hoodie. An army green sweater-hat cocked slightly to the left is pulled over my eyes. A black book bag is slung across my right shoulder.

When I took the picture of that ID, I felt so healthy. I felt so worthy of good love. I didn't feel delivered but I felt proud that I could take care of my Mississippi family. I felt that every beating I'd gotten with shoes, extension cords, switches, belts, belt buckles, fists, and the guns of police officers was worth it. I knew that our mamas and grandmamas and aunties beat us to remind us that there was a massive price to pay for being black, free, and imperfect. I knew they beat us partially so that we would one day have a chance to wield IDs like mine as a weapon and a shield.

Twelve years after getting my Vassar College faculty ID, I sit here and know that the nation can't structurally and emotionally assault black children and think they're going to turn out OK.

Vassar College can't structurally assault and neglect black children and think they're going to turn out OK.

I can't personally assault and neglect black children and think they're going to turn out OK.

I think about time travel and regret a lot. If I could go back and tell my Mama anything, I would tell her that I love her, and I thank her, and I see her and I know that white racial supremacy, poverty, heteropatriarchy, and a lifetime as a young black woman academic with a hardheaded son are whupping her ass, but black parents can't physically and emotionally assault their black children—even in an attempt to protect them from the worst of white folks—and think they are going to turn out OK.

We are not OK. We are not OK. We have to get better at organizing, strategizing, and patiently loving us because the people who issued my Vassar College ID, like the people who issued Darren Wilson and Robert McCulloch their badges, will never ever give a fuck about the inside of our lives.

I have a Vassar College Faculty ID. I write books that some people care about. I teach my students. I take care of my Grandma. I have more access to healthy choice than most of my cousins. And I, like a lot of you, am not OK. I am not subhuman. I am not superhuman. I am not a demon. I cannot walk through bullets. I am not a special nigger. I am not a fraud. I am not OK.

But.

Unlike Mike Brown and Aiyana Stanley-Jones and Tamir Rice, I am alive. We are alive.

And.

We are so much better than the sick part of our nation that murders an unarmed black boy like a rabid dog, before prosecuting him for being a nigger. We are so much better than powerful academic institutions, slick prosecutors, and the *innocent* practitioners of white racial supremacy in this nation who really believe that a handful of niggers with some special IDs, and a scar(r)ed black President on the wrong side of history, are proof of their—and really, our own—terrifying deliverance from American evil.

NOTES

1. Akinsiku, L. (2014, August 17.). *Gawker.com.* The Price of Blackness.
2. Hsu, H. (2014, December 1). *Newyorker.com.* The Civility Wars.
3. Hoffman, E. (2014, September 17). *miscellanynews.org.* VC Tops List of Economically Diverse Elite Colleges.

13 The Unbearable (In)visibility of Being Trans

Chase Strangio

During an internship in my second year of law school, I quickly realized that my trans-ness made me both hyper-visible and completely invisible.

I am noticed.

Innocuously, that visibility is a second glance when I use the bathroom, when I am walking down the street with my toddler, when I speak and my voice does not quite match up with people's expectations. But more insidiously that visibility is the older gentleman coming up behind me while I wait for a train at Penn Station, grabbing my crotch and asking, "how much?"; it is the receptionist at the gynecologist's office telling me I don't belong there, delaying my needed medical care for dangerous lengths of time; it is the unconsented to questions and declarations about my body.

At that internship in law school, where I first really felt this paradox of hyper-visibility and invisibility, there was something about the liminal gender space I occupied that invited attention. I didn't look quite right but no one could figure out what was "wrong." Everyone in the office knew my name and had their own way of asking (without asking)—"what are you?" Frequently this was in the form of unwanted and sexualized attention. I spent much of the internship managing questions about my body, how I had sex and from one staff member in the office, relentless requests to satisfy his own curiosity about both things.

At the same time, I walked into court every day—with relative ease because of my suit, my masculinity, my whiteness—through the separate security entrance for attorneys and law students. But once inside the courthouse, there was the constant suggestion that I was a young child accompanying my father to work every day. I would be yelled at if I didn't wear a tie—"young man, don't you understand professionalism"—but mocked if I did—"ties are not appropriate for women." One Judge joked flippantly that I was "Doogie Howser" and laughed in front of a courtroom full of people. This certainly didn't help me develop confidence in myself as a person and a lawyer but it paled in comparison to the humiliation and erasure levied upon those mostly black and brown bodies who sat in court awaiting sentencing or trial or more and endless court dates.

Make no mistake; none of these experiences are unique to trans-ness. Tragically few people go through the world without being surveilled and erased by the powerful and their power systems. And those who do—those who feel empowered and safe in powerful spaces—are disproportionately (if not exclusively) white,

Courtesy of Chase Strangio.

cis-, able-bodied, citizens with access to significant financial and social capital. They are the judges making jokes from the bench as they send young black men to prison for life.

Nor are the costs and consequences of this visibility evenly distributed and felt. Imagine what the cost is to those trans people who don't carry the powerful shield from systemic violence that comes with whiteness, masculinity, a legal education, a job doing LGBT work, at an organization with resources and cultural respect and recognition. If I can be erased and attacked, what about my friends and colleagues who are exposed to relentless surveillance, erasure and violence without such protection? What about the trans women of color for whom visibility does not lead to discomfort but to arrest or death?

There is unbearableness to being trans; so much visibility and so much invisibility.

I think of Ashley Arnold,[1] a 32 year-old white trans woman in federal prison in Virginia. She was hyper-visible to the officers who allegedly tormented[2] and harassed her daily. But she was invisible to the prison system and to the courts that systemically withheld her medical care. On February 25, Ashley died by suicide in her cell. When her trans sisters at FCI Petersburg tried to tell her story, make her visible on her own terms, they were punished by the prison. Disciplined for "acting as journalists."

I think of Islan Nettles,[3] a black trans woman, just 21 years old, who was brutally murdered for daring to exist in the world. When Islan walked down the street with her friends, the fact that she was trans evoked so much rage that a group of people beat her to death.

I think of CeCe McDonald,[4] a black trans woman, just 21 years old, when she almost suffered the same fate as Islan. Walking down the street in Minneapolis, her blackness and transness, prompted a group of white people to attack her and beat her. She fought back and survived. And what did she get for surviving against all odds—a manslaughter conviction and years in prison.

There is unbearableness but that unbearableness also binds us together. Amidst the scrutiny, the savage violence, the systemic discrimination, there are communities of resistance and resilience that hold each other up, that send letters and love to people in prison like Ashley's friends who are mourning her death, that organized for CeCe's release from prison, that tell stories of trans histories and leadership.

I am always struck by how many amazing trans people there are—mostly trans women of color—who don't work at big name organizations or appear in magazines or on television, but who make sure that other trans people are housed, fed, supported, and surviving.

Lorena Borjas,[5] Bamby Salcedo, Ruby Corado, Miss Major, Reina Gossett, and so many more. They are the connective tissue, the supportive framework, the breath that gives so many life and that makes trans survival beautiful and possible. Read about them, support them, donate to them.

NOTES

1. Lydon, J. (2015, March 25). *Blackandpink.org*. Prison Censorship in America: The Ashley Jean Arnold Case.

2. Zoukis, C. (2015, March 3). *Prisonlegalnews.org*. Transgender Prisoner Denied Adequate Treatment Hangs Herself.

3. Kellaway, M. (2015, March 4). *Advocate.com*. Suspect Indicted in Beating Death of N.Y. Trans Woman Islan Nettles.

4. Erdely, S. (2014, July 30). *Rollingstone.com*. The Transgender Crucible.

5. Cortes, Z. (2012, May 22). *Voicesofny.org*. Fund Seeks to Address Police Profiling of Transgender Women.

14 Black Bodies in Motion and in Pain

Edwidge Danticat

This past weekend, between not sleeping and constantly checking the news, I walked the long rectangular room at New York's Museum of Modern Art, where Jacob Lawrence's "Migration Series" is currently on display. I had seen many of the paintings before, in books and magazines, but never "in person." I'd somehow expected them to be as colossal as their subject, the fifty-five-year-plus mass migration of more than six million African-Americans from the rural south to urban centers in the northern United States. The sixty spare and, at times, appropriately stark tempera paintings in the series each measure twelve-by-eighteen inches and are underscored by descriptive captions written by the artist, whose parents moved from Virginia and South Carolina to New Jersey, where he was born. The size of the paintings quickly became inconsequential as I moved from panel to panel, the first one showing a crowd of people crammed into a train station and filing toward ticket windows marked Chicago, New York, Saint Louis, and the last panel returning us to yet another railroad station, showing that in spite of dangerous and unhealthy working conditions and race riots in the North, the migrants "kept coming."

At the end of a week when nine men and women were brutally assassinated by a racist young man in Charleston, South Carolina, and the possibility of two hundred thousand Haitians and Dominicans of Haitian descent being expelled from the Dominican Republic suddenly became very real,[1] I longed to be in the presence of Lawrence's migrants and survivors. I was yearning for their witness and fellowship, to borrow language from some of the churches that ended up being lifelines for the Great Migration's new arrivals. But what kept me glued to these dark silhouettes is how beautifully and heartbreakingly Lawrence captured black bodies in motion, in transit, in danger, and in pain. The bowed heads of the hungry and the curved backs of mourners helped the Great Migration to gain and keep its momentum, along with the promise of less abject poverty in the North, better educational opportunities, and the right to vote.

Human beings have been migrating since the beginning of time. We have always travelled from place to place looking for better opportunities, where they exist. We are not always welcomed, especially if we are viewed as different and dangerous, or if we end up, as the novelist Toni Morrison described in her Nobel lecture, on the edges of towns that cannot bear our company. Will we ever have a home in this place, or will we always be set adrift from the home we knew? Or the home we have never known.

The nine men and women who were senselessly murdered at Emanuel African Methodist Episcopal Church last Wednesday were home. They were in their own country, among family and friends, and they believed themselves to be in the presence

Edwidge Danticat/The New Yorker; © Conde Nast.

of God. And yet before they were massacred they were subjected to a variation of the same detestable vitriol that unwanted immigrants everywhere face: "You're taking over our country, and you have to go."

In the hateful manifesto posted on his Web site, the killer, Dylann Roof, also writes, "As an American we are taught to accept living in the melting pot, and black and other minorities have just as much right to be here as we do, since we are all immigrants. But Europe is the homeland of White people, and in many ways the situation is even worse there." I wonder if he had in mind Europe's most recent migrants, especially those who have been drowning by the hundreds in the waters of the Mediterranean Sea, brown and black bodies fleeing oppression and wars in sub-Saharan and northern Africa and the Middle East. Or maybe he was thinking of all those non-white people who are European citizens, though not by his standards. This bigoted young man charged himself with deciding who can stay and who can go, and the only uncontestable way he knew to carry out his venomous decree was to kill.

In "The Warmth of Other Suns," the Pulitzer Prize-winning journalist Isabel Wilkerson writes that, during the Great Migration, "The people did not cross the turnstiles of customs at Ellis Island. They were already citizens. But where they came from, they were not treated as such." Nearly every migrant Wilkerson interviewed justifiably resisted being called an immigrant. "The idea conjured up the deepest pains of centuries of rejection by their own country," she writes.

Tragically, we do not always get the final say on how our black bodies are labelled. Those fleeing the South during the Great Migration were sometimes referred to not only as immigrants but as refugees, just as the U.S. citizens who were internally displaced by Hurricane Katrina were given that label ten years ago.

Dominicans of Haitian descent also thought themselves to be at home in the Dominican Republic. The Dominican constitution, dating back to 1929, grants citizenship to all those who are born in the country, unless they are the children of people "in transit." Dominicans of Haitian descent who were born during the past eighty-six years are still considered to be in transit. Black bodies, living with "certain uncertainty," to use Frantz Fanon's words, can be in transit, it seems, for several generations.

White supremacists such as Dylann Roof like to speak of black bodies as though they are dangerous weapons. Xenophobes often speak of migrants and immigrants as though they are an invasion force or something akin to biological warfare. In an essay called "The Fear of Black Bodies in Motion," Wallace Best, a religion and Great Migration scholar writes that "a black body in motion is never without consequence. It is always a signifier of something, scripted and coded. And for the most part, throughout our history black bodies in motion have been deemed a threat."[2]

These days, it seems that black bodies are more threatened than they have ever been so far in this century. Or maybe we just have more ways to document the beatings, shootings, and other abuses that have been suffered in the recent past. As means of transportation have become more accessible, it also seems that we have more migration than ever. Even children are migrating by the thousands in our hemisphere, crossing several borders to flee gang violence in Central America, while hoping to be reunited with their U.S.-based parents. Still, we live in a world where, as the late Uruguayan writer Eduardo Galeano said, money can move freely, but people cannot.

Black bodies are increasingly becoming battlefields upon which horrors are routinely executed, each one so close to the last that we barely have the time to fully grieve and mourn. The massacre at Emanuel African Methodist Episcopal Church and the racist rant that preceded it highlight the hyper-vigilance required to live and love, work and play, travel and pray in a black body. These killings, and the potential mass expulsions from the Dominican Republic, remind us, as Baby Suggs reminds her out-of-doors congregation in Toni Morrison's "Beloved," that, both yonder and here, some do not love our flesh and are unwilling to acknowledge our humanity, much less our nationality or citizenship.

As many Haitian migrants and immigrants and Dominicans of Haitian descent now either go into hiding or leave the Dominican Republic out of fear, we are witnessing, once again, a sea of black bodies in motion, in transit, and in danger. And as Emanuel African Methodist Episcopal Church and the larger community of Charleston, South Carolina, prepare to bury their dead, we will once again be seeing black bodies in pain. And we will be expected to be exceptionally graceful mourners. We will be expected to stifle our rage. And we will keep asking ourselves, When will this end? When will it stop?

NOTES

1. Danticat, E. (2015, June 17). "Fear of Deportation in the Dominican Republic." *The New Yorker*.

2. Best, W. (2014, December 4). "The Fear of Black Bodies in Motion." *The Huffington Post*.

Suggestions for Further Reading

Adichie, Chimamanda Ngozi. *Americanah*. New York: Anchor Books, 2014.

Adichie, Chimamanda Ngozi. *We Should All Be Feminists*. New York: Anchor Books, 2015.

Anzaldúa, Gloria, ed. *Making Faces, Making Soul: Creative and Critical Perspectives by Women of Color*. San Francisco: Aunt Lute Books, 1990.

Azoulay, Katya Gibel. *Black, Jewish, and Interracial*. Durham, NC: Duke University Press, 1997.

Baca, Jimmy Santiago. *A Place to Stand*. New York: Grove, 2002.

Bahadur, Gaiutra. *Coolie Woman: The Odyssey of Indenture*. Chicago: University of Chicago Press, 2014.

Baumgardner, Jennifer. *Look Both Ways: Bisexual Politics*. New York: Farrar, Straus and Giroux, 2008.

Bayoumi, Moustafa. *This Muslim American Life: Dispatches from the War on Terror*. New York: New York University Press, 2015.

Bean, Joseph. *In the Life: A Black Gay Anthology*. Boston: Alyson Publications, 1986.

Brown, Rita Mae. *Rubyfruit Jungle*. New York: Bantam, 1977.

Clausen, Jan. *Apples and Oranges: My Journey to Sexual Identity*. Boston: Houghton Mifflin, 1999.

Coates, Ta-Nehisi. *Between the World and Me*. New York: Spiegel & Grau, 2015.

Cofer, Judith Ortiz. *The Latin Deli*. Athens, GA: University of Georgia Press, 1993.

Coltelli, Laura. *Winged Words: American Indian Writers Speak*. Lincoln, NE: University of Nebraska Press, 1990.

Crozier-Hogle, Lois, et al. *Surviving in Two Worlds: Contemporary Native American Voices*. Austin: University of Texas Press, 1997.

Danticat, Edwidge. *Breath, Eyes, Memory*. New York: Vintage Books, 1994.

Davis, Lennard. *The Disability Studies Reader*, 4th ed. New York: Routledge, 2013.

Delgado, Richard, and Jean Stefancic. *The Latino/a Condition: A Critical Reader*, 2nd ed. New York: New York University Press, 2010.

Eugenides, Jeffrey. *Middlesex: A Novel*. New York: Picador, 2003.

Findlen, Barbara. *Listen Up: Voices from the Next Feminist Generation*, 2nd ed. Berkeley, CA: Seal Press, 2001.

Fong, Timothy, and Larry Shinagawa. *Asian Americans: Experiences and Perspectives*. Englewood Cliffs, NJ: Prentice Hall, 2000.

Gay, Roxane. *Bad Feminist*. New York: Harper Perennial, 2014.

Gwaltney, John Langston. *Drylongso: A Self-Portrait of Black America*. New York: The New Press, 1993.

Halberstam, Judith. *In a Queer Place and Time: Transgender Bodies, Subcultural Lives*. New York: New York University Press, 2005.

Haley, Alex. *The Autobiography of Malcolm X*. New York: Grove Press, 1964.

Jackson, Naomi. *The Starside of Bird Hill: A Novel*. New York: Penguin Press, 2015.

James, Marlon. *A Brief History of Seven Killings*. New York: Riverhead Books, 2015.

Jen, Gish. *Typical American*. New York: Penguin, 1992.

Kim, Elaine H., Lilia V. Villanueva, and Asian Women United of California, eds. *Making More Waves: New Writings by Asian American Women*. Boston: Beacon Press, 1997.

Kimmel, Michael S., and Michael A. Messner, eds. *Men's Lives*, 9th ed. New York: Prentice Hall, 2012.

Kingston, Maxine Hong. *The Woman Warrior*. New York: Vintage Books, 1981.

Lahiri, Jhumpa. *The Namesake*. New York: Mariner Books, 2003.

Linton, Simi. *My Body Politic*. Ann Arbor: University of Michigan Press, 2005.

Moody, Anne. *Coming of Age in Mississippi*. New York: Dell, 1968.

Moraga, Cherríe L. *A Xicana Codex of Changing Consciousness: Writings, 2000–2010*. Durham, NC: Duke University Press, 2011.

Moraga, Cherríe, and Gloria Anzaldúa, eds. *This Bridge Called My Back*. New York: Kitchen Table: Women of Color Press, 1983.

Nam, Vickie. *Yell-Oh Girls!* New York: HarperCollins, 2001.

Obama, Barack. *Dreams of My Father*. New York: Three Rivers Press, 2004.

Portes, Alejandro, and Rubén G. Rumbaut. *Legacies: The Story of the Immigrant Second Generation*. Berkeley: University of California Press, 2001.

Rankine, Claudia. *Citizen*. Minneapolis, MN: Graywolf Press, 2014.

Rebolledo, Tey Diana, and Eliana S. Rivero, eds. *Infinite Divisions: An Anthology of Chicana Literature*. Tucson: University of Arizona Press, 1993.

Rehman, Bushra. *Corona*. Little Rock, AK: Sibling Rivalry Press, 2013.

Reid, John. *The Best Little Boy in the World*. New York: G.P. Putnam's Sons, 1973.

Rivera, Edward. *Family Installments: Memories of Growing Up Hispanic*. New York: Penguin, 1983.

Rubin, Lillian B. *Worlds of Pain: Life in the Working-Class Family*. New York: Basic Books, 1976.

Santiago, Esmeralda. *When I Was Puerto Rican: A Memoir*. New York: Vintage Books, 1993.

Savage, Dan. *The Commitment: Love, Sex, Marriage, and My Family*. New York: Plume, 2006.

Shulman, Alix Kates. *Memoirs of an Ex-Prom Queen*. New York: Knopf, 1972.

Silko, Leslie Marmon. *Ceremony*. New York: New American Library, 1972.

Smith, Barbara, ed. *Home Girls: A Black Feminist Anthology*. New York: Kitchen Table: Women of Color Press, 1983.

Terkel, Studs. *Working*. New York: Avon Books, 1972.

Warshaw, Robin. *I Never Called It Rape*. New York: Harper & Row, 1988.

Wu, Frank H. *Yellow: Race in America Beyond Black and White*. New York: Basic Books, 2003.

Zahava, Irene, ed. *Speaking for Ourselves: Short Stories by Jewish Lesbians*. Freedom, CA: Crossing Press, 1990.

Zhou, Min, and James V. Gatewood, eds. *Contemporary Asian Americans: A Multidisciplinary Reader*. New York: New York University Press, 2000.

Zia, Helen. *Asian American Dreams: The Emergence of an American People*. New York: Farrar, Straus and Giroux, 2000.

PART VII

How It Happened: Race and Gender Issues in U.S. Law

History can be written from many different perspectives. The life stories of so-called great men will vary greatly depending on whether the biographers are their mothers, their wives, their lovers, their peers, their children, or their servants.

It is commonly believed that history involves collecting and studying facts. But what counts as a "fact," and who decides which facts are important? Whose interests are served or furthered by these decisions? For many years, one of the first "facts" that children learned was that Christopher Columbus "discovered" America. Yet this "history" is neither clear nor incontrovertible. Native Americans might well ask how Columbus could have discovered America in 1492 if they had already been living here for thousands of years. Teaching children that Columbus was a hero served to render Native Americans invisible and thus tacitly excuse or deny the genocide carried out by European settlers.

Traditional historians adopted a fairly narrow, Eurocentric perspective and used it as the basis for writing what was alleged to provide an "objective" and "universal" picture of the past. These texts left out important information and consigned the majority of people in U.S. society to the margins of history. This approach failed to reflect the ways in which women, people of all colors, and working people created the wealth and culture of this country.

Today, many new approaches to history have arisen to remedy the omissions and distortions of the past. Women's history, black history, lesbian and gay history, ethnic history, labor history, and other studies all transform traditional history so that it more accurately reflects the reality of people's lives, both past and present.

Part VII does not attempt to provide a comprehensive history of the American Republic since its beginning. Rather, it traces the legal status of people of color and women since the first Europeans came to this land. After a preliminary reading (Selection 1) that presents an overview of legal issues as they apply to Native Americans in particular, this part presents documents that highlight developments in legal status. In a few cases, these documents are supplemented with materials that help paint a clearer picture of the issues involved in these legal decisions and their implications.

Much is left out by adopting this framework for our study. Most significant, discussions of the political and social movements that brought about the changes in the legal realm are omitted. For this reason, students are urged to supplement their study of the legal documents with the rich accounts of social history from the "Suggestions for Further Reading" list at the end of Part VII. Nonetheless, the legal documents themselves are fascinating. They make it possible to reduce hundreds of years of history to a manageable size. We can thus form a picture of the rights and status of many so-called minority groups in this country, a picture that contrasts sharply with the one usually offered in high school social studies classes. Most importantly, the documents can help us answer the question raised by material in the first six parts of this text: How is it that all women and all people of color have had such limited access to power and opportunity?

The readings here show that from the country's inception, the laws and institutions of the United States were designed to create and maintain the privileges of wealthy white males. The discrimination documented in the early parts of this book is no accident. It has a long and deliberate history. Understanding this history is essential if we are to create a more just and democratic society.

Unequal Laws, Unequal Treatment

On July 4, 1776, the thirteen colonies set forth a declaration of independence from Great Britain. In that famous document, the founders of the Republic explained their reasons for separating from the homeland and expressed their hopes for the new republic. In lines that are rightly famous and often quoted, the signatories proclaimed that "all men are created equal, that they are endowed by their Creator with certain unalienable Rights, that among these are Life, Liberty and the pursuit of Happiness." They went on to assert that "to secure these rights, Governments are instituted among Men, deriving their just Powers from the consent of the governed."

When these words were written, however, a large portion of the population of the United States had no legal rights whatsoever. Native Americans, women, indentured servants, poor white men who did not own property, and, of course, black people held as slaves could not vote, nor were they free to exercise their liberty or pursue their happiness in the same way that white men with property could. When the authors of the Declaration of Independence proclaimed that all men were created equal and endowed with unalienable rights, they meant "men" quite literally, and specifically white men. Black people held in slavery, as it turned out, were worth "three fifths of all other Persons," a figure stipulated in Article 1, Section 2, of the United States Constitution (Selection 3).

Black people were not the only, nor even the first, to be systematically oppressed by the European settlers. The deliberate and severe mistreatment of many groups—including poor white men, women, and children who were brought from Europe as indentured servants—ensued as soon as European settlers landed on these shores three centuries earlier. But the indigenous people of North America suffered the most egregious and most tragic abuse. Faced with the need for an enormous workforce to cultivate the land, the European settlers almost immediately tried to enslave the indigenous population.

When the early European settlers came to this country, there were approximately 2.5 million Native Americans living on the land that was to become the United States. These peoples were divided among numerous separate and autonomous tribes, each with its own highly developed culture and history. The white settlers quickly lumped these diverse peoples into a single and inferior category, "Indians," and set about destroying their cultures and seizing their lands. The Indian Removal Act of 1830 was fairly typical of the kinds of law that were passed to carry out the appropriation of Indian lands. Believing the Indians to be inherently inferior to whites, the U.S. government did not hesitate to legislate the removal of the Indians from valuable ancestral lands to ever more remote and barren reservations. The dissolution of the Indian tribal system was further advanced by the General Allotment Act of 1887 (the Dawes Act), which divided tribal landholdings among individual Indians and thereby successfully undermined the tribal system and the culture of which it was a part. In addition, this act opened up lands within the reservation area for purchase by the U.S. government, which then made those lands available to white settlers for homesteading. Many supporters of the allotment policy, who were considered "friends" of the Indians, argued that the benefits of individual ownership would have a "civilizing effect" on them.[1] Instead, it ensured a life of unrelenting poverty for most because it was usually impossible for a family to derive subsistence from a single plot of land and without the support of the tribal community.

Shortly after the European settlers began stripping land and rights away from the Native Americans, they also began doing the same to the people of Africa in an effort to meet their labor needs. Records show that the first enslaved African people were brought to this country as early as 1526. Initially, the enslaved Africans appear to have had the same status as the poor, white indentured servants brought over from Europe, but the laws reflect a fairly rapid distinction between the two groups. Maryland law made this distinction as early as 1640; Massachusetts legally recognized slavery in 1641; Virginia passed a law making "Negroes" slaves for life in 1661; and so it went until the number of slaves grew to roughly 600,000 at the time of the signing of the Declaration of Independence.[2] Numerous legal documents—such as An Act for the Better Ordering and Governing of Negroes and Slaves, passed in South Carolina in 1712 and excerpted in Selection 2—prescribed the existence of the slaves, as did the acts modeled on An Act

Prohibiting the Teaching of Slaves to Read, a nineteenth-century North Carolina statute reprinted here in Selection 4.

Women were also subject to this system of white male oppression. While John Adams was involved in writing the Declaration of Independence, his wife, Abigail Adams, took him to task for failing to accord women the same rights and privileges as men: "I cannot say that you are very generous to the ladies; for whilst you are proclaiming peace and good will to men, emancipating all nations, you insist upon retaining an absolute power over wives."[3] Although law and custom consistently treated women as if they were physically weaker and mentally inferior to men, the reality of their lived lives was very different. Black female slaves were forced to perform the same inhumane fieldwork as black male slaves and were expected to do so even in the final weeks of pregnancy. They were routinely beaten and abused without regard for the supposed biological fragility of the female sex. White women settlers gave birth to large numbers of children—10 and 12 in a family were quite common, and as many as 20 not unusual—and they did so in addition to working side by side with men to perform all those duties necessary to ensure survival in a new and unfamiliar environment. When her husband died, a woman often assumed his responsibilities as well. It was not until well into the 1800s, primarily as a result of changes brought about by the Industrial Revolution, that significant class differences began to affect the lives and work of white women.

As women, both black and white, became increasingly active in the antislavery movement during the 1800s, many saw similarities between the legal status of women and the legal status of people held as slaves. Participants at the first women's rights convention, held at Seneca Falls, New York, in 1848, listed women's grievances and specified their demands. At this time, married women were regarded as property of their husbands and had no direct legal control over their own wages, their property, or even their children. The Declaration of Sentiments issued at Seneca Falls (Selection 5) was modeled on the Declaration of Independence in the hope that men would extend the declaration's rights to women.

In a more famous case, *Dred Scott* v. *Sandford*, 1857 (Selection 7), the U.S. Supreme Court was asked to decide whether Dred Scott, a black man, was a citizen of the United States with the rights that that implied. Scott, a slave who had been taken from Missouri, a slave state, into the free state of Illinois for a period of time, argued that because he was free and had been born in the United States, he was therefore a citizen. The Court ruled that this was not the case and, using reasoning that strongly parallels *People* v. *Hall* decided two years before, offered a survey of U.S. law and custom to show that black people were never considered a part of the people of the United States.

The abysmal legal status of women and people of color in the United States during the nineteenth century is graphically documented in a number of court decisions reproduced in this part. In *People* v. *Hall*, 1854 (excerpted in Selection 6), the California Supreme Court decided that a California statute barring Indians and black people from testifying in court cases involving whites also applied to Chinese

Americans. The judges asserted that the Chinese were "a race of people whom nature has marked as inferior, and who are incapable of progress or intellectual development beyond a certain point." The extent of anti-Chinese feeling in parts of the United States was further institutionalized through the Chinese Exclusion Act (Selection 11), which remained U.S. policy from 1882 to 1943. A parallel arena of legal inquiry was concerned with whether immigrants were eligible for citizenship. These cases were often based on either "scientific" evidence that assigned the plaintiff a racial category or what the courts understood to be "common sense," a lay person's understanding of race. The case of Bhagat Singh Thind (Selection 15) is significant in that the court conceded that Thind, an Indian Sikh immigrant, could be racially Caucasian, but held that this designation was not equivalent to a common-sense understanding of "whiteness." Here, the common-sense understanding, how a lay person would interpret Thind's race, was the more powerful determinant of his racial assignment than any appeal to science, ancestry, or history.

The Abolitionist Period and the Struggle for Legal Status under the Law

During the period in which these and other court cases were brought, the United States moved toward and ultimately fought a bloody civil war. Allegedly fought to "free the slaves," much more was at stake. The Civil War reflected a struggle to the death between the Southern aristocracy, whose wealth was based on land and whose power rested on a kind of feudal economic and political order, and the Northern capitalists, who rose through the Industrial Revolution and who wished to restructure the nation's economic and political institutions to better serve the needs of the new industrial order. Chief among these needs was a large and mobile workforce for the factories in the North. Hundreds of thousands of soldiers died in the bloody conflict while wealthy Northern men were able to purchase deferments from the Union army for $300; on the Confederate side, men who owned 50 or more slaves were exempt from serving. Among those who purchased deferments and went on to become millionaires as a result of war profiteering were John D. Rockefeller, Andrew Carnegie, J. Pierpont Morgan, Philip Armour, James Mellon, and Jay Gould.[4]

In September 1862, President Abraham Lincoln signed the Emancipation Proclamation (Selection 8) as part of his efforts to bring the Civil War to an end by forcing the Southern states to concede. The proclamation did not free all slaves; it freed only those in states or parts of states in rebellion against the federal government. Only in September 1865, after the war, were all people held as slaves freed by the Thirteenth Amendment (Selection 9). However, Southern whites did not yield their privileges easily. Immediately after the war, the Southern states began to pass laws known as "Black Codes," which attempted to reestablish the conditions of slavery. Some of these codes are described in Selection 10, written by the historian W. E. B. Du Bois.

In the face of such efforts to deny the rights of citizenship to black men, Congress passed the Fourteenth Amendment (in Selection 9) in July 1868. This amendment, which plays a major role in contemporary legal battles over discrimination, includes a number of important provisions. It explicitly extended citizenship to all those born or naturalized in the United States and guaranteed all citizens "due process" and "equal protection" of the law. In addition, it canceled all debts incurred by the Confederacy in its unsuccessful rebellion, while recognizing the validity of the debts incurred by the federal government. This meant that wealthy Southerners who had extended large sums of money or credit to the Confederacy would lose it, whereas wealthy Northern industrialists would be repaid.

Southern resistance to extending the rights and privileges of citizenship to black men persisted, and the Southern states used all their powers, including unbridled terror and violence, to subvert the intent of the Thirteenth and Fourteenth Amendments. The Fifteenth Amendment (in Selection 9), which explicitly granted the vote to black men, was passed in 1870 but was received by the Southern states with as little enthusiasm as had greeted the Thirteenth and Fourteenth Amendments.

Even after the passage of the Fifteenth Amendment, voting rights continued to be contested, as shown by *Elk* v. *Wilkins,* 1884 (Selection 12). John Elk, a Native American who had left his tribe and lived among whites, argued that he was a citizen by virtue of the Fourteenth Amendment and should not be denied the right to vote by the state of Nebraska. The Supreme Court ruled that neither the Fourteenth nor Fifteenth Amendment applied to Elk. Native Americans became citizens of the United States three years later, under one of the provisions of the Dawes Act of 1887.

Likewise, the struggle for equal status in the social sphere of people's everyday lives continued to be contested. Unsuccessful in their attempts to reinstate some form of forced servitude by passage of the Black Codes, Southern states began to legalize the separation of the races in all aspects of public and private life. In *Plessy* v. *Ferguson,* 1896 (Selection 13), the Supreme Court was asked to rule on whether segregation by race in public facilities violated the Thirteenth and Fourteenth Amendments. In a ruling that was to cruelly affect several generations of black Americans, the Supreme Court decided that restricting black people to the use of "separate but equal" public accommodations did not deny them equal protection of the law. This decision remained in effect for almost 60 years, until *Brown* v. *Board of Education of Topeka,* 1954 (Selection 16). In the historic Brown decision, the Court ruled that "[se]parate educational facilities are inherently unequal." Nonetheless, abolishing segregation on paper was one thing; actually bringing about the integration of schools, and other public facilities, was another. The integration of public schools, housing, and employment in both the North and the South has been a long and often bloody struggle that continues to this day.

As has often been the case throughout American history, the rights and status of women took a back seat. As the abolitionist movement grew and the Civil War became inevitable, many women's rights activists, also engaged in the struggle to end slavery, argued that the push for women's rights should temporarily defer to the issue of slavery. After February 1861, no women's rights conventions were held until the end of the war. Although black and white women had long worked together in both movements, the question of which struggle took precedence created serious splits among women's rights activists, including such strong black allies as Frederick Douglass and Sojourner Truth. Some argued that the evils of slavery were so great that they took priority over the legal discrimination experienced by middle class white women. They resented attempts by Elizabeth Cady Stanton and others to equate the condition of white women with that of black people held in slavery and argued, moreover, that the women's rights movement had never been concerned with the extraordinary suffering of black women or the special needs of working women. The explicitly racist appeals made by some white women activists as they sought white men's support for women's suffrage did nothing to repair this schism. Black men received the vote in 1868, at least on paper, but women would have to continue their fight until the passage of the Nineteenth Amendment (Selection 14) in 1920. As a result, many women and blacks saw each other as adversaries or obstacles in their struggle for legal equality, deflecting their attention from the privileged white men who provoked the conflict and whose power was reinforced by it.

The Struggle Continues

The latter part of the twentieth century witnessed the growth of large and diverse movements for race and gender justice that are still rigorously championing not only equal laws but also equal treatment under those laws. These movements precipitated the creation of a number of commissions and government agencies, which were to research and enforce equal treatment for people of color and women; they also forced the passage of a number of statutes to this end and a series of Supreme Court decisions. For women, one of the most significant Court decisions of the recent past was *Roe* v. *Wade,* 1973 (Selection 17), which for the first time gave women the unconditional right to terminate pregnancy by abortion. Rather than affirming a woman's right to control her body, however, the Roe decision is based on the right to privacy. The impact of Roe was significantly blunted by *Harris* v. *McRae,* 1980, in which the Court ruled that the right to privacy did not require public funding of medically necessary abortions for women who could not afford them. In practice, this meant that middle class women who chose abortion could exercise their right but that many poor white women and women of color could not. The single biggest defeat for the women's movement of this period was the failure to pass the much misunderstood Equal Rights Amendment, which is reproduced in Selection 18.

Part VII concludes with an excerpt from the recent Supreme Court ruling in *Obergefell* v. *Hodges,* 2015 (Selection 19), that legalized same-sex marriage in all states. After many years of challenges to the bans on legal recognition of these relationships, the civil right to marry has been extended to lesbian and gay couples.

NOTES

1. U.S. Commission on Civil Rights, *Indian Tribes: A Continuing Quest for Survival,* a report of the United States Commission on Civil Rights, June 1981, p. 34.

2. W. Z. Foster, *The Negro People in American History* (New York: International Publishers, 1954), p. 37.

3. Letter to John Adams, May 7, 1776.

4. H. Wasserman, *Harvey Wasserman's History of the United States* (New York: Harper & Row, 1975), p. 3.

1 Indian Tribes

A Continuing Quest for Survival

U.S. Commission on Human Rights

Traditional civil rights, as the phrase is used here, include those rights that are secured to individuals and are basic to the United States system of government. They include the right to vote and the right to equal treatment without discrimination on the basis of race, religion, or national origin, among others, in such areas as education, housing, employment, public accommodations, and the administration of justice.

In order to understand where American Indians stand today with respect to these rights, it is important to look at historical developments of the concept of Indian rights along with the civil rights movement in this country. The consideration given to these factors here will not be exhaustive, but rather a brief look at some of the events that are most necessary to a background understanding of this area.

A basic and essential factor concerning American Indians is that the development of civil rights issues for them is in reverse order from other minorities in this country. Politically, other minorities started with nothing and attempted to obtain a voice in the existing economic and political structure. Indians started with everything and have gradually lost much of what they had to an advancing alien civilization. Other minorities have had no separate governmental institutions. Their goal primarily has been and continues to be to make the existing system involve them and work for them. Indian tribes have always been separate political entities interested in maintaining their own institutions and beliefs. Their goal has been to prevent the dismantling of their own systems. So while other minorities have sought integration into the larger society, much of Indian society is motivated to retain its political and cultural separateness.

Although at the beginning of the colonization process Indian nations were more numerous and better adapted to survival on this continent than the European settlers, these advantages were quickly lost. The colonization period saw the rapid expansion of non-Indian communities in numbers and territory covered and a shift in the balance of strength from Indian to non-Indian communities and governments. The extent to which Indians intermingled with non-Indian society varied by time period, geographical location, and the ability of natives and newcomers to get along with one another. As a general matter, however, Indians were viewed and treated as members of political entities that were not part of the United States. The Constitution acknowledges this by its separate provision regarding trade with the Indian tribes.[1] Indian tribes today that have not been forcibly assimilated, extinguished, or legally terminated still consider themselves to be, and are viewed in American law, as separate political units.

Indian Tribes: A Continuing Quest for Survival, a report of the United States Commission on Civil Rights, June 1981, p. 34. Reprinted by permission.

The Racial Factor

An important element in the development of civil rights for American Indians today goes beyond their legal and political status to include the way they have been viewed racially. Since colonial times Indians have been viewed as an "inferior race"; sometimes this view is condescendingly positive—the romanticized noble savage—at other times this view is hostile—the vicious savage—at all times the view is racist. All things Indian are viewed as inherently inferior to their counterparts in the white European tradition. Strong racist statements have appeared in congressional debates, Presidential policy announcements, court decisions, and other authoritative public utterances. This racism has served to justify a view now repudiated, but which still lingers in the public mind, that Indians are not entitled to the same legal rights as others in this country. In some cases, racism has been coupled with apparently benevolent motives, to "civilize" the "savages," to teach them Christian principles. In other cases, the racism has been coupled with greed; Indians were "removed" to distant locations to prevent them from standing in the way of the development of the new Western civilization. At one extreme the concept of inferior status of Indians was used to justify genocide; at the other, apparently benevolent side, the attempt was to assimilate them into the dominant society. Whatever the rationale or motive, whether rooted in voluntary efforts or coercion, the common denominator has been the belief that Indian society is an inferior lifestyle.

> It sprang from a conviction that native people were a lower grade of humanity for whom the accepted cannons [sic] of respect need not apply; one did not debase oneself by ruining a native person. At times, this conviction was stated explicitly by men in public office, but whether expressed or not, it generated decision and action.[2]

Early assimilationists like Thomas Jefferson proceeded from this assumption with benevolent designs.

> Thus, even as they acknowledged a degree of political autonomy in the tribes, their conviction of the natives' cultural inferiority led them to interfere in their social, religious, and economic practices. Federal agents to the tribes not only negotiated treaties and tendered payments; they pressured husbands to take up the plow and wives to learn to spin. The more conscientious agents offered gratuitous lectures on the virtues of monogamy, industry, and temperance.

The same underlying assumption provided the basis for Andrew Jackson's attitude. "I have long viewed treaties with the Indians an absurdity not to be reconciled to the principles of our government," he said. As President he refused to enforce the decisions of the U.S. Supreme Court upholding Cherokee tribal autonomy, and he had a prominent role in the forced removal of the Cherokees from Georgia and the appropriation of their land by white settlers. Other eastern tribes met a similar fate under the Indian Removal Act of 1830.[3]

Another Federal Indian land policy, enacted at the end of the 19th century and followed until 1934, that shows the virulent effect of racist assumptions was the allotment of land parcels to individual Indians as a replacement for tribal ownership.

Many proponents of the policy were considered "friends of the Indians," and they argued that the attributes of individual land ownership would have a great civilizing and assimilating effect on American Indians. This action, undertaken for the benefit of the Indians, was accomplished without consulting them. Had Congress heeded the views of the purported beneficiaries of this policy, allotment might not have been adopted. Representatives of 19 tribes met in Oklahoma and unanimously opposed the legislation, recognizing the destructive effect it would have upon Indian culture and the land base itself, which was reduced by 90 million acres in 45 years.

An important principle established by the allotment policy was that the Indian form of land ownership was not "civilized," and so it was the right of the Government to invalidate that form. It is curious that the principle of the right to own property in conglomerate form for the benefit of those with a shareholder's undivided interest in the whole was a basis of the American corporate system, then developing in strength. Yet a similar form of ownership when practiced by Indians was viewed as a hallmark of savagery. Whatever the explanation for this double standard, the allotment policy reinforced the notion that Indians were somehow inferior, that non-Indians in power knew what was best for them, and that these suppositions justified the assertion that non-Indians had the power and authority to interfere with the basic right to own property.

Religion is another area in which non-Indians have felt justified in interfering with Indian beliefs. The intent to civilize the natives of this continent included a determined effort to Christianize them. Despite the constitutional prohibition, Congress, beginning in 1819, regularly appropriated funds for Christian missionary efforts. Christian goals were visibly aligned with Federal Indian policy in 1869 when a Board of Indian Commissioners was established by Congress under President Grant's administration. Representative of the spectrum of Christian denominations, the independently wealthy members of the Board were charged by the Commissioner of Indian Affairs to work for the "humanization, civilization and Christianization of the Indians." Officials of the Federal Indian Service were supposed to cooperate with this Board.

The benevolent support of Christian missionary efforts stood in stark contrast to the Federal policy of suppressing tribal religions. Indian ceremonial behavior was misunderstood and suppressed by Indian agents. In 1892 the Commissioner of Indian Affairs established a regulation making it a criminal offense to engage in such ceremonies as the sun dance. The spread of the Ghost Dance religion, which promised salvation from the white man, was so frightening to the Federal Government that troops were called in to prevent it, even though the practice posed no threat to white settlers.

The judiciary of the United States, though it has in many instances forthrightly interpreted the law to support Indian legal claims in the face of strong, sometimes violent opposition, has also lent support to the myth of Indian inferiority. For example, the United States Supreme Court in 1883, in recognizing the right of tribes to govern themselves, held that they had the exclusive authority to try Indians for criminal offenses committed against Indians. In describing its reasons for refusing to find jurisdiction in a non-Indian court in such cases, the Supreme Court said:

> It [the non-Indian court] tries them, not by their peers, nor by the customs of their people, nor the law of their land, but by *superiors* of a different race, according to the

> law of a social state of which they have an imperfect conception, and which is opposed
> to the traditions of their history, to the habits of their lives, to the strongest prejudices
> of their *savage nature*; one which measures the red man's revenge by the maxims of the
> white man's morality.[4] (emphasis added)

In recognizing the power of the United States Government to determine the right
of Indians to occupy their lands, the Supreme Court expressed the good faith of the
country in such matters with these words: "the United States will be governed by
such considerations of justice as will control a Christian people in their treatment of
an ignorant and dependent race."[5]

Another example of racist stereotyping to be found in the courts is this example
from the Supreme Court of Washington State:

> The Indian was a child, and a dangerous child, of nature, to be both protected and
> restrained. . . . True, arrangements took the form of treaty and of terms like "cede," "re-
> linquish," "reserve." But never were these agreements between equals . . . [but rather]
> that "between a superior and an inferior."[6]

This reasoning, based on racism, has supported the view that Indians are wards
of the Government who need the protection and assistance of Federal agencies and
it is the Government's obligation to recreate their governments, conforming them to
a non-Indian model, to establish their priorities, and to make or approve their decisions for them.

Indian education policies have often been examples of the Federal Government
having determined what is "best" for Indians. Having judged that assimilation could
be promoted through the indoctrination process of white schools, the Federal Government began investing in Indian education. Following the model established by
army officer Richard Pratt in 1879, boarding schools were established where Indian
children were separated from the influences of tribal and home life. The boarding
schools tried to teach Indians skills and trades that would be useful in white society,
utilizing stern disciplinary measures to force assimilation. The tactics used are within
memory of today's generation of tribal leaders who recall the policy of deterring
communication in native languages. "I remember being punished many times for . . .
singing one Navajo song, or a Navajo word slipping out of my tongue just in an un-
planned way, but I was punished for it."

Federal education was made compulsory, and the policy was applied to tribes that
had sophisticated school systems of their own as well as to tribes that really needed
assistance to establish educational systems. The ability of the tribal school to educate
was not relevant, given that the overriding goal was assimilation rather than education.

Racism in Indian affairs has not been sanctioned recently by political or religious
leaders or other leaders in American society. In fact, public pronouncements over
the last several decades have lamented past evils and poor treatment of Indians.[7]
The virulent public expressions of other eras characterizing Indians as "children" or
"savages" are not now acceptable modes of public expression. Public policy today is
a commitment to Indian self-determination. Numerous actions of Congress and the
executive branch give evidence of a more positive era for Indian policy.[8] Beneath

the surface, however, the effects of centuries of racism still persist. The attitudes of the public, of State and local officials, and of Federal policymakers do not always live up to the positive pronouncements of official policy. Some decisions today are perceived as being made on the basis of precedents mired in the racism and greed of another era. Perhaps more important, the legacy of racism permeates behavior and that behavior creates classic civil rights violations. . . .

NOTES

1. U.S. Const. Art. 1, §8.
2. D'Arcy McNickel, *Native American Tribalism* (New York: Oxford University Press, 1973), p. 56.
3. Act of May 28, 1830, ch. 148, 4 Stat. 411.
4. *Ex Parte Crow Dog*, 109 U.S. 556, 571 (1883).
5. *Missouri, Kansas, and Texas Railway Co. v. Roberts*, 152 U.S. 114, 117 (1894).
6. *State v. Towessnute*, 154 P. 805, 807 (Wash. Sup. Ct. 1916), quoting *Choctaw Nation v. United States*, 119 U.S. 1, 27 (1886).
7. See, e.g., President Nixon's July 8, 1970, Message to the Congress, Recommendations for Indian Policy, H. Doc. No. 91–363, 91st Cong., 2d sess.
8. Ibid; Indian Self-Determination and Education Assistance Act, Pub. L. No. 93–638, 88 Stat. 2203 (1975); Indian Child Welfare Act of 1978, Pub. L. No. 95–608, 92 Stat. 3096; U.S. Department of the Interior, *Report on the Implementation of the Helsinki Final Act* (1979).

2 An Act for the Better Ordering and Governing of Negroes and Slaves, South Carolina, 1712

Colonial America had a role for the Negro. But the presence of a servile population, presumably of inferior stock, made it necessary to adopt measures of control. As might be expected, the southern colonies had the most highly developed codes governing Negroes. In 1712 South Carolina passed "An Act for the better ordering and governing of Negroes and Slaves." This comprehensive measure served as a model for slave codes in the South during the colonial and national periods. Eight of its thirty-five sections are reproduced below.

Whereas, the plantations and estates of this province cannot be well and sufficiently managed and brought into use, without the labor and service of negroes and other slaves; and forasmuch as the said negroes and other slaves brought unto the people of this Province for that purpose, are of barbarous, wild, savage natures, and such as renders them wholly unqualified to be governed by the laws, customs, and practices of this Province; but that it is absolutely necessary, that such other constitutions, laws and orders, should in this Province be made and enacted, for the good regulating and ordering of them, as may restrain the disorders, rapines and inhumanity, to which they are naturally prone and inclined, and may also tend to the safety and security of the people of this Province and their estates; to which purpose,

I. *Be it therefore enacted*, by his Excellency William, Lord Craven, Palatine, and the rest of the true and absolute Lords and Proprietors of this Province, by and with the advice and consent of the rest of the members of the General Assembly, now met at Charlestown, for the South-west part of this Province, and by the authority of the same, That all negroes, mulatoes, mustizoes or Indians, which at any time heretofore have been sold, or now are held or taken to be, or hereafter shall be bought and sold for slaves, are hereby declared slaves; and they, and their children, are hereby made and declared slaves, to all intents and purposes; excepting all such negroes, mulatoes, mustizoes or Indians, which heretofore have been, or hereafter shall be, for some particular merit, made and declared free, either by the Governor and council of this Province, pursuant to any Act or law of this Province, or by their respective owners or masters; and also, excepting all such negroes, mulatoes, mustizoes or Indians, as can prove they ought not to be sold for slaves. And in case any negro, mulatoe, mustizoe or Indian, doth lay claim to his or her freedom, upon all or any of the said accounts, the same shall be finally heard and determined by the Governor and council of this Province.

From Thomas Cooper and David J. McCord, eds., *Statutes at Large of South Carolina* (10 vols., Columbia, 1836–1841), VII, 352–357.

II. And for the better ordering and governing of negroes and all other slaves in this Province, *Be it enacted* by the authority aforesaid, That no master, mistress, overseer, or other person whatsoever, that hath the care and charge of any negro or slave, shall give their negroes and other slaves leave, on Sundays, hollidays, or any other time, to go out of their plantations, except such negro or other slave as usually wait upon them at home or abroad, or wearing a livery; and every other negro or slave that shall be taken hereafter out of his master's plantation, without a ticket, or leave in writing, from his master or mistress, or some other person by his or her appointment, or some white person in the company of such slave, to give an account of his business, shall be whipped; and every person who shall not (when in his power) apprehend every negro or other slave which he shall see out of his master's plantation, without leave as aforesaid, and after apprehended, shall neglect to punish him by moderate whipping, shall forfeit twenty shillings, the one half to the poor, to be paid to the church wardens of the Parish where such forfeiture shall become due, and the other half to him that will inform for the same, within one week after such neglect; and that no slave may make further or other use of any one ticket than was intended by him that granted the same, every ticket shall particularly mention the name of every slave employed in the particular business, and to what place they are sent, and what time they return; and if any person shall presume to give any negro or slave a ticket in the name of his master or mistress, without his or her consent, such person so doing shall forfeit the sum of twenty shillings; one half to the poor, to be disposed of as aforesaid, the other half to the person injured, that will complain against the person offending, within one week after the offence committed. And for the better security of all such persons that shall endeavor to take any runaway, or shall examine any slave for his ticket, passing to and from his master's plantation, it is hereby declared lawful for any white person to beat, maim or assult, and if such negro or slave cannot otherwise be taken, to kill him, who shall refuse to shew his ticket, or, by running away or resistance, shall endeavor to avoid being apprehended or taken.

III. *And be it further enacted* by the authority aforesaid, That every master, mistress or overseer of a family in this Province, shall cause all his negro houses to be searched diligently and effectually, once every fourteen days, for fugitive and runaway slaves, guns, swords, clubs, and any other mischievous weapons, and finding any, to take them away, and cause them to be secured; as also, for clothes, goods, and any other things and commodities that are not given them by their master, mistress, commander or overseer, and honestly come by; and in whose custody they find any thing of that kind, and suspect or know to be stolen goods, the same they shall seize and take into their custody, and a full and ample description of the particulars thereof, in writing, within ten days after the discovery thereof, either to the provost marshall, or to the clerk of the parish for the time being, who is hereby required to receive the same, and to enter upon it the day of its receipt, and the particulars to file and keep to himself; and the clerk shall set upon the posts of the church door, and the provost marshall upon the usual public places, or places of notice, a short brief, that such lost goods are found; whereby, any person that hath lost his goods may the better come to the knowledge where they are; and the owner going to the marshall or clerk, and proving, by marks or otherwise, that the goods lost belong to him, and paying twelve pence for the entry and declaration of the same, if the marshall or clerk be convinced that any part of the goods certified by him to be found, appertains to the party inquiring, he is to direct the said party inquiring to the place and party where the goods be, who is hereby required to make restitution of what is in being to the true owner; and every master, mistress or overseer, as also the provost marshall or clerk, neglecting his duty in any the particulars aforesaid, for every neglect shall forfeit twenty shillings.

IV. And for the more effectual detecting and punishing such persons that trade with any slave for stolen goods, *Be it further enacted* by the authority aforesaid, That where any person shall be suspected to trade as aforesaid, any justice of the peace shall have power to take from him suspected, sufficient recognizance, not to trade with any slave contrary to the laws of this Province; and if it shall afterwards appear to any of the justices of the peace, that such person hath, or hath had, or shipped off, any goods, suspected to be unlawfully come by, it shall be lawful for such justice of the peace to oblige the person to appear at the next general sessions, who shall there be obliged to make reasonable proof, of whom he brought, or how he came by, the said goods, and unless he do it, his recognizance shall be forfeited. . . .

VII. And *whereas*, great numbers of slaves which do not dwell in Charlestown, on Sundays and holidays resort thither, to drink, quarrel, fight, curse and swear, and profane the Sabbath, and using and carrying of clubs and other mischievous weapons, resorting in great companies together, which may give them an opportunity of executing any wicked designs and purposes, to the damage and prejudice of the inhabitants of this Province; for the prevention whereof, *Be it enacted* by the authority aforesaid, That all and every the constables of Charlestown, separately on every Sunday, and the holidays at Christmas, Easter and Whitsonside [*sic*], together with so many men as each constable shall think necessary to accompany him, which he is hereby empowered for that end to press, under the penalty of twenty shillings to the person that shall disobey him, shall, together with such persons, go through all or any the streets, and also, round about Charlestown, and as much further on the neck as they shall be informed or have reason to suspect any meeting or concourse of any such negroes or slaves to be at that time, and to enter into any house, at Charlestown, or elsewhere, to search for such slaves, and as many of them as they can apprehend, shall cause to be publicly whipped in Charlestown, and then to be delivered to the marshall, who for every slave so whipped and delivered to him by the constable, shall pay the constable five shillings, which five shillings shall be repaid the said marshall by the owner or head of that family to which the said negro or slave, doth belong, together with such other charges as shall become due to him for keeping runaway slaves; and the marshall shall in all respects keep and dispose of such slave as if the same was delivered to him as a runaway, under the same penalties and forfeiture as hereafter in that case is provided; and every constable of Charlestown which shall neglect or refuse to make search as aforesaid, for every such neglect shall forfeit the sum of twenty shillings. . . .

IX. *And be it further enacted* by the authority aforesaid, That upon complaint made to any justice of the peace, of any heinous or grievous crime, committed by any slave or slaves, as murder, burglary, robbery, burning of houses, or any lesser crimes, as killing or stealing any meat or other cattle, maiming one the other, stealing of fowls, provisions, or such like trespasses or injuries, the said justice shall issue out his warrant for apprehending the offender or offenders, and for all persons to come before him that can give evidence; and if upon examination, it probably appeareth, that the apprehended person is guilty, he shall commit him or them to prison, or immediately proceed to tryal of the said slave or slaves, according to the form hereafter specified, or take security for his or their forthcoming, as the case shall require, and also to certify to the justice next to him, the said cause, and to require him, by virtue of this Act, to associate himself to him, which said justice is hereby required to do, and they so associated, are to issue their summons to three sufficient freeholders, acquainting them with the matter, and appointing them a day, hour and place, when and where the same shall be heard and determined, at which day, hour and place, the said justices and freeholders shall cause the offenders and evidences to come before them, and if they, on hearing the matter, the said freeholders being by the said justices first sworn to judge uprightly and according to evidence, and diligently weighing and examining all evidences, proofs and testimonies (and in case of murder only, if on violent presumption and circumstances), they shall find such negro or other slave or slaves guilty thereof, they shall give sentence of death, if the crime by law deserve the same, and forthwith by their warrant cause immediate execution to be done, by the common or any other executioner, in such manner as they shall think fit, the kind of death to be inflicted to be left to their judgment and discretion; and if the crime committed shall not deserve death, they shall then condemn and adjudge the criminal or criminals to any other punishment, but not extending to limb or disabling him, without a particular law directing such punishment, and shall forthwith order execution to be done accordingly.

X. And in regard great mischiefs daily happen by petty larcenies committed by negroes and slaves of this Province, *Be it further enacted* by the authority aforesaid, That if any negro or other slave shall hereafter steal or destroy any goods, chattels, or provisions whatsoever, of any other person than his master or mistress, being under the value of twelve pence, every negro or other slave so offending, and being brought before some justice of the peace of this Province, upon complaint of the party injured, and shall be adjudged guilty by confession, proof, or probable circumstances, such negro or slave so offending, excepting children, whose punishment is left wholly to the discretion of the said justice, shall be adjudged by such justice to be publicly and severely whipped, not exceeding forty lashes; and if such negro or other slave punished as aforesaid, be afterwards, by two justices of the peace, found guilty of the like crimes, he or they, for such his or their second offence, shall either have one of his ears cut off, or be branded in the forehead with a hot iron, that the mark thereof may remain; and if after such punishment, such negro or slave for his third offence, shall have his nose slit; and if such negro or other slave, after the third time as aforesaid, be accused of petty larceny, or of any of the offences before mentioned, such negro or other slave shall be tried in such manner as those accused of murder, burglary, *etc.* are before by this Act provided for to be tried, and in case they shall be found guilty a fourth time, of any of the offences before mentioned, then such negro or other slave shall be adjudged to suffer death, or other punishment, as the said justices shall think fitting; and any judgment given for the first offence, shall be a sufficient conviction for the first offence; and any after judgment after the first judgment, shall be a sufficient conviction to bring the offender within the penalty of the second offence, and so for inflicting the rest of the punishments; and in case the said justices and freeholders, and any or either of them, shall neglect or refuse to perform the duties by this Act required of them, they shall severally, for such their defaults, forfeit the sum of twenty-five pounds. . . .

XII. *And it is further enacted* by the authority aforesaid, That if any negroes or other slaves shall make mutiny or insurrection, or rise in rebellion against the authority and government of this Province, or shall make preparation of arms, powder, bullets or offensive weapons, in order to carry on such mutiny or insurrection, or shall hold any counsel or conspiracy for raising such mutiny, insurrection or rebellion, the offenders shall be tried by two justices of the peace and three freeholders, associated together as before expressed in case of murder, burglary, *etc.*, who are hereby empowered and required to try the said slaves so offending, and inflict death, or any other punishment, upon the offenders, and forthwith by their warrant cause execution to be done, by the common or any other executioner, in such manner as they shall think fitting; and if any person shall make away or conceal any negro or negroes, or other slave or slaves, suspected to be guilty of the beforementioned crimes, and not upon demand bring forth the suspected offender or offenders, such person shall forfeit for every negro or slave so concealed or made away, the sum of fifty pounds; *Provided, nevertheless,* that when and as often as any of the beforementioned crimes shall be committed by more than one negro, that shall deserve death, that then and in all such cases, if the Governor and council of this Province shall think fitting, and accordingly shall order, that only one or more of the said criminals should suffer death as exemplary, and the rest to be returned to the owners, that then, the owners of the negroes so offending, shall bear proportionably the loss of the said negro or negroes so put to death, as shall be allotted them by the said justices and freeholders; and if any person shall refuse his part so allotted him, that then, and in all such cases, the said justices and freeholders are hereby required to issue out their warrant of distress upon the goods and chattels of the person so refusing, and shall cause the same to be sold by public outcry, to satisfy the said money so allotted him to pay, and to return the overplus, if any be, to the owner; *Provided, nevertheless,* that the part allotted for any person to pay for his part or proportion of the negro or negroes so put to death, shall not exceed one sixth part of his negro or negroes so excused and pardoned; and in case that shall not be sufficient to satisfy for the negro or negroes that shall be put to death, that the remaining sum shall be paid out of the public treasury of this Province.

3 The "Three-Fifths Compromise"
The U.S. Constitution, Article I, Section 2

One of the major debates in the Constitutional Convention hinged on the use of slaves in computing taxes and fixing representation. Southern delegates held that slaves should be computed in determining representation in the House, but that they should not be counted in determining a state's share of the direct tax burden. The northern delegates' point of view was exactly the opposite. A compromise was reached whereby three-fifths of the slaves were to be counted in apportionment of representation and in direct taxes among the states. Thus the South was victorious in obtaining representation for its slaves, even though delegate Luther Martin might rail that the Constitution was an insult to the Deity "who views with equal eye the poor African slave and his American master." The "three-fifths compromise" appears in Article I, Section 2.

Representatives and direct Taxes shall be apportioned among the several States which may be included within this Union, according to their respective Numbers, which shall be determined by adding to the whole Number of free Persons, including those bound to Service for a Term of Years, and excluding Indians not taxed, three fifths of all other Persons.

4 An Act Prohibiting the Teaching of Slaves to Read

To keep the slaves in hand, it was deemed necessary to keep them innocent of the printed page. Otherwise, they might read abolitionist newspapers that were smuggled in, become dissatisfied, forge passes, or simply know too much. Hence most states passed laws prohibiting anyone from teaching slaves to read or write. The North Carolina statute was typical.

An Act to Prevent All Persons from Teaching Slaves to Read or Write, the Use of Figures Excepted

Whereas the teaching of slaves to read and write, has a tendency to excite dissatisfaction in their minds, and to produce insurrection and rebellion, to the manifest injury of the citizens of this State:

Therefore,

Be it enacted by the General Assembly of the State of North Carolina, and it is hereby enacted by the authority of the same, That any free person, who shall hereafter teach, or attempt to teach, any slave within the State to read or write, the use of figures excepted, or shall give or sell to such slave or slaves any books or pamphlets, shall be liable to indictment in any court of record in this State having jurisdiction thereof, and upon conviction, shall, at the discretion of the court, if a white man or woman, be fined not less than one hundred dollars, nor more than two hundred dollars, or imprisoned; and if a free person of color, shall be fined, imprisoned, or whipped, at the discretion of the court, not exceeding thirty-nine lashes, nor less than twenty lashes.

II. *Be it further enacted,* That if any slave shall hereafter teach, or attempt to teach, any other slave to read or write, the use of figures excepted, he or she may be carried before any justice of the peace, and on conviction thereof, shall be sentenced to receive thirty-nine lashes on his or her bare back.

III. *Be it further enacted,* That the judges of the Superior Courts and the justices of the County Courts shall give this act in charge to the grand juries of their respective counties.

From *Acts Passed by the General Assembly of the State of North Carolina at the Session of 1830–1831* (Raleigh, 1831), 11.

5 Declaration of Sentiments and Resolutions, Seneca Falls Convention, 1848

The Declaration of Sentiments, adopted in July 1848 at Seneca Falls, New York, at the first woman's rights convention, is the most famous document in the history of feminism. Like its model, the Declaration of Independence, it contains a bill of particulars. Some people at the meeting thought the inclusion of disfranchisement in the list of grievances would discredit the entire movement, and when the resolutions accompanying the Declaration were put to a vote, the one calling for the suffrage was the only one that did not pass unanimously. But it did pass and thus inaugurated the woman's suffrage movement in the United States.

Declaration of Sentiments

When, in the course of human events, it becomes necessary for one portion of the family of man to assume among the people of the earth a position different from that which they have hitherto occupied, but one to which the laws of nature and of nature's God entitle them, a decent respect to the opinions of mankind requires that they should declare the causes that impel them to such a course.

We hold these truths to be self-evident: that all men and women are created equal; that they are endowed by their Creator with certain inalienable rights; that among these are life, liberty, and the pursuit of happiness; that to secure these rights governments are instituted, deriving their just powers from the consent of the governed. Whenever any form of government becomes destructive of these ends, it is the right of those who suffer from it to refuse allegiance to it, and to insist upon the institution of a new government, laying its foundation on such principles, and organizing its powers in such form, as to them shall seem most likely to effect their safety and happiness. Prudence, indeed, will dictate that governments long established should not be changed for light and transient causes; and accordingly all experience hath shown that mankind are more disposed to suffer, while evils are sufferable, than to right themselves by abolishing the forms to which they were accustomed. But when a long train of abuses and usurpations, pursuing invariably the same object, evinces a design to reduce them under absolute despotism, it is their duty to throw off such government, and to provide new guards for their future security. Such has been the patient sufferance of the women under this government, and such is now the necessity which constrains them to demand the equal station to which they are entitled.

The history of mankind is a history of repeated injuries and usurpations on the part of man toward woman, having in direct object the establishment of an absolute tyranny over her. To prove this, let facts be submitted to a candid world.

He has never permitted her to exercise her inalienable right to the elective franchise.

He has compelled her to submit to laws, in the formation of which she had no voice.

He has withheld from her rights which are given to the most ignorant and degraded men—both natives and foreigners.

Having deprived her of this first right of a citizen, the elective franchise, thereby leaving her without representation in the halls of legislation, he has oppressed her on all sides.

He has made her, if married, in the eye of the law, civilly dead.

He has taken from her all right in property, even to the wages she earns.

He has made her, morally, an irresponsible being, as she can commit many crimes with impunity, provided they be done in the presence of her husband. In the covenant of marriage, she is compelled to promise obedience to her husband, he becoming, to all intents and purposes, her master—the law giving him power to deprive her of her liberty, and to administer chastisement.

He has so framed the laws of divorce, as to what shall be the proper causes, and in case of separation, to whom the guardianship of the children shall be given, as to be wholly regardless of the happiness of women—the law, in all cases, going upon the false supposition of the supremacy of man, and giving all power into his hands.

After depriving her of all rights as a married woman, if single, and the owner of property, he has taxed her to support a government which recognizes her only when her property can be made profitable to it.

He has monopolized nearly all the profitable employments, and from those she is permitted to follow, she receives but a scanty remuneration. He closes against her all the avenues to wealth and distinction which he considers most honorable to himself. As a teacher of theology, medicine, or law, she is not known.

He has denied her the facilities for obtaining a thorough education, all colleges being closed against her.

He allows her in Church, as well as State, but a subordinate position, claiming Apostolic authority for her exclusion from the ministry, and, with some exceptions, from any public participation in the affairs of the Church.

He has created a false public sentiment by giving to the world a different code of morals for men and women, by which moral delinquencies which exclude women from society, are not only tolerated, but deemed of little account in man.

He has usurped the prerogative of Jehovah himself, claiming it as his right to assign for her a sphere of action, when that belongs to her conscience and to her God.

He has endeavored, in every way that he could, to destroy her confidence in her own powers, to lessen her self-respect, and to make her willing to lead a dependent and abject life.

Now, in view of this entire disfranchisement of one-half the people of this country, their social and religious degradation—in view of the unjust laws above mentioned, and because women do feel themselves aggrieved, oppressed, and fraudulently deprived of their most sacred rights, we insist that they have immediate admission to all the rights and privileges which belong to them as citizens of the United States.

In entering upon the great work before us, we anticipate no small amount of misconception, misrepresentation, and ridicule; but we shall use every instrumentality within our power to effect our object. We shall employ agents, circulate tracts, petition the State and National legislatures, and endeavor to enlist the pulpit and the press in our behalf. We hope this Convention will be followed by a series of Conventions embracing every part of the country.

Resolutions

WHEREAS, The great precept of nature is conceded to be, that "man shall pursue his own true and substantial happiness." Blackstone in his Commentaries remarks, that this law of Nature being coeval with mankind, and dictated by God himself, is of course superior in obligation to any other. It is binding over all the globe, in all countries and at all times; no human laws are of any validity if contrary to this, and such of them as are valid, derive all their force, and all their validity, and all their authority, mediately and immediately, from this original; therefore,

Resolved, That such laws as conflict, in any way, with the true and substantial happiness of woman, are contrary to the great precept of nature and of no validity, for this is "superior in obligation to any other."

Resolved, That all laws which prevent woman from occupying such a station in society as her conscience shall dictate, or which place her in a position inferior to that of man, are contrary to the great precept of nature, and therefore of no force or authority.

Resolved, That woman is man's equal—was intended to be so by the Creator, and the highest good of the race demands that she should be recognized as such.

Resolved, That the women of this country ought to be enlightened in regard to the laws under which they live, that they may no longer publish their degradation by declaring themselves satisfied with their present position, nor their ignorance, by asserting that they have all the rights they want.

Resolved, That inasmuch as man, while claiming for himself intellectual superiority, does accord to woman moral superiority, it is pre-eminently his duty to encourage her to speak and teach, as she has an opportunity, in all religious assemblies.

Resolved, That the same amount of virtue, delicacy, and refinement of behavior that is required of woman in the social state, should also be required of man, and the same transgressions should be visited with equal severity on both man and woman.

Resolved, That the objection of indelicacy and impropriety, which is so often brought against woman when she addresses a public audience, comes with a very ill-grace from those who encourage, by their attendance, her appearance on the stage, in the concert, or in feats of the circus.

Resolved, That woman has too long rested satisfied in the circumscribed limits which corrupt customs and a perverted application of the Scriptures have marked out for her, and that it is time she should move in the enlarged sphere which her great Creator has assigned her.

Resolved, That it is the duty of the women of this country to secure to themselves their sacred right to the elective franchise.

Resolved, That the equality of human rights results necessarily from the fact of the identity of the race in capabilities and responsibilities.

Resolved, therefore, That, being invested by the Creator with the same capabilities, and the same consciousness of responsibility for their exercise, it is demonstrably the right and duty of woman, equally with man, to promote every righteous cause by every righteous means; and especially in regard to the great subjects of morals and religion, it is self-evidently her right to participate with her brother in teaching them, both in private and in public, by writing and by speaking, by any instrumentalities proper to be used, and in any assemblies proper to be held; and this being a self-evident truth growing out of the divinely implanted principles of human nature, any custom or authority adverse to it, whether modern or wearing the hoary sanction of antiquity, is to be regarded as a self-evident falsehood, and at war with mankind. [All the preceding resolutions had been drafted by Elizabeth Cady Stanton. At the last session of the convention Lucretia Mott offered the following, which, along with all the other resolutions except the ninth, was adopted unanimously.—*Ed.*]

Resolved, That the speedy success of our cause depends upon the zealous and untiring efforts of both men and women, for the overthrow of the monopoly of the pulpit, and for the securing to woman an equal participation with men in the various trades, professions, and commerce.

6 *People* v. *Hall*, 1854

Bias against Chinese and other colored "races" was endemic in nineteenth-century California, but perhaps no single document so well demonstrates that bias as this majority opinion handed down by the Chief Justice of the California Supreme Court. Since Chinese miners lived in small, segregated groups, the practical effect of this decision was to declare "open season" on Chinese, since crimes against them were likely to be witnessed only by other Chinese.

The People, *Respondent,* v. *George W. Hall, Appellant*

The appellant, a free white citizen of this State, was convicted of murder upon the testimony of Chinese witnesses.

The point involved in this case, is the admissibility of such evidence.

The 394th section of the Act Concerning Civil Cases, provides that no Indian or Negro shall be allowed to testify as a witness in any action or proceeding in which a White person is a party.

The 14th section of the Act of April 16th, 1850, regulating Criminal Proceedings, provides that "No Black, or Mulatto person, or Indian, shall be allowed to give evidence in favor of, or against a white man."

The true point at which we are anxious to arrive, is the legal signification of the words, "Black, Mulatto, Indian and White person," and whether the Legislature adopted them as generic terms, or intended to limit their application to specific types of the human species.

Before considering this question, it is proper to remark the difference between the two sections of our Statute, already quoted, the latter being more broad and comprehensive in its exclusion, by use of the word "Black," instead of Negro.

Conceding, however, for the present, that the word "Black," as used in the 14th section, and "Negro," in 394th, are convertible terms, and that the former was intended to include the latter, let us proceed to inquire who are excluded from testifying as witnesses under the term "Indian."

When Columbus first landed upon the shores of this continent, in his attempt to discover a western passage to the Indies, he imagined that he had accomplished the object of his expedition, and that the Island of San Salvador was one of those Islands of the Chinese sea, lying near the extremity of India, which had been described by navigators.

Acting upon this hypothesis, and also perhaps from the similarity of features and physical conformation, he gave to the Islanders the name of Indians, which appellation was universally adopted, and extended to the aboriginals of the New World, as well as of Asia.

From that time, down to a very recent period, the American Indians and the Mongolian, or Asiatic, were regarded as the same type of human species. . . .

. . . That this was the common opinion in the early history of American legislation, cannot be disputed, and, therefore, all legislation upon the subject must have borne relation to that opinion. . . .

. . . In using the words, "No Black, or Mulatto person, or Indian shall be allowed to give evidence for or against a White person," the Legislature, if any intention can be ascribed to it, adopted the most comprehensive terms to embrace every known class or shade of color, as the apparent design was to protect the White person from the influence of all testimony other than that of persons of the same caste. The use of these terms must, by every sound rule of construction, exclude every one who is not of white blood. . . .

. . . We have carefully considered all the consequences resulting from a different rule of construction, and are satisfied that even in a doubtful case we would be impelled to this decision on grounds of public policy.

The same rule which would admit them to testify, would admit them to all the equal rights of citizenship, and we might soon see them at the polls, in the jury box, upon the bench, and in our legislative halls.

This is not a speculation which exists in the excited and overheated imagination of the patriot and statesman, but it is an actual and present danger.

The anomalous spectacle of a distinct people, living in our community, recognizing no laws of this State except through necessity, bringing with them their prejudices and national feuds, in which they indulge in open violation of law; whose mendacity is proverbial; a race of people whom nature has marked as inferior, and who are incapable of progress or intellectual development beyond a certain point, as their history has shown; differing in language, opinions, color, and physical conformation; between whom and ourselves nature has placed an impassible difference, is now presented, and for them is claimed, not only the right to swear away the life of a citizen, but the further privilege of participating with us in administering the affairs of our Government. . . .

. . . For these reasons, we are of opinion that the testimony was inadmissible. . . .

7 *Dred Scott* v. *Sandford*, 1857

The question is simply this: Can a negro, whose ancestors were imported into this country, and sold as slaves, become a member of the political community formed and brought into existence by the Constitution of the United States, and as such become entitled to all the rights, and privileges, and immunities, guarantied by that instrument to the citizen? One of which rights is the privilege of suing in a court of the United States in the cases specified in the Constitution.

It will be observed, that the plea applies to that class of persons only whose ancestors were negroes of the African race, and imported into this country, and sold and held as slaves. The only matter in issue before this court, therefore, is whether the descendants of such slaves, when they shall be emancipated, or who are born of parents who had become free before their birth, are citizens of a State, in the sense in which the word citizen is used in the Constitution of the United States. And this being the only matter in dispute on the pleadings, the court must be understood as speaking in his opinion of that class only, that is, of those persons who are the descendants of Africans who were imported into this country, and sold as slaves.

It becomes necessary, therefore, to determine who were citizens of the several States when the Constitution was adopted. And in order to do this, we must recur to the Governments and institutions of the thirteen colonies, when they separated from Great Britain and formed new sovereignties, and took their places in the family of independent nations. We must inquire who, at that time, were recognised as the people or citizens of a State, whose rights and liberties had been outraged by the English Government; and who declared their independence, and assumed the powers of Government to defend their rights by force of arms.

In the opinion of the court, the legislation and histories of the times, and the language used in the Declaration of Independence, show, that neither the class of persons who had been imported as slaves, nor their descendants, whether they had become free or not, were then acknowledged as a part of the people, nor intended to be included in the general words used in that memorable instrument.

It is difficult at this day to realize the state of public opinion in relation to that unfortunate race, which prevailed in the civilized and enlightened portions of the world at the time of the Declaration of Independence, and when the Constitution of the United States was formed and adopted. But the public history of every European nation displays it in a manner too plain to be mistaken.

They had for more than a century before been regarded as beings of an inferior order, and altogether unfit to associate with the white race, either in social or political relations; and so far inferior, that they had no rights which the white man was bound to respect; and that the negro might justly and lawfully be reduced to slavery for his benefit. He was bought and sold, and treated as an ordinary article of merchandise

From Benjamin C. Howard, *Report of the Decision of the Supreme Court of the United States in the Case Dred Scott* . . . (Washington, 1857), 9, 13–14, 15–17, 60.

and traffic, whenever a profit could be made by it. This opinion was at that time fixed and universal in the civilized portion of the white race. It was regarded as an axiom in morals as well as in politics, which no one thought of disputing, or supposed to be open to dispute; and men in every grade and position in society daily and habitually acted upon it in their private pursuits, as well as in matters of public concern, without doubting for a moment the correctness of this opinion.

And in no nation was this opinion more firmly fixed or more uniformly acted upon than by the English Government and English people. They not only seized them on the coast of Africa, and sold them or held them in slavery for their own use, but they took them as ordinary articles of merchandise to every country where they could make a profit on them, and were far more extensively engaged in this commerce than any other nation in the world.

The opinion thus entertained and acted upon in England was naturally impressed upon the colonies they founded on this side of the Atlantic. And, accordingly, a negro of the African race was regarded by them as an article of property, and held, and bought and sold as such, in every one of the thirteen colonies which united in the Declaration of Independence, and afterwards formed the Constitution of the United States. The slaves were more or less numerous in the different colonies, as slave labor was found more or less profitable. But no one seems to have doubted the correctness of the prevailing opinion of the time.

The legislation of the different colonies furnishes positive and indisputable proof of this fact.

The language of the Declaration of Independence is equally conclusive:

It begins by declaring that, "when in the course of human events it becomes necessary for one people to dissolve the political bands which have connected them with another, and to assume among the powers of the earth the separate and equal station to which the laws of nature and nature's God entitle them, a decent respect for the opinions of mankind requires that they should declare the causes which impel them to the separation."

It then proceeds to say: "We hold these truths to be self-evident: that all men are created equal; that they are endowed by their Creator with certain unalienable rights; that among them is life, liberty, and the pursuit of happiness; that to secure these rights, Governments are instituted, deriving their just powers from the consent of the governed."

The general words above quoted would seem to embrace the whole human family, and if they were used in a similar instrument at this day would be so understood. But it is too clear for dispute, that the enslaved African race were not intended to be included, and formed no part of the people who framed and adopted this declaration; for if the language, as understood in that day, would embrace them, the conduct of the distinguished men who framed the Declaration of Independence would have been utterly and flagrantly inconsistent with the principles they asserted; and instead of the sympathy of mankind, to which they so confidently appealed, they would have deserved and received universal rebuke and reprobation.

Yet the men who framed this declaration were great men—high in literary acquirements—high in their sense of honor, and incapable of asserting principles inconsistent with those on which they were acting. They perfectly understood the meaning of the language they used, and how it would be understood by others; and they knew that it would not in any part of the civilized world be supposed to embrace the negro race, which, by common consent, had been excluded from civilized Governments and the family of nations, and doomed to slavery. They spoke and acted according to the then established doctrines and principles, and in the ordinary language of the day, and no one misunderstood them. The unhappy black race were separated from the white by indelible marks, and laws long before established, and were never thought of or spoken of except as property, and when the claims of the owner or the profit of the trader were supposed to need protection.

The state of public opinion had undergone no change when the Constitution was adopted, as is equally evident from its provisions and language.

This brief preamble sets forth by whom it was formed, for what purposes, and for whose benefit and protection. It declares that it is formed by the *people* of the United States; that is to say, by those who were members of the different political communities in the several States; and its great object is declared to be to secure the blessings of liberty to themselves and their posterity. It speaks in general terms of the *people* of the United States, and of *citizens* of the several States, when it is providing for the exercise of the powers granted or the privileges secured to the citizen. It does not define what description of persons are intended to be included under these terms, or who shall be regarded as a citizen and one of the people. It uses them as terms so well understood, that no further description or definition was necessary.

But there are two clauses in the Constitution which point directly and specifically to the negro race as a separate class of persons, and show clearly that they were not regarded as a portion of the people or citizens of the Government then formed.

One of these clauses reserves to each of the thirteen States the right to import slaves until the year 1808, if it thinks proper. And the importation which it thus sanctions was unquestionably of persons of the race of which we are speaking, as the traffic in slaves in the United States had always been confined to them. And by the other provision the States pledge themselves to each other to maintain the right of property of the master, by delivering up to him any slave who may have escaped from his service, and be found within their respective territories. By the first above-mentioned clause, therefore, the right to purchase and hold this property is directly sanctioned and authorized for twenty years by the people who framed the Constitution. And by the second, they pledge themselves to maintain and uphold the right of the master in the manner specified, as long as the Government they then formed should endure. And these two provisions show, conclusively, that neither the description of persons therein referred to, nor their descendants, were embraced in any of the other provisions of the Constitution, for certainly these two clauses were not intended to confer on them or their posterity the blessings of liberty, or any of the personal rights so carefully provided for the citizen.

Upon the whole, therefore, it is the judgment of this court, that it appears by the record before us that the plaintiff in error is not a citizen of Missouri, in the sense in which that word is used in the Constitution; and that the Circuit Court of the United States, for that reason, had no jurisdiction in the case, and could give no judgment in it. Its judgment for the defendant must, consequently, be reversed, and a mandate issued, directing the suit to be dismissed for want of jurisdiction.

8 The Emancipation Proclamation

Abraham Lincoln

January 1, 1863

Whereas, on the twenty-second day of September, in the year of our Lord one thousand eight hundred and sixty two, a proclamation was issued by the President of the United States, containing, among other things, the following, to wit:

"That on the first day of January, in the year of our Lord one thousand eight hundred and sixty-three, all persons held as slaves within any State or designated part of a State, the people whereof shall then be in rebellion against the United States, shall be then, thenceforward, and forever free; and the Executive Government of the United States, including the military and naval authority thereof, will recognize and maintain the freedom of such persons, and will do no act or acts to repress such persons, or any of them, in any efforts they may make for their actual freedom.

"That the Executive will, on the first day of January aforesaid, by proclamation, designate the States and parts of States, if any, in which the people thereof, respectively, shall then be in rebellion against the United States; and the fact that any State, or the people thereof, shall on that day be, in good faith, represented in the Congress of the United States by members chosen thereto at elections wherein a majority of the qualified voters of such State shall have participated, shall, in the absence of strong countervailing testimony, be deemed conclusive evidence that such State, and the people thereof, are not then in rebellion against the United States."

Now, therefore I, Abraham Lincoln, President of the United States, by virtue of the power in me vested as Commander-in-Chief, of the Army and Navy of the United States in time of actual armed rebellion against authority and government of the United States, and as a fit and necessary war measure for suppressing said rebellion, do, on this first day of January, in the year of our Lord one thousand eight hundred and sixty-three, and in accordance with my purpose so to do publicly proclaimed for the full period of one hundred days, from the day first above mentioned, order and designate as the States and parts of States wherein the people thereof respectively, are this day in rebellion against the United States, the following, to wit:

Arkansas, Texas, Louisiana (except the Parishes of St. Bernard, Plaquemines, Jefferson, St. Johns, St. Charles, St. James[,] Ascension, Assumption, Terrebonne, Lafourche, St. Mary, St. Martin, and Orleans, including the City of New-Orleans), Mississippi, Alabama, Florida, Georgia, South-Carolina, North-Carolina, and Virginia (except the forty-eight counties designated as West Virginia, and also the counties of Berkley, Accomac, Northampton, Elizabeth-City, York, Princess Ann, and Norfolk, including the cities of Norfolk & Portsmouth [)]; and which excepted parts are, for the present, left precisely as if this proclamation were not issued.

And by virtue of the power, and for the purpose aforesaid, I do order and declare that all persons held as slaves within said designated States, and parts of States, are, and henceforward shall be free; and that the Executive Government of the United States, including the military and naval authorities thereof, will recognize and maintain the freedom of said persons.

And I hereby enjoin upon the people so declared to be free to abstain from all violence, unless in necessary self-defence; and I recommend to them that, in all cases when allowed, they labor faithfully for reasonable wages.

And I further declare and make known, that such persons of suitable condition, will be received into the armed service of the United States to garrison forts, positions, stations, and other places, and to man vessels of all sorts in said service.

And upon this act, sincerely believed to be an act of justice, warranted by the Constitution, upon military necessity, I invoke the considerate judgment of mankind, and the gracious favor of Almighty God.

In witness whereof, I have hereunto set my hand and caused the seal of the United States to be affixed.

Done at the City of Washington, this first day of January, in the year of our Lord one thousand eight hundred and sixty-three, and of the Independence of the United States of America the eighty-seventh.

By the President:
Abraham Lincoln

William H. Seward,
Secretary of State

9 United States Constitution
Thirteenth (1865), Fourteenth (1868), and Fifteenth (1870) Amendments

Amendment XIII (Ratified December 6, 1865). *Section 1.* Neither slavery nor involuntary servitude, except as a punishment for crime whereof the party shall have been duly convicted, shall exist within the United States, or any place subject to their jurisdiction.

Section 2. Congress shall have power to enforce this article by appropriate legislation. *Amendment XIV* (Ratified July 9, 1868). *Section 1.* All persons born or naturalized in the United States, and subject to the jurisdiction thereof, are citizens of the United States and of the state wherein they reside. No State shall make or enforce any law which shall abridge the privileges or immunities of citizens of the United States; nor shall any State deprive any person of life, liberty, or property, without due process of law; nor deny to any person within its jurisdiction the equal protection of the laws.

Section 2. Representatives shall be apportioned among the several states according to their respective numbers, counting the whole number of persons in each state, excluding Indians not taxed. But when the right to vote at any election for the choice of Electors for President and Vice-President of the United States, Representatives in Congress, the executive and judicial officers of a State, or the members of the Legislature thereof, is denied to any of the male inhabitants of such State, being twenty-one years of age, and, citizens of the United States, or in any way abridged, except for participation in rebellion, or other crime, the basis of representation therein shall be reduced in the proportion which the number of such male citizens shall bear to the whole number of male citizens twenty-one years of age in such State.

Section 3. No person shall be a Senator or Representative in Congress, or elector of President and Vice-President, or hold any office, civil or military, under the United States, or under any State, who, having previously taken an oath, as a member of Congress, or as an officer of the United States, or as an executive or judicial officer of any State, to support the Constitution of the United States, shall have engaged in insurrection or rebellion against the same, or given aid or comfort to the enemies thereof. But Congress may by a vote of two-thirds of each House, remove such disability.

Section 4. The validity of the public debt of the United States, authorized by law, including debts incurred for payment of pensions and bounties for services in suppressing insurrection or rebellion, shall not be questioned. But neither the United States nor any State shall assume or pay any debt or obligation incurred in aid of insurrection or rebellion against the United States, or any claim for the loss or emancipation of any slave; but all such debts, obligations, and claims, shall be held illegal and void.

Section 5. The Congress shall have power to enforce, by appropriate legislation, the provisions of this article.

Amendment XV (Ratified February 3, 1870). *Section 1.* The right of citizens of the United States to vote shall not be denied or abridged by the United States or by any State on account of race, color, or previous condition of servitude.

Section 2. The Congress shall have power to enforce this article by appropriate legislation.

10 The Black Codes

W. E. B. Du Bois

The whole proof of what the South proposed to do to the emancipated Negro, unless restrained by the nation, was shown in the Black Codes passed after [President Andrew] Johnson's accession, but representing the logical result of attitudes of mind existing when Lincoln still lived. Some of these were passed and enforced. Some were passed and afterward repealed or modified when the reaction of the North was realized. In other cases, as for instance, in Louisiana, it is not clear just which laws were retained and which were repealed. In Alabama, the Governor induced the legislature not to enact some parts of the proposed code which they overwhelmingly favored.

The original codes favored by the Southern legislatures were an astonishing affront to emancipation and dealt with vagrancy, apprenticeship, labor contracts, migration, civil and legal rights. In all cases, there was plain and indisputable attempt on the part of the Southern states to make Negroes slaves in everything but name. They were given certain civil rights: the right to hold property, to sue and be sued. The family relations for the first time were legally recognized. Negroes were no longer real estate.

Yet, in the face of this, the Black Codes were deliberately designed to take advantage of every misfortune of the Negro. Negroes were liable to a slave trade under the guise of vagrancy and apprenticeship laws; to make the best labor contracts, Negroes must leave the old plantations and seek better terms; but if caught wandering in search of work, and thus unemployed and without a home, this was vagrancy, and the victim could be whipped and sold into slavery. In the turmoil of war, children were separated from parents, or parents unable to support them properly. These children could be sold into slavery, and "the former owner of said minors shall have the preference." Negroes could come into court as witnesses only in cases in which Negroes were involved. And even then, they must make their appeal to a jury and judge who would believe the word of any white man in preference to that of any Negro on pain of losing office and caste.

The Negro's access to the land was hindered and limited; his right to work was curtailed; his right of self-defense was taken away, when his right to bear arms was stopped; and his employment was virtually reduced to contract labor with penal servitude as a punishment for leaving his job. And in all cases, the judges of the Negro's guilt or innocence, rights and obligations were men who believed firmly, for the most part, that he had "no rights which a white man was bound to respect."

Making every allowance for the excitement and turmoil of war, and the mentality of a defeated people, the Black Codes were infamous pieces of legislation.

Reprinted with the permission of Scribner, a division of Simon & Schuster, Inc., from *Black Reconstruction in America, 1860–1880* by W.E.B. DuBois. Copyright © 1935 by W.E.B. DuBois Copyright renewed 1962 by W.E.B. DuBois. All rights reserved.

Let us examine these codes in detail.[1] They covered, naturally, a wide range of subjects. First, there was the question of allowing Negroes to come into the state. In South Carolina the constitution of 1865 permitted the Legislature to regulate immigration, and the consequent law declared "that no person of color shall migrate into and reside in this State, unless, within twenty days after his arrival within the same, he shall enter into a bond, with two freeholders as sureties . . . in a penalty of one thousand dollars, conditioned for his good behavior, and for his support."

Especially in the matter of work was the Negro narrowly restricted. In South Carolina, he must be especially licensed if he was to follow on his own account any employment, except that of farmer or servant. Those licensed must not only prove their fitness, but pay an annual tax ranging from $10–$100. Under no circumstances could they manufacture or sell liquor. Licenses for work were to be granted by a judge and were revocable on complaint. The penalty was a fine double the amount of the license, one-half of which went to the informer.

Mississippi provided that "every freedman, free Negro, and mulatto shall on the second Monday of January, one thousand eight hundred and sixty-six, and annually thereafter, have a lawful home or employment, and shall have written evidence thereof . . . from the Mayor . . . or from a member of the board of police . . . which licenses may be revoked for cause at any time by the authority granting the same."

Detailed regulation of labor was provided for in nearly all these states.

Louisiana passed an elaborate law in 1865, to "regulate labor contracts for agricultural pursuits." Later, it was denied that this legislation was actually enacted but the law was published at the time and the constitutional convention of 1868 certainly regarded this statute as law, for they formally repealed it. The law required all agricultural laborers to make labor contracts for the next year within the first ten days of January, the contracts to be in writing, to be with heads of families, to embrace the labor of all the members, and to be "binding on all minors thereof." Each laborer, after choosing his employer, "shall not be allowed to leave his place of employment, until the fulfillment of his contract, unless by consent of his employer, or on account of harsh treatment, or breach of contract on the part of the employer; and if they do so leave, without cause or permission, they shall forfeit all wages earned to the time of abandonment. . . .

"In case of sickness of the laborer, wages for the time lost shall be deducted, and where the sickness is feigned for purposes of idleness, . . . and also should refusal to work be continued beyond three days, the offender shall be reported to a justice of the peace, and shall be forced to labor on roads, levees, and other public works, without pay, until the offender consents to return to his labor. . . .

"When in health, the laborer shall work ten hours during the day in summer, and nine hours during the day in winter, unless otherwise stipulated in the labor contract; he shall obey all proper orders of his employer or his agent; take proper care of his work mules, horses, oxen, stock; also of all agricultural implements; and employers shall have the right to make a reasonable deduction from the laborer's wages for injuries done to animals or agricultural implements committed to his care, or for bad or negligent work. Bad work shall not be allowed. Failing to obey reasonable orders, neglect of duty and leaving home without permission, will be deemed disobedience. . . . For any disobedience a fine of one dollar shall be imposed on the offender. For all lost time from work hours, unless in case of sickness, the laborer shall be fined twenty-five cents per hour. For all absence from home without leave, the laborer will be fined at the rate of two dollars per day. Laborers will not be required to labor on the Sabbath except to take the necessary care of stock and other property on plantations and do the necessary cooking and household duties, unless by special contract. For all thefts of the laborers from the employer of agricultural products, hogs, sheep, poultry or any other property of the employer, or willful destruction of property or injury, the laborer shall pay the employer double the amount of the value of the property stolen, destroyed or injured, one half to be paid to the employer, and the other half to be placed in the general fund provided for in this section. No live stock shall be allowed to laborers without the permission of the employer. Laborers shall not receive visitors during work hours. All difficulties arising between the employers and laborers, under this section, shall be settled, and all fines be imposed, by the former; if not satisfactory to the laborers, an appeal may be had to the nearest justice of the peace and two freeholders, citizens, one of said citizens to be selected by the employer and the other by the laborer; and all fines imposed and collected under this section shall be deducted from the wages due, and shall be placed in a common fund, to be divided among the other laborers employed on the plantation at the time when their full wages fall due, except as provided for above."

Similar detailed regulations of work were in the South Carolina law. Elaborate provision was made for contracting colored "servants" to white "masters." Their masters were given the right to whip "moderately" servants under eighteen. Others were to be whipped on authority of judicial officers. These officers were given authority to return runaway servants to their masters. The servants, on the other hand, were given certain rights. Their wages and period of service must be specified in writing, and they were protected against "unreasonable" tasks, Sunday and night work, unauthorized attacks on their persons, and inadequate food.

Contracting Negroes were to be known as "servants" and contractors as "masters." Wages were to be fixed by the judge, unless stipulated. Negroes of ten years of age or more without a parent living in the district might make a valid contract for a year or less. Failure to make written contracts was a misdemeanor, punishable by a fine of $5 to $50; farm labor to be from sunrise to sunset, with intervals for meals; servants to rise at dawn, to be careful of master's property and answerable for property lost or injured. Lost time was to be deducted from wages. Food and clothes might be deducted. Servants were to be quiet and orderly and to go to bed at reasonable hours. No night work or outdoor work in bad weather was to be asked, except in cases of necessity, visitors not allowed without the master's consent. Servants leaving employment without good reason must forfeit wages. Masters might discharge servants for disobedience, drunkenness, disease, absence, etc. Enticing away the services of a servant was punishable by a fine of $20 to $100. A master could command a servant to aid him in defense of his own person, family or property. House servants at all hours of the day and night, and at all days of the weeks, "must answer promptly all calls and execute all lawful orders. . . ."

Mississippi provided "that every civil officer shall, and every person may, arrest and carry back to his or her legal employer any freedman, free Negro, or mulatto who shall have quit the service of his or her employer before the expiration of his or her term of service without good cause; and said officer and person shall be entitled to receive for arresting and carrying back every deserting employee aforesaid the sum of five dollars, and ten cents per mile from the place of arrest to the place of delivery, and the same shall be paid by the employer and held as a set-off for so much against the wages of said deserting employee."

It was provided in some states, like South Carolina, that any white man, whether an officer or not, could arrest a Negro. "Upon view of a misdemeanor committed by a person of color, any person present may arrest the offender and take him before a magistrate, to be dealt with as the case may require. In case of a misdemeanor committed by a white person toward a person of color, any person may complain to a magistrate, who shall cause the offender to be arrested, and according to the nature of the case, to be brought before himself, or be taken for trial in the district court."

On the other hand, in Mississippi, it was dangerous for a Negro to try to bring a white person to court on any charge. "In every case where any white person has been arrested and brought to trial, by virtue of the provisions of the tenth section of the above recited act, in any court in this State, upon sufficient proof being made to the court or jury, upon the trial before said court, that any freedman, free Negro or mulatto has falsely and maliciously caused the arrest and trial of said white person or persons, the court shall render up a judgment against said freedman, free Negro or mulatto for all costs of the case, and impose a fine not to exceed fifty dollars, and imprisonment in the county jail not to exceed twenty days; and for a failure of said freedman, free Negro or mulatto to pay, or cause to be paid, all costs, fines and jail fees, the sheriff of the county is hereby authorized and required, after giving ten days' public notice, to proceed to hire out at public outcry, at the courthouse of the county, said freedman, free Negro or mulatto, for the shortest time to raise the amount necessary to discharge said freedman, free Negro or mulatto from all costs, fines, and jail fees aforesaid."

Mississippi declared that: "Any freedman, free Negro, or mulatto, committing riots, routs, affrays, trespasses, malicious mischief and cruel treatment to animals, seditious speeches, insulting gestures, language or acts, or assaults on any person, disturbance of the peace, exercising the functions of a minister of the gospel without a license from some regularly organized church, vending spirituous or intoxicating liquors, or committing any other misdemeanor, the punishment of which is not specifically provided for by law, shall, upon conviction thereof, in the county court, be fined not less than ten dollars, and not more than one hundred dollars, and may be imprisoned, at the discretion of the court, not exceeding thirty days. . . ."

The most important and oppressive laws were those with regard to vagrancy and apprenticeship. Sometimes they especially applied to Negroes; in other cases, they were drawn in general terms but evidently designed to fit the Negro's condition and to be enforced particularly with regard to Negroes.

The Virginia Vagrant Act enacted that "any justice of the peace, upon the complaint of any one of certain officers therein named, may issue his warrant for the apprehension of any person alleged to be a vagrant and cause such person to be apprehended and brought before him; and that if upon due examination said justice of the peace shall find that such person is a vagrant within the definition of vagrancy contained in said statute, he shall issue his warrant, directing such person to be employed for a term not exceeding three months, and by any constable of the county wherein the proceedings are had, be hired out for the best wages which can be procured, his wages to be applied to the support of himself and his family. The said statute further provides, that in case any vagrant so hired shall, during his term of service, run away from his employer without sufficient cause, he shall be apprehended on the warrant of a justice of the peace and returned to the custody of his employer, who shall then have, free from any other hire, the services of such vagrant for one month in addition to the original term of hiring, and that the employer shall then have power, if authorized by a justice of the peace, to work such vagrant with ball and chain. The said statute specified the persons who shall be considered vagrants and liable to the penalties imposed by it. Among those declared to be vagrants are all persons who, not having the wherewith to support their families, live idly and without employment, and refuse to work for the usual and common wages given to other laborers in the like work in the place where they are."

In Florida, January 12, 1866: "It is provided that when any person of color shall enter into a contract as aforesaid, to serve as a laborer for a year, or any other specified term, on any farm or plantation in this State, if he shall refuse or neglect to perform the stipulations of his contract by willful disobedience of orders, wanton impudence or disrespect to his employer, or his authorized agent, failure or refusal to perform the work assigned to him, idleness, or abandonment of the premises or the employment of the party with whom the contract was made, he or she shall be liable, upon the complaint of his employer or his agent, made under oath before any justice of the peace of the county, to be arrested and tried before the criminal court of the county, and upon conviction shall be subject to all the pains and penalties prescribed for the punishment of vagrancy."

In Georgia, it was ruled that "All persons wandering or strolling about in idleness, who are able to work, and who have no property to support them; all persons leading an idle, immoral, or profligate life, who have no property to support them and are able to work and do not work; all persons able to work having no visible and known means of a fair, honest, and respectable livelihood; all persons having a fixed abode, who have no visible property to support them, and who live by stealing or by trading in, bartering for, or buying stolen property; and all professional gamblers living in idleness, shall be deemed and considered vagrants, and shall be indicated as such, and it shall be lawful for any person to arrest said vagrants and have them bound over for trial to the next term of the county court, and upon conviction, they shall be fined and imprisoned or sentenced to work on the public works, for not longer than a year, or shall, in the discretion of the court, be bound out to some person for a time not longer than one year, upon such valuable consideration as the court may prescribe."

Mississippi provided "That all freedmen, free Negroes, and mulattoes in this state over the age of eighteen years, found on the second Monday in January, 1866, or thereafter, with no lawful employment or business, or found unlawfully assembling themselves together, either in the day or night time, and all white persons so assembling with freedmen, free Negroes or mulattoes, or usually associating with freedmen, free Negroes or mulattoes on terms of equality, or living in adultery or fornication with a freedwoman, free Negro or mulatto, shall be deemed vagrants, and on conviction thereof shall be fined in the sum of not exceeding, in the case of a freedman, free Negro or mulatto, fifty dollars, and a white man two hundred dollars and imprisoned, at the discretion of the court, the free Negro not exceeding ten days, and the white men not exceeding six months."

Sec. 5 provides that "all fines and forfeitures collected under the provisions of this act shall be paid into the county treasury for general county purposes, and in case any freedman, free Negro or mulatto, shall fail for five days after the imposition of any fine or forfeiture upon him or her, for violation of any of the provisions of this act to pay the same, that it shall be, and is hereby made, the duty of the Sheriff of the proper county to hire out said freedman, free Negro or mulatto, to any person who will, for the shortest period of service, pay said fine or forfeiture and all costs; *Provided*, a preference shall be given to the employer, if there be one, in which case the employer shall be entitled to deduct and retain the amount so paid from the wages of such freedman, free Negro or mulatto, then due or to become due; and in case such freedman, free Negro or mulatto cannot be hired out, he or she may be dealt with as a pauper. . . ."

In Alabama, the "former owner" was to have preference in the apprenticing of a child. This was true in Kentucky and Mississippi.

Mississippi "provides that it shall be the duty of all sheriffs, justices of the peace, and other civil officers of the several counties in this state to report to the probate courts of their respective counties semi-annually, at the January and July terms of said courts, all freedmen, free Negroes and mulattoes, under the age of eighteen, within their respective counties, beats, or districts, who are orphans, or whose parent or parents have not the means, or who refuse to provide for and support said minors, and thereupon it shall be the duty of said probate court to order the clerk of said court to apprentice said minors to some competent and suitable person, on such terms as the court may direct, having a particular care to the interest of said minors; *Provided*, that the former owner of said minors shall have the preference when, in the opinion of the court, he or she shall be a suitable person for that purpose. . . ."

"Capital punishment was provided for colored persons guilty of willful homicide, assault upon a white woman, impersonating her husband for carnal purposes, raising an insurrection, stealing a horse, a mule, or baled cotton, and housebreaking. For crimes not demanding death Negroes might be confined at hard labor, whipped, or transported; 'but punishments more degrading than imprisonment shall not be imposed upon a white person for a crime not infamous.'"[2]

In most states Negroes were allowed to testify in courts but the testimony was usually confined to cases where colored persons were involved, although in some states, by consent of the parties, they could testify in cases where only white people were involved. . . .

Mississippi simply reenacted her slave code and made it operative so far as punishments were concerned. "That all the penal and criminal laws now in force in this State, defining offenses, and prescribing the mode of punishment for crimes and misdemeanors committed by slaves, free Negroes or mulattoes, be and the same are hereby reenacted, and declared to be in full force and effect, against freedmen, free Negroes, and mulattoes, except so far as the mode and manner of trial and punishment have been changed or altered by law."

North Carolina, on the other hand, abolished her slave code, making difference of punishment only in the case of Negroes convicted of rape. Georgia placed the fines and costs of a servant upon the master. "Where such cases shall go against the servant, the judgment for costs upon written notice to the master shall operate as a garnishment against him, and he shall retain a sufficient amount for the payment thereof, out of any wages due to said servant, or to become due during the period of service, and may be cited at any time by the collecting officer to make answer thereto."

The celebrated ordinance of Opelousas, Louisiana, shows the local ordinances regulating Negroes. "No Negro or freedman shall be allowed to come within the limits of the town of Opelousas without special permission from his employer, specifying the object of his visit and the time necessary for the accomplishment of the same.

"Every Negro freedman who shall be found on the streets of Opelousas after ten o'clock at night without a written pass or permit from his employer, shall be imprisoned and compelled to work five days on the public streets, or pay a fine of five dollars.

"No Negro or freedman shall be permitted to rent or keep a house within the limits of the town under any circumstances, and anyone thus offending shall be ejected, and compelled to find an employer or leave the town within twenty-four hours.

"No Negro or freedman shall reside within the limits of the town of Opelousas who is not in the regular service of some white person or former owner, who shall be held responsible for the conduct of said freedman.

"No Negro or freedman shall be permitted to preach, exhort, or otherwise declaim to congregations of colored people without a special permission from the Mayor or President of the Board of Police, under the penalty of a fine of ten dollars or twenty days' work on the public streets.

"No freedman who is not in the military service shall be allowed to carry firearms, or any kind of weapons within the limits of the town of Opelousas without the special permission of his employer, in writing, and approved by the Mayor or President of the Board.

"Any freedman not residing in Opelousas, who shall be found within its corporate limits after the hour of 3 o'clock, on Sunday, without a special permission from his employer or the Mayor, shall be arrested and imprisoned and made to work two days on the public streets, or pay two dollars in lieu of said work."[3]

Of Louisiana, Thomas Conway testified February 22, 1866: "Some of the leading officers of the state down there—men who do much to form and control the opinions of the masses—instead of doing as they promised, and quietly submitting to the authority of the government, engaged in issuing slave codes and in promulgating them to their subordinates, ordering them to carry them into execution, and this to the knowledge of state officials of a higher character, the governor and others. And the men who issued them were not punished except as the military authorities punished them. The governor inflicted no punishment on them while I was there, and I don't know that, up to this day, he has ever punished one of them. These codes were simply the old black code of the state, with the word 'slave' expunged, and 'Negro' substituted. The most odious features of slavery were preserved in them. . . ."[4]

NOTES

1. Quotations from McPherson, *History of United States during Reconstruction,* pp. 29–44.
2. Simkins and Woody, *South Carolina during Reconstruction,* pp. 49, 50.
3. Warmoth, *War, Politics and Reconstruction,* p. 274.
4. *Report on the Joint Committee on Reconstruction,* 1866, Part IV, pp. 78–79.

11 The Chinese Exclusion Act

An Act to Execute Certain Treaty Stipulations Relating to Chinese

Whereas, in the opinion of the Government of the United States the coming of Chinese laborers to this country endangers the good order of certain localities within the territory thereof: Therefore,

Be it enacted by the Senate and House of Representatives of the United States of America in Congress assembled, That from and after the expiration of ninety days next after the passage of this act, and until the expiration of ten years next after the passage of this act, the coming of Chinese laborers to the United States be, and the same is hereby, suspended; and during such suspension it shall not be lawful for any Chinese laborer to come, or having so come after the expiration of said ninety days, to remain within the United States.

SEC. 2. That the master of any vessel who shall knowingly bring within the United States on such vessel, and land or permit to be landed, any Chinese laborer, from any foreign port or place, shall be deemed guilty of a misdemeanor, and on conviction thereof shall be punished by a fine of not more than $500 for each and every such Chinese laborer so brought, and may be also imprisoned for a term not exceeding one year.

SEC. 3. That the two foregoing sections shall not apply to Chinese laborers who were in the United States on the 17th day of November, 1880, or who shall have come into the same before the expiration of ninety days next after the passage of this act . . .

SEC. 4. That for the purpose of properly identifying Chinese laborers who were in the United States on the 17th day of November, 1880, or who shall have come into the same before the expiration of ninety days next after the passage of this act, and in order to furnish them with the proper evidence of their right to go from and come to the United States of their free will and accord, as provided by the treaty between the United States and China dated November 17, 1880, the collector of customs of the district from which any such Chinese laborer shall depart from the United States shall, in person or by deputy, go on board each vessel having on board any such Chinese laborer and cleared or about to sail from his district for a foreign port, and on such vessel make a list of all such Chinese laborers, which shall be entered in registry-books to be kept for that purpose, in which shall be stated the name, age, occupation, last place of residence, physical marks or peculiarities, and all facts necessary for the identification of each of such Chinese laborers, which books shall be safely kept in the custom-house; and every such Chinese laborer so departing from the United States shall be entitled to, and shall receive, free of any charge or cost upon application therefor, from the collector or his deputy, at the time such list is taken a certificate, signed by the collector or his deputy and attested by his seal of office, in such form as the Secretary of the Treasury shall prescribe, which certificate shall contain a statement of the name, age, occupation, last place of residence, personal description, and facts of identification of the Chinese laborer to whom the certificate is issued, corresponding with the said list and registry in all particulars . . .

SEC. 5. That any Chinese laborer mentioned in section four of this act being in the United States, and desiring to depart from the United States by land, shall have the right to demand and receive, free of charge or cost, a certificate of identification similar to that provided for in section four of this act to be issued to such Chinese laborers as may desire to leave the United States by water; and it is hereby made the duty of the collector of customs of the district next adjoining the foreign country to which said Chinese laborer desires to go to issue such certificate, free of charge or cost, upon application by such Chinese laborer, and to enter the same upon registry-books to be kept by him for the purpose, as provided for in section four of this act.

SEC. 6. That in order to the faithful execution of articles one and two of the treaty in this act before mentioned, every Chinese person other than a laborer who may be entitled by said treaty and this act to come within the United States, and who shall be about to come to the United States, shall be identified as so entitled by the Chinese Government in each case, such identity to be evidenced by a certificate issued under the authority of said government, which certificate shall be in the English language or (if not in the English language) accompanied by a translation into English, stating such right to come, and which certificate shall state the name, title, or official rank, if any, the age, height, and all physical peculiarities, former and present occupation or profession, and place of residence in China of the person to whom the certificate is issued and that such person is entitled conformably to the treaty in this act mentioned to come within the United States . . .

SEC. 7. That any person who shall knowingly and falsely alter or substitute any name for the name written in such certificate or forge any such certificate, or knowingly utter any forged or fraudulent certificate, or falsely personate any person named in any such certificate, shall be deemed guilty of a misdemeanor; and upon conviction thereof shall be fined in a sum not exceeding $1,000, and imprisoned in a penitentiary for a term of not more than five years.

SEC. 8. That the master of any vessel arriving in the United States from any foreign port or place shall, at the same time he delivers a manifest of the cargo, and if there be no cargo, then at the time of making a report, of the entry of the vessel pursuant to law, in addition to the other matter required to be reported, and before landing, or permitting to land, any Chinese passengers, deliver and report to the collector of customs of the district in which such vessels shall have arrived a separate list of all Chinese passengers taken on board his vessel at any foreign port or place, and all such passengers on board the vessel at that time . . .

SEC. 9. That before any Chinese passengers are landed from any such vessel, the collector, or his deputy, shall proceed to examine such passengers, comparing the certificates with the list and with the passengers; and no passenger shall be allowed to land in the United States from such vessel in violation of law . . .

SEC. 11. That any person who shall knowingly bring into or cause to be brought into the United States by land, or who shall knowingly aid or abet the same, or aid or abet the landing in the United States from any vessel of any Chinese person not lawfully entitled to enter the United States, shall be deemed guilty of a misdemeanor, and shall, on conviction thereof, be fined in a sum not exceeding $1,000, and imprisoned for a term not exceeding one year.

SEC. 12. That no Chinese person shall be permitted to enter the United States by land without producing to the proper officer of customs the certificate in this act required of Chinese persons seeking to land from a vessel . . .

SEC. 13. That this act shall not apply to diplomatic and other officers of the Chinese Government traveling upon the business of that government, whose credentials shall be taken as equivalent to the certificate in this act mentioned, and shall exempt them and their body and household servants from the provisions of this act as to other Chinese persons.

SEC. 14. That hereafter no State court or court of the United States shall admit Chinese to citizenship; and all laws in conflict with this act are hereby repealed.

SEC. 15. That the words "Chinese laborers," wherever used in this act, shall be construed to mean both skilled and unskilled laborers and Chinese employed in mining.

Approved, May 6, 1882.

12 *Elk* v. *Wilkins,* 1884

John Elk, an Indian who had voluntarily separated himself from his tribe and taken up residence among the whites, was denied the right to vote in Omaha, Nebraska, on the grounds that he was not a citizen. The Supreme Court considered the question of whether Elk had been made a citizen by the Fourteenth Amendment and decided against him.

. . . The plaintiff, in support of his action, relies on the first clause of the first section of the Fourteenth Article of Amendment of the Constitution of the United States, by which "all persons born or naturalized in the United States, and subject to the jurisdiction thereof, are citizens of the United States and of the State wherein they reside"; and on the Fifteenth Article of Amendment, which provides that "the right of citizens of the United States to vote shall not be denied or abridged by the United States or by any State on account of race, color, or previous condition of servitude." . . .

The petition, while it does not show of what Indian tribe the plaintiff was a member, yet, by the allegations that he "is an Indian, and was born within the United States," and that "he had severed his tribal relation to the Indian tribes," clearly implies that he was born a member of one of the Indian tribes within the limits of the United States, which still exists and is recognized as a tribe by the government of the United States. Though the plaintiff alleges that he "had fully and completely surrendered himself to the jurisdiction of the United States," he does not allege that the United States accepted his surrender, or that he has ever been naturalized, or taxed, or in any way recognized or treated as a citizen, by the State or by the United States. Nor is it contended by his counsel that there is any statute or treaty that makes him a citizen.

The question then is, whether an Indian, born a member of one of the Indian tribes within the United States, is, merely by reason of his birth within the United States, and of his afterwards voluntarily separating himself from his tribe and taking up his residence among white citizens, a citizen of the United States, within the meaning of the first section of the Fourteenth Amendment of the Constitution. . . .

Indians born within the territorial limits of the United States, members of, and owing immediate allegiance to, one of the Indian tribes (an alien, though dependent, power), although in a geographical sense born in the United States, are no more "born in the United States and subject to the jurisdiction thereof," within the meaning of the first section of the Fourteenth Amendment, than the children of subjects of any foreign government born within the domain of that government, or the children born within the United States, of ambassadors or other public ministers of foreign nations.

This view is confirmed by the second section of the Fourteenth Amendment, which provides that "representatives shall be apportioned among the several States

From *Elk* v. *Wilkins,* 112 *United States Reports: Cases Adjudged in the Supreme Court* (New York: Banks & Brothers).

according to their respective numbers, counting the whole number of persons in each State, excluding Indians not taxed." Slavery having been abolished, and the persons formerly held as slaves made citizens, this clause fixing the apportionment of representatives has abrogated so much of the corresponding clause of the original Constitution as counted only three-fifths of such persons. But Indians not taxed are still excluded from the count, for the reason that they are not citizens. Their absolute exclusion from the basis of representation, in which all other persons are now included, is wholly inconsistent with their being considered citizens. . . .

The plaintiff, not being a citizen of the United States under the Fourteenth Amendment of the Constitution, has been deprived of no right secured by the Fifteenth Amendment, and cannot maintain this action.

After the collapse of Reconstruction governments, Southern whites began gradually to legalize the informal practices of segregation which obtained in the South. One such law was passed by the Louisiana legislature in 1890 and provided that "all railway companies carrying passengers . . . in this State shall provide separate but equal accommodations for the white and colored races."

Plessy v. Ferguson tested the constitutionality of this recent trend in Southern legislation. Plessy was a mulatto who, on June 7, 1892, bought a first-class ticket on the East Louisiana Railway for a trip from New Orleans to Covington, Louisiana, and sought to be seated in the "white" coach. Upon conviction of a violation of the 1890 statute, he appealed to the Supreme Court of Louisiana, which upheld his conviction, and finally to the U.S. Supreme Court, which pronounced the Louisiana law constitutional, on May 18, 1896. The defense of Plessy and attack on the Louisiana statute was in the hands of four men, the most famous of whom was Albion W. Tourgée. M. J. Cunningham, attorney general of Louisiana, was assisted by two other lawyers in defending the statute. The majority opinion of the Court was delivered by Justice Henry B. Brown. John Marshall Harlan dissented and Justice David J. Brewer did not participate, making it a 7-1 decision.

In his dissent to this decision Harlan asserted that "Our Constitution is color-blind, and neither knows nor tolerates classes among citizens. In respect of civil rights, all citizens are equal before the law." He offered the prophecy that "the judgment rendered this day will, in time, prove to be quite as pernicious as the decision made by this tribunal in the Dred Scott case."

The constitutionality of this act is attacked upon the ground that it conflicts both with the Thirteenth Amendment of the Constitution, abolishing slavery, and the Fourteenth Amendment, which prohibits certain restrictive legislation on the part of the States.

1. That it does not conflict with the Thirteenth Amendment, which abolished slavery and involuntary servitude, except as a punishment for crime, is too clear for argument. Slavery implies involuntary servitude—a state of bondage: the ownership of mankind as a chattel, or at least the control of the labor and services of one man for the benefit of another, and the absence of a legal right to the disposal of his own person, property and services. . . .

A statute which implies merely a legal distinction between the white and colored races—a distinction which is founded in the color of the two races, and which must always exist so long as white men are distinguished from the other race by color—has

From *Plessy* v. *Ferguson,* 163 U.S. 537 *United States Reports: Cases Adjudged in the Supreme Court* (New York, Banks & Brothers, 1896).

no tendency to destroy the legal equality of the two races, or reestablish a state of involuntary servitude. Indeed, we do not understand that the Thirteenth Amendment is strenuously relied upon by the plaintiff in error in this connection.

2. By the Fourteenth Amendment, all persons born or naturalized in the United States, and subject to the jurisdiction thereof, are made citizens of the United States and of the State wherein they reside; and the States are forbidden from making or enforcing any law which shall abridge the privileges or immunities of citizens of the United States, or shall deprive any person of life, liberty or property without due process of law, or deny to any person within their jurisdiction the equal protection of the laws. . . .

The object of the amendment was undoubtedly to enforce the absolute equality of the two races before the law, but in the nature of things it could not have been intended to abolish distinctions based upon color, or to enforce social, as distinguished from political equality, or a commingling of the two races upon terms unsatisfactory to either. Laws permitting, and even requiring, their separation in places where they are liable to be brought into contact do not necessarily imply the inferiority of either race to the other, and have been generally, if not universally, recognized as within the competency of the state legislatures in the exercise of their police power. The most common instance of this is connected with the establishment of separate schools for white and colored children, which has been held to be a valid exercise of the legislative power even by courts of States where the political rights of the colored race have been longest and most earnestly enforced. . . .

While we think the enforced separation of the races, as applied to the internal commerce of the State, neither abridges the privileges or immunities of the colored man, deprives him of his property without due process of law, nor denies him the equal protection of the laws, within the meaning of the Fourteenth Amendment, we are not prepared to say that the conductor, in assigning passengers to the coaches according to their race, does not act at his peril, or that the provision of the second section of the act, that denies to the passenger compensation in damages for a refusal to receive him into the coach in which he properly belongs, is a valid exercise of the legislative power. Indeed, we understand it to be conceded by the State's attorney, that such part of the act as exempts from liability the railway company and its officers is unconstitutional. The power to assign to a particular coach obviously implies the power to determine to which race the passenger belongs, as well as the power to determine who, under the laws of the particular State, is to be deemed a white, and who a colored person. . . .

It is claimed by the plaintiff in error that, in any mixed community, the reputation of belonging to the dominant race, in this instance the white race, is *property*, in the same sense that a right of action, or of inheritance, is property. Conceding this to be so, for the purposes of this case, we are unable to see how this statute deprives him of, or in any way affects his right to, such property. If he be a white man and assigned to a colored coach, he may have his action for damages against the company for being deprived of his so called property. Upon the other hand, if he be a colored man and be so assigned, he has been deprived of no property, since he is not lawfully entitled to the reputation of being a white man.

In this connection, it is also suggested by the learned counsel for the plaintiff in error that the same argument that will justify the state legislature in requiring railways to provide separate accommodations for the two races will also authorize them to require separate cars to be provided for the people whose hair is of a certain color, or who are aliens, or who belong to certain nationalities, or to enact laws requiring colored people to walk upon one side of the street, and white people upon the other, or requiring white men's houses to be painted white, and colored men's black, or their vehicles or business signs to be of different colors, upon the theory that one side of the street is as good as the other, or that a house or vehicle of one color is as good as one of another color. The reply to all this is that every exercise of the police power must be reasonable, and extend only to such laws as are enacted in good faith for the promotion of the public good, and not for the annoyance or oppression of a particular class. . . .

We consider the underlying fallacy of the plaintiff's argument to consist in the assumption that the enforced separation of the two races stamps the colored race with a badge of inferiority. If this be so, it is not by reason of anything found in the act, but solely because the colored race chooses to put that construction upon it. The argument necessarily assumes that if, as has been more than once the case, and is not unlikely to be so again, the colored race should become the dominant power in the state legislature, and should enact a law in precisely similar terms, it would thereby relegate the white race to an inferior position. We imagine that the white race, at least, would not acquiesce in this assumption. The argument also assumes that social prejudices may be overcome by legislation, and that equal rights cannot be secured to the negro except by an enforced commingling of the two races. We cannot accept this proposition. If the two races are to meet upon terms of social equality, it must be the result of natural affinities, a mutual appreciation of each other's merits and a voluntary consent of individuals.

14 United States Constitution
Nineteenth Amendment (1920)

Amendment XIX (ratified August 18, 1920). *Section 1.* The right of citizens of the United States to vote shall not be denied or abridged by the United States or by any State on account of sex.

Section 2. Congress shall have power to enforce this Article by appropriate legislation.

15   *U.S.* v. *Bhagat Singh Thind*, 1923

Argued Jan. 11, 12, 1923.
Decided Feb. 19, 1923.
Mr. Solicitor General Beck, of Washington, D. C., for the United states.
Mr. Will R. King, of Washington, D. C., for Thind.
Mr. Justice SUTHERLAND delivered the opinion of the Court.
This cause is here upon a certificate from the Circuit Court of appeals requesting the instruction of this Court in respect of the following questions:

1. Is a high-caste Hindu, of full Indian blood, born at Amritsar, Punjab, India, a white person within the meaning of section 2169, Revised Statutes?
2. Does the Act of February 5, 1917 (39 Stat. 875, 3), disqualify from naturalization as citizens those Hindus now barred by that act, who had lawfully entered the United States prior to the passage of said act?'

Section 2169, Revised Statutes (Comp. St. 4358), provides that the provisions of the Naturalization Act 'shall apply to aliens being free white persons and to aliens of African nativity and to persons of African descent.'

If the applicant is a white person, within the meaning of this section, he is entitled to naturalization; otherwise not. In Ozawa v. United States, 260 U.S. 178, 43 Sup. Ct. 65, 67 L. Ed.—, decided November 13, 1922, we had occasion to consider the application of these words to the case of a cultivated Japanese and were constrained to hold that he was not within their meaning. As there pointed out, the provision is not that any particular class of persons shall be excluded, but it is, in effect, that only white persons shall be included within the privilege of the statute. 'The intention was to confer the privilege of citizenship upon that class of persons whom the fathers knew as white, and to deny it to all who could not be so classified. It is not enough to say that the framers did not have in mind the brown or yellow races of Asia. It is necessary to go farther and be able to say that had these particular [261 U.S. 204, 208] races been suggested the language of the act would have been so varied as to include them within its privileges'—citing Dartmouth College v. Woodward, 4 Wheat. 518, 644. Following a long line of decisions of the lower Federal courts, we held that the words imported a racial and not an individual test and were meant to indicate only persons of what is popularly known as the Caucasian race. But, as there pointed out, the conclusion that the phrase 'white persons' and the word 'Caucasian' are synonymous does not end the matter. It enabled us to dispose of the problem as it was there presented, since the applicant for citizenship clearly fell outside the zone of debatable ground on the negative side; but the decision still left the question to be dealt with, in doubtful and different cases, by the 'process of judicial inclusion and exclusion.' Mere ability on the part of an applicant for naturalization to establish a line of descent from a Caucasian ancestor will not ipso facto to and necessarily conclude the inquiry. 'Caucasian' is a conventional word of much flexibility, as a study of the literature dealing with racial questions will disclose, and while it and the words 'white persons' are treated as synonymous for the purposes of that case, they are not of identical meaning-idem per idem.

In the endeavor to ascertain the meaning of the statute we must not fail to keep in mind that it does not employ the word 'Caucasian,' but the words 'white persons,' and these are words of common speech and not of scientific origin. The word 'Caucasian' not only was not employed in the law, but was probably wholly unfamiliar to the original framers of the statute in 1790. When we employ it, we do so as an aid to the ascertainment of the legislative intent and not as an invariable substitute for the statutory words. Indeed, as used in the science of ethnology, the connotation of the word is by no means clear, and the use of it in its scientific sense as an equivalent [261 U.S. 204, 209] for the words of the statute, other considerations aside, would simply mean the substitution of one perplexity for another. But in this country, during the last half century especially, the word by common usage has acquired a popular meaning, not clearly defined to be sure, but sufficiently so to enable us to say that its popular as distinguished from its scientific application is of appreciably narrower scope. It is in the popular sense of the word, therefore, that we employ is as an aid to the construction of the statute, for it would be obviously illogical to convert words of common speech used in a statute into words of scientific terminology when neither the latter nor the science for whose purposes they were coined was within the contemplation of the framers of the statute or of the people for whom it was framed. The words of the statute are to be interpreted in accordance with the understanding of the common man from whose vocabulary they were taken. See Maillard v. Lawrence, 16 How. 251, 261.

They imply, as we have said, a racial test; but the term 'race' is one which, for the practical purposes of the statute, must be applied to a group of living persons now possessing in common the requisite characteristics, not to groups of persons who are supposed to be or really are descended from some remote, common ancestor, but who, whether they both resemble him to a greater or less extent, have, at any rate, ceased altogether to resemble one another. It may be true that the blond Scandinavian and the brown Hindu have a common ancestor in the dim reaches of antiquity, but the average man knows perfectly well that there are unmistakable and profound differences between them to-day; and it is not impossible, if that common ancestor could be materialized in the flesh, we should discover that he was himself sufficiently differentiated from both of his descendants to preclude his racial classification with either. The question for determination [261 U.S. 204, 210] is not, therefore, whether by the speculative processes of ethnological reasoning we may present a probability to the scientific mind that they have the same origin, but whether we can satisfy the common understanding that they are now the same or sufficiently the same to justify the interpreters of a statute—written in the words of common speech, for common understanding, by unscientific men—in classifying them together in the statutory category as white persons.

. . . We are unable to agree with the District Court, or with other lower federal courts, in the conclusion that a native Hindu is eligible for naturalization under section 2169. The words of familiar speech, which were used by the original framers of the law, were intended to include only the type of man whom they knew as white. The immigration of that day was almost exclusively from the British Isles and Northwestern Europe, whence they and their forebears had come. When they extended the privilege of American citizenship to 'any alien being a free white person' it was these immigrants—bone of their bone and flesh of their flesh—and their kind whom they must have had affirmatively in mind. The succeeding years brought immigrants from Eastern, Southern and Middle Europe, among them the Slavs and the dark-eyed, swarthy people of Alpine and Mediterranean stock, and these were received as unquestionably akin to those already here and readily amalgamated with them. It was the descendants of these, and [261 U.S. 204, 214] other immigrants of like origin, who constituted the white population of the country when section 2169, re-enacting the naturalization test of 1790, was adopted, and, there is no reason to doubt, with like intent and meaning.

What we now hold is that the words 'free white persons' are words of common speech, to be interpreted in accordance with the understanding of the common man, synonymous with the word 'Caucasian' only as that [261 U.S. 204, 215] word is popularly understood. As so understood and used, whatever may be the speculations of the ethnologist, it does not include the body of people to whom the appellee belongs. It is a matter of familiar observation and knowledge that the physical group characteristics of the Hindus render them readily distinguishable from the various groups of persons in this country commonly recognized as white. The children of English, French, German, Italian, Scandinavian, and other European parentage quickly merge into the mass of our population and lose the distinctive hallmarks of their European origin. On the other hand, it cannot be doubted that the children born in this country of Hindu parents would retain indefinitely the clear evidence of their ancestry. It is very far from our thought to suggest the slightest question of racial superiority or inferiority. What we suggest is merely racial difference, and it is of such character and extent that the great body of our people instinctively recognize it and reject the thought of assimilation.

It is not without significance in this connection that Congress, by the Act of February 5, 1917, 39 Stat. 874, c. 29, 3 (Comp. St. 1918, Comp. St. Ann. Supp. 1919, 4289 1/4b), has now excluded from admission into this country all natives of Asia within designated limits of latitude and longitude, including the whole of India. This not only constitutes conclusive evidence of the congressional attitude of opposition to Asiatic immigration generally, but is persuasive of a similar attitude toward Asiatic naturalization as well, since it is not likely that Congress would be willing to accept as citizens a class of persons whom it rejects as immigrants.

It follows that a negative answer must be given to the first question, which disposes of the case and renders an answer to the second question unnecessary, and it will be so certified.

Answer to question No. 1, No.

16 Brown v. Board of Education of Topeka, 1954

Mr. Chief Justice Warren delivered the opinion of the Court.

These cases come to us from the States of Kansas, South Carolina, Virginia, and Delaware. They are premised on different facts and different local conditions, but a common legal question justifies their consideration together in this consolidated opinion.[1]

In each of the cases, minors of the Negro race, through their legal representatives, seek the aid of the courts in obtaining admission to the public schools of their community on a nonsegregated basis. In each instance, they had been denied admission to schools attended by white children under laws requiring or permitting segregation according to race. This segregation was alleged to deprive the plaintiffs of the equal protection of the laws under the Fourteenth Amendment. In each of the cases other than the Delaware case, a three-judge federal district court denied relief to the plaintiffs on the so-called "separate but equal" doctrine announced by this Court in *Plessy v. Ferguson*, 163 U.S. 537. Under that doctrine, equality of treatment is accorded when the races are provided substantially equal facilities, even though these facilities be separate. In the Delaware case, the Supreme Court of Delaware adhered to that doctrine, but ordered that the plaintiffs be admitted to the white schools because of their superiority to the Negro schools.

The plaintiffs contend that segregated public schools are not "equal" and cannot be made "equal," and that hence they are deprived of the equal protection of the laws. Because of the obvious importance of the question presented, the Court took jurisdiction.[2] Argument was heard in the 1952 Term, and reargument was heard this Term on certain questions propounded by the Court.[3] . . .

In approaching this problem, we cannot turn the clock back to 1868 when the Amendment was adopted, or even to 1896 when *Plessy v. Ferguson* was written. We must consider public education in the light of its full development and its present place in American life throughout the Nation. Only in this way can it be determined if segregation in public schools deprives these plaintiffs of the equal protection of the laws.

Today, education is perhaps the most important function of state and local governments. Compulsory school attendance laws and the great expenditures for education both demonstrate our recognition of the importance of education to our democratic society. It is required in the performance of our most basic public responsibilities, even service in the armed forces. It is the very foundation of good citizenship. Today it is a principal instrument in awakening the child to cultural values, in preparing him for later professional training, and in helping him to adjust normally to his environment. In these days, it is doubtful that any child may reasonably be expected to succeed in life if he is denied the opportunity of an education. Such an opportunity, where the state has undertaken to provide it, is a right which must be made available to all on equal terms.

We come then to the question presented: Does segregation of children in public schools solely on the basis of race, even though the physical facilities and other "tangible" factors may be equal, deprive the children of the minority group of equal educational opportunities? We believe that it does.

In *Sweatt* v. *Painter*, in finding that a segregated law school for Negroes could not provide them equal educational opportunities, this Court relied in large part on "those qualities which are incapable of objective measurement but which make for greatness in a law school." In *McLaurin* v. *Oklahoma State Regents*, the Court, in requiring that a Negro admitted to a white graduate school be treated like all other students, again resorted to intangible considerations: ". . . his ability to study, to engage in discussions and exchange views with other students, and in general, to learn his profession." Such considerations apply with added force to children in grade and high schools. To separate them from others of similar age and qualifications solely because of their race generates a feeling of inferiority as to their status in the community that may affect their hearts and minds in a way unlikely ever to be undone. The effect of this separation on their educational opportunities was well stated by a finding in the Kansas case by a court which nevertheless felt compelled to rule against the Negro plaintiffs:

> Segregation of white and colored children in public schools has a detrimental effect upon the colored children. The impact is greater when it has the sanction of the law; for the policy of separating the races is usually interpreted as denoting the inferiority of the negro group. A sense of inferiority affects the motivation of a child to learn. Segregation with the sanction of law, therefore, has a tendency to [retard] the educational and mental development of negro children and to deprive them of some of the benefits they receive in a racial[ly] integrated school system.[4]

Whatever may have been the extent of psychological knowledge at the time of *Plessy* v. *Ferguson*, this finding is amply supported by modern authority.[5] Any language in *Plessy* v. *Ferguson* contrary to this finding is rejected.

We conclude that in the field of public education the doctrine of "separate but equal" has no place. Separate educational facilities are inherently unequal. Therefore, we hold that the plaintiffs and others similarly situated for whom the actions have been brought are, by reason of the segregation complained of, deprived of the equal protection of the laws guaranteed by the Fourteenth Amendment. This disposition makes unnecessary any discussion whether such segregation also violates the Due Process Clause of the Fourteenth Amendment.

Because these are class actions, because of the wide applicability of this decision, and because of the great variety of local conditions, the formulation of decrees in these cases presents problems of considerable complexity. On reargument, the consideration of appropriate relief was necessarily subordinated to the primary question—the constitutionality of segregation in public education. We have now announced that such segregation is a denial of the equal protection of the laws. In order that we may have the full assistance of the parties in formulating decrees, the cases will be restored to the docket, and the parties are requested to present further argument on Questions 4 and 5 previously propounded by the Court for the reargument this Term.[6] The Attorney General of the United States is again invited to participate. The Attorneys General of the states requiring or permitting segregation in public education will also be permitted to appear as amici curiae upon request to do so by September 15, 1954, and submission of the briefs by October 1, 1954.

It is so ordered.

NOTES

1. In the Kansas case, *Brown* v. *Board of Education*, the plaintiffs are Negro children of elementary school age residing in Topeka. They brought this action in the United States District Court for the District of Kansas to enjoin enforcement of a Kansas statute which permits, but does not require, cities of more than 15,000 population to maintain separate school facilities for Negro and white students. Kan. Gen. Stat. §72-1724 (1949). Pursuant to that authority, the Topeka Board of Education elected to establish segregated elementary schools. Other public schools in the community, however, are operated on a nonsegregated basis. The three-judge District Court, convened under 28 U.S.C. §§2281 and 2284, found that segregation in public education has a detrimental effect upon Negro children, but denied relief on the ground that the Negro and white schools were substantially equal with respect to buildings, transportation, curricula, and educational qualifications of teachers. 98 F. Supp. 797. The case is here on direct appeal under 28 U.S.C. §1253. [The Topeka, Kansas, case would be analogous to a northern school case inasmuch as the school segregation that existed in Topeka was not mandated by state law, and some of the system was integrated. It would be eighteen years before the Court would accept another such case for review. *Keyes* v. *School District No. 1, Denver*, 445 F.2d 990 (10th Cir. 1971), *cert. granted*, 404 U.S. 1036 (1972)].

In the South Carolina case, *Briggs* v. *Elliot*, the plaintiffs are Negro children of both elementary and high school age residing in Clarendon County. They brought this action in the United States District Court for the Eastern District of South Carolina to enjoin enforcement of provisions in the state constitution and statutory code which require the segregation of Negroes and whites in public schools. S.C. Const., Art. XI, §7; S.C. Code §5377 (1942). The three-judge District Court, convened under 28 U.S.C. §§2281 and 2284, denied the requested relief. The court found that the Negro schools were inferior to the white schools and ordered the defendants to begin immediately to equalize the facilities. But the court sustained the validity of the contested provisions and denied the plaintiffs admission to the white schools during the equalization program. 98 F. Supp. 529. This Court vacated the District Court's judgment and remanded the case for the purpose of obtaining the court's views on a report filed by the defendants concerning the progress made in the equalization program. 342 U.S. 350. On remand, the District Court found that substantial equality had been achieved except for buildings and that the defendants were proceeding to rectify this inequality as well. 103 F. Supp. 920. The case is again here on direct appeal under 28 U.S.C. §1253.

In the Virginia case, *Davis* v. *County School Board*, the plaintiffs are Negro children of high school age residing in Prince Edward County. They brought this action in the United States District Court for the Eastern District of Virginia to enjoin enforcement of provisions in the state constitution and statutory code which require the segregation of Negroes and whites in public schools. Va. Const., §140; Va. Code §22-221 (1950). The three-judge District Court, convened under 28 U.S.C. §§2281 and 2284, denied the requested relief. The court found the Negro school inferior in physical plant, curricula, and transportation, and ordered the defendants forthwith to provide substantially equal curricula and transportation and to "proceed with all reasonable diligence and dispatch to remove" the inequality in physical plant. But, as in the South Carolina case, the court sustained the validity of the contested provisions and denied the plaintiffs admission to the white schools during the equalization program. 103 F. Supp. 337. The case is here on direct appeal under 28 U.S.C. §1253.

In the Delaware case, *Gebhart* v. *Belton*, the plaintiffs are Negro children of both elementary and high school age residing in New Castle County. They brought this action in the Delaware Court of Chancery to enjoin enforcement of provisions in the state constitution and statutory code which require the segregation of Negroes and whites in public schools. Del. Const., Art. X, §2; Del. Rev. Code §2631 (1935). The Chancellor gave judgment for the plaintiffs and ordered their immediate admission to schools previously attended only by white children, on the ground that the Negro schools were inferior with respect to teacher training, pupil-teacher ratio, extracurricular activities, physical plant, and time and distance involved in travel. 87 A.2d 862. The Chancellor also found that segregation itself results in an inferior education for Negro children (see note 4, infra), but did not rest his decision on that ground. Id., at 865. The Chancellor's decree was affirmed by the Supreme Court of Delaware, which intimated, however, that the defendants might be able to obtain a modification of the decree after equalization of the Negro and white schools had been accomplished. 91 A.2d 137, 152. The defendants, contending only that the Delaware courts had erred in ordering the immediate admission of the Negro plaintiffs to the white schools, applied to this Court for certiorari. The writ was granted, 344 U.S. 891. The plaintiffs, who were successful below, did not submit a cross-petition.

2. 344 U.S. 1, 141, 891.

3. 345 U.S. 972. The Attorney General of the United States participated both Terms as amicus curiae.

4. A similar finding was made in the Delaware case: "I conclude from the testimony that in our Delaware Society, State-imposed segregation in education itself results in the Negro children, as a class, receiving educational opportunities which are substantially inferior to those available to white children otherwise similarly situated." 87 A.2d 862, 865.

5. K. B. Clark, Effect of Prejudice and Discrimination on Personality Development (Midcentury White House Conference on Children and Youth, 1950); Witmer and Kotinsky, Personality in the Making (1952), c. VI; Deutscher and Chein, The Psychological Effects of Enforced Segregation: A Survey of Social Science Opinion, 26 J. Psychol. 259 (1948); Chein, What Are the Psychological Effects of Segregation Under Conditions of Equal Facilities?, 3 Int. J. Opinion and Attitude Res. 229 (1949); Brameld, Educational Costs, in Discrimination and National Welfare (MacIver, ed., 1949), 44–48; Frazier, The Negro in the United States (1949), 674–681. And see generally Myrdal, An American Dilemma (1944).

6. "4. Assuming it is decided that segregation in public schools violates the Fourteenth Amendment

"(a) would a decree necessarily follow providing that, within the limits set by normal geographic school districting, Negro children should forthwith be admitted to schools of their choice, or "(b) may this Court, in the exercise of its equity powers, permit an effective gradual adjustment to be brought about from existing segregated systems to a system not based on color distinctions?

"5. On the assumption on which questions 4(a) and (b) are based, and assuming further that this Court will exercise its equity powers to the end described in question 4(b),

"(a) should this Court formulate detailed decrees in these cases;

"(b) if so, what specific issues should the decrees reach;

"(c) should this Court appoint a special master to hear evidence with a view to recommending specific terms for such decrees;

"(d) should this Court remand to the courts of first instance with directions to frame decrees in these cases, and if so what general directions should the decrees of this Court include and what procedures should the courts of first instance follow in arriving at the specific terms of more detailed decrees?"

17 Roe v. Wade, 1973

This historic decision legalized a woman's right to terminate her pregnancy by abortion. The ruling was based upon the right of privacy founded on both the Fourteenth and Ninth Amendments to the Constitution. The Court ruled that this right of privacy protected the individual from interference by the state in the decision to terminate a pregnancy by abortion during the early portion of the pregnancy. At the same time, it recognized the interest of the state in regulating decisions concerning the pregnancy during the latter period as the fetus developed the capacity to survive outside the woman's body.

18 The Equal Rights Amendment (Defeated)

Section 1. Equality of Rights under the law shall not be denied or abridged by the United States or any state on account of sex.

Section 2. The Congress shall have the power to enforce, by appropriate legislation, the provisions of this article.

Section 3. This amendment shall take effect two years after the date of ratification.

First introduced in Congress in 1923, the ERA was finally passed in 1972. However, because it failed to be ratified by the requisite number of states by its July 1982 deadline, the ERA never became part of the Constitution.

19 *Obergefell* v. *Hodges*, 2015

CERTIORARI TO THE UNITED STATES COURT OF APPEALS FOR THE SIXTH CIRCUIT

No. 14–556. Argued April 28, 2015—Decided June 26, 2015*

Michigan, Kentucky, Ohio, and Tennessee define marriage as a union between one man and one woman. The petitioners, 14 same-sex couples and two men whose same-sex partners are deceased, filed suits in Federal District Courts in their home States, claiming that respondent state officials violate the Fourteenth Amendment by denying them the right to marry or to have marriages lawfully performed in another State given full recognition. Each District Court ruled in petitioners' favor, but the Sixth Circuit consolidated the cases and reversed.

Held: The Fourteenth Amendment requires a State to license a marriage between two people of the same sex and to recognize a marriage between two people of the same sex when their marriage was lawfully licensed and performed out-of-State. Pp. 3–28.

(a) Before turning to the governing principles and precedents, it is appropriate to note the history of the subject now before the Court. Pp. 3–10.

(1) The history of marriage as a union between two persons of the opposite sex marks the beginning of these cases. To the respondents, it would demean a timeless institution if marriage were extended to same-sex couples. But the petitioners, far from seeking to devalue marriage, seek it for themselves because of their respect—and need—for its privileges and responsibilities, as illustrated by the petitioners' own experiences. Pp. 3–6.

(2) The history of marriage is one of both continuity and change. Changes, such as the decline of arranged marriages and the abandonment of the law of coverture, have worked deep transformations in the structure of marriage, affecting aspects of marriage once viewed as essential. These new insights have strengthened, not weakened, the institution. Changed understandings of marriage are characteristic of a Nation where new dimensions of freedom become apparent to new generations.

This dynamic can be seen in the Nation's experience with gay and lesbian rights. Well into the 20th century, many States condemned same-sex intimacy as immoral, and homosexuality was treated as an illness. Later in the century, cultural and political developments allowed same-sex couples to lead more open and public lives. Extensive public and private dialogue followed, along with shifts in public attitudes. Questions about the legal treatment of gays and lesbians soon reached the courts, where they could be discussed in the formal discourse of the law. In 2003, this Court overruled its

*Together with No. 14–562, *Tanco et al.* v. *Haslam, Governor of Tennessee, et al.,* No. 14–571, *DeBoer et al.* v. *Snyder, Governor of Michigan, et al.,* and No. 14–574, *Bourke et al.* v. *Beshear, Governor of Kentucky,* also on certiorari to the same court.

1986 decision in *Bowers* v. *Hardwick*, 478 U.S. 186, which upheld a Georgia law that criminalized certain homosexual acts, concluding laws making same-sex intimacy a crime "demea[n] the lives of homosexual persons." *Lawrence* v. *Texas*, 539 U.S. 558, 575. In 2012, the federal Defense of Marriage Act was also struck down. *United States* v. *Windsor*, 570 U.S. ___. Numerous same-sex marriage cases reaching the federal courts and state supreme courts have added to the dialogue. Pp. 6–10.

(b) The Fourteenth Amendment requires a State to license a marriage between two people of the same sex. Pp. 10–27.

(1) The fundamental liberties protected by the Fourteenth Amendment's Due Process Clause extend to certain personal choices central to individual dignity and autonomy, including intimate choices defining personal identity and beliefs. See, *e.g.,* *Eisenstadt* v. *Baird*, 405 U.S. 438, 453; *Griswold* v. *Connecticut*, 381 U.S. 479, 484–486. Courts must exercise reasoned judgment in identifying interests of the person so fundamental that the State must accord them its respect. History and tradition guide and discipline the inquiry but do not set its outer boundaries. When new insight reveals discord between the Constitution's central protections and a received legal stricture, a claim to liberty must be addressed.

Applying these tenets, the Court has long held the right to marry is protected by the Constitution. For example, *Loving* v. *Virginia*, 388 U.S. 1, 12, invalidated bans on interracial unions, and *Turner* v. *Safley*, 482 U.S. 78, 95, held that prisoners could not be denied the right to marry. To be sure, these cases presumed a relationship involving opposite-sex partners, as did *Baker* v. *Nelson*, 409 U.S. 810, a one-line summary decision issued in 1972, holding that the exclusion of same-sex couples from marriage did not present a substantial federal question. But other, more instructive precedents have expressed broader principles. See, *e.g.,* *Lawrence, supra,* at 574. In assessing whether the force and rationale of its cases apply to same-sex couples, the Court must respect the basic reasons why the right to marry has been long protected. See, *e.g., Eisenstadt, supra,* at 453–454. This analysis compels the conclusion that same-sex couples may exercise the right to marry. Pp. 10–12.

(2) Four principles and traditions demonstrate that the reasons marriage is fundamental under the Constitution apply with equal force to same-sex couples. The first premise of this Court's relevant precedents is that the right to personal choice regarding marriage is inherent in the concept of individual autonomy. This abiding connection between marriage and liberty is why *Loving* invalidated interracial marriage bans under the Due Process Clause. See 388 U.S., at 12. Decisions about marriage are among the most intimate that an individual can make. See *Lawrence, supra,* at 574. This is true for all persons, whatever their sexual orientation.

A second principle in this Court's jurisprudence is that the right to marry is fundamental because it supports a two-person union unlike any other in its importance to the committed individuals. The intimate association protected by this right was central to *Griswold* v. *Connecticut*, which held the Constitution protects the right of married couples to use contraception, 381 U.S., at 485, and was acknowledged in *Turner, supra,* at 95. Same-sex couples have the same right as opposite-sex couples to enjoy intimate association, a right extending beyond mere freedom from laws making same-sex intimacy a criminal offense. See *Lawrence, supra,* at 567.

A third basis for protecting the right to marry is that it safeguards children and families and thus draws meaning from related rights of childrearing, procreation, and education. See, *e.g., Pierce* v. *Society of Sisters,* 268 U.S. 510. Without the recognition, stability, and predictability marriage offers, children suffer the stigma of knowing their families are somehow lesser. They also suffer the significant material costs of being raised by unmarried parents, relegated to a more difficult and uncertain family life. The marriage laws at issue thus harm and humiliate the children of same-sex couples. See *Windsor, supra,* at ___. This does not mean that the right to marry is less meaningful for those who do not or cannot have children. Precedent protects the right of a married couple not to procreate, so the right to marry cannot be conditioned on the capacity or commitment to procreate.

Finally, this Court's cases and the Nation's traditions make clear that marriage is a keystone of the Nation's social order. See *Maynard* v. *Hill,* 125 U.S. 190, 211. States have contributed to the fundamental character of marriage by placing it at the center of many facets of the legal and social order. There is no difference between same- and opposite-sex couples with respect to this principle, yet same-sex couples are denied the constellation of benefits that the States have linked to marriage and are consigned to an instability many opposite-sex couples would find intolerable. It is demeaning to lock same-sex couples out of a central institution of the Nation's society, for they too may aspire to the transcendent purposes of marriage.

The limitation of marriage to opposite-sex couples may long have seemed natural and just, but its inconsistency with the central meaning of the fundamental right to marry is now manifest. Pp. 12–18.

(3) The right of same-sex couples to marry is also derived from the Fourteenth Amendment's guarantee of equal protection. The Due Process Clause and the Equal Protection Clause are connected in a profound way. Rights implicit in liberty and rights secured by equal protection may rest on different precepts and are not always coextensive, yet each may be instructive as to the meaning and reach of the other. This dynamic is reflected in *Loving,* where the Court invoked both the Equal Protection Clause and the Due Process Clause; and in *Zablocki* v. *Redhail,* 434 U.S. 374, where the Court invalidated a law barring fathers delinquent on child-support payments from marrying. Indeed, recognizing that new insights and societal understandings can reveal unjustified inequality within fundamental institutions that once passed unnoticed and unchallenged, this Court has invoked equal protection principles to invalidate laws imposing sex-based inequality on marriage, see, *e.g., Kirchberg* v. *Feenstra,* 450 U.S. 455, 460–461, and confirmed the relation between liberty and equality, see, *e.g., M. L. B.* v. *S. L. J.,* 519 U.S. 102, 120–121.

The Court has acknowledged the interlocking nature of these constitutional safeguards in the context of the legal treatment of gays and lesbians. See *Lawrence,* 539 U.S., at 575. This dynamic also applies to same-sex marriage. The challenged laws burden the liberty of same-sex couples, and they abridge central precepts of equality. The marriage laws at issue are in essence unequal: Same-sex couples are denied benefits afforded opposite-sex couples and are barred from exercising a fundamental right. Especially against a long history of disapproval of their relationships, this denial works a grave and continuing harm, serving to disrespect and subordinate gays and lesbians. Pp. 18–22.

(4) The right to marry is a fundamental right inherent in the liberty of the person, and under the Due Process and Equal Protection Clauses of the Fourteenth Amendment couples of the same-sex may not be deprived of that right and that liberty. Same-sex couples may exercise the fundamental right to marry. *Baker* v. *Nelson* is overruled. The State laws challenged by the petitioners in these cases are held invalid to the extent they exclude same-sex couples from civil marriage on the same terms and conditions as opposite-sex couples. Pp. 22–23.

(5) There may be an initial inclination to await further legislation, litigation, and debate, but referenda, legislative debates, and grassroots campaigns; studies and other writings; and extensive litigation in state and federal courts have led to an enhanced understanding of the issue. While the Constitution contemplates that democracy is the appropriate process for change, individuals who are harmed need not await legislative action before asserting a fundamental right. *Bowers,* in effect, upheld state action that denied gays and lesbians a fundamental right. Though it was eventually repudiated, men and women suffered pain and humiliation in the interim, and the effects of these injuries no doubt lingered long after *Bowers* was overruled. A ruling against same-sex couples would have the same effect and would be unjustified under the Fourteenth Amendment. The petitioners' stories show the urgency of the issue they present to the Court, which has a duty to address these claims and answer these questions. Respondents' argument that allowing same-sex couples to wed will harm marriage as an institution rests on a counterintuitive view of opposite-sex couples' decisions about marriage and parenthood. Finally, the First Amendment ensures that religions, those who adhere to religious doctrines, and others have protection as they seek to teach the principles that are so fulfilling and so central to their lives and faiths. Pp. 23–27.

(c) The Fourteenth Amendment requires States to recognize same-sex marriages validly performed out of State. Since same-sex couples may now exercise the fundamental right to marry in all States, there is no lawful basis for a State to refuse to recognize a lawful same-sex marriage performed in another State on the ground of its same-sex character. Pp. 27–28.

772 F. 3d 388, reversed.

KENNEDY, J., delivered the opinion of the Court, in which GINSBURG, BREYER, SOTOMAYOR, and KAGAN, JJ., joined. ROBERTS, C. J., filed a dissenting opinion, in which SCALIA and THOMAS, JJ., joined. SCALIA, J., filed a dissenting opinion, in which THOMAS, J., joined. THOMAS, J., filed a dissenting opinion, in which SCALIA, J., joined. ALITO, J., filed a dissenting opinion, in which SCALIA and THOMAS, JJ., joined.

Suggestions for Further Reading

Acuña, Rudolpho. *Occupied America: A History of Chicanos*, 7th ed. New York: Prentice Hall, 2010.

Alexander, Michelle. *The New Jim Crow*. New York: The New Press, 2012.

Anderson, Karen. *Changing Women: A History of Racial Ethnic Women in Modern America*. New York: Oxford University Press, 1997.

Aptheker, Bettina. *Woman's Legacy: Essays on Race, Sex, and Class in American History*. Amherst, MA: University of Massachusetts Press, 1982.

Baxandall, Rosalyn F., Linda Gordon, and Susan Reverby, eds. *America's Working Women: A Documentary History—1600 to the Present*, rev. ed. New York: W. W. Norton, 1995.

Berry, Mary Frances. *Justice for All: The United States Commission on Civil Rights and the Continuing Struggle for Freedom in America*. New York: Knopf, 2009.

Cacho, Lisa Marie. *Social Death: Racialized Rightlessness and the Criminalization of the Unprotected*. New York: New York University Press, 2012.

Cluster, Dick, ed. *They Should Have Served That Cup of Coffee*. Boston: South End Press, 1999.

Cott, Nancy F. *Root of Bitterness: Documents of the Social History of American Women*, 2nd edition. Boston: Northeastern Press, 1996.

Crenshaw, et al. *Critical Race Theory: The Key Writings That Formed the Movement*. New York: The New Press, 1996.

Davis, Mike. *Prisoners of the American Dream: Politics and Economics in the History of the U.S. Working Class*. New York: Verso, 2000.

D'Emilio, John, and Estelle B. Freedman. *Intimate Matters: A History of Sexuality in America*, 2nd ed. Chicago: University of Chicago Press, 1998.

Dray, Philip. *There Is Power in the Union: The Epic Story of Labor in America*. New York: Anchor, 2012.

Duberman, Martin Baum, Martha Vicinus, and George Chauncey, Jr., eds. *Hidden from History: Reclaiming the Gay and Lesbian Past*. New York: New American Library, 1989.

Fleischer, Doris Zames, and Frieda Zames. *The Disability Rights Movement from Charity to Confrontation*. Philadelphia: Temple University Press, 2001.

Flexner, Eleanor, and Ellen Fitzpatrick. *Century of Struggle: The Woman's Rights Movement in the United States*, 3rd ed. Cambridge, MA: Harvard University Press, 1996.

Freedman, Estelle B. *No Turning Back: The History of Feminism and the Future of Women*. New York: Ballantine, 2003.

Giddings, Paula. *When and Where I Enter: The Impact of Black Women on Race and Sex in America*. New York: William Morrow, 1996.

Gilmore, Ruth Wilson. *Golden Gulag: Prisons, Surplus, Crisis, and Opposition in Globalizing California*. Berkeley: University of California Press, 2007.

Katz, Jonathan. *Gay American History: Lesbians and Gay Men in the U.S.: A Documentary History*, rev. ed. New York: Plume, 1992.

Kessler-Harris, Alice. *In Pursuit of Equity: Women, Men, and the Quest for Economic Citizenship in 20th-Century America*, rev. ed. New York: Oxford University Press, 2003.

Meyer, Doug. *Violence against Queer People: Race, Class, Gender, and the Persistence of Anti-LGBT Discrimination*. New Brunswick, N.J.: Rutgers University Press, 2015.

Mogul, Joey L., Andrea J. Ritchie, and Kay Whitlock. *Queer (In)Justice: The Criminalization of LGBT People in the United States*. New York: Beacon, 2012.

Murolo, Priscilla, A. B. Chitty, and Joe Sacco. *From the Folks Who Brought You the Weekend: A Short, Illustrated History of Labor in the United States*. New York: The New Press, 2003.

Pérez, Emma. *The Decolonial Imaginary: Writing Chicanas into History*. Bloomington, IN: Indiana University Press, 1999.

Richie, Beth. *Arrested Justice: Black Women, Violence and America's Prison Nation.* New York: New York University Press, 2012.

Rios, Victor. *Punished: Policing the Lives of Black and Latino Boys.* New York: New York University Press 2011.

Robson, Ruthann. *Lesbian (Out)Law: Survival Under the Rule of Law.* Ithaca, NY: Firebrand Books, 1992.

Ruiz, Vicki L., and Ellen Carol DuBois, eds. *Unequal Sisters: An Inclusive Reader in U.S. Women's History,* 4th ed. New York: Routledge and Kegan Paul, 2007.

Silliman, Jael, and Anannya Bhattacharjee. *Policing the National Body: Race, Gender, and Criminalization.* Boston: South End Press, 2002.

Spade, Dean. *Normal Life: Administrative Violence, Critical Trans Politics and the Limits of Law.* Boston: South End Press, 2011.

Stanley, Eric. *Captive Genders : Trans Embodiment and the Prison Industrial Complex.* Oakland, CA: AK Press, 2011.

Stevenson, Bryan. *Just Mercy: A Story of Justice and Redemption.* New York: Spiegel & Grau, 2015.

Takaki, Ronald. *A Different Mirror: Multicultural American History.* Boston: Little, Brown, 1993.

———. *From Different Shores: Perspectives on Race and Culture in America,* 2nd edition. New York: Oxford University Press, 1994.

Tang, Eric. *Unsettled: Cambodian Refugees in the New York City Hyperghetto.* Philadelphia: Temple University Press, 2015.

United States Commission on Human Rights. *Indian Tribes: A Continuing Quest for Survival.* Washington, DC: United States Commission on Human Rights, 1981.

Wagenheim, Kal, and Olga Jiménez de Wagenheim, eds. *The Puerto Ricans: A Documentary History,* rev. ed. New York: Markus Wiener, 2008.

Zinn, Howard. *A People's History of the United States.* New York: Harper Perennial Modern Classics, 2010.

PART VIII

Maintaining Race, Class, and Gender Hierarchies: Reproducing "Reality"

In the end, the most effective forms of social control are invisible. Tanks in the streets and armed militia are obvious reminders that people are not free, and they provide a focus for anger and an impetus for rebellion. More effective by far are the beliefs and attitudes a society fosters to rationalize and reinforce prevailing distributions of power and opportunity. It is here that stereotypes and ideology have an important role to play. They shape how we see ourselves and others; they affect how we define social issues; and they determine whom we hold responsible for society's ills. If distorted, each plays a part in persuading people that differences in wealth, power, and opportunity are reflections of natural differences among people, not the results of the economic and political organization of society. If the distortions are truly effective, they go beyond rationalizing inequality to rendering it invisible. Once again we find that the social constructions of gender, race, and class are hierarchies at the heart of a belief system that makes the prevailing distribution of wealth and opportunity appear natural and inevitable rather than arbitrary and alterable. In U.S. society, the stereotypes and values transmitted through education and the media have played a critical role in perpetuating racism, sexism, heterosexism, and class privilege even at those times when the law has been used as a vehicle to fight discrimination rather than maintain it.

The selections in Part VIII examine some of the ways in which we are socialized to buy into belief systems that reinforce existing social roles and class positions and blunt social criticism. Stereotypes and discriminatory ideology are perpetuated by the institutions in which we live and grow and which provide us with information and values: Education, religion, and our families, along with the media, encourage us to adopt a particular picture of the world and our place in it. These institutions shape our perceptions of others and give us a sense of our own future. In effect, they construct what we take to be "reality."

The mass media selectively provides information, promotes values, and teaches us who and what we should regard as important. Along with other institutions, it shapes our definition of community, painting a picture of society divided between "us" and "them." By making inequities and suffering appear to be the result of personal or group deficiency rather than the consequences of injustice, the representations of race, class, and gender often depicted in mass media tend to reconcile people to the status quo and prevent them from seeking change. Violence and the threat of violence reinforce ideology and threaten with pain or death those who challenge the prevailing system or its conventions and prescriptions.

In the first selection in Part VIII, Mark Snyder uses examples from psychological research to show how important people's expectations are in shaping their perceptions of others and in determining how they behave. In particular, these studies raise serious questions about the "objectivity" of interviewers' evaluations of job candidates and applicants for admission to educational programs; the studies suggest that how we see others often says more about our own unconscious stereotyping and expectations than about the individuals being evaluated. As Snyder points out, some of the most interesting studies in education show that teachers' expectations are at least as important as a child's innate ability in determining how well the child does in school. The unconscious beliefs that people harbor can have powerful consequences for the life chances and well-being of others.

While men in our society continue to be judged by the jobs they hold and their earning power, women continue to be judged according to a narrow and rigid standard of beauty. The messages that bombard young women from an early age foster the belief that a tiny waist is infinitely more important than an advanced degree or a technical skill. Although many women have made considerable strides in the world of work, the prevailing ideology continues to assert that being attractive (read "thin") enough to capture the right man is the real way to success. Aside from its heterosexist bias, this emphasis on physical appearance (and, consequently, on unhealthy standards for body weight) is simply one more way in which women are distracted from their own self-interest and achieving true power and status in society. In Selection 2, Sharlene Hesse-Biber explores some of the consequences of the ways in which women have been encouraged to internalize an artificial and generally unattainable standard of beauty.

In Selection 3, Michael Parenti offers an account of our society as a plutocracy, a system of rule by and for the rich, rather than a democracy, a system of rule by and for the people. In this book excerpt, Parenti discusses the ways in which our social institutions are organized to perpetuate rule by the rich and the ways in which we are socialized to embrace a system of beliefs that reinforces the existing social hierarchy. He suggests that all of us are getting both a clear message that material success is the measure of a person's worth and the related suggestion that, by implication, the poor aren't worth very much and so we should not waste society's resources on them.

While Gregory Mantsios, the author of Selection 4, would undoubtedly agree with Parenti's conclusion, he argues that in addition to playing a major role in fostering racial, ethnic, gender, and class stereotypes, the media's programming and perspectives affect our ability to "see" class at all. "By ignoring the poor and blurring the lines between working people and the upper class," he writes, "the news media creates a universal middle class." By adopting the perspective of those who are most privileged, the media distorts the realities of daily life and encourages most of us to identify with the needs and interests of a privileged few.

It would be difficult if not impossible to underestimate the role that education plays in reproducing the social hierarchy (for more on this, see Annette Lareau in Part II). Jonathan Kozol has written numerous books about this role. In Selection 5, he describes what he calls "the governmentally administered diminishment in the value of children of the poor." Kozol's thesis is that education in the United States continues to be separate and unequal to such an extent that it both constitutes and perpetuates a system of apartheid.

While Gregory Mantsios's selection talks about the media's ability to make class issues disappear, Angela Davis suggests in Selection 6 that the criminal justice system in the United States performs a similarly magical feat by making social problems disappear. In her essay, Davis examines the recent trend toward privatizing the nation's prison system and argues that imprisonment has become the government's response to social problems. She writes: "Homelessness, unemployment, drug addiction, mental illness, and illiteracy are only a few of the problems that disappear from public view when the human beings contending with them are relegated to cages."

For an altogether different take on the perpetuation of stereotypes, the next two selections examine the influence of the entertainment industries of Hollywood and professional sports. Jon Ronson writes in Selection 7 about typecasting and the role of the entertainment industry in fueling the conflation of Islam and terrorism. He speaks with Muslim actors about how they negotiate the ethics of playing one-dimensional stereotypic roles with the pragmatic concerns of finding work and needing to pay the bills. Ronson notes that the public that consumes television and films that perpetuate these stereotypes is complicit in this. He asks, Where is the outrage? David Zirin offers another example, from the world of professional sports, in Selection 8. Zirin compares the Washington Redskins to the Florida Seminoles, asking why there has been so much public opposition to the Washington team's use of a slur against Native Americans in their name while silence has surrounded the Florida team's appropriation of a tribal name which is accompanied by "interactive minstrelsy" such as fans' war chanting, doing the "Tomahawk chop," and wearing feather headdresses. He explores the myth that actual Seminoles have agreed to this usage and shows how this "agreement" is constituted as part of a larger economic project. Zirin suggests that both team names and the continued imagery and stereotypes that are associated with them are forms of institutionalized racism that the public helps propagate.

The final selections turn to the very real and very tragic consequences of stereotyping in relation to law enforcement, and how such stereotyping is ultimately condoned in the mass media. Ta-Nehisi Coates and Tressie McMillan Cottom's pieces (Selections 9 and 10) both look at the recent cases of police violence against young unarmed black men. Coates's article reflects that by casting Michael Brown as "no angel," the *New York Times* sets an impossible standard for morality: does one need to be angelic to be safe from violence? Cottom takes this question of morality a step further by asking whether targeted groups or individuals are responsible to keep themselves safe by signaling that they are not threatening. Adapting behavior to mediate assumptions and stereotypes is a common coping practice used by different marginalized groups. Cottom asks us to consider the toll that this takes and the consequences of this stress.

1 Self-Fulfilling Stereotypes

Mark Snyder

Gordon Allport, the Harvard psychologist who wrote a classic work on the nature of prejudice, told a story about a child who had come to believe that people who lived in Minneapolis were called monopolists. From his father, moreover, he had learned that monopolists were evil folk. It wasn't until many years later, when he discovered his confusion, that his dislike of residents of Minneapolis vanished.

Allport knew, of course, that it was not so easy to wipe out prejudice and erroneous stereotypes. Real prejudice, psychologists like Allport argued, was buried deep in human character, and only a restructuring of education could begin to root it out. Yet many people whom I meet while lecturing seem to believe that stereotypes are simply beliefs or attitudes that change easily with experience. Why do some people express the view that Italians are passionate, blacks are lazy, Jews materialistic, and lesbians mannish in their demeanor? In the popular view, it is because they have not learned enough about the diversity among these groups and have not had enough contact with members of the groups for their stereotypes to be challenged by reality. With more experience, it is presumed, most people of good will are likely to revise their stereotypes.

My research over the past decade convinces me that there is little justification for such optimism—and not only for the reasons given by Allport. While it is true that deep prejudice is often based on the needs of pathological character structure, stereotypes are obviously quite common even among fairly normal individuals. When people first meet others, they cannot help noticing certain highly visible and distinctive characteristics: sex, race, physical appearance, and the like. Despite people's best intentions, their initial impressions of others are shaped by their assumptions about such characteristics.

What is critical, however, is that these assumptions are not merely beliefs or attitudes that exist in a vacuum; they are reinforced by the behavior of both prejudiced people and the targets of their prejudice. In recent years, psychologists have collected considerable laboratory evidence about the processes that strengthen stereotypes and put them beyond the reach of reason and good will.

My own studies initially focused on first encounters between strangers. It did not take long to discover, for example, that people have very different ways of treating those whom they regard as physically attractive and those whom they consider physically unattractive, and that these differences tend to bring out precisely those kinds of behavior that fit with stereotypes about attractiveness.

In an experiment that I conducted with my colleagues Elizabeth Decker Tanke and Ellen Berscheid, pairs of college-age men and women met and became acquainted

Psychology Today © Copyright 1982. www.Psychologytoday.com

in telephone conversations. Before the conversations began, each man received a Polaroid snapshot, presumably taken just months before, of the woman he would soon meet. The photograph, which had actually been prepared before the experiment began, showed either a physically attractive woman or a physically unattractive one. By randomly choosing which picture to use for each conversation, we insured that there was no consistent relationship between the attractiveness of the woman in the picture and the attractiveness of the woman in the conversation.

By questioning the men, we learned that even before the conversations began, stereotypes about physical attractiveness came into play. Men who looked forward to talking with physically attractive women said that they expected to meet decidedly sociable, poised, humorous, and socially adept people, while men who thought that they were about to get acquainted with unattractive women fashioned images of rather unsociable, awkward, serious, and socially inept creatures. Moreover, the men proved to have very different styles of getting acquainted with women whom they thought to be attractive and those whom they believed to be unattractive. Shown a photograph of an attractive woman, they behaved with warmth, friendliness, humor, and animation. However, when the woman in the picture was unattractive, the men were cold, uninteresting, and reserved.

These differences in the men's behavior elicited behavior in the women that was consistent with the men's stereotyped assumptions. Women who were believed (unbeknown to them) to be physically attractive behaved in a friendly, likeable, and sociable manner. In sharp contrast, women who were perceived as physically unattractive adopted a cool, aloof, and distant manner. So striking were the differences in the women's behavior that they could be discerned simply by listening to tape recordings of the woman's side of the conversations. Clearly, by acting upon their stereotyped beliefs about the women whom they would be meeting, the men had initiated a chain of events that produced *behavioral confirmation* for their beliefs.

Similarly, Susan Anderson and Sandra Bem have shown in an experiment at Stanford University that when the tables are turned—when it is women who have pictures of men they are to meet on the telephone—many women treat the men according to their presumed physical attractiveness, and by so doing encourage the men to confirm their stereotypes. Little wonder, then, that so many people remain convinced that good looks and appealing personalities go hand in hand.

Sex and Race

It is experiments such as these that point to a frequently unnoticed power of stereotypes: the power to influence social relationships in ways that create the illusion of reality. In one study, Berna Skrypnek and I arranged for pairs of previously unacquainted students to interact in a situation that permitted us to control the information that each one received about the apparent sex of the other. The two people were seated in separate rooms so that they could neither see nor hear each other. Using a system of signal lights that they operated with switches, they negotiated a division of labor, deciding which member of the pair would perform each of several tasks that differed in sex-role connotations. The tasks varied along the dimensions of masculinity and femininity: sharpen a hunting knife (masculine), polish a pair of shoes (neutral), iron a shirt (feminine).

One member of the team was led to believe that the other was, in one condition of the experiment, male; in the other, female. As we had predicted, the first member's belief about the sex of the partner influenced the outcome of the pair's negotiations. Women whose partners believed them to be men generally chose stereotypically masculine tasks; in contrast, women whose partners believed that they were women usually chose stereotypically feminine tasks. The experiment thus suggests that much sex-role behavior may be the product of other people's stereotyped and often erroneous beliefs.

In a related study at the University of Waterloo, Carl von Baeyer, Debbie Sherk, and Mark Zanna have shown how stereotypes about sex roles operate in job interviews. The researchers arranged to have men conduct simulated job interviews with women supposedly seeking positions as research assistants. The investigators informed half of the women that the men who would interview them held traditional views about the ideal woman, believing her to be very emotional, deferential to her husband, home-oriented, and passive. The rest of the women were told that their interviewer saw the ideal woman as independent, competitive, ambitious, and dominant. When the women arrived for their interviews, the researchers noticed that most of them had dressed to meet the stereotyped expectations of their prospective interviewers. Women who expected to see a traditional interviewer had chosen very feminine-looking makeup, clothes, and accessories. During the interviews (videotaped through a one-way mirror) these women behaved in traditionally feminine ways and gave traditionally feminine answers to questions such as "Do you have plans to include children and marriage with your career plans?"

Once more, then, we see the self-fulfilling nature of stereotypes. Many sex differences, it appears, may result from the images that people create in their attempts to act out accepted sex roles. The implication is that if stereotyped expectations about sex roles shift, behavior may change, too. In fact, statements by people who have undergone sex-change operations have highlighted the power of such expectations in easing adjustment to a new life. As the writer Jan Morris said in recounting the story of her transition from James to Jan: "The more I was treated as a woman, the more woman I became."

The power of stereotypes to cause people to confirm stereotyped expectations can also be seen in interracial relationships. In the first of two investigations done at Princeton University by Carl Word, Mark Zanna, and Joel Cooper, white undergraduates interviewed both white and black job applicants. The applicants were actually confederates of the experimenters, trained to behave consistently from interview to interview, no matter how the interviewers acted toward them.

To find out whether or not the white interviewers would behave differently toward white and black job applicants, the researchers secretly videotaped each interview and then studied the tapes. From these, it was apparent that there were substantial differences in the treatment accorded blacks and whites. For one thing, the interviewers' speech deteriorated when they talked to blacks, displaying more errors in grammar and pronunciation. For another, the interviewers spent less time with blacks than with whites and showed less "immediacy," as the researchers called it, in their manner. That is, they were less friendly, less outgoing, and more reserved with blacks.

In the second investigation, white confederates were trained to approximate the immediate or the nonimmediate interview styles that had been observed in the first investigation as they interviewed white job applicants. A panel of judges who evaluated the tapes agreed that applicants subjected to the nonimmediate styles performed less adequately and were more nervous than job applicants treated in the immediate style. Apparently, then, the blacks in the first study did not have a chance to display their qualifications to the best advantage. Considered together, the two investigations suggest that in interracial encounters, racial stereotypes may constrain behavior in ways to cause both blacks and whites to behave in accordance with those stereotypes.

Rewriting Biography

Having adopted stereotyped ways of thinking about another person, people tend to notice and remember the ways in which that person seems to fit the stereotype, while resisting evidence that contradicts the stereotype. In one investigation that I conducted with Seymour Uranowitz, student subjects read a biography of a fictitious woman named Betty K. We constructed the story of her life so that it would fit the stereotyped images of both lesbians and heterosexuals. Betty, we wrote, never had a steady boyfriend in high school, but did go out on dates. And although we gave her a steady boyfriend in college, we specified that he was more of a close friend than anything else. A week after we had distributed this biography, we gave our subjects some new information about Betty. We told some students that she was now living with another woman in a lesbian relationship; we told others that she was living with her husband.

To see what impact stereotypes about sexuality would have on how people remembered the facts of Betty's life, we asked each student to answer a series of questions about her life history. When we examined their answers, we found that the students had reconstructed the events of Betty's past in ways that supported their own stereotyped beliefs about her sexual orientation. Those who believed that Betty was a lesbian remembered that Betty had never had a steady boyfriend in high school, but tended to neglect the fact that she had gone out on many dates in college. Those who believed that Betty was now a heterosexual tended to remember that she had formed a steady relationship with a man in college, but tended to ignore the fact that this relationship was more of a friendship than a romance.

The students showed not only selective memories but also a striking facility for interpreting what they remembered in ways that added fresh support for their stereotypes. One student who accurately remembered that a supposedly lesbian Betty never had a steady boyfriend in high school confidently pointed to the fact as an early sign of her lack of romantic or sexual interest in men. A student who correctly remembered that a purportedly lesbian Betty often went out on dates in college was sure that these dates were signs of Betty's early attempts to mask her lesbian interests.

Clearly, the students had allowed their preconceptions about lesbians and heterosexuals to dictate the way in which they interpreted and reinterpreted the facts of Betty's life. As long as stereotypes make it easy to bring to mind evidence that supports them and difficult to bring to mind evidence that undermines them, people will cling to erroneous beliefs.

Stereotypes in the Classroom and Work Place

The power of one person's beliefs to make other people conform to them has been well demonstrated in real life. Back in the 1960s, as most people well remember, Harvard psychologist Robert Rosenthal and his colleague Lenore Jacobson entered elementary-school classrooms and identified one out of every five pupils in each room as a child who could be expected to show dramatic improvement in intellectual achievement during the school year. What the teachers did not know was that the children had been chosen on a random basis. Nevertheless, something happened in the relationships between teachers and their supposedly gifted pupils that led the children to make clear gains in test performance.

It can also do so on the job. Albert King, now a professor of management at Northern Illinois University, told a welding instructor in a vocational training center that five men in his training program had unusually high aptitude. Although these five had been chosen at random and knew nothing of their designation as high-aptitude workers, they showed substantial changes in performance. They were absent less often than were other workers, learned the basics of the welder's trade in about half the usual time, and scored a full 10 points higher than other trainees on a welding test. Their gains were noticed not only by the researcher and by the welding instructor, but also by other trainees, who singled out the five as their preferred coworkers.

Might not other expectations influence the relationships between supervisors and workers? For example, supervisors who believe that men are better suited to some jobs and women to others may treat their workers (wittingly or unwittingly) in ways that encourage them to perform their jobs in accordance with stereotypes about differences between men and women. These same stereotypes may determine who gets which job in the first place. Perhaps some personnel managers allow stereotypes to influence, subtly or not so subtly, the way in which they interview job candidates, making it likely that candidates who fit the stereotypes show up better than job seekers who do not fit them.

Unfortunately, problems of this kind are compounded by the fact that members of stigmatized groups often subscribe to stereotypes about themselves. That is what Amerigo Farina and his colleagues at the University of Connecticut found when they measured the impact upon mental patients of believing that others knew their psychiatric history. In Farina's study, each mental patient cooperated with another person in a game requiring teamwork. Half of the patients believed that their partners knew they were patients, the other half believed that their partners thought they were nonpatients. In reality, the nonpatients never knew a thing about anyone's psychiatric history. Nevertheless, simply believing that others were aware of their history led the patients to feel less appreciated, to find the task more difficult, and to perform poorly. In addition, objective observers saw them as more tense, more anxious, and more poorly adjusted than patients who believed that their status was not known. Seemingly, the belief that others perceived them as stigmatized caused them to play the role of stigmatized patients.

Consequences for Society

Apparently, good will and education are not sufficient to subvert the power of stereotypes. If people treat others in such a way as to bring out behavior that supports stereotypes, they may never have an opportunity to discover which of their stereotypes are wrong.

I suspect that even if people were to develop doubts about the accuracy of their stereotypes, chances are they would proceed to test them by gathering precisely the evidence that would appear to confirm them.

The experiments I have described help to explain the persistence of stereotypes. But, as is so often the case, solving one puzzle only creates another. If by acting as if false stereotypes were true, people lead others, too, to act as if they were true, why do the stereotypes not come to *be* true? Why, for example, have researchers found so little evidence that attractive people are generally friendly, sociable, and outgoing and that unattractive people are generally shy and aloof?

I think that the explanation goes something like this: Very few among us have the kind of looks that virtually everyone considers either very attractive or very unattractive. Our looks make us rather attractive to some people but somewhat less attractive to other people. When we spend time with those who find us attractive, they will tend to bring out our more sociable sides, but when we are with those who find us less attractive, they will bring out our less sociable sides. Although our actual physical appearance does not change, we present ourselves quite differently to our admirers and to our detractors. For our admirers we become attractive people, and for our detractors we become unattractive. This mixed pattern of behavior will prevent the development of any consistent relationship between physical attractiveness and personality.

Now that I understand some of the powerful forces that work to perpetuate social stereotypes, I can see a new mission for my research. I hope, on the one hand, to find out how to help people see the flaws in their stereotypes. On the other hand, I would like to help the victims of false stereotypes find ways of liberating themselves from the constraints imposed on them by other members of society.

2 Am I Thin Enough Yet?

Sharlene Hesse-Biber

"Ever since I was ten years old, I was just a very vain person. I always wanted to be the thinnest, the prettiest. 'Cause I thought, if I look like this, then I'm going to have so many boyfriends, and guys are going to be so in love with me, and I'll be taken care of for the rest of my life. I'll never have to work, you know?"

—DELIA, COLLEGE SENIOR

What's Wrong with This Picture?

Pretty, vivacious, and petite, Delia was a picture of fashionable perfection when she first walked into my office. Her tight blue jeans and fringed Western shirt showed off her thin, 5-ft frame; her black cowboy boots and silver earrings completed a presentation that said, "Look at me!"

The perfect picture had a serious price. Delia had come to talk about her "problem." She is bulimic. In secret, she regularly binges on large amounts of food, then forces herself to vomit. It has become a powerful habit, one that she is afraid to break because it so efficiently maintains her thin body. For Delia, as for so many others, being thin is everything.

"I mean, how many bumper stickers have you seen that say 'No Fat Chicks,' you know? Guys don't like fat girls. Guys like little girls. I guess because it makes them feel bigger and, you know, they want somebody who looks pretty. Pretty to me is you have to be thin and you have to have like good facial features. It's both. My final affirmation of myself is how many guys look at me when I go into a bar. How many guys pick up on me. What my boyfriend thinks about me."

Delia's Story

Delia is the eldest child, and only girl, in a wealthy Southern family. Her father is a successful dentist and her mother has never worked outside the home. They fought a lot when she was young—her father was an alcoholic—and they eventually divorced. According to Delia, both parents doted on her.

"I've never been deprived of anything in my entire life. I was spoiled, I guess, because I've never felt any pressure from my parents to do anything. My Dad would say, 'Whatever you want to do, if you want to go to Europe, if you want to go to law

Am I Thin Enough Yet? The Cult of Thinness and the Commercialization of Identity by Sharlene Hesse-Biber (1996): Extracts totaling 3,820 words from 7–9, 12–14, 32, 34, 35, 36, 39, 42 & 43. Copyright © 1996 by Oxford University Press, Inc. Used by permission of Oxford University Press, USA.

school, if you don't want to do anything . . . whatever you want to do, just be happy.' No pressure."

He was unconcerned about her weight, she said, but emphasized how important it was to be pretty. Delia quickly noticed this message everywhere, especially in the media.

"I am so affected by *Glamour* magazine and *Vogue* and all that, because that's a line of work I want to get into. I'm looking at all these beautiful women. They're thin. I want to be just as beautiful. I want to be just as thin. Because that is what guys like."

When I asked what her mother wanted for her, she recited, "To be nice and pretty and sweet and thin and popular and smart and successful and have everything that I could ever want and just to be happy." "Sweet and pretty and thin" meant that from the age of ten she was enrolled in a health club, and learned to count calories. Her mom, who at 45 is "beautiful, gorgeous, thin," gave her instructions on how to eat.

"'Only eat small amounts. Eat a thousand calories a day; don't overeat.' My mom was never critical like, 'You're fat.' But one time, I went on a camping trip and I gained four pounds and she said, 'You've got to lose weight.' I mean, she watched what I ate. Like if I was going to get a piece of cake she would be, 'Don't eat that.'"

At age 13 she started her secret bingeing and vomiting. "When I first threw up I thought, well, it's so easy," she told me. "I can eat and not get the calories and not gain weight. And I was modeling at the time, and I wanted to look like the girls in the magazines."

Delia's preoccupation with thinness intensified when she entered high school. She wanted to be a cheerleader, and she was tiny enough to make it. "When I was sixteen I just got into this image thing, like tiny, thin . . . I started working out more. I was Joe Healthy Thin Exercise Queen and I'd just fight eating because I was working out all the time, you know? And so I'm going to aerobics two or three times a day sometimes, eating only salad and a bagel, and like, no fat. I just got caught up in this circle."

College in New England brought a new set of social pressures. She couldn't go running every day because of the cold. She hated the school gym, stopped working out, and gained four pounds her freshman year. Her greatest stress at college had nothing to do with academics. "The most stressful thing for me is whether I'm going to eat that day, and what am I going to eat," she told me, "more than getting good grades."

After freshman year Delia became a cheerleader again. "Going in, I know I weighed like 93 or 94 pounds, which to me was this enormous hang-up, because I'd never weighed more than 90 pounds in my entire life. And I was really freaked out. I knew people were going to be looking at me in the crowd and I'm like, I've got to lose this weight. So I would just not eat, work out all the time. I loved being on the squad, but my partner was a real jerk. He would never work out, and when we would do lifts he'd always be, 'Delia, go run. Go run, you're too heavy.' I hadn't been eating that day. I had already run seven or eight miles and he told me to run again. And I was surrounded by girls who were all so concerned about their weight, and it was just really this horrible situation."

College life also confirmed another issue for Delia, a cultural message from her earliest childhood. She did *not* want to be a breadwinner. She put it this way, "When

I was eight I wanted to be President of the United States. As I grew older and got to college I was like, wow, it's hard for women. I mean, I don't care what people say. If they say the society's liberated, they're wrong. It's still really hard for women. It's like they look through a glass window [sic]. They're vice presidents, but they aren't the president. And I just figured, God, how much easier would it be for me to get married to somebody I know is going to make a lot of money and just be taken care of . . . I want somebody else to be the millionaire." . . .

Economic and career achievement is a primary definition of success for men. (Of course, men can also exhibit some self-destructive behaviors in pursuit of this success, such as workaholism or substance abuse.) Delia's upbringing and environment defined success for her in a different way. She was not interested in having a job that earned $150,000 a year, but in marrying the guy who did. She learned to use any tool she could to stay thin, to look good, and to have a shot at her goal.

No wonder she was reluctant to give up her behavior. She was terrified of losing the important benefits of her membership in the Cult of Thinness. She knew she was hurting psychologically and physically, but, in the final analysis, being counted among "the chosen" justified the pain.

"God forbid anybody else gets stuck in this trap. But I'm already there, and I don't really see myself getting out, because I'm just so obsessed with how I look. I get personal satisfaction from looking thin, and receiving attention from guys."

I told Delia about women who have suggested other ways of coping with weight issues. There are even those who advocate fat liberation, or who suggest that fat is beautiful. She was emphatic about these solutions.

"Bullshit. They live in la-la land . . . I can hold onto my boyfriend because he doesn't need to look anywhere else. The bottom line is that appearance counts. And you can sit here and go, 'I feel good about myself twenty pounds heavier,' but who is the guy going to date?"

A Woman's Sense of Worth

Delia's devotion to the rituals of beauty work involved a great deal of time and energy. She weighed herself three times a day. She paid attention to what she put in her mouth; when she had too much, she knew she must get rid of it. She had to act and look a certain way, buy the right clothes, the right makeup. She also watched out for other women who might jeopardize her chances as they vied for the rewards of the system.

A woman's sense of worth in our culture is still greatly determined by her ability to attract a man. Social status is largely a function of income and occupation. Women's access to these resources is generally indirect, through marriage.[1] Even a woman with a successful and lucrative career may fear that her success comes at the expense of her femininity. . . .

Cultural messages on the rewards of thinness and the punishments of obesity are everywhere. Most women accept society's standards of beauty as "the way things are," even though these standards may undermine self-image, self-esteem, or physical well-being. Weight concerns or even obsessions are so common among women and girls that they escape notice. Dieting is not considered abnormal behavior, even among women who are not overweight. But only a thin line separates "normal" dieting from an eating disorder.[2] . . .

Profiting from Women's Bodies

Because women feel their bodies fail the beauty test, American industry benefits enormously, continually nurturing feminine insecurities. Ruling patriarchal interests, like corporate culture, the traditional family, the government, and the media also benefit. If women are so busy trying to control their bodies through dieting, excessive exercise, and self-improvement activities, they lose control over other important aspects of selfhood that might challenge the status quo.[3] In the words of one critic, "A secretary who bench-presses 150 pounds is still stuck in a dead-end job; a housewife who runs the marathon is still financially dependent on her husband."[4]

In creating women's concept of the ideal body image, the cultural mirror is more influential than the mirror reflecting peer group attitudes. Research has shown that women overestimate how thin a body their male and female peers desire. In a recent study using body silhouettes, college students of both sexes were asked to indicate an ideal female figure, the one that they believed most attractive to the same-sex peer and other-sex peer. Not only did the women select a thinner silhouette than the men,[5] but when asked to choose a *personal* ideal, rather than a peer ideal, the women selected an even skinnier model.

Advertisements and Beauty Advice: Buy, Try, Comply

Capitalism and patriarchy most often use the media to project the culturally desirable body to women. These images are everywhere—on TV, in the movies, on billboards, in print. Women's magazines, with their glossy pages of advertising, advertorials, and beauty advice, hold up an especially devious mirror. They offer "help" to women, while presenting a standard nearly impossible to attain. As one college student named Nancy noted in our interviews,

> The advertisement showed me exactly what I should be, not what I was. I wasn't tall, I wasn't blonde, I wasn't skinny. I didn't have thin thighs, I didn't have a flat stomach. I am short, have brown curly hair, short legs. They did offer me solutions like dyeing my hair or a workout or the use of this cream to take away cellulite. . . .

Not everyone is taken in, of course. One student I interviewed dismissed the images she saw in the advertising pages of magazines as "constructed people."

> I just stopped buying women's magazines. They are all telling you how to dress, how to look, what to wear, the type of clothes. And I think they are just ridiculous. . . . You

can take the most gorgeous model and make her look terrible. Just like you can take a person who is not that way and make them look beautiful. You can use airbrushing and many other techniques. These are not really people. They are constructed people.

Computer-enhanced photography has advanced far beyond the techniques that merely airbrushed blemishes, added highlights to hair, and lengthened the legs with a camera angle. The September 1994 issue of *Mirabella* featured as a cover model "an extraordinary image of great American beauty." According to the magazine, the photographer "hints that she's something of a split personality . . . it wasn't easy getting her together. Maybe her identity has something to do with the microchip floating through space, next to that gorgeous face . . . true American beauty is a combination of elements from all over the world." In other words, the photo is a computerized composite. It is interesting that *Mirabella's* "melting pot" American beauty has white skin and predominantly Caucasian features, with just a hint of other ethnicities.

There are a number of industries that help to promote image, weight, and body obsession, especially among women. If we examine the American food and weight loss industries, we'll understand how their corporate practices and advertising campaigns perpetuate the American woman's dissatisfaction with her looks.

The American Food Industry: Fatten Up and Slim Down

. . . It is not uncommon for the average American to have a diet cola in one hand and high-fat fries and a burger in the other. Food and weight loss are inescapably a key part of the culture of the 1990s. The media bombard us with images of every imaginable type of food—snack foods, fast foods, gourmet foods, health foods, and junk foods. Most of these messages target children, who are very impressionable, and women, who make the purchasing decisions for themselves and their families. At the same time women are subjected to an onslaught of articles, books, videos, tapes, and TV talk shows devoted to dieting and the maintenance of sleek and supple figures. The conflicting images of pleasurable consumption and an ever leaner body type give us a food consciousness loaded with tension and ambivalence.

Social psychologist Brett Silverstein explains that the food industry, like all industries under capitalism, is always striving to maximize profit, growth, concentration, and control. It does so at the expense of the food consumer. "[It] promotes snacking so that consumers will have more than three opportunities a day to consume food, replaces free water with purchased soft drinks, presents desserts as the ultimate reward, and bombards women and children with artificially glamorized images of highly processed foods."[6]

Diet foods are an especially profitable segment of the business. . . .

In 1983, the food industry came up with a brilliant marketing concept, and introduced 91 new "lite" fat-reduced or calorie-reduced foods.[7] The success of lite products has been phenomenal. The consumer equated "lightness" with health. The food industry seemed to equate it with their own expenses—lite foods have lower production costs than "regular" lines, but they are often priced higher. . . .

The Diet and Weight-Loss Industry: We'll Show You the Way

. . . Increasingly, American women are told that they can have the right body if only they consume more and more products. They can change the color of their eyes with tinted contacts, they can have a tanned skin by using self-tanning lotion. They can buy cellulite control cream, spot firming cream, even contouring shower and bath firming gel to get rid of the "dimpled" look. One diet capsule on the market is supposed to be the "fat cure." It is called Anorex-eck, evoking the sometimes fatal eating disorder known as anorexia. It promises to "eliminate the cause of fat formation . . . so quickly and so effectively you will know from the very start why it has taken more than 15 years of research . . . to finally bring you . . . an ultimate cure for fat!"[8] . . .

There are currently more than 17,000 different diet plans, products, and programs from which to choose.[9] Typically, these plans are geared to the female market. They are loaded with promises of quick weight loss and delicious low-calorie meals. . . .

Many of these programs produce food products that they encourage the dieter to buy. The Jenny Craig member receives a set of pre-packaged meals that cost about $10 per day. (It allows for some outside food as well.) Some diet companies are concerned with the problem of gaining weight back and have developed "maintenance" products. Maintenance programs are often expensive and their long-term outcomes are unproven. What *can* be proven are bigger profits and longer dependence on their programs.

The Dis-eased Body: Medicalizing Women's Body Issues

The therapeutic and medical communities tend to categorize women's eating and weight problems as a disease.[10] In this view, behavior like self-starvation or compulsive eating is often called an addiction. An addiction model of behavior assumes that the cause and the cure of the problem lies within the individual. Such an emphasis fails to examine the larger mirrors that society holds up to the individual.[11]

. . . While a disease model lessens the burden of guilt and shame and may free people to work on change, it also has political significance. According to feminist theorist Bette S. Tallen, "The reality of oppression is replaced with the metaphor of addiction." It places the problem's cause within a biological realm, away from outside social forces.[12] Issues such as poverty, lack of education and opportunity, racial and gender inequality remain unexamined. More important, a disease-oriented model of addiction, involving treatment by the health care system, results in profits for the medical-industrial complex. Addiction, Tallen notes, suggests a solution that is personal—"Get treatment!"—rather than political—"Smash patriarchy!" It replaces the feminist view, that the personal is political, with the attitude of "therapism," that the "political is personal."[13] One of Bette Tallen's students told her that she had learned a lot from reading *Women Who Love Too Much* after her divorce from a man who had beaten her. Tallen suggested that "perhaps the best book to read would not be about women who love too much but about men who hit too much."[14]

The idea that overweight is a disease, and overeating represents an addiction, reinforces the dis-ease that American women feel about their bodies. The capitalist and patriarchal mirror held before them supports and maintains their obsession and insecurity. . . .

Women continue to follow the standards of the ideal thin body because of how they are rewarded by being in the right body. Thinness gives women access to a number of important resources: feelings of power, self-confidence, even femininity; male attention or protection; and the social and economic benefits that can follow. . . .

NOTES

1. Pauline B. Bart, "Emotional and Social Status of the Older Woman," in *No Longer Young: The Older Woman in America. Proceedings of the 26th Annual Conference on Aging,* ed. Pauline Bart et al. (Ann Arbor: University of Michigan Institute of Gerontology, 1975), pp. 3–21; Daniel Bar-Tal and Leonard Saxe, "Physical Attractiveness and Its Relationship to Sex-Role Stereotyping," *Sex Roles* 2 (1976): 123–133; Peter Blumstein and Pepper W. Schwartz, *American Couples: Money, Work and Sex* (New York: Willian Morrow, 1983); Glen H. Elder, "Appearance and Education in Marriage Mobility," *American Sociological Review* 34 (1969): 519–533; Susan Sontag, "The Double Standard of Aging," *Saturday Review* (September, 1972), pp. 29–38.

2. J. Polivy and C. P. Herman, "Dieting and Binging: A Causal Analysis," *American Psychologist* 40 (1985):193–201.

3. Ilana Attie and J. Brooks-Gunn, "Weight Concerns as Chronic Stressors in Women," in *Gender and Stress,* eds. Rosalind K. Barnett, Lois Biener, and Grace Baruch (New York: Free Press, 1987), pp. 218–252.

4. Katha Pollitt, "The Politically Correct Body," *Mother Jones* (May 1982): 67. I don't want to disparage the positive benefits of exercising and the positive self-image that can come from feeling good about one's body. This positive image can spill over into other areas of one's life, enhancing, for example, one's self-esteem, or job prospects.

5. See Lawrence D. Cohn and Nancy E. Adler, "Female and Male Perceptions of Ideal Body Shapes: Distorted Views Among Caucasian College Students," *Psychology of Women Quarterly* 16 (1992): 69–79; A. Fallon and P. Rozin, "Sex Differences in Perceptions of Desirable Body Shape," *Journal of Abnormal Psychology* 94 (1985): 102–105.

6. Brett Silverstein, *Fed Up!* (Boston: South End Press, 1984), pp. 4, 47, 110. Individuals may be affected in many different ways, from paying too much (in 1978, concentration within the industry led to the overcharging of consumers by $12 to $14 billion [p. 47]) to the ingestion of unhealthy substances.

7. Warren J. Belasco, "'Lite' Economics: Less Food, More Profit," *Radical History Review* 28–30 (1984): 254–278; Hillel Schwartz, *Never Satisfied* (New York: Free Press, 1986), p. 241.

8. Advertised in *Parade* magazine (December 30, 1984).

9. Deralee Scanlon, *Diets That Work* (Chicago: Contemporary Books, 1991), p. 1.

10. See Stanton Peele, *Diseasing of America: Addiction Treatment Out of Control* (Lexington, MA: D.C. Heath and Co., 1989).

11. There are a few recovery books that point to the larger issues of the addiction model. Anne Wilson Schaef's book, *When Society Becomes an Addict,* looks at the wider institutions of society that perpetuate addiction. She notes that society operates on a scarcity model. This is the "Addictive System." This model assumes that there is never enough of anything to go around and we need to get what we can. Schaef sees society as made up of three systems: A White Male System (the Addictive System), A Reactive Female System (one where women respond passively to men by being subject to their will), and the Emerging Female System (a system where women lead with caring and sensitivity). Society needs to move in the direction of the Emerging Female System in order to end addiction. Another important book is Stanton Peele's *Love and Addiction.* Another book by Stanton Peele, *The Diseasing of America: How the Addiction Industry Captured Our Soul* (Lexington, MA: Lexington Books, 1989), stresses the importance of social change in societal institutions and advocates changing the given distribution of resources and power within the society as a way to overcome the problem of addiction. See Anne Wilson Schaef, *When Society Becomes an Addict* (New York: Harper & Row, 1987), and Stanton Peele, *Love and Addiction* (New York: New American Library, 1975).

12. Bette S. Tallen, "Twelve Step Programs: A Lesbian Feminist Critique," *NWSA Journal* 2 (1990): 396.

13. Tallen, "Twelve Step Programs: A Lesbian Feminist Critique," 404–405.

14. Tallen, "Twelve Step Programs: A Lesbian Feminist Critique," 405.

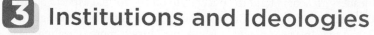 3 Institutions and Ideologies
Michael Parenti

Corporate Plutocracy

American capitalism represents more than just an economic system; it is a *plutocracy*, that is, a social order ruled mostly for and by the rich. Along with business enterprises and banks, the nation's *cultural institutions*—that is, its universities, publishing houses, mass-circulation magazines, newspapers, television and radio stations, professional sports teams, foundations, hospitals, churches, private museums, and charities— are mostly chartered as corporations, ruled by boards of directors (or "trustees" or "regents" as they might be called) composed overwhelmingly of affluent business people who exercise final judgment over institutional matters.

Consider the university. Private and public institutions of higher education are run by boards of trustees with authority over all matters of capital funding and budget; curriculum and tuition; degree awards; and hiring, firing, and promotion of faculty and staff. Daily decision-making power is delegated to administrators but can be easily recalled by the trustees when they choose. Most trustees are successful business people who have no administrative or scholarly experience in higher education. As trustees, they take no financial risks because their decisions are covered by insurance paid out of the university budget. Their main function seems to be to exercise oligarchic control over the institution.

Almost all of "our" cultural institutions are ruled by nonelected self-perpetuating boards of affluent corporate representatives who are answerable to no one but themselves. We the people have no vote, no portion of the ownership, and no legal decision-making power within these institutions.

We are taught to think that capitalism breeds democracy and prosperity. The private-enterprise system, it is said, creates equality of opportunity, rewards those who show ability, relegates the slothful to the lower rungs, creates national prosperity, and bolsters democracy. Little is said about how capitalism has supported and flourished under some of the most repressive regimes and impoverished Third World nations.

The corporate enterprise system places a great deal of emphasis on commercial worth: how to compete and get ahead. As Ralph Nader notes, the free market "only stimulates one value in society—the acquisitive, materialistic, profit value." What about the values relating to justice, health, occupational and consumer safety, regard for future generations, and equitable social relations?[1]

Among the key purveyors of plutocratic culture is our educational system. From grade school onward, students are given a positive picture of America's history,

Republished with permission of Cengage Learning, from *Democracy for the Few*, Michael Parenti, 9th edition © 2010. Permission conveyed through Copyright Clearance Center, Inc.

institutions, and leaders. Teachers tend to concentrate on the formal aspects of government and accord scant attention to the influence that wealthy, powerful groups exercise over political life. Instructors who wish to introduce a more revealing view invite critical attention from their superiors. High school students who attempt to explore controversial issues in student newspapers have frequently been overruled by administrators and threatened with disciplinary action.[2]

School texts seldom give more than passing mention to the courageous history of labor struggle or the corporate exploitation of working people at home and abroad. Almost nothing is said of the struggles of indigenous Americans (or Native American "Indians"), indentured servants, small farmers, and Latino, Asian, Middle Eastern, and European immigrants. The history of resistance to slavery, racism, and U.S. expansionist wars goes largely untaught in our classrooms.[3]

Schools and media are inundated with informational materials provided free by the Pentagon and large corporations to promote a highly favorable view of the military and to boost privatization, deregulation of industry, and other blessings of the free market.[4] Numerous conservative think tanks and academic centers have emerged, along with conservative journals, conferences, and endowed chairs, all funded by right-wing foundations, big corporations, and superrich individuals.

Many universities and colleges have direct investments in corporate America, holding stock portfolios worth billions of dollars. Such bountiful endowments are to be found especially in elite Ivy League schools like Yale, Harvard, Brown, Columbia, and others. More and more college presidents and other top administrators are drawn directly from corporate America with no experience in teaching, research, or university administration. Their salaries are skyrocketing and their fringe benefits are increasingly lavish, including such things as year-long paid leaves at full salary. Some administrators and faculty earn handsome sums as business consultants. Corporate logos are appearing in classrooms and student union buildings. Academic-based scientific research is being increasingly funded and defined by corporations that have a vested interest in the results of the research. With its financing of chairs and study programs, private industry is influencing who is hired and what is taught.[5]

Meanwhile library budgets, scholarships, course offerings, teaching staff, and student services are being cut back. At most universities and colleges, tuition has climbed more than 30 percent in the last decade years. Tenured and other full-time faculty positions are being replaced with underpaid part-time adjuncts. Some 40 percent of all college teachers are adjuncts, working for no benefits, and carrying heavy teaching loads for paltry pay.[6]

Ideological Orthodoxy

In academia, politically radical faculty, and even students, have suffered politically motivated negative evaluations and loss of stipends, grants, and jobs. Professors, journalists, managers, bureaucrats, and most other professionals who wish to advance their careers learn to go along with things as they are and avoid espousing radical views that conflict with the dominant economic interests of capitalist society.[7] . . .

Although we are often admonished to think for ourselves, we might ask if our socialization process puts limits on doing so. Ideological orthodoxy so permeates the plutocratic culture that it is often not felt as indoctrination. The most effective forms of tyranny are those so deeply ingrained, so thoroughly controlling, as not even to be consciously experienced as constraints.

In a capitalist society, mass advertising sells not only particular products but a way of life, a glorification of consumer acquisitiveness. Born of a market economy, the capitalist culture downplays cooperative efforts and human interdependence. People are expected to operate individually but toward rather similar goals. Everyone competes against everyone else, but for the same things. "Individualism" in this corporate-dominated culture refers to acquisitiveness and careerism. We are expected to get what we can for ourselves and not be too troubled by the problems faced by others. This attitude, considered inhuman in some societies, is labeled approvingly as "ambition" in our own and is treated as a quality of great social value.

Whether or not this "individualism" allows one to have much control over one's own life is another story. The decisions about the quality of the food we eat, the goods we buy, the air we breathe, the prices we pay, the wages we earn, the way work tasks are divided, the modes of transportation available to us, and the images we are fed by the media are usually made by people other than ourselves.

People who occupy privileged positions within the social hierarchy become committed to the hierarchy's preservation and hostile toward demands for a more equitable social order. Economically deprived groups are seen as a threat because they want more, and more for the have-nots might mean less for the haves. Class bigotry is one of the widely held forms of prejudice in American society and the least examined.

The plutocratic culture teaches that material success is a measure of one's worth, and because the poor are not worth much, then society's resources should not be squandered on them. In capitalist society, the poor are generally seen as personally deficient, the authors of their own straitened circumstances. Rarely are they considered to be the victims of poverty-creating economic forces: high rents, underemployment, low wages, unattended illnesses, disabilities, and other such features of the free market. As the American humorist Will Rogers once said, "It's no crime to be poor, but it might as well be."

In a society where money is the overriding determinant of one's life chances, the drive for material gain is not merely a symptom of a greed-driven culture but a factor in one's very survival. As corporate power tightens its grip over the political economy, many people have to work still harder to keep their heads above water. Rather than grasping for fanciful luxuries, they struggle to provide basic necessities. If they need more money than was essential in earlier days, it is partly because essentials cost so much more.

Because human services are based on ability to pay, money becomes a matter of life and death. To have a low or modest income is to run a higher risk of insufficient medical care, homelessness, and job insecurity, and to have less opportunity for education, recreation, travel, and comfort. Thus, the desire to "make it," even at the expense of others, is not merely a wrong-headed attitude but a reflection of the material conditions of capitalist society wherein no one is ever really economically secure except the superrich, and even they forever seek to secure and advance their fortunes through further capital accumulation.

For those who enjoy the best of everything, the existing politico-economic system is a smashing success. For those who are its hapless victims, or who are concerned about the well-being of all and not just themselves, the system leaves a great deal to be desired. . . .

Public Opinion: Which Direction?

The opinions most Americans have about socioeconomic issues are decidedly more progressive than what is usually enunciated by political leaders and right-wing media pundits. Surveys show substantial majorities strongly favoring public funding for Social Security, nursing home care, and lower-priced prescription drugs. Substantial majorities support unemployment insurance, disability assistance, job retraining, child care, price supports for family farms, and food stamps for the needy, while opposing tax cuts for the very rich and privatization of social services. Large majorities want improvements in managed health care and favor a universal health insurance program run by the government and funded by taxpayers. The public generally supports a stronger, not a weaker, social safety net. By nearly three to one, the public rejects cutbacks in Medicare and Social Security.[8]

Large majorities feel that the gap between rich and poor is growing, and that government has a responsibility to try to do away with poverty and hunger, that abortion should be a decision made by a woman and her doctor, and that racial minorities should be given fair treatment in employment—but not special preferences in hiring and promotion. After many years of strong support for organized labor, Americans became much less positive toward unions during the grim days of the 2009 recession.[9]

Sixty percent agree that large corporations wield too much power. A majority believes that corporate executives care very little about the environment, are given to falsifying company accounts, and are lining their own pockets. Large majorities say that corporations have too much influence over government. Most Americans are concerned about the environment. A majority also favors the death penalty and being "tough" on crime. Yet 60 percent agree that the president has no right to suspend the Bill of Rights in time of war or national emergency. By a five-to-three majority, Americans support the idea of a public health plan to compete with private insurance. Only 25 percent of Americans say banks are honest and trustworthy.[10]

In sum, on many important issues, a majority seems to hold positions at variance with those maintained by ideological conservatives and reactionaries and closer to the ones enunciated by liberals and progressives.

Opinion polls are only part of the picture. There is the whole history of democratic struggle that continues to this day and remains largely untaught in the schools and unreported in the media. It is expressed in mass demonstrations, strikes, boycotts, and civil disobedience—targeting such things as poverty, unemployment, unsafe nuclear reactors, nuclear missile sites, and U.S. wars abroad. There have been mass mobilizations in support of legalized abortion, women's rights, gay and lesbian rights, and environmental protections. There have been organized housing takeovers for the homeless, protests against police brutality, and noncompliance with draft registration. The Selective Service System admitted that over the years some 800,000 young men have refused to register (the actual number is probably higher).[11] At the same time, major strikes have occurred in a wide range of industries, showing that labor militancy is not a thing of the past.

This is not to deny that there remain millions of Americans, including many of relatively modest means, who succumb to the culture of fear propagated by right-wing reactionaries. They fear and resent gays, ethnic minorities, feminists, immigrants, intellectuals, liberals, peace activists, environmentalists, evolutionary scientists, communists, socialists, labor unions, Muslims, and atheists. They swallow the reactionary line that government is the enemy (not the powerful interests it serves), and they are readily whipped into jingoistic fervor when their leaders go to war against vastly weaker nations.

Yet this society does not produce large numbers of conservative activists. There are no mass demonstrations demanding tax cuts for the rich, more environmental devastation, more wars, more tax cuts for the rich, or more corporate accumulation of wealth.

Despite the mind-numbing distractions of a mass culture and the propaganda and indoctrination by plutocratic institutions, Americans still have concerns about important issues. Political socialization often produces contradictory and unexpected spin-offs. When opinion makers indoctrinate us with the notion that we are a free and prosperous people, we, in fact, begin to demand the right to be free and prosperous. The old trick of using democratic rhetoric to cloak an undemocratic class order can backfire when people begin to take the rhetoric seriously and translate it into democratic demands.

There are those who love justice more than they love money, those who do not long for more acquisitions but for a better quality of life for all.

Democracy: Form and Content

Americans of all political persuasions profess a dedication to democracy, but they tend to mean different things by the term. . . . *Democracy* refers to a system of governance that represents in both *form* and *content* the interests of the broad populace. Decision makers are to govern for the benefit of the many, not for the advantages of the privileged few. The people hold their representatives accountable by subjecting them to open criticism, the periodic check of elections, and, if necessary, recall and removal from office. Democratic government is limited government, the antithesis of despotic absolutism. . . .

We are taught that capitalism and democracy go together. The free market supposedly creates a pluralistic society of manifold groups, a "civic society" that acts independently of the state and provides the basis for political freedom and prosperity. In fact, many capitalist societies—from Nazi Germany to today's Third World dictatorships—have private-enterprise systems but no political freedom, and plenty of mass destitution. And the more open to free-market capitalism they become, the poorer they seem to get. In such systems, economic freedom means the freedom to exploit the labor of the poor and get endlessly rich. Transnational corporate capitalism is no guarantee of a meaningful political democracy, neither in Third World countries nor in the United States itself.

When it works with any efficacy, democracy is dedicated to protecting the well-being of the many and rolling back the economic oppressions and privileges that serve the few. Democracy seeks to ensure that even those who are not advantaged by wealth or extraordinary talent can earn a decent livelihood. The contradictory nature of "capitalist democracy" is that it professes egalitarian political principles while generating enormous disparities in material well-being and actual political influence.

Some people think that if you are free to say what you like, you are living in a democracy. But freedom of speech is not the sum total of democracy, only one of its necessary conditions. Too often we are free to say what we want, while those of wealth and power are free to do what they want to us regardless of what we say. Democracy is not a seminar but a system of power, like any other form of governance. Freedom of speech, like freedom of assembly and freedom of political organization, is meaningful only if it is heard and if it keeps those in power responsive to those over whom power is exercised.

Nor are elections a sure test of democracy. Some electoral systems are so thoroughly controlled by well-financed like-minded elites or rigged by dishonest officials that they discourage meaningful dialogue and broad participation. Whether a political system is democratic or not depends not only on its procedures but on the actual material benefits and the social justice or injustice it propagates. A government that pursues policies that by design or neglect are so steeply inequitable as to damage the life chances of large sectors of the population is not democratic no matter how many elections it holds.

It should be repeated that when we criticize the lack of democratic substance in the United States, we are not attacking or being disloyal to our nation itself. Quite the contrary. A democratic citizenry should not succumb to state idolatry but should remain critical of the powers that work against the democratic interests of our nation and its people.

NOTES

1. Nader quotes in *Home and Gardens*, August 1991.

2. For examples of censorship of high-school newspapers, see http://www.ioerror.us /2005/11/30/two-high-school-newspapers-censored/ and http://www.beverly-underground .com/editorials.htm.

3. On the biases of textbooks, see Michael Parenti, *History as Mystery* (City Lights, 1999), 11–21.

4. Mark Maier, "High-School Economics: Corporate Sponsorship and Pro-Market Bias," *Dollars and Sense*, May/June 2002.

5. Jennifer Washburn, *University Inc.: The Corporate Corruption of Higher Education* (Basic Books, 2005); also report in *Chronicle of Higher Education,* 17 November 2008.

6. *San Francisco Chronicle*, 13 November 2005.

7. Stephen Best, Anthony J. Nocella II, and Peter McLaren (eds.), *Academic Repression: Reflections from the Academic Industrial Complex* (AK Press, 2009).

8. Economic Policy Institute, www.epinet.org/pulse; *New York Times,* 24 May 2005; Public Citizen's Health Research Group, *Health Letter,* June 2004.

9. Gallup Polls, http://www.gallup.com/.

10. http://harrisinteractive.com/harris_poll/HarrisPoll.

11. Stephen Kohn, *The History of American Draft Law Violations 1658–1985* (Greenwood Press, 1986).

4 Media Magic: Making Class Invisible

Gregory Mantsios

Of the various social and cultural forces in our society, the mass media is arguably the most influential in molding public consciousness. Americans spend an average twenty-eight hours per week watching television. They also spend an undetermined number of hours reading periodicals, listening to the radio, and going to the movies. Unlike other cultural and socializing institutions, ownership and control of the mass media is highly concentrated. Twenty-three corporations own more than one-half of all the daily newspapers, magazines, movie studios, and radio and television outlets in the United States.[1] The number of media companies is shrinking and their control of the industry is expanding. And a relatively small number of media outlets is producing and packaging the majority of news and entertainment programs. For the most part, our media is national in nature and single-minded (profit-oriented) in purpose. This media plays a key role in defining our cultural tastes, helping us locate ourselves in history, establishing our national identity, and ascertaining the range of national and social possibilities. In this essay, we will examine the way the mass media shapes how people think about each other and about the nature of our society.

The United States is the most highly stratified society in the industrialized world. Class distinctions operate in virtually every aspect of our lives, determining the nature of our work, the quality of our schooling, and the health and safety of our loved ones. Yet remarkably, we, as a nation, retain illusions about living in an egalitarian society. We maintain these illusions, in large part, because the media hides gross inequities from public view. In those instances when inequities are revealed, we are provided with messages that obscure the nature of class realities and blame the victims of class-dominated society for their own plight. Let's briefly examine what the news media, in particular, tells us about class.

About the Poor

The news media provides meager coverage of poor people and poverty. The coverage it does provide is often distorted and misleading.

The Poor Do Not Exist

For the most part, the news media ignores the poor. Unnoticed are forty million poor people in the nation—a number that equals the entire population of Maine, Vermont, New Hampshire, Connecticut, Rhode Island, New Jersey, and New York combined. Perhaps even more alarming is that the rate of poverty is increasing twice as fast as the population growth in the United States. Ordinarily, even a calamity of much smaller

Copyright © by Gregory Mantsios. Reprinted by permission of the author.

proportion (e.g., flooding in the Midwest) would garner a great deal of coverage and hype from a media usually eager to declare a crisis, yet less than one in five hundred articles in the *New York Times* and one in one thousand articles listed in the *Readers' Guide to Periodic Literature* are on poverty. With remarkably little attention to them, the poor and their problems are hidden from most Americans.

When the media does turn its attention to the poor, it offers a series of contradictory messages and portrayals.

The Poor Are Faceless

Each year the Census Bureau releases a new report on poverty in our society and its results are duly reported in the media. At best, however, this coverage emphasizes annual fluctuations (showing how the numbers differ from previous years) and ongoing debates over the validity of the numbers (some argue the number should be lower, most that the number should be higher). Coverage like this desensitizes us to the poor by reducing poverty to a number. It ignores the human tragedy of poverty—the suffering, indignities, and misery endured by millions of children and adults. Instead, the poor become statistics rather than people.

The Poor Are Undeserving

When the media does put a face on the poor, it is not likely to be a pretty one. The media will provide us with sensational stories about welfare cheats, drug addicts, and greedy panhandlers (almost always urban and Black). Compare these images and the emotions evoked by them with the media's treatment of middle-class (usually white) "tax evaders," celebrities who have a "chemical dependency," or wealthy businesspeople who use unscrupulous means to "make a profit." While the behavior of the more affluent offenders is considered an "impropriety" and a deviation from the norm, the behavior of the poor is considered repugnant, indicative of the poor in general, and worthy of our indignation and resentment.

The Poor Are an Eyesore

When the media does cover the poor, they are often presented through the eyes of the middle class. For example, sometimes the media includes a story about community resistance to a homeless shelter or storekeeper annoyance with panhandlers. Rather than focusing on the plight of the poor, these stories are about middle-class opposition to the poor. Such stories tell us that the poor are an inconvenience and an irritation.

The Poor Have Only Themselves to Blame

In another example of media coverage, we are told that the poor live in a personal and cultural cycle of poverty that hopelessly imprisons them. They routinely center on the Black urban population and focus on perceived personality or cultural traits that doom the poor. While the women in these stories typically exhibit an "attitude" that leads to trouble or a promiscuity that leads to single motherhood, the men possess a need for immediate gratification that leads to drug abuse or an unquenchable greed that leads to the pursuit of fast money. The images that are seared into our mind are sexist, racist, and classist. Census figures reveal that most of the poor are white, not Black or Hispanic, that they live in rural or suburban areas, not urban centers, and hold jobs at least part of the year.[2] Yet, in a fashion that is often framed in an understanding and sympathetic tone, we are told that the poor have inflicted poverty on themselves.

The Poor Are Down on Their Luck

During the Christmas season, the news media sometimes provides us with accounts of poor individuals or families (usually white) who are down on their luck. These stories are often linked to stories about soup kitchens or other charitable activities and sometimes call for charitable contributions. These "Yule time" stories are as much about the affluent as they are about the poor: they tell us that the affluent in our society are a kind, understanding, giving people—which we are not.* The series of unfortunate circumstances that have led to impoverishment are presumed to be a temporary condition that will improve with time and a change in luck.

• • •

Despite appearances, the messages provided by the media are not entirely disparate. With each variation, the media informs us what poverty is not (i.e., systemic and indicative of American society) by informing us what it is. The media tells us that poverty is either an aberration of the American way of life (it doesn't exist, it's just another number, it's unfortunate but temporary) or an end product of the poor themselves (they are a nuisance, do not deserve better, and have brought their predicament upon themselves).

By suggesting that the poor have brought poverty upon themselves, the media is engaging in what William Ryan has called "blaming the victim."[3] The media identifies in what ways the poor are different as a consequence of deprivation, then defines those differences as the cause of poverty itself. Whether blatantly hostile or cloaked in sympathy, the message is that there is something fundamentally wrong with the victims—their hormones, psychological makeup, family environment, community, race, or some combination of these—that accounts for their plight and their failure to lift themselves out of poverty.

---

*American households with incomes of less than $10,000 give an average of 5.5 percent of their earning to charity or to a religious organization, while those making more than $100,000 a year give only 2.9 percent. After changes in the 1986 tax code reduced the benefits of charitable giving, taxpayers earning $500,000 or more slashed their average donation by nearly one-third. Furthermore, many of these acts of benevolence do not help the needy. Rather than provide funding to social service agencies that aid the poor, the voluntary contributions of the wealthy go to places and institutions that entertain, inspire, cure, or educate wealthy Americans—art museums, opera houses, theaters, orchestras, ballet companies, private hospitals, and elite universities. (Robert Reich, "Secession of the Successful," *New York Times Magazine*, February 17, 1991, p. 43.)

But poverty in the United States is systemic. It is a direct result of economic and political policies that deprive people of jobs, adequate wages, or legitimate support. It is neither natural nor inevitable: there is enough wealth in our nation to eliminate poverty if we chose to redistribute existing wealth or income. The plight of the poor is reason enough to make the elimination of poverty the nation's first priority. But poverty also impacts dramatically on the nonpoor. It has a dampening effect on wages in general (by maintaining a reserve army of unemployed and underemployed anxious for any job at any wage) and breeds crime and violence (by maintaining conditions that invite private gain by illegal means and rebellion-like behavior, not entirely unlike the urban riots of the 1960s). Given the extent of poverty in the nation and the impact it has on us all, the media must spin considerable magic to keep the poor and the issue of poverty and its root causes out of the public consciousness.

About Everyone Else

Both the broadcast and the print news media strive to develop a strong sense of "we-ness" in their audience. They seek to speak to and for an audience that is both affluent and like-minded. The media's solidarity with affluence, that is, with the middle and upper class, varies little from one medium to another. Benjamin DeMott points out, for example, that the *New York Times* understands affluence to be intelligence, taste, public spirit, responsibility, and a readiness to rule and "conceives itself as spokesperson for a readership awash in these qualities."[4] Of course, the flip side to creating a sense of "we," or "us," is establishing a perception of the "other." The other relates back to the faceless, amoral, undeserving, and inferior "underclass." Thus, the world according to the news media is divided between the "underclass" and everyone else. Again the messages are often contradictory.

The Wealthy Are Us

Much of the information provided to us by the news media focuses attention on the concerns of a very wealthy and privileged class of people. Although the concerns of a small fraction of the populace, they are presented as though they were the concerns of everyone. For example, while relatively few people actually own stock, the news media devotes an inordinate amount of broadcast time and print space to business news and stock market quotations. Not only do business reports cater to a particular narrow clientele, so do the fashion pages (with $2,000 dresses), wedding announcements, and the obituaries. Even weather and sports news often have a class bias. An all news radio station in New York City, for example, provides regular national ski reports. International news, trade agreements, and domestic policy issues are also reported in terms of their impact on business climate and the business community. Besides being of practical value to the wealthy, such coverage has considerable ideological value. Its message: the concerns of the wealthy are the concerns of us all.

The Wealthy (as a Class) Do Not Exist

While preoccupied with the concerns of the wealthy, the media fails to notice the way in which the rich as a class of people create and shape domestic and foreign policy. Presented as an aggregate of individuals, the wealthy appear without special interests, interconnections, or unity in purpose. Out of public view are the class interests of the wealthy, the interlocking business links, the concerted actions to preserve their class privileges and business interests (by running for public office, supporting political candidates, lobbying, etc.). Corporate lobbying is ignored, taken for granted, or assumed to be in the public interest. (Compare this with the media's portrayal of the "strong arm of labor" in attempting to defeat trade legislation that is harmful to the interests of working people.) It is estimated that two-thirds of the U.S. Senate is composed of millionaires.[5] Having such a preponderance of millionaires in the Senate, however, is perceived to be neither unusual nor antidemocratic; these millionaire senators are assumed to be serving "our" collective interests in governing.

The Wealthy Are Fascinating and Benevolent

The broadcast and print media regularly provide hype for individuals who have achieved "super" success. These stories are usually about celebrities and superstars from the sports and entertainment world. Society pages and gossip columns serve to keep the social elite informed of each others' doings, allow the rest of us to gawk at their excesses, and help to keep the American dream alive. The print media is also fond of feature stories on corporate empire builders. These stories provide an occasional "insider's" view of the private and corporate life of industrialists by suggesting a rags to riches account of corporate success. These stories tell us that corporate success is a series of smart moves, shrewd acquisitions, timely mergers, and well thought out executive suite shuffles. By painting the upper class in a positive light, innocent of any wrongdoing (labor leaders and union organizations usually get the opposite treatment), the media assures us that wealth and power are benevolent. One person's capital accumulation is presumed to be good for all. The elite, then, are portrayed as investment wizards, people of special talent and skill, whom even their victims (workers and consumers) can admire.

The Wealthy Include a Few Bad Apples

On rare occasions, the media will mock selected individuals for their personality flaws. Real estate investor Donald Trump and New York Yankees owner George Steinbrenner, for example, are admonished by the media for deliberately seeking publicity (a very un-upper class thing to do); hotel owner Leona Helmsley was caricatured for her personal cruelties; and junk bond broker Michael Milkin was condemned because he had the audacity to rob the rich. Michael Parenti points out that by treating business wrongdoings as isolated deviations from the socially beneficial system of "responsible capitalism," the media overlooks the features of the system that produce such abuses and the regularity with which they occur. Rather than portraying them as predictable and frequent outcomes of corporate power and the business system, the media treats abuses as if they were isolated and atypical. Presented as an occasional aberration, these incidents serve not to challenge, but to legitimate, the system.[6]

The Middle Class Is Us

By ignoring the poor and blurring the lines between the working people and the upper class, the news media creates a universal middle class. From this perspective, the size of one's income becomes largely irrelevant: what matters is that most of "us" share an intellectual and moral superiority over the disadvantaged. As *Time* magazine once concluded, "Middle America is a state of mind."[7] "We are all middle class," we are told, "and we all share the same concerns": job security, inflation, tax burdens, world peace, the cost of food and housing, health care, clean air and water, and the safety of our streets. While the concerns of the wealthy are quite distinct from those of the middle class (e.g., the wealthy worry about investments, not jobs), the media convinces us that "we [the affluent] are all in this together."

The Middle Class Is a Victim

For the media, "we" the affluent not only stand apart from the "other"—the poor, the working class, the minorities, and their problems—"we" are also victimized by the poor (who drive up the costs of maintaining the welfare roles), minorities (who commit crimes against us), and workers (who are greedy and drive companies out and prices up). Ignored are the subsidies to the rich, the crimes of corporate America, and the policies that wreak havoc on the economic well-being of middle America. Media magic convinces us to fear, more than anything else, being victimized by those less affluent than ourselves.

The Middle Class Is Not a Working Class

The news media clearly distinguishes the middle class (employees) from the working class (i.e., blue collar workers) who are portrayed, at best, as irrelevant, outmoded, and a dying breed. Furthermore, the media will tell us that the hardships faced by blue collar workers are inevitable (due to progress), a result of bad luck (chance circumstances in a particular industry), or a product of their own doing (they priced themselves out of a job). Given the media's presentation of reality, it is hard to believe that manual, supervised, unskilled, and semiskilled workers actually represent more than 50 percent of the adult working population.[8] The working class, instead, is relegated by the media to "the other."

• • •

In short, the news media either lionizes the wealthy or treats their interests and those of the middle class as one in the same. But the upper class and the middle class do not share the same interests or worries. Members of the upper class worry about stock dividends (not employment), they profit from inflation and global militarism, their children attend exclusive private schools, they eat and live in a royal fashion, they call on (or are called upon by) personal physicians, they have few consumer problems, they can escape whenever they want from environmental pollution, and they live on streets and travel to other areas under the protection of private police forces.*[9]

The wealthy are not only a class with distinct life-styles and interests, they are a ruling class. They receive a disproportionate share of the country's yearly income, own a disproportionate amount of the country's wealth, and contribute a disproportionate number of their members to governmental bodies and decision-making groups—all traits that William Domhoff, in his classic work *Who Rules America,* defined as characteristic of a governing class.[10]

This governing class maintains and manages our political and economic structures in such a way that these structures continue to yield an amazing proportion of our wealth to a minuscule upper class. While the media is not above referring to ruling classes in other countries (we hear, for example, references to Japan's ruling elite),[11] its treatment of the news proceeds as though there were no such ruling class in the United States.

Furthermore, the news media inverts reality so that those who are working class and middle class learn to fear, resent, and blame those below, rather than those above, them in the class structure. We learn to resent welfare, which accounts for only two cents out of every dollar in the federal budget (approximately $10 billion) and provides financial relief for the needy,** but learn little about the $11 billion the federal government spends on individuals with incomes in excess of $100,000 (not needy),[12] or the $17 billion in farm subsidies, or the $214 billion (twenty times the cost of welfare) in interest payments to financial institutions.

Middle-class whites learn to fear African Americans and Latinos, but most violent crime occurs within poor and minority communities and is neither interracial*** nor interclass. As horrid as such crime is, it should not mask the destruction and violence perpetrated by corporate America. In spite of the fact that 14,000 innocent people are killed on the job each year, 100,000 die prematurely, 400,000 become seriously ill, and 6 million are injured from work-related accidents and diseases, most Americans fear government regulation more than they do unsafe working conditions.

Through the media, middle-class—and even working-class—Americans learn to blame blue collar workers and their unions for declining purchasing power and

---

*The number of private security guards in the United States now exceeds the number of public police officers. (Robert Reich, "Secession of the Successful," *New York Times Magazine,* February 17, 1991, p. 42.)

**A total of $20 billion is spent on welfare when you include all state funding. But the average state funding also comes to only two cents per state dollar.

***In 92 percent of the murders nationwide the assailant and the victim are of the same race (46 percent are white/white, 46 percent are black/black), 5.6 percent are black on white, and 2.4 percent are white on black. (FBI and Bureau of Justice Statistics, 1985–1986, quoted in Raymond S. Franklin, *Shadows of Race and Class,* University of Minnesota Press, Minneapolis, 1991, p. 108.)

economic security. But while workers who managed to keep their jobs and their unions struggled to keep up with inflation, the top 1 percent of American families saw their average incomes soar 80 percent in the last decade.[13] Much of the wealth at the top was accumulated as stockholders and corporate executives moved their companies abroad to employ cheaper labor (56 cents per hour in El Salvador) and avoid paying taxes in the United States. Corporate America is a world made up of ruthless bosses, massive layoffs, favoritism and nepotism, health and safety violations, pension plan losses, union busting, tax evasions, unfair competition, and price gouging, as well as fast buck deals, financial speculation, and corporate wheeling and dealing that serve the interests of the corporate elite, but are generally wasteful and destructive to workers and the economy in general.

It is no wonder Americans cannot think straight about class. The mass media is neither objective, balanced, independent, nor neutral. Those who own and direct the mass media are themselves part of the upper class, and neither they nor the ruling class in general have to conspire to manipulate public opinion. Their interest is in preserving the status quo, and their view of society as fair and equitable comes naturally to them. But their ideology dominates our society and justifies what is in reality a perverse social order—one that perpetuates unprecedented elite privilege and power on the one hand and widespread deprivation on the other. A mass media that did not have its own class interests in preserving the status quo would acknowledge that inordinate wealth and power undermines democracy and that a "free market" economy can ravage a people and their communities.

NOTES

1. Martin Lee and Norman Solomon, *Unreliable Sources,* Lyle Stuart (New York, 1990), p. 71. See also Ben Bagdikian, *The Media Monopoly,* Beacon Press (Boston, 1990).
2. Department of Commerce, Bureau of the Census, "Poverty in the United States: 1992," *Current Population Reports, Consumer Income,* Series P60–185, pp. xi, xv, 1.
3. William Ryan, *Blaming the Victim,* Vintage (New York, 1971).
4. Benjamin Demott, *The Imperial Middle,* William Morrow (New York, 1990), p. 123.
5. Fred Barnes, "The Zillionaires Club," *The New Republic,* January 29, 1990, p. 24.
6. Michael Parenti, *Inventing Reality,* St. Martin's Press (New York, 1986), p. 109.
7. *Time,* January 5, 1979, p. 10.
8. Vincent Navarro, "The Middle Class—A Useful Myth," *The Nation,* March 23, 1992, p. 1.
9. Charles Anderson, *The Political Economy of Social Class,* Prentice Hall (Englewood Cliffs, N.J., 1974), p. 137.
10. William Domhoff, *Who Rules America,* Prentice Hall (Englewood Cliffs, N.J., 1967), p. 5.
11. Lee and Solomon, *Unreliable Sources,* p. 179.
12. *Newsweek,* August 10, 1992, p. 57.
13. *Business Week,* June 8, 1992, p. 86.

5 Still Separate, Still Unequal
America's Educational Apartheid
Jonathan Kozol

Many Americans who live far from our major cities and who have no firsthand knowledge of the realities to be found in urban public schools seem to have the rather vague and general impression that the great extremes of racial isolation that were matters of grave national significance some thirty-five or forty years ago have gradually but steadily diminished in more recent years. The truth, unhappily, is that the trend, for well over a decade now, has been precisely the reverse. Schools that were already deeply segregated twenty-five or thirty years ago are no less segregated now, while thousands of other schools around the country that had been integrated either voluntarily or by the force of law have since been rapidly resegregating. . . .

"There are expensive children and there are cheap children," writes Marina Warner, an essayist and novelist who has written many books for children, "just as there are expensive women and cheap women." The governmentally administered diminishment in value of the children of the poor begins even before the age of five or six, when they begin their years of formal education in the public schools. It starts during their infant and toddler years, when hundreds of thousands of children of the very poor in much of the United States are locked out of the opportunity for preschool education for no reason but the accident of birth and budgetary choices of the government, while children of the privileged are often given veritable feasts of rich developmental early education.

In New York City, for example, affluent parents pay surprisingly large sums of money to enroll their youngsters, beginning at the age of two or three, in extraordinary early-education programs that give them social competence and rudimentary pedagogic skills unknown to children of the same age in the city's poorer neighborhoods. The most exclusive of the private preschools in New York, which are known to those who can afford them as "Baby Ivies," cost as much as $24,000 for a full-day program. Competition for admission to these pre-K schools is so extreme that private counselors are frequently retained, at fees as high as $300 an hour, to guide the parents through the application process.

At the opposite extreme along the economic spectrum in New York are thousands of children who receive no preschool opportunity at all. Exactly how many thousands are denied this opportunity in New York City and in other major cities is almost impossible to know. Numbers that originate in governmental agencies in many states are incomplete and imprecise and do not always differentiate with clarity between authentic pre-K programs that have educative and developmental substance

Adapted from *The Shame of the Nation* (Crown Publishers, 2005). Reprinted by permission of the author.

and those less expensive child-care arrangements that do not. But even where states do compile numbers that refer specifically to educative preschool programs, it is difficult to know how many of the children who are served are of low income, since admissions to some of the state-supported programs aren't determined by low income or they are determined by a complicated set of factors of which poverty is only one.

There are remarkable exceptions to this pattern in some sections of the nation. In Milwaukee, for example, virtually every four-year-old is now enrolled in a preliminary kindergarten program, which amounts to a full year of preschool education, prior to a second kindergarten year for five-year-olds. More commonly in urban neighborhoods, large numbers of low-income children are denied these opportunities and come into their kindergarten year without the minimal social skills that children need in order to participate in class activities and without even such very modest early-learning skills as knowing how to hold a crayon or a pencil, identify perhaps a couple of shapes and colors, or recognize that printed pages go from left to right.

Three years later, in third grade, these children are introduced to what are known as "high-stakes tests," which in many urban systems now determine whether students can or cannot be promoted. Children who have been in programs like those offered by the "Baby Ivies" since the age of two have, by now, received the benefits of six or seven years of education, nearly twice as many as the children who have been denied these opportunities; yet all are required to take, and will be measured by, the same examinations. Which of these children will receive the highest scores? The ones who spent the years from two to four in lovely little Montessori programs and in other pastel-painted settings in which tender and attentive and well-trained instructors read to them from beautiful storybooks and introduced them very gently for the first time to the world of numbers and the shapes of letters, and the sizes and varieties of solid objects, and perhaps taught them to sort things into groups or to arrange them in a sequence, or to do those many other interesting things that early childhood specialists refer to as prenumeracy skills? Or the ones who spent those years at home in front of a TV or sitting by the window of a slum apartment gazing down into the street? There is something deeply hypocritical about a society that holds an eight-year-old inner-city child "accountable" for her performance on a high-stakes standardized exam but does not hold the high officials of our government accountable for robbing her of what they gave their own kids six or seven years earlier.

Perhaps in order to deflect these recognitions, or to soften them somewhat, many people, even while they do nor doubt the benefit of making very large investments in the education of their own children, somehow—paradoxical as it may seem—appear to be attracted to the argument that money may not really matter that much at all. No matter with what regularity such doubts about the worth of spending money on a child's education are advanced, it is obvious that those who have the money, and who spend it lavishly to benefit their own kids, do not do it for no reason. Yet shockingly large numbers of well-educated and sophisticated people whom I talk with nowadays dismiss such challenges with a surprising ease. "Is the answer really to throw money into these dysfunctional and failing schools?" I'm often asked. "Don't we have some better ways to make them 'work'?" The question is posed in a variety of forms. "Yes, of course, it's not a perfectly fair system as it stands. But money alone is surely not the sole response. The values of the parents and the kids themselves must have a role in this as well you know, housing, health conditions, social factors." "Other factors"—a term of overall reprieve one often hears—"have got to be considered, too." These latter points are obviously true but always seem to have the odd effect of substituting things we know we cannot change in the short run for obvious solutions like cutting class size and constructing new school buildings or providing universal preschool that we actually could put in place right now if we were so inclined.

Frequently these arguments are posed as questions that do not invite an answer because the answer seems to be decided in advance. "Can you really buy your way to better education for these children?" "Do we know enough to be quite sure that we will see an actual return on the investment that we make?" "Is it even clear that this is the right starting point to get to where we'd like to go? It doesn't always seem to work, as I am sure that you already know," or similar questions that somehow assume I will agree with those who ask them.

Some people who ask these questions, although they live in wealthy districts where the schools are funded at high levels, don't even send their children to these public schools but choose instead to send them to expensive private day schools. At some of the well-known private prep schools in the New York City area, tuition and associated costs are typically more than $20,000 a year. During their children's teenage years, they sometimes send them off to very fine New England schools like Andover or Exeter or Groton, where tuition, boarding, and additional expenses rise to more than $30,000. Often a family has two teenage children in these schools at the same time, so they may be spending more than $60,000 on their children's education every year. Yet here I am one night, a guest within their home, and dinner has been served and we are having coffee now; and this entirely likeable, and generally sensible, and beautifully refined and thoughtful person looks me in the eyes and asks me whether you can really buy your way to better education for the children of the poor.

As racial isolation deepens and the inequalities of education finance remain unabated and take on new and more innovative forms, the principals of many inner-city schools are making choices that few principals in public schools that serve white children in the mainstream of the nation ever need to contemplate. Many have been dedicating vast amounts of time and effort to create an architecture of adaptive strategies that promise incremental gains within the limits inequality allows.

New vocabularies of stentorian determination, new systems of incentive, and new modes of castigation, which are termed "rewards and sanctions," have emerged. Curriculum materials that are alleged to be aligned with governmentally established goals and standards and particularly suited to what are regarded as "the special needs and learning styles" of low-income urban children have been introduced. Relentless emphasis on raising test scores, rigid policies of nonpromotion and nongraduation, a new empiricism and the imposition of unusually detailed lists of named and numbered "outcomes" for each isolated parcel of instruction, an oftentimes fanatical insistence upon uniformity of teachers in their management of time, an openly conceded emulation of the rigorous approaches of the military and a frequent use of terminology that comes out of the world of industry and commerce—these are just a few of the familiar aspects of these new adaptive strategies.

Although generically described as "school reform," most of these practices and policies are targeted primarily at poor children of color; and although most educators speak of these agendas in broad language that sounds applicable to all, it is understood that they are valued chiefly as responses to perceived catastrophe in deeply segregated and unequal schools.

"If you do what I tell you to do, how I tell you to do it, when I tell you to do it, you'll get it right," said a determined South Bronx principal observed by a reporter for the *New York Times.* She was laying out a memorizing rule for math to an assembly of her students. "If you don't, you'll get it wrong." This is the voice, this is the tone, this is the rhythm and didactic certitude one hears today in inner-city schools that have embraced a pedagogy of direct command and absolute control. "Taking their inspiration from the ideas of B. F. Skinner . . . ," says the *Times,* proponents of scripted rote-and-drill curricula articulate their aim as the establishment of "faultless communication" between "the teacher, who is the stimulus," and "the students, who respond."

The introduction of Skinnerian approaches (which are commonly employed in penal institutions and drug-rehabilitation programs), as a way of altering the attitudes and learning styles of black and Hispanic children, is provocative, and it has stirred some outcries from respected scholars. To actually go into a school where you know some of the children very, very well and see the way that these approaches can affect their daily lives and thinking processes is even more provocative.

On a chilly November day four years ago in the South Bronx, I entered P.S. 65, a school I had been visiting since 1993. There had been major changes since I'd been there last. Silent lunches had been instituted in the cafeteria, and on days when children misbehaved, silent recess had been introduced as well. On those days the students were obliged to sit in rows and maintain perfect silence on the floor of a small indoor room instead of going out to play. The words SUCCESS FOR ALL, the brand name of a scripted curriculum—better known by its acronym, SFA—were prominently posted at the top of the main stairway and, as I would later find, in almost every room. Also frequently displayed within the halls and classrooms were a number of administrative memos that were worded with unusual didactic absoluteness. "Authentic Writing," read a document called "Principles of Learning" that was posted in the corridor close to the principal's office, "is driven by curriculum and instruction." I didn't know what this expression meant. Like many other undefined and arbitrary phrases posted in the school, it seemed to be a dictum that invited no interrogation.

I entered the fourth grade of a teacher I will call Mr. Endicott, a man in his mid-thirties who had arrived here without training as a teacher, one of about a dozen teachers in the building who were sent into this school after a single summer of short-order preparation. Now in his second year, he had developed a considerable sense of confidence and held the class under a tight control.

As I found a place to sit in a far corner of the room, the teacher and his young assistant, who was in her first year as a teacher, were beginning a math lesson about building airport runways, a lesson that provided children with an opportunity for measuring perimeters. On the wall behind the teacher, in large letters, was written: "Portfolio Protocols: 1. You are responsible for the selection of [your] work that enters your portfolio. 2. As your skills become more sophisticated this year, you will want to revise, amend, supplement, and possibly replace items in your portfolio to reflect your intellectual growth." On the left side of the room: "Performance Standards Mathematics Curriculum: M-5 Problem Solving and Reasoning. M-6 Mathematical Skills and Tools . . ."

My attention was distracted by some whispering among the children sitting to the right of me. The teacher's response to this distraction was immediate: his arm shot out and up in a diagonal in front of him, his hand straight up, his fingers flat. The young co-teacher did this, too. When they saw their teachers do this, all the children in the classroom did it, too.

"Zero noise," the teacher said, but this instruction proved to be unneeded. The strange salute the class and teachers gave each other, which turned out to be one of a number of such silent signals teachers in the school were trained to use, and children to obey, had done the job of silencing the class.

"Active listening!" said Mr. Endicott. "Heads up! Tractor beams!" which meant, "Every eye on me."

On the front wall of the classroom, in handwritten words that must have taken Mr. Endicott long hours to transcribe, was a list of terms that could be used to praise or criticize a student's work in mathematics. At Level Four, the highest of four levels of success, a child's "problem-solving strategies" could be described, according to this list, as "systematic, complete, efficient, and possibly elegant," while the student's capability to draw conclusions from the work she had completed could be termed "insightful" or "comprehensive." At Level Two, the child's capability to draw conclusions was to be described as "logically unsound"; at Level One, "not present." Approximately 50 separate categories of proficiency, or lack of such, were detailed in this wall-sized tabulation.

A well-educated man, Mr. Endicott later spoke to me about the form of classroom management that he was using as an adaptation from a model of industrial efficiency. "It's a kind of 'Taylorism' in the classroom," he explained, referring to a set of theories about the management of factory employees introduced by Frederick Taylor in the early 1900s. "Primitive utilitarianism" is another term he used when we met some months later to discuss these management techniques with other teachers from the school. His reservations were, however, not apparent in the classroom. Within the terms of what he had been asked to do, he had, indeed, become a master of control. It is one of the few classrooms I had visited up to that time in which almost nothing even hinting at spontaneous emotion in the children or the teacher surfaced while I was there.

The teacher gave the "zero noise" salute again when someone whispered to another child at his table. "In two minutes you will have a chance to talk and share this with your partner." Communication between children in the class was not prohibited but was afforded time slots and, remarkably enough, was formalized in an expression that I found included in a memo that was posted on the wall beside the door: "An opportunity . . . to engage in Accountable Talk."

Even the teacher's words of praise were framed in terms consistent with the lists that had been posted on the wall. "That's a Level Four suggestion," said the teacher when a child made an observation other teachers might have praised as simply "pretty good" or "interesting" or "mature." There was, it seemed, a formal name for every cognitive event within this school: "Authentic Writing," "Active Listening," "Accountable Talk." The ardor to assign all items of instruction or behavior a specific name was unsettling me. The adjectives had the odd effect of hyping every item of endeavor. "Authentic Writing" was, it seemed, a more important act than what the children in a writing class in any ordinary school might try to do. "Accountable Talk" was some thing more self-conscious and significant than merely useful conversation.

Since that day at P.S. 65, I have visited nine other schools in six different cities where the same Skinnerian curriculum is used. The signs on the walls, the silent signals, the curious salute, the same insistent naming of all cognitive particulars, became familiar as I went from one school to the next.

"Meaningful Sentences," began one of the many listings of proficiencies expected of the children in the fourth grade of an inner-city elementary school in Hartford (90 percent black, 10 percent Hispanic) that I visited a short time later. "Noteworthy Questions," "Active Listening," and other designations like these had been posted elsewhere in the room. Here, too, the teacher gave the kids her outstretched arm, with hand held up, to reestablish order when they grew a little noisy, but I noticed that she tried to soften the effect of this by opening her fingers and bending her elbow slightly so it did not look quite as forbidding as the gesture Mr. Endicott had used. A warm and interesting woman, she later told me she disliked the regimen intensely.

Over her desk, I read a "Mission Statement," which established the priorities and values for the school. Among the missions of the school, according to the printed statement, which was posted also in some other classrooms of the school, was "to develop productive citizens" who have the skills that will be needed "for successful global competition," a message that was reinforced by other posters in the room. Over the heads of a group of children at their desks, a sign anointed them BEST WORKERS OF 2002.

Another signal now was given by the teacher, this one not for silence but in order to achieve some other form of class behavior, which I could not quite identify. The students gave exactly the same signal in response. Whatever the function of this signal, it was done as I had seen it done in the South Bronx and would see it done in other schools in months to come. Suddenly, with a seeming surge of restlessness and irritation—with herself, as it appeared, and with her own effective use of all the tricks that she had learned—she turned to me and said, "I can do this with my dog."

"There's something crystal clear about a number," says a top adviser to the U.S. Senate committee that has jurisdiction over public education, a point of view that is reinforced repeatedly in statements coming from the office of the U.S. education secretary and the White House. "I want to change the face of reading instruction across the United States from an art to a science," said an assistant to Rod Paige, the former education secretary, in the winter of 2002. This is a popular position among advocates for rigidly sequential systems of instruction, but the longing to turn art into science doesn't stop with reading methodologies alone. In many schools it now extends to almost every aspect of the operation of the school and of the lives that children lead within it. In some schools even such ordinary acts as children filing to lunch or recess in the hallways or the stairwells are subjected to the same determined emphasis upon empirical precision.

"Rubric For Filing" is the printed heading of a lengthy list of numbered categories by which teachers are supposed to grade their students on the way they march along the corridors in another inner-city district I have visited. Someone, in this instance, did a lot of work to fit the filing proficiencies of children into no more and no less than thirty-two specific slots:

"Line leader confidently leads the class. . . . Line is straight. . . . Spacing is right. . . . The class is stepping together. . . . Everyone shows pride, their shoulders high . . . no slumping," according to the strict criteria for filing at Level Four.

"Line is straight, but one or two people [are] not quite in line," according to the box for Level Three. "Line leader leads the class," and "almost everyone shows pride."

"Several are slumping. . . . Little pride is showing," says the box for Level Two. "Spacing is uneven. . . . Some are talking and whispering."

"Line leader is paying no attention," says the box for Level One. "Heads are turning every way. . . . Hands are touching. . . . The line is not straight. . . . There is no pride."

The teacher who handed me this document believed at first that it was written as a joke by someone who had simply come to be fed up with all the numbers and accounting rituals that clutter up the day in many overregulated schools. Alas, it turned out that it was no joke but had been printed in a handbook of instructions for the teachers in the city where she taught.

In some inner-city districts, even the most pleasant and old-fashioned class activities of elementary schools have now been overtaken by these ordering requirements. A student teacher in California, for example, wanted to bring a pumpkin to her class on Halloween but knew it had no ascertainable connection to the California standards. She therefore had developed what she called "The Multi-Modal Pumpkin Unit" to teach science (seeds), arithmetic (the size and shape of pumpkins, I believe—this detail wasn't clear), and certain items she adapted out of language arts, in order to position "pumpkins" in a frame of state proficiencies. Even with her multi-modal pumpkin, as her faculty adviser told me, she was still afraid she would be criticized because she knew the pumpkin would not really help her children to achieve expected goals on state exams.

Why, I asked a group of educators at a seminar in Sacramento, was a teacher being placed in a position where she'd need to do preposterous curricular gymnastics to enjoy a bit of seasonal amusement with her kids on Halloween? How much injury to state-determined "purpose" would it do to let the children of poor people have a pumpkin party once a year for no other reason than because it's something fun that other children get to do on autumn days in public schools across most of America?

"Forcing an absurdity on teachers does teach something," said an African-American professor. "It teaches acquiescence. It breaks down the will to thumb your nose at pointless protocols to call absurdity 'absurd.'" Writing out the standards with the proper numbers on the chalkboard has a similar effect, he said; and doing this is "terribly important" to the principals in many of these schools. "You *have* to post the standards, and the way you know the children know the standards is by asking them to *state* the standards. And they do it—and you want to be quite certain that they do it if you want to keep on working at that school."

In speaking of the drill-based program in effect at P.S. 65, Mr. Endicott told me he tended to be sympathetic to the school administrators, more so at least than the other teachers I had talked with seemed to be. He said he believed his principal had little choice about the implementation of this program, which had been mandated for all elementary schools in New York City that had had rock-bottom academic records over a long period of time. "This puts me into a dilemma," he went on, "because I love the kids at P.S. 65." And even while, he said, "I know that my teaching SFA is a charade . . . if I don't do it I won't be permitted to teach these children."

Mr. Endicott, like all but two of the new recruits at P.S. 65—there were about fifteen in all—was a white person, as were the principal and most of the administrators at the school. As a result, most of these neophyte instructors had had little or no prior contact with the children of an inner-city neighborhood; but, like the others I met, and despite the distancing between the children and their teachers that resulted from the scripted method of instruction, he had developed close attachments to his students and did not want to abandon them. At the same time, the class- and race-specific implementation of this program obviously troubled him. "There's an expression now," he said. "The rich get richer, and the poor get SFA." He said he was still trying to figure out his "professional ethics" on the problem that this posed for him.

White children made up "only about one percent" of students in the New York City schools in which this scripted teaching system was imposed,[1] according to the *New York Times,* which also said that "the prepackaged lessons" were intended "to ensure that all teachers—even novices or the most inept"—would be able to teach reading. As seemingly pragmatic and hardheaded as such arguments may be, they are desperation strategies that come out of the acceptance of inequity. If we did not have a deeply segregated system in which more experienced instructors teach the children of the privileged and the least experienced are sent to teach the children of minorities, these practices would not be needed and could not be so convincingly defended. They are confections of apartheid, and no matter by what arguments of urgency or practicality they have been justified, they cannot fail to further deepen the divisions of society.

There is no misery index for the children of apartheid education. There ought to be; we measure almost everything else that happens to them in their schools. Do kids who go to schools like these enjoy the days they spend in them? Is school, for most of them, a happy place to be? You do not find the answers to these questions in reports about achievement levels, scientific methods of accountability, or structural revisions in the modes of governance. Documents like these don't speak of happiness. You have to go back to the schools themselves to find an answer to these questions. You have to sit down in the little chairs in first and second grade, or on the reading rug with kindergarten kids, and listen to the things they actually say to one another and the dialogue between them and their teachers. You have to go down to the basement with the children when it's time for lunch and to the playground with them, if they have a playground, when it's time for recess, if they still have recess at their school. You have to walk into the children's bathrooms in these buildings. You have to do what children do and breathe the air the children breathe. I don't think that there is any other way to find out what the lives that children lead in school are really like.

High school students, when I first meet them, are often more reluctant than the younger children to open up and express their personal concerns; but hesitation on the part of students did not prove to be a problem when I visited a tenth-grade class at Fremont High School in Los Angeles. The students were told that I was a writer, and they took no time in getting down to matters that were on their minds.

"Can we talk about the bathrooms?" asked a soft-spoken student named Mireya.

In almost any classroom there are certain students who, by the force of their directness or the unusual sophistication of their way of speaking, tend to capture your attention from the start. Mireya later spoke insightfully about some of the serious academic problems that were common in the school, but her observations on the physical and personal embarrassments she and her schoolmates had to undergo cut to the heart of questions of essential dignity that kids in squalid schools like this one have to deal with all over the nation.

Fremont High School, as court papers filed in a lawsuit against the state of California document, has fifteen fewer bathrooms than the law requires. Of the limited number of bathrooms that are working in the school, "only one or two . . . are open and unlocked for girls to use." Long lines of girls are "waiting to use the bathrooms," which are generally "unclean" and "lack basic supplies," including toilet paper. Some of the classrooms, as court papers also document, "do not have air conditioning," so that students, who attend school on a three-track schedule that runs year-round, "become red-faced and unable to concentrate" during "the extreme heat of summer." The school's maintenance records report that rats were found in eleven classrooms. Rat droppings were found "in the bins and drawers" of the high school's kitchen, and school records note that "hamburger buns" were being "eaten off [the] bread-delivery rack."

No matter how many tawdry details like these I've read in legal briefs or depositions through the years, I'm always shocked again to learn how often these unsanitary physical conditions are permitted to continue in the schools that serve our poorest students—even after they have been vividly described in the media. But hearing of these conditions in Mireya's words was even more unsettling, in part because this student seemed so fragile and because the need even to speak of these indignities in front of me and all the other students was an additional indignity.

"The problem is this," she carefully explained. "You're not allowed to use the bathroom during lunch, which is a thirty-minute period. The only time that you're allowed to use it is between your classes." But "this is a huge building," she went on. "It has long corridors. If you have one class at one end of the building and your next class happens to be way down at the other end, you don't have time to use the bathroom and still get to class before it starts. So you go to your class and then you ask permission from your teacher to go to the bathroom and the teacher tells you, 'No. You had your chance between the periods . . .'

"I feel embarrassed when I have to stand there and explain it to a teacher."

"This is the question," said a wiry-looking boy named Edward, leaning forward in his chair. "Students are not animals, but even animals need to relieve themselves sometimes. We're here for eight hours. What do they think we're supposed to do?"

"It humiliates you," said Mireya, who went on to make the interesting statement that "the school provides solutions that don't actually work," and this idea was taken up by several other students in describing course requirements within the school. A tall black student, for example, told me that she hoped to be a social worker or a doctor but was programmed into "Sewing Class" this year. She also had to take another course, called "Life Skills," which she told me was a very basic course—"a retarded class," to use her words—that "teaches things like the six continents," which she said she'd learned in elementary school.

When I asked her why she had to take these courses, she replied that she'd been told they were required, which as I later learned was not exactly so. What was required was that high school students take two courses in an area of study called "The Technical Arts," and which the Los Angeles Board of Education terms "Applied Technology." At schools that served the middle class or upper-middle class, this requirement was likely to be met by courses that had academic substance and, perhaps, some relevance to college preparation. At Beverly Hills High School, for example, the technical-arts requirement could be fulfilled by taking subjects like residential architecture, the designing of commercial structures, broadcast journalism, advanced computer graphics, a sophisticated course in furniture design, carving and sculpture, or an honors course in engineering research and design. At Fremont High, in contrast, this requirement was far more often met by courses that were basically vocational and also obviously keyed to low-paying levels of employment.

Mireya, for example, who had plans to go to college, told me that she had to take a sewing class last year and now was told she'd been assigned to take a class in hairdressing as well. When I asked her teacher why Mireya could not skip these subjects and enroll in classes that would help her to pursue her college aspirations, she replied, "It isn't a question of what students want. It's what the school may have available. If all the other elective classes that a student wants to take are full, she has to take one of these classes if she wants to graduate."

A very small girl named Obie, who had big blue-tinted glasses tilted up across her hair, interrupted then to tell me with a kind of wild gusto that she'd taken hairdressing twice! When I expressed surprised that this was possible, she said there were two levels of hairdressing offered here at Fremont High. "One is in hairstyling," she said. "The other is in braiding."

Mireya stared hard at this student for a moment and then suddenly began to cry. "I don't want to take hairdressing. I did not need sewing either. I knew how to sew.

My mother is a seamstress in a factory. I'm trying to go to college. I don't need to sew to go to college. My mother sews. I hoped for something else."

"What would you rather take?" I asked.

"I wanted to take an AP class," she answered.

Mireya's sudden tears elicited a strong reaction from one of the boys who had been silent up till now: a thin, dark-eyed student named Fortino, who had long hair down to his shoulders. He suddenly turned directly to Mireya and spoke into the silence that followed her last words.

"Listen to me," he said. "The owners of the sewing factories need laborers. Correct?"

"I guess they do," Mireya said.

"It's not going to be their own kids. Right?" "Why not?" another student said.

"So they can grow beyond themselves," Mireya answered quietly. "But we remain the same."

"You're ghetto," said Fortino, "so we send you to the factory." He sat low in his desk chair, leaning on one elbow, his voice and dark eyes loaded with a cynical intelligence. "You're ghetto—so you sew!"

"There are higher positions than these," said a student named Samantha.

"You're ghetto," said Fortino unrelentingly. "So sew!"

Admittedly, the economic needs of a society are bound to be reflected to some rational degree within the policies and purposes of public schools. But, even so, there must be *something* more to life as it is lived by six-year-olds or by teenagers, for that matter, than concerns about "successful global competition." Childhood is not merely basic training for utilitarian adulthood. It should have some claims upon our mercy, not for its future value to the economic interests of competitive societies but for its present value as a perishable piece of life itself.

Very few people who are not involved with inner-city schools have any real idea of the extremes to which the mercantile distortion of the purposes and character of education have been taken or how unabashedly proponents of these practices are willing to defend them. The head of a Chicago school, for instance, who was criticized by some for emphasizing rote instruction that, his critics said, was turning children into "robots," found no reason to dispute the charge. "Did you ever stop to think that these robots will never burglarize your home?" he asked, and "will never snatch your pocketbooks. . . . These robots are going to be producing taxes."

Corporate leaders, when they speak of education, sometimes pay lip-service to the notion of "good critical and analytic skills," but it is reasonable to ask whether they have in mind the critical analysis of *their* priorities. In principle, perhaps some do; but, if so, this is not a principle that seems to have been honored widely in the schools I have been visiting. In all the various business-driven inner-city classrooms that I have observed in the past five years, plastered as they are with corporation brand names and managerial vocabularies, I have yet to see the two words "labor unions." Is this an oversight? How is that possible? Teachers and principals themselves, who are almost always members of a union, seem to be so beaten down that they rarely even question this omission.

It is not at all unusual these days to come into an urban school in which the principal prefers to call himself or herself "building CEO" or "building manager." In some of the same schools teachers are described as "classroom managers."[2] I have never been in a suburban district in which principals were asked to view themselves or teachers in this way. These terminologies remind us of how wide the distance has become between two very separate worlds of education.

It has been more than a decade now since drill-based literacy methods like Success For All began to proliferate in our urban schools. It has been three and a half years since the systems of assessment that determine the effectiveness of these and similar practices were codified in the federal legislation, No Child Left Behind, that President Bush signed into law in 2002. Since the enactment of this bill, the number of standardized exams children must take has more than doubled. It will probably increase again after the year 2006, when standardized tests, which are now required in grades three through eight, may be required in Head Start programs and, as President Bush has now proposed, in ninth, tenth, and eleventh grades as well.

The elements of strict accountability, in short, are solidly in place; and in many states where the present federal policies are simply reinforcements of accountability requirements that were established long before the passage of the federal law, the same regimen has been in place since 1995 or even earlier. The "tests-and-standards" partisans have had things very much their way for an extended period of time, and those who were convinced that they had ascertained "what works" in schools that serve minorities and children of the poor have had ample opportunity to prove that they were right.

What, then, it is reasonable to ask, are the results?

The achievement gap between black and white children, which narrowed for three decades up until the late years of the 1980s—the period in which school segregation steadily decreased—started to widen once more in the early 1990s when the federal courts began the process of resegregation by dismantling the mandates of the *Brown* decision. From that point on, the gap continued to widen or remained essentially unchanged; and while recently there has been a modest narrowing of the gap in reading scores for fourth-grade children, the gap in secondary school remains as wide as ever.

The media inevitably celebrate the periodic upticks that a set of scores may seem to indicate in one year or another in achievement levels of black and Hispanic children in their elementary schools. But if these upticks were not merely temporary "testing gains" achieved by test-prep regimens and were instead authentic education gains, they would carry over into middle school and high school. Children who know how to read—and read with comprehension—do not suddenly become nonreaders and hopelessly disabled writers when they enter secondary school. False gains evaporate; real gains endure. Yet hundreds of thousands of the inner-city children who have made what many districts claim to be dramatic gains in elementary school, and whose principals and teachers have adjusted almost every aspect of their school days and school calendars, forfeiting recess, canceling or cutting back on all the so-called frills (art, music, even social sciences) in order to comply with state demands, those students, now in secondary school, are sitting in subject-matter classes where they cannot comprehend the texts and cannot set down their ideas in the kind of sentences expected of most fourth- and fifth-grade students in the suburbs. Students in this painful situation, not surprisingly, tend to be most likely to drop out of school.

In 48 percent of high schools in the nation's 100 largest districts, which are those in which the highest concentrations of black and Hispanic students tend to be enrolled, less than half the entering ninth-graders graduate in four years. Nationwide, from 1993 to 2002, the number of high schools graduating less than half their ninth-grade class in four years has increased by 75 percent. In the 94 percent of districts in New York State where white children make up the majority, nearly 80 percent of students graduate from high school in four years. In the 6 percent of districts where black and Hispanic students make up the majority, only 40 percent do so. There are 120 high schools in New York, enrolling nearly 200,000 minority students, where less than 60 percent of entering ninth-graders even make it to twelfth grade.

The promulgation of new and expanded inventories of "what works," no matter the enthusiasm with which they're elaborated, is not going to change this. The use of hortatory slogans chanted by the students in our segregated schools is not going to change this. Desperate historical revisionism that romanticizes the segregation of an older order (this is a common theme of many separatists today) is not going to change this. Skinnerian instructional approaches, which decapitate a child's capability for critical reflection, are not going to change this. Posters about "global competition" will certainly not change this. Turning six-year-olds into examination soldiers and denying eight-year-olds their time for play at recess will not change this.

"I went to Washington to challenge the soft bigotry of low expectations," said President Bush in his campaign for reelection in September 2004. "It's working. It's making a difference." Here we have one of those deadly lies that by sheer repetition is at length accepted by surprisingly large numbers of Americans. But it is not the truth; and it is not an innocent misstatement of the facts. It is a devious appeasement of the heartache of the parents of the black and brown and poor, and if it is not forcefully resisted it will lead us further in a very dangerous direction.

Whether the issue is inequity alone or deepening resegregation or the labyrinthine intertwining of the two, it is well past the time for us to start the work that it will take to change this. If it takes people marching in the streets and other forms of adamant disruption of the governing civilities, if it takes more than litigation, more than legislation, and much more than resolutions introduced by members of Congress, these are prices we should be prepared to pay. "We do not have the things you have," Alliyah told me when she wrote to ask if I would come and visit her school in the South Bronx. "Can you help us?" America owes that little girl and millions like her a more honorable answer than they have received.

Notes

1. SFA has since been discontinued in the New York City public schools, though it is still being used in 1,300 U.S. schools, serving as many as 650,000 children. Similar scripted systems are used in schools (overwhelmingly minority in population) serving several million children.

2. A school I visited three years ago in Columbus, Ohio, was littered with "Help Wanted" signs. Starting in kindergarten, children in the school were being asked to think about the jobs that they might choose when they grew up. In one classroom there was a poster that displayed the names of several retail stores: J. C. Penney, Wal-Mart, Kmart, Sears, and a few others. "It's like working in a store," a classroom aide explained. "The children are learning to pretend they're cashiers." At another school in the same district, children were encouraged to apply for jobs in their classrooms. Among the job positions open to the children in this school, there was an "Absence Manager" and a "Behavior Chart Manager," a "Form Collector Manager," a "Paper Passer Outer Manager," a "Paper Collecting Manager," a "Paper Returning Manager," an "Exit Ticket Manager," even a "Learning Manager," a "Reading Corner Manager," and a "Score Keeper Manager." I asked the principal if there was a special reason why those two words "management" and "manager" kept popping up throughout the school. "We want every child to be working as a manager while he or she is in this school," the principal explained. "We want to make them understand that, in this country, companies will give you opportunities to work, to prove yourself, no matter what you've done." I wasn't sure what she meant by "no matter what you've done," and asked her if she could explain it. "Even if you have a felony arrest," she said, "we want you to understand that you can be a manager someday."

6 Masked Racism
Reflections on the Prison Industrial Complex
Angela Davis

Imprisonment has become the response of first resort to far too many of the social problems that burden people who are ensconced in poverty. These problems often are veiled by being conveniently grouped together under the category "crime" and by the automatic attribution of criminal behavior to people of color. Homelessness, unemployment, drug addiction, mental illness, and illiteracy are only a few of the problems that disappear from public view when the human beings contending with them are relegated to cages.

Prisons thus perform a feat of magic. Or rather the people who continually vote in new prison bonds and tacitly assent to a proliferating network of prisons and jails have been tricked into believing in the magic of imprisonment. But prisons do not disappear problems, they disappear human beings. And the practice of disappearing vast numbers of people from poor, immigrant, and racially marginalized communities has literally become big business.

The seeming effortlessness of magic always conceals an enormous amount of behind-the-scenes work. When prisons disappear human beings in order to convey the illusion of solving social problems, penal infrastructures must be created to accommodate a rapidly swelling population of caged people. Goods and services must be provided to keep imprisoned populations alive. Sometimes these populations must be kept busy and at other times—particularly in repressive super-maximum prisons and in INS detention centers—they must be deprived of virtually all meaningful activity. Vast numbers of handcuffed and shackled people are moved across state borders as they are transferred from one state or federal prison to another.

All this work, which used to be the primary province of government, is now also performed by private corporations, whose links to government in the field of what is euphemistically called "corrections" resonate dangerously with the military industrial complex. The dividends that accrue from investment in the punishment industry, like those that accrue from investment in weapons production, only amount to social destruction. Taking into account the structural similarities and profitability of business–government linkages in the realms of military production and public punishment, the expanding penal system can now be characterized as a "prison industrial complex."

This article was first published in *ColorLines* magazine (now Colorlines.com), Fall 1998. Reprinted by permission of the author.

The Color of Imprisonment

Almost two million people are currently locked up in the immense network of U.S. prisons and jails. More than 70 percent of the imprisoned population are people of color. It is rarely acknowledged that the fastest growing group of prisoners are black women and that Native American prisoners are the largest group per capita. Approximately five million people—including those on probation and parole—are directly under the surveillance of the criminal justice system.

Three decades ago, the imprisoned population was approximately one-eighth its current size. While women still constitute a relatively small percentage of people behind bars, today the number of incarcerated women in California alone is almost twice what the nationwide women's prison population was in 1970. According to Elliott Currie, "[t]he prison has become a looming presence in our society to an extent unparalleled in our history—or that of any other industrial democracy. Short of major wars, mass incarceration has been the most thoroughly implemented government social program of our time."

To deliver up bodies destined for profitable punishment, the political economy of prisons relies on racialized assumptions of criminality—such as images of black welfare mothers reproducing criminal children—and on racist practices in arrest, conviction, and sentencing patterns. Colored bodies constitute the main human raw material in this vast experiment to disappear the major social problems of our time. Once the aura of magic is stripped away from the imprisonment solution, what is revealed is racism, class bias, and the parasitic seduction of capitalist profit. The prison industrial system materially and morally impoverishes its inhabitants and devours the social wealth needed to address the very problems that have led to spiraling numbers of prisoners.

As prisons take up more and more space on the social landscape, other government programs that have previously sought to respond to social needs—such as Temporary Assistance to Needy Families—are being squeezed out of existence. The deterioration of public education, including prioritizing discipline and security over learning in public schools located in poor communities, is directly related to the prison "solution."

Profiting from Prisoners

As prisons proliferate in U.S. society, private capital has become enmeshed in the punishment industry. And precisely because of their profit potential, prisons are becoming increasingly important to the U.S. economy. If the notion of punishment as a source of potentially stupendous profits is disturbing by itself, then the strategic dependence on racist structures and ideologies to render mass punishment palatable and profitable is even more troubling.

Prison privatization is the most obvious instance of capital's current movement toward the prison industry. While government-run prisons are often in gross violation of international human rights standards, private prisons are even less accountable. In March of this year, the Corrections Corporation of America (CCA), the largest U.S. private prison company, claimed 54,944 beds in 68 facilities under contract or development in the U.S., Puerto Rico, the United Kingdom, and Australia. Following the global trend of subjecting more women to public punishment, CCA recently opened a women's prison outside Melbourne. The company recently identified California as its "new frontier."

Wackenhut Corrections Corporation (WCC), the second largest U.S. prison company, claimed contracts and awards to manage 46 facilities in North America, the United Kingdom, and Australia. It boasts a total of 30,424 beds as well as contracts for prisoner health care services, transportation, and security.

Currently, the stocks of both CCA and WCC are doing extremely well. Between 1996 and 1997, CCA's revenues increased by 58 percent, from $293 million to $462 million. Its net profit grew from $30.9 million to $53.9 million. WCC raised its revenues from $138 million in 1996 to $210 million in 1997. Unlike public correctional facilities, the vast profits of these private facilities rely on the employment of non-union labor.

The Prison Industrial Complex

But private prison companies are only the most visible component of the increasing corporatization of punishment. Government contracts to build prisons have bolstered the construction industry. The architectural community has identified prison design as a major new niche. Technology developed for the military by companies like Westinghouse are being marketed for use in law enforcement and punishment.

Moreover, corporations that appear to be far removed from the business of punishment are intimately involved in the expansion of the prison industrial complex. Prison construction bonds are one of the many sources of profitable investment for leading financiers such as Merrill Lynch. MCI charges prisoners and their families outrageous prices for the precious telephone calls which are often the only contact prisoners have with the free world.

Many corporations whose products we consume on a daily basis have learned that prison labor power can be as profitable as third world labor power exploited by U.S.-based global corporations. Both relegate formerly unionized workers to joblessness and many even wind up in prison. Some of the companies that use prison labor are IBM, Motorola, Compaq, Texas Instruments, Honeywell, Microsoft, and Boeing. But it is not only the hi-tech industries that reap the profits of prison labor. Nordstrom department stores sell jeans that are marketed as "Prison Blues," as well as t-shirts and jackets made in Oregon prisons. The advertising slogan for these clothes is "made on the inside to be worn on the outside." Maryland prisoners inspect glass bottles and jars used by Revlon and Pierre Cardin, and schools throughout the world buy graduation caps and gowns made by South Carolina prisoners.

"For private business," write Eve Goldberg and Linda Evans (a political prisoner inside the Federal Correctional Institution at Dublin, California) "prison labor is like a pot of gold. No strikes. No union organizing. No health benefits, unemployment insurance, or workers' compensation to pay. No language barriers, as in foreign countries. New leviathan prisons are being built on thousands of eerie acres of factories inside the walls. Prisoners do data entry for Chevron, make telephone reservations for TWA, raise hogs, shovel manure, make circuit boards, limousines, waterbeds, and lingerie for Victoria's Secret—all at a fraction of the cost of 'free labor.' "

Devouring the Social Wealth

Although prison labor—which ultimately is compensated at a rate far below the minimum wage—is hugely profitable for the private companies that use it, the penal system as a whole does not produce wealth. It devours the social wealth that could be used to subsidize housing for the homeless, to ameliorate public education for poor and racially marginalized communities, to open free drug rehabilitation programs for people who wish to kick their habits, to create a national health care system, to expand programs to combat HIV, to eradicate domestic abuse—and, in the process, to create well-paying jobs for the unemployed.

Since 1984 more than twenty new prisons have opened in California, while only one new campus was added to the California State University system and none to the University of California system. In 1996–97, higher education received only 8.7 percent of the State's General Fund while corrections received 9.6 percent. Now that affirmative action has been declared illegal in California, it is obvious that education is increasingly reserved for certain people, while prisons are reserved for others. Five times as many black men are presently in prison as in four year colleges and universities. This new segregation has dangerous implications for the entire country.

By segregating people labeled as criminals, prison simultaneously fortifies and conceals the structural racism of the U.S. economy. Claims of low unemployment rates—even in black communities—make sense only if one assumes that the vast numbers of people in prison have really disappeared and thus have no legitimate claims to jobs. The numbers of black and Latino men currently incarcerated amount to two percent of the male labor force. According to criminologist David Downes, "[t]reating incarceration as a type of hidden unemployment may raise the jobless rate for men by about one-third, to 8 percent. The effect on the black labor force is greater still, raising the [black] male unemployment rate from 11 percent to 19 percent."

Hidden Agenda

Mass incarceration is not a solution to unemployment, nor is it a solution to the vast array of social problems that are hidden away in a rapidly growing network of prisons and jails. However, the great majority of people have been tricked into believing in the efficacy of imprisonment, even though the historical record clearly demonstrates that prisons do not work. Racism has undermined our ability to create a popular critical discourse to contest the ideological trickery that posits imprisonment as key to public safety. The focus of state policy is rapidly shifting from social welfare to social control.

Black, Latino, Native American, and many Asian youth are portrayed as the purveyors of violence, traffickers of drugs, and as envious of commodities that they have no right to possess. Young black and Latina women are represented as sexually promiscuous and as indiscriminately propagating babies and poverty. Criminality and deviance are racialized. Surveillance is thus focused on communities of color, immigrants, the unemployed, the undereducated, the homeless, and in general on those who have a diminishing claim to social resources. Their claim to social resources continues to diminish in large part because law enforcement and penal measures increasingly devour these resources. The prison industrial complex has thus created a vicious cycle of punishment which only further impoverishes those whose impoverishment is supposedly "solved" by imprisonment.

Therefore, as the emphasis of government policy shifts from social welfare to crime control, racism sinks more deeply into the economic and ideological structures of U.S. society. Meanwhile, conservative crusaders against affirmative action and bilingual education proclaim the end of racism, while their opponents suggest that racism's remnants can be dispelled through dialogue and conversation. But conversations about "race relations" will hardly dismantle a prison industrial complex that thrives on and nourishes the racism hidden within the deep structures of our society.

The emergence of a U.S. prison industrial complex within a context of cascading conservatism marks a new historical moment, whose dangers are unprecedented. But so are its opportunities. Considering the impressive number of grassroots projects that continue to resist the expansion of the punishment industry, it ought to be possible to bring these efforts together to create radical and nationally visible movements that can legitimize anti-capitalist critiques of the prison industrial complex. It ought to be possible to build movements in defense of prisoners' human rights and movements that persuasively argue that what we need is not new prisons, but new health care, housing, education, drug programs, jobs, and education. To safeguard a democratic future, it is possible and necessary to weave together the many and increasing strands of resistance to the prison industrial complex into a powerful movement for social transformation.

7 You May Know Me from Such Roles as Terrorist #4

Jon Ronson

The right-wing action hero gave Maz Jobrani hope. This was 2001. Maz had been trying to make it as an actor in Hollywood for three years, but things were going badly for him. He was earning peanuts as an assistant at an advertising agency. But then his agent telephoned: Did Maz want to play a terrorist in a Chuck Norris movie? So Maz read the screenplay for *The President's Man: A Line in the Sand,* and he found within it a moment of promising subtlety.

"Chuck Norris plays a professor of Middle Eastern studies," Maz tells me. We're sitting in a coffee shop in Westwood, Los Angeles. Maz is a goateed man in his early forties who was born in Tehran but moved with his family to the San Francisco Bay Area when he was 6. "There's a scene where he's talking to his students about Afghanistan. One of the students raises his hand and says something like, 'Uh, professor, they're all fanatics, so why don't we just kill them all?' And the Chuck Norris character goes, 'Now, now. They're not all bad.' And I thought, 'Wow! A nuance!'"

The nuance gave Maz hope. Did this mean they'd allow him to make his character nuanced? Maz was aware that fixating on this one line might have been self-deluding, like a drowning man clutching driftwood in a hurricane. But he agreed to take the part. Then, at the wardrobe fitting, they handed him his turban.

"I said, 'Whoa, whoa! No! Afghans in America don't wear turbans. Plus, this guy's a terrorist. He's not going to draw attention to himself. You tell the producers I want to bring authenticity to this character.' The wardrobe supervisor replied, 'All right, all right, I'll talk to them.'"

The message came back from Chuck Norris's people that the turban was mandatory.

And then came Maz's death. It was the one thing he'd been excited about, because the script alluded to a short fight immediately preceding it. Hand-to-hand combat with Chuck Norris!

"But on the day of the scene," Maz says, "Chuck Norris told his son, who was the director, 'Oh, I'll just take a gun and I'll shoot him.' Oh, great! I don't even get a fight!"

"So how exactly did you get shot?" I ask Maz.

"Okay, so I'm about to set off a bomb at a refinery," he replies. "Chuck Norris runs in. I run away, because I'm scared. He gets behind the computer and starts dismantling the bomb, because he's a genius. I come running back in carrying an Uzi. And I try to shoot him. But he takes out his gun and shoots me." Maz shrugs. "I start to yell, '*Allah—*' Bang! I'm down. I don't even get 'Allahu Akbar!' out. It was horrible, man."

Republished with permission of Jon Ronson/GQ.

Maz shakes his head at the memory. It was humiliating. Actually, it was worse than humiliating—it was a harbinger. Maz understood, as he lay dead in that refinery, that Hollywood didn't want him to be an actor. Hollywood wanted him to be a caricature. "I started acting in junior high," he says. "I was in *Guys and Dolls.* I was Stanley Kowalski. In my head, before coming to Hollywood, I thought, 'I can play anything.'" But instead he'd become the latest iteration in Hollywood's long history of racist casting, reducing his religion and culture to a bunch of villainous, cartoonish psychopaths. He knew he had to get out.

I glance at my phone. It's 1 P.M. We're running late to meet three of Maz's friends at a nearby Lebanese restaurant. We jump into Maz's car.

Maz refuses to take terrorist parts nowadays. He's primarily a stand-up comedian instead, a very funny and successful one. In fact, he's just published a memoir, *I'm Not a Terrorist, But I've Played One on TV.* But Maz's friends at the restaurant haven't been so lucky. They still make their livings as actors, which means they still play terrorists all the time.

Maz and I hurry into the restaurant, apologizing for being late. We order a *mezze* plate for five. These men have been killed while committing acts of terrorism on *Homeland* and *24,* in *The Kingdom* and *Three Kings* and *True Lies,* and in too many other films and shows to list. We've barely sat down when Waleed Zuaiter, a Palestinian-American actor in his early forties, recounts for me his death scene on *Law & Order: Criminal Intent.* This was about a year after September 11. "I play a guy from a sleeper cell," Waleed says. "I'm checking my e-mails. I hear the cops come in, and the first thing I go for is my box cutter. There's literally a box cutter in the scene."

"Was this in an office?" I ask Waleed.

"It was in my home!" he replies. "I just *happened* to have a box cutter lying around." Waleed shakes his head, bemused. "The cops burst in, and next thing you know I've got the box cutter to some guy's neck. And then one of the cops shoots me."

"I die in *Iron Man,*" says Sayed Badreya, an Egyptian man with a salt-and-pepper beard. "I die in *Executive Decision.* I get shot at by—what's his name?—Kurt Russell. I get shot by everyone. George Clooney kills me in *Three Kings.* Arnold blows me up in *True Lies . . .*"

As Sayed and Waleed and the others describe their various demises, it strikes me that the key to making a living in Hollywood if you're Muslim is to be good at dying. If you're a Middle Eastern actor and you can die with charisma, there is no shortage of work for you.

Here's another irony in the lives of these men: While they profoundly wish they didn't have to play terrorists, much of our lunch is taken up with them swapping tips on clever ways to stand out at terrorist auditions.

"If I'm going in for the role of a nice father, I'll talk to everybody," Sayed tells the table. "But if you're going for a terrorist role, don't fucking smile at all those white people sitting there. Treat them like shit. The minute you say hello, you break character."

"But it's smart at the end of the audition to break it," adds Hrach Titizian, who at 36 is the youngest actor here. " 'Oh, thanks, guys.' So they know it's okay to have you on set for a couple of weeks."

Then Waleed says something you don't often hear actors say, because most actors regard their competition with dread: "Whenever it's that kind of role and we see each other at the auditions, it's so comforting. We're not in this alone. We're in this together."

We're in this together. By this Waleed is referring to a uniquely demeaning set of circumstances. I'm sure practically *all* actors, Muslim or otherwise, feel degraded. Most have no power over their careers—what roles they can play, how their performances are edited. But Muslim actors are powerless in unusually hideous ways. The last time one became a big star in America was back in 1962—Omar Sharif in *Lawrence of Arabia.* These days they get offered terrorist roles and little else. And we—the paying public—barely even notice, much less worry about it. Where's the outrage? There is none, except from the actors themselves. These roles are ethically nightmarish for them, and the stress can wreak havoc on their lives. Waleed's father, for instance, threatened never to talk to him again if he ever played a terrorist. I thought that was bad enough. But then I meet another actor who had it much worse.

• • •

Ahmed Ahmed was raised a strict Muslim in Riverside, California, by his Egyptian-immigrant parents—a mother who learned English from watching soap operas, and a gas-station-attendant father who ended up buying an automotive shop. The day Ahmed told them he was quitting college to try his luck in Hollywood, his father asked if he was gay and didn't speak to him for seven years.

When I meet Ahmed at the French Roast Café in downtown New York City, he echoes Waleed's thoughts about the camaraderie among these actors. "It's always the same guys at every audition. Waleed, Sayed Badreya . . . You're all sitting in a row in the waiting room. Oftentimes the casting offce is right next to you. The door's shut, but you can hear what's going on."

"What do you hear?" I ask him.

"Oh, you know," he says. "'ALLAHU AKBAR!' And then . . ." Ahmed switches to the voice of a bubbly casting director. "'Thank you! That was *great!*' And the guy walks out, sweating. And you walk in and they're, 'Hey! Thanks for coming in! Whenever you're ready!' And you're thinking, 'How do I do it differently from the guy before me? Do I go louder?'"

When he auditioned for *Executive Decision,* he went louder. *Executive Decision* is, I realize as I talk to people from this world, considered the ground zero (as it were) of ludicrous portrayals of Islamic terrorists. This was 1996, and Ahmed was in his mid-twenties. "My agent had called me. 'There's this film. It's a $55 million action suspense thriller starring Kurt Russell, Halle Berry, and Steven Seagal. They want to bring you in to read for one of the parts.' I said, 'What's the part?' She said, 'Terrorist Number Four.' I said, 'I don't want to do it.' She said, 'It's three weeks of work. It pays $30,000.'"

And so Ahmed read for the part. "My lines were 'Sit down and obey or I will kill you in the name of Allah.' And the director goes, 'Brilliant! Do it again. But this time, can you give me more of that Middle Eastern, you know . . .' I go, 'Anger?' He goes, 'Yes! Yes! Angry!'"

Feeling a flash of actual anger, Ahmed decided to ridicule the process by going stupidly over-the-top.

"And the next day," he says, "my agent calls me up: 'You booked it.'"

By the time *Executive Decision* came out later that year, Ahmed says, his life had "become dark. Boozing on the Sunset Strip. After-hours parties. I'd wake up at 2 P.M. and do it all over again. It's the same people in the clubs every night. Everyone's trying to fill a void."

"Were you doing all that boozing because you felt guilty for playing terrorists?" I ask him.

"There was an element of that," he replies. "There was an element of not working between those parts. And then I had an epiphany. I called my agent: 'Hey! Don't send me out on these terrorist parts anymore. I'll be open for anything else, but not the terrorist stuff.'" Ahmed pauses. "After that, she never called."

"How often did she call before then?" I ask him.

"Oh, three or four times a week."

And so Ahmed made a decision: "Get the fuck out of Hollywood." He went to Mecca. And what he saw there were "four and a half million people dressed in white—rich, poor, walking side by side, asking for blessings from God."

For ten solid years after his trip to Mecca, Ahmed quit acting and became a stand-up comedian. He still performs regularly, but he says he'll take a terrorist role from time to time if a good one comes along. After all, he notes, nobody accuses Robert De Niro of betraying other Italian-Americans when he plays a mobster.

● ● ●

The evening after our lunch in Westwood, I visit Sayed Badreya, the older Egyptian actor, at his Santa Monica apartment. When I arrive, he's online, looking at photographs of Arabian horses.

"I'm involved in breeding them," he says, "because I don't know if I can keep playing these same parts." He says his daughter was once asked at school what her father did for a living and she replied, "He hijacks airplanes."

Sayed takes his work seriously and has always gone to great lengths to research his roles. In 1991, he started attending a mosque in Culver City, one that was known to attract some militant worshippers, so he could study Islamic radicalism up close. A few years later, some of the mosque's worshippers went to a movie and recognized Sayed. Back at the mosque after Friday prayers, they surrounded him. "They were yelling, right in my face: 'You're helping the Zionist Jews of Hollywood in their agenda to make Islam look bad. For money, you're giving up your heritage.'"

"How were you responding?" I ask.

"I felt guilty," he says. "I knew they were sort of right. But I yelled back at them, 'We have to take their money to make our own movie and tell our own story!' We were yelling so hard we were showering each other with spit."

"What was the movie of yours they saw?" I ask him.

"*Executive* fucking *Decision*," he says.

Sayed says he does all he can to intersperse his terrorist roles with more helpful portrayals of Muslims. He wrote and starred in a well-regarded film, *AmericanEast,* charting the struggles of Muslims in America post-9/11. But he has to play terrorists to pay the bills, so he at least tries to be a realistic one. He does side work as a technical consultant, advising directors on the accuracy of their films. He worked in this capacity on *Executive Decision*. "We had a really beautiful moment in an Arabic wedding scene," Sayed says. "And the producer, Joel Silver, saw it and said, 'No, no. This is nice. I want a fucking bad Arab. We don't want a good Arab.'"

Almost all of the wedding scene was cut from the film, Sayed says. But here's a scene that wasn't cut: One of the terrorists takes a quick break from killing people to read the Koran. "If I'm playing a guy chosen to hijack a plane, that means I'm one of the top soldiers. I'm going on a mission. I'm not going to Mecca. He might recite something in his head if he's religious, but he's not going to open the Bible. But producers get really sensitive if you say, 'No, that's not accurate.'"

In an e-mailed statement, Joel Silver denied the "bad Arab" incident, adding, "Any editorial decisions, made twenty years ago, were strictly creative, and not to perpetuate any stereotypes." I didn't hear back from any of the other producers or directors I approached. Not Peter Berg (*The Kingdom*, another film that has a bad reputation with Muslim actors for its portrayal of the Islamic world), nor Stephen McEveety (Mel Gibson's collaborator on *The Passion of the Christ* and the producer of the *The Stoning of Soraya M.*, in which an Iranian husband has his wife stoned to death), nor Joel Surnow, the co-creator of *24*. Maz told me that his most offensive acting offer ever was for a Joel Surnow production—Fox's short-lived comedy *The 1/2 Hour News Hour*. Maz says he was asked to audition for a sketch about a Middle Eastern architect pitching to rebuild the Twin Towers. The joke was that his design included a bull's-eye right on the building. Howard Gordon, the man behind *Homeland* and *24*, is the only producer I persuade to talk to me. He calls me from his car.

"I came to this issue when I was accused of having Islamophobia in *24*," he says. "We had a family, essentially, of terrorists on the show. The Muslim Public Affairs Council provided an education for me on the power of images."

"What did they say?"

"They asked me to imagine what it might be like to be a Muslim, to have people fear my faith," he replies. "I felt very sympathetic. I didn't want to be a midwife to xenophobia."

Since then, he says, he has done his best. And people have noticed. When I was having lunch with Maz and the other actors at the Lebanese restaurant in Westwood, Howard was one of the only mainstream producers they praised. (*Three Kings'* David O. Russell was another.)

"Anyone with a conscience has to take this seriously," Howard tells me. "I'd often hidden behind the defense that *24* was a counterterrorism show. We rationalized to ourselves that our primary task was to tell a compelling story." But the truth, he knew, was darker than that: "We all have our personal biases and fears—I suspect we're wired to feel threatened by the 'other.' And I include myself in that category."

• • •

In the lobby of a chichi old hotel in Midtown Manhattan, Anthony Azizi warns me that this interview might get heated. And indeed it does. If you want to know the impact that a lifetime of doing these movies can have on a man, spend some time with Anthony Azizi.

Anthony is a veteran of various *CSIs* and *NCISs* and *24*. His death scene in *24*, he says, made it onto a Yahoo list of best deaths ever. (His throat gets slit with a credit card.) He's a big, handsome, intense man who is not, by the way, a Muslim. He's a member of the Iranian spiritualist faith the Bahá'í.

"Hollywood has the power to snap its fingers and make whoever it wants a star," he begins. "It specifically and purposefully doesn't want to see an Arab or a Middle Eastern star. There's too much prejudice and racism—and the people running it, I don't need to go into the specifics of their backgrounds. . . ."

I think I know what he's getting at. But all sorts of producers—not just Jews—are behind insensitive movie portrayals of Muslims. There's Chuck Norris. There's John Musker, director of 1992's *Aladdin*, in which all the "good Arabs" have American accents and all the "bad Arabs" have pseudo-Middle Eastern accents. Stephen McEveety (*The Stoning of Soraya M.*) is Catholic.

Anthony carries on, turning his anger toward Jon Stewart's *Rosewater*, in which the Mexican actor Gael García Bernal plays the Iranian-Canadian reporter Maziar Bahari. "Man, if I saw Jon Stewart, you'd have to hold me back. How dare you hire a Mexican-American to play an Iranian-American, with all these amazing Iranian-American artists. I can't stand it. I'm sick of it. I speak Spanish fluently. . . ."

He effortlessly slides into perfect Spanish for a few seconds, then returns to being Anthony. "Why am I not being hired for Mexican or Latino roles?" he says. "You play my roles, but I can't play yours, and I speak Spanish just as well? Go fuck yourself." Anthony picks up my recorder. "Go fuck yourself, Jon Stewart!" he yells. "Have me on your show if you have the balls! You don't have the balls!"

He's really shouting now. The hotel receptionists keep glancing nervously over at us, wondering whether to intervene. "Hollywood people are pussies!" he rants. "They're racist! They don't want to say, 'I just built a Middle Eastern star!' Here's how I see it—and this is probably the most controversial thing I'll ever say: The only Middle Eastern star was Omar Sharif. The minute he had a relationship with a Jewish-American woman named Barbra Streisand was the death knell for any other Arab-American actor's career. Hear it again! The minute he had a sexual relationship with a Jewish . . ."

"I don't underst—" I start to say.

"How dare you make that an incident where no Arab-American actor can ever get a career again!"

Finally I get my question out, or at least some of it: "But what's the connection between Omar Sharif purportedly having an affair with Barbra Streisand and—"

"I think there's a certain type of producer that doesn't want to see that happen," he says. "They don't want their gem—Barbra Streisand was the gem of the Jewish community—sleeping with the Arab heathen! It caused huge riots in Egypt, too. I'd say the same thing to the Egyptian community. . . ."

Sure, Anthony's Barbra Streisand outburst is crazy. If there *is* a racist conspiracy in Hollywood to rob Middle Eastern actors of roles, it's not a great idea to rail against it with a racist-conspiracy theory of one's own. But think about what Anthony has been subjected to in his career. He and the other men in this story are going through something that future generations will regard as outrageous. They're the bloodthirsty Red Indians surrounding the settlers' wagons in *Stagecoach*. They're the black savages in *The Birth of a Nation* (who were played by white actors in blackface). They are the people Hollywood will be apologizing to tomorrow.

"Don't question my talent," Anthony says. "I should be a star by now. But I'm not. So you explain why."

Perhaps the closest this community has to a star is Navid Negahban. He played, most famously, Abu Nazir in *Homeland* and also the Iraqi in *American Sniper* who helps the U.S. military locate "the butcher." He was Ali, the stoner in *The Stoning of Soraya M.*

"Everyone I've met seems really talented," I tell Anthony. "So why do you think Navid, of all of you . . .?"

"He's hot right now, playing bad guys," Anthony replies. "He loves to play those roles. I love Navid. He's my brother. But there's no longevity in those roles. You always get whacked. Everybody who's still alive in *Homeland* is white! Where is Abu Nazir? He got whacked, 'cause he's brown."

• • •

Getting to meet Navid isn't easy. One minute he's filming in upstate New York, the next he's doing motion capture as a video-game character in Los Angeles before flying off to shoot a movie in Morocco. But I manage to catch him for an hour at a coffee shop near Columbus Circle in New York City. He's already there, chatting with another on-screen terrorist, Herzl Tobey (*The Shield, 24, Homeland*). They've been working on a movie together upstate, so Navid has brought him along to meet me. Navid is very dashing, with an old-fashioned matinee-idol air to him.

"I'm sure you've had a few of the others say, 'I won't do terrorists anymore,'" he says as I sit down.

"Yes," I say.

"I've told them that's the biggest mistake," says Navid. "If we don't play those roles, the character becomes a caricature. [The producers] might get some actor from a different background who looks Middle Eastern." Herzl nods, adding, "The writer is sitting here in America, writing about a world he's completely unfamiliar with. So of course he won't be able to write it with the full depth and sensuality that comes with that world. It's up to us to bring that depth."

I tell Navid that I've noticed that the more prominent the Middle Eastern actor, the more awesome the death. Back when Maz was just starting out, he barely got 'Allah' out before Chuck Norris shot him. But Navid is at the top of the pecking order, the closest thing we have to the late Omar Sharif. I ask him to remind me how Abu Nazir died on *Homeland*.

"Oh, he was graceful," Navid replies. "It was so . . ." He smacks his lips. "He's sitting very gracefully on the floor. On his knees. He's ready. The soldiers run in. Everybody's yelling. But he's calm. He's just looking at all of them very, very calmly. And then he reaches into his pocket and they shoot him. And there's a Koran in his pocket." Navid smiles wistfully. "That was beautiful," he says. "I die well."

8 The Florida State Seminoles: The Champions of Racist Mascots

Dave Zirin

It's easy to oppose the name of the Washington Redskins and call for owner Dan Snyder to change his beloved bigoted brand. After all, it's a dictionary-defined slur bestowed on the NFL franchise by their arch-segregationist, minstrel-loving founder.[1] When you have Native American organizations, leading sportswriters, Republicans as well as Democrats in Congress and even the president say the time has come to change the name, it is not exactly difficult to get on board.

But what about the Florida State Seminoles, whose football team on Monday night won the Vizio/Dow Chemical/Blackwater/Vivid Video BCS National Championship Game? The NCAA, since 2005, has had formal restrictions against naming teams after Native American tribes, and yet there were the Seminole faithful: thousands of overwhelmingly Caucasian fans with feathers in their hair, doing the Tomahawk chop and whooping war chants on national television. Their passions were stirred into a frenzy by a white person, face smeared with war paint, dressed as the legendary chief Osceola riding out on a horse. As Stewart Mandel of *Sports Illustrated* gushed, "Chief Osceola plants the flaming spear in the Rose Bowl. Awesome." (Osceola was adopted after the school quietly retired their previous Native American mascot "Sammy Seminole.")

I have been to dozens of Redskins game and have never seen anything close to this kind of mass interactive minstrelsy. Yet there are no protests against this spectacle, no angry editorials and no politicians jumping on the issue. Why is that? Because as any Florida State fanatic will shout at you, the university has "a formal agreement with Seminole Nation" and that makes everything all right. Fans treat this much-touted agreement like they have a "racism amnesty card" in their back pocket. The approval of the Seminole Nation, they will tell you makes it all A-okay. Actually it doesn't. It doesn't first and foremost because the existence of this "agreement with the Seminole Nation" is a myth.

The agreement is with the Florida Seminole Tribal Council and not the Seminole Nation. The majority of Seminoles don't even live in Florida. They live in Oklahoma, one of the fruits of the Seminole Wars, the Indian Removal Act and The Trail of Tears. These Oklahoma Seminoles—who, remember, are the majority—oppose the name. On October 26, 2013, the Seminole Nation of Oklahoma's governing body passed a resolution that read in part, "The Seminole Nation condemns the use of all American Indian sports team mascots in the public school system, by college and university level and by professional teams."

From *The Nation*, January 7, 2014. © 2014 The Nation Company, LLC. All rights reserved. Used by permission and protected by the Copyright Laws of the United States. The printing, copying, redistribution, or retransmission of this Content without express written permission is prohibited.

As for the Florida Seminole Tribal Council, it is the owner of a series of luxury casino hotels throughout the state where the Seminole "brand" is prominently on display. The Tribal Council also bought the Hard Rock Cafe for $965 million in cash in 2006, which thanks to the Seminoles' "first-nation status" now also offers gambling in its Florida locales. Hard Rock corporate called this "the perfect marriage of two kindred spirits." Seminole Nation Hard Rock Hotel and Casino T-shirts are available for purchase.

For the wealthy and powerful Florida Seminole tribal leaders, the cultural elevation of the football program is a part of their extremely lucrative gaming operation. Defending the school's use of the name is about defending its brand. That is why the chairman of the Florida Seminole Tribe of Florida, James Billie, said, "Anybody come here into Florida trying to tell us to change the name, they better go someplace else, because we're not changing the name."

Some might say that this is fine with them. After all, given the incalculable wealth stolen from Native American tribes over the centuries, what is wrong with them getting some of it back? That would be fine, except for the stubborn fact that gambling wealth flows into very few hands. The majority of Native Americans languish in dire poverty, with reservation poverty listed at 50 percent in the last census.

Another argument for the Florida State Seminoles' keeping their name is that it actually educates people and keeps the history from being eradicated. This is self-serving codswallop, like saying a Muhammad Ali mousepad teaches people about his resistance to the war in Vietnam. Branding and cultural appropriation is not history. It's anti-history. Take school mascot Chief Osceola as an example. If people in the stands and at home actually knew who Osceola was, the ritual of his riding a horse and throwing a spear before games would be an outrage, and not just because the Seminoles, who lived and fought in swampy everglades, tended not to ride horses. Chief Osceola was a great resistance fighter and leader of the Second Seminole War in Florida.

As written in the terrific book *101 Changemakers: Rebels and Radicals Who Changed US History*, "Osceola became an international symbol of the Seminole Nation's refusal to surrender. He was a renowned public speaker and a fierce fighter who was also an opponent of the US slave system. One of his two wives was a woman of African descent and it was not uncommon for escaped slaves to become a part of Seminole Nation. Osceola's army frustrated the entire US Government, five separate Army generals, at a cost to the US Treasury of more than 20 million dollars. . . . On October 21, 1837, Osceola met with US government officials to discuss a peace treaty. When he arrived, he was captured and imprisoned. Osceola's respect was so widespread that this maneuver was widely condemned and viewed as a dishonorable way to bring down the great warrior."[2]

Osceola was nothing less than the American Mandela, but a Nelson Mandela who did not survive Robben Island. Imagine before a South African soccer game, a white person in black face, dressed like Mandela, running out to midfield to psyche up the crowd. Not even Rick Reilly would say that this was somehow educating people about African resistance to apartheid.[3] No one is getting educated about Osceola or the Seminole Wars. Instead their heroic resistance has been translated for football purposes to being "tough." This "respect" for their toughness not only reduces a rich and varied Seminole culture to a savage culture of war, it is also an unspoken way to to praise our own ability to engineer their conquest.

The last argument, which is perhaps the most common, is, "Changing the name of the Redskins or the Seminoles . . . where does the politically correct madness end? Do we stop using 'Giants' because it offends tall people? Or 'Cowboys' because it offends cowboys?" This kind of witticism is actually profoundly insulting because there was this thing called "history" that happened, and in this "history" giants were not subject to mass displacement and genocide. Once 100 percent of this country, Native Americans are now 0.9 percent, and we play sports on their graves. Their rituals and dress are our own commercialized entertainment. We turn our eyes to the field and away from the way institutionalized racism continues to define the lives of the overwhelming majority to Native Americans who do not own a stake in the Hard Rock Cafe. That gets us to the final problem with Seminole nation and all Native American mascoting. It makes us more ignorant about our own collective history. I'm not sure we can afford it.

NOTES

1. Tomasky, Michael. (2011, November 10). "The Racist Redskins" [Review of the book *Showdown: JFK and the Integration of the Washington Redskins* by Thomas G. Smith]. *The New York Review of Books*.

2. Michelle Bollinger and Dao X. Tran (eds.), *101 Changemakers: Rebels and Radical Who Changed US History*. Haymarket Books © 2012.

3. Zirin, D. (2013, September 18). "Rick Reilly and the Most Irredeemably Stupid Defense of the Redskins Name You Will Ever Read." *The Nation*.

9 Michael Brown's Unremarkable Humanity

Ta-Nehisi Coates

The New York Times has a feature[1] today looking at the brief life of Michael Brown, informing us that he was "no angel." The reasons for this are many. Brown smoked marijuana. He lived in a community that "had rough patches." He wrote rap songs that were "by turns contemplative and vulgar." He shoplifted and pushed a store clerk who tried to stop him. These details certainly paint a portrait of a young man who failed to be angelic. That is because no person is angelic—least of all teenagers—and there is very little in this piece that distinguishes Brown from any other kid his age.

What horrifies a lot of us beholding the spectacle of Ferguson, beholding the spectacle of Sanford,[2] of Jacksonville,[3] is how easily we could see ourselves in these kids. I shudder to think of my reaction, at 17, to some strange dude following me through my own housing development. I shudder to think of my reaction, at 17, to some other strange dude pulling up next to me and telling me to turn down my music.

And if Michael Brown was not angelic, I was practically demonic. I had my first drink when I was 11. I once brawled in the cafeteria after getting hit in the head with a steel trash can. In my junior year I failed five out of seven classes. By the time I graduated from high school, I had been arrested for assaulting a teacher and been kicked out of school (twice). And yet no one who knew me thought I had the least bit of thug in me. That is because I also read a lot of books, loved my Commodore 64, and ghostwrote love notes for my friends. In other words, I was a human being. A large number of American teenagers live exactly like Michael Brown. Very few of them are shot in the head and left to bake on the pavement.

The "angelic" standard was not one created by the reporter. It was created by a society that cannot face itself, and thus must employ a dubious "morality" to hide its sins. It is reinforced by people who have embraced the notion of "twice as good" while avoiding the circumstances which gave that notion birth. Consider how easily living in a community "with rough patches" becomes part of a list of ostensible sins. Consider how easily "black-on-black crime" becomes not a marker of a shameful legacy of segregation but a moral failing.

We've been through this before.[4] We will almost certainly go through it again.

© 2014 The Atlantic Media Co., as first published in *The Atlantic Magazine*. All rights reserved. Distributed by Tribune Content Agency, LLC.

NOTES

1. Eligon, J. (2014, August 24). Michael Brown Spent Last Weeks Grappling With Problems and Promise. *The New York Times.*

2. Coates, T. (2013, July 13). On the Killing of Trayvon Martin by George Zimmerman. *The Atlantic.*

3. Coates, T. (2014, February 17). Black Boy Interrupted. *The Atlantic.*

4. Touré. (2014). Black America and the burden of the perfect victim. The *Washington Post.*

10 When You Forget to Whistle Vivaldi

Tressie McMillan Cottom

Last week Johnathan Ferrell had a horrible car crash. He broke out the back window to escape and walked, injured, to the nearest home hoping for help. Ferrell may have been too hurt, too in shock to remember to whistle Vivaldi. Ferrell is dead.[1]

Social psychologist Claude Steele revolutionized our understanding of the daily context and cognitive effects of stereotypes and bias. The title of his book alludes to a story his friend, *New York Times* writer Brent Staples, once shared.[2] An African American man, Staples, recounts how his physical presence terrified whites as he moved about Chicago as a free citizen and graduate student. To counter the negative effects of white fear he took to whistling a classical music piece by Italian composer Vivaldi. It was a signal to the victimless victims of his blackness that he was safe. Dangerous black men do not listen to classical music, or so the hope goes. The incongruence between Staples' musical choices and the stereotype of him as a predator were meant to disrupt the implicit, unexamined racist assumptions of him. It seems trite perhaps, an attempt to make whites feel at ease unless we recall the potential consequences of white disease for black lives.

I do not know many black people who do not have a similar coping mechanism. I have been known to wear university branded clothing when I am shopping for real estate. A friend straightens her hair when she is job seeking. Another friend, a Hispanic male, told me that he shaves all his facial hair when entertaining white clients to signal that he is respectable. While stereotype threat can occur to any member of any group, it occurs most frequently and with more dangerous consequences for groups for whom there are more and stronger negative beliefs.

Of course, the oft-quoted idiom that respectability politics will not save you is true. Just as wearing long johns is not a preventative measure against rape for women, affecting middle class white behaviors is not a protective measure but a talisman. In exerting any measure of control over signaling that we are not dangerous or violent or criminal we are mostly assuaging the cognitive stress that constant management of social situations causes.

That stress has real consequences. Steele inspired an entire body of research on those effects. When the object of a stereotype is aware of the negative perception of her, that awareness constrains all manner of ability and performance. From testing scores of women who know the others in the room believe women cannot do math to missing a sports play when one is reminded that Asians don't have hops, the effects of stereotype threat are real.

Republished with permission of Tressie McMillan Cottom.

Perhaps more interesting to me is what Steele described as the constant background processing that stereotyped people engage. It's like running too many programs in the background of your computer as you try to play a YouTube video. Just as the extra processing, invisible to the naked eye, impacts the video experience the cognitive version compromises the functioning of our most sophisticated machines: human bodies.

I mentioned just today to a colleague that for all we social scientists like to talk about structural privilege it might be this social-psychological privilege that is the most valuable. Imagine the productivity of your laptop when all background programs are closed. Now imagine your life when those background processes are rarely, if ever, activated because of the social position your genetic characteristics afford you.

Of course, privilege is sometimes structural. But the murder of Johnathan Ferrell reminds us that activation of stereotype threat in daily interactions can be aided and abetted by organizational processes like the characterization of a police call to 911 and structural legitimacy like the authority of the police to shoot first and ask questions later. I am choosing to ignore how that process was set in motion. Perhaps better feminist scholars than myself can explore the historical, cultural gendered fear that legitimizes the unconscious bias of black men as sexual and criminal predators. I find I do not have the stomach for it today.

I just read an article that quotes Ferrell's family at length. His family's attorney did not just want us to know that Ferrell was a friend and son but that: "He's engaged to be married, he has a dog and a cat, he was driving a Toyota Camry, he survived an accident, had 3.7 GPA, a chemistry major. This is not someone who posed a threat to the officers or anyone else, this is an everyday American."

A 3.7 GPA.

They want us to know that their murdered friend, son, brother and cousin had a 3.7 GPA.

Ferrell may have been too injured, too shocked to whistle Vivaldi to all he encountered the night he was shot. It may not have helped if he had through slammed doors, over police sirens, and gunfire. But even in death his family cannot help but signal to us all that he was a student and, by extension, a human being whose death should matter.

Whistling Vivaldi in tribute, a talisman and hope that justice will hear what its executor's did not.

NOTES

1. Lee, T. (2013, September 25). The 911 call that led to Jonathan Ferrell's death.
2. Pronin, E. (2010, May 1). Not Just Whistling Vivaldi.

Suggestions for Further Reading

Cole, David. *No Equal Justice: Race and Class in the American Criminal Justice System*. New York: The New Press, 2000.

Fraser, Steve, and Gary Gerstle. *Ruling America: A History of Wealth and Power in a Democracy*. Cambridge, MA: Harvard University Press, 2005.

Goings, Kenneth W. *Mammy and Uncle Mose: Black Collectibles and American Stereotyping*. Bloomington, IN: Indiana University Press, 1994.

Harding, Sandra, and Merrill B. Hintikka. *Discovering Reality: Feminist Perspectives on Epistemology, Metaphysics, Methodology, and Philosophy of Science,* 2nd ed. New York: Springer, 2007.

Harvey, David. *Spaces of Global Capitalism: A Theory of Uneven Geographical Development*. New York: Verso, 2006.

Holtzman, Linda. *Media Messages: What Film, Television, and Popular Music Teach Us About Race, Class, Gender, and Sexual Orientation*. Armonk, NY: M. F. Sharp, 2000.

hooks, bell. *Teaching to Transgress: Education as the Practice of Freedom*. New York: Routledge, 1994.

Jhalley, Sut. *The Spectacle of Accumulation: Essays in Culture, Media and Politics*. New York: Peter Lang International Academic Publishers, 2011.

Kimmel, Michael. *Guyland: The Perilous World Where Boys Become Men*. New York: Harper, 2009.

Klein, Naomi. *No Logo: 10th Anniversary Edition*. New York: Picador, 2009.

Lewis, Amanda E. *Race in the Schoolyard*. New Brunswick, NJ: Rutgers University Press, 2003.

Loewen, James. *Lies My Teacher Told Me: Everything Your American History Textbook Got Wrong,* Rev. ed. New York: New Press, 2008.

Madrick, Jeff. *The Case for Big Government*. Princeton, NJ: Princeton University Press, 2008.

Mazzocco, Dennis W. *Networks of Power: Corporate TV's Threat to Democracy*. Boston: South End Press, 1999.

Orenstein, Peggy. *Cinderella Ate My Daughter: Dispatches from the Frontlines of the New Girlie-Girl Culture*. New York: Harper, 2012.

———. *Schoolgirls: Young Women, Self-Esteem, and the Confidence Gap*. New York: Anchor, 1995.

Parenti, Michael. *Inventing Reality,* 2nd ed. New York: St. Martin's Press, 1992.

Sadker, David, Myra Sadker, and Karen Zittleman. *Still Failing at Fairness: How Gender Bias Cheats Boys and Girls in School and What We Can Do About It*. New York: Scribner, 2009.

Schor, Juliet B. *Born to Buy: The Commercialized Child and the New Consumer Culture*. New York: Scribner, 2004.

Steele, Claude. *Whistling Vivaldi: How Stereotypes Affect Us and What We Can Do*. New York: Norton, 2011.

Thompson, Becky W. *A Hunger So Wide and So Deep,* 2nd ed. Minneapolis, MN: University of Minnesota Press, 1996.

Valenti, Jessica. *The Purity Myth: How America's Obsession with Virginity Is Hurting Young Women*. Berkeley, CA: Seal Press, 2009.

Yates, Michael D., ed. *More Unequal: Aspects of Class in the United States*. New York: Monthly Review Press, 2007.

PART IX

Social Change: Revisioning the Future and Making a Difference

An adequate understanding of the nature and causes of race, class, and gender oppression is a critical first step toward moving beyond these issues. Solutions to problems are generated, at least in part, by the way we pose them. That is why so much of this book is devoted to defining and analyzing the nature of these systems of oppression. Only when we appreciate the subtle and complex factors that combine to create a society in which wealth, privilege, and opportunity are unequally apportioned will we be able to formulate viable proposals for bringing about social change.

What, then, have the selections in this book told us about racism, sexism, heterosexism, and class divisions? First, that there is no single cause. Eliminating these forms of oppression will involve changes at the personal, social, political, and economic level. It will require us to think differently about ourselves and others and to see the world through new lenses and using new categories. We will have to learn to pay close attention to our attitudes and behavior and ask what values and what kinds of relationship they create and maintain, both consciously and unconsciously. We will have to reevaluate virtually every institution in society and critically appraise the ways in which those institutions, intentionally or unintentionally, privilege some and disadvantage others in what we take to be their normal course of operations. As we identify the ways in which our society reproduces the forms of inequality and privilege that we have been studying, we will have to act to change them. In short, we must scrutinize every aspect of economic, political, and social life with a view to asking whose interests are served and whose are denied when the world is organized in this way.

In Selection 1, poet and writer Audre Lorde suggests that we will need to begin by redefining and rethinking the meaning of difference. While acknowledging that real differences of race, age, and sexuality exist, Lorde argues that it is not these differences in themselves that separate us as much as it is our refusal to acknowledge them and the role they play in shaping our relationships and social institutions. Denying or distorting those differences keeps us apart; embracing them can provide a new starting point from which to work together to reconstruct our world.

In Selection 2, bell hooks joins Audre Lorde in urging us to rethink difference. At the same time, she continues another of the major themes of this book: understanding the ways in which sex, race, and class function as interlocking, mutually supportive, systems of domination. While acknowledging past failures of much feminist theory to adequately address issues of race, racism, and class, hooks argues that a revisioned feminism can provide the most comprehensive perspective from which to challenge all forms of oppression and domination. This is true, she maintains, because sexism is the form of oppression we confront daily: "Sexism directly shapes and determines relations of power in our private lives, in familiar social spaces, in that most intimate context 'home' and in that most intimate sphere of relations 'family.'" hooks envisions a process of education and consciousness raising whereby women from diverse backgrounds come together in small groups to talk about feminism and to learn from one another, and she calls on men as well to commit themselves to overthrowing patriarchal domination.

Cooper Thompson picks up the challenge in Selection 3. A new vision of society will require new choices and options for men as well as women. In his essay, Thompson is profoundly critical of the ways in which boys are socialized to believe that violence is an acceptable, "even desirable" way to establish their manhood and to negotiate difference. He believes that this socialization leads to both misogyny and homophobia and makes it difficult for men to form warm and loving friendships with members of both sexes. Because the social costs of prevailing conceptions of masculinity are so high, Thompson urges us to develop a new vision of the word "man," one that allows boys to claim many of the qualities previously defined as "feminine." Thompson concludes with a warning: "The survival of our society may rest on the degree to which we are able to teach men to cherish life."

Confronted by the enormous scale of the work to be done, many of us feel overwhelmed and disheartened. But significant and lasting change in our society will only come about when each of us assumes responsibility for making a difference. In Selection 4, Andrea Ayvazian suggests that one way to overcome a sense of immobilization and despair is to become an ally of those who are oppressed. According to Ayvazian, "An ally is a member of a dominant group in our society who works to dismantle any form of oppression from which she or he receives the benefit." By acting consciously and deliberately to challenge oppression and to make privilege visible, allies provide role models for us all and demonstrate ways in which each of us can act as a powerful agent of change. Several of the articles that follow provide concrete examples of what this might mean.

Selection 4 is by Matthew Rothschild, former editor of *The Progressive*, and like many of the other authors in this section, he makes no pretense of neutrality. The stakes are too high and the possibilities of disaster are ever more severe. The time is now, and we must fight for equality and justice for all people everywhere. Rothschild makes clear that to see the social change we want, we must "demand the impossible"—the title of his piece.

In Selection 6, Tasbeeh Hewees writes about the black feminist founders of the Black Lives Matter movement, which began in response to the police violence in black communities. This movement against state-authorized discrimination and brutality emerges from a history of organizing among women of color and queer people that takes the intersectionality of oppression as a starting point. This piece demonstrates how in "addressing the specific struggles of black queer women . . . they [the founders of Black Lives Matter] are confronting a system that subjugates everyone."

Scot Nakagawa's piece, Selection 7, expands the discussion of what it means to be an ally by asking how Asian Americans can put a challenge to anti-blackness at the center of their work for racial justice. Nakagawa argues that the role of Asian Americans in this political moment is to acknowledge the leadership of the Black Lives Matter movement and to connect to organized resistance to the varied forms of oppression that are produced by an ideology of white supremacy. For Nakagawa, this is a time to tell complex stories that can lead to greater understanding of the ways in which racial injustice is created, sustained, and disrupted, and that centering black liberation in activist work requires us to make connections and see intersections, not ignore them for the sake of simplicity.

1 Age, Race, Class, and Sex

Women Redefining Difference

Audre Lorde

Much of Western European history conditions us to see human differences in simplistic oppression to each other: dominant/subordinate, good/bad, up/down, superior/inferior. In a society where the good is defined in terms of profit rather than in terms of human need, there must always be some group of people who, through systematized oppression, can be made to feel surplus, to occupy the place of the dehumanized inferior. Within this society, that group is made up of Black and Third World people, working-class people, older people, and women.

As a forty-nine-year-old Black lesbian feminist socialist mother of two, including one boy, and a member of an interracial couple, I usually find myself a part of some group defined as other, deviant, inferior, or just plain wrong. Traditionally, in american society, it is the members of oppressed, objectified groups who are expected to stretch out and bridge the gap between the actualities of our lives and the consciousness of our oppressor. For in order to survive, those of us for whom oppression is as american as apple pie have always had to be watchers, to become familiar with the language and manners of the oppressor, even sometimes adopting them for some illusion of protection. Whenever the need for some pretense of communication arises, those who profit from our oppression call upon us to share our knowledge with them. In other words, it is the responsibility of the oppressed to teach the oppressors their mistakes. I am responsible for educating teachers who dismiss my children's culture in school. Black and Third World people are expected to educate white people as to our humanity. Women are expected to educate men. Lesbians and gay men are expected to educate the heterosexual world. The oppressors maintain their position and evade responsibility for their own actions. There is a constant drain of energy which might be better used in redefining ourselves and devising realistic scenarios for altering the present and constructing the future.

Institutionalized rejection of difference is an absolute necessity in a profit economy which needs outsiders as surplus people. As members of such an economy, we have *all* been programmed to respond to the human differences between us with fear and loathing and to handle that difference in one of three ways: ignore it, and if that is not possible, copy it if we think it is dominant, or destroy it if we think it is subordinate. But we have no patterns for relating across our human differences as equals. As a result, those differences have been misnamed and misused in the service of separation and confusion.

Certainly there are very real differences between us of race, age, and sex. But it is not those differences between us that are separating us. It is rather our refusal to

From *Sister Outsider*, by Audre Lorde, published by Crossing Press. Copyright © 1984, 2007 by Audre Lorde. Used herein by permission of the Charlotte Sheedy Literary Agency.

recognize those differences, and to examine the distortions which result from our misnaming them and their effects upon human behavior and expectation.

Racism, the belief in the inherent superiority of one race over all others and thereby the right to dominance. Sexism, the belief in the inherent superiority of one sex over the other and thereby the right to dominance. Ageism. Heterosexism. Elitism, Classism.

It is a lifetime pursuit for each one of us to extract these distortions from our living at the same time as we recognize, reclaim, and define those differences upon which they are imposed. For we have all been raised in a society where those distortions were endemic within our living. Too often, we pour the energy needed for recognizing and exploring difference into pretending those differences are insurmountable barriers, or that they do not exist at all. This results in a voluntary isolation, or false and treacherous connections. Either way, we do not develop tools for using human difference as a springboard for creative change within our lives. We speak not of human difference, but of human deviance.

Somewhere, on the edge of consciousness, there is what I call a *mythical norm,* which each one of us within our hearts knows "that is not me." In america, this norm is usually defined as white, thin, male, young, heterosexual, christian, and financially secure. It is with this mythical norm that the trappings of power reside within society. Those of us who stand outside that power often identify one way in which we are different, and we assume that to be the primary cause of all oppression, forgetting other distortions around difference, some of which we ourselves may be practicing. By and large within the women's movement today, white women focus upon their oppression as women and ignore differences of race, sexual preference, class, and age. There is a pretense to a homogeneity of experience covered by the word *sisterhood* that does not in fact exist.

Unacknowledged class differences rob women of each others' energy and creative insight. Recently a women's magazine collective made the decision for one issue to print only prose, saying poetry was a less "rigorous" or "serious" art form. Yet even the form our creativity takes is often a class issue. Of all the art forms, poetry is the most economical. It is the one which is the most secret, which requires the least physical labor, the least material, and the one which can be done between shifts, in the hospital pantry, on the subway, and on scraps of surplus paper. Over the last few years, writing a novel on tight finances, I came to appreciate the enormous differences in the material demands between poetry and prose. As we reclaim our literature, poetry has been the major voice of poor, working class, and Colored women. A room of one's own may be a necessity for writing prose, but so are reams of paper, a typewriter, and plenty of time. The actual requirements to produce the visual arts also help determine, along class lines, whose art is whose. In this day of inflated prices for material, who are our sculptors, our painters, our photographers? When we speak of broadly based women's culture, we need to be aware of the effect of class and economic differences on the supplies available for producing art.

As we move toward creating a society within which we can each flourish, ageism is another distortion of relationship which interferes with our vision. By ignoring the past, we are encouraged to repeat its mistakes. The "generation gap" is an important social tool for any repressive society. If the younger members of a community view the older members as contemptible or suspect or excess, they will never be able to join hands and examine the living memories of the community, nor ask the all important question, "Why?" This gives rise to a historical amnesia that keeps us working to invent the wheel every time we have to go to the store for bread.

We find ourselves having to repeat and relearn the same old lessons over and over that our mothers did because we do not pass on what we have learned, or because we are unable to listen. For instance, how many times has this all been said before? For another, who would have believed that once again our daughters are allowing their bodies to be hampered and purgatoried by girdles and high heels and hobble skirts?

Ignoring the differences of race between women and the implications of those differences presents the most serious threat to the mobilization of women's joint power.

As white women ignore their built-in privilege of whiteness and define woman in terms of their own experience alone, then women of Color become "other," the outsider whose experience and tradition is too "alien" to comprehend. An example of this is the signal absence of the experience of women of Color as a resource for women's studies courses. The literature of women of Color is seldom included in women's literature courses and almost never in other literature courses, nor in women's studies as a whole. All too often, the excuse given is that the literatures of women of Color can only be taught by Colored women, or that they are too difficult to understand, or that classes cannot "get into" them because they come out of experiences that are "too different." I have heard this argument presented by white women of otherwise quite clear intelligence, women who seem to have no trouble at all teaching and reviewing work that comes out of the vastly different experiences of Shakespeare, Molière, Dostoyefsky, and Aristophanes. Surely there must be some other explanation.

This is a very complex question, but I believe one of the reasons white women have such difficulty reading Black women's work is because of their reluctance to see Black women as women and different from themselves. To examine Black women's literature effectively requires that we be seen as whole people in our actual complexities—as individuals, as women, as human—rather than as one of those problematic but familiar stereotypes provided in this society in place of genuine images of Black women. And I believe this holds true for the literatures of other women of Color who are not Black.

The literatures of all women of Color recreate the textures of our lives, and many white women are heavily invested in ignoring the real differences. For as long as any difference between us means one of us must be inferior, then the recognition of any difference must be fraught with guilt. To allow women of Color to step out of stereotypes is too guilt provoking, for it threatens the complacency of those women who view oppression only in terms of sex.

Refusing to recognize difference makes it impossible to see the different problems and pitfalls facing us as women.

Thus, in a patriarchal power system where whiteskin privilege is a major prop, the entrapments used to neutralize Black women and white women are not the same. For example, it is easy for Black women to be used by the power structure against

Black men, not because they are men, but because they are Black. Therefore, for Black women, it is necessary at all times to separate the needs of the oppressor from our own legitimate conflicts within our communities. This same problem does not exist for white women. Black women and men have shared racist oppression and still share it, although in different ways. Out of that shared oppression we have developed joint defenses and joint vulnerabilities to each other that are not duplicated in the white community, with the exception of the relationship between Jewish women and Jewish men.

On the other hand, white women face the pitfall of being seduced into joining the oppressor under the pretense of sharing power. This possibility does not exist in the same way for women of Color. The tokenism that is sometimes extended to us is not an invitation to join power; our racial "otherness" is a visible reality that makes that quite clear. For white women there is a wider range of pretended choices and rewards for identifying with patriarchal power and its tools.

Today, with the defeat of ERA, the tightening economy, and increased conservatism, it is easier once again for white women to believe the dangerous fantasy that if you are good enough, pretty enough, sweet enough, quiet enough, teach the children to behave, hate the right people, and marry the right men, then you will be allowed to co-exist with patriarchy in the relative peace, at least until a man needs your job or the neighborhood rapist happens along. And true, unless one lives and loves in the trenches it is difficult to remember that the war against dehumanization is ceaseless.

But Black women and our children know the fabric of our lives is stitched with violence and with hatred, that there is no rest. We do not deal with it only on the picket lines, or in dark midnight alleys, or in the places where we dare to verbalize our resistance. For us, increasingly, violence weaves through the daily tissues of our living—in the supermarket, in the classroom, in the elevator, in the clinic and the schoolyard, from the plumber, the baker, the saleswoman, the bus driver, the bank teller, the waitress who does not serve us.

Some problems we share as women, some we do not. You fear your children will grow up to join the patriarchy and testify against you, we fear our children will be dragged from a car and shot down in the street, and you will turn your backs upon the reasons they are dying.

The threat of difference has been no less blinding to people of Color. Those of us who are Black must see that the reality of our lives and our struggle does not make us immune to the errors of ignoring and misnaming difference. Within Black communities where racism is a living reality, differences among us often seem dangerous and suspect. The need for unity is often misnamed as a need for homogeneity, and a Black feminist vision mistaken for betrayal of our common interests as a people. Because of the continuous battle against racial erasure that Black women and Black men share, some Black women still refuse to recognize that we are also oppressed as women, and that sexual hostility against Black women is practiced not only by the white racist society, but implemented within our Black communities as well. It is a disease striking the heart of Black nationhood, and silence will not make it disappear. Exacerbated by racism and the pressures of powerlessness, violence against Black women and children often becomes a standard within tour communities, one by which manliness can be measured. But these woman-hating acts are rarely discussed as crimes against Black women.

As a group, women of Color are the lowest paid wage earners in america. We are the primary targets of abortion and sterilization abuse, here and abroad. In certain parts of Africa, small girls are still being sewed shut between their legs to keep them docile and for men's pleasure. This is known as female circumcision, and it is not a cultural affair as the late Jomo Kenyatta insisted, it is a crime against Black women.

Black women's literature is full of the pain of frequent assault, not only by a racist patriarchy, but also by Black men. Yet the necessity for and history of shared battle have made us, Black women, particularly vulnerable to the false accusation that anti-sexist is anti-Black. Meanwhile, womanhating as a recourse of the powerless is sapping strength from Black communities, and our very lives. Rape is on the increase, reported and unreported, and rape is not aggressive sexuality, it is sexualized aggression. As Kalamu ya Salaam, a Black male writer, points out, "As long as male domination exists, rape will exist. Only women revolting and men made conscious of their responsibility to fight sexism can collectively stop rape."[1]

Differences between ourselves as Black women are also being misnamed and used to separate us from one another. As a Black lesbian feminist comfortable with the many different ingredients of my identity, and a woman committed to racial and sexual freedom from oppression, I find I am constantly being encouraged to pluck out some one aspect of myself and present this as the meaningful whole, eclipsing or denying the other parts of self. But this is a destructive and fragmenting way to live. My fullest concentration of energy is available to me only when I integrate all the parts of who I am, openly, allowing power from particular sources of my living to flow back and forth freely through all my different selves, without the restrictions of externally imposed definition. Only then can I bring myself and my energies as a whole to the service of those struggles which I embrace as part of my living.

A fear of lesbians, or of being accused of being a lesbian, has led many Black women into testifying against themselves. It has led some of us into destructive alliances, and others into despair and isolation. In the white women's communities, heterosexism is sometimes a result of identifying with the white patriarchy, a rejection of that interdependence between women-identified women which allows the self to be, rather than to be used in the service of men. Sometimes it reflects a diehard belief in the protective coloration of heterosexual relationships, sometimes a self-hate which all women have to fight against, taught us from birth.

Although elements of these attitudes exist for all women, there are particular resonances of heterosexism and homophobia among Black women. Despite the fact that woman-bonding has a long and honorable history in the African and African-american communities, and despite the knowledge and accomplishments of many strong and creative women-identified Black women in the political, social and cultural fields, heterosexual Black women often tend to ignore or discount the existence and work of Black lesbians. Part of this attitude has come from an understandable terror of Black male attack within the close confines of Black society, where the punishment for any female self-assertion is still to be accused of being a lesbian and therefore unworthy of the attention or support of the scarce Black male. But part of this need to misname and ignore Black lesbians comes from a very real fear that openly women-identified Black women who are no longer dependent upon men for their self-definition may well reorder our whole concept of social relationships.

Black women who once insisted that lesbianism was a white woman's problem now insist that Black lesbians are a threat to Black nationhood, are consorting with the enemy, are basically un-Black. These accusations, coming from the very women to whom we look for deep and real understanding, have served to keep many Black lesbians in hiding, caught between the racism of white women and the homophobia of their sisters. Often, their work has been ignored, trivialized, or misnamed, as with the work of Angelina Grimke, Alice Dunbar-Nelson, Lorraine Hansberry. Yet women-bonded women have always been some part of the power of Black communities, from our unmarried aunts to the amazons of Dahomey.

And it is certainly not Black lesbians who are assaulting women and raping children and grandmothers on the streets of our communities.

Across this country, as in Boston during the spring of 1979 following the unsolved murders of twelve Black women, Black lesbians are spearheading movements against violence against Black women.

What are the particular details within each of our lives that can be scrutinized and altered to help bring about change? How do we redefine difference for all women? It is not our differences which separate women, but our reluctance to recognize those differences and to deal effectively with the distortions which have resulted from the ignoring and misnaming of those differences.

As a tool of social control, women have been encouraged to recognize only one area of human difference as legitimate, those differences which exist between women and men. And we have learned to deal across those differences with the urgency of all oppressed subordinates. All of us have had to learn to live or work or coexist with men, from our fathers on. We have recognized and negotiated these differences, even when this recognition only continued the old dominant/subordinate mode of human relationship, where the oppressed must recognize the masters' difference in order to survive.

But our future survival is predicated upon our ability to relate within equality. As women, we must root our internalized patterns of oppression within ourselves if we are to move beyond the most superficial aspects of social change. Now we must recognize differences among women who are our equals, neither inferior nor superior, and devise ways to use each others' difference to enrich our visions and our joint struggles.

The future of our earth may depend upon the ability of all women to identify and develop new definitions of power and new patterns of relating across difference. The old definitions have not served us, nor the earth that supports us. The old patterns, no matter how cleverly rearranged to imitate progress, still condemn us to cosmetically altered repetitions of the same old exchanges, the same old guilt, hatred, recrimination, lamentation, and suspicion.

For we have, built into all of us, old blueprints of expectation and response, old structures of oppression, and these must be altered at the same time as we alter the living conditions which are a result of those structures. For the master's tools will never dismantle the master's house.

As Paulo Freire shows so well in *The Pedagogy of the Oppressed*,[2] the true focus of revolutionary change is never merely the oppressive situations which we seek to escape, but that piece of the oppressor which is planted deep within each of us, and which knows only the oppressor's tactics, the oppressors' relationships.

Change means growth, and growth can be painful. But we sharpen self-definition by exposing the self in work and struggle together with those whom we define as different from ourselves, although sharing the same goals. For Black and white, old and young, lesbian and heterosexual women alike, this can mean new paths to our survival.

We have chosen each other
and the edge of each others battles
the war is the same
if we lose
someday women's blood will congeal
upon a dead planet
if we win
there is no telling
we seek beyond history
for a new and more possible meaning.[3]

NOTES

1. From "Rape: A Radical Analysis, An African-American Perspective" by Kalamu ya Salaam in *Black Books Bulletin,* vol. 6, no. 4 (1980).

2. Seabury Press, New York, 1970.

3. From "Outlines," unpublished poem.

2 Feminism

A Transformational Politic
bell hooks

We live in a world in crisis—a world governed by politics of domination, one in which the belief in a notion of superior and inferior, and its concomitant ideology—that the superior should rule over the inferior—affects the lives of all people everywhere, whether poor or privileged, literate or illiterate. Systematic dehumanization, world-wide famine, ecological devastation, industrial contamination, and the possibility of nuclear destruction are realities which remind us daily that we are in crisis. Contemporary feminist thinkers often cite sexual politics as the origin of this crisis. They point to the insistence on difference as that factor which becomes the occasion for separation and domination and suggest that differentiation of status between females and males globally is an indication that patriarchal domination of the planet is the root of the problem. Such an assumption has fostered the notion that elimination of sexist oppression would necessarily lead to the eradication of all forms of domination. It is an argument that has led influential Western white women to feel that feminist movement should be *the* central political agenda for females globally. Ideologically, thinking in this direction enables Western women, especially privileged white women, to suggest that racism and class exploitation are merely the offspring of the parent system: patriarchy. Within feminist movement in the West, this has led to the assumption that resisting patriarchal domination is a more legitimate feminist action than resisting racism and other forms of domination. Such thinking prevails despite radical critiques made by black women and other women of color who question this proposition. To speculate that an oppositional division between men and women existed in early human communities is to impose on the past, on these non-white groups, a world view that fits all too neatly within contemporary feminist paradigms that name man as the enemy and woman as the victim.

Clearly, differentiation between strong and weak, powerful and powerless, has been a central defining aspect of gender globally, carrying with it the assumption that men should have greater authority than women, and should rule over them. As significant and important as this fact is, it should not obscure the reality that women can and do participate in politics of domination, as perpetrators as well as victims—that we dominate, that we are dominated. If focus on patriarchal domination masks this reality or becomes the means by which women deflect attention from the real conditions and circumstances of our lives, then women cooperate in suppressing and promoting false consciousness, inhibiting our capacity to assume responsibility for transforming ourselves and society.

Copyright 2014 from *Talking Back: Thinking Feminist, Thinking Black,* by bell hooks. Reproduced by permission of Taylor and Francis Group, LLC, a division of Informa plc.

Thinking speculatively about early human social arrangement, about women and men struggling to survive in small communities, it is likely that the parent–child relationship with its very real imposed survival structure of dependency, of strong and weak, of powerful and powerless, was a site for the construction of a paradigm of domination. While this circumstance of dependency is not necessarily one that leads to domination, it lends itself to the enactment of a social drama wherein domination could easily occur as a means of exercising and maintaining control. This speculation does not place women outside the practice of domination, in the exclusive role of victim. It centrally names women as agents of domination, as potential theoreticians, and creators of a paradigm for social relationships wherein those groups of individuals designated as "strong" exercise power both benevolently and coercively over those designated as "weak."

Emphasizing paradigms of domination that call attention to woman's capacity to dominate is one way to deconstruct and challenge the simplistic notion that man is the enemy, woman the victim; the notion that men have always been the oppressors. Such thinking enables us to examine our role as women in the perpetuation and maintenance of systems of domination. To understand domination, we must understand that our capacity as women and men to be either dominated or dominating is a point of connection, of commonality. Even though I speak from the particular experience of living as a black woman in the United States, a white-supremacist, capitalist, patriarchal society, where small numbers of white men (and honorary "white men") constitute ruling groups, I understand that in many places in the world oppressed and oppressor share the same color. I understand that right here in this room, oppressed and oppressor share the same gender. Right now as I speak, a man who is himself victimized, wounded, hurt by racism and class exploitation is actively dominating a woman in his life—that even as I speak, women who are ourselves exploited, victimized, are dominating children. It is necessary for us to remember, as we think critically about domination, that we all have the capacity to act in ways that oppress, dominate, wound (whether or not that power is institutionalized). It is necessary to remember that it is first the potential oppressor within that we must resist—the potential victim within that we must rescue—otherwise we cannot hope for an end to domination, for liberation.

This knowledge seems especially important at this historical moment when black women and other women of color have worked to create awareness of the ways in which racism empowers white women to act as exploiters and oppressors. Increasingly this fact is considered a reason we should not support feminist struggle even though sexism and sexist oppression is a real issue in our lives as black women (see, for example, Vivian Gordon's *Black Women, Feminism, Black Liberation: Which Way?*). It becomes necessary for us to speak continually about the convictions that inform our continued advocacy of feminist struggle. By calling attention to interlocking systems of domination—sex, race, and class—black women and many other groups of women acknowledge the diversity and complexity of female experience, of our relationship to power and domination. The intent is not to dissuade people of color from becoming engaged in feminist movement. Feminist struggle to end patriarchal domination should be of primary importance to women and men globally not because it is the foundation of all other oppressive structure but because it is that form of domination we are most likely to encounter in an ongoing way in everyday life.

Unlike other forms of domination, sexism directly shapes and determines relations of power in our private lives, in familiar social spaces, in that most intimate context—home—and in that most intimate sphere of relations—family. Usually, it is within the family that we witness coercive domination and learn to accept it, whether it be domination of parent over child, or male over female. Even though family relations may be, and most often are, informed by acceptance of a politic of domination, they are simultaneously relations of care and connection. It is this convergence of two contradictory impulses—the urge to promote growth and the urge to inhibit growth—that provides a practical setting for feminist critique, resistance, and transformation.

Growing up in a black, working-class, father-dominated household, I experienced coercive adult male authority as more immediately threatening, as more likely to cause immediate pain than racist oppression or class exploitation. It was equally clear that experiencing exploitation and oppression in the home made one feel all the more powerless when encountering dominating forces outside the home. This is true for many people. If we are unable to resist and end domination in relations where there is care, it seems totally unimaginable that we can resist and end it in other institutionalized relations of power. If we cannot convince the mothers and/or fathers who care not to humiliate and degrade us, how can we imagine convincing or resisting an employer, a lover, a stranger who systematically humiliates and degrades?

Feminist effort to end patriarchal domination should be of primary concern precisely because it insists on the eradication of exploitation and oppression in the family context and in all other intimate relationships. It is that political movement which most radically addresses the person—the personal—citing the need for transformation of self, of relationships, so that we might be better able to act in a revolutionary manner, challenging and resisting domination, transforming the world outside the self. Strategically, feminist movement should be a central component of all other liberation struggles because it challenges each of us to alter our person, our personal engagement (either as victims or perpetrators or both) in a system of domination.

Feminism, as liberation struggle, must exist apart from and as a part of the larger struggle to eradicate domination in all its forms. We must understand that patriarchal domination shares an ideological foundation with racism and other forms of group oppression, that there is no hope that it can be eradicated while these systems remain intact. This knowledge should consistently inform the direction of feminist theory and practice. Unfortunately, racism and class elitism among women has frequently led to the suppression and distortion of this connection so that it is now necessary for feminist thinkers to critique and revise much feminist theory and the direction of feminist movement. This effort at revision is perhaps most evident in the current widespread acknowledgement that sexism, racism, and class exploitation constitute interlocking systems of domination—that sex, race, and class, and not sex alone, determine the nature of any female's identity, status, and circumstance, the degree to which she will or will not be dominated, the extent to which she will have the power to dominate.

   While acknowledgement of the complex nature of woman's status (which has been most impressed upon everyone's consciousness by radical women of color) is a significant corrective, it is only a starting point. It provides a frame of reference which must serve as the basis for thoroughly altering and revising feminist theory and practice. It challenges and calls us to re-think popular assumptions about the nature of feminism that have had the deepest impact on a large majority of women, on mass consciousness. It radically calls into question the notion of a fundamentally common female experience which has been seen as the prerequisite for our coming together, for political unity. Recognition of the inter-connectedness of sex, race, and class highlights the diversity of experience, compelling redefinition of the terms of unity. If women do not share "common oppression," what then can serve as a basis for our coming together?

   Unlike many feminist comrades, I believe women and men must share a common understanding—a basic knowledge of what feminism is—if it is ever to be a powerful mass-based political movement. In *Feminist Theory: From Margin to Center,* I suggest that defining feminism broadly as "a movement to end sexism and sexist oppression" would enable us to have a common political goal. We would then have a basis on which to build solidarity. Multiple and contradictory definitions of feminism create confusion and undermine the effort to construct feminist movement so that it addresses everyone. Sharing a common goal does not imply that women and men will not have radically divergent perspectives on how that goal might be reached. Because each individual starts the process of engagement in feminist struggle at a unique level of awareness, very real differences in experience, perspective, and knowledge make developing varied strategies for participation and transformation a necessary agenda.

   Feminist thinkers engaged in radically revisioning central tenets of feminist thought must continually emphasize the importance of sex, race, and class as factors which *together* determine the social construction of femaleness, as it has been so deeply ingrained in the consciousness of many women active in feminist movement that gender is the sole factor determining destiny. However, the work of education for critical consciousness (usually called consciousness-raising) cannot end there. Much feminist consciousness-raising has in the past focused on identifying the particular ways men oppress and exploit women. Using the paradigm of sex, race, and class means that the focus does not begin with men and what they do to women, but rather with women working to identify both individually and collectively the specific character of our social identity.

   Imagine a group of women from diverse backgrounds coming together to talk about feminism. First they concentrate on working out their status in terms of sex, race, and class using this as the standpoint from which they begin discussing patriarchy or their particular relations with individual men. Within the old frame of reference, a discussion might consist solely of talk about their experiences as victims in relationship to male oppressors. Two women—one poor, the other quite wealthy—might describe the process by which they have suffered physical abuse by male partners and find certain commonalities which might serve as a basis for bonding. Yet if these same two women engaged in a discussion of class, not only would the social construction and expression of femaleness differ, so too would their ideas about how to confront and change their circumstances. Broadening the discussion to include an analysis of race and class would expose many additional differences even as commonalities emerged.

Clearly the process of bonding would be more complex, yet this broader discussion might enable the sharing of perspectives and strategies for change that would enrich rather than diminish our understanding of gender. While feminists have increasingly given "lip service" to the idea of diversity, we have not developed strategies of communication and inclusion that allow for the successful enactment of this feminist vision.

Small groups are no longer the central place for feminist consciousness-raising. Much feminist education for critical consciousness takes place in Women's Studies classes or at conferences which focus on gender. Books are a primary source of education, which means that already masses of people who do not read have no access. The separation of grassroots ways of sharing feminist thinking across kitchen tables from the spheres where much of that thinking is generated, the academy, undermines feminist movement. It would further feminist movement if new feminist thinking could be once again shared in small group contexts, integrating critical analysis with discussion of personal experience. It would be useful to promote anew the small group setting as an arena for education for critical consciousness, so that women and men might come together in neighborhoods and communities to discuss feminist concerns.

Small groups remain an important place for education for critical consciousness for several reasons. An especially important aspect of the small group setting is the emphasis on communicating feminist thinking, feminist theory, in a manner that can be easily understood. In small groups, individuals do not need to be equally literate or literate at all because the information is primarily shared through conversation, in dialogue which is necessarily a liberatory expression. (Literacy should be a goal for feminists even as we ensure that it not become a requirement for participation in feminist education.) Reforming small groups would subvert the appropriation of feminist thinking by a select group of academic women and men, usually white, usually from privileged class backgrounds.

Small groups of people coming together to engage in feminist discussion, in dialectical struggle make a space where the "personal is political" as a starting point for education for critical consciousness can be extended to include politicization of the self that focusses on creating understanding of the ways sex, race, and class together determine our individual lot and our collective experience. It would further feminist movement if many well known feminist thinkers would participate in small groups, critically re-examining ways their works might be changed by incorporating broader perspectives. All efforts at self-transformation challenge us to engage in ongoing, critical self-examination and reflection about feminist practice, about how we live in the world. This individual commitment, when coupled with engagement in collective discussion, provides a space for critical feedback which strengthens our efforts to change and make ourselves new. It is in this commitment to feminist principles in our words and deeds that the hope of feminist revolution lies.

Working collectively to confront difference, to expand our awareness of sex, race, and class as interlocking systems of domination, of the ways we reinforce and perpetuate these structures, is the context to which we learn the true meaning of solidarity. It is this work that must be the foundation of feminist movement. Without it, we cannot effectively resist patriarchal domination; without it, we remain estranged and alienated from one another. Fear of painful confrontation often leads women and men active in feminist movement to avoid rigorous critical encounter, yet if we cannot engage dialectically in a committed, rigorous, humanizing manner, we cannot hope to change the world. True politicization—coming to critical consciousness—is a difficult, "trying" process, one that demands that we give up set ways of thinking and being, that we shift our paradigms, that we open ourselves to the unknown, the unfamiliar. Undergoing this process, we learn what it means to struggle and in this effort we experience the dignity and integrity of being that comes with revolutionary change. If we do not change our consciousness, we cannot change our actions or demand change from others.

Our renewed commitment to a rigorous process of education for critical consciousness will determine the shape and direction of future feminist movement. Until new perspectives are created, we cannot be living symbols of the power of feminist thinking. Given the privileged lot of many leading feminist thinkers, both in terms of status, class, and race, it is harder these days to convince women of the primacy of this process of politicization. More and more, we seem to form select interest groups composed of individuals who share similar perspectives. This limits our capacity to engage in critical discussion. It is difficult to involve women in new processes of feminist politicization because so many of us think that identifying men as the enemy, resisting male domination, gaining equal access to power and privilege is the end of feminist movement. Not only is it not the end, it is not even the place we want revitalized feminist movement to begin. We want to begin as women seriously addressing ourselves, not solely in relation to men, but in relation to an entire structure of domination of which patriarchy is one part. While the struggle to eradicate sexism and sexist oppression is and should be the primary thrust of feminist movement, to prepare ourselves politically for this effort we must first learn how to be in solidarity, how to struggle with one another.

Only when we confront the realities of sex, race, and class, the ways they divide us, make us different, stand us in opposition, and work to reconcile and resolve these issues will we be able to participate in the making of feminist revolution, in the transformation of the world. Feminism, as Charlotte Bunch emphasizes again and again in *Passionate Politics,* is a transformational politics, a struggle against domination wherein the effort is to change ourselves as well as structures. Speaking about the struggle to confront difference, Bunch asserts:

> A crucial point of the process is understanding that reality does not look the same from different people's perspective. It is not surprising that one way feminists have come to understand about differences has been through the love of a person from another culture or race. It takes persistence and motivation—which love often engenders—to get beyond one's ethnocentric assumptions and really learn about other

perspectives. In this process and while seeking to eliminate oppression, we also discover new possibilities and insights that come from the experience and survival of other peoples.

Embedded in the commitment to feminist revolution is the challenge to love. Love can be and is an important source of empowerment when we struggle to confront issues of sex, race, and class. Working together to identify and face our differences—to face the ways we dominate and are dominated—to change our actions, we need a mediating force that can sustain us so that we are not broken in this process, so that we do not despair.

Not enough feminist work has focussed on documenting and sharing ways individuals confront differences constructively and successfully. Women and men need to know what is on the other side of the pain experienced in politicization. We need detailed accounts of the ways our lives are fuller and richer as we change and grow politically, as we learn to live each moment as committed feminists, as comrades working to end domination. In reconceptualizing and reformulating strategies for future feminist movement, we need to concentrate on the politicization of love, not just in the context of talking about victimization in intimate relationships, but in a critical discussion where love can be understood as a powerful force that challenges and resists domination. As we work to be loving, to create a culture that celebrates life, that makes love possible, we move against dehumanization, against domination. In *Pedagogy of the Oppressed*, Paulo Freire evokes this power of love, declaring:

> I am more and more convinced that true revolutionaries must perceive the revolution, because of its creative and liberating nature, as an act of love. For me, the revolution, which is not possible without a theory of revolution—and therefore science—is not irreconcilable with love . . . The distortion imposed on the word "love" by the capitalist world cannot prevent the revolution from being essentially loving in character, nor can it prevent the revolutionaries from affirming their love of life.

That aspect of feminist revolution that calls women to love womanness, that calls men to resist dehumanizing concepts of masculinity, is an essential part of our struggle. It is the process by which we move from seeing ourselves as objects to acting as subjects. When women and men understand that working to eradicate patriarchal domination is a struggle rooted in the longing to make a world where everyone can live fully and freely, then we know our work to be a gesture of love. Let us draw upon that love to heighten our awareness, deepen our compassion, intensify our courage, and strengthen our commitment.

3 A New Vision of Masculinity

Cooper Thompson

I was once asked by a teacher in a suburban high school to give a guest presentation on male roles. She hoped that I might help her deal with four boys who exercised extraordinary control over the other boys in the class. Using ridicule and their status as physically imposing athletes, these four wrestlers had succeeded in stifling the participation of the other boys, who were reluctant to make comments in class discussions.

As a class we talked about the ways in which boys got status in that school and how they got put down by others. I was told that the most humiliating put-down was being called a "fag." The list of behaviors which could elicit ridicule filled two large chalkboards, and it was detailed and comprehensive; I got the sense that a boy in this school had to conform to rigid, narrow standards of masculinity to avoid being called a fag. I, too, felt this pressure and became very conscious of my mannerisms in front of the group. Partly from exasperation, I decided to test the seriousness of these assertions. Since one of the four boys had some streaks of pink in his shirt, and since he had told me that wearing pink was grounds for being called a fag, I told him that I thought he was a fag. Instead of laughing, he said, "I'm going to kill you."

Such is the stereotypic definition of strength that is associated with masculinity. But it is a very limited definition of strength, one based on dominance and control and acquired through the humiliation and degradation of others.

Contrast this with a view of strength offered by Pam McAllister in her introduction to *Reweaving the Web of Life*:

> The "Strength" card in my Tarot deck depicts, not a warrior going off to battle with his armor and his mighty sword, but a woman stroking a lion. The woman has not slain the lion nor maced it, not netted it, nor has she put on it a muzzle or a leash. And though the lion clearly has teeth and long sharp claws, the woman is not hiding, nor has she sought a protector, nor has she grown muscles. She doesn't appear to be talking to the lion nor flattering it, nor tossing it fresh meat to distract its hungry jaws. The woman on the "Strength" card wears a flowing white dress and a garland of flowers. With one hand she cups the lion's jaws, with the other she caresses its nose. The lion on the card has big yellow eyes and a long red tongue curling out of its mouth. One paw is lifted and the mane falls in thick red curls across its broad torso. The woman. The lion. Together they depict strength.

This image of strength stands in direct contrast to the strength embodied in the actions of the four wrestlers. The collective strength of the woman and the lion is a strength unknown in a system of traditional male values. Other human qualities are equally

From Franklin Abbot and Cooper Thompson, *New Men, New Minds*. Copyright © 1987 by Cooper Thompson. Reprinted by permission of the author.

foreign to a traditional conception of masculinity. In workshops I've offered on the male role stereotype, teachers and other school personnel easily generate lists of attitudes and behaviors which boys typically seem to not learn. Included in this list are being supportive and nurturant, accepting one's vulnerability and being able to ask for help, valuing women and "women's work," understanding and expressing emotions (except for anger), the ability to empathize with and empower other people, and learning to resolve conflict in nonagressive, noncompetitive ways.

Learning Violence

All of this should come as no surprise. Traditional definitions of masculinity include attributes such as independence, pride, resiliency, self-control, and physical strength. This is precisely the image of the Marlboro man, and to some extent, these are desirable attributes for boys and girls. But masculinity goes beyond these qualities to stress competitiveness, toughness, aggressiveness, and power. In this context, threats to one's status, however small, cannot be avoided or taken lightly. If a boy is called a fag, it means that he is perceived as weak or timid—and therefore not masculine enough for his peers. There is enormous pressure for him to fight back. Not being tough at these moments only proves the allegation.

Violence is learned not just as a way for boys to defend allegations that they are feminized, but as an effective, appropriate way for them to normally behave. In "The Civic Advocacy of Violence" [M., Spring 1982] Wayne Ewing clearly states:

> I used to think that we simply tolerated and permitted male abusiveness in our society. I have now come to understand rather, that we advocate physical violence. Violence is presented as effective. Violence is taught as the normal, appropriate and necessary behavior of power and control. Analyses which interweave advocacy of male violence with "SuperBowl Culture" have never been refuted. Civic expectations—translated into professionalism, financial commitments, city planning for recreational space, the raising of male children for competitive sport, the corporate ethics of business ownership of athletic teams, profiteering on entertainment—all result in the monument of the National Football League, symbol and reality at once of the advocacy of violence.

Ultimately, violence is the tool which maintains what I believe are the two most critical socializing forces in a boy's life: *homophobia,* the hatred of gay men (who are stereotyped as feminine) or those men believed to be gay, as well as the fear of being perceived as gay; and *misogyny,* the hatred of women. The two forces are targeted at different classes of victims, but they are really just the flip sides of the same coin. Homophobia is the hatred of feminine qualities in men while misogyny is the hatred of feminine qualities in women. The boy who is called a fag is the target of other boys' homophobia as well as the victim of his own homophobia. While the overt message is the absolute need to avoid being feminized, the implication is that females—and all that they traditionally represent—are contemptible. The United States Marines have a philosophy which conveniently combines homophobia and misogyny in the belief that "When you want to create a group of male killers, you kill 'the woman' in them."

The pressures of homophobia and misogyny in boys' lives have been poignantly demonstrated to me each time that I have repeated a simple yet provocative activity with students. I ask them to answer the question, "If you woke up tomorrow and discovered that you were the opposite sex from the one you are now, how would you and your life be different?" Girls consistently indicate that there are clear advantages to being a boy—from increased independence and career opportunities to decreased risks of physical and sexual assault—and eagerly answer the question. But boys often express disgust at this possibility and even refuse sometimes to answer the question. In her reports of a broad-based survey using this question, Alice Baumgartner reports the following responses are typical of boys: "If I were a girl, I'd be stupid and weak as a string"; "I would have to wear makeup, cook, be a mother, and yuckky stuff like that"; "I would have to hate snakes. Everything would be miserable"; "If I were a girl, I'd kill myself."

The Costs of Masculinity

The costs associated with a traditional view of masculinity are enormous, and the damage occurs at both personal and societal levels. The belief that a boy should be tough (aggressive, competitive, and daring) can create emotional pain for him. While a few boys experience short-term success for their toughness, there is little security in the long run. Instead, it leads to a series of challenges which few, if any, boys ultimately win. There is no security in being at the top when so many other boys are competing for the same status. Toughness also leads to increased chances of stress, physical injury, and even early death. It is considered manly to take extreme physical risks and voluntarily engage in combative, hostile activities.

The flip side of toughness—nurturance—is not a quality perceived as masculine and thus not valued. Because of this boys and men experience a greater emotional distance from other people and few opportunities to participate in meaningful interpersonal relationships. Studies consistently show that fathers spend very small amounts of time interacting with their children. In addition, men report that they seldom have intimate relationships with other men, reflecting their homophobia. They are afraid of getting too close and don't know how to take down the walls that they have built between themselves.

As boys grow older and accept adult roles, the larger social costs of masculinity clearly emerge. Most women experience male resistance to an expansion of women's roles; one of the assumptions of traditional masculinity is the belief that women should be subordinate to men. The consequence is that men are often not willing to accept females as equal, competent partners in personal and professional settings. Whether the setting is a sexual relationship, the family, the streets, or the battlefield, men are continuously engaged in efforts to dominate. Statistics on child abuse consistently indicate that the vast majority of abusers are men, and that there is no "typical" abuser. Rape may be the fastest growing crime in the United States. And it is men, regardless of nationality, who provoke and sustain war. In short, traditional masculinity is life threatening.

New Socialization for Boys

Masculinity, like many other human traits, is determined by both biological and environmental factors. While some believe that biological factors are significant in shaping some masculine behavior, there is undeniable evidence that cultural and environmental factors are strong enough to override biological impulses. What is it, then, that we should be teaching boys about being a man in a modern world?

- Boys must learn to accept their vulnerability, learn to express a range of emotions such as fear and sadness, and learn to ask for help and support in appropriate situations.

- Boys must learn to be gentle, nurturant, cooperative and communicative, and in particular, learn nonviolent means of resolving conflicts.

- Boys must learn to accept those attitudes and behaviors which have traditionally been labeled feminine as necessary for full human development—thereby reducing homophobia and misogyny. This is tantamount to teaching boys to love other boys and girls.

Certain qualities like courage, physical strength, and independence, which are traditionally associated with masculinity, are indeed positive qualities for males, provided that they are not manifested in obsessive ways nor used to exploit or dominate others. It is not necessary to completely disregard or unlearn what is traditionally called masculine. I believe, however, that the three areas above are crucial for developing a broader view of masculinity, one which is healthier for all life.

These three areas are equally crucial for reducing aggressive, violent behavior among boys and men. Males must learn to cherish life for the sake of their *own* wholeness as human beings, not just *for* their children, friends, and lovers. If males were more nurturant, they would be less likely to hurt those they love.

Leonard Eron, writing in the *American Psychologist,* puts the issue of unlearning aggression and learning nurturance in clear-cut terms:

> Socialization is crucial in determining levels of aggression. No matter how aggression is measured or observed, as a group males always score higher than females. But this is not true for all girls. There are some girls who seem to have been socialized like boys who are just as aggressive as boys. Just as some females can learn to be aggressive, so males can learn *not* to be aggressive. If we want to reduce the level of aggression in society, we should also discourage boys from aggression very early on in life and reward them too for others' behaviors; in other words, we should socialize boys more like girls, and they should be encouraged to develop socially positive qualities such as tenderness, cooperation, and aesthetic appreciation. The level of individual aggression in society will be reduced only when male adolescents and young adults, as a result of socialization, subscribe to the same standards of behavior as have been traditionally encouraged for women.

Where will this change in socialization occur? In his first few years, most of a boy's learning about masculinity comes from the influences of parents, siblings and images of masculinity such as those found on television. Massive efforts will be needed to make changes here. But at older ages, school curriculum and the school environment provide powerful reinforcing images of traditional masculinity. This reinforcement occurs through a variety of channels, including curriculum content, role modeling, and extracurricular activities, especially competitive sports.

School athletics are a microcosm of the socialization of male values. While participation in competitive activities can be enjoyable and healthy, it too easily becomes a lesson in the need for toughness, invulnerability, and dominance. Athletes learn to ignore their own injuries and pain and instead try to injure and inflict pain on others in their attempts to win, regardless of the cost to themselves or their opponents. Yet the lessons learned in athletics are believed to be vital for full and complete masculine development, and as a model for problem-solving in other areas of life.

In addition to encouraging traditional male values, schools provide too few experiences in nurturance, cooperation, negotiation, nonviolent conflict resolution, and strategies for empathizing with and empowering others. Schools should become places where boys have the opportunity to learn these skills; clearly, they won't learn them on the street, from peers, or on television.

Setting New Examples

Despite the pressures on men to display their masculinity in traditional ways, there are examples of men and boys who are changing. "Fathering" is one example of a positive change. In recent years, there has been a popular emphasis on child-care activities, with men becoming more involved in providing care to children, both professionally and as fathers. This is a clear shift from the more traditional view that child rearing should be delegated to women and is not an appropriate activity for men.

For all of the male resistance it has generated, the Women's Liberation Movement has at least provided a stimulus for some men to accept women as equal partners in most areas of life. These are the men who have chosen to learn and grow from women's experiences and together with women are creating new norms for relationships. Popular literature and research on male sex roles is expanding, reflecting a wider interest in masculinity. Weekly news magazines such as *Time* and *Newsweek* have run major stories on the "new masculinity," suggesting that positive changes are taking place in the home and in the workplace. Small groups of men scattered around the country have organized against pornography, battering, and sexual assault. Finally there is the National Organization for Changing Men which has a pro-feminist, pro-gay, pro–"new man" agenda, and its ranks are slowly growing.

In schools where I have worked with teachers, they report that years of efforts to enhance educational opportunities for girls have also had some positive effects on boys. The boys seem more tolerant of girls' participation in coed sports activities and in traditionally male shops and courses. They seem to have a greater respect for the accomplishments of women through women's contributions to literature and history. Among elementary school aged males, the expression of vulnerable feelings is gaining acceptance. In general, however, there has been far too little attention paid to redirecting male role development.

Boys Will Be Boys

I think back to the four wrestlers and the stifling culture of masculinity in which they live. If schools were to radically alter this culture and substitute for it a new vision of masculinity, what would that look like? In this environment, boys would express a full range of behaviors and emotions without fear of being chastised. They would be permitted and encouraged to cry, to be afraid, to show joy, and to express love in a gentle fashion. Extreme concern for career goals would be replaced by a consideration of one's need for recreation, health, and meaningful work. Older boys would be encouraged to tutor and play with younger students. Moreover, boys would receive as much recognition for artistic talents as they do for athletics, and, in general, they would value leisure-time, recreational activities as highly as competitive sports.

In a system where maleness and femaleness were equally valued, boys might no longer feel that they have to "prove" themselves to other boys; they would simply accept the worth of each person and value those differences. Boys would realize that it is permissible to admit failure. In addition, they would seek out opportunities to learn from girls and women. Emotional support would be commonplace, and it would no longer be seen as just the role of the female to provide the support. Relationships between boys and girls would no longer be based on limited roles, but instead would become expressions of two individuals learning from and supporting one another. Relationships between boys would reflect their care for one another rather than their mutual fear and distrust.

Aggressive styles of resolving conflicts would be the exception rather than the norm. Girls would feel welcome in activities dominated by boys, knowing that they were safe from the threat of being sexually harassed. Boys would no longer boast of beating up another boy or of how much they "got off" of a girl the night before. In fact, the boys would be as outraged as the girls at rape or other violent crimes in the community. Finally, boys would become active in efforts to stop nuclear proliferation and all other forms of military violence, following the examples set by activist women.

The development of a new conception of masculinity based on this vision is an ambitious task, but one which is essential for the health and safety of both men and women. The survival of our society may rest on the degree to which we are able to teach men to cherish life.

4 Interrupting the Cycle of Oppression

The Role of Allies as Agents of Change

Andrea Ayvazian

Many of us feel overwhelmed when we consider the many forms of systemic oppression that are so pervasive in American society today. We become immobilized, uncertain about what actions we can take to interrupt the cycles of oppression and violence that intrude on our everyday lives. One way to overcome this sense of immobilization is to assume the role of an ally. Learning about this role—one that each and every one of us is capable of assuming—can offer us new ways of behaving and a new source of hope.

Through the years, experience has taught us that isolated and episodic actions—even dramatic, media-grabbing events—rarely produce more than a temporary blip on the screen. What does seem to create real and lasting change is highly-motivated individuals—usually only a handful at first—who are so clear and consistent on an issue that they serve as a heartbeat in a community, steadily sending out waves that touch and change those in their path. These change agents or allies have such a powerful impact because their actions embody the values they profess: their behavior and beliefs are congruent.

What Is an Ally?

An ally is a member of a dominant group in our society who works to dismantle any form of oppression from which she or he receives the benefit. Allied behavior means taking personal responsibility for the changes we know are needed in our society, and so often ignore or leave to others to deal with. Allied behavior is intentional, overt, consistent activity that challenges prevailing patterns of oppression, makes privileges that are so often invisible visible, and facilitates the empowerment of persons targeted by oppression.

I use the term "oppression" to describe the combination of prejudice plus access to social, political, and economic power on the part of a dominant group. Racism, a core component of oppression, has been defined by David Wellman as a system of advantage based on race. Wellman's definition can be altered slightly to describe every other form of oppression. Hence we can say that sexism is a system of advantage based on gender, that heterosexism is a system of advantage based on sexual orientation, and so on. In each form of oppression there is a dominant group—the one that receives

From *Fellowship* (January/February 1995). Reprinted by permission of Rev. Dr. Andrea Ayvazian, Pastor of the Haydenville Congregational Church.

the unearned advantage, benefit, or privilege—and a targeted group—the one that is denied that advantage, benefit, or privilege. We know the litany of dominants: white people, males, Christians, heterosexuals, able-bodied people, those in their middle years, and those who are middle or upper class.

We also know that everyone has multiple social identities. We are all dominant and targeted simultaneously. I, for instance, am simultaneously dominant as a white person and targeted as a woman. A white able-bodied man may be dominant in those categories, but targeted as a Jew or Muslim or as a gay person. Some people are, at some point in their lives, entirely dominant; but if they are, they won't be forever. Even a white, able-bodied, heterosexual, Christian male will literally grow out of his total dominance if he reaches old age.

When we consider the different manifestations of systematic oppression and find ourselves in any of the categories where we are dominant—and therefore receive the unearned advantages that accrue to that position of advantage—we have the potential to be remarkably powerful agents of change as allies. Allies are whites who identify as anti-racists, men who work to dismantle sexism, able-bodied people who are active in the disability rights movement, Christians who combat anti-Semitism and other forms of religious prejudice. Allied behavior usually involves talking to other dominants about their behavior: whites confronting other whites on issues of racism, men organizing with other men to combat sexism, and so on. Allied behavior is clear action aimed at dismantling the oppression of others in areas where you yourself benefit—it is proactive, intentional, and often involves taking a risk.

To tether these principles to everyday reality, just think of the group Parents, Families and Friends of Lesbians and Gays (PFLAG) as the perfect example of allied behavior. PFLAG is an organization of (mainly) heterosexuals who organize support groups and engage in advocacy and education among other heterosexuals around issues of gay and lesbian liberation. PFLAG speakers can be heard in houses of worship, schools, and civic organizations discussing their own commitment to securing gay and lesbian civil rights. Because they are heterosexuals speaking (usually) to other heterosexuals, they often have a significant impact.

The anti-racism trainer Kenneth Jones, an African-American, refers to allied behavior as "being at my back." He has said to me, "Andrea, I know you are at my back on the issue of race equity—you're talking to white people who cannot hear me on this topic, you're out there raising these issues repeatedly, you're organizing with other whites to stand up to racism. And I'm at your back. I'm raising issues of gender equity with men, I am talking to men who cannot hear you, I've made a commitment to combat sexism."

Available to each one of us in the categories where we are dominant is the proud and honorable role of ally: the opportunity to raise hell with others like us and to interrupt the cycle of oppression. Because of our very privilege, we have the potential to stir up good trouble, to challenge the status quo, and to inspire real and lasting change. William Stickland, an aide to Jesse Jackson, once said: "When a critical mass of white people join together, rise up, and shout a thunderous 'No' to racism, we will actually alter the course of history."

Reducing Violence

When I ponder the tremendous change a national network of allies can make in this country, I think not only of issues of equity and empowerment, but also of how our work could lead to diminishing levels of violence in our society. Let us consider for a moment the critical connection between oppression and violence on one hand, and the potential role of allied behavior in combating violence on the other.

A major source of violence in our society is the persistent inequity between dominant and targeted groups. Recall that oppression is kept in place by two factors:

1. Ideology, or the propagation of doctrines that purport to legitimize inequality; and
2. Violence (or the threat of violence) by the dominant group against the targeted group.

The violence associated with each form of systemic oppression noticeably decreases when allies (or dominants) rise up and shout a thunderous "No" to the perpetuation of these inequities. Because members of the dominant group are conferred with considerable social power and privilege, they carry significant authority when confronting perpetrators of violence in their own group—when whites deter other whites from using violence against people of color, when heterosexuals act to prevent gay bashing, and so on.

Research studies have confirmed what observers and allies have been saying for years: that when a woman is the victim of ongoing, violent domestic abuse, it makes no difference to her chances of survival if she has counseling, takes out a restraining order, or learns to fight back. According to the studies, the only factor that statistically increases a woman's chances of survival is if the victimizer himself is exposed to direct and ongoing anti-battering intervention.

These studies have inspired the creation of model mentoring programs in places like Quincy, Massachusetts, Duluth, Minnesota, and New York City—programs in which men prone to violence against women work with other men through a series of organized interventions. The success of these programs has demonstrated that it is actually possible to interrupt and stop the cycle of violence among batterers. In 1992, for instance, the model program in Quincy helped cut the incidence of domestic homicide to zero. The Batterers Anonymous groups, in which men who are former perpetrators work with men who are current batterers, have also had remarkable success in breaking the habit of violence. These groups are allied behavior made manifest; their success in reducing the incidence of violence against women is now statistically proven.

In our society, oppression and violence are woven together: one leads to the other, one justifies the other. Furthermore, members of the dominant group who are not perpetrators of violence often collude, through their silence and inactivity, with those who are. Allied behavior is an effective way of interrupting the cycle of violence by breaking the silence that reinforces the cycle, and by promoting a new set of behavior through modeling and mentoring.

Providing Positive Role Models

Not only does allied behavior contribute to an increase in equity and a decrease in violence, but allies provide positive role models that are sorely needed by today's young people. The role of ally offers young people who are white, male, and in other dominant categories a positive, proactive, and proud identity. Rather than feeling guilty, shameful, and immobilized as the "oppressor," whites and other dominants can assume the important and useful role of social change agent. There have been proud allies and change agents throughout the history of this nation, and there are many alive today who can inspire us with their important work.

I often speak in high school classes and assemblies, and in recent years I have taken to doing a little informal survey from the podium. I ask the students if they can name a famous living white racist. Can they? Yes. They often name David Duke—he ran for President in their lifetime—or they sometimes name Senator Jesse Helms; and when I was in the midwest, they named Marge Schott, the owner of the Cincinnati Reds. It does not take long before a hand shoots up, or someone just calls out one of those names.

Following that little exercise, I ask the students, "Can you name a famous living white anti-racist (or civil rights worker, or someone who fights racism)?" Can they? Not very often. Sometimes there is a whisper or two, but generally the room is very quiet. So, recently, I have been saying: forget the famous part. Just name for me any white person you know in your community, or someone you have heard of, who has taken a stand against racism. Can they? Sometimes. Occasionally someone says "my mom," or "my dad." I have also heard "my rabbi, my teacher, my minister." But not often enough.

I believe that it is difficult for young people to grow up and become something they have never heard of. It is hard for a girl to grow up and become a commercial airline pilot if it has never occurred to her that woman can and do fly jet planes. Similarly, it is hard for young people to grow up and fight racism if they have never met anyone who does.

And there *are* many remarkable role models whom we can claim with pride, and model ourselves after. People like Laura Haviland, who was a conductor on the Underground Railroad and performed unbelievably brave acts while the slave-catchers were right on her trail; Virginia Foster Durr, a southern belle raised with great wealth and privilege who, as an adult, tirelessly drove black workers to and from their jobs during the Montgomery bus boycott; the Rev. James Reeb, who went south during the Mississippi Freedom Summer of 1964 to organize and march; Hodding Carter, Jr., editor and publisher of a newspaper in the Mississippi Delta who used his paper to battle for racial equity and who took considerable heat for his actions. And more: the Grimke sisters, Lucretia Mott, William Lloyd Garrison, John Brown, Viola Liuzzo.

There are also many contemporary anti-racists like Morris Dees, who gave up a lucrative law practice to start the Southern Poverty Law Center and Klan Watch in Alabama and bring white supremacists to trial; Anne Braden, active for decades in the civil rights struggle in Kentucky; Rev. Joseph Barndt, working within the religious community to make individual churches and entire denominations proclaim themselves as anti-racist institutions. And Peggy McIntosh, Judith Katz, and Myles Horton. And so many others. Why don't our young people know these names? If young people knew more about these dedicated allies, perhaps they would be inspired to engage in more anti-racist activities themselves.

Choosing Our Own Roles

We also need to consider our role as allies. In our own communities, would young people, if asked the same questions, call out our names as anti-racists? In areas where we are dominant, is our struggle for equity and justice evident? When we think about our potential role as allies, we need to recall a Quaker expression: "Let your life be your teaching." The Quakers understand that our words carry only so much weight, that it is our actions, our daily behaviors, that tell the true story.

In my own life I struggle with what actions to take, how to make my beliefs and my behaviors congruent. One small step that has had interesting repercussions over the last decade is the fact that my partner (who is male) and I have chosen not to be legally married until gay and lesbian couples can be married and receive the same benefits and legal protection that married heterosexual couples enjoy. A small step, but it has allowed us to talk with folks at the YMCA about their definition of "family" when deciding who qualifies for their "family plan"; to challenge people at Amtrak about why some "family units" receive discounts when traveling together and others do not; and to raise questions in the religious community about who can receive formal sanction for their loving unions and who cannot. These are not earth-shattering steps in the larger picture, but we believe that small steps taken by thousands of people will eventually change the character of our communities.

When we stop colluding and speak out about the unearned privileges we enjoy as members of a dominant group—privileges we have been taught for so long to deny or ignore—we have the potential to undergo and inspire stunning transformation. Consider the words of Gandhi: "As human beings, our greatness lies not so much in being able to remake the world, as in being able to remake ourselves."

In my own community, I have been impressed by the efforts of three middle-aged males who have remade themselves into staunch allies for women. Steven Botkin established the Men's Resource Center in Amherst, Massachusetts twelve years ago and put a commitment to eliminating sexism in its very first mission statement. Another Amherst resident, Michael Burkart, travels nationwide and works with top executives in Fortune 500 companies on the issue of gender equity in their corporations. And Geoff Lobenstine, a social worker who identifies as an anti-sexist male, brings these issues to his work in Holyoke, Massachusetts.

Charlie Parker once said this about music: "Music is your own experience, your thoughts, your wisdom. If you don't live it, it won't come out of your horn." I think the same is true about us in our role as allies—it is our own experience, our thoughts, our wisdom. If we don't live it, it won't come out of our horn.

Preparing for the Long Haul

Now I would be the first to admit that personally and professionally the role of ally is often exhausting. I know that it involves challenges—being an ally is difficult work, and it can often be lonely. We must remember to take care of ourselves along this journey, to sustain our energy and our zest for those ongoing challenges.

We must also remember that it is hard to go it alone: allies need allies. As with any other struggle in our lives, we need supportive people around us to help us to persevere. Other allies will help us take the small, daily steps that will, in time, alter the character of our communities. We know that allied behavior usually consists of small steps and unglamorous work. As Mother Teresa once said: "I don't do any great things. I do small things with great love."

Finally two additional points about us in our role as allies: First, we don't always see the results of our efforts. Sometimes we do, but often we touch and even change lives without ever knowing it. Consequently, we cannot measure our success in quantitative terms. Like waves upon the shore, we are altering the landscape—but exactly how, may be hard to discern.

Doubts inevitably creep up about our effectiveness, about our approach, about the positions we assume or the actions we take. But we move forward, along with the doubts, the uncertainty, and often the lack of visible results. In our office, we have a famous William James quote on the wall to sustain us: "I will act as though what I do makes a difference." And, speaking personally, although my faith gets rattled, I try to act as though what I do does make a difference.

Second, there is no such thing as a perfect ally. Perfection is not our goal. When I asked my colleague Kenneth Jones what stood out for him as the most important characteristic of a strong ally, he said simply: "being consistently conscious." He didn't say "never stumbling," or "never making mistakes." He said: "being consistently conscious." And so we do our best: taking risks, being smart, making errors, feeling foolish, doing what we believe is right, based on our best judgment at the time. We are imperfect, but we are steady. We are courageous but not faultless. As Lani Guinier said: "It is better to be vaguely right than precisely wrong." If we obsess about looking good instead of doing good, we will get caught in a spiral of ineffective action. Let's not get side-tracked or defeated because we are trying to be perfect.

And so we move ahead, pushing ourselves forward on our growing edge. We know that although none of us are beginners in dealing with issues of oppression and empowerment, none of us are experts either. These issues are too complex, too painful, and too pervasive for us to achieve a state of clarity and closure once and for all. The best we can hope for is to strive each day to be our strongest and clearest selves, transforming the world one individual at a time, one family at a time, one community at a time. May we summon the wisdom to be devoted allies today. May we walk the walk, living as though equity, justice and freedom for all have already arrived.

Like most activists, I carry a dream inside me. As I travel nationwide for my work, I can actually see signs of it becoming true. The dream is that we will create in this country a nonviolent army of allies that will challenge and break the cycle of oppression and usher in a new era of liberation, empowerment, and equity for persons historically targeted by systemic oppression. Within each individual is the potential to effect enormous change. May we move foward, claiming with pride our identities as allies, interrupting the cycle of oppression, and modeling a new way of behaving and believing.

5 Demand the Impossible
Matthew Rothschild

The brazenness of the ruling class is a sight to behold. The people who run this country—the Wall Street tycoons and the CEOs of America's largest corporations—are not content with the extraordinary amount of lucre they've grabbed already. They're insatiable. And they don't give a damn about anyone else.

Their Republican servants in Congress, and their contract employees among the Democrats, have so rigged the legislative process that the vast majority of the American people can't get what they desperately want and need. And the plight of the sixteen million Americans without work right now does not get the attention it deserves—or the remedy. Instead, Congress protects the prerogatives of those at the top.

Meanwhile, President Obama readies the public for cutbacks in Social Security and Medicare.

In the midst of an agonizing economy, Republicans in Congress slammed the door on any serious proposal to generate jobs. They concocted the debt-ceiling crisis, and then used it as a way to extort massive cuts to social programs, which will only make the unemployment picture more dire. And even after Hurricane Irene took its toll on the East Coast, they were in no mood to approve government spending for devastated areas like Vermont.

Through it all, they made sure that no rich person or corporation would have to pay a dime more in taxes. Their priorities could not be clearer. In the August debate of the Republican Presidential candidates, they all said that even a budget deal that included ten dollars in cuts for every dollar in tax increases would not be acceptable. They've made the money-grab by the rich a matter of the highest principle.

And what a money-grab it's been.

"After remaining relatively constant for much of the postwar era, the share of total income accrued by the wealthiest 10 percent of households jumped from 34.6 percent in 1980 to 48.2 percent in 2008," according to a report last year by the Joint Economic Committee of Congress. "Much of the spike was driven by the share of total income accrued by the richest 1 percent of households. Between 1980 and 2008, their share rose from 10.0 percent to 21.0 percent, making the United States one of the most unequal countries in the world."

It's even worse when you look at wealth, not income, as the top 1 percent now accounts for 40 percent of the nation's wealth, up from 33 percent in the 1980s.

"All the growth in recent decades—and more—has gone to those at the top," Nobel Prize–winning economist Joseph Stiglitz wrote in *Vanity Fair* earlier this year in an article entitled "Of the 1%, By the 1%, For the 1%." He went on to explain how

From *The Progressive*, October 2011. Reprinted by permission of The Progressive, Inc., www.progressive.org.

this growth in inequality leads directly to an unwillingness by the powerful to address common needs.

"The rich don't need to rely on government for parks or education or medical care or personal security—they can buy all these things for themselves," he noted. "In the process, they become more distant from ordinary people, losing whatever empathy they may once have had. They also worry about strong government: one that could use its powers to adjust the balance, take some of their wealth, and invest it for the common good. The top 1 percent may complain about the kind of government we have in America, but in truth they like it just fine: too gridlocked to redistribute, too divided to do anything but lower taxes."

And when government wasn't too gridlocked or too divided, that is, when President Obama had both houses of Congress and enormous popularity in the first months of his term, he failed to come forward with a sufficient jobs program and he backed off his effort to make the rich pay a little more in taxes.

Not only do the rich not have empathy for those below them, many U.S. multinationals no longer rely on U.S. consumers for the bulk of their profits. They can find buyers now all over the world, especially in booming markets like India and China. They don't need us anymore.

We're peons now.

What to do? An old slogan of the surrealists applies here: "Be Realistic: Demand the Impossible." It was a slogan that the French students adopted in their uprising in 1968. We should adopt it again today.

Instead of going along with the neoliberal acquiescence that so typifies the Obama Administration, we should put forward robust demands that will lead us toward the kind of society we want to build and inhabit.

Instead of letting Obama and the Republicans raise the retirement age for Social Security, we should demand lowering the retirement age to fifty-five.

Instead of going along with crimping Social Security benefits, we should raise them, as the labor writer Thomas Geoghegan recommends, from their current level of, on average, 39 percent of pre-retirement earnings to 50 percent.

Instead of defending the minimum wage of $7.25, we should insist on a living wage of at least $10 an hour and then peg that to the inflation rate, as Ralph Nader has proposed.

Instead of allowing the unemployment rate to hover around 9 percent, we should demand that the government directly employ people until everyone who wants a job can get one.

Instead of working longer and longer hours, including forced overtime, we should insist on a shorter workweek of thirty hours.

Instead of being coerced back into the workplace shortly after we have a kid, we should demand one-year paid family leave, as they have in Europe.

Instead of letting the rightwing cut back on school funding so that class sizes, K–12, exceed thirty pupils in many places, we should limit them to a maximum of twenty.

Instead of accepting the loan burden for students going to college, we should demand—as students are doing in Chile—free quality college education for all.

Instead of allowing a child poverty rate of 21 percent, we should demand that no child live in poverty.

Instead of accepting the role of the private health-insurance industry, we should demand Medicare for all.

None of this is too much to ask. Nor is an economy freed from fossil and nuclear fuels.

"We can't afford it," people will say.

I refuse to believe this. Whenever a President wants to go wage a war somewhere, he can always find $3 trillion to do it. Whenever the banks need bailing out, suddenly trillions more become available.

So don't tell me we can't afford it.

There are ways to get it done.

Yes, redistribute the wealth. Yes, increase the top marginal income tax rates. Yes, increase the estate tax. Yes, increase the capital gains tax so it at least equals that on earned income. Yes, make corporations pay their fair share. And yes, cut way back on Pentagon spending.

If this is the society we want, then this is the society we're going to have to fight for.

I'm heartened by the fighting spirit I've witnessed all year in Madison, Wisconsin, and seen elsewhere in Michigan, New Jersey, and Ohio, among other places.

I'm heartened by the massive civil disobedience at the White House recently over the tar sands pipeline.

And I'm heartened by the plans for more civil disobedience in Washington on October 6 to protest the tenth anniversary of the Afghanistan War and to demand, as the organizers say, "that America's resources be invested in human needs and environmental protection instead of war and exploitation."

The impossible always seems unrealistic until people start going for it. It's like a tennis ball that seems unreachable until you hustle. Let us start going for it now.

6 The Motivating Forces Behind Black Lives Matter

Tasbeeh Herwees

. . . When activists Patrisse Cullors, Alicia Garza and Opal Tometi first hashtagged the phrase #BlackLivesMatter on social media in 2013, it was just an emotional response to the news of George Zimmerman's acquittal in the Trayvon Martin case. But the phrase has since become the banner slogan for a movement that has permanently altered the political consciousness of the nation.

Last year, after thousands of protesters took to the streets in Ferguson, Missouri, braving tear gas and rubber bullets, the movement, began growing at a rapid pace. Black Lives Matter chapters materialized all over the country—there are now 26 chapters in North America. . . .

• • •

"What I've been focused on is making sure that black women are empowered to reshape the economy and reshape our democracy in their image," says Garza, speaking to me from Oakland, where she works as special projects director for the National Domestic Workers Alliance. In many ways, Garza serves as Black Lives Matter's narrator. Her op-eds and articles appear in publications like *The Feminist Wire, Truthout* and, more recently, *Those People,* often functioning as declarative statements about the role and direction of the movement. There is a constant effort in her writing to re-center the conversation on black women, particularly those who identify as queer or trans.

"We were all heavily influenced by the writings of Barbara Smith and Cherríe Moraga and Gloria Anzaldúa, and this kind of notion that as women of color, and as queer women of color, we faced multiple oppressions at once," she says.

In Oakland, Garza witnessed the rise of a strong Occupy movement, one that would overtake the city. Although the death of Oscar Grant helped set the stage for the rise of Occupy Oakland, critics like Garza say that those in the encampment failed to make substantial considerations of race and gender in their critiques of economic injustice and police violence. Many argue that this failure contributed to its downfall—its inability, mostly, to galvanize a broader community.

Black Lives Matter, Garza hoped, would succeed where the Occupy movement had faltered. This meant establishing a broad but singular mission statement, one that addressed all intersecting injustices afflicting the black community. The phrase "Black Lives Matter," which Garza posted to Facebook for the first time two years ago as a "love note to black people," embodied the specificity of this political purpose.

This article was originally published at *Good: A Magazine for the Global Citizen.* Republished with permission of Good Worldwide Inc.

It began, first, as a hashtag. It could have lived and died as a hashtag, as many modern campaigns do. But Garza and Cullors, a community organizer from Southern California, wanted more from the project. And when Tometi, an immigration activist from Arizona, stepped in, their advocacy began taking the shape of a movement. Suddenly, they had a Facebook page. A Tumblr blog. A Twitter account. All over the country—in Los Angeles, Oakland, New York City—protesters carried posters emblazoned with "Black Lives Matter." One year later, demonstrators in Ferguson and Baltimore used the phrase as a rallying cry—then it began to show up at protests in Paris, Delhi, and Tokyo. In Israel, Ethiopian Jews chanted the words in a challenge to police violence there.

But while the larger movement might draw its power from its broad appeal and inclusiveness, its slogan operates against the notion of a post-racial society. To say "Black Lives Matter" is to recognize that we live in a world in which that statement is not true.

"It says we're unapologetically black," says Tometi. "We're going to name it. We're going to name how acutely social issues impact black people. You can't deny it.". . .

• • •

If [Patrisse] Cullors has a particular passion for the subversive brand of activism she practices, it comes from a very personal place. She grew up in Van Nuys, California, where the threat of police violence pervaded everyday life in the neighborhood. "I remember LAPD lining up my siblings—and they were probably like 12, 13—just stopping and frisking them daily," says Cullors. Her brother was jailed for a while, and he describes waking up in a pool of his own blood after being assaulted by a police officer. Her father, too, was incarcerated—a casualty of the war on drugs, he was in and out of jail for substance abuse. He had no support. He had no treatment. At 51, she says, his body was "done." He died three days before the death of Oscar Grant.

In high school, Cullors read feminist writers like bell hooks for the first time. "It was my first introduction to putting language to my suffering and my family's suffering," she says. Racism, classism, patriarchy, homophobia—these words helped her contextualize her pain. But they also energized her activism.

When she was 18, she organized her first demonstration. She was at a park, kissing her girlfriend when a man approached them, yelling at them to stop spreading "lesbianism." They left, hand in hand, unsettled by the interaction. When they got home, they called their friends and made protest signs. About 10 people showed up to the park and they marched down Ventura Boulevard. "It was about reclaiming space, you know? It feels so funny now."

The reclamation of space has always been an important protest tool for marginalized people in the U.S. It means reinscribing places that are stained with the memory of trauma with stories of resistance and resilience. It's a strategy that Black Lives Matter implements in both symbolic and practical ways. . . .

• • •

In 1977, the Combahee River Collective, a radical black lesbian women's liberation group, released what it called its "Black Feminist Statement." The manifesto, written by Barbara Smith, Beverly Smith and Demita Frazier, became legendary. "If Black women were free, it would mean that everyone else would have to be free since our freedom would necessitate the destruction of all the systems of oppression," they wrote.

Several decades later, Garza and Cullors stood on stage at Dëmos' Transforming America Awards in New York City, being honored for their work and echoing the sentiments of their feminist forbears. "This generation is really pushing and challenging the old civil rights establishment that has in large part looked like heterosexual, cis, Christian, black men. And women who were doing amazing hard work but were not getting any credit for it," said Cullors.

By addressing the specific struggles of black queer women, the Black Lives Matters founders argue, echoing their Combahee predecessors, that they are confronting a system that subjugates everyone. "Because we know that black women, cis and trans, are really like the canaries in the coal mine, right? What's happening to black women is the future of everybody else," says Garza. . . .

7 On Solidarity, "Centering Anti-Blackness," and Asian Americans

Scot Nakagawa

As a long-time racial justice worker—a grey head in a movement mainly made up of young people—earnest young Asian Americans, anxious to acknowledge the pivotal role anti-Black racism plays in the perpetuation of white supremacy, often ask me how to "center anti-Blackness" in Asian American racial justice activism. I am as often asked that question by white progressives who aspire to become allies in the Movement for Black Lives.

My answer is simple. Acknowledge the leadership of Black Lives Matter and use the political space and opportunity the movement has created—including the 24/7 media coverage that has finally changed the dominant news narratives about Black crime to one of crimes against Black bodies—to ask ourselves, how does this movement serve me and those like me, whether they be Asian or Latino, Native or white? And then make those connections and tell your story.

Some tell me doing so "de-centers anti-Blackness." But "centering anti-Blackness" requires us to tell the stories of the many oppressions that hold it in that central role, as the fulcrum of white supremacy, and of the many levers without which elites, who are the ultimate beneficiaries of white supremacy, cannot continue to use that fulcrum to continue to propel us toward racial dystopia.

White supremacy, after all, originated as a labor exploitation system. Racism wasn't its primary product. No. Cotton, sugar, tobacco, produce for our markets, and chattel slaves, these were the commodities around which it was built, and these commodities were created for the sake of profit. Racism and white supremacy were the means, not the end.

In today's more complex economy, the hand that picks the strawberry isn't the same as the one that packages it for market, but both are exploited for the sake of profit.

Still others tell me that telling such complex stories—stories about connections and intersections, and common cause being rooted in multiple self-interests is too much for most people. Only those already ready to hear it will listen. That it's preaching to the choir.

To them, I say this—

Those who say activists for racial justice ought not preach to the choir are too personally invested in the people doing the singing to hear what they sound like to those for whom they are strangers or even the "other." To them, the lack of harmony among

This article was originally published at Race Files: A project of ChangeLab. Republished with permission of Scot Nakagawa.

our voices makes us sound confusing at best, and like nothing more than noise, even an angry din, at worst. And this has been true for a very long time.

Now, finally, a clear, compelling voice—an Aretha in the form of the Movement for Black Lives—has risen in our midst, cutting through the noise and turning heads everywhere. Our job is not to stop singing in order to hear her, nor to try to copy her and sing along.

To silence ourselves diminishes the potential power and reach of our combined voices. To simply sing along threatens to drown her voice out.

Instead, we need to find our way to harmony, weaving our various voices together while retaining the integrity of each voice. We are, after all, there to sing, to have our voices heard, too. If not, why show up? And our singing is of stories that are clearly deeply intertwined, if only we can sing in harmony.

To help people understand relationship, the social nature of what we have been, are now, and will be in the future we create together, not singly but together, whether we do so with conscious intent or not is the most important message of our music.

Harmony is our goal. Not amalgamation or appropriation or imitation. We need to use the political space and cultural opportunity that the Movement for Black Lives has created for us and use it for this purpose, picking up the diverse threads of our lives and weaving them into a powerful, prophetic cry for justice.

This after all, is the true self-interest we all share in the cause of Black liberation. Black liberation has always been the teacher, the prophet, the true hope for the liberation of us all.

Suggestions for Further Reading

Boggs, Grace Lee, and Scott Kurasighe. *The Next American Revolution: Sustainable Activism for the 21st Century.* Berkeley: University of California Press, 2012.

Colby, Anne, and William Damon. *Some Do Care: Contemporary Lives of Moral Commitment.* New York: Free Press, 1992. Dees, Morris. *A Season for Justice: A Lawyer's Own Story of Victory Over America's Hate Groups.* New York: Touchstone Books, 1991.

Eisenstein, Zillah R. *The Color of Gender: Reimaging Democracy.* Berkeley: University of California Press, 1994.

Featherstone, Liza. *Selling Women Short: The Landmark Battle for Workers' Rights at Wal-Mart.* New York: Basic Books, 2004.

Fletcher, Bill, Jr. *"They're Bankrupting Us!" And 20 Other Myths about Unions.* Boston: Beacon Press, 2012.

Gitlin, Todd. *Occupy Nation: The Roots, the Spirit, and the Promise of Occupy Wall Street.* New York: Harper, 2012.

Imarisha, Walidah. *Octavia's Brood: Science Fiction Stories from Social Justice Movements.* Oakland, CA: AK Press, 2015.

Iyer, Deepa. *We Too Sing America: South Asian, Arab, Muslim and Sikh Immigrants Shape our Multiracial Future.* New York: The New Press, 2015.

Kivel, Paul. *Uprooting Racism: How White People Can Work for Racial Justice,* 3rd edition. New York: New Society Publishers, 2011.

Marable, Manning. *The Great Wells of Democracy: The Meaning of Race in American Life.* New York: Basic Books, 2003.

McCarthy, Timothy Patrick, ed. *The Radical Reader: A Documentary History of the American Radical Tradition.* New York: The New Press, 2003.

Nadasen, Premilla. *Household Workers Unite: The Untold Story of African American Women Who Built a Movement.* Boston: Beacon Press, 2015.

Reddy, Maureen T., ed. *Everyday Acts Against Racism: Raising Children in a Multiracial World.* Seattle: Seal Press, 1996.

Reich, Robert B. *Beyond Outrage: What Has Gone Wrong with Our Economy and Our Democracy, and How to Fix It.* New York: Vintage, 2012.

Savage, Dan, and Terry Miller, eds. *It Gets Better: Coming Out, Overcoming Bullying, and Creating a Life Worth Living.* New York: Plume, 2012.

Solnit, Rebecca. *Hope in the Dark: Untold Histories, Wild Possibilities.* New York: Nation Books, 2005.

Spring, Joel. *Deculturalization and the Struggle for Equality: A Brief History of the Education of Dominated Cultures in the United States,* 7th ed. New York: McGraw-Hill, 2012.

Stansell, Christine. *The Feminist Promise: 1792 to the Present.* New York: Modern Library, 2011.

Stoltenberg, John. *The End of Manhood: A Book for Men of Conscience.* New York: Dutton, 1993.

Thompson, Becky. *A Promise and a Way of Life: White Antiracist Activism.* Minneapolis, MN: University of Minnesota Press, 2001.

INDEX